Individual Behaviors and Technologies for Financial Innovations

Wesley Mendes-Da-Silva
Editor

Individual Behaviors and Technologies for Financial Innovations

Springer

Editor
Wesley Mendes-Da-Silva
Sao Paulo School of Business
Administration (FGV/EAESP)
Sao Paulo, SP, Brazil

University of Texas at Austin
Austin, TX, USA

ISBN 978-3-030-06325-2 ISBN 978-3-319-91911-9 (eBook)
https://doi.org/10.1007/978-3-319-91911-9

Printed on acid-free paper

This Springer imprint is published by the registered company Springer Nature Switzerland AG
The registered company address is: Gewerbestrasse 11, 6330 Cham, Switzerland

Foreword

Worldwide, the Internet has increasingly provided predicted, as well as unforeseen opportunities in communication through diminishing distance, including expanded participation in financial landscapes.

New research is needed to help us better understand these important changes in context. This volume is such a text as it provides relevant insights to relevant topics in different regions at different levels of analysis around interactions between individuals, technologies and financial innovations. This discussion is developed focusing on the topic of crowdfunding and corporate finance to *guanxi*, students' credit card habits, and beyond.

This collection of research perspectives makes a substantial and important contribution to understanding the many faceted aspects of economic patterns that present insights into mature as well as emerging economies.

The volume is at once relevant and academically thorough, making it valuable for policy makers and the financial community. The methodologies are described in detail and provide a quintessential guide to solid research in this field, by including different approaches that reveal data in its most salient forms. These qualities also make it an appropriate text for students in different fields, linking finance, psychology, and technology to understand various topics and methodologies for data-driven, empirical financial research in various contexts.

Propositions for further research are present in each chapter, and practical suggestions for pursuing empirical studies in the field of financial innovation based on the convergence of various domains are offered.

The Visiting Scholars Program at IC^2 Institute, The University of Texas at Austin, is pleased to have hosted Professor Wesley Mendes-Da-Silva, São Paulo School of Business Administration of the Fundação Getulio Vargas during his research and writing to complete this important volume on *Individual Behaviors and Technologies for Financial Innovations*.

Austin, TX, USA David V. Gibson

Preface

Innovation significantly implies value creation, besides new products creation. Emerging problems, as a consequence, need new solutions in any field. In the context of one of the most competitive sectors, the financial industry, financial innovation has received significant attention since the recent international 2008/2009 economic crisis. As a result of the crisis, financial innovation has become a focus in a time of reevaluation. Yet despite this importance, the sources of financial innovation remain surprisingly poorly understood. Besides, at that particular moment in time, we witnessed the rise of financial instruments and institutions that did not even exist at the end of the 1970s.

Financial innovation has been defined as the action of creating and popularizing new financial instruments as well as new financial technologies, markets, and institutions. In recent years, economists recognized as leaders of the academic community have championed the idea that "finance is really technology that works toward reducing inequality." Inequalities, on the other hand, have motivated crises of diverse types around the world, with serious damages to the well-being of the world population. In this context, financial innovations can help the society, notably through new technologies that address inequality problems by offering new assets for risk diversification, insurance that provides protection against emerging risks (such as climate risks), and informational apparatus available for making financial decisions at different levels of interest, among other innovations that collaborate for the democratization of finance.

It is necessary to consider that all of us have behaviors shaped according to our life trajectory, which implies a set of emotions and impulses, widely studied by neuroscience researchers. And this implies two sides of our brain: one altruistic and one selfish, with whom we live. This notion impacts our lives in the various spheres. On a personal level, our propensity to save and spend, the choice for certain investment assets, the propensity to buy insurance, the recurrence to family members to borrow money – all emphasize reciprocal relationships. On the other hand, at the business level, we can best understand the willingness to turn to friends and family to fund a business. And in the financial and capital markets, corporate governance mechanisms, including board composition, propensity for corruption, and illegal or unethical behavior, can be anticipated through the use of technology to address the consequences of mismanagement in companies.

Why study financial innovation? The answer could be as simple as it may seem: because it creates value! At least that is what recent papers have assumed as a title. But it is indeed a field whose complexity reminds us of an exciting research agenda, ranging from personal aspects to SMEs and large listed corporations, in both developed and emerging markets – especially the last. That is, to the extent that a country's GDP can depend heavily on the individual's behavior of the citizen, it is understood that financial innovation is important for understanding the behavior of the economy at the aggregate level. That is why the theme of financial innovation is interesting for researchers from different areas, policy makers, and the business community, especially the financial industry.

Faced with these arguments, there is a growing need for a book that summarizes research results and points out directions for future research. *Individual Behaviors and Technology for Financial Innovations* responds to this demand by referring relevant social and psychological issues to the reflection about financial innovations, their antecedents, and their consequences at different levels of analysis, in different theoretical and methodological approaches, with a particular focus on emerging markets but emphasizing the relevance of financial innovation to the global context. This content directly helps finance researchers interested in financial innovation, policy makers, educators, and practitioners in the design, implementation, and evaluation of financial innovation initiatives.

The connection between technology and finance is not something recent. Financial innovations, at their various levels, can be more efficient and more contributory as the use of technology is oriented toward value creation. A recent example is the fintech and crowdfunding industry, which allows democratizing finances, since it promotes the sale of parts of a company to a broad set of investors, who would rigorously be venture capitalists. Recent empirical evidence suggests that financial innovation often increases the complexity of transactions, resulting in opportunities to explore questions of interest to the consumers of financial services. Thus, in the long term, financial liberalization likely has negative effects and does not result in an innovative process. However, there are also many financial innovations that have already produced significantly positive effects, such as opportunities for venture capital and other financial innovations that are still in the early stages of development. Thus, research on financial innovation can introduce new evidence to important economic issues such as financial crises, economic growth, and system instability. Hence, there are clear opportunities for future research in this finance subdiscipline, whether at the corporate level or at the transaction level. These types of opportunities suggest that researchers interested in financial innovation can provide valuable evidence in other areas of modern finance and help develop financial technologies.

Financial innovation enhances sustainability of institutions and their outreach to the poor. A useful distinction between the different types of financial innovations include: first, financial system/institutional innovations – such innovations can affect the financial sector as a whole, relating to changes in business structures, to the establishment of new types of financial intermediaries, or to changes in the legal and supervisory framework. Important examples include the use of the group mechanism to retail financial services, formalizing informal finance systems, reducing the access barriers for women, or setting up a completely new service structure. Second, process innovations – such innovations cover the introduction of new business processes, leading to increased efficiency, market expansion, etc. Examples include office automation and use of computers with accounting and client data management software. Third, product innovations – such innovations include the introduction of new credit, deposit, insurance, leasing, hire purchase, and other financial products. Product innovations are introduced to respond better to changes in market demand or to improve the efficiency of the market.

While this agenda has been transformed in recent years, it has never failed to consider what was already pointed to at the end of the 1980s. An example of this movement is the growing interest in new financial products that will help solve emerging problems, such as climate change and the ever-accelerating aging of the population. The explicit and growing speed of the spread of new technologies has also led to the emergence of innovation in the field of finance. Topics like blockchain, Internet of Things (IoT), semantic computing, and Big Data Finance are motivating the reconstruction of financial tools that translate into new financial mechanisms that are in their maturing phase. One of the main motivations put forward by the finance community to write about financial innovation is to provide arguments for financial industry professionals not to apologize, but to assume their personal responsibility as well as their role in promoting market efficiency.

All the chapters are based on work conducted by experienced and knowledgeable researchers who are active in multidisciplinary research in financial innovation. They contributed with chapters that provide an overview of the current research. In each chapter these authors initially present the relevant literature regarding the topic of the discussion, in order to attest the research status. In addition, the authors compile search results and make them accessible to people not necessarily experts in the field. Given the particular relevance that financial innovations have for emerging markets, as well as their relevance to global stability, we discuss financial innovation from emerging market evidence. As a result of this, we understand that discussing and pointing out a research agenda about financial innovation with a focus on emerging markets is an important element in the international research agenda, given the notion that finance is really a technology that works toward reducing inequality.

The book is organized in three parts, with 16 chapters. Part I has eight chapters that review the research on gender differences in attitudes about risk and propensity to purchase automobile insurance, financial literacy models for college students, wellness and attitude of university students in the use of credit cards, impact of programs on income distribution and propensity to remain in employment, financial literacy and propensity to resort to informal financing channels, and risk behavior in the use of credit cards by students. Part II reviews the research on financing for startups and SMEs, exploring funding through crowdfunding platform, operating credit unions, and using networks of friends to finance small businesses outside the domestic market. The four chapters of Part III describe the contexts of financial innovation in listed companies, including society's demands on their behavior – we discuss motivations for companies to participate in corporate sustainability indexes, corporate performance through their profile of socially responsible investments, the influence of networks of social relations in the formation of boards, and management of companies, and also the precariousness of financial decisions in large companies, as well as the role of the internet in corporate communication with the market.

This volume is the first to offer a comprehensive picture of research on the relevance of individual behavior and technology to financial innovations. Therefore, it represents a contribution to the literature, insofar as it presents the basis on which quality research on financial innovation can be developed. The book also contributes to providing useful information to researchers and policy makers interested in initiatives that have the potential to reduce inequalities and increase people's quality of life and well-being. Overall, the book contributes to the literature on finance, business, human development, technology, and related fields.

Austin, TX, USA Wesley Mendes-Da-Silva

Acknowledgments

This book is one of the results of years of research on financial innovations and related topics, where several people, institutions, and organizations are worthy to be acknowledged for their support, comments, and especially cooperation. I appreciate the financial support and endorsement from the São Paulo Research Foundation (FAPESP) and National Council for Scientific and Technological Development (CNPq). I wish to acknowledge the IC^2 Institute of The University of Texas at Austin for its unrestricted support in the development of this work, as well as the School of Business Administration of São Paulo of Fundação Getulio Vargas (FGV/EAESP). A special mention is given to my colleagues from FGV/EAESP, The University of Texas at Austin, Marriott School of Management at Brigham Young University, and the University of Georgia: Arthur Ridolfo Neto, Bruce Kellison, Cesar Caselani, David V. Gibson, Fabio G. Garcia, Gregory Pogue, João C. Douat, José Evaristo, Luiz A.L. Brito, Maria T.L. Fleury, Oscar Malvessi, Paulo R.S. Terra, Rafael R. Schiozer, Rodrigo Bandeira de Mello, Samy Dana, Tales Andreassi, Ted Christensen, and Walter Fernando Araújo de Moraes.

Moreover, I acknowledge some colleagues from other universities with whom I have had the pleasure to work, whose conversations, comments, and presentations provided precious insights for this volume: among others, Abraham Yu, University of São Paulo; Alexandre Silveira, FECAP; André Oda, University of São Paulo; Andrea Minardi, Insper; Antonio Lopo Martinez, FUCAPE; Carlo Drago, University of Rome; Celso Roberto Perez, Federal University of Santa Catarina; Cesar Cruz, Federal University of São Carlos; Cesare Fracassi, McCombs School of Business/The University of Texas at Austin; Cristiana Leal, University of Minho; Dany Rogers, Federal University of Uberlândia; David Wood, Marriott School of Management at BYU; Denísio Liberato, FAAP; Denize Grzybovski, University of Passo Fundo; Edison Simoni, FECAP; Elin Merethe Oftedal, University of Tromsø; Fabio Frezatti, University of São Paulo; Fernando Moreira, University of Edinburgh; Flávio Hourneaux Junior, University of São Paulo; Florêncio Absalão, FIR; Francisco Cassano, Mackenzie Presbyterian University; Franz Fuerst, University of Cambridge; Fuad G. Sobrinho, SDPS; Gilnei Luiz de Moura, Federal University of Santa Maria; Guilherme Silveira, Insper; Gustavo Araújo, Ibmec Rio; Heber Silveira, FECAP; Herbert Kimura, University of Brasília; Hideo Hori, Mackenzie Presbyterian University; Jairo Dornelas, Federal University of Pernambuco; Jairo L. Procianoy, Federal University of Rio Grande do Sul; José Mauro Ferraz Andrade, Mackenzie Presbyterian University; José R. Securato, University of São Paulo; Joséte Florencio dos Santos, Federal University of Pernambuco; Josilmar C. Cia, Mackenzie Presbyterian University; Julian Cardenas, Freie Universität Berlin; Karen Perrotta, Mackenzie Presbyterian University; Kay Stice, Marriott School of Management at BYU; Leonardo Pontual, FIR; Lucas Barros, University of São Paulo; Luiz Eduardo Brandão, PUC/Rio; Luis Eduardo Carvalheira de Mendonça, Catholic University of Pernambuco; Luiz Eduardo Gaio, Unicamp; Manuel Rocha Armada, University of Minho; Marcelo Phelippe, Mackenzie Presbyterian University; Margaret Cotrofeld, IC^2; Maria Sylvia Macchione Saes, University of São Paulo; Matthew Dixon, University of San Francisco; Michelle Helena Kovacs, NHTV Breda University of Applied Sciences; Odilon Costa, Pontifical Catholic University of São Paulo; Oliviero Roggi, University of Florence; Pablo Rogers, Federal University of Uberlândia; Patricia Vidal, Mackenzie Presbyterian University; Patti Fisher, College of Liberal Arts and Human Sciences/Virginia Tech; Paulo Glício da Rocha, Federal University of Pernambuco; Phillip Sheu, University of California at Irvine; Rafael Bastos, Ateneu; Raquel Oliveira, Central Bank of Brazil; Raymond Yeh, SDPS; Ricardo P.C. Leal, Federal University of Rio de Janeiro; Robert Iquiapaza, Federal University of Minas Gerais; Roberto Borges Kerr, Mackenzie Presbyterian University; Roberto Ricciuti, Università degli Studi di Verona; Roy Martelanc, University of São Paulo; Rubens Famá, University of São Paulo; Rubens Ricupero, FAAP; Scott Summers, Marriott School of Management at BYU; Sergio Lex, Mackenzie Presbyterian University; Sílvio Parodi Oliveira Camilo, UNESC; Sirkka Jarvenpaa, McCombs School of Business at The University of Texas at Austin; Spenser Robinson, Central Michigan University; Taiguara Langrafe, FECAP; Thiago Barros, Federal University of Ouro Preto; Wilson Toshiro Nakamura, Mackenzie Presbyterian University.

Furthermore, I want to gratefully acknowledge all companies that have collaborated with my research program, in particular: ADM do Brasil Ltda, Agrale, ALL, AES Eletropaulo, Arcos Dourados, Aurora, Austin Rating, Bahiagas, Banco do Brasil, Banco Itaú, Batavo, Belagricola, BFRE, Blumenau, Brasil Foods, Broota, C. Vale Cooperativa, Caramuru Alimentos, Carioca Christiani-Nielsen, Casan, Catarse, CBMM, Cedro, CESP, Cia Metalurgica Prada, COAMO S/A, Cocamar, Coelce, Conces Rod ViaOeste, Construtora Barbosa Mello, Cooxupé, Corretora de Valores Souza Barros, CPTM, CTA Continental Tobaccos Alliance, Cummins, Curitiba, Drogaria Pacheco, Duke Energy, Duratex, EISA, Elektro, Embraer, Estácio, Etc, Even, EZB, Fras Le, Gafor, Grazziotin, Grupo ADP Energias, Grupo CCR, Grupo IMC, Iharabras S/A Ind Quimicas, Ind Romi, Instituto Brasileiro de Inovação Financeira (IBRIF)®, Instituto Brasileiro de Executivos de Finanças (IBEF), Instituto Brasileiro de Governança Corporativa (IBGC), Ipiranga Produtos Petr, Josapar, Liberum Ratings, Locamerica, Lojas Renner, Mapfre, McDonalds Comércio Alimentos, Mercedes-Benz, Mongeral Aegon, Monteiro Aranha,

Multigrain, Multiplan, Nadir, NAMISA, NET Serviços, OGX, OHL Brasil S/A, Paraná Equipamentos, Paranapanema, Petrobrás, Porto Seguro, Profarma, Providencia, Prysmian Energia Cab, Qualicorp, Redecard, Refrescos Guararapes, RV Tecnologia, São Martinho, Schulz S/A, Senior Solutions, Servimed Ltda, SLC Agricola, Souza Cruz, SPTuris, Stefanini consultoria, STIHL, Trisul S/A, Ultra, VLI Logística, Wetzel.

I would especially like to acknowledge all the people that have supported me during these years with insights and suggestions. I learned so much from them, and their ideas and competences have inspired my research work: Adilson Gomes da Silva, Brazilian Army; Alberto Monteiro Alves Junior, Brazilian Army; Antonio Gabriel Esper, Brazilian Army; Antônio Nogueira Leitão, Mongeral Aegon; Antônio Sérgio Farias, AES Eletropaulo; Bradley Schurman, AARP; Catherine Collinson, Transamerica Institute; Cassius Guerra Varejão de Alcântara, Brazilian Army; Cristovam Buarque, Brazilian Senate; Décio Baptista, Diretor Liberum Rating; Pedro Melo, KPMG; Eduardo Chehab, IBGC; Fausto Augusto de Sousa Pontes, Brazilian Army; Fernando Manguinho, Brazilian Army; Genilson Vilela Silva, FedEx; George Henrique Vasconcelos, Brazilian Army; Guilherme de Mauro Favaron, AES Eletropaulo; Henrique Noya, Mongeral Aegon; Jairo Araújo, Riachuelo; João Edson Minnicelli, Brazilian Army; José Cláudio Securato, Saint Paul; Leonardo Barros Brito de Pinho, IBEF; Leonardo Mussel Bracaglia, Brazilian Army; Luiz F.D. Martha, IBGC; Luis R. Callado, IBEF; Mauro Motoryn; Mike Mansfield, Aegon; Paulo Cruvinel, Embrapa; Paulo Oliveira Magalhães Filho, Infraero; Pedro Severo da Costa Leite Filho, Brazilian Army; Renée de Vries, ANBO; Sandra Guerra, Vale, Eletropaulo; Severino do Carmo Filho, Brazilian Army; Sunny Jonathan, AES Eletropaulo.

Finally, I acknowledge my family whose constant support and patience made this book happen, and all my co-authors who collaborated for this volume.

Wesley Mendes-Da-Silva

Contents

About the Editor

Wesley Mendes-Da-Silva is a Visiting Professor of Business Finance at University of Texas at Austin. He has academic and professional expertise in corporate governance mechanisms, and in corporate and personal finance. Currently, he is actively involved in a graduate program on financial management at one of the most prestigious and accredited Business Schools in South America, São Paulo School of Business Administration of The Fundação Getulio Vargas (FGV/EAESP) at São Paulo/Brazil. His main research interests include funding mechanisms such as crowdfunding, financial innovation, behavioral finance, as well as corporate governance. Wesley has collaborated with many academic, professional, and governmental institutions from Brazil, Portugal, the USA, Italy, the UK, Australia, Mexico, Chile, Norway, and France. He also has collaborated with different board of directors of listed and nonlisted companies and governments in different spheres.

Contributors

Daniel Reed Bergmann University of São Paulo, São Paulo, SP, Brazil

Danilo Braun Santos Federal University of Sao Paulo (UNIFESP), Osasco, SP, Brazil

Aureliano Angel Bressan Department of Business Economics, Federal University of Minas Gerais, Belo Horizonte/MG, MG, Brazil

Valéria Gama Fully Bressan Department of Business Economics, Federal University of Minas Gerais, Belo Horizonte/MG, MG, Brazil

Eduardo da Silva Flores University of São Paulo, São Paulo, SP, Brazil

Israel José dos Santos Felipe Department of Business Economics, Federal University of Ouro Preto, Mariana, Minas Gerais, Brazil

Economic Policies Research Unit – NIPE, University of Minho, Braga, Portugal

Eduardo Francisco Department of Business Economics, Fundação Getulio Vargas at São Paulo (FGV/EAESP), Sao Paulo, SP, Brazil

Alexandre S. Garcia Centro Universitario Fecap, Sao Paulo, SP, Brazil

Cristiane C. Gattaz IC² Institute/University of Texas at Austin, Austin, TX, USA

Lauro Gonzalez Columbia University and Fundação Getulio Vargas, Sao Paulo, SP, Brazil

Alexandre Ribeiro Leichsenring University of São Paulo (USP), São Paulo, SP, Brazil

Edimilson Costa Lucas Department of Business Economics, Federal University of São Paulo, Osasco, SP, Brazil

Angela Christine Lyons University of Illinois at Urbana Champaign, Urbana, IL, USA

Wesley Mendes-Da-Silva Sao Paulo School of Business Administration (FGV/EAESP), Sao Paulo, SP, Brazil

University of Texas at Austin, Austin, TX, USA

Naercio Aquino Menezes Filho University of São Paulo (USP) and Insper, São Paulo, SP, Brazil

Jill M. Norvilitis State University of New York, Buffalo, NY, USA

Renato J. Orsato Department of Operations Management, Fundação Getulio Vargas at São Paulo (FGV/EAESP), Sao Paulo, Brazil

Ani Caroline Grigion Potrich Department of Business Administration, Federal University of Santa Catarina, Florianópolis, SC, Brazil

Luciano Rossoni Department of Management, UniGranRio, Rio de Janeiro, RJ, Brazil

Richard Saito Department of Finance, Fundação Getulio Vargas at São Paulo (FGV/EAESP), Sao Paulo, Brazil

Kelmara Mendes Vieira Department of Business Administration, Federal University of Santa Maria, Santa Maria, RS, Brazil

Laís Karlina Vieira Department of Business Economics, Federal University of Minas Gerais, Belo Horizonte/MG, Brazil

List of Figures

List of Tables

Part I
Financial Innovation in the Personal Level

Chapter 1
Introduction: The Context of Financial Innovations

Wesley Mendes-Da-Silva

The main function of the financial system is to facilitate the allocation of financial resources, distributing them well in terms of time and space within an uncertain context. In performing this function, the financial system permits the transfer of financial resources from savers to borrowers as well as the reduction of risk through insurance and diversification (Merton 1992). Since there are uncertainties involved in the future states of many resources, individuals can modify their behavior depending on their aversion to the risk that results from these uncertainties. However, these risks can frequently be addressed through financial instruments that satisfy the demands voiced by participants in the financial system. These financial instruments can contribute as much to the economy as the technologies that support them.

Based on this view, Frame and White (2012) define financial innovation as something new that reduces costs, reduces risk, or offers some improvement in a product, service, or instrument that better satisfies the demands of the participants of the financial system. Tufano (2003, p. 310) assumes that, broadly speaking, financial innovation is the act of creating and then popularizing new financial instruments as well as new financial technologies, institutions, and markets. In turn, according to Llewellyn (2009), the context of financial innovation defines the characteristics of the financial system. In terms of the nature of financial innovations, Llewellyn (2009) also identifies and details three alternatives for classifying them: by type, function, and motive.

First in terms of types, financial innovations can be product innovations (the creation of new financial instruments, contracts, techniques, and markets), risk-shifting innovations (unbundling the separate characteristics and risks of individual instruments – such as credit risk and interest rate risk – and repackaging

W. Mendes-Da-Silva (✉)
Sao Paulo School of Business Administration (FGV/EAESP), Sao Paulo, SP, Brazil

University of Texas at Austin, Austin, TX, USA

W. Mendes-Da-Silva (ed.), *Individual Behaviors and Technologies for Financial Innovations*, https://doi.org/10.1007/978-3-319-91911-9_1

them in different combinations), or process innovations (process improvements typified by new means of, e.g., distributing securities and processing or pricing transactions).

In terms of functions, Llewellyn (2009) argues that they can be classified according to their contributions to the main role played by the financial system: transferring risk, pricing risk, enhancing liquidity, enhancing credit generation (e.g., CDSs, CDOs), generating equity, insurance (e.g., CDSs), asset and liability management (e.g., CDSs and CDOs), and the funding of financial institutions.

In respect to the motives why financial innovations occur, Llewellyn (2009) believes that they can be organized into four categories: (i) defensive, when they occur as a response to changes in regulation; (ii) aggressive, when financial institutions create new financial instruments believing that they have the potential to attract market interest; (iii) responsive, when a financial instrument is developed to make changes requested by clients in terms of their portfolios; or (iv) protective, when institutions adopt techniques that are derived from their own portfolio restrictions.

Keeping in mind the nature of the technological innovation process, this book prioritizes the debate between theory and practice, exploring empirical evidence related to the essence of certain innovations. Thus, when considering the contribution of practical examples, we need to remember that they may last for only a limited period of time, which is why the focus of this book is on the rationale behind various models of financial innovation and not innovations themselves per se. Therefore, in conducting the discussion of models of how financial innovations originate, this book will also be relevant for policy makers and the business community, in addition to being a natural reference for researchers interested in discussing the fundamental principles, motivations, and consequences of financial innovations from the point of view of various levels of analysis (Fig. 1.2).

Technological changes have occurred with increasing frequency during recent years, especially since 1990 with the arrival of the Internet. This phenomenon has had such a great effect that four of the five largest American companies listed on the stock market were high-tech firms at the end of 2017 as was pointed out by Jerome H. Powell at the 41st Annual Central Banking Seminar in New York. Parallel to this, the globalization of the financial markets and the expansion of financial innovations have led to an increase in the velocity and flexibility of transactions, which has affected people's daily lives. Since the 1950s, we've witnessed the growth and increased sophistication of financial innovations such as credit cards, mobile payments, weather derivatives, subprime mortgages, debit cards, prepaid cards, online banking, ATMs, automated clearing houses, CDOs, CDSs, and small business credit scoring. All of these financial innovations have radically transformed the routines of banks and a number of nonfinancial firms. In addition, other changes are being established such as robo-advising, equity crowdfunding, as well as other emerging ones, such as the Internet of Things (IoT) and high-performance computers known as quantum computers, and it is hoped that they will be capable of executing tasks that have not been thought viable due to the time required and the high costs incurred (MIT Technology Review 2018, p. 24; Marsal-Llacuna 2018).

These changes induce new behavior on the part of individuals and organizations and demand new mechanisms, making it necessary for the finance industry to adapt to these new technologies (Schierz et al. 2010; Kim et al. 2016; Chen et al. 2016). In this way, when people use services offered by companies such as Uber and Lyft, when they participate in collective financing networks, or even when they make instant electronic transfers of funds, they contribute to the transformations that technology and behavior are implementing all over the world to reduce friction that can compromise market efficiency – such as a lack of transparency, elevated operational costs, or fraud. This has created a need for other advanced technologies, including fraudulent transaction detection and consumer identification procedures such as fingerprints and face scans, IP addresses, and geolocation data.

The field literature has considered financial innovation to be a permanent and irreversible phenomenon, which therefore needs to be constantly studied to improve our understanding of it (Gubler 2011). The financial innovation research agenda is essentially made up of its antecedents and consequences, as well as its positive and negative externalities. In addition, given that financial innovation can be seen as a complex phenomenon, which cannot be characterized as a zero sum game, special attention needs to be paid to two aspects of it. First, attention must be paid to research and the accumulation of knowledge to identify the best practices in the creation and sharing of value in the financial innovation ecosystem (Fig. 1.2). The second is the role of the guardians of the financial system, which are responsible for planning and maintaining the proper functioning of financial mechanisms through the definition of the apparatus of rules that govern them, in order to guarantee market efficiency by preventing opportunistic behavior and preserving adequate levels of transparency (Mottura 2009). Moreover, according to Thaler and Tucker (2013), consumers are increasingly immersed in contexts in which they have to consider information to make their consumption decisions. Therefore, individual selection behavior is more and more dependent on technology, given that it presents itself as the key to accessing information that is relevant to decision-making.

From the theoretical point of view in regard to individuals, according to Shiller (2006), financial theory over the past few decades has been characterized by an apparent dissociation between the theoretical conceptions reflected by two currents of thought. The first is the neoclassic revolution in finance which began in the 1960s with the efficient market theory and the capital asset pricing model (CAPM). The second is the behavioral revolution which has accelerated since the 1980s with the work of Kahneman and Tversky (1979), through a discussion of the volatility of financial markets and a profound study of different market anomalies. It happens that, also according to Shiller (2006), that these two currents of thought should not be seen as necessarily incompatible, because they should be applied together in relevant fields of finance. One illustration of this point of view is mentioned by Shiller (2006), when he goes back to the thinking found in the seminal work of Samuelson (1937), which represents the maximum present value of utility, subject to budgetary restrictions, as being formalized by (1.1).

$$J = \int_0^b U(x)e^{-\pi t}dt \tag{1.1}$$

Subject to (1.2):

$$S = \int_0^b x(t)e^{-rt}dt \tag{1.2}$$

where J is the present value of instantaneous utility U of consumption x of an individual, discounting rate π, S is the wealth of the individual at time 0, r is the market interest rate, and b is the individual's presumed date of death. This model – dedicated to making it possible to understand consumption and saving behavior – would later be criticized by Samuelson himself, but at the same time, it would go on to serve as the inspiration for contemporary authors of behavioral finance such as Shefrin and Thaler (1981).

If on one hand there is skepticism regarding the contributions of the behavioral approach to the theory and practice of finance, on the other there are arguments that point to unequivocal contributions, especially in terms of financial innovations, as discussed by Kunreuther et al. (2013) and Abreu and Mendes (2018). The academic community has recognized these initiatives, at least in terms of recent Nobel Prizes for Economics given to Daniel Kahneman and Vernon Smith in 2002, Robert Shiller in 2013, and Richard Thaler in 2017. No matter from which angle the field of behavioral finance is viewed, one thing that is obvious is its potential to solve complex problems based on a similarly complex apparatus of knowledge.

This leads to a discussion of the modern inducer of innovation – convergence, i.e., a transdisciplinary approach to solving problems. It is a human, interactive process aimed at breaking through artificial domain boundaries that limit innovation. Convergence is an approach to problem solving that integrates expertise from life sciences with physical, mathematical, and computational sciences, as well as medicine and engineering to form comprehensive synthetic frameworks that merge areas of knowledge from multiple fields to address specific challenges. In other words, convergence occurs when problems are resolved based on various fields of knowledge, rather than disciplinary approaches which are inherently more simplistic. The interaction between financial innovation and individual behavior, treated on a complex level by research, is related to issues regarding the role played by technology in this context (Frame and White 2012).

Technology and Financial Innovation

The role played by technological changes in stimulating the emergence of financial innovations has been discussed ever since the work of Schmookler (1967), and since then it has been the subject of new works such as Bloomestein (2000) and White (2000), and most recently Frame and White (2012), which have reviewed the field literature, with a particular focus on the United States, describing the way in which technological changes influence financial innovations, and in turn induce changes in the dynamics of the finance industry. The availability of technology is the key aspect in the emergence of financial innovations. In this sense, in terms of the concept of technology, a portion of the field literature assumes that the dynamic nature of technology has contributed to the existence of various definitions and concepts of technology.

A discussion of the concept of technology is crucial to getting a clear understanding of the nature of technology and examining what technology consists of, which is not assumed to be a simple task according to the field literature (Reddy and Zhoa 1990). According to Kumar et al. (1999), technology consists of two primary components: its physical component which is composed of items such as products, tools, equipment, blueprints, techniques, and processes and its informational component which consists of knowledge in terms of the areas of management, marketing, production, quality control, reliability, skilled labor, and functionality.

During recent decades, researchers who study technology transfer have linked technology directly to knowledge and have given more attention to the process of research and development (Dunning 1994, 1981). Technology always has to do with obtaining a certain result, resolving certain problems, completing certain tasks using particular skills, as well as employing knowledge and exploiting assets (Lan and Young 1996). This view appears to be close to the idea of financial innovation presented by Frame and White (2012) and shared by Gubler (2011), to whom financial innovation should incorporate improvements to products, services, or instruments that satisfy market demands. The concept of technology is not only related to the technology that the product embodies but also the knowledge regarding its use and application and the product development process (Lovell 1998; Bozeman 2000). The old concept of technology as information holds that a technology should be broadly applicable and easy to reproduce and reuse (Arrow 1962, 1969).

In order to broaden the concept of technology, the need for financial innovations, and the basis upon which consumer preferences are used in certain innovations, a company's motivations to innovate have also become an essential subject of research with the appearance of successful financial innovations (BIS 1986). Before the more explicit effects of the Internet, Allen and Gale (1994), in supplying a broad vision of the fundamental theoretical principles of financial innovation, pointed out that an important incentive for innovation can be supplied by changes in the value of pre-existing assets. Even though, for example, a large part of innovation in certain industries, such as the automobile industry, does not rely on patents to ensure profitability, companies make an effort to innovate, because if a company does not manage to come up with any innovations, it runs a greater risk of quickly losing its market share, and as a result, its market value will also probably be affected.

The potential of generating business deals between companies through investments of this type should also be emphasized. In this respect, if on one hand companies in the automobile industry, like Ford, have invested in automobiles using IoT technology, attracting consumers interested in the benefits of technology, on the other hand, these owners can try out insurance offered at prices that reflects its risk in a more reliable fashion. In essence, the value of automobile manufacturing companies can increase, driven by sales to consumers who are interested in more accessible insurance, since the insurer will have more information to better estimate the insurance risk, based on technologies like IoT and machine learning.

In the financial innovation theory that Allen and Gale (1994) describe, the idea that companies innovate to maximize their value is revealed to be important. In other words, it is the effect on a company's value that provides the incentive to innovate. To promote investments directed toward innovation, the main source of financial resources that a company relies on is its cash flows, and the financial problem that the firm confronts is deciding how to use these cash flows so that they will maximize value.

Allen and Gale (1994, p. 72) establish that the incentive comes from the desire of the original owners of the company to maximize the value of their assets. It should be emphasized that investments to promote innovation need to be characterized by a vision supported by the notion of convergence, which by using knowledge from various areas, increases the potential of innovations that can affect society. This thinking is reflected in the understanding of the scientific community. According to the National Academy of Sciences (NRC 2014), convergence has great potential to accelerate discoveries and innovations. In addition, it is expected that discoveries and innovations will be guided by the interaction between science and society, which implies that they will have some level of social consequences. Thus, research activities ranging from basic science to applied science should be part of a virtuous cycle which seeks the interaction between knowledge and social relevance as summarized in Fig. 1.1.

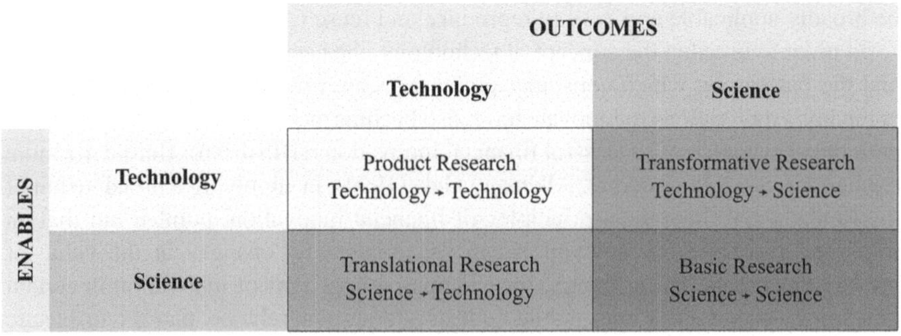

Fig. 1.1 Innovation through convergence. (Source: Adapted from SDPS 2017, p. 6)

Methods and Fieldwork

This volume offers content organized to offer a diversified but systematic vision of themes relevant to the antecedents of financial innovations, especially individual behavior and its consequences for the functioning of financial management mechanisms as seen through three main levels of analysis. In this respect, every chapter of this book offers, in addition to content dedicated to each chapter's theme and an updated review of the literature, empirical evidence derived from the employment of different methods of analysis, utilizing a wide array of data, ranging from the first data collected through surveys to secondary data collected from a variety of sources. Data relative to large or small firms is also utilized as well as data that reflects the behavior of individuals of different ages.

The content of this volume is the result of efforts undertaken over an 8-year period from 2010 to 2017 to explore problems and themes relevant to a wide range of contexts. This work was mainly developed while I was a visiting scholar at the Marriott School of Management of Brigham Young University in Provo, Utah (in 2014), and more recently during my collaboration with the University of Texas at Austin at the IC^2 Institute. During both of these opportunities, I received unconditional support from the Getulio Vargas Foundation (FGV/EAESP), and during the second opportunity, I also received partial support from two agencies of the Brazilian government: the National Council for Scientific and Technological Development (CNPq) through the federal government of Brazil and the São Paulo Research Foundation (FAPESP) through the state government of São Paulo. Each chapter is the result of a collaboration between colleagues from research institutions including the University of Illinois, State University of New York, University of California at Irvine, and SDPS in the United States and the Federal University of Minas Gerais, Federal University of Santa Maria, UniGranRio, Federal University of Sao Paulo, and University of Sao Paulo in Brazil.

In each of the three component parts of this volume, the theme of financial innovation is addressed on a specific level of analysis: the individual, small- and medium-sized businesses, and businesses listed on the stock exchange. The first part, besides this introduction, is composed of seven chapters dedicated to the behavior of adults in relation to financial innovations, such as insurance, credit cards, loans in informal markets, and income distribution programs. In this manner, we will analyze in the first part, everything from the propensity to acquire car insurance to the propensity to save during a crisis.

The second part of this volume is dedicated to four studies of small- and medium-sized companies. In regard to this, we discuss the relevance of personal relations to the financing of businesses in their embryonic stages. We address issues such as financing via crowdfunding, informal financing used by Chinese entrepreneurs through the influence of the guanxi phenomenon of the Confucian culture; and we discuss empirical evidence of the importance of friendship in business transactions. The trust present in relationship networks is one of the fundamental principles of credit unions, and they are also the subject of a case study in one of the chapters.

Finally, the third part is made up of four chapters and is focused on a discussion of financial innovations in companies that are listed on the stock exchange. We address the relevance and complexity of corporate networks formed by the relationships between board members to the creation of a firm's value; the propensity of listed companies to prioritize performance in terms of environmental, social, and governance criteria (ESG); and the use of Internet technology to report relevant market information and their impact on the cost of a firm's capital, and we also discuss the propensity of financial executives to use investment analysis techniques for more or less complex real assets. The content of this volume is organized according to the concept of a model of the financial innovation ecosystem which is illustrated in Fig. 1.2.

According to Lee and Shin (2018), the phenomenon of financial innovation occurs within the environment of an ecosystem formed by relevant stakeholders. With respect to the content of this volume, it is understood that the targets of financial innovation typically belong to three spheres, the individual, small- and medium-sized companies, and large companies, as can be seen in Fig. 1.2. In essence, today financial innovations can satisfy individual needs, from methods of payment to even financial products dedicated to retirement. At the same time, the operations of small- to medium-sized companies can benefit from financial innovations of various types ranging from fundraising to instruments which facilitate the relationships between companies and their customers and suppliers.

Within the context of companies listed on the stock exchange, opportunities for financial innovation still merit more discussion, given their complexity, and corporate relations with the market are already being affected by innovations such as the ESG report (Costa et al. 2018; Flores et al. 2018) and the refinement of corporate governance practices (Yermack 2017; Morabito 2017; Rossoni et al. 2018). In fact, a better understanding of individual behavior, combined with access to technology that is relevant to financial innovation, constitute determinant aspects for traditional financial institutions such as banks, fintech startups, and big tech companies, such as Facebook and Google, to create value for individuals and companies, by offering financial innovations in an increasingly unregulated environment, though they are still subject to the actions of policy makers.

Over the last few decades, we have witnessed the appearance and disappearance of financial innovations. Credit cards, credit unions, informal credit, and derivatives of various types are widely known, but other innovations are still relatively unknown to a large group of countries around the world. And certainly the emergence of technologies will induce innovations which will provoke changes in industry and the behavior of individuals. Being a pioneer in knowledge and intelligence certainly will offer conditions to take advantage of opportunities. Later on we will discuss future avenues for research on financial innovation. It is hoped that the use of technologies, as well as the development of convergence studies in this area – contemplating the behavior of agents – will be reflected more explicitly in the field literature in the coming years.

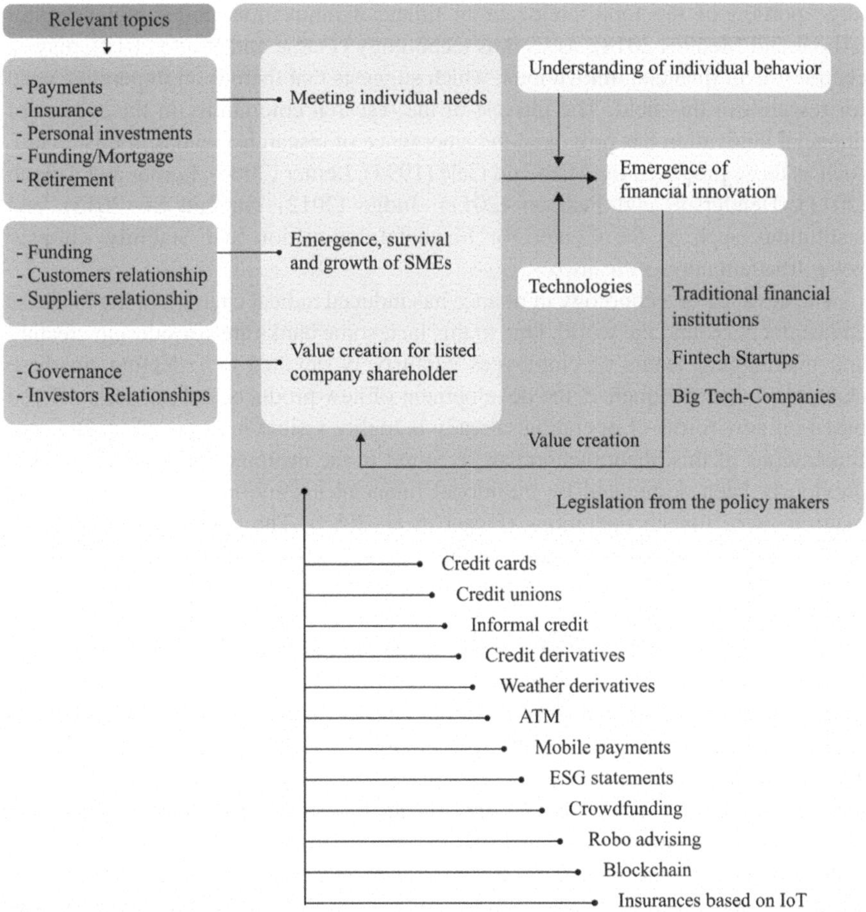

Fig. 1.2 Model of the financial innovation ecosystem. (Source: Prepared by the author. This figure presents the financial innovation ecosystem that this volume is based on. The left portion of the figure lists examples of financial innovation themes which are relevant to the three levels of analysis proposed in our ecosystem model, i.e., individuals, small- and medium-sized companies, and companies listed on the stock exchange. The right side of the figure lists sources of financial innovation, i.e., traditional financial institutions as well as fintechs and big tech companies, which propose financial innovations based on available technologies and their knowledge of individual behavior. The bottom part of the figure lists examples of financial innovation that result from the ecosystem, ranging from the oldest, e.g., credit and debit cards, to the most recent, e.g., robo-advising and insurance based on IoT)

Future Directions

In as far as this book examines financial innovations through individual behavior and technology, the dynamics of this industry have led to changes at such a rate that sufficiently broad empirical evidence still has not been documented in terms of a large portion of the topics relevant to financial innovation. Individual behavior (Abreu and Mendes 2018), as well as technology (Frame and White 2012), plays a central role in financial innovations, which suggests that there is an imperative need for research in this field. The interest of the research community in the subject of financial innovation has provoked the emergence of research agendas in this regard, such as those proposed by Allen and Gale (1994), Lerner (2006), Lerner and Tufano (2011), Henderson and Pearson (2011), Judge (2012), Su and Si (2015), and institutions such as the Center for Financial Innovation and Stability <https://www.frbatlanta.org/cenfis.aspx>.

The advance of technology in finance has induced radical changes in the business environment around the world. Due to this fact, some banks are considering creating and maintaining teams of employees exclusively devoted to reflecting on these changes. As a consequence, the development of new products and services, offered based on new forms of operating, already is highly visible in financial institutions. Illustrations of this phenomenon can be found in the insurance area, which having previously been dominated by traditional financial institutions, is now one of the main areas of fintech operations (Fuster et al. 2018). The operations of financial institutions themselves have gone through great transformations due to financial innovations, including the use of robo-advisors used by banks to relate to some of their customers (IMF 2017).

However, whether they're large financial institutions or financial services startups (of the most diverse known types or new ones that soon will appear), all of these firms need to know the demands and preferences of household decision-makers or even the management of different sized companies (Abreu and Mendes 2018; Li et al. 2018; Kunreuther et al. 2013). This places the study of financial innovation on the individual level under the spotlight, to the extent that the bottom line is that people make institutions, as argued by Li et al. (2018). For example, crowdfunding platforms (in their various forms) work because they have a heightened interest in promoting the success of their fundraising campaigns, and the literature has documented how the success of these campaigns is strongly dependent on the commitment of the people who support them.

Financial innovations have found a place to proliferate in the growing deregulation of markets and relationships. Therefore, issues related to trust between agents occupy center stage, since regulation has ceased to act as the gatekeeper, ceding its spot to the social capital implicit in relationships which form individual networks. The absence of, or at least the reduction of, centralized regulation has made room for the autoregulation practiced by fintechs. As a result of this movement, nonfinancial companies are being affected by innovations in financial services to the extent that the demands of society are presented more explicitly and exert growing pressures on these companies.

This phenomenon can induce changes in a company's internal mechanisms to the extent that the company responds adequately to external pressures, which can influence the company's level of performance, provoking changes in company behavior, for example, the adoption of an ESG report by some of the listed companies, or the use of crowdfunding platforms by startups interested in raising funds related to business prospecting. In terms of internal mechanisms, it is understood that governance practices and the management of supplier relationship networks, for example, can be influenced by the adoption of technologies such as a blockchain.

Blockchain

In essence, a blockchain is a relatively recent technology which offers the chance to create relevant new financial products with a heightened potential for disruptive transformation in the urban context, as discussed by Marsal-Llacuna (2018). As pointed out by Friedlob and Plewa (1996), for more than 7000 years humanity has used ledgers (here assumed to be the complete register of financial transactions during the life of an organization) to archive economic transactions. Since then, the technology supporting the registration and archiving of financial documents has undergone great changes, above all in terms of the sophistication of information technology. As a consequence, issues related to digital databases, organizational transparency, and data security have taken on a central role, which is where blockchain technology comes in Morabito (2017). Allayannis and Fernstrom (2017) state that blockchain technology makes it possible for user networks to track and trade virtually anything of value.

According to Liebenau and Elaluf-Calderwood (2016), blockchain technology can be seen both as a technical and as an economic innovation – and it is touted as one of the most significant technical innovations in the digitalization of asset ownership. In addition, blockchains have been demonstrated to be a flexible programmable platform for managing contracts and ownership and providing an audit trail that cannot easily be tampered with and can be distributed in real time. And, if we consider the initial words of Roger Wattenhofer, in the preface of *The Science of the Blockchain*, published in 2016, "Some fintech colleagues seem to understand the blockchain as a magic piece of code that allows the participants of a distributed system to agree on a common view of the system, to track changes in the system." But blockchain, the technology bitcoin is built on, is what matters. It's set to become the foundation for everything from public records to medical data to insurance.

There is an understanding that blockchain is a significant disruptor. Because of this understanding, business leaders in many different industries need to figure out what it means for them. Blockchain is different from every data system that has come before it, not least because it removes the need for an intermediary, a central authority, or any kind of trusted third party in transactions. Most ledgers are centralized; e.g., the Federal Reserve regulates the supply of money in the economy, and health-care records are stored in large private centralized servers, but a blockchain is a distributed database that stores records in blocks (Portion C of Fig. 1.3).

Every block is linked to the next in chronological order using a unique cryptographic signature. These chains of transactions form a permanent ledger, openly

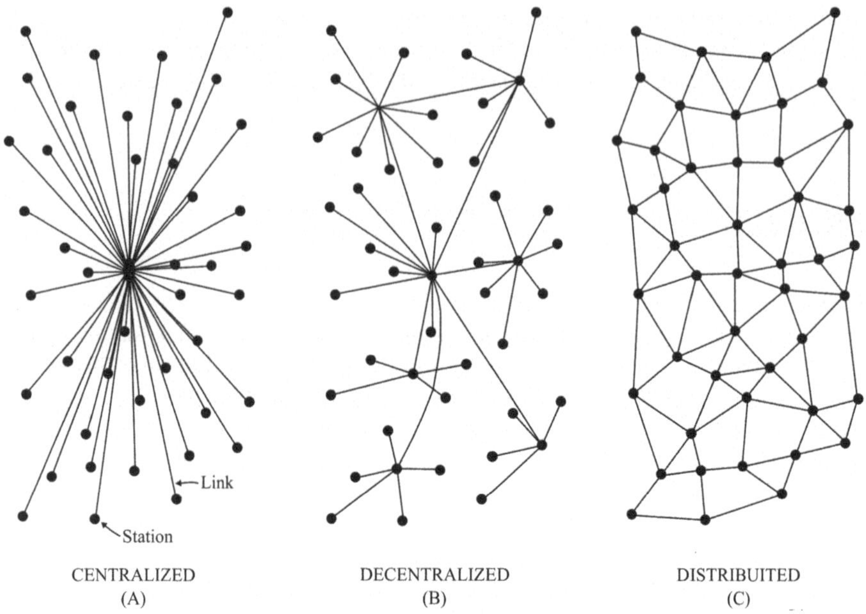

Fig. 1.3 Centralized, decentralized, and distributed ledgers

distributed among multiple parties in a peer-to-peer network. Once information is stored in the blockchain, no one can revise it or tamper with it: Attempted changes are easily detected and rejected. In a blockchain, there's no need for a central authority because the system makes it almost impossible to interfere with the data. That immutability – the guarantee that information on the blockchain can be trusted – takes the potential of blockchains way beyond cryptocurrencies. The demands for future research regarding blockchains, according to Lindman et al. (2017) revolve around three main axes: organizational issues, the competitive environment, and the design of the technology. The potential applications of blockchains are ample and can include business, health care, and private and public organizations, as can be seen in Table 1.1. In finance, the applications of blockchains are mainly associated with fintechs.

Fintechs

In the progression of financial innovations, financial technology companies, known as fintechs, have led to calls for caution in terms of the financial system, given that they represent a global phenomenon oriented toward the offering of financial service industry innovations which can pose risks to the system (Fuster et al. 2018). This is why fintechs represent an important area of research within the area of financial

Table 1.1 Potential applications of blockchains

Finance	Policy making	Internet of Things (IoT)	Health care	Business and science
Banking	P2P bonds	Connected vehicles	Health tokens	Mortgages
Crowdfunding	Voting	Self-driving cars	Databanks	Artificial intelligence
Currencies	Contract automation	Agricultural networks		P2P
Fintech	Tax receipts	Drones	Smart properties	Smart contracts
Insurance		Smart homes sensors		Community supercomputing
Payments		Robotics		
Procurement				
Corporate governance				

Source: Elaborated by the author based on Nicoletti (2017), Morabito (2017), Yermack (2017), and Bambara and Allen (2018)

innovation. In turn, these innovations imply new technologies that stimulate the elimination of intermediaries in these transactions, which is a role that has traditionally been played by financial institutions. And this process occurs essentially through digital channels. The typical activity of a fintech has led to the emergence of companies focused on big data analytics, robotics, mobility, and tech organizations, which have figured in the disruptive processes within the finance industry.

According to BIS (2017), although fintechs are only the latest wave of innovation to affect the banking industry, the rapid adoption of enabling technologies and the emergence of new business models pose an increasing challenge to traditional banks in almost all the scenarios considered. Banking standards and supervisory expectations should be able to adapt to new innovations while maintaining appropriately prudent standards. Against this background, the Basel Committee on Banking Supervision (BCBS) has identified ten key observations and related recommendations on the following supervisory issues to be considered by banks and bank supervisors:

- The overarching need to ensure safety and soundness and high compliance standards without inhibiting beneficial innovations in the banking sector
- The key risks for banks related to fintech developments, including strategic/profitability risks, operational, cyber, and compliance risks
- The implications for banks of the use of innovative enabling technologies
- The implications for banks of the growing use of third parties, via outsourcing and/or partnerships
- Cross-sectoral cooperation between supervisors and other relevant authorities
- International cooperation between banking supervisors
- Adaptability of the skill sets of supervisors

- Potential opportunities for supervisors to use innovative technologies ("suptech")
- Relevance of existing regulatory frameworks for new innovative business models
- Key features of regulatory initiatives set up to facilitate fintech innovation

Fintechs leverage the explosion of big data in terms of individuals and firms, advances in artificial intelligence, computing power, cryptography, and the reach of the Internet. The strong complementary characteristics of these technologies are giving rise to an impressive array of new applications touching on services ranging from payments to financing, asset management, insurance, and financial advice, reinforcing the relevance of convergence (NRC 2014). The possibility now looms that entities driven by fintechs may emerge as competitive alternatives to traditional financial intermediaries, markets, and infrastructure (He et al. 2017). Given that this is a recent phenomenon which at the same time is surrounded by growing expectations, fintechs require research relating to these open issues.

Among the financial service opportunities within the context of the financial innovation ecosystem, Fig. 1.4 depicts the three product sectors, as well as market support services, that reflect the enabling technologies which support these innovative products. The three sectors relate directly to core banking services, while the market support services relate to innovations and new technologies that are not specific to the financial sector but also play a significant role in fintech developments.

The growing elimination of intermediaries in financial services promoted by fintechs is helping make transactions in the financial system more efficient, especially because they permit greater flexibility, transparency, liquidity, and a reduction in transaction costs (Fuster et al. 2018) in mature markets, but even more so in developing markets, in which companies that offer financial services operate using

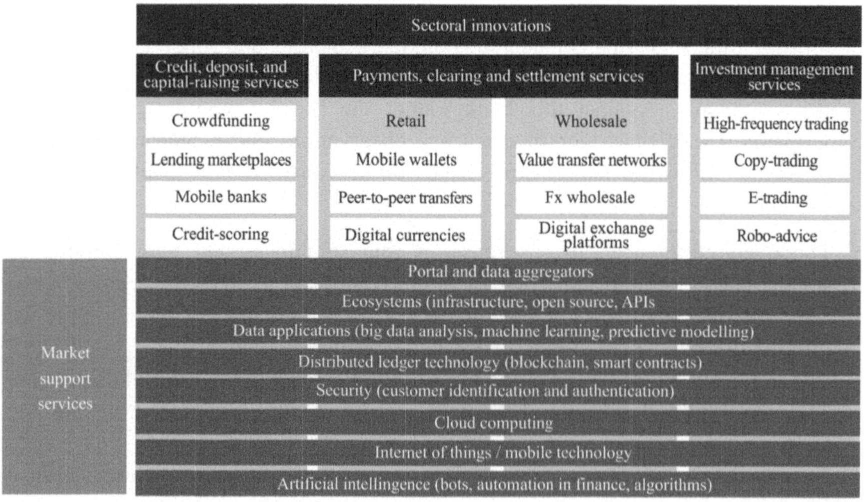

Fig. 1.4 Innovative service sectors. (Source: Adapted from the BIS-Bank for International Settlements 2017, p. 9)

more fragile and less efficient mechanisms, creating economic friction that requires attention. That is, financial technology and innovation have the potential to restore trust in the financial markets, especially by reducing friction caused by low levels of transparency, which implies adverse selection and moral hazards (Gubler 2011). Thus, the identification of fraud – through the employment of technologies such as big data and machine learning, the reduction of volatility through the better risk management that IoT offers, and the increase of transparency and fairness that has been verified in the transactions supported by blockchains, are typical examples of the contributions that technology provides to the field of finance.

The growing role of fintechs, compared to traditional financial institutions that offer insurance, financing, investments, and methods of making payments, has resulted in radical changes in the behavior of various players, ranging from policy makers and the finance industry to consumers (Fuster et al. 2018). The consequences of this process can be seen in the reduction in the number of commercial bank branches all over the world, which are expected to decrease during the period of 2015–2025 by 33% in the United States and 50% in the Nordic countries, according to the World Bank and Citi Research. This reduction of commercial bank branches between 2015 and 2025 may lead to a large reduction in the number of bank employees, roughly 40% of full-time employees according to recent estimates by the US Bureau of Labor Statistics. In fact, fintechs occupy a central role in the reconfiguration of the competitive arena within the finance industry, but these startups have rarely been acquired by large financial institutions, which apparently are initiating a new industry movement characterized by heavy investments in developing in-house technology.

According to Cesare Fracassi, professor at the McCombs School of Business, as of January 2018, of the 50 top banks operating in the United States (by total asset value), such as the Bank of America, Wells Fargo, Citibank, and Morgan Stanley, 80% of them have not acquired a single fintech startup. At the same time, banks like Morgan Stanley have already launched their own robo-advisor services. Goldman Sachs, in addition to launching robo-advisor services, is considering launching its own platform for online lending. On the other hand, the large technology companies like Google, Microsoft, Facebook, and Amazon are continually sending out signals that they are disposed to compete in the offering of financial services, side by side with traditional financial institutions.

Financial Networks

As argued by Allen and Gale (1994), the sharing of risks and opportunities within the highly complex environment that characterizes financial networks constitutes a relevant research agenda which has received relatively little attention, which is a view shared by Wainwright (2013), Battiston et al. (2016), and Pollak and Guan (2017). Financial networks have been on the research agenda since the so-called subprime financial crisis of 2008/2009. Today, both regulators and academia in general recognize that interconnectedness was a crucial component which played a key role in the exacerbation of losses during this crisis. Therefore, understanding the structure of financial networks is important in assessing, monitoring, and regulating financial systems. In addition, this crisis washed away the belief that supervising banks operating individually would be able to guarantee the safety of the financial system, as networks can greatly amplify negative spillover effects.

It is inherently complex to analyze modern financial networks as economic agents that participate in a multiplex of interrelationships in several different markets (Rossoni et al. 2018; Anagnostou et al. 2018; Eberhard et al. 2017; Pollak and Guan 2017; He and Li 2017). Investigating this heterogeneity of interconnections is an important standing problem because each connection can potentially create channels that transmit contagion, which can thereby amplify losses. Financial institutions form multilayered networks by engaging in contracts with each other and by sharing exposure to assets they have in common (Engelmann et al. 2017).

Social Impact of Financial Innovations

The relationship between emerging technologies, such as blockchains, fintechs, and IoT, with the transformation of the urban context is something that is present in the recent literature (Marsal-Llacuna 2018). Considering the gamut of topics for future research within financial innovations, especially on an individual level and in terms of issues related to the role of technology, it is notable that no matter which of these topics we consider, their impact on the dynamics of society appears to be a particularly important field.

In respect to the social impact of innovations, Smilor et al. (1989) propose a conceptual model that they call the *technopolis wheel*, in which these authors point to financial incentives as the main medium for local development, using the city of Austin, Texas, as a case study. The model represented in Fig. 1.5 illustrates the integration of the seven main segments of the city's development based on technology. One of their most relevant impacts is their potential effects on the continuity of companies, whether they are in the financial sector or not, as well as their promotion of personal well-being.

Positive impacts on daily city life can be observed through the use of financial technology. To illustrate this point, the use of financial innovation technologies can contribute to attenuating the effects of crime in major cities in South America. Bank attacks and robberies are part of peoples' daily lives. During the first half of 2017, 880 attacks on banks were registered in Brazil, including 442 explosions, 284 robberies, and 174 assaults, distributed throughout the country (Contrast 2017). In this aspect, beyond the simple definition of digital transformation, companies frequently find that their most difficult task is how to properly guide and align their organizations in terms of what their vision of digital transformation will be. Thus, it is not uncommon that executives do not seem to know how to conduct change so that it will help their organizations achieve their objectives in terms of creating value, cash

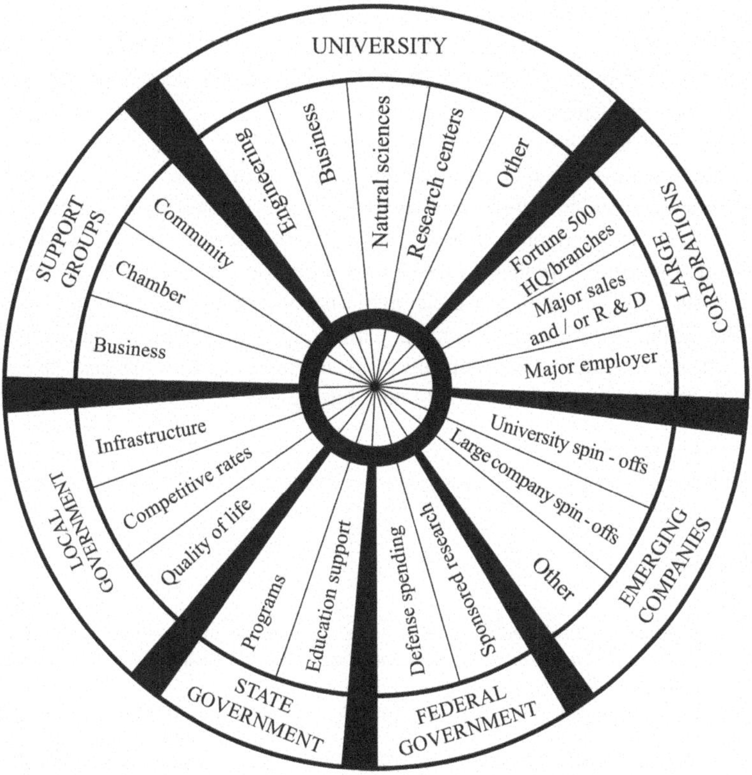

Fig. 1.5 The technopolis wheel. (Source: Adapted from Smilor et al. 1989, p. 51)

flow, and continuity within the context of disruptive change, which apparently will remain with us in the years ahead.

In the midst of this discussion, it seems important to consider that frequently managers are reluctant to align their organizations with new market practices, imposed by new technologies. In this way, it may be understood that financial innovations deserve special attention, given their potential to act as a player that induces development, and keeping in mind their resulting impacts on different levels, ranging from the individual, to the corporate, to the national level. Some cities are seen as centers for financial innovations. What are the typical attributes of a city considered to be a financial innovation center? Sassen (2005) suggests that global cities perform coordinating roles and functions instead of competing against rivals, which is an opinion shared by Wainwright (2013).

Continuing this line of thought, the CSFI (2003) discusses the reasons why certain cities, like New York, are viewed as financial innovation centers, just as London is viewed as an international banking and finance center, Tokyo is viewed as a key provider of unprocessed capital, and Paris is viewed as a global financial center due to the structural features of its banking and financial systems. At the same time, this vision of global cities admits that large cities, such as these, usually also have characteristics that can compromise the quality of life for their residents and visitors, given that most have high costs of living, a large degree of competition for top positions, and great stress.

Nonetheless, technology makes it possible to offer financial services in a decentralized manner, frequently eliminating intermediaries, which can facilitate the emergence of cities with a high quality of life, which at the same time are relevant players in the finance industry. In addition, researchers such as Macomber (2016) have identified financial innovations as a way to address an issue that is central to our civilization: how we can avoid becoming a planet of informal slums, just as the digital revolution is occurring, which represents the most significant event of the past few decades? The maturing of these emerging technologies may be the key to this process of promoting well-being throughout the cities of the world (Jaffe et al. 2017).

References

Abreu, M., & Mendes, V. (2018). The investor in structured retail products: advice driven or gambling oriented? *Journal of Behavioral and Experimental Finance, 17*, 1–9. https://doi.org/10.1016/j.jbef.2017.12.001.

Allayannis, Y., & Fernstrom, A. (2017). *An introduction to blockchain*. Background Note Harvard #UV7356.

Allen, F., & Gale, D. (1994). *Financial innovation and risk sharing*. Cambridge, MA: MIT Press.

Anagnostou, I., Sourabh, S., & Kandhai, D. (2018). Incorporating contagion in portfolio credit risk models using network theory. *Complexity*. Article ID 6076173. https://doi.org/10.1155/2018/6076173.

Arrow, K. (1962). Economic Welfare and the Allocation of Resources for Invention, in Universities-National Bureau Committee for Economic Research, Committee on Economic Growth of the Social Science Research Council (eds), The Rate and Direction of Inventive Activity: Economic and Social Factors, Princeton University Press, pp. 609–626. ISBN: 0-87014-304-2. Available at: http://papers.nber.org/books/univ62-1

Arrow, K. (1969). Classificatory notes on the production and transmission of technological knowledge. *American Economic Review, 59*(2), 29–35.

Bambara, J. J., & Allen, P. R. (2018). *Blockchain: A practical guide to developing business, law, and technology solutions*. New York: McGrawHill.

Battiston, S., Caldarelli, G., May, R. M., Roukny, T., & Stiglitz, J. E. (2016). The price of complexity in financial networks. *Social Sciences – Economic Sciences – Physical Sciences – Physics, 113*(36), 10031–10036. https://doi.org/10.1073/pnas.1521573113.

BIS-Bank for International Settlements. (1986). *Recent innovations in international banking*. Basel: BIS.

BIS-Bank for International Settlements. (2017). *Sound practices: Implications of fintech developments for banks and bank supervisors*. Basel: BIS Available at: https://www.bis.org/bcbs/publ/d415.pdf.

Bloomestein, H. (2000). *The changing nature of risk and the challenges to sound risk management in the new global financial landscape*. Paris: OECD.

Bozeman, B. (2000). Technology transfer and public policy: A review of research and theory. *Research Policy, 29*(4–5), 627–655. https://doi.org/10.1016/S0048-7333(99)00093-1.

Chen, M. C., Chen, S. S., Yeh, H. M., & Tsaur, W. G. (2016). The key factors influencing internet finances services satisfaction: An empirical study in Taiwan. *American Journal of Industrial and Business Management, 6*(6), 748–762. https://doi.org/10.4236/ajibm.2016.66069.

Contrast-Confederacao dos Trabalhadores de Seguranca Privada. (2017). *Pesquisa Nacional de Ataques a Bancos Primeiro Semestre de 2017*. Available at: http://contrasp.org.br/wp-content/uploads/2017/08/BANCOS2017.pdf.

Costa, O., Fuerst, F., Robinson, S. J., & Mendes-Da-Silva, W. (2018). Green label signals in an emerging real estate market. A case study of Sao Paulo, Brazil. *Journal of Cleaner Production, 184*, 660–670.

CSFI-Centre for the Study of Financial Innovation. (2003). *Sizing up the city – London's ranking as a financial centre*. Available at: http://www.longfinance.net/FCF/SizingUpTheCity.pdf. Acessed February 27, 2018.

Dunning, J. H. (1981). Alternative channels and modes of international resource transmission. In T. Sagafi-Nejad, H. Perlmutter, & R. Moxon (Eds.), *Controlling international technology transfer: Issues, perspectives and implications*. New York: Permagon.

Dunning, J. H. (1994). Multinational enterprises and the globalization of innovatory capacity. *Research Policy, 23*(1), 67–88

Eberhard, J., Lavin, J. F., & Montecinos-Pearce, A. (2017). A network-based dynamic analysis in an equity stock market. *Complexity*. Article ID 3979836. https://doi.org/10.1155/2017/3979836.

Engelmann, F., Kopp, H., Kargl, F., Glaser, F., & Weinhardt, C. (2017). Toward and economic analysis of routing in payment channel networks. In *Proceedings... SERIAL 2017 Conference*.

Flores, E., Mendes-Da-Silva, W., & Fasan, M. (2018). The improvement effect of the integrated reporting adoption on the accuracy of capital market analysts. In *Proceedings... BALAS 2018, San Diego. Bridging Borders for Peace and Prosperity*

Frame, W. S., & White, L. J. (2012). Technological change, financial innovation, and diffusion in banking. In A. N. Berger, P. Mlyneux, & J. O. S. Wilson (Eds.), *Oxford handbooks online*. Oxford: Oxford University Press. https://doi.org/10.1093/oxfordhb/9780199640935.013.0019.

Friedlob, G. T., & Plewa, F. J. (1996). *Understanding balance sheets*. New York: Wiley.

Fuster, A., Plosser, M., Schnabl, P., & Vickery, J. (2018). *The role of technology on mortgage lending*. Federal Reserve Bank of New York Staff Reports, no. 836.

Gubler, Z. J. (2011). The Financial Innovation Process: Theory and Application (2011). *Delaware Journal of Corporate Law (DJCL), 36*(1), 55–119. Available at SSRN: https://ssrn.com/abstract=1905458.

He, L., & Li, S. (2017). Network entropy and systemic risk in dynamic banking systems. *Complexity*. Article ID 1852897. https://doi.org/10.1155/2017/1852897.

He, D., Leckow, R., Haksar, V., Mancini-Griffoli, T., Jenkinson, N., Kashima, M., Khiaonarong, T., Rochon, C., & Tourpe, H. (2017). *Fintech and financial services: Initial considerations*. IMF staff discussion note SDN/17/05.

Henderson, B. J., & Pearson, N. D. (2011). The dark side of financial innovation: A case study of the pricing of a retail financial product. *Journal of Financial Economics, 100*(2), 227–247. https://doi.org/10.1016/j.jfineco.2010.12.006.

IMF. (2017). Fintech and financial services: Initial considerations, IMF staff discussion notes no. 17/05. Available at: https://www.imf.org/en/Publications/Staff-Discussion-Notes/Issues/2017/06/16/Fintech-and-Financial-Services-Initial-Considerations-44985.

Jaffe, C., Mata, C., & Kamvar, S. (2017). Motivating urban cycling through a blockchain-based financial incentives system. In *Proceedings... UniCamp 2017* (pp. 81–87).

Judge, K. (2012). Fragmentation nodes: A study in financial innovation, complexity, and systemic risk. *Stanford Law Review, 64*(3), 657–725.

Kahneman, D., & Tversky, A. (1979). Prospect Theory: An Analysis of Decision under Risk. *Econometrica, 47*(2), 263.

Kim, Y., Park, Y. J., & Choi, J. (2016). The adoption of mobile payment services for fintech. *International Journal of Applied Engineering Research, 11*(2), 1058–1061.

Kumar, V., Kumar, U., & Persaud, A. (1999). Building technological capability through importing technology: The case of Indonesian manufacturing industry. *Journal of Technology Transfer, 24*, 81–96.

Kunreuther, D. H. C., Pauly, M. V., & McMorrow, S. (2013). *Insurance & Behavioral Economics: Improving decisions in the most misunderstood industry*. Cambridge: Cambridge University Press.

Lan, Y., & Young, S. (1996). International technology transfer examined at technology component level: a case study in China. *Technovation, 16*(6), 277–286.

Lee, I., & Shin, Y. J. (2018). Fintech: Ecosystem, business models, investment decisions, and challenges. *Business Horizons, 61*, 35–46.

Lerner, J. (2006). The new new financial thing: The origins of financial innovations. *Journal of Financial Economics, 79*(2), 223–255. https://doi.org/10.1016/j.jfineco.2005.01.004.

Lerner, J., & Tufano, P. (2011). The consequences of financial innovation: A counterfactual research agenda. *Annual Review of Financial Economics, 3*(1), 41–85.

Li, X., Subrahmanyam, A., & Yang, X. (2018). Can financial innovation succeed by catering to behavioral preferences? Evidence from a callable options market. *Journal of Financial Economics, 128*(1), 38–65. https://doi.org/10.1016/j.jfineco.2018.01.010.

Liebenau, J., & Elaluf-Calderwood, S. M. (2016). *Blockchain innovation beyond bitcoin and banking*. Available at SSRN 2749890.

Lindman, J., Rossi, M., & Tuunainen, V. K. (2017). Opportunities and risks of blockchain technologies in payments-a research agenda. In *Proceedings of the 50th Hawaii International Conference on system Sciences*.

Llewellyn, D. T. (2009). Financial innovation and the economics of banking and the financial system. In L. Anderloni, D. T. Llewellyn, & R. H. Schmidt (Eds.), *Financial innovation in retail and corporate banking: New horizons in money and finance*. Northampton, MA: Edward Elgar.

Lovell, S. A. (1998). Technology Transfer: Testing a Theoretical Model of the Human, Machine, Mission, Management and Medium Components. Unpublished Msc. thesis. Cranfield: College of Aeronautics, Cranfield University.

Macomber, J. D. (2016). The future of cities depends on innovative financing. *Harvard Business Review*. Web Article Product #: H02L7R-PDF-ENG. Available at: https://hbr.org/2016/01/the-future-of-cities-depends-on-innovative-financing.

Marsal-Llacuna, M.-L. (2018). Future living framework: Is blockchain the next enabling network? *Technological Forecasting and Social Change, 128*, 226–234. https://doi.org/10.1016/j.techfore.2017.12.005.

Merton, R. C. (1992). Financial innovation and the management and regulation of financial institutions. *Journal of Banking & Finance, 19*(3–4), 461–481. https://doi.org/10.1016/0378-4266(94)00133-N.

MIT Technology Review. (2018). *Upfront, 121*(1), 24.

Morabito, V. (2017). *Business innovation through blockchain: The B^3 perspective*. New York: Springer.

Mottura, P. (2009). *Financial innovation in retail and corporate banking: New horizons in money and finance*. Cheltenham/Northampton: Edward Elgar.

Nicoletti, B. (2017). The Future of FinTech: Integrating Finance and Technology in Financial Services. Springer Nature. ISBN-13: 978-3319514147

NRC-National Research Council. (2014). *Convergence: Facilitating transdisciplinary integration of life sciences, physical sciences, engineering, and beyond*. Washington, DC: The National Academies Press. https://doi.org/10.17226/18722.

Pollak, M., & Guan, Y. (2017). Partially overlapping ownership and contagion in financial networks. *Complexity*. Article ID 9895632. https://doi.org/10.1155/2017/9895632.

Reddy, N. M., & Zhao, L. (1990). International technology transfer: A review. *Research Policy, 19*, 285–307.

Rossoni, L., Aranha, C. E., & Mendes-Da-Silva, W. (2018). The complexity of social capital: The influence of board and ownership interlocks on implied cost of capital in an emerging market. *Complexity*. Article ID 6248427. https://doi.org/10.1155/2018/6248427.

Samuelson, P. A. (1937). A note on the measurement of utility. *The Review of Economic Studies, 4*, 155–161.

Sassen, S. (2005). The global city: Introducing a concept. *Brown Journal of World Affairs, 11*(2), 27–43.

Schierz, P. G., Schilke, O., & Wirtz, B. (2010). Understanding customer acceptance of mobile payment services: An empirical analysis. *Electronic Commerce Research and Applications, 9* (3), 209–216.

Schmookler, J. A. (1967). *Intervention and economic growth*. Cambridge, MA: Harvard University Press.

SDPS-Society for Design and Process Science. (2017). In *22nd International Conference Emerging Trends and Technologies in Convergence Solutions*. Final Program, Available at: https://www.sdpsnet.org/sdps/documents/sdps-2017/advanced-program-low.pdf. Accessed 25 March 2018.

Shefrin, H. M., & Thaler, R. H. (1981). An economic theory of self control. *Journal of Political Economy, 89*, 392–406.

Shiller, R. (2006). Tools for financial innovation: The neoclassical versus behavioral finance. *The Financial Review, 41*, 1–8.

Smilor, R. W., Gibson, D. V., & Kozmetsky, G. (1989). Creating the technopolis: high-technology development in Austin, Texas. *Journal of Business Venturing, 4*(1), 49–67.

Su, Y., & Si, S. (2015). What motivates financial innovation across countries? The influences of performance aspiration and economic freedom. *Management International Review, 55*(4), 563–587.

Thaler, R. H., & Tucker, W. (2013). Smarter information, smarter consumers. *Harvard Business Review* Available at: https://hbr.org/.

Tufano, P. (2003). Financial innovation. In G. M. Constatinides, M. Harris, & R. M. Stulz (Eds.), *Handbook of the economics of finance* (Vol. 1A). New York: Elsevier.

Wainwright, T. (2013). Finance's outsiders?: Networks, knowledge and power beyond the city. *Journal of Economic Geography, 13*(6), 1041–1058. https://doi.org/10.1093/jeg/lbs051.

Wattenhofer, R. (2016). *The science of the blockchain*. Charleston: Inverted Forest Publishing.

White, L. J. (2000). Technological change, financial innovation, and financial regulation in the US: The challenge for public policy. In D. Harker & S. Zenios (Eds.), *Performance of financial innovations* (pp. 80–91). Cambridge: Cambridge University Press.

Yermack, D. (2017). Corporate governance and blockchains. *Review of Finance, 21*(1), 7–31. https://doi.org/10.1093/rof/rfw074.

Chapter 2
Gender Differences and Automobile Insurance Acquisition

Edimilson Costa Lucas, Wesley Mendes-Da-Silva, and Angela Christine Lyons

Abstract This chapter examines the associations between driver gender, risk behavior when driving motor vehicles, and the inclination to acquire automobile insurance. To inform this investigation, a random survey was conducted of 566 middle-class adults. By using nonparametric tests and logit models, the results suggest that even when controlling for other variables, women feel a greater need than men to have automobile insurance in the event of possible accidents under rainy conditions and to have access to driver support services. Women also tend to have more respect for speed limits in various situations, such as during the rush hour, on local roads and on highways. The results also showed that men feel safer than women when driving in more precarious situations: at night, in unfamiliar areas, after drinking, or when they are tired. These results, while contributing to the theoretical development of road traffic and transportation safety, are of special relevance to the financial industry and the regulatory agency. The insurance industry may find these results particularly helpful in designing future policies and setting premiums.

Keywords Gender differences · Risk taking · Attitude toward driving · Insurance · Traffic safety

JEL Code G22 · J16 · L62

Portions of this chapter appeared in the 2017 paper "Gender differences in attitudes towards driving and demand for private Insurance: Evidence from middle class drivers," *Transportation Research Part F-Traffic Psychology and Behaviour*, vol 47, pp 72–85.

E. C. Lucas
Department of Business Economics, Federal University of São Paulo, Osasco, SP, Brazil

W. Mendes-Da-Silva (✉)
Sao Paulo School of Business Administration (FGV/EAESP), Sao Paulo, SP, Brazil

University of Texas at Austin, Austin, TX, USA

A. C. Lyons
University of Illinois at Urbana Champaign, Urbana, IL, USA
e-mail: anglyons@uiuc.edu

W. Mendes-Da-Silva (ed.), *Individual Behaviors and Technologies for Financial Innovations*, https://doi.org/10.1007/978-3-319-91911-9_2

Are men more inclined to assume risks than women? This question is immediately relevant to various economic issues, including human behavior with regard to traffic and transportation safety (Friedl et al. 2017; Nunen et al. 2016). The theoretical lines in the field of traffic and transportation safety point to the predominance of the inclination for men to take risks. Literature has empirically documented the recklessness of men, especially young men (Møller and Haustein 2014). One of the ten main causes of death worldwide is traffic accidents (WHO 2013), and countries with emerging economies have the largest number of traffic-related deaths. In absolute terms this list of countries is led by China, India, Nigeria, and Brazil, the latter being the country with the second highest number of deaths caused by traffic accidents per 100,000 inhabitants (Table 2.1).

Gender-based differences in taking risks while driving have been of interest to industry, policy makers, and the international academic community (Bergdahl 2005; Falk and Montgomery 2009; González-Iglesias et al. 2012; Obst et al. 2011; Özkan and Lajunen 2006; WIIT 2014). Various industries (e.g., insurance, tourism, education, vehicles, and health care) seek understanding of this phenomenon, and the insurance industry has keen interest in studying human behavior while driving.

Kunreuther and Michel-Kerjan (2013) advocate that the insurance industry, while not well understood by individuals, is highly relevant to the resilience of society. Kunreuther and Michel-Kerjan (2013) also emphasize the gap that exists when policy makers are unable to reduce this apparent distance between the supply of and demand for insurance services, which leads to both diminished opportunity for industry and the well-being of consumers.

This study addresses an issue of utmost importance to policy makers, to the financial industry, and to the resilience society as a whole. This research is particularly relevant as it offers evidence of driver behaviors in Brazil, a country with one of the largest populations in the world and one of the highest death rates related to

Table 2.1 Countries with the largest number of traffic deaths in absolute numbers (2013)

Country	Population (millions)[a]	#Total deaths[b]	Deaths/100,000 inhabitants[b]	Licensed vehicles (million)[b]	Deaths/motor vehicles (‰)[b]
China	1348.03	275,983	20.5	207.06	1.33
India	1224.61	231,027	18.9	114.95	2.01
Nigeria	158.42	53,339	33.7	12.55	4.25
Brazil[c]	194.95	42,844	22.5[c]	64.82	0.66[c]
Indonesia	239.87	42,734	17.7	72.69	0.59
United States	310.38	35,490	11.4	258.96	0.14
Pakistan	173.59	30,131	17.4	7.85	3.84
Russia	142.96	26,567	18.6	43.33	0.61

Sources: [a]Population Division of the United Nations Organization. [b]*Global Report on Road Safety 2013* from the WHO. [c]Datasus 2010

Note: This table shows the countries with the largest number of traffic deaths in absolute terms. Base year: 2010 traffic accidents (see Table 2.1). Both theoretical and empirical research show, according to Efrat and Shoham (2013), that aggressive driving is a growing problem worldwide. This underscores the value that this work brings to the literature (Cross et al. 2011; Charness and Gneezy 2012), in line with the aspects of theoretical contributions indicated by Wacker (1998) and Whetten (1989).

Based on these arguments, i.e., the distance between consumers and insurance companies, poor actions by policy makers, and the few studies carried out in Brazil (Velloso and Jacques 2012), this chapter presents research highlights and analyzes the associations between gender and risk behavior when driving motor vehicles including the likelihood to acquire insurance. The findings from this research provide insight into how financial professionals and policy makers might provide more effective financial products to society. The chapter concludes with recommendations for research that might further this field of inquiry.

Background

On a global scale, traffic and transportation safety in Brazil are of particular interest. Table 2.1 reports key transportation and safety statistics for the eight countries with the largest number of traffic-related deaths. These statistics show that Brazil ranks second worldwide, in terms of deaths per 100,000 inhabitants. Also, while Brazil has only 25% of the number of vehicles as does the United States, the number of traffic-related deaths in Brazil is 10% higher than in the United States, resulting in a death rate by motor vehicle that is more than four times higher in Brazil (0.66) than in the United States (0.14).

To place our findings in context, it is important also to provide a brief description of the Brazilian insurance industry. There are two types of insurance in Brazil: public insurance which is compulsory (Personal Injury Caused by Vehicles – DPVAT (government administered)) and insurance offered by private companies. Since 1974, vehicle owners in Brazil have been required by law to have DPVAT insurance (Federal Law 6.194/74). In the event of an accident, this insurance covers death, permanent partial or total disability, as well as medical expenses for accident victims. However, under the law, DPVAT's compensation limits are relatively small (US$ 3970 for death, up to US$ 3970 for disability, and up to US$ 795 for medical and hospital expenses, in 2014).

In addition, other risks are not covered by DPVAT, such as theft, natural disasters, and collisions. This has resulted in increased consumer demand for private insurance that offers protection around the total value of the vehicle, in addition to allowing for greater damages to third parties. Further, it is interesting to note that the Brazilian population is comprised almost equally of men (49%) and women (51%) (IBGE 2013). Yet, in 2013, DPVAT paid out 633,845 claims, of which 24% were to women and 76% were to men. Of the death claims (8.64%), 82% of the victims were men.

Of the five regions in Brazil, the southeast shows the highest number of traffic-related deaths (almost 36% of the cases), but it must also be noted that this region accounts for 56% of the country's automobile fleet. The total number of automobiles in Brazil is approximately 45.4 million, almost one automobile for every 4.4 Brazilians (Denatran 2014). Ten years ago the proportion was 7.4 inhabitants per automobile. The purchase of automobile insurance grew by 80% between 2006 and 2013, and between 2003 and 2012, the number of claims grew by around 107% (SUSEP 2013; DPVAT 2013).

Gender and Attitudes Toward Driving

A number of studies have looked at differences in risk-related driving behaviors between men and women (e.g., Cross et al. 2011; Charness and Gneezy 2012; Zuckerman 1988). Some of these studies reveal that men tend to feel safer than women when driving in risky situations, such as driving in snowstorms, in densely populated areas, or at high speeds (Farrow and Brissing 1990; Fergunson and Braitman 2006; Wieczorek et al. 1994). Some findings further suggest that men tend to assume more risk than women when at the wheel, thus causing more fatal events (Bergdahl and Norris 2002; Mannering 1993; Møller and Haustein 2014; Wolf et al. 2010). Bergdahl (2005) used nonparametric techniques on data collected from 198 university students in Texas.

He found that men tend to trust their driving skills more than women. Other researchers around the world have also focused on gender-based differences in behavior when driving vehicles. Özkan and Lajunen (2006) studied the phenomenon based on data collected in Turkey, and Oltedal and Rundmo (2006) analyzed the effects of personality traits and gender on risk behavior and involvement in accidents among Norwegian teenager drivers.

According to the main findings of Schwebel et al. (2006), the search for extreme sensations, i.e., feeling of excitement in risk conditions while driving motor vehicles, is one of the main predictors of traffic violations. This line of thinking is shared by Özkan and Lajunen (2006), who suggest that women tend to exhibit better safety skills in traffic, which is corroborated by the work of Lonczak et al. (2007). In analyzing the effect of age, Oltedal and Rundmo (2006) and Machin and Sankey (2008) obtained results that suggest that anxiety and the excitement of younger drivers are significantly associated with risk-related driving behavior and collisions.

Wolf et al. (2010) analyzed vehicle parking skills and the results indicated that men park faster and more accurately than women. However, younger male drivers tend to disrespect speed limits as compared to other drivers (Cestac et al. 2011). Based on a repertoire of evolutionist, development, and personality theories, Cross et al. (2011) conclude that risk activities are predominantly found in men. The presence of passengers can sometimes mitigate a driver's risk behaviors that violate traffic laws, especially if that passenger has a degree of relationship with the driver

(Johnson et al. 2012; Møller and Haustein 2014; Scott-Parker et al. 2012; Simons-Morton et al. 2011).

A literature review shows that despite Brazil's population size and considerable market for automobiles, there are relatively few studies that investigate gender differences among Brazilian drivers, even while recent years have shown significant growth in the automobiles fleet (155.4% from 2000 to 2016, a growth eight times that of the country's population increase over the same period), and the reduced use of private insurance, with high rates of disrespect for traffic legislation and the number of traffic accidents nationwide (Table 2.1), as well argued by Velloso and Jacques (2012) and Campos et al. (2013).

In order to provide an ethnographic explanation of male/female differences around issues including general attitudes toward law and order, when we examine the specific Brazilian context, it is interesting to consider that according to SIRC (2004), there is a strong consensus in the research literature that males are more likely to exceed speed limits and commit other traffic offenses than females. Official statistics support this general tendency in Brazil. According to Hautzinger (1997) and Renzetti et al. (2013), in Brazil a male is more likely than a female to commit crime. In 2014, when Brazil still had a woman as president, the Brazilian Justice Department verified explicit growth of the number of women punished by incarceration, 248.3% in the last 13 years, compared to a growth rate 145.3% among men, yet the population of prison inmates remains 15 times higher for men than women (DEPEN 2014).

Other countries with high rates of traffic-related deaths also document gender-based differences toward taking risk while driving. In China, Li et al. (2016) collected data by self-reported questionnaire that revealed gender-based differences in driving behaviors. This work expands on the analysis carried out by Bergdahl (2005) and others and contributes to the existing literature in at least four aspects: (i) in addition to nonparametric tests, multivariable analysis is used by way of binary response models; (ii) data was collected from residents in 66 different towns and cities; (iii) a larger set of subjects were surveyed than in previous studies; (iv) the dataset was expanded to analyze the inclination to acquire vehicle insurance. This research also deals with a different institutional environment of considerable size, the high traffic accident rates in Brazil, of which little research can be found.

Data and Variables

In January and February 2014, a traffic questionnaire used by Bergdahl (2005) was adapted for the Brazilian context with characteristics based on recommendations from Fowler (1998). This study implemented a self-reported survey based on a direct self-rating (Paulhus and Vazire 2011) that was administered via printed form to a nonrandom sample of 566 adults living in 66 Brazilian cities and towns. The 566 respondents were selected based on whether they were primarily responsible for the insurance decisions related to their own vehicle. The cities that took part in the survey were mostly located in the southeast region of Brazil (where most of the country's vehicle fleet is located).

These cities included São Paulo (15.34%), Bauru (14.72%), Osasco (7.06%), Ribeirão Preto (6.75%), and Santo André (5.21%). Other cities near these were included, while a few cities were also included in the region of Brasília and Goiânia (10.43%) near the center of Brazil. Respondents were selected from diverse cities of origin to reduce selection biases arising from demographic and geographical patterns since they can sometimes influence driver behavior (Schroeder et al. 2013). Further, the regions of São Paulo and Brasília both attract people from all five major regions of Brazil, who migrate in search of opportunity. It is therefore reasonable to assume that São Paulo and Brasília represent the general profile of the Brazilian population (Baer 2014; Zhang 2010). The questionnaire included four parts: (i) respondent profile, (ii) situations for which the driver perceives the need to have insurance on the vehicle, (iii) driver's inclination to obey speed limits in different situations, and (iv) perception of safety when driving the vehicle in various situations. Table 2.2 presents the survey questions that were used in this study.

Analysis Strategy

The analysis procedure is organized in two parts: (i) univariate analysis, which presents the descriptive statistics and nonparametric tests for each variable, in an attempt to identify the existence of differences between male and female drivers, and (ii) multivariable analysis, using logit models that made it possible to compare eventual differences in behavior in traffic by way of the gender of the driver, taking into consideration other variables jointly. Eighteen logistic regression models were estimated.

Univariate Analysis

The sample consisted of 566 respondents. However, 100 observations were dropped to ensure sample robustness, following procedure from Inouei and Kilian (2005) and Patton (2004). The final sample was 466 subjects in which 60% were men with an average age of 33% and 40% were women with an average age of 31. Most of the respondents (72%) held managerial positions, and all were enrolled in postgraduate studies in various degree programs. Because the individuals were all postgraduate students and the majority held managerial positions, it is fair to say these were among the more educated and potentially wealthy members of the Brazilian population. For this reason, we must be somewhat cautious in generalizing our findings to the population of Brazilian drivers as a whole.

Most of the responses (83.05%) came from the state of São Paulo, which represents some 33% of the Brazilian gross domestic product. Around 85% of the

Table 2.2 Definition of the independent variables used in this study

Variables	Operational definition
1. Profile of the respondent	
Gender	= Dummy variable that identifies the gender of the respondent received value = 1 if a female and value = 0 otherwise
Age	= Continuous variable that gives the age of the respondent, expressed by the ln of the number of years
Region	= Dummy variable that expresses the region in which the respondent lives had a value = 1 if in the capital or metropolitan area and value = 0 if lived in upstate region according to *IBGE* criteria
Marital status	= Dummy variable that denotes the marital status of the respondent had a value = 1 if married and value = 0 otherwise
Time driving	= Time the respondent had been driving vehicles, expressed by the ln of the number of years
Do they have private insurance	= Dummy variable that denotes that the respondent has private automobile insurance had the value = 1 if yes and value = 0 otherwise
Frequency use of insurance	
Rate of motorization for city	
2. I feel the need to have the vehicle insured in these situations	The possible replies for each item were shown in a five-point Likert scale: always; frequently; sometimes; rarely; or never
Robbery; collision; accident involving personal injury to a third party; excessive rainfall; assistance services (tow truck and the like)	
3. I obey the speed limit in these situations	The possible responses for each item were presented in the form of a five-point Likert scale: always; frequently; sometimes; rarely; never
At night; in the rush hour; on main roads; on local streets and highways; close to my home; school zones; bad weather	
4. How I feel about driving in the following situations	The possible responses were presented as very safe, safe, indifferent, unsafe, and very unsafe
At night; in unfamiliar areas; in the city; in bad weather; after drinking alcohol; when tired; in an unfamiliar automobile; when I'm angry; at 37.3 mph; and at 68.4 mph	

men reported that they had vehicle insurance, compared with 82% of the women, thus not representing a significant difference ($p = 0.438$). Among the women who reported not having insurance, 64% indicated the main reason was because they had never needed to use insurance. Among the male respondents who reported not having insurance, some 56% attributed this to the price or the reduced chance of needing to use it in any type of situation.

Table 2.3 shows the frequency with which the respondents reported feeling the need to have insurance on their vehicles based on certain situations. No significant difference was found at the 10% level between the genders. In other words, the results suggest that there is no difference between men and women as far as it concerns situations in which there might be a preference to have automobile insurance.

Table 2.3 Situations in which use of insurance is desired (% respondents)

	Always		Frequently		Sometimes		Rarely		
Situation/use of insurance	M	F	M	F	M	F	M	F	*p*-value
Theft	80	85	6	4	8	2	3	5	0.153
Excessive rainfall	19	29	7	7	24	21	26	21	0.375
Hitting third party with car knocking over	46	46	5	10	13	11	21	17	0.467
Assistance services	42	50	8	11	28	19	14	14	0.200

The questions were asked as to the respondents' need to have automobile insurance because of theft, excessive rainfall, hitting a third party with the vehicle, and assistance services (e.g., a tow truck). The possible responses were always, frequently, sometimes, rarely, and never. *M* male and *F* female. A chi-square test for independence was conducted between gender and the relevance of having insurance in each of the four risk situations (the results of the test are reported in the final column of this table). No result was significant at the 10% significance level

Table 2.4 Respect for speed limits in various situations (% of respondents)

	Always		Frequently		Sometimes		Rarely		Never		
Situation	M	F	M	F	M	F	M	F	M	F	*p*-value
At night	26	31	29	30	29	30	13	5	3	5	*
In the rush hour	50	59	31	29	12	11	5	2	3	0	0.136
Close to home	42	43	30	33	18	16	7	8	3	1	0.750
School zones	64	70	26	21	8	8	1	1	2	0	0.425
In bad weather	57	72	32	22	8	2	1	3	2	0	***
In the city	27	40	42	34	24	20	6	5	2	1	0.176
Highway	18	40	28	33	30	17	21	8	3	2	0.125

The questions were in relation to the speed limits in driving situations: at night, in the rush hour, close to where they live, in school zones, in bad weather, on local streets, and on highways. The possible responses were always, frequently, sometimes, rarely, and never. M represents male respondents and F female respondents. A chi-square comparison test of the averages between the genders of the respondents was carried out. The *p*-values of the tests were reported in the final column

*p-value < 0.1; **p-value < 0.05; ***p-value < 0.01

Table 2.4 presents the results for the following question related to risky driving behaviors: "I obey the speed limit in these situations: (1) at night, (2) in the rush hour, (3) close to home, (4) school zones, (5) in bad weather, (6) in the city, and (7) on the highway." A significant gender-based difference was found only in situations where the vehicle was being driven at night and in cases of bad weather. Respect for speed limits at night and in adverse weather conditions, both in the study of Bergdahl (2005) and in this research, was dependent on the driver's gender, indicating that male drivers may have greater confidence in their own skills. These results also support the arguments of Cross et al. (2011), for whom men are impulsive and are more inclined to look for risk sensations than women.

Table 2.5 describes the responses relating to safety perceptions when driving vehicles in different situations. Of the nine situations presented to the respondents,

Table 2.5 Safety perceptions in different situations (% of respondents)

	Very safe		Safe		Neither		Unsafe		Very unsafe		
Situation	M	F	M	F	M	F	M	F	M	F	*p*-value
At night	17	7	45	30	21	17	14	37	3	9	***
In unfamiliar area	3	2	22	9	28	9	44	62	4	18	***
In the city	18	17	51	44	24	24	8	15	0	0	0.177
In bad weather	3	2	28	15	27	16	40	59	2	8	***
After drinking	1	1	14	5	33	21	27	29	25	45	***
In unfamiliar car	2	1	24	11	43	33	29	44	3	11	***
When angry	3	3	23	15	52	37	21	35	2	10	***
At 60 kph (37.3 mph)	47	34	37	52	15	14	1	1	1	0	0.400
At 110 kph (68.4 mph)	23	18	51	45	20	19	6	16	0	2	0.350

The questions explored drivers' safety perceptions in the following situations: at night, in an unfamiliar area, in the city, in adverse weather conditions, after drinking, when driving an unfamiliar car, when angry, driving at 60 kph (37.3 mph), and driving at 110 kph (68.4 mph). The responses were very safe, safe, neither, unsafe, and very unsafe. *M* male respondents and *F* female respondents. A comparative chi-square test was carried out of the averages between the genders of the respondents (the results of the test are reported in the final column)
$^{*}p$-value < 0.1; $^{**}p$-value < 0.05; $^{***}p$-value < 0.01

there was no significant difference found for three of the nine vehicle driving situations: in the city, at 60 kph (37.3 mph), and at 110 kph (68.4 mph). However, significant differences were found for the remaining situations: at night, in unfamiliar areas, in bad weather conditions, after drinking, driving unfamiliar vehicles, or when they are angry. Also, Table 2.5 shows that in all these situations men reported a greater safety perception than women. These findings support those of Farrow and Brissing (1990), who found that men feel reasonably safe when driving at high speeds in highly populated areas and even after drinking.

These findings help to shed light on gender differences in driving attitudes and behaviors. Yet, one might be concerned about potential biases in differences between male and female responses since the responses to these survey questions were self-reported. While this is a reasonable concern, the literature suggests that these types of self-reported responses are often valid and can serve as good proxy measures for driving attitudes and behaviors (West et al. 1993). For example, West et al. (1993) show that self-reported speed is a good proxy for the probability of being involved in an accident. Parker et al. (1995) also argue that the tendency to get involved in accidents may be estimated from the traffic violations referred to by the drivers themselves.

Multivariable Analysis

Using the sample of 466 respondents, 17 logit models were initially estimated, in which the co-variables all relate to the driver's profile (see Table 2.2). These models were organized into three groups: (i) reason for having insurance (Table 2.3),

(ii) respect for speed limits (Table 2.4), and (iii) feeling of safety when driving (Table 2.5). The last two columns of Table 2.6 in the last two columns show that women are more inclined to acquire insurance to protect themselves against excessive rainfall ($\widehat{\beta} = 0.4849; p < 0.05$) and in cases when they need assistance services ($\widehat{\beta} = 0.5869; p < 0.01$). We tested the significance of an interaction term $Age * Gender$ and did not find any significant result for that term in any model.

With regard to the magnitude of the findings, female respondents (gender = 1) were 62.40% and 79.84% more likely than men to have the need to insure their vehicle for situations of excessive rainfall and for assistance services, respectively. The estimated coefficient for the *age* variable was significant and positive in *collision conditions* ($\widehat{\beta} = 1.988; p < 0.05$), *excessive rainfall* ($\widehat{\beta} = 0.532; p < 0.05$), and *assistance services* ($\widehat{\beta} = 1.5659; p < 0.05$). This suggests that younger respondents perceive less need for vehicle insurance with regard to the conditions presented (Machin and Sankey 2008).

Table 2.6 also shows that respondents living in the capital or other metropolitan areas that are not part of the upstate urban centers were significantly less inclined to purchase automobile insurance to protect themselves against *vehicle theft* ($\widehat{\beta} = 0.7629; p - value < 0.05$) and losses caused by *excessive rainfall* ($\widehat{\beta} = 0.5327; p < 0.05$). These results reflect the greater risk sensation people have with regard to having their vehicle stolen in bigger cities and the possible flooding and traffic chaos situations experienced in large cities at times of heavy rainfall.

Brazilian public safety statistics indicate that in 2015 more than half a million vehicles were stolen, a rate of 562 per 100,000 vehicles in Brazil (FBSP 2016). Considering the context in the city of São Paulo, this rate was 711.7, and in the Federal District (Brasília), it was 684.9 (FBSP 2016). The results suggest that being a resident of the capital increases by 114% the chance of buying insurance ($\widehat{\beta} = 0.7629; p < 0.05$); this result can suggest the perception of the risk of having the vehicle stolen. This result reflects the feeling of insecurity that major cities like São Paulo cause in people, especially when the driver is female, according to recent data collection by the policy makers in Brazil (SUSEP 2016). This was found in recent surveys into satisfaction with living conditions in this city (Mendes-Da-Silva et al. 2014, p. 27). Female respondents were 62.40% more inclined than men to buy insurance because of extreme rainfall situations ($\widehat{\beta} = 0.4849; p < 0.05$). This percentage increases to being almost 80% more inclined than men when the women feel the need to use the assistance services ($\widehat{\beta} = 0.5869; p < 0.01$) which are provided by insurance companies.

Table 2.7 gives the results regarding the inclination to respect speed limits in various situations. Because we are here dealing with behavioral differences between men and women, the results suggest that women in four of the six situations given: *in the rush hour* ($\widehat{\beta} = 0.5315; p < 0.1$), *on main roads* ($\widehat{\beta} = 0.9645; p < 0.01$), *on local streets* ($\widehat{\beta} = 0.5513; p < 0.01$), and *on highways* ($\widehat{\beta} = 1.314; p < 0.01$), tend to be more inclined to respect speed limits. This result is seen even when controlling for the other variables of the driver profile. It also needs to be pointed out that on the highway the fact that the driver is a female contributes more to respect for the speed

Table 2.6 Respondent profile and desire for insurance for specific situations

	Reason for having automobile insurance									
Driver profile	Theft		Collision		Hit third party		Rain		Services	
Gender[a]	0.2915		0.0319		0.2725		0.4849	**	0.5869	***
Age[b]	0.2587		1.9889	**	0.4346		1.9571	**	1.5659	**
Region[c]	0.7629	**	−0.3085		−0.1016		0.5327	**	0.1258	
Marital status[d]	−0.1025		−0.277		−0.069		−0.0154		0.0622	
Time driving[e]	0.0994		−0.2638		0.0334		−0.3279		−0.4373	*
Has insurance[f]	2.0251	***	0.7304	*	1.2125	***	0.7084	*	0.6412	*
Freq. use of ins.[g]	−0.3007		0.1815		−0.1196		0.0202		0.2529	*
Motorization of city[h]	−2.0735		−0.6601		−2.3366		−2.5269		−0.6729	
Constant	0.1057		−5.0768		−1.3783		−6.8127		−5.0498	**
Adj. measures										
Log-likelihood	−156.829	***	−223.747	**	−310.993	***	−279.158	***	−304.718	***
H-L (p-value)	0.353		0.666		0.07		0.183		0.519	
Correct rating class	0.877		0.802		0.596		0.695		0.603	
Somer's D	0.46		0.27		0.25		0.3		0.27	
N	466		466		466		466		466	

Note: Each column represents the results of a logistic regression associated with the question "I feel the need to have the vehicle insured in these situations." The value = 1 was attributed to responses always and frequently and value = 0 to the three possible responses sometimes, rarely, or never. In this way the response variables were associated with theft, collision, hitting a third party with the vehicle, excessive rainfall, and assistance services (e.g., use of tow truck). In the *region* variable, the cities were grouped into capital and metropolitan region (value 1) and upstate (value 0), according to *IBGE* criteria

*p-value < 0.1; **p-value < 0.05; ***p-value < 0.01

[a]Dummy variable, which indicates the gender of the respondent, was given the value = 1 if female and value = 0 otherwise

[b]Age of the respondent expressed by the ln of the number of years

[c]Dummy variable that expresses the region in which the respondent lives was given the value = 1 if in the capital, and value = 0 otherwise

[d]Dummy variable, which indicates the marital status of the respondent, was given the value = 1 if married and the value = 0 otherwise

[e]Time that the respondent has been driving vehicles, expressed by the ln of the number of years

[f]Dummy variable, which indicates that the respondent has automobile insurance, was given the value = 1 if yes and the value = 0 otherwise

[g]Number of times the respondent has already needed to use insurance

[h]Rate of motorization of the city, calculated by the number of vehicle divided by the number of inhabitants in the city in 2013, according to the *IBGE*

Table 2.7 Profile of the respondent and inclination to respect speed limits in certain situations under which they are driving

	Context in which the respondent needs to respect the speed limit											
Driver profile	At night		In the rush hour		School		Main road		Local road		Highway	
Gender[a]	0.3041		0.5315	*	0.162		0.9645	***	0.5513	***	1.3144	***
Age[b]	2.1991	***	3.7509	***	5.2065	***	6.1946	***	2.8874	***	2.0405	**
Region[c]	−0.4024	**	0.8778	***	0.2366		0.1017		0.3959	*	0.9614	***
Marital status[d]	0.444	**	0.2711		0.9306	**	0.1919		0.7238	***	0.3316	
Time driving[e]	−0.4138	*	−0.7648	*	−1.1586	*	−1.3646	***	−0.3455		−0.3236	
Has insurance[f]	−0.7143	**	−0.0039		0.7986		0.1593		−0.0113		−0.6246	*
Freq. use of insurance[g]	−0.0007		−0.1901		−0.6084	***	−0.3286	**	−0.2652	*	0.0033	
Motoriz. of city[h]	−0.7554		−3.7835		0.2074		−0.8264		−3.6375	*	−4.0436	*
Constant	−5.5756	**	−8.3241	**	−13.0916	**	−16.5553	***	−7.1525	***	−5.0563	**
Adjustment measures												
Log-likelihood	−305.521	***	−193.615	***	−126.054	***	−224.318	***	−261.618	***	−280.7	***
H-L (*p*-value)	0.821		0.932		0.675		0.455		0.811		0.41	
Correct class. rate	0.596		0.836		0.907		0.766		0.699		0.654	
Somer's D	0.28		0.41		0.48		0.46		0.42		0.46	
N	466		466		466		466		466		466	

NB: Each column represents the results of a logistic regression associated with the statement "I obey the speed limit in these situations." Value = 1 was attributed to replies always and frequently and value 0 to the other possible replies sometimes, rarely, or never. The variable responses were associated with at night, in the rush hour, school (school areas), main roads, local roads, and highways. In the "region" variable, cities were grouped into capital and metropolitan region (value 1) and upstate (value = 0), according to *IBGE* criteria

*p-value < 0.1; **p-value < 0.05; ***p-value < 0.01

[a]Dummy variable that indicates the gender of the respondent had the value = 1 if female and value = 0 otherwise

[b]Age of the respondent expressed by the ln of the number of years

[c]Dummy variable, which expresses the region in which the respondent lives, was given the value = 1 if in the capital and value = 0 otherwise

[d]Dummy variable, which denotes the marital status of the respondent, was given the value = 1 if married and the value = 0 otherwise

[e]Time the respondent has been driving vehicles, expressed by the ln of the number of years

[f]Dummy variable, which indicates that the respondent has automobile insurance, was given the value = 1 if yes and the value = 0 otherwise

[g]Number of times the respondent has needed to use insurance

[h]Motorization rate of the city, calculated by the number of vehicles divided by the number of inhabitants in the city in 2013, according to the IBGE

limit when compared with the other situations. This result supports the arguments and results obtained by Özkan and Lajunen (2006) and Fergunson and Braitman (2006); for these authors sex (being male) predicted the number of total, active, and passive accidents and perceptual motor skills.

Also with regard to the inclination to respect speed limits in certain situations, the age of the respondent proved to be positive and associated with all the situations presented. This result strengthens the argument that younger male individuals tend to systematically show a greater inclination to disregard speed limits (Cestac et al. 2011). The residents of urban centers (*Region* = 1), when compared with the inhabitants of more distant cities, tend to respect the speed limit in various situations: *at night* ($\widehat{\beta} = -0.4024; p < 0.05$), *in the rush hour* ($\widehat{\beta} = 0.877; p < 0.01$), *on local streets* ($\widehat{\beta} = 0.3959; p < 0.1$), and *on highways* ($\widehat{\beta} = 0.961; p < 0.01$). However, with regard to driving at night, for those who live in the capital and metropolitan region, there is a 33% reduction in the chance of obeying the speed limit when compared with those who live in cities that are not close to urban centers.

Table 2.8 gives the results of safety perception when driving in different situations. In addition to being less inclined to respect speed limits, male respondents have a greater feeling of safety in the situations presented, when compared with female respondents, according to the arguments of Bergdahl (2005), Cross et al. (2011), Møller and Haustein (2014), and Wolf et al. (2010). The estimated coefficients enable us to infer that the females participating in this survey have a 64.94% reduction in the feeling of safety when driving after drinking alcohol when compared with male respondents. It should be emphasized that over the last few years policy makers in Brazil have emphasized the forbidding of driving after drinking alcohol over a certain level and after taking drugs (De Boni et al. 2013; Campos et al. 2013).

Also in Table 2.8 we can see that the older the individual is, the less likely they are to feel safe when driving: at night ($\widehat{\beta} = -1.2861; p < 0.1$), after drinking ($\widehat{\beta} = -3.405; p < 0.1$), and driving at around 68.4 mph ($\widehat{\beta} = -1.8068; p < 0.05$). The search for a feeling of excitement in risk conditions at the wheel of motor vehicles tends to be more common in younger individuals, as Oltedal and Rundmo (2006) and Machin and Sankey (2008) suggest. It seems to us that it is worth registering that the fact of living in urban centers is significant for four of the six situations presented, which supports the arguments of the recent study carried out by Schroeder et al. (2013).

As well as main findings from Schwebel et al. (2006), Schroeder et al. (2013) assume that the search for extreme sensations, i.e., feeling of excitement in risk conditions at the wheel of motor vehicles, is one of the main predictors of violations when driving vehicles. This line of thinking is shared by Özkan and Lajunen (2006), who suggest that women tend to have more safety skills in traffic, which is corroborated by the work of Lonczak et al. (2007).

In this respect the estimated coefficients allow us to check a counterintuitive result. Respondents who live upstate have a 57.16% and 50% increased feeling of safety when they drive after drinking and at 110 kph (68.4 mph), respectively, compared with drivers from larger cities. It is probable that because of the reduced

Table 2.8 Parameters estimated for the feeling of safety at the wheel in different situations

	How do you feel driving in this situation											
Driver profile	At night		In unfamiliar areas		After drinking		When tired		Unfamiliar automobile		At around 110 kph (68.4 mph)	
Gender[a]	−0.7697	***	−0.8893	***	−1.0481	***	−0.9517	**	−0.9171	***	−0.2418	
Age[b]	−1.2861	*	−0.4477		−3.405	*	0.4003		−0.2847		−1.8068	**
Region[c]	−0.5821	***	−0.6165	**	−0.8477	***	0.2777		0.2699		−0.6929	***
Marital status[d]	−0.2902		−0.0735		−0.3373		−0.2202		0.2166		0.1451	
Time driving[e]	0.7191	***	0.5476		1.3105	*	0.0146		0.1469		0.4194	*
Has insurance[f]	−0.0381		−0.0497		−0.0525		−0.3302		−0.8164	**	0.2953	
Freq. use of insurance[g]	0.0604		0.1326		−0.0762		−0.1199		0.3171	*	0.1963	
Motoriz. of city[h]	−1.7812		−1.8809		3.0514		4.6464		−3.535		−1.5029	
Constant	4.1769	*	−0.1392		6.0633		−5.2033		0.8927		6.5988	***
Adjustment measures												
Log-likelihood	−298.526	***	−205.578	***	−144.08	***	−114.5		−216.889	***	−269.96	***
H-L (*p*-value)	0.829		0.729		0.491		0.448		0.316		0.171	
Correct class. rate	0.641		0.819		0.894		0.929		0.809		0.706	
Somer's D	0.37		0.36		0.42		0.32		0.3		0.31	
N	466		466		466		466		466		466	

Each column represents the results of a logistic regression associated with the question "How do you feel driving." The value = 1 was attributed to the replies very safe and safe and value = 0 to the other possible replies (indifferent, unsafe, and very unsafe). The response variables were associated with at night, in unfamiliar areas, alcohol (after drinking), being tired, unfamiliar (unfamiliar automobile), and at 68.4 mph

*p-value < 0.1; **p-value < 0.05; ***p-value < 0.01

[a]Dummy variable, which indicates the gender of the respondent, was given the value = 1 if female and value = 0 otherwise

[b]Age of the respondent expressed by the ln of the number of years

[c]Dummy variable, which expresses the region in which the respondent lives, was given the value = 1 if in the capital, and value = 0 otherwise

[d]Dummy variable, which indicates the marital status of the respondent, was given the value = 1 if married and the value = 0 otherwise

[e]Time the respondent has been driving vehicles, expressed by the number of years

[f]Dummy variable, which indicates the respondent has automobile insurance, was given the value = 1 if yes and the value = 0 otherwise

[g]Number of times the respondent has already needed to use insurance

[h]Motorization rate of the city, calculated by the number of vehicles divided by the number of inhabitants of the city in 2013, according to *IBGE*

traffic law enforcement in regions that are far from Brazil's urban centers, individuals who live upstate have a feeling of being less exposed to the penalties for traffic violations, which gives them a greater appetite for driving in more risky conditions (Campos et al. 2013; De Boni et al. 2013).

Robustness Test

To check the fit level of the models, a logit model was estimated using the stepwise variable selection method, with 466 randomly selected questionnaires. The significant variables were *age*, *services* (e.g., assistance services, like a tow truck), *I obey the speed limit close to the place where I live*, *I obey the speed limit on local streets*, and *I obey the speed limit on highways*, and the other selected variables correspond to the feeling of people when they are driving at night, in unfamiliar areas, in the city, in an unfamiliar automobile, after drinking, and at 110 kph (68.4 mph).

To identify the discriminating capacity of the model, based on this estimated model, the Kolmogorov-Sminorv (KS) and Gini coefficients were calculated, the values being 0.47 and 0.65, respectively, indicating a significant discriminating power of the model when dealing with male or female individuals. To check the robustness of this model, the responses of the 100 remaining individuals were used to carry out an out-of-sample adjustment test, as Inouei and Kilian (2005) and Patton (2004) recommend. The model initially estimated was used for these new data, and the KS and GINI coefficients were recalculated. Therefore, the model was reasonably discriminating between the genders, since the new KS was 0.53 and the new Gini coefficient was the same at 0.63, reflecting that these estimated coefficients are stable. This being so, there are reasons to consider this logistic regression model as suitable to discriminate gender-based differences in the respondents' driving habits, as is reflected in the significant variables.

In addition our additional results suggest that female respondents have a greater feeling of safety when driving in the city. On highways and on local streets, women reported that they respected the established speed limits more than men. With regard to drinking alcohol, the greater the feeling of safety the smaller the chance of the driver being a woman. From the model found, as the feeling of safety increases when the driver drinks and drives, the probability that the driver is male increases by around 18%. Women are more likely to feel the need to have vehicle insurance to guarantee access to assistance services, such as tow truck services. When driving close to home, men are least likely to obey the speed limit. The greater perception of safety when driving at night, unfamiliar vehicles, or at 110 kph (68.4 mph), the fewer the chances are that the respondent drivers are female, providing evidence yet again of increased aggressive behavior with men at the wheel compared with women. Regarding risk behavior in traffic, we reference again the personality theory proposed by Zuckerman (1988).

Among the personality traits described by this author is "the search for strong sensations," characterized by a preference for things new and by the desire to take personal risks to experience them. Analysis of this survey shows that male respondents adopt more risky driving behaviors than women. It is important to point out that in the variables that were studied, the greater the feeling of driver safety, the lower the probability that the driver was female and the higher the probability for the driver being male, offering statistical support to the theory that men are more risk-inclined than women (Møller and Haustein 2014). According to the estimated model, a driver engaging in risk behavior is 86% more likely to be male than female. (MC note: would it also be true to state that "a male driver is 86% more likely to engage in risk behavior than a female driver"?).

Concluding Remarks

According to Charness and Gneezy (2012), a relevant question that deserves more investigation for a broad range of economic issues is are men more willing to assume risks than women? Part of the literature has analyzed individual behavior in terms of traffic and transportation safety based on a comparative approach according to driver gender. This chapter examines this argument to analyze the associations between driver profile and risk behavior when driving motor vehicles and the inclination to purchase vehicle insurance. A survey was administered to 566 adults from 66 cities in Brazil, which has one of the largest populations worldwide and ranks second in the world for the rate of traffic-related deaths and where little is known with regard to the evidence of driver behavior.

From the data that were collected, the nonparametric tests, and the 18 estimated binary response models in this article, male respondents exhibited higher levels of risk-inclined behavior when driving, which is in line with previous studies (Bergdahl 2005; Wolf et al. 2010). It was also possible to see that women tend to behave more cautiously in traffic and with greater responsibility than men, which also supports previous arguments, like those presented by Özkan and Lajunen (2006). In this regard, the results obtained from the logit models suggest that the greater the feeling of driver safety, the smaller the chance of it being a woman and the greater the chance of it being a man; the study shows a 66% increase of probability that the driver is male, as the feeling of driver safety in various possible risk situations increases, like driving (i) at night, (ii) in unfamiliar areas, (iii) in the city, (iv) after drinking, and (v) at a speed close to 110 kph (68.4 mph).

The study revealed results worth highlighting regarding driving while intoxicated, which is one of Brazil's largest determinants of traffic accidents. Safety perceptions with driving while under the influence of alcohol increases the probability of the driver being male by 18%. In addition, drivers living in cities that are more distant from urban centers tend to feel safer after drinking alcohol than drivers who live in urban centers, probably because traffic control agents are less in evidence and there is less policing in these areas.

Women are more likely to want insurance to ensure access to assistance services (like tow truck services). With regard to the demand to acquire financial products that protect against possible losses arising from traffic accidents, 82% of the women had some type of insurance on their vehicle. Of the women who reported they did not have insurance, 64% indicated that the reason is because they never needed to use insurance coverage or other reasons. However, among male respondents who did not have insurance (15%), around 56% replied that the reason was because of the price or a reduced chance of using insurance.

Future Directions

According to the recommendations proposed by Wacker (1998) and Whetten (1989), the results of this study have potential to add value to the development of theories associated with traffic and transportation safety. Inasmuch as the study verifies the persistence of results in other institutional environments, with new variables, the research has potential to make contribution to theory development, as it offers new evidence. Policy makers and industry can also benefit from these results. One immediate implication of this study is that the findings might assist industry, especially insurance companies, to develop product concepts and strategies that more closely align to the customer needs. In the public sphere, government education programs could address gender-based driving behavior differences, e.g., the male drivers' search for greater risk sensations in traffic. A result of better driver education and greater enforcement of traffic laws would theoretically contribute to a reduction in traffic-related injury and death and the many direct and indirect costs of traffic accidents (Campos et al. 2013).

This work has some limitations that are worth recording. Among these it cannot be assumed that the whole of the population is represented by the dataset collected, despite dealing with the region that has the biggest proportion of the Brazilian vehicle fleet. Furthermore, bearing in mind the scope chosen for the work, tests were not carried out that segregated the types of vehicle (Bacchieri et al. 2011). Finally, the relevance of the theme, the lack of other research, and also the potential of the social impact of new research join with the arguments, documented evidence, and limitations of this study and point to a promising research agenda. For future research, we suggested that similar studies are needed in different institutional environments (with particular interest regarding other countries where the rates of motorization are high, as well as China and India) that might explore additional questions to provide a deeper understanding of the behavior differences between men and women, as previous work recommends, i.e., Gurin (1981), Meyer (2006), and Özkan and Lajunen (2006).

The propensity of individuals to acquire automobile insurance as well as driver behavior should impact more strongly the premiums charged by insurance companies. This is because new technologies will allow data access at the individual level, rather than based on a niche. The growing number of connected sensors is allowing insurance companies to collect enough data to offer usage-based insurance (UBI) models,[1] which effectively identify a *one segment*, implying individualized premiums, where costs depend on continuously compiled data from a single customer. UBI has become popular in the automobile insurance market, as risk assessments are based on data collected from connected cars that generate real drivers' behaviors, such as speed acceleration, average time, and distance traveled, among other relevant parameters. When effectively implemented, UBI providers can reduce claims costs by 40%, reduce policy administration by 50%, and reduce acquisition costs.

References

Bacchieri, G., Barros, A. J., Santos, J. V., & Gigante, D. P. (2011). Cycling to work in Brazil: Users profile, risk behaviors, and traffic accident occurrence. *Accident Analysis & Prevention, 43*, 1408–1413.

Baer, W. (2014). *The Brazilian economy: Growth & development* (7th ed.). London: Lynne Rienner Publishers.

Bergdahl, J. (2005). Sex differences in attitudes toward driving: A survey. *The Social Science Journal, 42*, 595–601. https://doi.org/10.1016/j.soscij.2005.09.006.

Bergdahl, J., & Norris, M. R. (2002). Sex differences in single vehicle fatal crashes: A research note. *The Social Science Journal, 39*, 287–293. https://doi.org/10.1016/S0362-3319(02)00169-6.

Campos, V. R., Silva, R. S., Dualibi, S., Santos, J. F., Laranjeira, R., & Pinsky, I. (2013). The effect of the new traffic law on drinking and driving in São Paulo. *Accident Analysis & Prevention, 50*, 622–627.

Cestac, J., Paran, F., & Delhomme, P. (2011). Young drivers sensation seeking, subjective norms, and perceived behavioural control and their roles in predicting speeding intention: How risk-taking motivations evolve with gender and driving experience. *Safety Science, 49*, 424–432. https://doi.org/10.1016/j.ssci.2010.10.007.

Charness, G., & Gneezy, U. (2012). Strong evidence for gender differences in risk taking. *Journal of Economic Behavior & Organization, 83*, 50–58. https://doi.org/10.1016/j.jebo.2011.06.007.

Cross, C. P., Copping, L. T., & Campbell, A. (2011). Sex differences in impulsivity: A meta-analysis. *Psychological Bulletin, 137*, 97–130. https://doi.org/10.1037/a0021591.

DATASUS (2010). Ministério da Saúde do Brasil. Available at: http://www.datasus.gov.br.

De Boni, R., Bastos, F. I., Vasconcellos, M., Oliveira, F., Limberger, R. P., & Pechansky, I. (2013). Drug use among drivers who drank on alcohol outlets from Porto Alegre, Brazil. *Accident Analysis & Prevention, 62*, 137–142.

Denatran. (2014). Departamento Nacional de Trânsito-Denatran. Available at: http://www.denatran.gov.br/frota.htm.

DEPEN-Departamento Penitenciário Nacional, Justice Department of Brazil. (2014). Levantamento Nacional de Informações Penitenciárias Info-Mulheres. Available at: https://www.justica.gov.br/noticias/estudo-traca-perfil-da-populacao-penitenciaria-feminina-no-brasil/relatorio-infopen-mulheres.pdf.

DPVAT. (2013). Seguro Obrigatório de Danos Pessoais Causados por Veículos Automotores de Via Terrestre-DPVAT. Available at: www.dpvatsegurodotransito.com.br.

Efrat, K., & Shoham, A. (2013). The theory of planned behavior, materialism, and aggressive driving. *Accident Analysis & Prevention, 59*, 459–465. https://doi.org/10.1016/j.aap.2013.06.023.

[1]For a discussion about UBI, see Wells, J.R., and Danskin, G. (2014). Progressive 2007–2013. *Harvard Cases* #9–715-427.

Falk, B., & Montgomery, H. (2009). Promoting traffic safety among young male drivers by means of elaboration-based interventions. *Transportation Research Part F, 12*, 1–11. https://doi.org/10.1016/j.trf.2008.06.001.

Farrow, J. A., & Brissing, P. (1990). Risk for DUI: A new look at gender differences in drinking and driving influences, experiences, and attitudes among new adolescent drivers. *Health Education Quarterly, 17*, 213–221. https://doi.org/10.1177/109019819001700207.

FBSP. (2016). Forum Brasileiro de Segurança Pública. *Anuário Brasileiro de Segurança Pública, 2016* Available at: http://www.forumseguranca.org.br/storage/download//anuario_site_18-11-2016-retificado.pdf.

Fergunson, S. A., Braitman, K. A. (2006). Women's issues in highway safety: Summary of the literature. In *Transportation Research Board Conference Proceedings 35*. Available at: http://onlinepubs.trb.org/onlinepubs/conf/CP35v1.pdf.

Fowler, F. J. (1998). Design and evaluation of survey questions. In L. Bickman & D. J. Rog (Eds.), *Handbook of applied social research methods* (pp. 343–374). Thousand Oaks, CA: Sage.

Friedl, A., Ring, P., & Schmidt, U. (2017). *Theory and Decision, 82*(2), 211–219. https://doi.org/10.1007/s11238-016-9565-9.

González-Iglesias, B., Gómez-Fraguela, J. A., & Luengo-Martín, M. A. (2012). Driving anger and traffic violations: Gender differences. *Transportation Research Part F, 15*, 404–412. https://doi.org/10.1016/j.trf.2012.03.002.

Gurin, D. B. (1981). Women's future travel, driving, and transit use. *Psychology of Women Quarterly, 6*, 72–84. https://doi.org/10.1111/j.1471-6402.1981.tb01061.x.

Hautzinger, S. J. (1997). "Calling a state a state": Feminist politics and the policing of violence against the women in Brazil. *Feminist Issues, 15*(1–2), 3–30.

IBGE. (2013). Instituto Brasileiro de Geografia e Estatística-IBGE. In Senso Demográfico 2010. ISBN: 9788524042812. Available at: http://biblioteca.ibge.gov.br/index.php/biblioteca-catalogo?view=detalhes&id=264529.

Inouei, A., & Kilian, L. (2005). In-sample or out-of-sample tests of predictability: Which one should we use? *Econometric Reviews, 23*, 371–402. https://doi.org/10.1081/ETC-200040785.

Johnson, M. B., Voas, R. B., & Miller, B. A. (2012). Driving decisions when leaving electronic music dance events: Driver, passenger, and group effects. *Traffic Injury Prevention, 13*, 577–584. https://doi.org/10.1080/15389588.2012.678954.

Kunreuther, H., & Michel-Kerjan, E. (2013). Managing Catastrophic Risks Through Redesigned Insurance: Challenges and Opportunities. In G. Dionne (Ed.), *Handbook of insurance* (Vol. XXVI., 1126p., 2nd ed., pp. 517–546). Springer Nature. ISBN: 978-1493908615.

Li, P., Shi, J., Liu, X., & Wang, H. (2016). The theory of planned behavior and competitive driving in China. *Procedia Engineering, 137*, 362–371. https://doi.org/10.1016/j.proeng.2016.01.270.

Lonczak, H. S., Neighbors, C., & Donovan, D. M. (2007). Predicting risky and angry driving as a function of gender. *Accident Analysis & Prevention, 39*, 536–545. https://doi.org/10.1016/j.aap.2006.09.010.

Machin, M. A., & Sankey, K. S. (2008). Relationships between young drivers' personality characteristics, risk perceptions, and driving behaviour. *Accident Analysis and Prevention, 40*, 541–547.

Mannering, F. L. (1993). Male/female driver characteristics and accident risk: Some new evidence. *Accident Analysis and Prevention, 25*, 77–84. https://doi.org/10.1016/0001-4575(93)90098-H.

Mendes-Da-Silva, W., Garcia, F. G., & Motoryn, M. (2014). *Survey well being Brasil: Cidade de São Paulo*. Available at: http://ag.taxi.br/projetos/myfuncity/WBB_RELATORIO_SP.pdf.

Meyer, M. D. (2006). Women's issues in transportation: Policy and planning. In Transportation Research Board Conference Proceedings 35, Proceedings, Available at: http://onlinepubs.trb.org/onlinepubs/conf/CP35v1.pdf.

Møller, M., & Haustein, S. (2014). Peer influence on speeding behaviour among male drivers aged 18 and 28. *Accident Analysis and Prevention, 64*, 92–99. https://doi.org/10.1016/j.aap.2013.11.009.

Nunen, K. V., Reniers, G., Ponnet, K., & Cozzani, V. (2016). Major accident prevention decision-making: A large-scale survey-based analysis. *Safety Science, 88*, 242–250.

Obst, P., Armstrong, K., Smith, S., & Banks, T. (2011). Age and gender comparisions of driving while sleepy: Behaviours and risk perceptions. *Transportation Research Part F, 14*, 539–542.
Oltedal, S., & Rundmo, T. (2006). The effects of personality and gender on risky driving behaviour and accident involvement. *Safety Science, 44*, 621–628. https://doi.org/10.1016/j.ssci.2005.12.003.
Özkan, T., & Lajunen, T. (2006). What causes the differences in driving between young men and women? The effects of gender roles and sex on young drivers, driving behaviour and self-assessment of skills. *Transportation Research Part F, 9*, 269–277. https://doi.org/10.1016/j.trf.2006.01.005.
Parker, D., Reason, J. T., Manstead, A. S. R., & Stradling, S. G. (1995). Driving errors, driving violations and accident involvement. *Ergonomics, 38*, 1036–1048. https://doi.org/10.1080/00140139508925170.
Patton, A. J. (2004). On the out-of-sample importance of skewness and asymmetric dependence for asset allocation. *Journal of Financial Econometrics, 2*(1), 130–168. https://doi.org/10.1093/jjfinec/nbh006.
Paulhus, D. L., & Vazire, S. (2011). The self-report method. In R. W. Robins, R. C. Fraley, & R. F. Krueger (Eds.), *Handbook of research methods in personality psychology*. New York: Guilford.
Renzetti, C. M., Miller, S. L., & Gover, A. R. (2013). *Routledge international handbook of crime and gender studies*. London: Routledge Taylor & Francis Group.
Schroeder, P., Meyers, M., & Kostyniuk, L. (2013). *National survey on distracted driving attitudes and behaviors*, 2012. Report no. DOT HS 811-729. Washington, DC: National Highway Trafic Safety Administration.
Schwebel, D. C., Severson, J., Ball, K. K., & Rizzo, M. (2006). Individual difference factors in risky driving: The roles of anger/hostility, conscientiousness, and sensation-seeking. *Accident Analysis and Prevention, 38*, 801–810. https://doi.org/10.1016/j.aap.2006.02.004.
Scott-Parker, B., Watson, B., King, M. J., & Hyde, M. K. (2012). "They're lunatics on the road": Exploring the normative influences of parents, friends, and police on young novices' risky driving decisions. *Safety Science, 50*, 1917–1928. https://doi.org/10.1016/j.ssci.2012.05.014.
Simons-Morton, B. G., Ouimet, M. C., Zhang, Z., Klauer, S. E., Lee, S. E., Wang, J., Chen, R., Albert, P., & Dingus, T. A. (2011). The effect of passengers and risk-taking friends on risky driving and crashes/near crashes among novice teenagers. *Journal of Adolescent Health, 49*, 587–593. https://doi.org/10.1016/j.jadohealth.2011.02.009.
SIRC-Social Issues Research Centre. (2004). Sex differences in driving and insurance risk: An analysis of the social and psychological differences between men and women that are relevant to their driving behavior. Available: http://www.sirc.org/publik/driving.pdf.
SUSEP (2013). Sistema de Estatísticas da SUSEP. Available at: http://www2.susep.gov.br/menuestatistica/SES/principal.aspx
SUSEP. (2016). Superintendência de Seguros Privados. Stolen Car Index (*Índice de Veículos Roubados*). Available at: http://blog.suhaiseguradora.com/consultar-indice-veiculos-roubados.
Velloso, M. S., & Jacques, M. A. P. (2012). On-the-spot study of pedestrian crashes on Brazilian Federal District rural highways crossing urban areas. *Transportation Research Part F, 15*, 588–599. https://doi.org/10.1016/j.trf.2012.06.001.
Wacker, J. G. (1998). A definition of theory: Research guidelines for different theory-building research methods in operations management. *Journal of Operations Management, 16*, 361–385.
West, R., French, D., Kemp, R., & Elander, J. (1993). Direct observation of driving, self reports of driver behaviour, and accident involvement. *Ergonomics, 36*, 557–567.
Whetten, D. A. (1989). What constitutes a theoretical contribution? *Academy of Management Review, 14*, 490–495.
WHO. (2013). *Global status report on road safety 2013: Supporting a decade of action*. World Health Organization-WHO. Available at: http://www.who.int/violence_injury_prevention/road_safety_status/2013/en/
Wieczorek, W. E., Mirand, A. L., & Callahan, C. P. (1994). Perception of the risk of arrest for drinking and driving. *Criminal Justice and Behavior, 21*, 312–326.

WIIT. (2014). In *Women's Issues in Transportation, Proceedings*, Paris. Available at: http://wiit-paris2014.sciencesconf.org/conference/wiit-paris2014/pages/Proceedings_The_5th_International_Conference_on_WIiT_1.pdf.
Wolf, C. C., Ocklenburg, S., Ören, B., Becker, C., Hofstätter, A., Bös, C., Popken, M., Thorstensen, T., & Güntürkün, O. (2010). Sex differences in parking are affected by biological and social factors. *Psychological Research, 74*, 429–435. https://doi.org/10.1007/s00426-009-0267-6.
Zhang, M. (2010). *Competitiveness and growth in Brazilian cities: Local policies and actions for innovation*. Washington, DC: The World Bank.
Zuckerman, M. (1988). What lies beyond E and N? Factor analyses of scales believed to measure basic dimensions of personality. *Journal of Personality and Social Psychology, 54*, 96–107.

Chapter 3
Economic Crisis and Saving Behavior

Israel José dos Santos Felipe

Abstract This study used data from the Survey of Consumer Finances (SCF), 2007 and 2013, to examine the propensity to savings of American households in the pre- and post-economic crisis, based on the two-period consumption/savings model described by Bowman et al. (J Econ Behav Organ 38, 1999. https://doi.org/10.1016/S0167-2681(99)00004-9). This model assumes that asymmetry occurs in agents' savings behavior in response to positive and negative shocks in income. Results obtained by logistic regression suggest that the 2008 global financial crisis has increased the relevance of factors such as the number of children, age, education level, income, and economic uncertainty, while other factors have diminished in relevance such as equity, financial risk tolerance, investment horizon, health, and home ownership. Evidence suggests that events of the magnitude of the crisis may lead to changes in the financial behavior of agents that are not entirely explained by the financial impacts suffered. The information discussed in this study may allow financial professionals and educators to provide recommendations that are more geared to the economic and financial reality of their countries. In addition, the discussions promoted here may offer opportunities for advancement in the study of savings determination.

Keywords Saving · Crisis · Consumer finances · Financial well-being

JEL code H12 · D14 · D12

In recent decades, researchers have shown increasing interest in the saving behavior of families and individuals (Mendes-Da-Silva et al. 2015), reflecting research efforts to produce knowledge about forming adequate savings to guarantee the power of

---

Portions of this chapter appeared in the 2017 paper "The Impact of Crisis on Household Savings Behavior in The United States", *Innovar*, vol 27, pp 137–151.

I. J. dos Santos Felipe (✉)
Department of Business Economics, Federal University of Ouro Preto, Mariana, Minas Gerais, Brazil

Economic Policies Research Unit – NIPE, University of Minho, Braga, Portugal

W. Mendes-Da-Silva (ed.), *Individual Behaviors and Technologies for Financial Innovations*, https://doi.org/10.1007/978-3-319-91911-9_3

consumption after retirement. From the works of Keynes (1936), Friedman (1957), Ando and Modigliani (1963), Shefrin and Statman (1985), Shefrin and Thaler (1988), Moore and Mitchell (1997), Kahneman and Tversky (2000), Shefrin and Statman (2000), Barberis and Thaler (2002), Fisher and Anong (2012), Babiarz and Robb (2014), Argento et al. (2015), Cobb-Clark et al. (2016), and Lusardi and Mitchell (2017), several works have contributed to the advancement of the theoretical-empirical literature in this field.

Friedman (1957) and Ando and Modigliani (1963) assume that economic agents make financial decisions about consumption, savings, investment, and financing rationally, intending to maximize utility over time. However, Shefrin and Thaler (1988) assume that the maximization of expected utility depends on the individuals' propensity to maintain a certain level of savings to ensure the capacity to consume at retirement. Shefrin and Statman (1985) assume that individuals are risk-averse to gains but risk-prone to losses. In this regard, Kahneman and Tversky (1979) concluded that individuals by nature are averse to lose. Thus, they more keenly feel a financial loss, compared to feeling the benefits that would be generated by the similar value in gain.

Interest in the topic of retirement savings is relevant because it reveals how families attempt to maintain the consumption pattern, when their livelihoods leave the productive phase, and enter the phase of emptiness (retirement). In the field of behavioral finance, these, and other, aspects of studying saving and retirement have motivated recent research and constitute a relevant research agenda (Mendes-Da-Silva et al. 2015; Potrich et al. 2016; Braun Santos et al. 2016; Dos-Santos-Felipe et al. 2017).

The knowledge generated in this academic field may be useful for public and private agents to help reduce the risks related to social security in the national context, which does not yet appear to be adequate. In addition, the imbalance in social security has been attributed to a lack of planning by key agents (public and private) and of the families themselves. In this regard, the Social Security Administration's report (SSA 2017) points out that US pension expenditures combined with expenditures in the health and human services department account for more than 53.2% of federal spending in 2017 (more of $ 2.1 trillion). The US government has reported concern to reduce this cost, through research and campaigns for American family financial management.

To address this important issue, this chapter analyzes a wide range of data provided by the Survey of Consumer Finances (SCF). The SCF is a survey conducted by the central bank of the United States throughout the country every 3 years to examine household financial information. Methodology for the present study is based on Bowman et al. (1999) two-period consumption and savings model, which incorporates the impact of shocks on households' propensity for saving by income. This model was used to analyze households' investment decisions in pre- and post-economic crisis of 2008 in the United States.

Based on a two-stage approach (precrisis and postcrisis), with the use of binary logistic regressions, it was possible to obtain two main results:

(i) The factors that contribute positively to the saving decision and are significant in both years include income, wealth, high and medium tolerance to financial risk, medium and long horizon of investments, and being Hispanic or belonging to another race that was not contemplated in the presented alternatives.
(ii) Similarly, the factors that contributed negatively to the savings decision in both periods were having children, age, earning below expected income, being separated or divorced, and having reported being compromised.

Overall, the subprime crisis has had a significant impact on the propensity for American households to set aside savings and seems to have led to greater concern for families and individuals to save money for the future.

This survey informs on the way that extreme events can change the saving behavior of individuals and families. At the end of this chapter, some recommendations are made, including suggestions for developing future research.

Savings

According to Fisher and Anong (2012), economists and social scientists define saving as net income, after deducting agent consumption. In the real world, savings is the financial resource withheld in order to protect the agent from adverse events or to secure purchasing power for future higher-value purchases. It is common to find a distinction between discretionary savings made deliberately and residual savings made when consumption in a given period is involuntarily lower than income earned in the same period. For the present study, savings follow the traditional economic concept of income above consumption in the previous period, excluding the exceptional expenses due to the home and vehicle, among others, and do not differentiate its purpose or its origin (discretionary or residual).

Despite the efforts of some countries, a considerable number of people (even among those who accumulate substantial resources during the productive phase) do not succeed in saving adequate funds for retirement. It should be noted that literature, especially theoretical literature, has mostly focused on developed countries and economies. It should be noted that there are poor social levels even in countries such as the United States and that these social strata were more severely affected by the crisis (Dos-Santos-Felipe et al. 2017). However, there is also theoretical literature in the context of developing countries, such as Deaton (1989), who has studied the relationship between consumption and savings in emerging countries.

In this regard, some literature that advocates saving is highly complex, considering the psychological and behavioral factors that influence personal planning ability, as well as the realization of those intentions (Economic Theory Classical). It is important to highlight that most individuals are poorly informed agents, which limits the ability to process information correctly and base their choices on purely economic factors (Mendes-Da-Silva et al. 2016). The research by Beshears et al. (2015) corroborates the premise of limiting the processing of people's information, and these authors argue that too much or too little information can lead households to save less.

Determinants of Savings

A portion of the studies indicates that the main variables to be investigated as determinants of savings are of several natures: financial, demographic, educational, and psychological profile, among others. Table 3.1 presents a summary of the

Table 3.1 Review of the literature and variables investigated

	Other studies											This study
Variables	(a)	(b)	(c)	(d)	(e)	(f)	(g)	(h)	(i)	(j)	(k)	(l)
Government assistance								✓				
Banking						✓		✓				
Own home		✓	✓	✓	✓	✓	✓				✓	✓
Shock on income	✓		✓	✓	✓				✓	✓		✓
Financial knowledge						✓		✓		✓		
Panel date	✓				✓			✓			✓	✓
Education	✓	✓		✓	✓	✓	✓	✓	✓	✓	✓	✓
Employment	✓				✓	✓	✓		✓	✓	✓	
Marital status	✓	✓	✓	✓	✓	✓			✓			✓
Income expectation		✓	✓	✓	✓							✓
Children	✓	✓	✓	✓	✓	✓	✓		✓		✓	✓
Future gain/expenses	✓	✓									✓	
Geography		✓							✓			
Investment horizon		✓	✓	✓		✓	✓				✓	✓
Age	✓	✓	✓	✓	✓	✓	✓	✓	✓	✓	✓	✓
Uncertainty			✓	✓			✓					
Psychological motivations		✓	✓			✓	✓	✓			✓	
Patrimony	✓	✓	✓	✓	✓	✓	✓	✓				✓
Race/ethnicity		✓	✓	✓	✓		✓	✓	✓	✓	✓	✓
Income		✓	✓	✓	✓	✓	✓	✓	✓	✓	✓	✓
Health	✓			✓	✓	✓	✓				✓	✓
Gender	✓			✓					✓	✓		
Risk tolerance	✓	✓	✓		✓				✓	✓	✓	✓

Source: Elaborated by the author from an empirical literature review

Notes: (a) Kennickell and Lusardi (2005); (b) Rha et al. (2006); (c) Fredrickson (2013); (d) Fisher and Montalto (2010); (e) Yuh and Hanna (2010); (f) Fisher and Hsu (2012); (g) Fisher and Anong (2012); (h) Heckman and Hanna (2012); (i) Whitaker et al. (2013); (j) Babiarz and Robb (2014); (k) Lee and Hanna (2015); (1) this paper empirically evaluates a good part of the variables available in the SCF (which does not occur systematically in the works found, so far, in the literature). Therefore, this is one of the contributions of this study.

independent variables found in the literature. Earlier studies, such as those of Keynes (1936), Katona (1975), and Sunden and Surette (1998), assume that one reason for family savings is to meet the financial needs of their children. However, in contemporary analyses such as Yuh and Hanna (2010), Fisher and Anong (2012), Fredrickson (2013), Babiarz and Robb (2014), and Lee and Hanna (2015), having children lessens the family's propensity to save. Despite this apparent paradox, it is important to distinguish two aspects: the will and the possibility of saving.

While having children can generate a greater demand of the family for preventive savings, the children themselves generate a considerable increase in expenses, which can impair the family's saving capacity. In turn, age is one of the factors most related to saving behavior and was called out in the theories of Modigliani and Brumberg (1954), Friedman (1957), and Shefrin and Thaler (1988) as one of the main determinants. Age also appears as a major factor in most current studies into savings determinants (Yuh and Hanna 2010; Babiarz and Robb 2014; Lee and Hanna 2015).

Comparing the behaviors of men and women can further inform financial professionals and educators, making gender another often-explored variable (Whitaker et al. 2013). Fisher (2010) argues that women are less likely to save in the short run. In addition, women tend to exhibit lower risk tolerance than men. Education is usually exploited as the ability to make financial decisions that maximize the income and financial security of the family. Yuh and Hanna (2010), Fisher and Montalto (2011), Fisher and Anong (2012), Heckman and Hanna (2012), and Babiarz and Robb (2014) found positive correlations between education and the propensity to save.

Regarding the financial condition of the families, most studies show that, if everything remains constant, an increase in income generates, in absolute terms, an increase in both consumption capacity and savings. Rha et al. (2006) argue that, under ideal conditions, retirement income derived from either equity or savings would be perfect substitutes, which should result in a negative correlation between these factors; yet their research points to the opposite. Recent literature shows that, in fact, increases in income also generate a decrease in the marginal propensity to consume, thus increasing the percentage of income that is earmarked for savings (Fisher and Montalto 2011; Babiarz and Robb 2014; Fredrickson 2013; Lee and Hanna 2015).

Both positive and negative associations between wealth and savings have been investigated by several authors. Fisher and Anong (2012) analyzed the factors that lead households to save regularly (discretionary savings) and irregularly (residual savings) and identified a positive association between equity and residual saving, which is not significant for discretionary savings. Bowman et al. (1999), Fisher and Montalto (2010), and Fredrickson (2013) show that the resistance to decrease consumption under lower than expected income conditions is greater than the resistance to increase consumption in higher than expected income conditions.

Regarding the investment horizon of the families, for Fisher and Montalto (2011), Fisher and Anong (2012), and Lee and Hanna (2015), the probability of saving is positively associated with both a medium horizon and a long financial planning. Fredrickson (2013) investigates how marital status influences the propensity to save and finds evidence that being married is a positively associated factor to saving. Similarly, Fisher and Montalto (2011) assumed "being married" as the base category and found significant negative coefficients for the categories "separated/divorced," "widowed," and "never married." The customs and habits derived from the cultural formation of families also seem to affect personal financial decisions, although challenges remain inadequately discriminating which effects arise from cultural differences and which arise from socioeconomic differences between the ethnic groups. In this regard, Babiarz and Robb (2014) found a negative association for minorities in relation to White respondents.

The results revealed by Fredrickson (2013) and Lee and Hanna (2015) suggest that, compared to Caucasians, Blacks are less likely to save, while other ethnicities, other than Blacks and Hispanics, are more likely to save than Caucasians. However, Fisher and Anong (2012) presented a positive and significant result for Black vis-à-vis Whites. Fisher and Hsu (2012) compared how the explanatory factors of savings behavior between Whites and Hispanics were modified and found that age was negatively associated with saving for Hispanics, but was not a significant factor for Whites. With a particular focus on low-income families, Heckman and Hanna (2012) found that all minorities were more likely to save than Whites.

For Fisher and Montalto (2011), Fisher and Anong (2012), and Lee and Hanna (2015), having medium or poor health was negatively related to savings. For Yuh and Hanna (2010), not owning a home implies a greater propensity for saving, since tenants need to save more for retirement, to possibly buy their own house in the future. However, Fisher and Montalto (2011) and Lee and Hanna (2015), suggest that home ownership significantly increases the likelihood of saving.

Bowman Model Fundamentals et al. (1999)

Bowman et al. (1999) extended the prospect theory (Kahneman and Tversky 1979) to assimilate how loss aversion affects the probability for savings of economic agents. This savings model considers the effects of loss aversion in scenarios of uncertainty. Bowman et al. (1999) postulate that agents measure utility by comparing their current level of consumption with their previous level of consumption.

Taking into account uncertainty about the economic future, loss-averse agents tend to be reluctant to reduce their level of consumption, even after negative shocks to their income. Bowman et al. (1999), Fisher and Montalto (2010), and Fredrickson (2013) conclude that shocks in household income generate asymmetric impacts on the decision to save, depending on the direction of the shock in the income. In addition, income shocks can cause transitory effects as consumers adapt to their new level of wealth (Carroll 1992, 2009). The model presented by Bowman et al. (1999) describes the utility of an individual by the function $U\ (\alpha,\ \beta)$. That is a function by which utility is expressed in terms of the current consumption level α and its reference consumption level β. This function is expressed by (1), where $\gamma\ (\cdot)$ is the utility function, and $\rho\ (\cdot)$ is the "reference function".

$$U(\alpha, \beta) = \rho(\beta) + \gamma(\alpha - \beta) \tag{3.1}$$

The function of utility v (·) is based on the assumptions of utility defined by Kahneman and Tversky (1979), which were:

- The utility is defined in terms of profit and loss, regardless of the original reference value. Values potentially below the reference level were computed as losses, and values above the reference level are earned.
- γ (x) is primarily increasing in x.
- The utility curve takes the form of S, that is, concave in the domain of gains and convex in the domain of losses.
- The function is not symmetric, since the curve of losses is more inclined than that of gains, indicating that losses and gains of equal magnitude are not canceled but instead generate a negative utility result, where $U(X)$ is the utility derived from the gain of X, and X as a positive real number, we have $|U(-X)| > U(+X)|$.

Impacts of the Crisis on the Propensity for Savings

Current literature suggests that the subprime crisis does not appear to have affected homogenous American households, as might be expected. Researchers in this field suggest that the greatest financial impacts were on lower-income individuals (Emmons and Noeth 2012; Kennickell 2012; Pfeffer et al. 2013; Necker and Ziegelmeyer 2016), Blacks and Hispanics (Taylor et al. 2011; Emmons and Noeth 2012; Pfeffer et al. 2013), those with less formal education (Emmons and Noeth 2012; Pfeffer et al. 2013), and those who were younger (Emmons and Noeth 2012).

Although the richest families suffered the largest absolute losses, in relative terms the crisis insinuated the greatest impact on lower-income families, belonging to minorities, with lower levels of education, who were younger. Wealth reduction among the wealthy was mainly due to the fall in stock prices and the investments maintained by the families. Households with fewer resources, despite not having a significant part of their equity in shares, suffered from falling property prices, which typically represent a considerable portion of their assets (Emmons and Noeth 2012).

Method

Data Collection and Description

This study references data from the 2007 and 2013 editions of the *Survey of Consumer Finances*[1](SCF), a survey conducted by the Federal Reserve (FED) every 3 years, covering a wide range of personal finance issues. Regarding the

[1]For more information on the SCF data set, it is recommended to see the works of Dettling and Hsu (2014) and Bricker and Kennickell (2017).

validity of the SCF, the EDF points out the following: "... SCF employs a sample design, essentially unchanged since 1989, consisting of two parts: a standard, geographically based random sample and a special oversample of relatively wealthy families. Weights are used to combine information from the two samples to make estimates for the full population." That is, it is assumed to be valid and representative of the population of the United States (FED 2014, p. 5). In 2007 (precrisis) and 2013 (postcrisis) editions, 4522 and 6026 families were interviewed, respectively, between May and December of both years (FED 2007, 2013). Families in which one of the members is retired were disregarded, an exclusion justified by the assumption that retirees tend to concentrate their investments primarily on fixed income assets and are in a state of disarray during their retirement years, as argued by Ando and Modigliani (1963) and Kennickell and Lusardi (2005). After excluding the retired group, the 2007 and 2013 samples included 3433 and 4603 families, respectively.

Adopted Model Specification

Our research objective is to compare the factors that lead a family to save or consume within a given year and to investigate how the economic crisis, which peaked in 2008, may have affected these factors. The dependent variable in this study is savings, a dummy variable that identifies whether the family in question was able to save money in the year before and after the economic crisis. Logistic regression modeling provided the statistical support for this investigation of households' propensity to save, as is widely recommended for cases in which the dependent variable is binary (Bohrnstedt et al. 2002). Table 3.2 presents the model's independent variables. Control variables were selected to reflect recent findings on the determinants of saving (Rha et al. 2006; Fisher and Montalto 2010; Yuh and Hanna 2010; Fisher and Hsu 2012; Fisher and Anong 2012; Heckman and Hanna 2012; Whitaker et al. 2013; Fredrickson 2013; Babiarz and Robb 2014); as summarized in Table 3.2.

The variables of shock with expectation of income and uncertainty differ from the other variables in as much as they deal with family expectations, not objective data. Its inclusion in the set of independent variables finds support in the arguments around the model of Bowman et al. (1999). For the continuous variables, the procedure of subtracting the average of each variable from its observations was adopted to guarantee normal distribution. In addition, the variance inflation factor (FIV) was used to verify the occurrence of multicollinearity, which pointed to the nonexistence of multicollinearity among the independent variables.

Table 3.2 Description of the variables used

Variable	Type	Description
Savings	Dummy	1 if the family managed to save in the previous year, excluding eventual acquisitions of own property and/or car
Children	Continuous	Number of children in the family
Age	Continuous	Respondent's age in years
Education	Continuous	Number of years of schooling, including primary, secondary and tertiary education
Income	Continuous	Income measured in the previous year, in dollars
Patrimony	Continuous	Property held by the family in dollars
Shock on income expectation		
Above expectation	Dummy	1 if the previous year's income was higher than the expected income for a normal year
Below expectation	Dummy	1 if the previous year's income was lower than the income expected for a normal year
Same expectation†	Dummy	1 if the previous year's income was equal to the income expected for a normal year
Uncertainty	Dummy	1 if the family is unsure about how much income they will have the following year
Financial risk tolerance		
High-risk tolerance	Dummy	1 if the family classifies its financial risk tolerance as high, as regards the management of its equity
Medium to low-risk tolerance	Dummy	1 if the family classifies its tolerance to financial risk as medium or low, as regards the management of its equity
No risk tolerance†	Dummy	1 if the family classifies its financial risk tolerance as null in relation to the management of its equity
Investment horizon		
Short†	Dummy	1 if the horizon considered for family financial planning is equal to or less than 1 year
Medium	Dummy	1 if the horizon considered for family financial planning is greater than 1 year and less than 10 years
Long	Dummy	1 if the horizon considered for family financial planning is greater than 10 years
Marital status		
Married†	Dummy	1 if the interviewee is married
Common-law marriage	Dummy	1 if the interviewee lives with his or her partner
Separated	Dummy	1 if the interviewee is separated/divorced
Widowed	Dummy	1 if the interviewee is a widow
Single	Dummy	1 if the interviewee is single
Race		
White†	Dummy	1 if the respondent's race is White, Caucasian, or Arab
Black	Dummy	1 if the race of the interviewee is Black or African-American
Hispanic	Dummy	1 if the respondent's race is Hispanic or Latin

(continued)

Table 3.2 (continued)

Variable	Type	Description
Other	Dummy	1 if the respondent's race is none of the above
Health		
Good†	Dummy	1 if the health of both the respondent and the spouse is excellent
Median	Dummy	1 if the health of the respondent and/or the spouse is fair
Weak	Dummy	1 if the health of the respondent and/or spouse is poor
Own home	Dummy	1 if the family lives in a property of their own

Source: Prepared by the author
Note: The variables were grouped into combinations and transformations of SCF questions. The baseline categories for each set of variables are †

Empirical Results

Descriptive Statistics

Table 3.3 presents the descriptive statistics of the investigated variables, for the pre- and postcrisis periods. With respect to the dependent variable (savings), it is noted that the percentage of savings of the American families was reduced by approximately 1.5%. There was also a reduction in the number of families that earned income above the expectation for a typical year, while the number of families that had income below expectations increased from 16.9% to 21.7%.

The risk profile and the financial horizon of the families also changed. In the postcrisis period, a larger portion of households declared that they did not tolerate any type of financial risk in the management of their assets and considered a shorter time horizon for their financial decisions. The respondents' age did not show significant bearing, but there was a considerable change in the marital status of the Americans. The proportion of married individuals declined by 4.4%; the same reduction effect was observed in the number of divorced persons (1.7%).

Alternatively, there was an increase in the number of single Americans, about 3.3%; widows, 0.8%; and common-law marriage (stable union), 1.9%. The health conditions of the population also worsened; according to the statements of the respondents, there was a reduction of 2.7% in the number of people who were judged to have good health. The average income increased only in nominal terms, since accumulated inflation for the period was 12.35%, resulting in a real variation in income of −5.7% (inflation of the period calculated by the consumer price index accumulated between January 2007 and December 2013). The share of families that owned the property in which they lived was also reduced, from 57.5% to 52.7% (a reduction of 4.9%). And finally, average family wealth declined by almost 15% in nominal terms, equivalent to a contraction of 24% in real terms.

Table 3.3 Descriptive statistics of variables

Variables	Mean (standard deviation)		Δ pp	
	Precrisis	Postcrisis		
Savings	44.6%	43.1%	−1.5 pp	***
Shock on income expectation				
Above expectation	9.8%	7.8%	−1.9 pp	***
Below expectation	16.9%	21.7%	4.8 pp	***
Same expectation	73.4%	70.5%	−2.9 pp	***
Uncertainty	34.4%	36.5%	2.1 pp	***
Financial risk tolerance				
High-risk tolerance	23.2%	19.9%	−3.3 pp	***
Medium- to low-risk tolerance	39.1%	37.5%	−1.6 pp	***
No risk tolerance	37.7%	42.6%	4.9 pp	***
Investment horizon				
Short	33.9%	42.8%	8.9 pp	***
Medium	51.5%	45.6%	−6.0 pp	***
Long	14.6%	11.6%	−3.0 pp	***
Children	1.03 (1.22)	1.01 (1.22)	−2.7 pp	**
Age	43.3 (12.7)	44.2 (13.3)	1.9 pp	***
Education (years)	13.4 (2.7)	13.6 (2.7)	1.5 pp	***
Marital status				
Married	51.0%	46.6%	−4.4 pp	***
Common-law marriage	9.3%	11.2%	1.9 pp	***
Separated	19.5%	17.8%	−1.7 pp	***
Widowed	3.3%	4.1%	0.8 pp	***
Single	16.9%	20.2%	3.3 pp	***
Race				
White	70.2%	66.7%	−3.5 pp	***
Black	13.9%	15.5%	1.6 pp	***
Hispanic	11.1%	12.5%	1.4 pp	***
Other	4.8%	5.3%	0.5 pp	**
Health				
Good	72.5%	69.8%	−2.7 pp	***
Median	21.9%	24.1%	2.2 pp	***
Weak	5.7%	6.1%	0.4 pp	*
Income (U$ thousand)	84.2 (362.9)	89.2 (370,5)	6.0 pp	—
Own home	57.5%	52.7%	−4.9 pp	***
Patrimony (U$ thousand)	542.4 (3579.3)	462.7 (3625.2)	—	**

Source: Research data

Note: $*p < 0.1$; $**p < 0.05$; $***p < 0.01$; *pp* percentage points

Binary Logistic Regression

Table 3.4 presents the logistic regression results for each period. The first important information is that no variable whose coefficient is seen as significant in both 2007 and 2013 changes signal between one period and another. The factors that contribute positively to the savings decision and which were significant in both years include income, equity, high and medium tolerance to financial risk, and medium and long horizon of investments and belong to the Hispanic race or to another race which was not included in the alternatives presented.

Equally, factors that contribute negatively to the savings decision in both periods are having children, age, earning below expected income, being separated or divorced, and having reported being compromised. In 2007, each additional child reduced the likelihood of savings by 16.8%, while in 2013 the probability reduction was 21.6% for each additional child.

The adjusted coefficients in the continuous variables were transformed into the natural logarithm of the original variable (age, education, income, and equity). In these, the adjusted coefficient indicates the relationship between the saving probability and the logarithm of the percentage change in the continuous independent variable. Table 3.5 shows the variation of the saving probability for each continuous variable, and it is noted that a 100% increase in the respondent's age would reduce its probability of saving in 2013 by 33.7% – the difference between a respondent of 25 and another of 50 years. In the traditional life cycle model (Modigliani and Brumberg 1954), age is related to savings according to the pattern of increase, and subsequent decrease, of income over a lifetime. However, if the income is constant, the life cycle model assumes that the optimal savings should be higher for the young (Yuh and Hanna 2010), corroborating the findings of the present study.

While education was a significant factor before the crisis ($\widehat{\psi} = -0.141, p < 0.1$), it became even more relevant and positive afterward ($\widehat{\psi} = 0.473, p < 0.01$). Rha et al. (2006) argue that more educated agents as young people may worry less about saving, on the belief that they will have a high income in the future, implying a negative coefficient between education and a propensity to save. However, Babiarz and Robb (2014) studied the relationship between financial proficiency and maintaining financial reserves for emergencies and concluded that the level of financial knowledge has significant effects on the existence of emergency reserves. It can be assumed that additional years of training reinforce awareness and financial discipline, which in turn contribute to the increase in the level of savings. Yuh and Hanna (2010), Fisher and Montalto (2011), Fisher and Anong (2012), and Heckman and Hanna (2012) also reported positive relationships between education and savings.

The last two continuous variables, income and equity, presented significant and positive coefficients in the 2 years. While the coefficient of income increased from 0.353 ($p < 0.01$) to 0.571 ($p < 0.01$), the equity ratio decreased from 0.104 ($p < 0.01$) to 0.078 ($p < 0.01$). Fisher and Anong (2012), in a study that included the reasons for saving among the control variables, showed that small variations in

Table 3.4 Statistical results

	Coefficients		Adjusted coefficients(‡)	
Independent variables	Precrisis	Postcrisis	2007	2013
Children	−0.184***	−0.244***	−16.8%	−21.6%
Age	−0.192** (0.077)	−0.667*** (0.066)	−17.5%	−48.7%
Education	−0.141* (0.080)	0.473*** (0.085)	−13.1%	60.5%
Income	0.353*** (0.019)	0.571*** (0.021)	42.3%	77.1%
Patrimony	0.104*** (0.007)	0.078*** (0.005)	11.0%	8.2%
Shock on income expectation				
Above expectation	0.016 (0.057)	−0.243*** (0.055)	1.6%	−21.6%
Below expectation	−0.371*** (0.052)	−0.251*** (0.042)	−31.0%	−22.2%
Uncertainty	−0.062 (0.038)	−0.395*** (0.033)	−6.0%	−32.6%
Financial risk tolerance				
High-risk tolerance	0.318*** (0.048)	0.043*** (0.043)	37.5%	4.4%
Medium- to low-risk tolerance	0.308*** (0.041)	0.119*** (0.035)	36.1%	12.7%
Investment horizon				
Medium	0.275*** (0.039)	0.238** (0.032)	31.7%	26.9%
Long	0.615*** (0.055)	0.596*** (0.052)	84.9%	81.6%
Status marital				
Common-law marriage (yes = 1; no = 0)	−0.204*** (0.070)	0.011 (0.054)	−18.5%	1.1%
Separated (yes = 1; no = 0)	−0.248*** (0.051)	−0.133*** (0.046)	−22.0%	−12.4%
Widowed (yes = 1; no = 0)	−0.052 (0.110)	0.234*** (0.088)	−5.1%	26.3%
Single (yes = 1; no = 0)	0.213*** (0.062)	0.094* (0.069)	23.7%	9.9%
Race				
Black (yes = 1; no = 0)	0.104* (0.060)	0.138*** (0.049)	10.9%	14.8%
Hispanic (yes = 1; no = 0)	0.242*** (0.066)	0.105* (0.052)	27.4%	11.1%
Other	0.199** (0.083)	0.146* (0.083)	22.0%	15.7%

(continued)

Table 3.4 (continued)

	Coefficients		Adjusted coefficients$^{(‡)}$	
Independent variables	Precrisis	Postcrisis	2007	2013
Health				
Median	−0.488*** (0.045)	−0.261*** (0.038)	−38.6%	−22.9%
Weak	−0.446***	−0.317***	−36.0%	−27.2%
Own home	−0.143***	0.007	−13.4%	0.7%
McFadden R-square	19.30%	21.80%		
Pearson's chi-square	15,631.64***	25,365.37***		
Hosmer-Lemeshow	204.59***	123.72***		
% of correct ratings	71.24%	71.87%		

Source: Research data

Note: *p < 0.1; **p < 0.05; ***p < 0.01. $^{(‡)}$ The adjusted coefficients aim to facilitate the interpretation of the binomial variables. The relationship between the regression coefficients and the adjusted coefficients is given by adjusted coefficient $= e^{\text{coefficient}} - 1$

Table 3.5 Estimation of adjusted coefficients of observed variables

		Δ%		
Variable	Subsample	10%	50%	100%
Age	Precrisis	−1.7%	−7.1%	−12.1%
	Postcrisis	−4.6%	−19.7%	−33.7%
Education	Precrisis	−1.3%	−5.3%	−9.1%
	Postcrisis	5.8%	24.5%	41.9%
Income	Precrisis	4.0%	17.1%	29.3%
	Postcrisis	7.3%	31.3%	53.4%
Patrimony	Precrisis	1.0%	4.4%	7.6%
	Postcrisis	0.8%	3.3%	5.7%

Source: Research data

Note: This table shows the adjusted coefficients of the continuous variables (see Table 3.4)

income were mainly associated with discretionary savings (regular and deliberate), while the relationship with residual savings appears only for greater variations in income. According to Fisher and Anong (2012), the variation in the income coefficient between 2007 and 2013 could be explained by an increase in discretionary savings in relation to residual savings. These same authors concluded that the variable equity is positively related to the residual savings, but has no significant relation with the discretionary saving.

The results obtained with the coefficient of the families that perceived lower incomes than expected converge with the findings of Bowman et al. (1999) and Fisher and Montalto (2011), who argue that, in situations where income declines below the levels expected by the agent, there is resistance to decrease consumption due to its aversion to loss. However, the coefficient associated with the families that realized income higher than what they expected became negative and significant in the postcrisis period ($\widehat{\psi} = -0.243$ ***), in contrast to the results presented by Bowman et al. (1999) and Fisher and Montalto (2011). One likely explanation for such evidence is that a significant increase in income, above family expectations, may also raise expectations of future family earnings and thereby lessen the sense of the need to save in the present.

The negative coefficient in this research may have been due to a side effect associated with positive shocks in family income. In this respect, Yuh and Hanna (2010) included the expectation of income variation as an independent variable in their model, and reported a positive relationship between savings and positive shocks in income, supporting this assumption.

In contrast to classical theories, more recent studies show that in situations of uncertainty, households resist decreasing consumption even when they expect to be unable to maintain their standard of living (Fisher and Montalto 2010; Fisher and Anong 2012; Fredrickson 2013). The results of the present study differed from Fisher and Montalto (2010) for the SCF 2007 ($\widehat{\psi} = -0.062$) but converged in the analysis of 2013 ($\widehat{\psi} = -0.395$; $p < 0.01$); strengthening the premise of uncertainty reduces the likelihood of household savings.

The results of the risk tolerance and the lower probability of saving are in accordance with the findings of Fisher and Montalto (2010). The research showed that the coefficients linked to risk tolerance reduced considerably between the pre- and postcrisis period (2007, $\widehat{\psi} = 0.318$, $p < 0.01$; 2013, $\widehat{\psi} = 0.043$, $p < 0.01$). A viable explanation for this result is that families with greater risk tolerance have a portfolio of assets with greater exposure to capital markets and other higher volatility assets, which performed better in the years prior to the 2008 crisis, and arguably worse performance in consecutive years.

White families' equity declined by 16%; Black and Hispanic families suffered a 53% and 66% devaluation, respectively. White families accounted for 7 times the share of Black families in 1995, rising to 11 times in 2004 and 19 times in 2009 (the highest since 1984, when the first edition of the SCF came out).

Minorities may have undergone more significant changes in their willingness to spare. For low-income populations, Heckman and Hanna (2012) found that minorities had a significantly higher probability of saving relative to White households, in line with the hypothesis presented, with the results of this study, and with the perception that socioeconomic differences between ethnic groups do not explain the distinct probabilities of saving.

On the other hand, contrary to expectations, Yuh and Hanna (2010) showed that families with Black members were 21.6% less likely to save than White families. The significant difference between the present research and the findings of Yuh and Hanna (2010) can be explained by the absence of variables in their study (investment horizon, risk tolerance, and uncertainty) or by the presence of the employment variable, which does not appear in this study.

The results of the positive relationship between good health and savings are in agreement with most of the related studies (Fisher and Montalto 2011; Fisher and Anong 2012; Lee and Hanna 2015). The decrease in health ratios between 2007 and

2013 indicates that during this period, health became a less important factor for household savings, and the variation can be explained by the sanction of the Patient Protection and Affordable Care Act in 2010 (as it increased coverage of public health plans for a larger portion of the population). Positive shocks in income, uncertainty about the economic future, age, educational level, income, and the number of children were the coefficients that increased in importance, while those that decreased in importance were owning a home, high- and medium- to low-risk tolerance, medium or poor health, and negative income shocks.

Figure 3.1 corroborates the estimates discussed throughout this section and highlights the marginal effects of the American households' propensity to save, comparing the pre- and post-economic crisis. The economic crisis of 2007/2008 seems to have induced a greater concern for families and individuals to save financial resources for the future. Figure 3.2 shows a marked reduction in the need for savings of American households after the economic crisis, which may indicate a greater financial awareness of people to prevent rare, unexpected, and striking events.

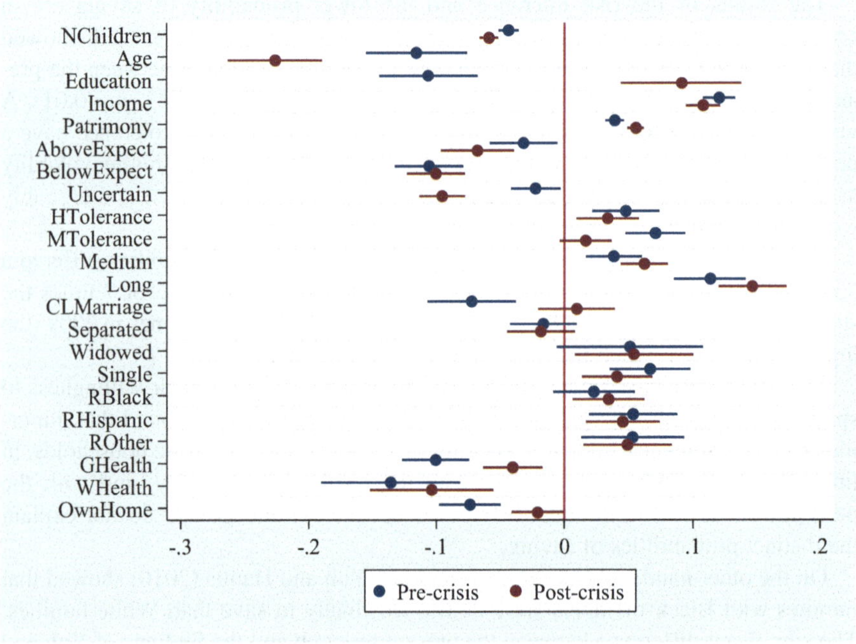

Fig. 3.1 Marginal effects of propensity to save before and after the economic crisis. Note: This figure shows the marginal effects of the American households' propensity to save before (2007) and after (2013) the economic crisis. Since it is possible to understand that there have been strong changes in people's saving behavior

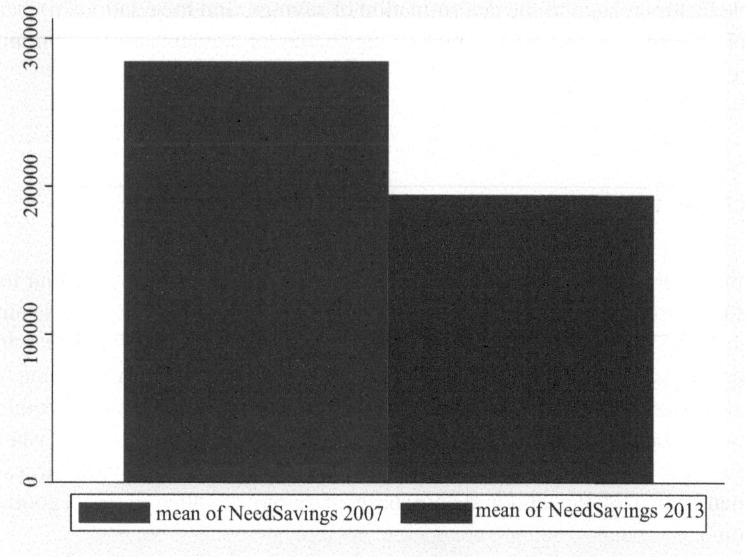

Fig. 3.2 Need for savings (in dollars) of American families before and after the economic crisis. Note: This figure shows the reduction in the financial need for resources to be saved by families and individuals after the period of economic recession in 2007/2008

Concluding Remarks

The empirical evidence presented in this paper suggests that the subprime crisis had a significant impact on the determinants of the propensity for saving in a developed economy country. In general, the findings point to a behavioral change between the two periods "before" and "after" the climax of the crisis. Despite the empirical assumption that the economic crisis has had significant impacts on the financial behavior of Americans, there remains the paradox documented in the literature about the relationship between some groups of determinants and the propensity to save. That is, factors such as ethnicity, wealth, income shocks, and uncertainty deserve further deepening with the intention of better understanding not only the existence of associations between these factors and savings but also the underlying motives that explain such associations. In addition, it was found that the financial need for household savings was greatly reduced after the crisis. That is, individuals and families may have gained some financial experience from the lesson they experienced during the country's severe economic and financial recession.

As contributions of the present study, it is understood that the results provide important information about the relations between factors determining the savings of American families, as specifically impacted by widespread economic crisis. These findings can inform financial professionals and educators in making recommendations for savings and provide guidelines that are more coherent with the economic and financial reality of their countries. It should be emphasized that there are other possible factors related to the determination of savings, and the relationship between these unexamined factors with actual savings behavior demands a deep continuation in the exhaustion of this issue.

Directions for Future Research

From the theoretical literature on the propensity for savings, we identify four lines of study that hold high potential for further research in this subject. The first is outlined by Fisher and Anong (2012) and Lee and Hanna (2015), to include psychological motives among the determinants of the propensity for saving. Lee and Hanna (2015) used an adaptation of the hierarchy of needs (basic needs, safety, comfort in retirement, social needs, self-esteem, and self-actualization), while Fisher and Anong supported the six categories proposed by Katona (1975) (basic necessities, retirement, need of the children, purchase of home or other durable goods, and vacations).

The second proposed line of study is based on the premise that the variables obtained in the regressions have complex and triangular relations between them, so that, for example, the coefficient attributed to age may differ between men and women, since in fact it was presented by Whitaker et al. (2013). The third line of research examines the distinction between potential and intention of saving. Once the data on savings are provided by the respondent, categorically, the willingness and awareness of the importance of saving can offset the answers. This differentiation is relevant in preparing consistent corrective measures. If the problem exists in the ability to save, and not in intention, then programs of awareness and financial education may provide little help. On the other hand, if insufficiency is identified in the will to save, then financial education programs will be more effective than debt reduction and household consumption programs.

This chapter recommends research efforts regarding the relation of financial literacy of families with their preparation for retirement. People's financial literacy is an indispensable prerequisite for the correction of family financial problems (Lusardi and Mitchell 2017). Some of these problems may be derived from people's temptation to consumption, lack of self-control, and limited financial knowledge (Cobb-Clark et al. 2016). Thus, it is believed that deepening research in this direction might reveal important economic information for planning public policies that encourage families to save, not only for retirement but also for eventual domestic financial needs. Finally, it is worth highlighting the existence of a latent need to create a database similar to SCF for several countries, because the variety of information available allows the development of research that may offer relevant implications for the formulation of public policies in financial education, as well as public and private strategies for the supply of financial products, as investment alternatives and savings for families (Grinstein-Weiss et al. 2015).

References

Ando, A., & Modigliani, F. (1963). The 'life-cycle' hypothesis of saving: Aggregate implications and tests. *American Economic Review, 53*(1), 55–84.

Argento, R., Bryant, V. L., & Sabelhaus, J. (2015). Early withdrawals from retirement accounts during the great recession. *Contemporary Economic Policy, 33*(1), 1–16.

Babiarz, P., & Robb, C. A. (2014). Financial literacy and emergency saving. *Journal of Family and Economic Issues, 35*. https://doi.org/10.1007/s10834-013-9369-9.

Barberis, N., & Thaler, R. (2002). *A survey of behavioral finance*. Cambridge: National Bureau of Economic Research. Available at: http://www.nber.org/papers/w9222. https://doi.org/10.3386/w9222.

Beshears, J., Choi, J. J., Laibson, D., Madrian, B. C., & Milkman, K. L. (2015). The effect of providing peer information on retirement savings decisions. *The Journal of Finance, 70*(3), 1161–1201.

Bohrnstedt, G. W., Knoke, D., & Mee, A. P. (2002). *Statistics for social data analysis* (4th ed.). Itasca, IL: Peacock.

Bowman, D., Minehart, D., & Rabin, M. (1999). Loss aversion in a consumption-savings model. *Journal of Economic Behavior and Organization, 38*. https://doi.org/10.1016/S0167-2681(99)00004-9.

Braun Santos, D., Mendes-Da-Silva, W., Flores, E., & Norvilitis, J. M. (2016). Predictors of credit card use and perceived financial well-being of female college students: A Brazil-United States comparative study. *International Journal of Consumer Studies, 40*, 133–142. https://doi.org/10.1111/ijcs.12234.

Bricker, J., & Kennickell, A. B. (2017). Shared understanding and data quality in the SCF. *Statistical Journal of the IAOS, 33*(1), 165–174.

Carroll, C. D. (1992). The buffer-stock theory of saving: Some macroeconomic evidence. *Brookings Papers on Economic Activity, 1992*(1), 61–156.

Carroll, C. D. (2009). Precautionary saving and the marginal propensity to consume out of permanent income. *Journal of Monetary Economics, 56*, 780–790.

Cobb-Clark, D. A., Kassenboehmer, S. C., & Sinning, M. G. (2016). Locus of control and savings. *Journal of Banking & Finance, 73*, 113–130.

Deaton, A. (1989). Saving in developing countries: Theory and review. In *Proceedings of The World Bank Annual Conference on Development Economics*.

Dettling, L. J., & Hsu, J. W. (2014). The state of young adults' balance sheets: Evidence from the survey of consumer finances. *Federal Reserve Bank of St. Louis Review, 96*(4), 305–330.

Dos-Santos-Felipe, I. J., Ermel, M. D. A., Cassius, L. F. P., & Mendes-Da-Silva, W. (2017). Efeito de Crise Econômica sobre Escolhas de Ativos para Investimentos Pessoais. *Revista de Administração Contemporânea, 21*, 84–109. https://doi.org/10.1590/1982-7849rac2017160087.

Emmons, W. R., & Noeth, B. J. (2012). Household financial stability: Who suffered the most from the crisis? *The Regional Economist*, (Jul).

Federal Reserve Board FED. (2014). Changes in U.S. Family finances from 2010 to 2013: Evidence from the survey of consumer finances. *Federal Reserve Bulletin, 100*(4). https://www.federalreserve.gov/pubs/bulletin/2014/pdf/scf14.pdf.

Federal Reserve Board FED. (2007). *Survey of consumer finances*. Available at: https://www.federalreserve.gov/econresdata/scf/scf_2007.htm.

Federal Reserve Board FED. (2013). *Survey of consumer finances*. Available at: https://www.federalreserve.gov/econresdata/scf/scfindex.htm.

Fisher, P. J. (2010). Gender differences in personal saving behaviors. *Journal of Financial Counseling and Planning, 21*(1), 14–24.

Fisher, P. J., & Anong, S. T. (2012). Relationship of saving motives to saving habits. *Journal of Financial Counseling and Planning, 23*(1), 63–79.

Fisher, P. J., & Hsu, C. (2012). Differences in household saving between non-Hispanic white and Hispanic households. *Hispanic Journal of Behavioral Sciences, 34*. https://doi.org/10.1177/0739986311428891.

Fisher, P. J., & Montalto, C. P. (2010). Effect of saving motives and horizon on saving behaviors. *Journal of Economic Psychology, 31*. https://doi.org/10.1016/j.joep.2009.11.002.

Fisher, P. J., & Montalto, C. P. (2011). Loss aversion and saving behavior: Evidence from the 2007 U.S. survey of consumer finance. *Journal of Family and Economic Issues, 32*. https://doi.org/10.1007/s10834-010-9196-1.

Fredrickson, J. E. (2013). Prospect theory and saving behaviors during the great recession: 2009 SCF panel survey results. *Journal of Behavioral Studies in Business, 6*(1), 1–17.

Friedman, M. (1957). *A theory of the consumption function*. Princeton: Princeton University Press.

Grinstein-Weiss, M., Guo, S., Reinertson, V., & Russell, B. (2015). Financial education and savings outcomes for low-income IDA participants: Does age make a difference? *Journal of Consumer Affairs, 49*(1), 156–185. https://doi.org/10.1111/joca.12061.

Heckman, S., & Hanna, S. D. (2012). Factors related to saving behavior among low-income households in the 1992–2007 survey of consumer finances. *Proceedings of the Academy of Financial Services* Available at SSRN: https://ssrn.com/abstract=2178264.

Kahneman, D., & Tversky, A. (1979). Prospect theory: An analysis of decision under risk. *Econometrica, 47*(2), 263–291. https://doi.org/10.2307/1914185.

Kahneman, D., & Tversky, A. (2000). Choices, values, and frames. In: Kahneman, D., Tversky, A (eds) Choices, values, and frames. Cambridge University Press, Cambridge, p. 1–16.

Katona, G. (1975). *Psychological economics*. Nova Iorque: Elsevier.

Kennickell, A. B. (2012). *The other, other half: Changes in the finances of the least wealthy 50 percent, 2007–2009*. *Finance & economic discussion paper*, Federal Reserve Board, Washington, DC

Kennickell, A., & Lusardi, A. (2005). *Disentangling the importance of the precautionary savings motive*. Center for Financial Studies Working Paper Series

Keynes, J. M. (1936). *The general theory of employment, interest, and money*. Londres: Macmillan.

Lee, J. M., & Hanna, S. D. (2015). Savings goals and saving behavior from a perspective of Maslow's hierarchy of needs. *Journal of Financial Counseling and Planning, 26*(2), 129–147.

Lusardi, A., & Mitchell, O. S. (2017). How ordinary consumers make complex economic decisions: Financial literacy and retirement readiness. *Quarterly Journal of Finance, 7*(03), 1750008.

Mendes-Da-Silva, W., Costa Junior, N. C., Barros, L. A. B. C., Armada, M. J. R., & Norvilitis, J. M. (2015). Behavioral finance: Advances in the last decade. *Revista de Administração de Empresas, 55*, 10–13. https://doi.org/10.1590/S0034-759020150102.

Mendes-Da-Silva, W., Gattaz, C. C., & Gibson, D. V. (2016). Decisão sob Ignorância e Disclosure de Produto: Implicações na Compra de Seguros. In *Proceedings of the 40° EnAnpad*.

Modigliani, F., & Brumberg, R. H. (1954). *Utility analysis and the consumption function: An interpretation of cross-section data* (K. K. Kurihara Ed.). New Brunswick: Post Keynesian Economics.

Moore, J. F., & Mitchell, O. S. (1997). *Projected retirement wealth and savings adequacy in the health and retirement study*. Cambridge, MA: National Bureau of Economic Research. https://doi.org/10.3386/w6240.

Necker, S., & Ziegelmeyer, M. (2016). Household risk taking after the financial crisis. *The Quarterly Review of Economics and Finance, 59*, 141–160.

Pfeffer, F. T., Danziger, S., & Schoeni, R. F. (2013). Wealth disparities before and after the great recession. *The ANNALS of the American Academy of Political and Social Science, 650*(1), 98–123.

Potrich, A. C. G., Vieira, K. M., & Mendes-Da-Silva, W. (2016). Development of a financial literacy model for university students. *Management Research Review, 39*, 356–376. https://doi.org/10.1108/MRR-06-2014-0143.

Rha, J. Y., Montalto, C., & Hanna, S. D. (2006). The effect of self-control mechanisms on household saving behavior. *Journal of Financial Counseling and Planning, 17*(2).

Shefrin, H. M., & Statman, M. (1985). The disposition to sell winners too early and ride losers too long: Theory and evidence. *The Journal of Finance, 40*(3), 777–790.

Shefrin, H. M., & Statman, M. (2000). Behavioral portfolio theory. *Journal of Financial and Quantitative Analysis, 35*(2), 127–151. https://doi.org/10.2307/2676187.

Shefrin, H. M., & Thaler, R. H. (1988). The behavioral life-cycle hypothesis. *Economic Inquiry, 26* (4). https://doi.org/10.1111/j.1465-7295.1988.tb01520.x.

Social Security Administration – SSA. (2017). Available at: https://www.ssa.gov/oact/TR/2017/tr2017.pdf.

Sunden, A. E., & Surette, B. J. (1998). Gender differences in the allocation of assets in retirement savings plans. *The American Economic Review, 88*(2), 207–211.

Taylor, P., Kochhar, R., Fry, R., Velasco, G., & Motel, S. (2011). *Wealth gaps rise to record highs between whites, blacks, and Hispanics*. Washington, DC: Pew Research Center.

Whitaker, E. A., Bokemeiner, J. L., & Loveridge, S. (2013). Interactional associations of gender on savings behavior: Showing gender continued influence on economic action. *Journal of Family and Economic Issues, 34*(1). https://doi.org/10.1007/s10834-012-9307-2.

Yuh, Y., & Hanna, S. D. (2010). Which households think they save? *The Journal of Consumer Affairs, 44*(1), 174–186. https://doi.org/10.1111/j.1745-6606.2010.01158.x.

Chapter 4
A Financial Literacy Model for University Students

Kelmara Mendes Vieira, Ani Caroline Grigion Potrich, and Wesley Mendes-Da-Silva

Abstract Financial literacy, understood as the mastery of a set of knowledge, attitudes, and behaviors, has assumed a fundamental role in allowing and enabling people to make responsible decisions as they strive to attain financial well-being. In this context, the objective of this chapter is to build and compare models that assess university students' financial literacy. To this end, models that integrate financial knowledge, behavior, and attitude are integrated. The models are subsequently estimated, and many comparative tests are performed. For an analysis of the collected data, structural equation modeling (SEM) was employed using two strategies. The findings indicate that, in the model estimation stage, the scales for behavior and attitude have been reduced. Among all of the models estimated, the best adjusted model indicates that financial knowledge and financial attitude have positive impacts on financial behavior. In practical terms, the financial behavior expresses the ability to establish long-term aims and savings aimed at future acquisitions and unexpected spending. This behavior is directly influenced by basic and advanced questions of financial knowledge and also by the importance attributed to attitude by establishing aims, control of spending and financial reserves.

Keywords Financial literacy · Structural equation modeling · Competing models

---

Portions of this chapter appeared in the 2016 paper "Development of a financial literacy model for university students," *Management Research Review*, vol 39, pp 356–376.

K. M. Vieira
Department of Business Administration, Federal University of Santa Maria, Santa Maria, RS, Brazil

A. C. G. Potrich (✉)
Department of Business Administration, Federal University of Santa Catarina, Florianópolis, SC, Brazil
e-mail: ani.potrich@ufsc.br

W. Mendes-Da-Silva
Sao Paulo School of Business Administration (FGV/EAESP), Sao Paulo, SP, Brazil

University of Texas at Austin, Austin, TX, USA

W. Mendes-Da-Silva (ed.), *Individual Behaviors and Technologies for Financial Innovations*, https://doi.org/10.1007/978-3-319-91911-9_4

JEL Code C91 · E51 · D9

Financial literacy is seen as a critical competence for the twenty-first century (Messy and Monticone 2016) and essential for the full participation of the individual in society (OECD 2015c). Decisions made and outcomes experienced matter not only at the household level but also for the economy as a whole; an extreme example is the subprime mortgage crisis which devastated household finances and triggered the last recession (Lusardi et al. 2017). Governments and international entities around the world are interested in finding effective approaches, and numerous studies have been dedicated to this theme: to create or improve national strategies for financial education that offer learning opportunities at various levels of education and thus improve a population's level of financial literacy. For example, the Organisation for Economic Co-operation and Development (OECD), recognizing the increasingly global nature of financial literacy and education issues, created the International Network on Financial Education (INFE) to benefit from and encompass the experience and expertise of developed and emerging economies. More than 240 public institutions from more than 110 countries and economies are members of the INFE (OECD 2017).

Despite such efforts, there is still no consensus on the concept and measurement of financial literacy. Many adhere to the definition offered by OECD, describing financial literacy as a combination of the consciousness, knowledge, ability, attitude, and behavior that are necessary to make financial decisions and, accordingly, to achieve individual financial wealth. In this context, financial education is a process of ability development that facilitates people to make correct decisions and to manage their personal finances successfully, while financial literacy is the capacity to use the knowledge and abilities acquired. In other words, the focus of financial education is knowledge, while financial literacy involves an individual attaining, apart from knowledge, successful financial attitudes, and behaviors (OECD 2015b).

As for the measures, different instruments have been proposed to assess financial literacy, including Chen and Volpe (1998), Murphy and Yetmar (2010), Lusardi (2015a) and Clark et al. (2015) in the USA. Studies examining families from the UK were conducted by Disney and Gathergood (2011), while Sekita (2011) conducted a similar study in Japan and Ansong (2011) with university students in Ghana. Van Rooij et al. (2011) and Bucher-Koenen et al. (2017) studied people in Holland and Gerrans and Heaney (2014) in Australia, in addition to comparative studies among several developed countries with the OECD (2015b) instrument. Among the emergent countries, it is still common to find works that discuss the themes explored in this article. In the Brazilian scenario, for example, Mendes-Da-Silva et al. (2012), Norvilitis and Mendes-Da-Silva (2013), Potrich et al. (2015), Silva et al. (2017), and Santos et al. (2018) have conducted studies regarding the subject of financial literacy.

Although many differences are found in conceptualizing and evaluating the dimensions related to financial literacy, there is a general consensus regarding its importance. Bucher-Koenen et al. (2017) affirmed financial literacy has been linked to economic behavior, including retirement planning and wealth accumulation. Disney et al. (2015) also emphasize that financial literacy can be seen as central to financial decision-making and financial independence, as well as significantly improve financial well-being (Atkinson and Messy 2015).

The literature contends that financial literacy is an interdisciplinary concept with many dimensions. In this way, the need to construct and validate models that consider the measures and their interrelations simultaneously is critical and is the theme of this study. In this context, this study builds and compares models that assess university student financial literacy. To this end, models that integrate financial knowledge, behavior, and attitude are integrated. The models are subsequently estimated, and many comparative tests are performed.

The principal contribution of this paper is the multidimensional measure of financial literacy. Some authors have suggested that financial literacy should be considered more broadly; there is not yet an operationally valid instrument to measure financial literacy in its totality (Remund 2010). According to Fernandes et al. (2014), there is a marked disconnect between such instruments and the conceptual definition of financial literacy, and the authors suggest that future works should develop measures that relate more directly to the conceptual definition of financial literacy and how it has been operationalized.

Background

Financial markets are increasingly complex even while they are more accessible to more people, and with this, the ability of individuals to manage their finances becomes essential. In this context, financial literacy is now a topic for national and international research, recognized as an important element to help prevent financial adversities (Opletalová 2015), providing an intellectual empowerment tool for better decision-making (Huston 2010).

The term financial literacy does not have a single and simple definition in the literature, and it has been frequently used as a synonym for financial education or financial knowledge. However, these constructs actually are conceptually different in that financial literacy is deeper than financial education; thus, using them synonymously can cause problems. Huston (2010) contends that financial literacy has two dimensions: understanding, which represents the personal financial knowledge of financial education, and use, which refers to the management of personal financial knowledge. In this context, the individual could have financial knowledge, but to be considered literate, he should have the ability and confidence to implement it when making decisions.

Therefore, financial literacy is deeper than the basic concept of financial education (Mccormick 2009; Huston 2010). Financial knowledge alone is not sufficient for the effective management of finances, as the influence of financial knowledge on behavior is measured through the student's financial attitudes (Norvilitis and Maclean 2010; Xiao et al. 2011). Having financial acumen goes beyond establishing future savings or managing the bank account; it further includes learning to choose an appropriate financial objective from among several alternatives (Criddle 2006).

In addition, according to Messy and Monticone (2016), financial literacy is a critical competence for individuals, since financial education is an essential complement to the protection and financial capacity of consumers, and efforts must be made to improve both in order to support economic growth in any world economy. Similarly, Fernandes et al. (2014) argue that financial education can be seen as an "information remedy" for a policy mix that includes offering more choices to individuals, providing better information, and, from these, providing incentives for consumers to change their behavior.

A study by Lusardi (2015a) wields a broad definition of financial literacy as the ability to process economic information and make informed decisions about financial planning, accumulation of wealth, debt, and retirement (although Lusardi's metrics only address questions of financial knowledge). In addition, Gerrans and Heaney (2014) define financial literacy as part of a "political arsenal" aimed to facilitate better outcomes for consumers.

Another research dilemma is the lack of models that present the dimensions involved. Remund (2010) has determined that while there is no uniformity among the definitions proposed, most definitions fit into one of the following categories: knowledge of financial concept, the ability to communicate financial concepts attitude to manage personal financial, the ability to make appropriate financial decisions, and the confidence to plan for future financial necessities. Hung et al. (2009) contend that financial literacy can be defined by four variables, financial knowledge, financial attitude, financial behavior, and financial ability, all of which are correlated with one another, and that financial knowledge coordinates the attitudes that influence financial management behavior. The OECD (2015b), Atkinson and Messy (2012), and Agarwalla et al. (2013) state that financial literacy is focused on three dimensions: financial knowledge, financial attitudes, and financial behavior.

Financial knowledge is a particular type of capital acquired through learning the ability to manage income, expenditure, and savings in a safe way (Delavande et al. 2008). For OECD, financial knowledge is essential to determine if the individual is financially literate, involving questions related to concepts such as simple and compound interest, risk and return, and inflation (Atkinson and Messy 2012). Financial attitudes are defined as a combination of concepts, information, and emotions about learning, which results in a readiness to react favorably (Shockey 2002). Financial behavior is defined as an essential (indeed, the most important) financial literacy element (OECD 2015b). In recent study findings, the financial behavior dimension has been found to be a determinant of financial literacy (Lusardi and Mitchell 2013).

The financial literacy measure poses an additional complex question. Lusardi and Mitchell (2011) posit that although it is important to evaluate the way in which people are literate, in a practical sense, it is difficult to explore the way in which people proceed with financial information and make decisions based on this knowledge. For Hudson, it would be important to determine not only if the person has the information but also whether the individual uses it in the correct way. Kempson (2011), conducting an investigation of financial literacy research, found great diversity in the way the subject was addressed and in the questions that were answered. Due to the difficulty in directly measuring financial literacy, Moore (2003) suggests

Table 4.1 The main concepts and dimensions of financial literacy

Concepts of financial literacy	Dimensions	Authors
Financial knowledge and application of this knowledge, with self-confidence in financial decision-making	Financial knowledge and application of knowledge	Huston (2010)
The ability to use knowledge and skills acquired for better management	Financial knowledge and skills	Jump$tart Coalition (2007) and Hung et al. (2009)
The ability to make simple decisions in the everyday context of financial choices	Daily decisions	Lusardi and Tufano (2009)
The ability to evaluate financial options and make informed judgments	Assessment and judgment	Schagen (1997) and Mandell (2007)
The ability to understand financial information and make effective decisions using this information	Understanding and decision	Noctor et al. (1992), Beal and Delpachitra (2003), ANZ (2008), and Servon and Kaestner (2008)
It goes beyond the basic idea of financial education, where the influence of financial knowledge on behavior is mediated by the student's financial attitudes	Knowledge, behavior, and attitudes	Norvilitis and MacLean (2010) and Xiao et al. (2011)
The choice of numerous alternatives for the establishment of financial goals	Effective choice	Criddle (2006)
It involves only financial knowledge	Financial knowledge	Hilgert et al. (2003)
It encompasses the financial experiences of individuals	Financial experiences	Moore (2003)
Making informed financial decisions	Financial decisions	Remund (2010)
Human capital measured through education or formal experience	Financial knowledge	Crook (2002) and Kerr and Dunn (2002)
More specific human capital measured through financial knowledge issues	Financial knowledge	Courchane and Zorn (2005) and Lusardi and Tufano (2009)
Measured through a set of questions that measure basic financial concepts, such as interest capitalization, inflation, and risk diversification	Financial knowledge	Lusardi and Mitchell (2013)
It is a combination of the consciousness, knowledge, ability, attitude, and behavior that are necessary to make financial decisions and, accordingly, to achieve individual financial wealth. It encompasses financial literacy in three dimensions: financial knowledge, financial behavior, and financial attitude	Financial knowledge, financial behavior, and financial attitude	Atkinson and Messy (2012) and OECD (2015a, b)

(continued)

Table 4.1 (continued)

Concepts of financial literacy	Dimensions	Authors
It is defined as part of a "political arsenal" aimed at facilitating better outcomes for consumers. However, it is measured with questions of financial knowledge	Financial knowledge	Gerrans and Heaney (2014)
It is seen as fundamental to financial decision-making and to financial independence, as measured by interest knowledge issues and debt repayment	Financial knowledge	Disney et al. (2015)
It is defined as the ability to process economic information and make informed decisions about financial planning, wealth accumulation, debt, and retirement. However, it is measured with questions of financial knowledge	Financial knowledge	Lusardi (2015a)
It is a critical competence in the twenty-first century for individuals and follows OECD guidance on the dimensions that measure it	Financial knowledge, financial behavior, and financial attitude	Messy and Monticone (2016)

the use of proxies. Table 4.1 summarizes the main concepts and dimensions of financial literacy.

In summary, several authors conceptualize financial literacy as synonymous with financial knowledge, since they measure it only with this construct. Others bring a broader definition, but when measuring it, they only address questions of financial knowledge. Such definitions guide, and can limit, concepts of knowledge; only a few researchers use the term more comprehensively and also measure it as applying of this knowledge. In addition, it is noted that some researchers describe this broad concept using other terms such as financial behavior, financial attitude, and financial experiences, among others.

Thus a major challenge for conducting research on financial literacy is the difficulty of determining appropriate metrics, in the absence of a standard definition in the literature (Hung et al. 2009; Huston 2010; Remund 2010; Lusardi and Mitchell 2014). Table 4.2 presents a summary of the main instruments and dimensions that measure financial literacy.

We conclude that, like the concepts, the instruments also measure the financial knowledge more preponderantly. It is noted that few studies propose scales with two or more dimensions to measure financial literacy. In addition, the aspects that are being investigated most are interest rates, inflation, risk diversification, savings, loans, and expenditure.

Table 4.2 Main instruments and dimensions that measure financial literacy

Instrument	Questions	Dimensions	Content	Authors/Organizations
Issues of Annamaria Lusardi and Olivia Mitchell	3	Financial knowledge	Interest rates, inflation, and risk diversification	Hastings and Tejeda-Ashton (2008), Hastings and Mitchell (2011), Lusardi and Mitchell (2011, 2014), Fornero and Monticone (2011), Klapper and Panos (2011), Brown and Graf (2013), Arrondel et al. (2013), Beckmann (2013), Clark et al. (2015), Grohmann et al. (2015), and Lusardi (2015a)
Financial literacy survey	25	Financial attitude and behavior	Budget, spending, savings, payment, credit and debit cards, knowledge of personal finances, and financial problems	*National Foundation for Credit counseling* (NFCC 2015)
National Financial Capability Study (NFCS)	5	Financial knowledge	Interest rates, inflation, risk diversification, bond prices, and mortgages	Lusardi and Mitchell (2011), Robb et al. (2012), Knoll and Houts (2012), NFCS (2013), and Mottola (2013)
American life panel in 2012	5	Financial knowledge, confidence, and self-efficacy	Self-efficacy, knowledge, and confidence for risk diversification	Lusardi et al. (2014)
OECD	19	Financial attitude, behavior, and knowledge	Interest, inflation, return, prices, risk, financial products, expenses, household budget, savings, loans, and financial expenditure	Atkinson and Messy (2012) and OECD (2015a)
FL-ABK	40	Financial attitude, behavior, and knowledge	Financial attitudes, financial behaviors, and knowledge about spending, debt, money management, savings, and investment	Shockey (2002)
Financial fitness quiz	20	Financial behavior	Budget, spending, and savings	O'Neill and Xiao (2012)
Klapper et al. (2013)	4	Financial knowledge	Simple interest, compound interest, inflation, and sales discounts	Klapper et al. (2013)

(continued)

Table 4.2 (continued)

Instrument	Questions	Dimensions	Content	Authors/Organizations
Bruine de Bruin et al. (2010)	16	Financial knowledge	Inflation, basic and advanced arithmetic	Bruine de Bruin et al. (2010)
Van Rooij et al. (2011)	16	Financial knowledge	Basic knowledge (numerical skills, inflation, simple and compound interest, and the value of money over time) and advanced knowledge (stocks, bonds, mutual funds, risk diversification, risk, and return)	Van Rooij et al. (2011)
Chen and Volpe (1998)	36	Financial knowledge	Savings, loans, insurance, and investments	Chen and Volpe (1998)
Potrich et al. (2015)	21	Financial attitude, behavior, and knowledge	Savings, concern for the future, inflation, interest rate, time value of money, risk, return, diversification, stock market, credit, and government securities	Potrich et al. (2015)
Gerrans and Heaney (2014)	12	Financial knowledge	1. Basics: composition, inflation, time value of money, and inflation. 2. Advanced: risk assets, long-term asset returns, long-term volatility, and diversification result. 3. Applied: ranking of the expected long-term returns, risks, cost of financing the car, and consumer goods	Gerrans and Heaney (2014)
Salleh (2015)	3	Financial knowledge	Financial management, emergency planning, and investment for goals	Salleh (2015)
Disney et al. (2015)	3	Financial knowledge	Simple interest, compound interest, and amortization	Disney et al. (2015)
FinLit survey	5	Financial knowledge	Interest rate, inflation, risk diversification, and fiscal contributions to retirement	Clark et al. (2015)
Programme for International Student Assessment (PISA)	40	Financial attitude, behavior, and knowledge	Money and transactions, financial planning and management, risk and reward, and financial picture	OECD (2015b) and Lusardi (2015b)

(continued)

Table 4.2 (continued)

Instrument	Questions	Dimensions	Content	Authors/Organizations
Lusardi (2015a)	11	Financial knowledge	Simple questions: interest rate, inflation, and risk diversification. Advanced issues: stock market function, knowledge of investment funds, relationship between interest rates and bond prices, risk diversification between company stock or funds if stocks or bonds have higher risk, long-term returns, greater fluctuations, and diversification of risks with different assets	Lusardi (2015a)

Method

Participants

This study investigated a random sample of 534 university students attending public and private universities in southern Brazil. The data were collected in an internal environment based on teacher availability and the contact with those students who were disposed to participate. The instrument, which consists of four groups of questions, was administered between April and May 2013. Initially, we attempted to identify student profiles related to eight socioeconomic and demographic variables: gender, age, civil status, dependent living, race, descent, occupation, and income.

Several points support the decision to use university students in southern Brazil for this study. (a) Financial literary is not widely explored in the academic environment as on the society level in general, especially when considering emergent markets such as Brazil. (b) Among the students, we chose university students because of evidence reported by Lusardi and Mitchell (2010), in which individuals with lower educational levels are less prone to answer the questions correctly and more prone to say that they do not know the answer. (c) University students currently have more responsibilities and are obliged to make decisions and engage in behaviors that will define their financial independence (Mendes-Da-Silva et al. 2012). (d) Among Brazilian regions, the south is listed first in the Human Development Index (HDI), and it exhibits superior indicators when compared to other regions of Brazil, where most cities (64.70%) are in high-development groups, according to the Atlas of Human Being Development in Brazil (2013).

Instrument

Given that there is not an operationally valid instrument to measure financial literacy in its totality (Remund 2010), a proxy was selected according to the procedures adopted by several prior studies (Knoll and Houts 2012; Shim et al. 2009; Shim et al. 2010; Atkinson and Messy 2012) that have evaluated literacy with various factors. In this study, financial literacy is defined by financial behavior, financial knowledge, and financial attitude, as recommended by the OECD (2012), Atkinson and Messy (2012), and Agarwalla et al. (2013).

First, to model financial behavior, several questions developed by Chen and Volpe (1998), Johnson (2001), and Shockey (2002) have been used and adapted to fit the Brazilian context. Composed of 20 questions, a five-point Likert scale (1-never and 5-always) was used to evaluate university student behavior regarding financial management as it pertains to the use of personal credit, planned consumption, investments, and savings. High scores on the scale indicate good financial behaviors.

To evaluate the academic level of financial knowledge, a factor from the average response of two groups of multiple choice questions adapted from Van Rooij et al. (2011) was constructed. The first group (basic knowledge) posits three questions to measure basic financial abilities with questions related to inflation, tax rates, and the value of money in time. The second group (advanced knowledge) initiates five questions to explore the level of knowledge in relation to complex financial instruments, such as shares, public bonds, and risk diversification. The differentiation between basic and advanced knowledge has been inspired by a study by Van Rooij et al. (2011), who took into consideration the difficulty level of the questions. Furthermore, in the stage of instrument validation, they have been confirmed by the analysis of specialists. Each correct answer from the basic knowledge group was awarded a score of 1.0, while each correct answer from the advanced knowledge group received a score of 2.0. Thus, a student who answered three questions correctly from the basic knowledge group received one point for each question (three points possible), while the student who correctly answered three questions in the advanced knowledge group received two points for each questions (six points possible). According to this scale, the higher the score, the better is the level of financial knowledge.

To measure financial attitude, the scale developed by Shockey (2002) was used. This scale is informed by nine questions organized around a five-point Likert scale (1-absolutely disagree and 5-absolutely agree). The aim of this scale is to identify how individuals evaluate their financial management. Accordingly, the higher the score, the better is the financial attitude of the individual. The scale choice has taken into consideration the best adjustment for the Brazilian context which is translated and the content validation of which is analyzed. These scales have been chosen for this study because they adapt to Brazilian reality best. Based on the model of Churchill (1979), scales were validated by two specialists and applied to 112 students to improve and refine measures through exploratory factorial analysis. The final questions are displayed in Appendix A. For an analysis of the collected data, descriptive statistics and the multivariate analysis technique were used, both of which were applied using Statistical Package for the Social Sciences (SPSS) 17.0® and Analysis of Moment Structures (AMOS) 18® software.

Models

Because there is no consolidated model to evaluate financial literacy in the literature, we have chosen to construct the three models displayed in Fig. 4.1. Model 1 reflects the argument that financial knowledge and attitude precede financial behavior, as Hayhoe et al. (2005) and Miller and C' de Baca (2001) determined that meaningful financial behavior change follows modifications in financial knowledge and attitude, apart from the fact that financial knowledge is correlated with financial attitude, as found by Hayhoe et al. (2005). Thus, in this model, it was assumed that knowledge imparts influence on financial behavior and attitude and that attitude and behavior will correlate.

Model 2 is a factorial in the second order, for which original constructs were maintained, and financial literacy was a second-order construct. This model presents the idea of OECD (2015b), Atkinson and Messy (2012), and Agarwalla et al. (2013) by measuring financial literacy as a combination of financial behavior, financial knowledge, and financial attitude, and this is the main reason to study these three components in combination. Model 3 assumed the existence of a unique financial literacy construct formed by all variables in the three constructs (financial behavior, financial knowledge, and financial attitude) built in a way that considers the arguments of Shockey (2002), whereby financial literacy would be measured from the variables of constructs financial behavior, financial knowledge, and financial attitude.

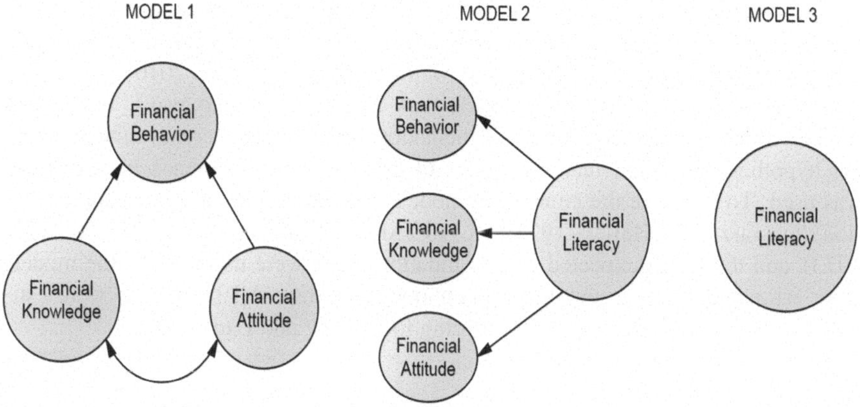

Fig. 4.1 Proposed models. Note: for simplicity, observed variables and errors have not been represented in the figure

Data Analysis

To analyze the models, structured equation modeling (SEM) was employed using two strategies. In the first strategy, competitor models have been applied using original scales and constructing a model in only one step. In the second strategy, confirmatory factor analysis (CFA) was used to validate financial behavior and financial attitude constructs, while in the second part, a structural model was used. In both strategies, correlations between errors from observed variables were introduced, as suggested by the AMOS 18 report, which makes logical theoretical sense (Models b). Kline (2011) states, "Correlations between residuals can be inserted when necessary." Furthermore, six models are initially presented, three of which are structured differently and two of which have different ways of measuring constructs.

The measurement modeling validity was evaluated through convergent validity, unidimensionality, and construct reliability. The convergent validity of each construct was analyzed according to the magnitude and meaningful statistics of its standardized coefficients, as well as the absolute fit indices, such as chi-square statistics (χ^2), root mean square residual (RMSR), root mean square error of approximation (RMSEA), and goodness-of-fit index (GFI), and the comparative fit indices, such as the comparative fit index (CFI), normed fit index (NFI), and Tucker-Lewis index (TLI). There is no consensus in the extant literature regarding acceptable values for these indices. For example, for the chi-square/degrees of freedom, recommendations vary from less than five to less than two (Hooper et al. 2008). For CFI, GFI, NFI, and TLI, it is suggested their values be less than 0.95, and for RMSR and RMSA, the recommendations suggest they be less than 0.05 and 0.08, respectively (Hooper et al. 2008).

To measure the construct reliability, extracted variance, score reliability, and Cronbach's alpha were used. The construct is considered reliable if the score reliability and extracted variance values are equal to or exceed to 0.7 and 0.5, respectively (Garver and Mentzer 1999; Hair et al. 2010). Alphas of approximately 0.7 are considered adequate (Kline 2011). The construct unidimensionality is verified through the evaluation of adjusted residuals. Absolute values below 2.5 suggest that there are no problems (Garver and Mentzer 1999; Hair et al. 2010).

The comparison of the two models was conducted in two ways. For nested models, models measuring financial behavior and attitude were evaluated under the hypothesis of equal factorial loads. In this case, the difference in chi-square was used. To compare the concurrent models, the BIC/Bayesian information criterion (Schwarz 1978; Raftery 1993), the AIC/Akaike's informational criteria (Akaike 1973), and the ECVI/expected cross-validation index were used. All of the models were estimated using a maximum likelihood bootstrap. All bootstraps were estimated with a sample size of 100 according to Cheung and Lau (2008).

Results

The sample was composed of 534 students, and of these, 49.25% completed subjects related to finance during their professional training. Therefore, it was concluded that these students have financial training. The remaining 50.75% did not have this training. It was verified that 56.93% of the respondent population were female, 86.89% were single, and the average age was approximately 24 years. The majority of the respondents (90.82%) did not have dependents and considered themselves of the white race (86.52%) and were of Brazilian descent (49.81%). With regard to occupation, 63.67% did not have a formal job, and the majority were students or scholarship students. More than half declared earnings below R$ 1300.00. According to the first strategy, the three conceptual models based on previous empirical evidence were estimated using the ML bootstrap. The results of this index fit are displayed in Table 4.3.

In the initial estimation, the models presented very low indices when compared to the desired indices. Following AMOS suggestions, correlations between observed variable errors were included, thereby making sense from a theoretical perspective. Despite some improvement, all the models continued to exhibit inadequate fit indices. Therefore, the three models, as well as the versions with insert correlations between errors, were adjusted. Given these results, we chose to adopt the second

Table 4.3 Fit indices of models with all variables

Fit indices	Model 1.1a	Model 1.1b	Model 2.1a	Model 2.1b	Model 3.1a	Model 3.1b
Chi-square (value)	1871.488	915.398	1871.488	915.398	2489.871	1146.460
Chi-square (probability)	$p - 0.000$	$p - 0.000$	$p - 0.000$	$p - 0.000$	$p - 0.000$	$p - 0.000$
Freedom degree	431	410	431	410	434	410
GFI/goodness-of-fit index	0.781	0.893	0.781	0.893	0.717	0.863
CFI/comparative fit index	0.668	0.884	0.668	0.884	0.526	0.830
NFI/normed fit index	0.610	0.809	0.610	0.809	0.482	0.761
TLI/Tucker-Lewis index	0.642	0.868	0.642	0.868	0.492	0.807
RMSR/root mean square residual	0.087	0.057	0.087	0.057	0.092	0.063
RMSEA/RMS error of approximation	0.081	0.049	0.081	0.049	0.097	0.060
AIC/Akaike's information criterion	2001.488	1087.398	2001.488	1087.398	2613.871	1318.460
BIC/Bayesian information criterion	2276.469	1451.220	2276.469	1451.220	2876.161	1682.281
ECVI/expected cross-validation index	3.948	2.145	3.948	2.145	5.156	2.601

Table 4.4 Fit model for financial behavior and financial attitude constructs

	Financial behavior		Financial attitude	
Fit indices	Proposed	Final	Proposed	Final
Chi-square (value)	1112.359	9.310	237.724	5.185
Chi-square (probability)	$p - 0.000$	$p - 0.054$	$p - 0.000$	$p - 0.075$
Freedom degree	170	4	27	2
GFI: goodness-of-fit index	0.792	0.993	0.888	0.995
CFI: comparative fit index	0.646	0.993	0.818	0.995
NFI: normed fit index	0.610	0.988	0.801	0.991
TLI: Tucker-Lewis index	0.604	0.982	0.758	0.984
RMSR: root mean square residual	0.123	0.028	0.034	0.008
RMSEA: RMS error of approximation	0.105	0.051	0.124	0.056
Extracted variance	0.227	0.441	0.317	0.483
Construct reliability	0.838	0.795	0.798	0.778
Cronbach's alpha	0.828	0.795	0.789	0.763

strategy, whereby modeling is applied in two steps. Initially, the measurement models were adjusted, and the baseline model (measurement model and structural model) was later evaluated. In this stage, the improvement strategy model is adopted, although several changes were necessary in the measurement of the model (Table 4.4).

For both constructs, the proposed models refer to the model with all variables in the original scale. The results indicate that both models are inadequate because the chi-square/degrees of freedom is greater than three; the fit for the GFI, CFI, NFI, and TLI does not achieve the minimum of 0.95; the RMSEA and RMSR are greater than 0.08 and 0.05, respectively; and the extracted variance is less than 0.5. To find more adequate measuring models, two additional measuring models were adopted after removing all of the variables that have presented standardized factor loadings with values below 0.3 and did not contribute significantly to the model (Hair et al. 2010) and include correlations between the variable errors. After these changes, both models presented adequate adjustment.

That is, the models exhibited (i) convergent validity, whereby the indices CFI, GFI, NFI, and TLI exceeded 0.95 and the RMSR and RMSEA were greater than 0.05; (ii) reliability, as all are greater than 0.7, although the medium variance is slightly below 0.50, and the Cronbach's alphas exceed 0.7, thereby indicating reliability; and (iii) unidimensionality, as evidenced by all standardized residuals falling below 2.5 ($p < 0.05$). Chi-square values were no longer significant at the 5% level. For each model, the hypothesis of equal factor loading is tested. Both the financial behavior model (CMIN 35.837; $p - 0.000$) and the financial attitude model (CMIN 102.309; $p - 0.000$) exhibit worsening results, indicating that factorial loans may differ for the various measures of the models. Figure 4.2 displays the original measuring models with all variables and the models after financial behavior and attitude constructs.

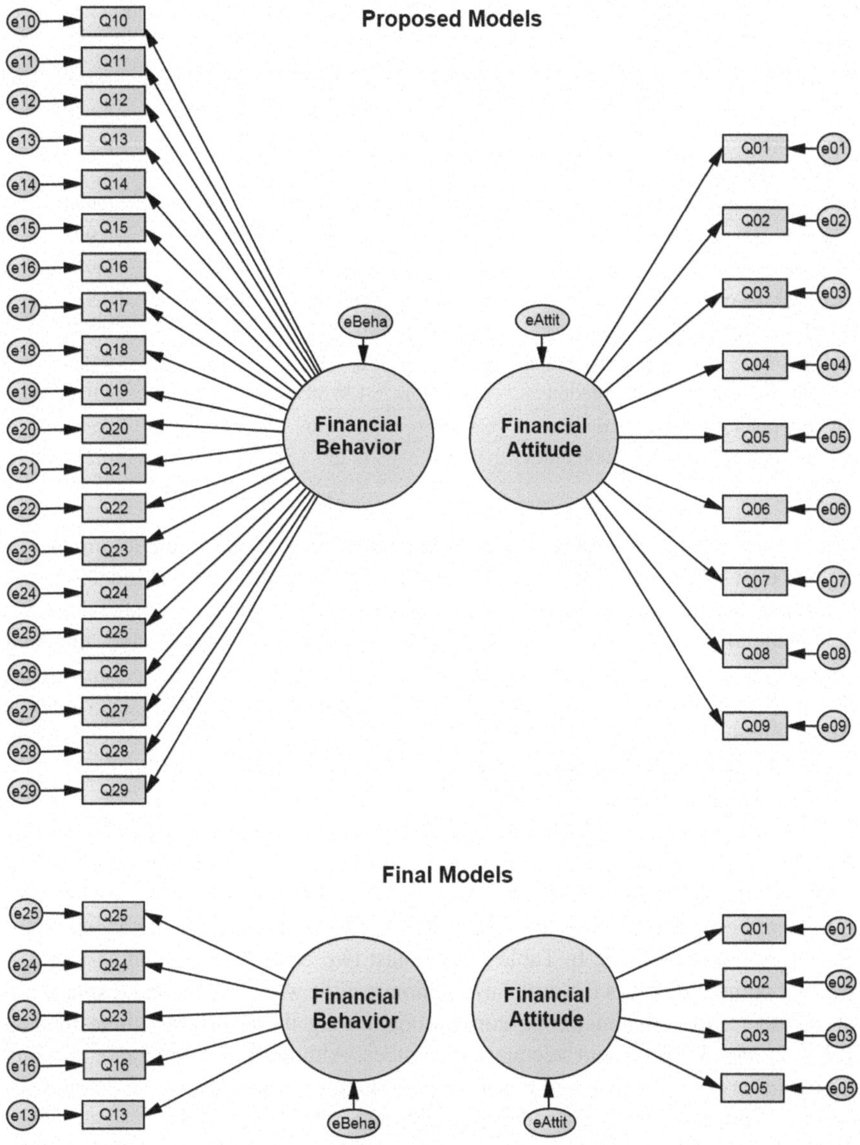

Fig. 4.2 Proposed and final models for financial behavior and attitude constructs. Note: for simplicity, the correlations between errors have not been shown, but they are in shown in Table 4.6

Financial knowledge was not adjusted, because it is not possible to adjust constructs formed by fewer than three variables. Therefore, based on the measurement models for financial behavior and financial attitude, the estimation of tree baseline models is conducted. The first model (Model 1.2) was constructed based on the argument that financial knowledge and attitude precede financial behavior, and

Table 4.5 Fit indices for financial behavior and financial attitude measuring adjusted construct models

Fit indices	Model 1.2	Model 2.2	Model 3.2a	Model 3.2b
Chi-square (value)	68.885	68.885	655.283	42.301
Chi-square (probability)	$p - 0.001$	$p - 0.001$	$p - 0.000$	$p - 0.105$
Freedom degree	37	37	43	32
GFI/goodness-of-fit index	0.976	0.976	0.786	0.985
CFI/comparative fit index	0.980	0.980	0.607	0.993
NFI/normed fit index	0.957	0.957	0.594	0.974
TLI/Tucker-Lewis index	0.970	0.970	0.497	0.989
RMSR/root mean square residual	0.033	0.033	0.072	0.022
RMSEA/RMS error of approximation	0.041	0.041	0.168	0.025
AIC/Akaike's information criterion	126.885	126.885	701.283	110.301
BIC/Bayesian information criterion	249.569	249.569	798.584	254.137
ECVI/expected cross-validation index	0.250	0.250	1.383	0.218

financial knowledge is correlated with financial attitude, based in the arguments of Hayhoe et al. (2005) and Miller and C' de Baca (2001). The second (Model 2.2) is a factorial in the second order, whereby the measurement models for financial behavior, financial attitude, and financial knowledge were maintained, and financial literacy was a second-order construct, according to OECD (2015b), Atkinson and Messy (2012), and Agarwalla et al. (2013). The last model (Model 3.2) determined a unique financial literacy construct formed by all variables in the three constructs (financial behavior, financial knowledge, and financial attitude), as Shockey (2002) affirmed. Table 4.5 reveals the results.

Table 4.5 highlights that Models 1.2 and 2.2 are not equals because the relations between the tree constructs are different, where Model 1.2 is a factorial in the first order and the other is a factorial in the second order. However, the models are equivalent because they have the same variables and constructs, which is why they present with equal values. In Table 4.5, the last two columns represent Model 3.2. The first column displays the initial estimation results, while the second displays the estimation results after including correlations among the errors. All three models (1.2, 2.2, and 3.2b) present adequate fit indices. Although the chi-square exhibits significant results, the results of the chi-square/degrees of freedom are less than two. Figure 4.3 presents the final Models 1.2, 2.2, and 3.2b.

All models present differences when compared to the proposed models. In Model 1.2, the correlation between financial knowledge and financial attitude is not significant. In Model 2.2, financial literacy, as a second-order construct, is not practical, because all categories related to knowledge and attitude constructs are not significant, and only the construct of financial behavior impacts on the level of financial literacy of university students. This result supports the findings of Lusardi and Mitchell (2013), OECD (2015b), Klapper et al. (2013), and Fernandes et al. (2014) when stating that financial behavior is an essential and determining element of financial literacy. Model 3.2b differs from the proposed model because it includes

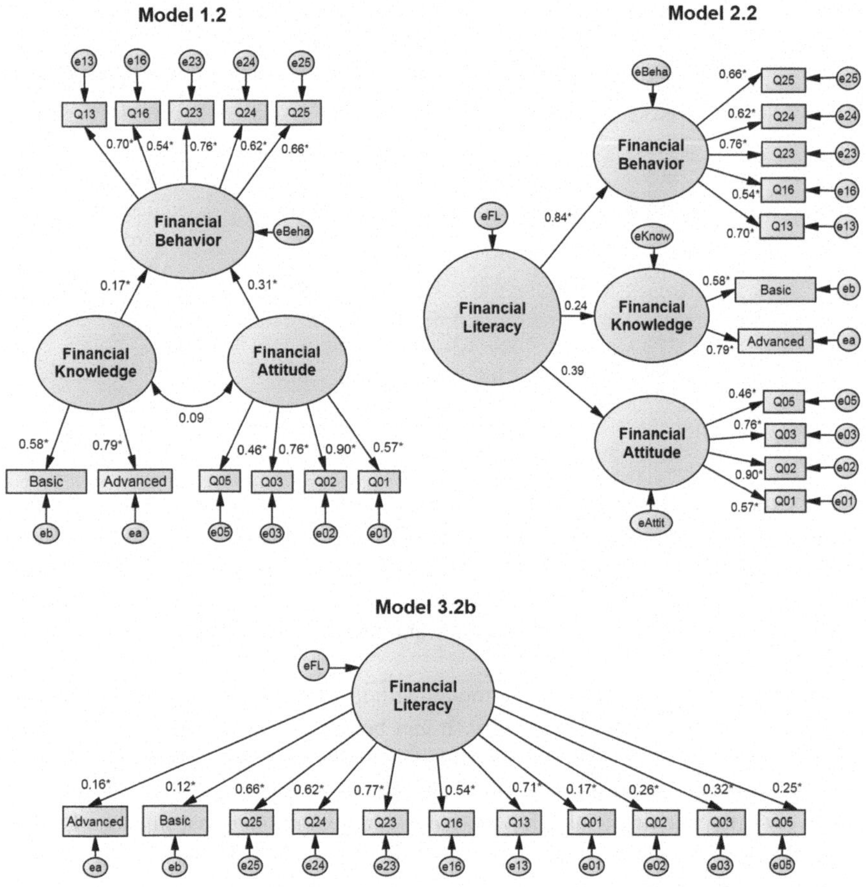

Fig. 4.3 Standardized coefficients for models 1.2, 2.2, and 3.2b. Note: $*p < 0.001$. For simplicity, the correlations among the errors have not been shown, but they are shown in Table 4.6

correlations between errors. Furthermore, because financial literacy is a first-order construct, it is necessary to verify its reliability. The extracted variance indices are 0.227, indicating that the model does not have sufficient reliability. For all models for which correlations among errors were included (Models 1.1b, 2.1b, 3.1b, 1.2, 2.2, and 3.2b), it is observed that the criteria may well have made theoretical sense, as suggested by many authors (Hooper et al. 2008; Kline 2011). Table 4.6 presents all correlations inserted.

It is observed that all correlations are significant and positive. Correlations in Models 1.2 and 2.2 are exactly the same because they address equivalent models, and all of them are classified as low correlations at approximately 0.200. However, correlations in Model 3.2b varied from very low to moderate. In an attempt to improve Model 3.2b, we applied the same techniques used when assessing the validity of the models, with the subsequent removal of variables with low loads

Table 4.6 Correlations among errors from observed variables in Models 1.2, 2.2, and 3.2b

Correlations			Model 1.2		Model 2.2		Model 3.2b	
e13	↔	e05	0.249	***	0.249	***	0.181	***
e23	↔	e03	0.228	***	0.228	***	0.134	***
e23	↔	e24	0.220	***	0.220	***	0.233	***
e23	↔	e05	0.201	***	0.201	***	0.149	***
e03	↔	e05					0.331	***
e02	↔	e03					0.658	***
e01	↔	e02					0.515	***
e02	↔	e05					0.360	***
Ea	↔	Eb					0.443	***
e01	↔	e05					0.216	***
e01	↔	e03					0.368	***

Note: ***$p < 0.001$

and insertion correlations, which made theoretical sense. The application of these techniques resulted in the withdrawal of all variables related to financial knowledge (both variables with the smallest information in Model 3.2b) and all variables related to financial attitude. Thus, as the model has the same structure as the measurement model for financial behavior, it is determined to be not viable as a measure for financial literacy.

Among all models estimated, the model with the lowest AIC (3.2b) is considered inadequate due to a lack of reliability. It can be concluded that Model 1.2, which reported the second lowest AIC, is the most adequate for evaluating financial literacy. This model presupposes that financial knowledge and financial attitude positively influence financial behavior, based on the argument that financial knowledge and attitude precede financial behavior (Miller and C' de Baca 2001; Hayhoe et al. 2005).

Our result supports the findings of Fernandes et al. (2014), which indicated that financial literacy, measured by the percentage of correct answers on financial knowledge tests, significantly predicted financial behavior, but this effect had a weak relationship. For this, according to Fernandes et al. (2014), the interventions studied so far clarify that different approaches to financial education are required if one expects to produce larger effects on behavior. A possibility, based on Hadar et al. (2013), is that future education should teach soft skills, such as the propensity to plan, confidence to be proactive, and willingness to take investment risks, more than content knowledge about compound interest and bonds, for example.

Aiming to provide robustness for Model 1.2, the research specialization tool from AMOS is used to test alternative structured models in different relations among the three constructs. Accordingly, the software generated and compared eight alternative models. Again, the results indicate that Model 1.2 provides the best fit for the intended purpose.

Conclusions

The environment in which the society is inserted requires contextually accurate self-sufficiency and responsibility, and financial literacy is an essential component to achieve a more successful adulthood. Therefore, the mastery of personal-finance skills plays a central role in attitudes and responsible knowledge formation when considering personal finance. Considering financial literacy's importance, this study's objective was to construct and compare financial literacy models. Three scales were used to model literacy: financial knowledge, financial behavior, and financial attitude. From these scales, three conceptual models were built that differed in relation to these scales.

This study used two different strategies in its evaluations. In the first, the original scales are applied under the assumption that they would be adequate, as they are already developed and have been used for evaluations in other studies. However, the results indicate the estimation made in only one step has been inadequate, and the estimation in two steps has presented the best indices; however, the problem consisted of reducing the measures proposed. From the 20 initial items on the financial behavior scale, only 5 were included, while on the attitude scale, the items have been reduced from 9 to 4, indicating instability in the scales chosen. These variables were excluded because it presented standardized factor loadings with values below 0.3, and therefore, it did not contribute significantly to the model (Hair et al. 2010). The results from these two scales indicate the need for the increased application of techniques, the use of more stringent criteria, and a refinement of scale items, to the point that the instruments to measure financial behavior and financial attitude are valid.

In the second stage, two out of the three models are considered inadequate, and both have explored the possibility of treating financial literacy as a first- or second-order model (Model 3 or Model 2, respectively). These results suggest that the creation of only one measure of financial literacy would be inadequate, at least based on the proposed variables. Thus, the construction of a multidisciplinary measure for financial literacy is still considered a challenge. However, there are possible alternative methods, such as creating a new scale or creating other models from existing scales.

Model 1.2 is determined to be the most adequate of the measurement tools analyzed. This model finds that financial knowledge and attitude provide positive impact on financial behavior, and these results are consistent with the conceptual models, other than the expectation regarding the correlation between knowledge and attitude.

The results are similar to those of Hilgert et al. (2003), Lyons (2004), and Servon and Kaestner (2008), indicating that higher financial knowledge scores coincide with higher standard of financial behavior, and people with positive attitudes are more prone to behave consistently. However, the evidence found by Hayhoe et al. (2005) has not been supported, in showing a correlation between financial knowledge and financial attitude. It is concluded that university student's financial literacy is preceded by financial behavior, financial knowledge, and financial attitude, with a higher impact from attitude.

In practical terms, Brazilian university students' financial behavior expresses the ability to establish long-term goals and savings for future acquisitions or unexpected spending. This behavior is directly influenced by basic questions (interest and inflation) and advanced questions (risk and return from different assets) of financial knowledge, as well as by the importance attributed to attitude in the form of establishing aims, controlling spending and financial reserves. These findings imply the urgent need to ratify and develop effective actions to minimize financial illiteracy. One possible measure might be requiring completion of courses in personal financial management and financial market literacy across all academic disciplines. An additional possible measure relates to the development and adoption of education programs in the effort to promote personal financial literacy in all sectors of society.

According to Lynch and Wood (2006), the public policy tools to help consumers make better decisions can be drawn from economics to present three broad classes of interventions: offering more choices, providing better information to consumers about options they might consider, and providing incentives for consumers or sellers to change their behavior. The use of new technologies might also contribute rapid improvement of global financial literacy levels. Government agencies, as well as financial and educational institutions, can help increase the financial literacy of young people and adults through smartphone applications, new Internet banking configurations, and the adoption of investment simulators and spreadsheets.

Future Research

It is important to note that the data were collected only in Brazil, which presents explicit peculiarities, such as an economic structure for services. Therefore, different countries should be researched using a larger sample. Furthermore, while three constructs were used for financial literacy, other scales may also be relevant. Model 1.2 indicated that attitude and knowledge influence behavior, which is an example that should be incorporated in the parental financial education scale developed by Norvilitis and MacLean (2010) for this model. This research confirms the hypothesis for a multidimensional metric of financial literacy by measuring financial behavior, financial knowledge, and financial attitude. This model reflects the broader conceptual definition of financial literacy and thus fills the research gap identified by Fernandes et al. (2014). While these findings have limitations, this study provides specific advances in modeling financial literacy. This topic must necessarily be improved as the creation of more complex financial products demands a more rigorous evaluation of financial literacy.

Questions Related to Financial Attitude, Financial Behavior, and Financial Knowledge

Financial attitude	01. It is important to control monthly expenses
	02. It is important to establish financial targets for the future
	03. It is important to save money on a monthly basis
	04. The way I manage my money today will affect my future
	05. It is important to have and follow a monthly expense plan
	06. It is important to pay the full value on credit cards
	07. When buying in installments, it is important to compare available credit offers
	08. It is important to stay within a budget
	09. It is important to invest regularly to achieve targets in the long term
Financial behavior	10. I always pay my credit cards on time to avoid extra charges
	11. I worry about how best to manage my money
	12. I take notes and control my personal expenses (e.g., expense and revenue spreadsheet)
	13. I establish financial targets for the long term that influence the managing of my expenses
	14. I follow a weekly or monthly plan for expenses
	15. I go more than 1 month without balancing my expenses
	16. I am satisfied with the way I control my finances
	17. I pay my bills without delay
	18. I can identify how much I pay when using credit
	19. I use credit cards and overdrafts when I do not have money for expenses
	20. When buying in installments, I compare the available credit options
	21. I use more than 10% of my monthly earnings to make payments on my credit cards (except car financing)
	22. I check my credit card invoices to avoid possible mistakes and debts
	23. I save monthly
	24. I save so I can buy something expensive (e.g., car)
	25. I have a financial reserve at least three times my monthly earnings, which can be used in unexpected moments (e.g., unemployment)
	26. I compare prices when buying something
	27. I analyze my financial situation before a major purchase
	28. I buy on impulse
	29. I prefer to buy a financial product to save money to buy in cash

(continued)

Basic financial knowledge	30. Imagine you have R$ 100.00 in the savings account and the tax rate is 10% a year. After 5 years, how much money will you have in this account? *More than R$ 150.00* *Exactly R$ 150.00* *Less than R$ 150.00* *Do not know*
	31. Imagine the tax rate applied to your savings account is 6% a year and the inflation tax is 10% a year. After 1 year, how much will you be able to buy with the money from this account? *More than today* *Exactly the same* *Less than today* *Do not know*
	32. Imagine Joseph inherits R$ 10000.00 today and Peter inherits R$ 10000.00 in 3 years. According to the time value of money, who is going to be wealthier? *Joseph* *Peter* *They are equally as wealthy* *Do not know*
Advanced financial knowledge	33. Which of the options below best describes the stock market's functions? *Allow for the meeting of people who want to buy and sell shares* *Predict gains of shares* *Increase the prices of shares* *Do not know*
	34. Considering a long time period, (e.g., 10 years). Which asset described below normally gives the highest rate of return? *Account* *Bond* *Stocks* *Do not know*
	35. Which statement is correct? *Once investing in investment refunds, it is not possible to take the money out in the first year* *Investment refunds can be invested in many assets, such as shares and securities* *Investment refunds pay assured return rates that depend on past behavior* *None of them* *Do not know*
	36. Normally, which asset exhibits higher oscillations over time? *Savings account* *Shares* *Public securities* *Do not know*
	37. When an investor diversifies, his investments are divided among different assets. The risk of losing money: *Increases* *Decreases* *Remains the same* *Do not know*

References

Agarwalla, S. K., Barua, S. K., Jacob, J., & Varma, J. R. (2013). *Financial literacy among working young in Urban India* (Working Paper/2013-10-02), Indian Institute of Management Ahmedabad.

Akaike, H. (1973). Information theory and an extension of the maximum likelihood principle. In Petrov, B. N. & Csaki, F. (Eds), *Proceedings of the 2nd International Symposium on Information Theory* (pp. 267–281). Budapest: Akademiai Kiado.

Ansong, A. (2011). Level of knowledge in personal finance by university freshmen business students. *African Journal of Business Management, 5*(22), 8933–8940.

ANZ. (2008). *ANZ survey of adult financial literacy in Australia.* Available at: http://www.anz.com/Documents/AU/Aboutanz/AN_5654_Adult_Fin_Lit_Report_08_Web_Report_full.pdf (Accessed November 05, 2013)

Arrondel, L., Debbich, M., & Savignac, F. (2013). Financial literacy and financial planning in France. *Numeracy, 6*(2). Article 8.

Atkinson, A., & Messy, F. (2012). *Measuring financial literacy: Results of the OECD/International Network on Financial Education (INFE) pilot study* (Working paper/15, OECD working papers on finance, insurance and private pensions). Paris: OECD Publishing.

Atkinson, A., & Messy, F. (2015). *Financial education for migrants and their families* (Working paper/38, OECD working papers on finance, insurance and private pensions). Paris: OECD Publishing.

Atlas of Human Being Development in Brazil. (2013). *Evolution of human development in the Brazilian municipalities.* Available at: http://www.atlasbrasil.org.br/2013/e n/destaques/faixas_idhm (Accessed November 15, 2013)

Beal, D. J., & Delpachitra, S. B. (2003). Financial literacy among Australian university students. *Economic Papers, 22*(1), 65–78.

Beckmann, E. (2013). Financial literacy and household savings in Romania. *Numeracy, 6*(2). Article 9.

Brown, M., & Graf, R. (2013). Financial literacy and retirement planning in Switzerland. *Numeracy, 6*(2). Article 6.

Bruine de Bruin, W., Van Derklaauw, W., Downs, J. S., Fischhoff, B., Topa, G., & Armantier, O. (2010). Expectations of inflation: The role of demographic variables, expectations formation, and financial literacy. *The Journal of Consumer Affairs, 44*(2), 381–402.

Bucher-Koenen, T., Lusardi, A., Alessie, R., & Van Rooij, M. (2017). How financially literate are women? An overview and new insights. *The Journal of Consumer Affairs, 51*(2), 255–283.

Chen, H., & Volpe, R. P. (1998). An analysis of personal financial literacy among college students. *Financial Services Review, 7*(2), 107–128.

Cheung, G. W., & Lau, R. S. (2008). Testing mediation and suppression effects of latent variables: Bootstrapping with structural equation models. *Organizational Research Methods, 11*(2), 296–325.

Churchill, G. A., Jr. (1979). A paradigm for developing better measures of marketing constructs. *Journal of Marketing Research, 16*(1), 64–73.

Clark, R., Lusardi, A., & Mitchell, O. S. (2015). *Employee financial literacy and retirement plan behavior: A case study* (NBER working paper/21461). Available at: http://www.nber.org/papers/w21461 (Accessed November 05, 2016).

Courchane, M., & Zorn, P. (2005). *Consumer literacy and credit worthiness.* Presented at Federal Reserve System Conference, Promises and Pitfalls: As Consumer Options Multiply, Who Is Being Served and at What Cost?.

Criddle, E. (2006). Financial literacy: Goals and values, not just numbers. *Alliance, 34*(4).

Crook, J. N. (2002). *Adverse selection and search in the US bank credit card market* (University of Edinburgh working paper/01/1), University of Edinburgh Credit Research Center.

Delavande, A., Rohwedder, S., & Willis, R.J. (2008). *Retirement planning and the role of financial literacy and cognition* (Working paper 2008-190), Michigan Retirement Research Center.

Disney, R.F., & Gathergood, J. (2011). *Financial literacy and indebtedness: New evidence for UK consumers, EconPapers* (Discussion papers), Centre for Finance, Credit and Macroeconomics (CFCM), University of Nottingham.
Disney, R., Gathergood, J., & Weber, J. (2015). Credit counseling: A substitute for consumer financial literacy? *Journal of Pension Economics and Finance, 14*(4), 466–491.
Fernandes, D., Lynch, J. G., & Netemeyer, R. G. (2014). Financial literacy, financial education, and downstream financial behaviors. *Manag Sci, 60*(8), 1861–1883.
Fornero, E., & Monticone, C. (2011). Financial literacy and pension plan participation in Italy. *Journal of Pension Economics and Finance, 10*(4), 547–564.
Garver, N. S., & Mentzer, J. T. (1999). Logistics research methods: Employing structural equation modeling to test for construct validity. *Journal of Business Logistics, 20*(1), 33–57.
Gerrans, P., & Heaney, R. A. (2014). The role of undergraduate personal finance education in financial literacy, financial attitudes and financial behaviours, *Social Sciense Research Network*. Available at: https://doi.org/10.2139/ssrn.2537344 (Accessed 29 Nov 2016).
Grohmann, A., Kouwenbergb, R., & Menkhoff, L. (2015). Childhood roots of financial literacy. *Journal of Economic Psychology, 51*, 114–133.
Hadar, L., Sood, S., & Fox, C. R. (2013). Subjective knowledge in consumer financial decisions. *Journal of Marketing Research, 50*(3), 303–316.
Hair, J. F., Black, W. C., Babin, B. J., & Anderson, R. E. (2010). *Multivariate data analysis* (7th ed.). Upper Saddle River: Pearson.
Hastings, J., & Mitchell, O. S. (2011). *How financial literacy and impatience shape retirement wealth and investment behaviors* (NBER working paper/16740).
Hastings, J., & Tejeda-Ashton, L. (2008). *Financial literacy, information, and demand elasticity: Survey and experimental evidence from Mexico* (NBER working paper/14538).
Hayhoe, C. R., Leach, L., Allen, M. W., & Edwards, R. (2005). Credit cards held by college students. *Financial Counseling and Planning, 16*(1), 1–10.
Hilgert, M. A., Hogart, J. M., & Beverly, S. G. (2003). Household financial management: The connection between knowledge and behavior. *Federal Reserve Bulletin, 89*(7), 309–322.
Hooper, D., Coughlan, J., & Mullen, M. R. (2008). Structural equation modelling: Guidelines for determining model fit. *The Electronic Journal of Business Research Methods, 6*(1), 53–60.
Hung, A. A., Parker, A. M., & Yoong, J. (2009). *Defining and measuring financial literacy* (Working paper/708), Social Science Research Network. Santa Monica, CA: RAND Corporation.
Huston, S. J. (2010). Measuring financial literacy. *The Journal of Consumer Affairs, 44*(2), 296–316.
Johnson, A. C. (2001). *Evaluating a financial assessment tool: The financial checkup*. Dissertation of Utah University, USA
Jump$Tart Coalition. (2007). *National standards in K-12 personal finance education*. Available at: http://www.jumpstart.org/guide.html (Accessed November 02, 2016).
Kempson, E. (2011). A framework for developing international financial literacy surveys. In OECD, Improving Financial Education Efficiency: OECD-Bank of Italy Symposium on Financial Literacy. Paris: OECD Publishing.
Kerr, S., & Dunn, L. (2002). *Consumer search behavior and the changing credit card market* (OSU working papers/02-03), Department of Economics, The Ohio State University.
Klapper, L., & Panos, G. A. (2011). Financial literacy and retirement planning: The Russian case. *Journal of Pension Economics and Finance, 10*, 599–618.
Klapper, L., Lusardi, A., & Panos, G. A. (2013). Financial literacy and its consequences: Evidence from Russia during the financial crisis. *Journal of Banking & Finance, 37*, 3904–3923.
Kline, R. B. (2011). *Principles and practice of structural equation modeling* (3rd ed.). New York: The Guilford Press.
Knoll, M. A. Z., & Houts, C. R. (2012). The financial knowledge scale: An application of item response theory to the assessment of financial literacy. *The Journal of Consumer Affairs, 46*(3), 381–410.

Lusardi, A. (2015a). Financial literacy: Do people know the ABCs of finance? *Public Understanding of Science, 24*(3), 260–271.
Lusardi, A. (2015b). Financial literacy skills for the 21st century: Evidence from PISA. *The Journal of Consumer Affairs, 49*(3), 639–659.
Lusardi, A., & Mitchell, O. S. (2010). *Financial literacy and planning: Implications for retirement wellbeing* (Working paper/17078). Cambridge, MA: National Bureau of Economic Research.
Lusardi, A., & Mitchell, O. S. (2011). Financial literacy and retirement planning in the United States. *Journal of Pension Economics and Finance, 10*(4), 509–525.
Lusardi, A., & Mitchell, O. S. (2013). *The economic importance of financial literacy: Theory and evidence* (Working paper/18952). Cambridge, MA: National Bureau of Economic Research.
Lusardi, A., & Mitchell, O. S. (2014). The economic importance of financial literacy: Theory and evidence. *Journal of Economic Literature, 52*(1), 5–44.
Lusardi, A., & Tufano, P. (2009). Debt literacy, financial experiences, and overindebtedness, National Bureau of Economic Research, Cambridge. Available at: http://www.nber.org/papers/w14808.pdf (Accessed November 04, 2016).
Lusardi, A., Samek, A. S., Kapteyn, A., Glinert, L., Hung, A., & Heinberg, A. (2014). *Visual tools and narratives: New ways to improve financial literacy* (NBER working paper/20229). Available at: http://www.nber.org/papers/w20229.pdf (Accessed 01 Nov 2016).
Lusardi, A., Oggero, N., & Yakoboski, P. J. (2017). *The TIAA Institute-GFLEC personal finance index: A new measure of financial literacy*, The TIAA Institute-GFLEC. Available at: https://www.tiaainstitute.org/sites/default/files/presentations /2017-04/TIAA%20Institute-GFLEC%20P-Fin%20Index%20Report_2.pdf (Accessed 15 Jan 2018).
Lynch, J. G., Jr., & Wood, W. (2006). Special issue editors' statement: Helping consumers help themselves. *Journal of Public Policy & Marketing, 25*(1), 1–7.
Lyons, A. C. (2004). A profile of financially at-risk college students. *Journal of Consumer Affairs, 38*(1), 56–80.
Mandell, L. (2007). Financial literacy of high schools students. In J. J. Xiao (Ed.), *Handbook of consumer finance research*. New York: Springer.
Mccormick, M. H. (2009). The effectiveness of youth financial education: A review of the literature. *Journal of Financial Counseling and Planning, 20*(1), 70–83.
Mendes-Da-Silva, W., Nakamura, W. T., & Moraes, D. C. (2012). Credit card risk behavior on college campuses: Evidence from Brazil. *BAR Brazilian Administration Review, 9*(3), 351–373.
Messy, F., & Monticone, C. (2016). *Financial education policies in Asia and the Pacific* (Working paper/40, OECD working papers on finance, insurance and private pensions). Paris: OECD Publishing.
Miller, W. R., & C' de Baca, J. (2001). *Quantum change: When epiphanies and sudden insights transform ordinary lives*. New York: Guilford Press.
Moore, D. (2003). *Survey of financial literacy in Washington State: Knowledge, behavior, attitudes, and experiences* (Technical report/03-39), Social and Economic Sciences Research Center, Washington State University.
Mottola, G. R. (2013). In our best interest: Women, financial literacy, and credit card behavior. *Numeracy, 6*(2). Article 4.
Murphy, D. S., & Yetmar, S. (2010). Personal financial planning attitudes: A preliminary study of graduate students. *Management Research Review, 33*(8), 811–817.
National Financial Capability Study – NFCS. (2013). *Financial capability in the United States – Report of findings from the 2012 national financial capability study*. Financial Industry Regulatory Authority (FINRA) Investor Education Foundation. Available at: http://www.usfinancialcapability.org/downloads/NFCS_2012_Report_Natl_Findings.pdf (Accessed April 07, 2015).
National Foundation For Credit Counseling – NFCC. (2015). *The 2015 consumer financial literacy survey*, Report of the Network Branded Prepaid Card Association. Available at: https://www.nfcc.org/wp-content/uploads/2015/04/NFCC_2015_Financial_Literacy_Survey_FINAL.pdf (Accessed November 28, 2016).

Noctor, M., Stoney, S., & Stradling, R. (1992). *Financial literacy: A discussion of concepts and competences of financial literacy and opportunities for its introduction into young people's learning, report prepared for the National Westminster Bank*. London: National Foundation for Education Research.
Norvilitis, J. M., & Maclean, M. G. (2010). The role of parents in college students' financial behaviors and attitudes. *Journal of Economic Psychology, 31*(1), 55–63.
Norvilitis, J. M., & Mendes-Da-Silva, W. (2013). Attitudes toward credit and finances among college students in Brazil and the United States. *Journal of Business Theory and Practice, 1*(1), 132–151.
O'Neill, B., & Xiao, J. (2012). Financial behaviors before and after the financial crisis: Evidence from an online survey. *Journal of Financial Counseling and Planning, 23*(1), 33–46.
Opletalová, A. (2015). Financial education and financial literacy in the Czech education system. *Procedia – Social and Behavioral Sciences, 171*(16), 1176–1184.
Organisation for Economic Co-operation and Development – OECD. (2012). *OECD/INFE high-level principles on national strategies for financial education*. Paris: OECD Publishing.
Organisation for Economic Co-operation and Development – OECD. (2015a). *2015 OECD/INFE toolkit for measuring financial literacy and financial inclusion*. Paris: OECD Publishing.
Organisation for Economic Co-operation and Development – OECD. (2015b). *PISA 2012 assessment and analytical framework: mathematics, reading, science, problem solving and financial literacy*. Paris: OECD Publishing.
Organisation for Economic Co-operation and Development – OECD. (2015c). *The ABC of gender equality in education: Aptitude, behaviour, confidence, PISA*. Paris: OECD Publishing.
Organisation for Economic Co-Operation and Development – OECD. (2017). *PISA 2015 assessment and analytical framework: science, reading, mathematic, financial literacy and collaborative problem solving*. Paris: OECD Publishing.
Potrich, A. C. G., Vieira, K. M., & Kirch, G. (2015). Determinants of financial literacy: Analysis of the influence of socioeconomic and demographic variables. *Revista Contabilidade & Finanças, 26*(69), 362–377.
Raftery, A. E. (1993). Bayesian model selection in structural equation models. In K. A. Bollen & J. S. Long (Eds.), *Testing structural equation models* (pp. 163–180). Newbury Park, CA: Sage Publications.
Remund, D. L. (2010). Financial literacy explicated: The case for a clearer definition in an increasingly complex economy. *The Journal of Consumer Affairs, 44*(2), 276–295.
Robb, C. A., Babiarz, P., & Woodyard, A. (2012). The demand for financial professionals' advice: The role of financial knowledge, satisfaction, and confidence. *Financial Services Review, 21*(4), 291–306.
Salleh, A. M. H. A. P. M. (2015). A comparison on financial literacy between welfare recipients and non-welfare recipients in Brunei. *International Journal of Social Economics, 42*(7), 598–613.
Santos, D. B., Mendes-Da-Silva, W., & Gonzalez, L. (2018). Lower financial literacy induces use of informal loan. *Revista de Administração de Empresas, 58*(1), 44–59.
Schagen, S. (1997). *The evaluation of NatWest face 2 face with finance*. National Foundation For Education Research, London.
Schwarz, G. (1978). Estimating the dimension of a model. *The Annals of Statistics, 6*(2), 461–464.
Sekita, S. (2011). Financial literacy and retirement planning in Japan. *Journal of Pension Economics and Finance, 10*(4), 637–656.
Servon, L. J., & Kaestner, R. (2008). Consumer financial literacy and the impact of online banking on the financial behavior of lower-income bank customers. *Journal of Consumer Affairs, 42*(2), 271–305.
Shim, S., Xiao, J. J., Barber, B. L., & Lyons, A. C. (2009). Pathways to life success: A conceptual model of financial well-being for young adults. *Journal of Applied Developmental Psychology, 30*(6), 708–723.

Shim, S., Barber, B. L., Card, N. A., Xiao, J. J., & Serido, J. (2010). Financial socialization of first-year college students: The roles of parents, work, and education. *Journal of Youth and Adolescence, 39*(12), 1457–1470.
Shockey, S. S. (2002). *Low-wealth adult's financial literacy. Money management behavior and associates factors, including critical thinking*. Unpublished doctoral dissertation, The Ohio State University (AAT 3039524).
Silva, T. P., Dal Magro, C. B., Gorla, M. C., & Nakamura, W. T. (2017). Financial education level of high school students and its economic reflections. *Revista de Administração, 52*(3), 285–303.
Van Rooij, M. C. J., Lusardi, A., & Alessie, R. J. M. (2011). Financial literacy and retirement planning in the Netherlands. *J Econ PsycholJournal of Economic Psychology, 32*(4), 593–608.
Xiao, J. J., Tang, C., Serido, J., & Shim, S. (2011). Antecedents and consequences of risky credit behavior among college students: Application and extension of the theory of planned behavior. *Journal of Public Policy & Marketing, 30*(2), 239–258.

Chapter 5
Credit Card and Financial Well-Being Among Females

Danilo Braun Santos, Wesley Mendes-Da-Silva, Jill M. Norvilitis, and Eduardo da Silva Flores

Abstract The literature documents the impact of credit card use on people's financial well-being, including special interest in women's credit card behavior. This chapter examines predictors of the financial well-being for female college students living in São Paulo City (Brazil) or New York City (United States), focusing upon behaviors regarding credit card use. The results of structural equation models, based on 784 participants, suggest that financial self-confidence and social comparison impact the respondents' habits surrounding credit card use and, more largely, influence financial well-being. Although social comparison is more strongly predictive of credit card use among Brazilian women, credit card use behavior has a greater impact on the well-being of American women.

Keywords Social comparison · Credit card use · Well-being · College students

JEL Code E51 · J16 · I31

Among the most popular financial innovations is the credit card. This popularization has been intensified as a result of the advantages (in relation to cash in kind)

Portions of this chapter appeared in the 2016 paper "Predictors of credit card use and perceived financial well-being in female college students: a Brazil-United States comparative study," *International Journal of Consumer Studies*, vol 40, pp 133–142.

D. B. Santos
Federal University of Sao Paulo (UNIFESP), Osasco, SP, Brazil

W. Mendes-Da-Silva (✉)
Sao Paulo School of Business Administration (FGV/EAESP), Sao Paulo, SP, Brazil

University of Texas at Austin, Austin, TX, USA

J. M. Norvilitis
State University of New York, Buffalo, NY, USA
e-mail: norviljm@buffalostate.edu

E. da Silva Flores
University of São Paulo, São Paulo, SP, Brazil
e-mail: eduardoflores@usp.br

W. Mendes-Da-Silva (ed.), *Individual Behaviors and Technologies for Financial Innovations*, https://doi.org/10.1007/978-3-319-91911-9_5

identified by the users of this financial instrument. Credit cards are easy to carry, lightweight, usually pocket-sized, and relatively safe and carry a value in and of themselves. Used mainly for travel and entertainment, the Diners Club Card claims the title of the first credit card in widespread use. In the early 1950s, its existence was inspired in a moment of need that awakened the creative genius of a client who forgot his wallet while attending a business dinner at New York's Major's Cabin Grill. Months later, this client, Frank McNamara, along with his partner, Ralph Schneider, returned to the restaurant with a small card and a proposal that resulted in the Diners Club Card.

Although your purchases were made with credit, the Diners Club was technically a charge card, which meant that the account was to be paid in full at the end of each month. In 1951, the Diners Club had 20,000 cardholders. The American Express card was released in 1958, with a different provenance. Formed in 1850 as a competitor to the United States Postal Service, American Express had introduced money orders in 1882, invented travelers' checks in 1891, and had begun contemplating a billing card in 1946, prior to the Diners Club. American Express would soon claim proprietary milestones, expanding its reach to other countries and presenting the first plastic card in 1959, replacing previous cardboard versions. Since then, credit cards have become popular around the world, especially among younger people, who often are not prepared to use a credit card responsibly (Friedline et al. 2017). Consumers are inevitably confronted with many complex financial decisions to handle while still young adults. The negative consequences of wrong financial decisions taken at the beginning of adulthood can extend for a considerable period of one's life (Lusardi et al. 2010). This realization has led researchers to examine predictors of debt and financial well-being in order to help students develop positive financial habits. One of the first tests that college students must face is when to use credit cards. Most students manage credit cards wisely. Research in the United States indicates that most students maintain relatively low balances, with 67% reporting a balance of less than $3000 and 22% paying off their credit cards monthly (Sallie Mae 2009). According to financial press, about 43 million Americans currently owe almost 1.4 trillion in federal student debt, the highest form of debt in United States, excluding mortgages (Mitchell 2018).

However, a significant minority find themselves in substantial debt, which is associated with a variety of negative consequences, including decreased confidence in one's money management skills, lower self-esteem, decreased financial well-being, and higher stress (Lange and Byrd 1998; Norvilitis et al. 2003). Of concern for colleges, students with high levels of debt are at risk of dropping out of college caused by their decreased financial well-being (Dwyer et al. 2013). Clearly, it is important to understand the factors predicting credit card use and financial well-being and to examine the universality of these predictors, given that most of the research to date has been conducted in North America, Western Europe, and Australia. Thus, the present study sought to explore college students' credit card use in both the United States and in Brazil.

Credit card debt is viewed as arising from multiple factors, including demographics, personality, and social and educational variables. In studies of American students, important demographic factors include year in college, with students reporting increasingly worse financial well-being with advancing year in school (Gutter and Copur 2011), and age, with older students self-reporting more problematic financial behavior (Lokken Worthy et al. 2010). Personality factors most frequently identified with this trend include more liberal attitudes toward credit use (Norvilitis et al. 2006), poor delay of gratification, more impulsiveness, and more compulsive spending (Joireman et al. 2010; Norvilitis et al. 2006; Palan et al. 2011; Pirog and Roberts 2007; Strayhorn 2002; Watson 2003). Social and educational factors are also predictive of financial well-being, although the role of financial knowledge is unclear, with some studies showing a protective effect (Norvilitis et al. 2006; Robb 2011) and others showing increased risk (Hirt and Nick 1999; Norvilitis and MacLean 2010).

However, it is not known if many of these same predictors for students in the United States apply to other cultures, including emerging markets (Norvilitis and Mendes-Da-Silva 2013). Brazil's credit market among university students has shown rapid growth, while in the United States, new legal restrictions have been imposed, such as provisions of the 2009 Credit CARD Act that have served to limit college student access to credit cards (Credit Card Accountability Responsibility and Disclosure Act 2009). Given the differences across the two countries, similar predictors of financial well-being would point toward the universality of these factors.

This study represents one of the most comprehensive overviews of college students' credit card behaviors. Data was collected from over 780 students in two large cities in South and North America, i.e., São Paulo and New York. This chapter presents highlights from this research and identifies predictors of financial well-being for female college students, focusing on their habits for credit card use. These findings offer insight into how financial professionals, educators, financial industry, and campus administrators can develop and provide students more effective financial education, especially those who are financially at risk. At the end of this chapter, some recommendations are made, and directions for future research are suggested.

Theoretical Background

In examining college student financial behavior, the present study combines two theories: the social comparison theory and the theory of planned behavior. According to social comparison theory (Festinger 1954), people evaluate themselves through comparisons with others. Such comparisons can influence self-confidence, self-esteem, and positive and negative feelings about oneself. In Lee's (2014) study of social media usage, individuals who were less certain about themselves were more likely to engage in social comparison. One area in which one is likely to find social comparison is that of spending and consumption. People may compare their possessions and their income with others. Indeed, even with similar levels of income, households who consider themselves to be better off than others report higher levels of consumption (Karlsson et al. 2004). Further, research has established that social comparison is linked with satisfaction with income and success (McBride 2010) and debt among adults (Lea et al. 1995), as well as to financial well-being among American college students (Norvilitis and Mao 2012).

Social comparison may also be the basis for subjective norms about financial behavior. Chudry et al. (2011) examined attitudes toward borrowing as an application of the theory of planned behavior. The theory of planned behavior (Ajzen 1991) conceptualizes behavior as the result of a combination of attitudes, subjective norms, and perceived behavioral control. Chudry et al. (2011) reported support for this model in a study involving student loans, for all three of these factors were found to affect intention to borrow. Also, students' beliefs about social norms are related to overspending on credit cards (Sotiropoulos and d'Astous 2013). In the present study, we conceptualized student financial behavior and perceived financial well-being as resulting from a combination of these influences. Thus, financial behavior, in this case credit card use, was expected to be predicted by subjective norms, as measured by social comparison. In addition, credit card use was also expected to be predicted by students' attitudes concerning financial self-confidence, and by perceived behavioral control, which is assumed to be related to parental modeling of financial behavior.

Financial Self-Confidence

In a study of 2008 first year college students, Shim et al. (2010) examined a financial socialization model using structural equations to explain how young people acquire financial attitudes, behaviors, and knowledge. The authors reported that greater parental participation, especially when performing a new financial management task, can help develop self-confidence and encourages young people to adopt healthier financial attitudes and behaviors. Similarly, Norvilitis and Mao (2012) reported that parental education was related to increased financial self-confidence. Further, financial self-confidence was linked to increased delay of gratification, suggesting that self-confidence is related to more positive outcomes. Conversely, anxiety is related to compulsive buying, indicating that a lack of self-confidence is related to negative outcomes (Roberts and Jones 2001).

Parental Education and Modeling

Positive parental modeling and instruction about money appear to decrease the risk of debt (Norvilitis and MacLean 2010; Norvilitis and Mao 2012; Pinto et al. 2001). In a study that examined the influence of parental interactions on credit card use behavior among students in seven universities, Hancock et al. (2013) identified the importance of parents as positive models. Limbu et al. (2012) further highlighted the importance of parents in terms of confidence and balanced management when it comes to credit card use, adding that those female students who are less influenced by their parents are subject to greater debt risk. In a study of 7417 Americans between 12 and 17 years of age, Lusardi et al. (2010) emphasized the importance of parental influence when it comes to young people acquiring financial knowledge before they get involved with contracts and begin making financial decisions. Thus, parental modeling is critical for college students to acquire perceived control over their finances.

Gender and Financial Behavior

Although the model described above should apply to both male and female college students, it is important to examine men and women separately because research on gender differences has been inconclusive, with some studies showing no differences (Davies and Lea 1995; Norvilitis et al. 2003; Norvilitis et al. 2006; Ha 2013) and others reporting increased risk among men or women. For example, Wang et al. (2011) stated that men tend to get into debt more frequently. Conversely, Lyons (2004) found that women are more likely not to pay the whole of their credit card bill for a period equal to or greater than 2 months.

Male college students are reported to be more risk-tolerant and make more financially risky decisions (Lemaster and Strough 2014). There may also be differences by gender in response to debt. Dwyer et al. (2013) report that, although student debt causes both male and female college students to slow down their progress toward graduation, males are more likely to drop out of school at lower levels of debt. In a study of 26,896 students from 10 North American universities, Yilmazer and Lyons (2010) found that women are more likely to have credit card debts in excess of $1000, not to pay the whole bill for a period equal to or greater than 2 months and to exceed their credit card limit. Similarly, O'Guinn and Faber (1989), d'Astous (1990), and Norum (2008) argue that women report more compulsive buying behavior, which may lead women to greater debt.

Given these conflicting results, it is evident that further research into women's use of credit is necessary, particularly in emerging markets such as Brazil. The credit industry has been growing rapidly in Brazil. Between January 2004 and January 2011, the volume of credit increased from about US$232.11 billion to about US $0.95trillion, largely due to personal credit (Depec 2011). This growth in the use of credit has been so rapid that growth in the credit market has outpaced research. Among the few studies, Mendes-Da-Silva et al. (2012) examined credit card risk behavior among 769 college students, finding that those with more credit cards were at increased likelihood of risky credit behavior and that those students who reported knowing their interest rates were at decreased risk, suggesting that knowledge may be protective. However, little work to date has examined men and women separately.

Brazilian authors have argued that Brazilian women's financial behavior should be investigated more fully since they do not have the financial autonomy as men. This is reflected in recently published information about the determinants of well-being in the city of São Paulo. When compared with men, women reported that they were less satisfied with their financial lives and with their savings for retirement (Well Being Brazil Index 2014). In addition, among the few studies that have been conducted, women's behavior has been examined without using control groups or data from other institutional contexts, thereby reducing the opportunity for more detailed explanations as to why certain behaviors are found in females (Ha 2013).

Model

Although components of this study have previously been examined in isolation, we are not aware of any studies that have simultaneously examined the influence of the three predictors on credit card use and financial well-being in female college students in a cross-cultural setting. More specifically, the research, which utilized Brazilian and American students, was carried out by constructing a structural equation model. This model was capable of capturing the dynamic between these three predictors through the use of a comparative approach to these two different institutional environments. According to Tenenhaus et al. (2004), structural equation modeling (SEM) allows for a simultaneous statistical regression of a group of different equations between themselves. This makes it possible to check the relationship of the two types of variable: latent and observable. Figure 5.1 shows the path diagram between the latent variables of the structural model.

Overall, it was expected that parental financial education and modeling would influence financial self-confidence and this combined with financial social comparison would predict credit card use. In turn, credit card use would predict financial well-being. Specifically, based on the prior research on predictors of debt and the social comparison and planned behavior theories, we identified four hypotheses:

H_1: The better the financial education transmitted by the parents (PFES), the greater the student's subsequent self-confidence in financial management (FSC).

H_2: The greater the self-confidence in financial management (FSC), the more responsible the student's credit card use behavior (CCUS).

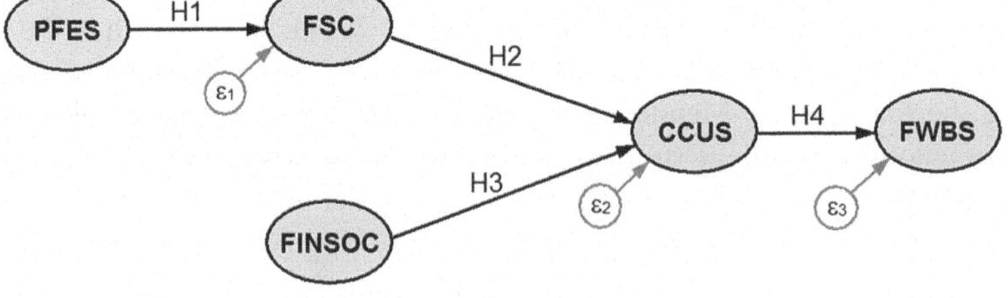

Fig. 5.1 Proposed structural model. Note: PFES – parent financial education scale; FSC – financial self-confidence; FINSOC – financial social comparison; CCUS – credit card use scale; FWBS – financial well-being scale

H_3: The greater the focus upon social comparisons (FINSOC), the less responsible with credit card use (CCUS).

H_4: The less responsible the credit card use (CCUS), the worse the financial well-being (FWBS).

Data

Data were collected in medium-large public universities located in São Paulo (Brazil) and New York (United States). A total of 784 female students took part: 436 Brazilians and 348 Americans. Of the North American female students, 71% consider themselves to be white, 8% said they were African American, 17% were of Hispanic origin, 3% were of Asian origin, and 1% was Native American. With regard to the Brazilian respondents, 75% said they were white, 10% were black, 7% were of Hispanic descent, 7% were of Asian origin, and 1% came from Brazilian indigenous tribes. With regard to the student profile of the respondents, in the sample of Brazilians, 12% were enrolled in the first undergraduate year, 31% in the second year, 23% in the third year, 19% in the fourth year, and 15% in the fifth year. Of the North Americans, 14% said they were first year college students, 25% in the second year, 34% in the third year, 18% in the fourth year, and 8% in the fifth year.

With regard to the frequency with which students used credit cards, 26% of the Brazilians indicated they only use credit cards in emergency situations, 20% said that they use them less than once a week, 13% said they use them at least once a week, and the remaining 40% of the respondents said they use their cards more than once a week. Approximately 38% of the North Americans, in their turn, reported that they only use credit cards in emergency situations, while 26% said they use them less than once per week, and 13% reported they make purchases with their cards at least once weekly. The remaining 23% disclosed a use frequency greater than once per week (Percentages may not add up to 100% due to rounding). Ten students from Brazil and 50 students from the United States left this item blank because they do not use credit cards.

Participants were recruited from a variety of departments and courses across each campus to assure that the samples were representative of each of the colleges. Both credit card users and noncredit card users participated. Instructors awarded extra credit for participation. Following a description of the study, students were given the opportunity to take a survey packet to complete. Surveys were completed outside of class and returned to the class in which they were distributed. Because students were not required to take a packet, it is impossible to determine the response rate. The information collected was hand-written on three printed documents: a consent form, a questionnaire, and a sheet for completing the replies. Upon return, consent forms were immediately separated from the answer sheet so that all responses were anonymous.

The constructs in the questionnaire formed five large question groups: financial well-being scale (FWBS; Norvilitis et al. 2003), financial self-confidence (FSC; Norvilitis and Mao 2012), modified credit card use scale (CCUS; Raghubir and Srivastava 2008), financial social comparison (FINSOC; Norvilitis and Mao 2012), and parental financial education scale (PFES; Norvilitis and MacLean 2010). Table 5.1 gives a brief definition of the constructs and the number of questions used to measure them. A 5-point Likert scale was used for all questions, with 1 meaning "strongly agree" and 5 meaning "strongly disagree." The scale was inverted for some variables so that high scores had the interpretation suggested in Table 5.1. The variables used in the reverse scale can be identified by the suffix *r* in Fig. 5.2 and the original questions in Table 5.1, with the observable variables remaining in the model.

Empirical Results

All estimations were carried out using Stata version 12 software. Whenever possible and to enhance the robustness of the results, we used three different estimation techniques: the asymptotic distribution-free (ADF) method, the maximum verisimilitude method (ML), and the maximum verisimilitude method, with missing values treatment (MLMV). In the order in which they were listed, these methods give gradually more restrictive hypotheses. The asymptotic distribution-free method is a generalized method of moments (GMM) estimator and makes no supposition of joint normality or even of symmetry in the data.

But ADF is less efficient than ML when the suppositions for ML are valid. Maximum verisimilitude is the estimation method most widely used in SEM analyses because it requires a smaller number of data for convergence and conditional normality is sufficient for obtaining consistent estimates. MLMV, conversely, requires all variables to be jointly normal, which is a very strong premise in most cases, particularly if the measurement scale is categorical, as is the case with this study. According to Mueller and Hancock (2007), the process of composition of the latent variable components of the structural model is based on the choice of indicators by the researcher. And this process of choice must rest on two main pillars, (i) the arguments underlying the model, in the literature on the subject studied, and the model fit measures. This procedure has already been used in recent studies about young adult attitudes to credit and money (Potrich et al. 2016).

Despite the fact that each construct initially contains a large number of observable variables (see Table 5.1), to achieve convergence in the estimation methods and satisfactory adjustments in the measurement, validity, and reliability models, it was necessary to reduce the number of indicators drastically. The question of the convergence of the estimation methods is linked to the identification hypothesis of the models and to sample size. Models with a large number of indicators need larger samples and estimation methods with fewer restrictive hypotheses (Thompson 2006). In this study, for example, if an indicator which was created to measure

Table 5.1 Constructs of the proposed structural model and observable variables remaining in the model

Label	Definition	Questions (latent variable indicators)	No. of indicators
FSC	Higher scores indicate higher self-confidence to manage financial assets	Financial self-confidence	10
	fsc1	I'm confident that I know how to handle my money	
	fsc4	I trust my capacity for handling credit cards	
	fsc5	I trust my capacity for handling bank accounts	
FINSOC	Higher scores indicate less desire to own the goods that others have	Financial social comparison	9
	finsoc1	When I see that others have nice things, like clothes or an automobile, I'd often like to have that too	
	finsoc2	I often compare what I have with what my friends have	
	finsoc3	I'm happy if I have nicer things than other people	
CCUS	Higher scores indicate greater responsibility in credit card use	Credit card use scale	30
	ccus6	Every month I'm afraid to receive my credit card bill	
	ccus11	I regret the amount of my credit card bills when it's time to pay them	
	ccus13	I buy unnecessary items when I use a credit card	
PFES	Higher scores indicate better financial education passed on by parents	Parental financial education scale	34
	pfes12	My parents helped teach me how to save money	
	pfes13	My parents talked to me about their financial priorities	
	pfes28	My parents helped me understand their financial priorities	
FWBS	Higher scores indicate high financial well-being	Subjective financial well-being	10
	fwbs1	I'm bothered about the debts I currently have	
	fwbs7	I think a lot about my current debts	
	fwbs9	I frequently catch myself thinking about my debts	

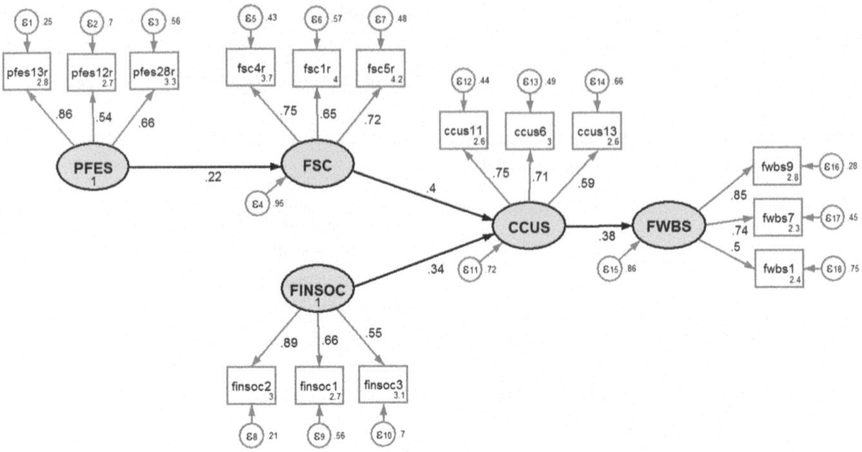

Fig. 5.2 Structural model (estimated for maximum verisimilitude). Note: This diagram shows the standardized estimates. The values in arrows represent the betas and the values within the rectangles, the constant. The values alongside the errors represent their variance

Table 5.2 Results of the validities and reliabilities of the constructs

		ADF method				ML method		
	CR[a]	AVE[b]	MSV[c]	ASV[d]	CR[a]	AVE[b]	MSV[c]	ASV[d]
FINSOC	0.787	0.561	0.097	0.038	0.747	0.507	0.114	0.031
FSC	0.803	0.579	0.081	0.031	0.749	0.500	0.148	0.066
FWBS	0.765	0.534	0.258	0 → 0.078	0.747	0.507	0.135	0.052
PFES	0.758	0.519	0.018	0.010	0.737	0.493	0.052	0.014
CCUS	0.729	0.477	0.258	0.114	0.721	0.465	0.148	0.099

Note: Recommended values [a]CR > 0.7; [b]AVE > 05; [ab]CR > AVE; [c]MSV < AVE; [d]ASV < AVE
ADF asymptotic distribution-free method, *ML* maximum verisimilitude method

PFES better explains the CCU, we have a divergent validity problem. And, if the set of indicators that measure PFES, for example, do not adequately correlate, we can have convergent validity and reliability problems. A convergent validity problem occurs when the indicators of a latent variable do not correlate sufficiently. And the lack of discriminant validity is when an indicator can better explain another factor than father factor.

To address both problems, the indicators were excluded one by one, from the most critical. With each step we calculated the measures of composite reliability (CR), average variance extracted (AVE), maximum shared variance (MSV), and shared average variance (ASV), until the adjustment is considered satisfactory. Therefore, our final model could only handle three indicators in each construct. The remaining observable variables are listed in Table 5.1. Table 5.2 contains the adjustments of the measurement model for the validity and reliability of the constructs, as estimated by the ADF and ML methods. The composite reliability (CR), average variance extracted (AVE), maximum shared variance (MSV), and average

Table 5.3 Adjustment metrics of the models

Model	N	χ^2	df	χ^2 /df[a]	RMS A[b]	pclose[c]	CFI[d]	SRMR[e]
CFA (ADF)	612	230.71*	80	2.88	0.055	0.135	0.856	0.108
CFA (ML)	612	216.04*	80	2.70	0.053	0.287	0.943	0.044
CFA (MLMV)	784	246.14*	80	3.07	0.051	0.359	0.943	
MG-CFA (ML)	612	497.38*	180	2.76	0.076		0.875	0.074
Brazil	374							0.070
United States	238							0.078
MG-CFA (MLMV)	784	596.50*	180	3.31	0.077		0.866	
SEM (ADF)	612	243.78*	86	2.83	0.055	0.160	0.849	0.114
SEM (ML)	612	225.38*	86	2.62	0.051	0.372	0.941	0.049
SEM (MLMV)	784	255.15*	86	2.97	0.050	0.479	0.942	
MG-SEM (ML)	612	555.87*	195	2.85	0.078		0.858	0.094
Brazil	374							0.076
United States	238							0.108
MG-SEM (MLMV)	784	655.66*	195	3.36	0.078		0.851	

Note: *CFA* confirmatory factorial analysis, *SEM* structural model, *MG* multigroup analysis. *ADF* asymptotic distribution-free estimation method, *ML* maximum verisimilitude method, *MLMV* maximum verisimilitude method with missing values treatment. *for the *p*-value (χ^2) < 0.05. Recommended values: [a]χ^2/df < 5 moderate <3 good. [b]RMSEA <0.10 moderate <0.05 good. [c]pclose >0.05. [d]CFI >0.80 moderate >0.90 good. [e]SRMR <0.08. SRMR is not calculated by the MLMV method and pclose is not calculated in multigroup analysis

shared variance (ASV) variables gave the values recommended in literature. The only exception was the AVE value for the CCUS construct, which, despite not exceeding the value recommended, gives a result that is very close to it.

The adjustment measures of the confirmatory factor analysis model (CFA) and the structural model (SEM) are shown in Table 5.3. We estimated both using the three methods previously mentioned: ADF, ML, and MLMV. With regard to the adjustments to the full sample, we saw that both CFA and SEM gave values within the recommended parameters. The exception was for the standardized root mean square residual (SRMR) value for the ADF method, which does not satisfy the criterion of remaining below 0.08 (Hu and Bentler 1999).

With regard to the structural model (SEM), a correlation was initially allowed between the exogenous latent variables, PFES and FINSOC. However, we obtained a nonsignificant correlation coefficient, and we chose, therefore, to restrict this correlation to zero. This led to obtaining a slight improvement in the adjustments of the model. It is worth noting that for the ML method the SRMR was less than 0.08 and the root mean square error of approximation (RMSEA) was less than 0.06, and thus Hu and Bentler's two-index strategy was satisfied. Generally speaking, the statistics calculated using the ML method gave better adjustments than the ADF and the MLMV methods. This is no reason, however, for one method to be selected in detriment to another since, as we have already discussed, the assumptions of each of them differ substantially. We preferred, therefore, to present the parameters as estimated by the three methods because we believe that the convergence or not of the results is important which leads us to a picture that is closer to reality.

Structural Model

Figure 5.2 presents the results of the estimation by the maximum verisimilitude method of the proposed structural model, and Table 5.4 shows the adjustments to the model. The standardized estimates of the parameters for the three estimation methods can be seen in Table 5.4 in "default model."

Before analyzing the results obtained for these parameters (Table 5.4) and checking the hypotheses of the models, a discussion on the construction of this model is in order. The hypotheses raised were based on studies in which the dynamic between the constructs was examined in isolation. In other words, when we formulated Hypothesis 1, which is that parental education has an impact in terms of financial self-confidence, we used studies that checked this implication without considering the effect of other variables. Testing this hypothesis in the structural model consists in analyzing up to what point this relationship is maintained in a broader context, where other dynamics are observed.

However, when we create a path from PFES to FSC and from the latter to CCUS, we are discarding a possible direct effect from PFES to CCUS. In other words, we might be basing this on research that is prior to the impact of financial self-confidence on credit card use behavior and to the impact of parental education on self-confidence; but this ignores that there might be a direct and relevant impact of

Table 5.4 Estimates of the parameters in the path model

Panel A: Default model	ADF	ML	MLMV
PFES → FSC	0.05	0.22***	0.16***
FSC → CCUS	0.34***	0.40***	0.41***
FINSOC → CCUS	0.33***	0.34***	0.33***
CCUS → FWBS	0.53***	0.38***	0.39***
Panel B: FSC mediation			
PFES → FSC	0.04	0.23***	0.17***
PFES → CCUS	−0.09*	−0.09*	−0.09*
FSC → CCUS	0.33***	0.43***	0.43***
FINSOC → CCUS	0.34***	0.34***	0.33***
CCUS → FWBS	0.51***	0.38***	0.39***
Panel C: CCUS mediation			
PFES → FSC	0.05	0.22***	0.16***
FSC → CCUS	0.34***	0.39***	0.40***
FINSOC → CCUS	0.33***	0.35***	0.33***
FSC → FWBS	0.01	0.12**	0.09
FINSOC → FWBS	0	−0.02	−0.02
CCUS → FWBS	0.53***	0.33***	0.36***

Note: Standardized estimates of the coefficients in the structural model
ADF asymptotic distribution-free estimation method, *ML* maximum verisimilitude method, *MLMV* maximum verisimilitude method, with missing values treatment
$^{*}p < 0.10$; $^{**}p < 0.05$; $^{***}p < 0.01$

Table 5.5 Direct, indirect, and total effects

Panel A: Direct effects	ADF	ML
PFES → FSC	0.04	0.16***
FSC → CCUS	0.38***	0.46***
FINSOC → CCUS	0.28***	0.32***
CCUS → FWBS	0.66***	0.43***
Panel B: Indirect effects		
PFES → CCUS	0.01	0.07***
PFES → FWBS	0.01	0.03***
FSC → FWBS	0.25***	0.19***
FINSOC → FWBS	0.19***	0.14***
Panel C: Total effects		
PFES → FSC	0.04	0.16***
PFES → CCUS	0.01	0.07***
FSC → CCUS	0.38***	0.46***
FINSOC → CCUS	0.28***	0.32***
PFES → FWBS	0.01	0.03***
FSC → FWBS	0.25***	0.20***
FINSOC → FWBS	0.19***	0.14***
CCUS → FWBS	0.66***	0.43***

Note: Standardized estimates of the coefficients in the structural model
ADF asymptotic distribution-free estimation method, *ML* maximum verisimilitude method
$*p < 0.10$; $**p < 0.05$; $***p < 0.01$

parental education on credit card use. To examine this type of concern, we tested the mediating effects of the constructs. These results are also presented in Table 5.4. To measure the mediation relationship exercised by FSC of PFES on CCUS, we included a new path between PFES and CCUS. Despite being statistically significant at 10%, we notice that the beta was very small, being estimated in the three methods at −0.09. Analogously, to test the mediation exercised by CCUS on FINSOC and FSC on FWBS, we included direct paths between them. We note that with the exception of the impact of FSC on FWBS by the ML method, all the estimates were statistically nonsignificant for all the estimation methods. These tests, therefore, corroborate the validity of the proposed model. Returning to the original model, we must first illustrate that we oriented the measurement scale in a way that (see Table 5.5) hypotheses confirmation is linked to finding positively significant coefficients between constructs.

We can check that the conclusions about the effects of PFES on FSC are doubtful. While the ML and MLMV methods estimated this effect at 0.22 and 0.16, respectively, significant at 1%, the ADF method did not reject the possibility of this effect being null. Therefore, hypothesis (H_1), that parental education positively affects self-confidence in financial management, cannot be satisfactorily demonstrated. What the results do allow us to state is that if the effect exists, it will be positive. On the other hand, hypotheses (H_2), that confidence in financial management leads to better credit card use; (H_3), that less inclination to social comparison implies a more rational credit card use; and (H_4), that less responsibility in credit card use results in a state of worse financial well-being were all supported by the model. Regardless of the estimation method used, all the coefficients are significant at 1% and positive.

As for the magnitudes of the estimated values, we note a convergence of the results with the maximum verisimilitude methods. The ADF method estimated the FINSOC on CCUS (H_3) coefficient with a result similar to the ML methods, but the FSC on CCUS (H_2) and CCUS on FWBS (H_4) coefficients with results that were different from those in the ML methods, at below (0.34 vs. 0.40) and above (0.53 vs. 0.38), respectively. Table 5.5 shows the direct, indirect, and total effects between all the constructs of the model. We note that the total effect of PFES both on CCUS and on FWBS is null or practically null, while FINSOC and FSC are significantly important for determining the financial well-being of women.

Comparison Between Brazil and the United States

To compare Brazilian and American women, it was first necessary to check the invariance in the measurement model, known in literature as factorial invariance (FI). FI procedures are well established and made increasingly easier by powerful statistical packages, but there is controversy regarding the acceptable levels of invariance and the preferred manner of testing them. Meredith and Horn (2001) propose that factorial invariance should be tested by forcing equality both of the coefficients and the intercepts of the indicators. This type of invariance is called strong factorial invariance, or metric and scalar factorial invariance.

Following this procedure we carried out a score test on the difference in chi-squares between the restricted and unrestricted model (Baseline) using the ML method, and we obtained a $X_{diff}(10) = 34{,}617$ for the CFA multigroup model and a $X_{diff}(10) = 34{,}884$ for the SEM multigroup model. Both gave statistically significant differences, which invalidate strong factorial invariance. The adjustment metrics for these models are shown in Table 5.4, along with the models with the whole sample. The ADF method did not converge in the group analysis and so there is nothing to report.

If strong factorial invariance should be required, analysis between the groups must be aborted. Some researchers, however, argue that in the absence of invariance, finding some factorial invariance is better than abandoning the analyses altogether (Byrne et al. 1989). In their work on partial measurement invariance (PMI), Byrne et al. (1989) argue that if two or more loadings are invariant, then the metric of the common factor can be considered equivalent between the groups, so that comparisons can still be made. If this methodology is adopted, a score test of the difference in the coefficients in our SEM comparison between groups rejected the restriction at 10% for items (*p-value* in parentheses): fwbs1 (0.0698), ccus6 (0.0003), finsoc3 (0.0083), fsc5r (0.0054), and pfes28r (0.0659). Considering that two of the three

Table 5.6 Results of the multigroup analysis

	ML			MLMV	
	BR	US	$\chi 2$ (1)	BR	US
PFES → FSC	0.23***	0.20**	0.65	0.18***	0.14**
FSC → CCUS	0.35***	0.46***	1.82	0.38***	0.44***
FINSOC → CCUS	0.43***	0.23***	5.66**	0.39***	0.22***
CCUS → FWBS	0.30***	0.48***	4.55**	0.34***	0.47***

Note: Standardized estimates of the coefficients in the structural model. *ML* maximum verisimilitude method, with treatment of missing values
*$p < 0.10$, **$p < 0.05$, ***$p < 0.01$

loadings of each construct were considered invariant, the PMI could be a defense for the validity of the comparison between groups.

However, we are not interested in pursuing this investigation into the factorial invariance of the model in any more depth and neither, based on the results we found, do we want to argue that this partial invariance is satisfactory, since we understand that this is still a problem under development that is both theoretical, since researchers have not reached any consensus, and empirical, since only a repeat of this study with new data can clarify this issue. According to Bontempo et al. (2007), what is needed is knowledge of the limit at which the lack of invariance presents a significant practical bias for a private study, but what is tested is only the difference in the coefficients.

Table 5.6 shows the estimates of the coefficients in the SEM multigroup analysis. The estimates were generated using the ML and MLMV methods; ADF did not converge, which is why there is nothing to show. For the ML method, we carried out a Wald test to test for equality of coefficients. The effects of PFES on FSC and FSC on CCUS were determined to be equal between the groups, implying that the value of parental education for confidence in financial management is the same among Americans and Brazilians, as is the effect of financial self-confidence on credit card use behavior. The FINSOC on CCUS and CCUS on FWBS coefficients, on the other hand, were determined to be different between the two countries.

The effect of social comparison practices on card use is stronger among Brazilian women. This result is in line with the larger rate of frequent and nonurgent use of credit cards by Brazilian women, while the impact of credit card use on financial well-being is greater for American females than for Brazilian women. The present study analyzed the effect of credit card use behavior on the financial well-being of college women living in São Paulo or in New York. To do so, structural equation models were used, based on a survey of 784 participants. We investigated the relationships that exist between financial social comparison, parental financial education, financial self-confidence, modified credit card use scale, and perceived financial well-being scale constructs. These effects have already been checked in isolation by other researchers. In this work we expanded the analysis by considering the joint dynamics of these factors. To do so we built a structural equation model in which the proposed relationships between the constructs are analyzed through four hypotheses.

To test the hypotheses, the same model was estimated in three different ways: (i) the asymptotic distribution-free method, (ii) the maximum verisimilitude method, and (iii) the maximum verisimilitude method, considering missing values. The four hypotheses that were formulated were confirmed; that is, the arguments used in proposing the empirical model found support in the data collected. However, doubts remained as to the magnitude of the effect of parental education on self-confidence in financial management.

The comparison between Brazilian and American female students identified similar effects for parental education and self-confidence in financial management. Credit card use behavior among Brazilian females seems to be more affected by social comparison than among American females. However, American women who reported more negative credit card behavior report lower levels of financial well-being than Brazilians. These results indicate that American and Brazilian college students use credit cards differently, that they are affected by their use in different ways, or a combination of these two factors. Clearly, this question warrants further research. However, results from the combined samples suggest more similarities across cultures than differences.

Overall, the results support the theoretical model in that social comparison appears to influence credit card behavior. Specifically, women who engage in more social comparison are more likely to report problematic credit card use. This suggests that students who more frequently compare their possessions and spending habits with others may use their credit cards to maintain the lifestyle that they aspire to have. The other portion of the model, the theory of planned behavior, was generally supported as well. The theory of planned behavior posits that intended behavior is predicted by social norms, attitudes, and perceived behavioral control. In this case, social comparison (representing social norms) and financial self-confidence (attitudes) both predicted credit card behavior. The third factor, parental modeling and education (leading to perceived behavioral control), was related in some models, but not all. It is noteworthy that these results were consistent across two countries, Brazil and the United States, indicating that these processes are not simply products of one culture.

Future Directions

Student debt in the United States has been a concern of government officials, families, the financial industry, and young students themselves, whose debts exceed $1 trillion, according to traditional American media (Cauchon 2011). Financial innovations in the means of payment, or even personal loans, should cause significant changes in the credit card industry. Therefore, knowledge of the users' behavior of this financial instrument may be essential for the construction of new financial products and processes. Therefore, the results presented in this chapter are contributory.

Despite our results, the present study had limitations. Most notably, it was assumed that parental modeling and education would lead to perceived behavioral control. Although this assumption is based upon prior research (e.g., Limbu et al. 2012), in the future, it would be helpful to include measures of both constructs in a future model to explicitly test this assumption. Further, the data were collected on just two campuses, one in each country. The two colleges are similar in that both are medium-large, public institutions, located in urban areas, and thus they are broadly comparable to one another. However, it is possible that different results might be found on campuses with different characteristics. Future research should examine this possibility.

Overall, the results highlight the need for interventions with college students that extend beyond simple financial education. Although financial literacy is important, the role of financial knowledge in predicting student debt is unclear, with some studies showing a protective effect (Norvilitis et al. 2006; Robb 2011) and others showing increased risk (Hirt and Nick 1999; Norvilitis and MacLean 2010). Given this, it may be that interventions to help students avoid debt and to promote perceived financial well-being should also address the social factors, such as social comparison, and attitudes, including financial self-confidence, that clearly play a role in student financial behavior.

Financial innovations in recent years may offer contributions to markets, whether mature or emerging. On one hand, in the personal online lending space in the United States, fintechs began to challenge traditional models of credit, e.g. credit cards, among those who could not access mainstream banking services. On the other hand, in emerging countries like Mexico, fintechs can contribute even more toward individual financial democratization, since an expressive part of the population does not have access to banking services. A wide range of business and research opportunities presents itself in today's world (Markovich and Achwal 2017). Finally, based on arguments from Collinson and Pettigrew (2009), this chapter can be contributive since in the field of international business, the differences between places that influence business activities and management behavior are important. This diversity demands adaptability in individuals and industries, in response to cultural, social, political, institutional, environmental, economic, industrial, and market variety.

References

Ajzen, I. (1991). The theory of planned behavior. *Organizational Behavior and Human Decision Processes, 50*, 179–211.

Bontempo, D. E., Hofer, S. M., & Lawrence, F. R. (2007). Assessing factorial invariance in cross-sectional and longitudinal studies. In A. D. Ong & M. H. M. van Dulmen (Eds.), *Handbook of methods in positive psychology* (pp. 153–175). New York: Oxford University Press.

Byrne, B. M., Shavelson, R. J., & Muthen, B. (1989). Testing for the equivalence of factor covariance and mean structures: The issue of partial measurement invariance. *Psychological Bulletin, 105*, 456–466.

Cauchon, D. (2011). Student loans outstanding will exceed $1 trillion this year. *USA Today*. 10 Oct 2011. Available at: http://college.usatoday.com/2017/02/21/student-loan-debt-now-totals-over-1-3-trillion/

Chudry, F., Foxall, G., & Pallister, J. (2011). Exploring attitudes and predicting intentions: Profiling student debtors using an extended theory of planned behavior. *Journal of Applied Social Psychology, 41*(1), 119–149.

Collinson, S. C., & Pettigrew, A. M. (2009). Comparative international business research methods: Pitfalls and practicalities. In A. M. Rugman (Ed.), *The Oxford handbook of international business* (2nd ed.). Oxford: Oxford University Press.

D'Astous, A. (1990). An inquiry into the compulsive side of "normal" consumers. *Journal of Consumer Policy, 13*(1), 15–31.

Davies, E., & Lea, S. E. G. (1995). Student attitudes to student debt. *Journal of Economic Psychology, 16*, 663–679.

Depec, Departamento De Pesquisas Econômicas Do Bradesco. (2011), DestaqueDepec, No. 10, Year IX, April.

Dwyer, R. E., Hodson, R., & McCloud, L. (2013). Gender, debt, and dropping out of college. *Gender and Society, 27*, 30–55.

Festinger, L. (1954). A theory of social comparison processes. *Human Relations, 7*, 117–140.

Friedline, T., West, S., Rosell, N., Serido, J., & Shim, S. (2017). Do community characteristics relate to young adult college students' credit card debt? The hypothesized role of collective institutional efficacy. *American Journal of Community Psychology, 59*(1–2), 80–93.

Gutter, M., & Copur, Z. (2011). Financial behavior and financial well-being of college students: Evidence from a national survey. *Journal of Family and Economic Issues, 32(4)*, 699–714. https://doi.org/10.1007/s10834-011-9255-2

H.R. 627-111th Congress. (2009). Credit card accountability responsibility and disclosure act of. [WWW document]. http://www.govtrack.us/congress/bills/111/hr627/text.

Ha, H. (2013). Credit card use and debt by female students: A case study in Melbourne, Australia. *Youth Studies Australia, 32*(4).

Hancock, A., Jorgensen, B., & Swanson, M. (2013). College students and credit card use: The role of parents, work experience, financial knowledge, and credit card attitudes. *Journal of Family and Economic Issues, 34*, 369–381.

Hirt, J. B., & Nick, H. (1999). How students manage money: Some developmental implications. *NASPA Journal, 37*, 349–360.

Hu, L., & Bentler, P. M. (1999). Cutoff criteria for fit indexes in covariance structure analysis: Conventional criteria versus new alternatives. *Structural Equation Modeling, 6*(1), 1–55.

Joireman, J., Kees, J., & Sprott, D. (2010). Concern with immediate consequences magnifies the impact of compulsive buying tendencies on college students' credit card debt. *Journal of Consumer Affairs, 44*, 155–178.

Karlsson, N., Dellgran, P., Klingander, B., & Garling, T. (2004). Household consumption: Influences of aspiration level, social comparison, and money management. *Journal of Economic Psychology, 25*, 753–769.

Lange, C., & Byrd, M. (1998). The relationship between perceptions of financial distress and feelings of psychological well-being in New Zealand university students. *International Journal of Adolescence and Youth, 7*, 193–209.

Lea, S. E. G., Webley, P., & Walker, C. M. (1995). Psychological factors in consumer debt: Money management, economic socialization, and credit use. *Journal of Economic Psychology, 16*, 681–701.

Lee, S. Y. (2014). How do people compare themselves with others on social network sites? The case of Facebook. *Computers in Human Behavior, 32*, 253–260.

Lemaster, P., & Strough, J. (2014). Beyond Mars and Venus: Understanding gender differences in financial risk tolerance. *Journal of Economic Psychology, 42*, 148–160.

Limbu, Y. B., Huhmann, B. A., & Xu, B. (2012). Are college students at greater risk of credit card abuse?: Age, gender, materialism and parental influence on consumer response to credit cards. *Journal of Financial Services Marketing, 17*(2), 148–162.

Lokken Worthy, S., Jonkman, J., & Blinn-Pike, L. (2010). Sensation-seeking, risk-taking, and problematic financial behaviors of college students. *Journal of Family and Economic Issues, 31*, 161–170.

Lusardi, A., Mitchell, O. S., & Curto, V. (2010). Financial literacy among the young. *Journal of Consumer Affairs, 44*, 358–380. https://doi.org/10.1111/j.1745-6606.2010.01173.x.

Lyons, A. C. (2004). A profile of financially at-risk college students. *Journal of Consumer Affairs, 38*(1), 56–80.

Markovich, S., & Achwal, N. (2017). Kueski: Revolutionizing consumer credit in Mexico. Harvard cases # KE1026.

McBride, M. (2010). Money, happiness, and aspirations: An experimental study. *Journal of Economic Behavior and Organization, 74*, 262–276.

Mendes-da-Silva, W., Nakamura, W. T., & Moraes, D. C. (2012). Credit card risk behavior on college campuses: Evidence from Brazil. *Brazilian Administration Review, 9*, 351–373.

Meredith, W., & Horn, J. (2001). The role of factorial invariance in modeling growth and change. In L. M. Collins & A. G. Sayer (Eds.), *New methods for the analysis of change. Decade of behavior* (pp. 203–240). Washington, DC: American Psychological Association.

Mitchell, J. (2018). Federal students-loan program looks set to start losing money. *Wall Street Journal*, A3. February (3–4), Saturday/Sunday.

Mueller, R. O., & Hancock, G. R. (2007). Best practices in structural equation modeling. In J. Osborve (Ed.), *Best practices in quantitative methods*. Thousand Oaks, CA: SAGE. https://doi.org/10.4135/9781412995627.

Norum, P. S. (2008). The role of time preference and credit card usage in compulsive buying behavior. *International Journal of Consumer Studies, 32*, 269–275.

Norvilitis, J. M., & MacLean, M. G. (2010). The role of parents in college students' financial behaviors and attitudes. *Journal of Economic Psychology, 31*, 55–63. https://doi.org/10.1016/j.joep.2009.10.003.

Norvilitis, J. M., & Mao, Y. (2012). Attitudes toward credit and finances in college students in China and the United States. *International Journal of Psychology, 48*, 389–398. https://doi.org/10.1080/00207594.2011.645486.

Norvilitis, J. M., & Mendes-Da-Silva, W. (2013). Attitudes toward credit and finances among college students in Brazil and the United States. *Journal of Business Theory and Practice, 1*(1), 132–151.

Norvilitis, J. M., Szablicki, P. B., & Wilson, S. D. (2003). Factors influencing levels of credit card debt in college students. *Journal of Applied Social Psychology, 33*, 935–947. https://doi.org/10.1111/j.1559-1816.2003.tb01932.x.

Norvilitis, J. M., Merwin, M. M., Osberg, T. M., Roehling, P. V., Young, P., & Kamas, M. M. (2006). Personality factors, money attitudes, financial knowledge and credit card debt in college students. *Journal of Applied Social Psychology, 36*, 1395–1413. https://doi.org/10.1111/j.0021-9029.2006.00065.x.

O'Guinn, T. C., & Faber, R. J. (1989). Compulsive buying: A phenomenological exploration. *Journal of Consumer Research, 16*(2), 147–157.

Palan, K. M., Morrow, P. C., Trapp, A., & Blackburn, V. (2011). Compulsive buying behavior in college students: The mediating role of credit card misuse. *Journal of Marketing Theory and Practice, 19*, 81–96.

Pinto, M. B., Parente, D. H., & Palmer, T. S. (2001). College student performance and credit card usage. *Journal of College Student Development, 42*(1), 49–58.

Pirog, S. F., & Roberts, J. A. (2007). Personality and credit card misuse among college students: The mediating role of impulsiveness. *Journal of Marketing Theory and Practice, 15*(1), 65–77.

Potrich, A. C., Vieira, K. M., & Mendes-Da-Silva, W. (2016). Development of a financial literacy model for university students. *Management Research Review, 39*(3), 356–376.

Raghubir, P., & Srivastava, J. (2008). Monopoly money: The effect of payment coupling and form on spending behavior. *Journal of Experimental Psychology. Applied, 14*, 213–225.

Robb, C. A. (2011). Financial knowledge and credit card behavior of college students. *Journal of Family and Economic Issues, 32*, 690–698. https://doi.org/10.1007/s10834-011-9259-y.

Roberts, J. A., & Jones, E. (2001). Money attitudes, credit card use, and compulsive buying among American college students. *Journal of Consumer Affairs, 35*, 213–240.

Sallie Mae (2009). *How undergraduate students use credit cards: Sallie Mae's national study of usage rates and trends 2009*. Wilkes-Barre, PA: Author Available at http://static.mgnetwork.com/rtd/pdfs/20090830_iris.pdf.

Shim, S., Barber, B. L., Card, N. A., Xiao, J. J., & Serido, J. (2010). Financial socialization of first-year college students: The roles of parents, work, and education. *Journal of Youth and Adolescence, 39*, 1457–1470.

Sotiropoulos, V., & d'Astous, A. (2013). Attitudinal, self-efficacy, and social norms determinants of young consumers' propensity to overspend on credit cards. *Journal of Consumer Policy, 36*, 179–196.

Strayhorn, J. M. (2002). Self-control: Theory and research. *Journal of the American Academy of Child and Adolescent Psychiatry, 41*, 7–16.

Tenenhaus, M., Amato, S., & Vinzi, V. E. (2004). A global goodness-of-fit index for PLS structural equation modeling. In *Proceedings of the Atti della Riunione Scientifica della Società Italiana di Statistica* (Vol. 62). Roma.

Thompson, B. (2006). Ten commandments of structural equation modeling. In L. G. Grimm & P. R. Yarnold (Eds.), *Reading and understanding more multivariate statistics* (pp. 261–284). Washington, DC: American Psychological Association.

Wang, L., Lu, W., & Malhotra, N. K. (2011). Demographics, attitude, personality and credit card features correlate with credit card debt: A view from China. *Journal of Economic Psychology, 32*, 179–193.

Watson, J. J. (2003). The relationship of materialism to spending tendencies, saving, and debt. *Journal of Economic Psychology, 24*, 723–739.

Well Being Brazil Index. (2014). *Survey well being Brasil – Cidade de São Paulo*. Available at: http://www.wbbindex.org (Accessed April 2014).

Yilmazer, T., & Lyons, A. C. (2010). Marriage and the allocation of assets in women's defined contribution plans. *Journal of Family and Economic Issues, 31*, 121–137.

Chapter 6
Income Distribution and Duration of Poverty-Level Employment

Danilo Braun Santos, Alexandre Ribeiro Leichsenring, Naercio Aquino Menezes Filho, and Wesley Mendes-Da-Silva

Abstract In this chapter we use microdata to examine employment duration for families receiving benefits from a distribution income. To achieve this goal, Cox proportional hazard models were used to estimate the job duration for program beneficiaries and non-beneficiaries, using a database of more than three million people. Our findings suggest that the risk of leaving work among beneficiaries of this program is 7–10% lower than the risk for non-beneficiaries. Parametric models were also adjusted to verify robustness, producing results equivalent to those of the Cox model. In all cases, program participation was observed through a covariate that varies over time, extracted directly from the program's payment records. These results are relevant for the definition of public policies regarding the risk of the income level of poor families, as well as for the financial industry, as it offers relevant empirical evidence for the design of new financial products.

Keywords Employment · Labor supply · Duration analysis · Income distribution, Income risk

JEL Code D31 · E24 · I32

Portions of this chapter appeared in the 2017 paper "The impact of the Bolsa Familia Program on the duration of formal employment for low income individuals," *Brazilian Journal of Public Administration*, vol 51, pp708–733.

D. B. Santos (✉)
Federal University of Sao Paulo (UNIFESP), Osasco, SP, Brazil

A. R. Leichsenring
University of São Paulo (USP), São Paulo, SP, Brazil
e-mail: alexandre.leichsenring@usp.br

N. A. Menezes Filho
University of São Paulo (USP) and Insper, São Paulo, SP, Brazil
e-mail: naercioamf@insper.edu.br

W. Mendes-Da-Silva
Sao Paulo School of Business Administration (FGV/EAESP), Sao Paulo, SP, Brazil

University of Texas at Austin, Austin, TX, USA

W. Mendes-Da-Silva (ed.), *Individual Behaviors and Technologies for Financial Innovations*, https://doi.org/10.1007/978-3-319-91911-9_6

According to the International Labour Organization (ILO), work is the fundamental path to climbing out of poverty, overcoming inequality and social exclusion, and is one of the most direct ways in which economic development benefits population well-being. The formal labor market, along with keeping families out of poverty, can also offer access to rights and warranties for workers and social security. The precarious position of low-income workers in the formal labor market ends up aggravating income volatility and high job turnover, which characterize this portion of the population. Within this context, it is important to understand the participation dynamic of economically vulnerable members of the population in the formal labor market. The accumulation of this type of knowledge may suggest the implementation of reforms to the current social protection system in a way that guarantees the promotion of population well-being and its adequacy to a variety of socioeconomic realities and stages of life.

It is expected that a program based on monetary transfers may lead to a reduction in employment, since it reduces economic necessity to work (income effect). Associated with this is the fact that programs focused on low-income public may discourage formal employment, given that the eligibility criterion based on family income may imply a decrease in the number of employed family members in order to avoid exceeding the established income ceiling. This supposed accommodation has been treated in the literature as *work-disincentive effect.*

On the other hand, an income transfer program that is conditioned on school attendance would lead to an increase in the amount of time allocated to school by children and a decrease in time spent on other activities such as work and leisure. Once there is reduction in the time children spend working, adults should supply substitution for this work. From the point of view of economic theory, therefore, the effect of a conditional transfer program on beneficiary labor supply is ambiguous. Besides the effects depend on individual preferences, the analyses should take into account the various members of the family, who have conflicting budgetary restrictions. Thus, this is an eminently empirical question. A more detailed discussion of the limitations of a microeconomic analysis in the evaluation of the impact of conditional cash transfer programs is presented by Oliveira and Soares (2012).

Various empirical strategies can be employed to investigate the effect of a cash transfer program on employment. Ideally, it would be desirable to have an experimental model in which the attribution of the benefit is randomized, or in other words, the treatment is randomly attributed to a fraction of the eligible population (the treatment group). If the selection of the individuals receiving the benefit is random, the treatment and control groups, if sufficiently large, should have uniformly similar characteristics. In this case, any differences observed in the results can be attributed to the effects of participating in this program. Unfortunately, this context is very rare in social science studies. The eligibility criterion for the Bolsa Familia Program is fundamentally based on family per capita income (as declared in the Federal Government's Unified Registry of Social Programs), which does not correspond to a randomized experimental model. This is a typical observational study, which requires nonexperimental methods. Generally, studies based on these methods use individual data to control for the differences between treatment and control groups, typically using measures that depend on a series of observable individual characteristics.

The current study is dedicated to specifying a particular regression model to identify the effect of the Bolsa Familia Program on the duration of employment in the formal labor market, an approach that has not yet been explored in publications on this subject. Among other techniques, the characterization of the beneficiary's status in the program is determined by a covariate that varies over time, making it possible to identify the months that a family was effectively benefitting from the program and the months that it was not. This study also uses a broad data set: (i) the Federal Government's Unified Registry of Social Programs (CadUnico) managed by the Ministry of Social Development and the Fight Against Hunger, considered to be a census of the low-income population of Brazil, containing approximately 80 million observations; (ii) the Annual Social Information Report (RAIS), prepared by the Ministry of Labor and Employment, which offers information about the entire universe of formal workers in Brazil and containing around 50 million observations/year; and (iii) the payment records for the Bolsa Familia Program (BFP), which include data for every month since its inception in 2004 and cover approximately 21 million families which in 2011 were or had been beneficiaries of the program.

This study provides one of the most comprehensive overviews of behaviors of employment duration among people in the income distribution program. Most research in this area has used small convenience samples or data from individual college campuses. This study collected official data from over 3,000,000 individuals. This chapter presents highlights from this research and uses this large data set to identify duration of employment determinants. The methodology used in this study is survival analysis. The findings from this research provide insight into how policy makers, employers, financial professionals, educators, and financial industry can develop and provide more effective income distribution programs and financial products dedicated to ensure income. At the end of this chapter, some recommendations are made. Directions for future research are also included.

About the Income Distribution Program

The Bolsa Familia Program (BFP) was instituted by the Brazilian federal government through Law No. 10,836 on January 9, 2004 and descends from other programs like Bolsa Escola (School Benefit) and Bolsa Alimentação (Food Benefit) (Cecchini and Atuesta 2017). According to the Ministry of Social Development and the Fight Against Hunger (MDS), the BFP is a direct cash transfer program that benefits families in poverty or extreme poverty. In 2011, poverty was characterized as family monthly per capita income between R$ 70 and R$ 140, and extreme poverty was characterized as family monthly per capita income of less than R$ 70. To participate in the program, a family needs to be characterized by either extreme poverty, or poverty with the additional requirement of having pregnant or nursing mothers or children between the ages of 0 and 17. In addition, the program requires at least 85%

school attendance from children between 6 and 15, and younger children have to be taken regularly to health units to keep them up to date with their vaccinations. The conditions and complementary activities associated with the program constitute long-term objectives about the construction of human capital aimed at interrupting the generational transmission of poverty (Britto 2005; Lindert et al. 2007).

With regard to the impact of cash transfer programs in general, Marshall and Hill (2014) reviewed the literature and observed effects in terms of an increase in school attendance and consequent increase in female labor supply. By directing transfer of resources to the mother, rather than to the father, these programs produce higher levels of well-being for the children and also contribute to the empowerment of female beneficiaries who take on more relevant role in decision-making of the household (Britto 2005). The reduction of child labor is also considered consensus for conditional cash transfer programs (De Hoop and Rosati 2014). There is also considerable consensus on the positive impact of the Bolsa Familia Program on school attendance (Araújo et al. 2010; Oliveira and Soares 2012; Soares et al. 2010; Chitolina et al. 2016; and Ferro et al. 2010). However, Oliveira et al. (2007) found that the BFP did not impact child vaccination. Since the program has led to greater consciousness about the need to access public health services for obtaining child immunization, through the conditions imposed, the absence of this impact suggests obstacles on the supply of these services (Soares et al. 2010).

Britto (2005) also points two other collateral effects: (i) incentives for the civil registry, since official documents are needed for the mothers to collect the benefit, and (ii) greater access to the financial system, because the beneficiaries receive these transfers through magnetic cards of individual bank accounts. Oliveira and Soares (2012) compiled a list of various articles that focus on investigating a possible *work-disincentive*. The study summarizes results of articles about employment for the population that benefits from conditional cash transfer programs, based on various national studies. Employment is measured through three prisms: participation in the work force, working hours, and efforts to obtain employment. In addition to Oliveira and Soares (2012), a range of other studies indicate that there is no significant effect of the Bolsa Familia on the labor supply of adult relatives, either from the statistical point of view or from the degree of magnitude (Ferro et al. 2010; Chitolina et al. 2016; Foguel and Barros 2010; Soares 2012). Most of the findings are related to the reduction of the number of working hours, especially by mothers and women.

Using data from the National Household Survey (PNAD), Tavares (2010) studied the BFP's effect on employment among mothers, a group that theoretically should be more affected by receiving the benefit, given that they have a greater reserve salary due to domestic care and time dedicated to children. The author finds an income effect associated with the value of the benefit (the greater the transfer received, the lower the mother's engagement in the labor market) and a substitution effect (mothers increase their labor supply to compensate the reduction of labor supply by the children, who increase school attendance). This result is in line with Teixeira's study (2010), which concludes that the benefit values are not large enough to generate an income effect capable of overriding the substitution effect.

The propensity of beneficiaries to transfer their activities to the informal labor market has been analyzed by Barbosa and Corseuil (2014). They also use PNAD data, but unlike the previous works which use the *propensity score matching methodology*, they use regression discontinuity analysis and conclude that the program does not affect the decision whether to enter the formal or the informal labor market. However, De Brauw et al. (2015) found different results concluding that, even though there is no effect on the total number of working hours for the household, the program causes a "substantial" reallocation of working hours from the formal to the informal market. They argue that this change may be induced by the use of income records in the formal market to verify whether the eligibility criterion is being met. Soares and Ribas (2011) found a reduction in the participation in the formal labor market by beneficiaries in large cities and report a decrease in the number of hours worked by beneficiaries in poor areas, even though the benefit tends to encourage greater participation in the formal labor market by other household members.

In terms of the effects of cash transfer programs on employment in other Latin American countries, the empirical results are, roughly speaking, similar to those seen in Brazil. The work of Skoufias and Di Maro (2008) about the Progresa do México concludes that, in general, the program does not have a significant effect on the participation rate of beneficiaries in the labor market. They identify exceptions for specific groups: men between the ages of 35 and 54 significantly increased their participation, even though of small magnitude, and women between the ages of 45 and 54 reduced their participation at the beginning of the program. On the other hand, it could not be stated that beneficiaries spent more time on leisure activities. Parker and Skoufias (2000) present similar results.

The most recent work of Alzúa et al. (2013) on conditional income programs in Mexico, Nicaragua, and Honduras reports comparable results in these three countries, which indicates that the effects of these programs on the labor market were slightly negative, in general, but small and not statistically significant. The results of Gonzalez-Rozada and Pinto (2011) and Barrientos and Villa (2013) for Ecuador and Colombia indicate an increase in participation in the former and a null effect in the latter. Garganta et al. (2017) examines the impact on the supply of female labor in a conditional income transfer program, Universal Child Allowance, launched in Argentina in 2009. The authors report a negative and economically significant effect of the program on labor force participation for married women, while the effect is not relevant for unmarried women with children. Finally Cepal (2014), in a survey of studies in a variety of countries such as Argentina, Brazil, Chile, Honduras, Mexico, Nicaragua, and Paraguay, did not find empirical evidence of the existence of disincentives created by these programs in terms of the beneficiaries' labor inclusion.

Job Duration

From 2000 on, the Brazilian labor market was marked by a net increase in formal employment according to the data from the General Employment and Unemployment Registry (CAGED). As illustrated in Fig. 6.1, during the 2-year period of

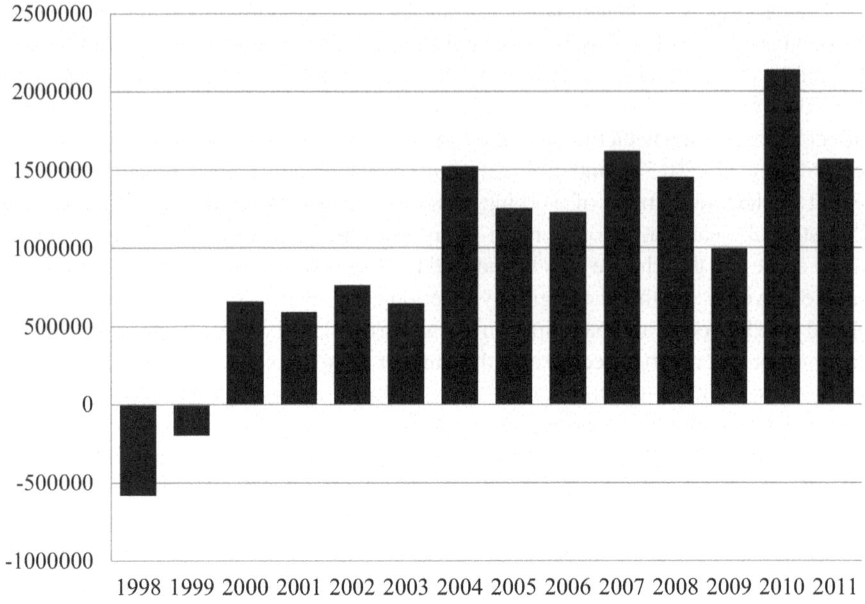

Fig. 6.1 Evolution of net formal job creation (1998–2011). (Source: Elaborated by the authors based on data from the Ministry of Labor and Employment—General Registry of Employment and Unemployment (CAGED))

1998–1999, more jobs were lost than created in the formal Brazilian economy, with 389 thousand people losing their jobs. However, in the 2000s, net job creation was positive in all years and improved substantially by the end of the decade. In the 2000s, 658 thousand new formal jobs were created in Brazil, while in 2008 almost 1.5 million jobs were created, and in 2011 almost 1.6 million jobs were created.

As pointed out by Menezes-Filho and Picchetti (2000) in relation to unemployment, the duration of employment is as important (and less studied) than the existence of employment. In other words, workers' characteristics determine the time that workers remain on a job. Jobs of short duration affect retirement for low-wage workers, given that they have more difficulty in requesting and proving the benefits that they are entitled to due to time of service, because of constant changes in employment and periods of unemployment or informal employment (Além et al. 1998).

Since retirement benefits, in general, are conceded to people who have had stable jobs or who have rarely changed jobs during their professional lives and are based on time of service (Além et al. 1998), the duration of formal employment serves as a measure of the quality of employment which affects the well-being of the worker. In this respect, Giambiagi and Afonso (2009) emphasize that retirement by age in Brazil has lower average benefits than retirement based on time of contribution. These authors observe that in December 2008 14,453,455 retirement benefits were issued, with 7,500,092 (51.9%) of these being based on age, 2,835,391 (19.6%)

based on disability, and 4,117,972 (28.5%) based on time of contribution. The average values of the benefits for disability and age were R$ 552.01 and R$ 432.97, respectively, while the average value of benefits based on time of contribution was R$ 1058.93.

Data and Procedure

The data used in this work comes from three main sources: the Unified Registry (CadUnico), the Annual Social Information Report (RAIS), and the Bolsa Familia Program (BFP) payment records. The CadUnico is an instrument of the Ministry of Social Development and the Fight Against Hunger (MDS) which identifies and characterizes low-income families, which are understood to be those with a monthly income up to half minimum wage per person or total monthly income of up to three minimum wages. To be eligible for benefits from federal government social programs like the BFP, recipients must be registered in the CadUnico. RAIS, on the other hand, is an annual data collection instrument, which is the responsibility of the Ministry of Labor and Employment, used in the public management of the labor sector. All companies are required to deliver the RAIS declaration, whether they have employees or not, and this includes public and individual companies; administrative bodies directly or indirectly administered by federal, state, or municipal governments; foundations; and rural employers.

To construct this database, we considered all individuals between the ages of 16 and 65 who were admitted to their jobs in 2008 and were registered in the CadUnico (as of December 2011). For individuals with more than one formal job, we used only the main one (with the largest salary). These jobs were accompanied for up to 4 years, using the information from RAIS for 2009, 2010, and 2011. For cases in which the job ended for any reason before December 2011, the individual was no longer followed. Thus, only one job per individual was followed and reentries were not observed. This procedure resulted in more than three million observations. Even though there was data from 2008 to 2011, only the most recent information (from the date of termination of employment) was kept in the registers. Differently, the presence of the individuals on the BFP was verified monthly. The relevance of considering the receiving of the benefit as a variable that varies over time will become clearer after the discussions in the following subsections of this chapter.

Descriptive Statistics

The data for each individual refers to the year in which the job terminated, or 2011, for those cases in which the individual was still employed. As shown in Table 6.1, 60% of the individuals were men, 87% resided in urban areas, for 24% this was their

Table 6.1 Descriptive statistics for quantitative and dichotomous variables

Variable	N	Average	Std deviation	Minimum	Maximum
Age	3,012,384	33.26	9.87	16	68
Male	3,012,384	0.60	0.49	0	1
Income_percap	3,012,384	89.88	63.42	0	311
Children	3,012,384	1.89	1.41	0	28
Minors	3,012,384	1.18	1.23	0	12
Salary	2,988,028	616.78	4249.12	0	3,934,232
Location	3,007,901	0.87	0.33	0	1
First_job	3,012,384	0.24	0.42	0	1
UnionMember	3,012,379	0.071	0.26	0	1
BFP_2011	3,012,384	0.47	0.50	0	1
Job_duration	3,012,384	12.99	13.06	0	48
Censored	3,012,384	0.18	0.39	0	1

Source: Elaborated by the authors

Note: The data for each individual refers to the year in which the job ended or 2011, if the individual still had this job; *Age* in years; *Male*, 1 yes, 0 no; *Income_percap* indicates family monthly per capita income in Brazilian reais, self-declared; *Children* indicates the number of children; *Minors* indicates the number of children under 18 years of age; *Salary* is the average annual salary for the year in which the job ended or 2011, if the individual still had this job, with values corrected by the consumer price index (INPC) for December 2011; *Location*, 1 urban, 0 rural; *First_job*, 1 first job, 0 no; *UnionMember*, 1 yes, 0 no; *BFP_2011*, 1 program beneficiary as of December 2011, 0 no; *Job_duration* indicates the duration of the job in months; *censored*, 1 still had this job as of December 2011, 0 didn't

first job, 7% were union members, and 47% were beneficiaries of the BFP in December 2011. The average age was 33 and each worker had an average of 1.89 children, with 1.18 being the average of children under the age of 18. These individuals remained at the job for 13 months on average, and just 18% were still employed on December 2011, and thus these observations are considered censored.

Family monthly per capita income, which is self-declared in the CadUnico, was approximately 90 reais on average, which is in line with the program eligibility criteria for the year 2011, namely, below R$ 140.00. The values for individual monthly salaries obtained from the RAIS database were corrected by the INPC consumer price index for December 2011. The average salary was calculated for the year in which the job ended or for those who still were working at this job, the year 2011. The averages and standard deviations found for the three million individuals were R$ 616.78 and R$ 4249.12, respectively. The largest observed salary, close to four million reais, suggests that attention should be paid to outliers for this variable as discussed later on in this section. Table 6.2 presents the descriptive statistics for polychotomous category variables. Note that 45% of the jobs were in the country's Southeast, followed by 23% in the Northeast, 18% in the South, 8.3% in the Central-West, and 5.7% in the North. An initial comparative examination between the groups of interest, beneficiaries and non-beneficiaries of BFP, is presented in Table 6.3.

Table 6.2 Descriptive statistics for polychotomous variables

Variable	N	Category	Average	Std deviation
Race	2,843,787	White	0.39	0.49
		Yellow	0.0027	0.052
		Indigenous	0.0034	0.058
		Brown	0.51	0.50
		Black	0.10	0.29
Education	2,313,213	No education	0.072	0.26
		Incomplete primary	0.58	0.49
		Complete primary	0.14	0.35
		Incomplete secondary	0.14	0.35
		Complete secondary	0.055	0.23
		Incomplete higher or more	0.0089	0.094
Region	3,012,384	Northeast	0.23	0.42
		North	0.057	0.23
		Central-West	0.083	0.28
		Southeast	0.45	0.50
		South	0.18	0.39
Size_city	3,012,384	(0, 10 thou]	0.089	0.29
		(10 thou, 100 thou]	0.42	0.49
		(100 thou, 1 million]	0.34	0.47
		(1 million, +]	0.15	0.36
Size_establishment	3,012,384	(0, 10]	0.16	0.37
		(10, 100]	0.35	0.48
		(100, 1000]	0.29	0.46
		(1000, 10,000]	0.17	0.38
		(10,000, +]	0.018	0.13
CBO	3,012,384	Farming and fishing	0.16	0.36
		Industry—Generalists	0.33	0.47
		Industry—Operators	0.051	0.22
		Maintenance and repair	0.023	0.15
		Services, commerce	0.28	0.45
		Administrative services	0.11	0.32
		Mid-level technicians	0.030	0.17
		Others	0.020	0.14
CNAE	3,012,250	Public administration	0.037	0.19
		Agriculture and livestock	0.14	0.34
		Administrative activities	0.10	0.31
		Vehicle sales and repair	0.21	0.41
		Contracting	0.13	0.33
		Industry	0.20	0.40
		Others	0.18	0.38
Reason_failure	2,465,298	Retirement	0.00038	0.019
		Death	0.0018	0.042

(continued)

Table 6.2 (continued)

Variable	N	Category	Average	Std deviation
		Term. w. j. c. in. Employee	0.0016	0.040
		Term. w. j. c. in. Employer	0.015	0.12
		Term. w/o j. c. in. Employee	0.18	0.39
		Term. w/o j. c. in. Employer	0.57	0.49
		Transfer	0.020	0.14
		End of contract	0.20	0.40
		Others	0.00021	0.014

Source: Elaborated by the authors
Note: *Size_city* provides the number of inhabitants of the employer city; *Size_establishment* provides the number of employees at the employer establishment; *CBO*, Brazilian Occupation Classification; *CNAE*, National Classification of Economic Activity; *Reason_failure* provides the reason for the job's ending (failure). *Term. w. j.c. in. Employee* means termination with just cause initiated by the employee; *Term. w. j.c. in. Employer* means termination with just cause initiated by the employer; *Term. w/o j.c. in. Employee* means termination without just cause initiated by the employee; *Term. w/o j.c. in. Employer* means termination without just cause initiated by the employer

Table 6.3 Comparison between beneficiaries and non-beneficiaries of the Bolsa Familia Program

Variable	Non-beneficiary	Beneficiary
Age	32.78	33.77
Male	0.605	0.597
Income_percap	107.30	70.32
Children	1.58	2.24
Minors	0.77	1.64
Salary	638.25	592.70
Urban_area	0.869	0.873
First_job	0.238	0.235
UnionMember	0.069	0.073
Job_duration	13.96	11.77
N	1,592,012	1,420,372

Source: Elaborated by the authors
Note: Average values of variables for BFP non-beneficiaries and beneficiaries in December 2011

It is important to note that these groups have been determined by an indicator variable of presence in the program on a specific date (December 2011). As expected, beneficiaries of the program have lower salaries and more children and therefore lower family per capita income. Obviously, it will be important to control for these characteristics when seeking to measure the specific effect of the BFP on job duration in order to eliminate endogeneity.

Some evidence about the work-disincentive effect is suggested by the 2 months longer job duration found for non-beneficiaries. However, this preliminary analysis carries a problem that should be noted: the fact that an individual was a beneficiary of the BFP in December 2011 does not mean that this individual was a beneficiary at the end of his or her job (see Table 6.1 which shows that only 18% of the individuals maintained their jobs until this date). Therefore, the comparison of job duration is not valid given that the allocation of the individuals in these groups is not random and the job duration variable is censored (i.e., the job is only followed until December 2011, and we do not know what happens afterward) and the participation in the program is analyzed at a fixed moment in time.

Thus, to achieve a correct specification, the model needs to overcome these three obstacles. Table 6.4 shows that 42.5% of the surveyed individuals remained in the program for the duration of the data term. We may also observe that roughly a third of the individuals were members of the program at some point in time, but after leaving the program, they did not return. Only 6.78% of the sample is comprised of individuals who returned to receive benefits from the program after having left it at some previous moment. Another relevant question in evaluating the impact of the BFP has to do with the individuals who are considered for the program. Even though the concession of the benefits is based on family per capita income and having pregnant women or children in the family, these facts are not sufficient to guarantee staying or even entering the program.

Even though a family may be eligible according to the BFP criteria, it must have an updated registration in the CadUnico in order to be considered. These issues may relate to the individual's predisposition or to the municipality's management efficiency (Coêlho and Fernandes 2017). Table 6.5 corroborates this analysis by showing that, among individuals who satisfied the BFP selection criteria in December 2011, only 43% received the benefit. The reasons for this can be diverse: receiving the benefit is not immediate after registration; CadUnico data can be out of date; the family could have been eliminated at some point during the auditing

Table 6.4 BFP entrance and exit dynamics

Dynamic	%
Entered and never left	42.53%
Left and never returned	33.06%
Never were BFP beneficiaries	17.64%
Left and later returned	6.78%

Source: Elaborated by the authors

Table 6.5 Considered and eligible

	BFP in 12/2011		
BFP criteria	No	Yes	Total
Satisfy	972,875	1,294,108	2,266,983
	43%	57%	100%
Do not satisfy	619,137	126,264	745,401
	83%	17%	100%
Total	1,592,012	1,420,372	3,012,384
	53%	47%	100%

Source: Elaborated by the authors

Note: Those with per capita income below R$ 70.00 or those with per capita income below R$ 140.00 and who also have one child of minor age within the family process or may not have fulfilled one of the conditions or may have declared incompatible income.

We should also remember that family per capita income is self-declared, which means that there can be fraud and households that might be considered outside the scope of a family unit. The MDS seeks to minimize the incidence of these cases through periodic audits in which salaries reported by the RAIS database are used to evaluate the trustworthiness of the reported values. Yet a considerable gap exists in this process, because the RAIS database is made available only 2 years later. In addition, a large proportion of the Brazilian economy is informal, and in order to qualify for the benefit, many individuals do not declare informal income since it can't be audited (Soares et al. 2010). The salary reported by the RAIS database is provided by the employer rather than the employee. Of the three million individuals in the sample, only 97 cases registered a salary above 10 thousand reais, of which 17 were above 50 thousand reais and just 9 above 100 thousand reais. There are three possible explanations for the presence of these observations in the database: (i) registration error, which is very probable in the case of a salary of four million reais; (ii) fraud, given that the CadUnico is self-reported; or (iii) individuals who later prospered, because the CadUnico database does not eliminate the individuals who were once registered in the database.

Low salaries have also been observed. Around 790 thousand records had salaries below 450 reais, which is less than the national minimum wage corrected by the consumer price index (INPC) for any of the years considered as shown in Table 6.6. This could be related to registration errors, temporary absences, or reduced workdays. Provisional Measure No. 2164-41 of August 24, 2001, governs the regime of part-time employment. Article 58-A, which was incorporated into the Consolidation of Work Laws (CLT), considers part-time employment that which does not exceed 25 h per week, and its first paragraph establishes that "the salary to be paid to employees under a part-time regime will be proportional to the workday performed by workers who perform the same functions in a full-time capacity."

To deal with high as well as low salaries in the database, the values have been separated into ten classes of salary (Table 6.7). In the main filter used in the estimates shown in Section 4, we use the 40% of the records that make up the most central classes of salaries, classes 4 through 7 in Table 6.7. It should be noted that this filter, in addition to analyzing only the more homogeneous salaries, disconsiders high salaries and those below the minimum wage.

Table 6.6 Brazilian monthly minimum wage

Year	Jan. 1st	Dec. 2011
2008	380	476
2009	415	488
2010	510	576
2011	510	541

Source: Elaborated by the authors
Note: R$ corrected by the INPC

Table 6.7 Separation into ten classes of salary

Class	Average	Class	Average
1	202.19	6	587.32
2	373.30	7	649.56
3	450.58	8	734.37
4	497.40	9	868.46
5	539.92	10	1390.35

Source: Elaborated by the authors

Survival Analysis

Survival analysis is a group of statistical procedures used to analyze data in which the variable of interest is the time until a given event. In the survival nomenclature, when the event occurs, "failure" is said to have been observed. If, on the other hand, the event of interest does not occur during the time under analysis, it is said that the information is "censored." For this study the analyzed variable is the job duration, and the event of interest is the termination (exit) of this job. The job durations for those who remained employed as of December 2011 are censored. Considering a random variable t, with probability density $f(t)$ and accumulated distribution $F(t)$, the survival function is defined by:

$$S(t) = 1 - F(t) = P(T > t)$$

and the hazard function is:

$$h(t) = \lim_{\Delta t \to 0} \frac{P(t \leq T < t + \Delta t | T \geq t)}{\Delta t} = \frac{f(t)}{1 - F(t)} = \frac{f(t)}{S(t)}.$$

While the survival function indicates the probability of remaining on the job for longer than a specific time t, the hazard function is a rate that represents the potential of a job to terminate at a determined instant, given that it has lasted up until that date. The survival function $S(t)$ can be estimated using the Kaplan-Meier method. This estimator orders the failure times and calculates the probability of surviving for each interval of time, taking into consideration only individuals at risk. Thus, this estimator deals with the issue of "censorship." This is a nonparametric procedure, because it does not impose a theoretical model for the failures (or censorship) observed in the sample. However, this method does not permit estimating of the collective effects of a group of covariates on job duration. To do this, other methods are needed to incorporate the explanatory variables into the model. The most common method is called the Cox proportional hazard model. The formula of the hazard function is:

$$h(t, \boldsymbol{X}) = h_0(t) e^{\sum_{i=1}^{p} \beta_i X_i},$$

where $X = (X_1, X_2, \ldots, X_p)$ is the vector of explanatory variables and $h_0(t)$ is the so-called baseline hazard function, common to all individuals. Thus, this model considers that individual characteristics determine the hazard for each element in the sample together with a hazard multiple common to all individuals. By not specifying function $h_0(t)$, this methodology is called semiparametric. In contrast, parametric models are those in which the functional formula of $h_0(t)$ is completely specified, except for the values of unknown parameters. For example, the Weibull hazard function is given by $h(t, X) = \lambda p t^{p-1}$, where $h_0(t) = p t^{p-1}$ and $\lambda = e^{\sum_{i=1}^{p} \beta_i X_i}$.

One of the main reasons for the popularity of the Cox model is that even though the baseline hazard function is not specified, it obtains good estimates of regression coefficients. That is, the model is robust in the sense that the results of the Cox model are close to the results of the correctly specified parametric model (Kleinbaum and Klein 2006). It should be noted that the hazard function involves the product of two functions, the baseline hazard ($h_0(t)$), which is a function of t but not of X, and the exponential function ($e^{\sum_{i=1}^{p} \beta_i X_i}$), which is a function of X but not of t. This is why the X characteristics are called time-invariant. The hazard function considering covariates that vary over time may be expressed as:

$$h(t, \boldsymbol{X}(t)) = \lim_{\Delta t \to 0} \frac{P(t \le T < t + \Delta t | T \ge t, \boldsymbol{X}(t + \Delta t))}{\Delta t}.$$

A detailed discussion of the existence of this limit can be found in Lancaster (1992). But, according to Wooldridge (2010), a sufficient condition occurs when $\boldsymbol{X}(t)$ assumes constant values during time intervals such as days, weeks, or months. In this study the *bfp* variable assumes values of 1 (for beneficiaries) or 0 (for non-beneficiaries), for time intervals of at least a month (the period between payments). The Cox model can be extended for covariates that vary over time:

$$h(t, \boldsymbol{X}(t)) = h_0(t) e^{\sum_{i=1}^{p} \beta_i X_i(t)}.$$

According to Kleinbaum and Klein (2006), an important assumption of the extended Cox model is that the effect of a variant variable over time on the survival probability at time t depends on the value of this variable at the same instant of time and not its past or future value. It seems reasonable that the decision to leave or not to leave a job at each instant is influenced by whether this individual is a BFP beneficiary at that moment and not whether he or she has been a beneficiary in the past or is expected to be one in the future.

Results

Figure 6.2, Panel A presents the estimated survival and hazard functions for the nonparametric Kaplan-Meier model. The average job duration was 597 days (20 months) with a median value of 424 days (14 months), which indicates that

Painel A: Kaplan-Meier Curves

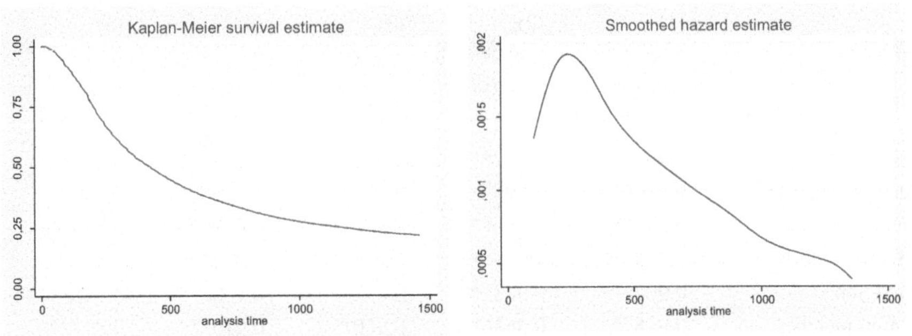

(a) (b)

Panel B: Kaplan-Meier Curves for BFP Beneficiaries and Non-Beneficiaries

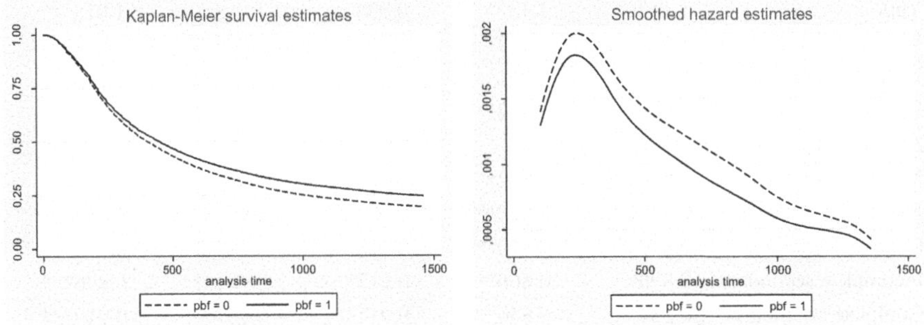

(a) (b)

Fig. 6.2 Kaplan-Meier curves. (**A**) Survival function. (**B**) Hazard function. (Source: Elaborated by the authors)

half of the individuals lost or left their jobs after less than a year and 2 months of work. Panel B shows the survival and hazard functions for beneficiaries ($bfp = 1$) and non-beneficiaries ($bfp = 0$) of the BFP. Note that the survival rate of beneficiaries is greater than that of non-beneficiaries. It should be noted that this variable indicates that their presence in the BFP varies over time. In this initial examination related to the Kaplan-Meier curves, the sample used was for all those admitted in 2008 who remained at their jobs through the end of 2011 or were terminated (for just cause or without just cause and by the initiative of the employee or the initiative of the employer) and which had remuneration that falls within salary classes 4 through 7, as shown in Table 6.7. Thus, the sample included 1,007,315 individuals, of which 771,634 presented failure (termination of employment) and the other 235,681 individuals remained at their jobs until December 2011 (censored data).

The Cox model (Table 6.8) is used to quantify the effect of the time-dependent BFP presence covariate on job duration, controlling for other factors which are time-invariant; this constitutes the main result of this article. The survival models consider the issue of censure and the BFP entrance and exit dynamics and controls for the differences between groups in terms of various individual characteristics. The

Table 6.8 Cox hazard regression ratios for job duration

	(1)	(2)	(3)	(4)	(5)
BFP	0.923***	0.929***	0.898***	0.904***	0.913***
Age	0.991***	0.993***	0.995***	0.996***	0.996***
Male	1.234***	1.214***	1.214***	1.196***	1.027***
Salary	0.997***	0.997***	0.997***	0.997***	0.999***
Income_per capita	0.999***	0.999***	0.999***	0.999***	0.999***
Children	0.976***	0.976***	0.981***	0.979***	0.985***
Minors	1.033***	1.035***	1.031***	1.032***	1.022***
First_job	0.902***	0.928***	0.897***	0.908***	0.926***
Union member	0.918***	0.863***	0.960***	0.916***	0.891***
Location	1.097***	1.096***	1.096***	1.092***	1.095***
Race (ref.: Black)					
Yellow	1.142*	1.133**	0.994	1.018	1.018
White	1.087***	1.092***	1.076***	1.074***	1.037***
Indigenous	1.059	1.256***	1.146***	1.210***	1.265***
Brown	1.018	1.042***	1.027***	1.029***	1.012***
Education (ref.: Incomplete higher or more)					
No education	0.871***	0.842***	0.885***	0.890***	0.917***
Incomplete primary	0.875***	0.852***	0.906***	0.908***	0.915***
Complete primary	0.890**	0.850***	0.918***	0.912***	0.913***
Incomplete secondary	0.896**	0.866***	0.917***	0.904***	0.896***
Complete secondary	0.881**	0.850***	0.911***	0.907***	0.910***
Region (ref.: South)					
Central-West	0.840***	0.976*	0.863***	0.975***	0.968***
Northeast	0.460***	0.592***	0.517***	0.638***	0.736***
North	0.612***	0.745***	0.707***	0.833***	0.866***
Southeast	0.826***	0.944***	0.860***	0.975***	1.016***
Size_city (ref.: (0, 10 thou])					
(10 thou,100 thou]	1.011	1.006	1.032***	1.023***	1.057***
(100 thou, **1** million]	1.097***	1.044***	1.078***	1.037***	1.066***
(1 million, +]	1.023	0.992	1.066***	1.024***	1.026***
Size_establishment (ref.: (0, 10]) (10, 100]	1.308***	1.260***	1.267***	1.231***	1.333***
(100, 1.000]	1.386***	1.295***	1.323***	1.246***	1.390***
(1.000, 10.000]	1.487***	1.411***	1.412***	1.327***	1.472***
(10.000, +]	1.238***	1.178***	1.107***	1.112***	1.306***
CBO (ref.: Farming and fishing) Industry—Generalists	0.883***	0.901***	0.880***	0.881***	0.804***
Industry—Operators	0.870***	0.821***	0.918***	0.866***	0.786***
Maintenance and repair	0.783***	0.786***	0.836***	0.829***	0.737***

(continued)

Table 6.8 (continued)

	(1)	(2)	(3)	(4)	(5)
Services, commerce	0.749***	0.762***	0.786***	0.765***	0.669***
Administrative services	0.743***	0.747***	0.787***	0.751***	0.628***
Mid-level technicians	0.760***	0.764***	0.825***	0.804***	0.710***
Others	0.837***	0.822***	0.837***	0.807***	0.731***
CNAE (ref.: Public administration) Agriculture, livestock	3.041***	3.316***	3.161***	3.048***	1.994***
Administrative activities	2.981***	3.083***	2.789***	2.656***	1.866***
Vehicle sales and repair	3.864***	3.681***	3.585***	3.239***	1.847***
Contracting	5.903***	5.638***	4.854***	4.418***	2.469***
Industry	3.457***	3.381***	3.385***	3.108***	1.727***
Others	3.699***	3.474***	3.466***	3.104***	1.689***
Admission	Jan/08	Jan/08	2008	2008	2008
Classes of salary	4–7	2–9	4–7	2–9	1–10
Reason for failure	Termination	Termination	Termination	Termination	All
Num. Observations	85,663	168,565	909,291	1,766,564	2,617,064
Num. Individuals	69,537	138,370	729,786	1,432,657	2,178,741
Num. Failures	56,386	114,933	565,040	1,136,191	1,805,839
Wald chi^2 (43)	11,398***	24,867***	80,857***	198,900***	146,435***

Source: Elaborated by the authors
Note: p-value * < 0.10; ** < 0.05; *** < 0.01

sample size makes it possible to include several controls, which favors our identification hypothesis: that the control for observable characteristics is sufficient to eliminate endogeneity. Table 6.8 presents the estimated hazard ratios for the five models in which the collected sample was altered.

The idea of altering the sample makes it possible to increase the robustness of the results, to the extent that the estimates converge. In Model 1 we considered only those admitted in January 2008 with salaries falling within classes 4–7 who left their jobs due to termination (with or without just cause and initiated by the employee or the employer). The restriction of admission in January 2008 allows us to analyze a group in which all of the individuals were exposed to the same macroeconomic conditions since the beginning of their employment. Concentrating the analysis on more homogeneous salaries also helps guarantee that the control and treatment groups really comprise of comparable individuals.

In Model 2 the salary restriction was relaxed to include classes 2–9. Models 3 and 4 follow the pattern of Models 1 and 2 but take into consideration all those admitted during the year 2008. Finally, Model 5 considers the entire sample with no restrictions in terms of salary or reason for failure. Note that the impact of the BFP, measured by the hazard ratio, varied between 0.898 and 0.929 for the various samples used. Even in the last regression, in which all the restrictions were relaxed, including the reason for failure, the finding was an intermediate value of 0.913. These results show that BFP beneficiaries had a 7–10% lower chance of leaving their jobs as compared to non-beneficiaries, which not only contradicts the hypothesis of a *work-disincentive* due to cash transfer but also opens the possibility that this extra income produced an incentive to remain in their jobs.

This finding of the effect for conditional cash transfers, in this case in relation to formal employment job duration, is in line with various other studies that have found evidence for increased employment for beneficiaries (Brito and Kerstenetzky 2011; Medeiros et al. 2007; Tavares 2010; Teixeira 2010). The argument is that, as children spend less time at home and attend school, their parents have more time available to work. However, this result can also be explained in a different manner that does not depend on the program's conditions, but by the benefit itself. In 2011, the average value of the benefit per family was R$ 120.19. However small this financial benefit may seem, for a family that lives on less than 140 reais per capita (or less than 70 reais), this extra income can make a big difference to the extent that it is used to give attention to the family's dependents.

This analysis is corroborated by Oliveira et al. (2007), who found that the BFP effect on the consumption of beneficiary families was related to spending on food, education, and clothing for children. The increase in expenses on child clothing is similar to the impacts witnessed in cash transfer programs in Mexico and Colombia and is related to the perception of these families that the benefit is a bonus to be spent in the best interest of their children (Soares et al. 2010). A simple but interesting exercise is to note (based on regression number 3 in Table 6.8) that the risk of leaving one's job is 3.1% greater for individuals who have a minor child (hazard ratio: $e^{0.030529} = 1.031$). When we look at an individual with three minor children, as compared to an individual without minor children, there is a 9.6% greater chance of leaving one's job (hazard ratio: $e^{3 \cdot 0.030529} = 1.096$).

Being a BFP beneficiary, however, is capable of nullifying this effect (hazard ratio: 1.096 0.898 = 0.984). In other words, suppose that an employer is choosing between a candidate who is not a BFP beneficiary and does not have a minor child and another candidate with three minor children. Ceteris paribus, if this other candidate with three minor children is a BFP beneficiary, he or she will have the same chances of remaining on the job as the first candidate. In relation to the control variables, it may be noted that there is a lower risk of leaving work for residents of the Northeast, rural residents, older individuals, women, those with higher salaries, those in their first job, and those working in public administration. It can also be seen that those who are Black have a lower chance of leaving their work than those who declared themselves to be white. As pointed out by Menezes-Filho et al. (2008) and Garcia and Dedecca (2013), union membership is related to stability in remaining in jobs, productivity, and salaries. The result for the *union member* variable indicates that employees who are union members are less likely to leave their jobs.

Greater risk of leaving jobs was observed for civil construction employees, for those living in the South, for individuals with more than secondary education, and for residents of large cities, with populations ranging from 100 thousand to a million individuals. Most of these results are in line with the literature related to the duration of employment and unemployment, covering various regions of the country: Menezes-Filho and Picchetti (2000), Penido and Machado (2002), Malbouisson and Menezes (2004), Menezes and Dedecca (2006), Antigo and Machado (2006), Oliveira and Carvalho Júnior (2009), Leichsenring (2010), and Lira (2011). In addition, we adjusted our parametric models, and their estimated coefficients are shown in Table 6.9. All of these models are in the form of accelerated failure time (AFT).

In this context, a positive coefficient indicates a greater chance of survival (greater job duration). Contrary to the Cox model, where e^{β} indicates the hazard ratio, in the AFT metric, the quantity e^{β} supplies the survival time ratio. For example, the estimated coefficient for the variable *bfp* in the Loglogístic model was 0.093. This value represents the survival time ratio of beneficiaries versus non-beneficiaries of $e^{0.093} = 1.097$, which means that BFP beneficiaries have job survival results which are 9.7% greater than non-beneficiaries. According to Akaike (AIC) and Bayesian (BIC) criteria, the best adjustment comes from the gamma function which has an estimated coefficient of 0.086, which is the most conservative effect among all the models. This value indicates that BFP beneficiaries stay in their jobs 8.95% longer than non-beneficiaries, with a 95% confidence interval of a result between 8.34% and 9.56%. Due to the demands related to data distribution of parametric models, the stability of the estimates demonstrates the robustness of the results. Regarding the convergence of the estimates, it should be noted that the estimated coefficient for the *bfp* variable in the exponential model using the AFT metric (0.117) corresponds to a hazard ratio of 0.889. This value is in line with the result obtained through the semiparametric Cox model (Model 3 in Table 6.8).

Concluding Remarks and Future Directions

This article analyzes the effect of the Bolsa Familia Program on formal employment in the poor portion of the Brazilian population according to the Unified Registry of Social Programs (CadUnico). Based on a unique combination of data with more than three million individuals, we have found that Bolsa Familia Program beneficiaries have greater chances of remaining in their jobs than non-beneficiaries. This finding not only contradicts the hypothesis of there being a *work-disincentive* associated with the concession of this benefit but also establishes an inverse effect, in which the financial benefit provided by the program contributes to the maintenance of employment.

In terms of public policy, this is a relevant result, given that the poor population of Brazil is characterized by considerable income volatility and job turnover, which compromise present and future well-being and make it difficult to retire based on time of contribution. This study contributes to the literature and is innovative in that it analyzes the effect of cash transfer on job duration, in contrast to most studies that

Table 6.9 Estimated coefficients for the parametric models

	Exponential	Weibull	Loglogístic	Lognormal	Gamma
BFP	0.117***	0.114***	0.093***	0.095***	0.086***
Age	0.006***	0.006***	0.004***	0.004***	0.003***
Male	−0.202***	−0.198***	−0.223***	−0.216***	−0.214***
Salary	0.004***	0.004***	0.004***	0.004***	0.003***
Income_percap	0.001***	0.001***	0.001***	0.001***	0.001***
Children	0.020***	0.020***	0.023***	0.022***	0.022***
Minors	−0.032***	−0.032***	−0.031***	−0.030***	−0.029***
First_job	0.109***	0.107***	0.126***	0.118***	0.115***
UnionMember	0.036***	0.036***	0.053***	0.058***	0.070***
Location	−0.094***	−0.092***	−0.108***	−0.100***	−0.096***
Race (ref.: Black)					
Yellow	0.007	0.007	0.002	0.005	0.006
White	−0.077***	−0.076***	−0.081***	−0.079***	−0.079***
Indigenous	−0.130***	−0.129***	−0.132***	−0.127***	−0.123***
Brown	−0.028***	−0.028***	−0.026***	−0.027***	−0.027***
Education (ref.: Incomplete higher or more)					
No education	0.126***	0.123***	0.137***	0.131***	0.130***
Incomplete primary	0.101***	0.099***	0.124***	0.119***	0.122***
Complete primary	0.085***	0.083***	0.115***	0.109***	0.115***
Incomplete secondary	0.085***	0.083***	0.119***	0.113***	0.120***
Complete secondary	0.089***	0.087***	0.135***	0.126***	0.135***
Region (ref.: South)					
Central-West	0.163***	0.161***	0.130***	0.131***	0.116***
Northeast	0.704***	0.690***	0.707***	0.691***	0.666***
North	0.378***	0.372***	0.355***	0.351***	0.329***

Southeast	0.162***	0.160***	0.143***	0.136***	0.119***
Size_city (ref.: (0, 10 thou])					
(10 thou,100 thou]	−0.037***	−0.036***	−0.023***	−0.027***	−0.025***
(100 thou, 1 million]	−0.087***	−0.086***	−0.066***	−0.067***	−0.061***
(1 million,+]	−0.078***	−0.077***	−0.055***	−0.063***	−0.060***
Size_establishment (ref.: (0, 10])					
(10, 100]	−0.356***	−0.350***	−0.365***	−0.364***	−0.357***
(100, 1.000]	−0.108***	−0.108***	−0.045***	−0.074***	−0.069***
(1.000, 10.000]	−0.247***	−0.242***	−0.262***	−0.262***	−0.261***
(10.000, +]	−0.289***	−0.284***	−0.307***	−0.308***	−0.307***
CBO (ref.: Farming and fishing) Industry—Generalists	0.123***	**0.120*****	0.182***	0.150***	0.148***
Industry—Operators	0.076***	0.074***	0.139***	0.115***	0.119***
Maintenance and repair	0.168***	0.164***	0.274***	0.237***	0.243***
Services, commerce	0.232***	0.226***	0.339***	0.308***	0.317***
Administrative services	0.223***	0.218***	0.352***	0.315***	0.331***
Mid-level technicians	0.182***	0.178***	0.283***	0.245***	0.250***
Others	0.168***	0.165***	0.244***	**0.200*****	**0.200*****
CNAE (ref.: Public administration) Agriculture, livestock	−1.251***	−1.219***	−1.077***	−0.960***	−0.861***
Administrative activities	−1.107***	−1.077***	**−1.011*****	−0.877***	−0.793***
Vehicle sales and repair	−1.383***	−1.348***	−1.226***	−1.088***	−0.976***
Contracting	−1.674***	−1.633***	−1.629***	−1.449***	−1.336***
Industry	−1.327***	−1.293***	−1.131***	−0.997***	−0.877***
Others	**−1.341*****	−1.306***	**−1.212*****	−1.074***	−0.970***
Constant	5.490***	5.501***	4.773***	4.794***	4.630***
Wald chi^2 (43)	84,321***	87,453***	117,348***	105,869***	91,278***

(continued)

Table 6.9 (continued)

	Exponential	Weibull	Loglogístic	Lognormal	Gamma
AIC	2,129,206	2,127,993	2,043,432	2,037,241	2,030,510
BIC	2,129,721	2,128,520	2,043,959	2,037,768	2,031,050

Source: Elaborated by the authors

Note: The sample is comprised of all those admitted in 2008 who remained in their jobs through December 2011 or who terminated their contracts with or without just cause by the initiative of the employee or the employer, considering salary classes 4 through 7. The total number of observations was 909,291, with 729,786 individuals. The number of failures was 565,040. All of the models use the AFT (accelerated time failure) metric

p-value: * < 0.10; ** < 0.05; *** < 0.01

address this issue from the point of view of participation and the length of the workday (Oliveira and Soares 2012; Ferro et al. 2010; Chitolina et al. 2016; Foguel and Barros 2010; Soares 2012; Tavares 2010) and treat the participation in the Bolsa Familia Program as a time-dependent variable.

Using the semiparametric Cox model, we estimate the risk of leaving one's job to be 7% to 10% less for beneficiaries as compared to non-beneficiaries. To illustrate this point, we can compare it with the effect caused by having minor children in the family, which increases the chances of the parents leaving their jobs. In the main regression, the presence of three children in the household increased the chances of leaving employment by 9.6%. However, this probability was nullified when the individual received a BFP payment. The parametric models corroborated this result, indicating that BFP beneficiaries remain in their jobs at least 9% longer than non-beneficiaries.

The described effect is supported by the financial benefit itself to the extent that it is used to take care of the family's children under the conditions imposed by the program, which requires school attendance and the children's visits to health units. Thus, the results point to the prevalence of a substitution effect over the income effect, giving the BFP a positive impact on maintaining employment. The budgetary restrictions that BFP has been facing due to the recent Brazilian fiscal and political crisis, besides the labor reform, implemented by Law No. 13,467 of July 13, 2017, which flexibilizes Labor Laws, raise interesting questions for future investigations. How was employment affected by the fiscal crisis? What is the effect of the program amid a scenario of rising unemployment and withdrawal of labor rights? These are just a few questions that justify reanalysis of the problem with current data.

References

Além, A. C., Pastoriza, F., & Giambiagi, F. (1998). A aposentadoria por tempo de serviço no Brasil: Estimativa do subsídio recebido pelos seus beneficiários. *Revista Brasileira de Economia, 52* (1), 169–206.

Alzúa, M. L., Cruces, G., & Ripani, L. (2013). Welfare programs and labor supply in developing countries: Experimental evidence from Latin America. *Journal of Population Economics, 26*(4), 1255–1284.

Antigo, M. F., & Machado, A. F. (2006). Transições e duração do desemprego: Uma revisão da literatura com novas evidências para Belo Horizonte. *Nova Eeconomia, 16*(3), 375–406.

Araújo, G. S., Ribeiro, R., & Neder, H. D. (2010). Impactos do Programa Bolsa Família sobre o trabalho de crianças e adolescentes residentes na área urbana em 2006. *Economia, 11*(4), 57–102.

Barrientos, A., & Villa, J. (2013). *Antipoverty transfers and labor force participation effects* (BWPI), The University of Manchester.

Brito, A. S., & Kerstenetzky, CL. (2011). Programa Bolsa Família E Mercado De Trabalho: Considerações Metodológicas E Substantivas. In *Anais do XXXVIII Encontro Nacional de Economia* [Proceedings of the 38th Brazilian Economics Meeting] (No. 185). ANPEC-Associação Nacional dos Centros de Pósgraduação em Economia [Brazilian Association of Graduate Programs in Economics].

Britto, T. (2005). Recent trends in the development agenda of Latin America: An analysis of conditional cash transfers. In *Conference on Social Protection for Chronic Poverty Hosted by the Institute for Development Policy and Management and the Chronic Poverty Research Centre*, Manchester (pp. 23–24).

Cecchini, S. and Atuesta, B. (2017). Conditional cash transfer programmes in Latin America and the Caribbean. Coverage and investment trends'. Social Policy Series No. 224. ECLAC, Santiago.

Cepal, N. (2014). The employment situation in Latin America and the Caribbean: Conditional transfer programmes and the labour market. ILO Bulletin No. 10. ECLAC, Santiago. http://repository.eclac.org/handle/11362/40700?locale-attribute=en.

Chitolina, L., Foguel, M. N., & Menezes-Filho, N. A. (2016). The impact of the expansion of the Bolsa Família program on the time allocation of youths and their parents. *Revista Brasileira de Economia, 70*(2), 183–202.

Coêlho, D. B., & Fernandes, A. S. A. (2017). Rules matter: Determinants of bureaucratic control in the Bolsa Família program. *Revista de Administração Pública, 51*(5), 689–707.

de Barbosa, A. L. N. H., & Corseuil, C. H. L. (2014). *Bolsa Família, escolha ocupacional e informalidade no Brasil* (Texto para Discussão), Instituto de Pesquisa Econômica Aplicada (Ipea).

De Brauw, A., et al. (2015). Bolsa Família and household labor supply. *Economic Development and Cultural Change, 63*(3), 423–457.

De Hoop, J., & Rosati, F. C. (2014). Cash transfers and child labor. *The World Bank Research Observer, 29*(2), 202–234.

de Oliveira, P. F. A., & de Carvalho Júnior, J. R. A. (2009). Desigualdade de gênero na duração do desemprego e seus efeitos sobre os salários aceitos no Brasil. *Revista Econômica do Nordeste, 40*(4), 833–850.

Ferro, A. R., Lúcia Kassouf, A., & Levison, D. (2010). The impact of conditional cash transfer programs on household work decisions in Brazil. In *Child labor and the transition between school and work* (pp. 193–218). Emerald Group Publishing Limited.

Foguel, M. N., & de Barros, R. P. (2010). The effects of conditional cash transfer programmes on adult labor supply: An empirical analysis using a time-series-cross-section sample of Brazilian municipalities. *Estudos Econômicos, São Paulo, 40*(2), 259–293.

Garcia, C. H., & Dedecca, C. S. (2013). A heterogeneidade do mercado de trabalho e a desigualdade na representação sindical. *Sociologia & Antropologia, 3*(5), 223–243.

Garganta, S., Gasparini, L., & Marchionni, M. (2017). Cash transfers and female labor force participation: The case of AUH in Argentina. *IZA Journal of Labor Policy, 6*(1), 10.

Giambiagi, F., & Afonso, L. E. (2009). Cálculo da alíquota de contribuição previdenciária atuarialmente equilibrada: Uma aplicação ao caso brasileiro. *Revista Brasileira de Economia, 63*(2), 153–179.

Gonzalez-Rozada, M., & Pinto, F. L. (2011). *The effects of a conditional transfer program on the labor market: The human development bonus in Ecuador*. Washington, DC: Inter-American Development Bank, Mimeografado.

Kleinbaum, D. G., & Klein, M. (2006). *Survival analysis: A self-learning text.* Nova York: Springer Science & Business Media.

Lancaster, T. (1992). *The econometric analysis of transition data*. Nova York: Cambridge University Press.

Leichsenring, A. R. (2010). Precariedade laboral e o Programa Bolsa Família. In J. A. De Castro & L. Modesto (Eds.), *Bolsa Família 2003–2010: Avanços e desafios* (Vol. 1, pp. 271–300). Brasília: Ipea.

Lindert, K., et al. (2007). *The nuts and bolts of Brazil's Bolsa Família program: Implementing conditional cash transfers in a decentralized context* (Social protection discussion paper).

Lira, S. A. (2011). Duração do desemprego na região metropolitana de Curitiba. *Revista Paranaense de Desenvolvimento-RPD, 109*, 139–160.

Malbouisson, C. S., & Menezes, W. F. (2004). Duração do desemprego na Região Metropolitana de Salvador: mensuração e análise. In *Encontro Nacional de Economia* (Vol. 32, p. 2004). João Pessoa, PB. Anais... Belo Horizonte: ANPEC 2004.

Marshall, C., & Hill, P. S. (2014). Ten best resources on conditional cash transfers. *Health Policy and Planning, 30*(6), 742–746.

Medeiros, M., Britto, T., & Soares, F. (2007). *Programas focalizados de transferência de renda: Contribuições para o debate, Texto para discussão* (Vol. 1283). Brasília: Ipea jun.

Menezes, W. F., & Dedecca, C. S. (2006). Avaliação da duração do desemprego nas regiões metropolitanas de Salvador e de São Paulo. *Revista Economia Contemporânea, 10*(1), 35–60.

Menezes-Filho, N. A., & Picchetti, P. (2000). Os determinantes da duração do desemprego em São Paulo. *Pesquisa e Planejamento Econômico, 30*(1), 23–47.

Menezes-Filho, N. A., et al. (2008). Trade unions and the economic performance of Brazilian establishments. *Estudos Econômicos, 38*(1), 55–72.

Oliveira, L. F. B., & Soares, S. S. D. O (2012). *Que se sabe sobre os efeitos das transferências de renda sobre a oferta de trabalho* (Texto para Discussão), Instituto de Pesquisa Econômica Aplicada (Ipea).

Oliveira, A. M. H., et al. (2007). The first results of the baseline impact evaluation of Bolsa Família. In: Vaitsman, J. & Paes-Souza, R. (Ed.). *Evaluation of MDS' programs and policies-results.* Brasília: Sagi/MDS. v. 2, p. 19–64.

Parker, S., & Skoufias, E. (2000). *The impact of Progresa on work, leisure and time allocation.* Washington, DC: International Food Policy Research Institute.

Penido, M., & Machado, A. (2002). Desemprego: Evidências da duração no Brasil metropolitano. In *Encontro Da Associação Brasileira De Estudos Populacionais – Abep, XIII*, Ouro Preto.

Skoufias, E., & Di Maro, V. (2008). Conditional cash transfers, adult work incentives, and poverty. *The Journal of Development Studies, 44*(7), 935–960.

Soares, S. S. D. (2012). *Bolsa Família, its design, its impacts and possibilities for the future* (Working paper 89), International Policy, Centre for Inclusive Growth.

Soares, F. V., & Ribas, R. P. (2011). Is the effect of conditional transfers on labor supply negligible everywhere? In *6th Iza/World Bank Conference: Employment and Development*, Cidade do México.

Soares, F. V., Ribas, R. P., & Osório, R. G. (2010). Evaluating the impact of Brazil's Bolsa Família: Cash transfer programs in comparative perspective. *Latin American Research Review, 45*(2), 173–190.

Tavares, P. A. (2010). Efeito do Programa Bolsa Família sobre a oferta de trabalho das mães. *Revista Economia e Sociedade, 19*(3), 613–635.

Teixeira, C. G. (2010). *A heterogeneity analysis of the Bolsa Familía Programme effect on men and women's work supply* (Working paper), International Policy Centre for Inclusive Growth.

Wooldridge, J. M. (2010). *Econometric analysis of cross section and panel data.* Cambridge: MIT Press.

Chapter 7
Financial Literacy and Informal Loan

Danilo Braun Santos, Wesley Mendes-Da-Silva, and Lauro Gonzalez

Abstract The finance literature documents associations between family financial literacy and their propensity to borrow. However, there is a predominance of studies that focus exclusively on formal loan markets. In this chapter, based on 2023 observations about financial behavior of families, we examined the impacts of financial literacy on borrowing in informal markets, such as loans obtained from friends or acquaintances or even moneylenders. Using multinomial logit models, we measured the effects of financial literacy on the propensity to take informal loans, comparing two groups: families that did not take any type of loan and those took bank loans. The proxy adopted for the level of financial literacy is the consumption of a particular financial product called capitalization bond. The results suggest that financial literacy may have greater relevance in the propensity for informal loans compared to the formal credit constraint.

Keywords Financial literacy · Informal loan · Shadow economy · Emerging economies

JEL Code H81 · E26 · I22

The phenomenon of informality in the economy is seen with varied intensity in most countries around the world. Schneide et al. (2010) estimated what they called the

---

Portions of this chapter appeared in the 2018 paper "Lower Financial Literacy Induces Use of Informal Loans," *Revista de Administracao de Empresas*, vol 58, pp 44–59.

D. B. Santos (✉)
Federal University of Sao Paulo (UNIFESP), Osasco, SP, Brazil

W. Mendes-Da-Silva
Sao Paulo School of Business Administration (FGV/EAESP), Sao Paulo, SP, Brazil

University of Texas at Austin, Austin, TX, USA

L. Gonzalez
Columbia University and Fundação Getulio Vargas, Sao Paulo, SP, Brazil
e-mail: lauro.gonzalez@fgv.br

W. Mendes-Da-Silva (ed.), *Individual Behaviors and Technologies for Financial Innovations*, https://doi.org/10.1007/978-3-319-91911-9_7

shadow economy as a percentage of the GDP for a group of 162 countries, from 1999 to 2007. The estimated informal economy in Brazil grew monotonically over that period. The average rate of growth was 40.5%, and the last reading in 2007 was 43%. To this effect, the level of informality of the Brazilian economy is more explicitly similar to that (average) of countries like Colombia (41%), Uruguay (51.5%), Ecuador (36.6%), and Venezuela (33.4%) than that of economies like China (13.5%), India (24%), or other South American nations, such as Argentina (25.5%) and Chile (20.3%).

The informal economy not only compromises tax revenue but also distorts official figures on unemployment, income, consumption, and other indicators, which jeopardizes public policies that rely on such data. Moreover, Schneider et al. (2010) discuss the potential effects a growing informal economy can have on the official economy. If, on the one hand, the informal economy competes for labor, on the other hand, it has a positive effect on the formal economy, since at least two thirds of the earnings from informal work are immediately spent in the official economy. The shadow economy is also linked to higher levels of corruption, especially in the poorest countries (Borlea et al. 2017). Cole et al. (2011) believe that one of the fastest ways of promoting financial development in emerging markets is attracting individuals and businesses to the formal financial sector.

According to Pagano (2001), efficient credit depends on a series of support institutions that can provide (i) a reasonable rate of return for the creditors, (ii) a constant flow of information from the borrowers to the creditors, and (iii) the legal means to foreclose on the guarantees. Yet these institutions require borrowers to present evidence of their earnings, proof of address, and the ownership of foreclosable property. At least in the Brazilian market, there are no explicit hurdles for a worker holding an informal job to secure credit from official sources. In practice, however, this worker will face difficulties either because he or she cannot produce proper documentation related neither to income nor to assets that could be used as collateral. The flip side is higher risk and interest rates.

It is a known fact that the feasibility of guarantee mechanisms is associated with the quality of the legal institutions. La Porta, Lopez-de-Silanes, and Schleifer (1999) point out that emerging nations tend to have institutional environments that are less favorable to the transfer of ownership of collateralized assets. An informal economy exacerbates these disadvantages to the extent that without formal title the market value of assets is reduced drastically. Bertrand and Morse (2011) studied the behavioral bias in choosing payday loans and concluded that individuals can be fully informed regarding the interest rate charged by payday loans, can have no problems controlling themselves, and may not have overly optimistic expectations regarding their capacity to repay such loans. Nonetheless, they choose to take payday loans with high interest rates because they may have a pressing need for cash and no other loan alternatives. In other words, their decision is not necessarily irrational, but reflects a choice to maximize utility vis-à-vis the limitations they face.

An alternative, but not excluding, viewpoint claims that low financial literacy acts as an important barrier in the demand for financial services and products (Cole et al. 2011). If individuals have no knowledge of the available products, or even if they cannot differentiate between the possible alternatives, they will not pursue the best alternatives. Lusardi (2008) points out that while credit has become more accessible, most individuals still cannot make simple calculations to compound interest.

As financial products become more abundant and complex, the issue of financial literacy also becomes increasingly important. Lusardi and Mitchell (2014) argue that the development of financial markets brought advantages, bringing customized contracts and improving access to credit. On the other hand, it imposed more responsibility on households, which had to manage their finances responsibly. Some researchers suggest the possibility of a predatory *marketing* industry (Campbell 2006; Gabaix and Laibson 2006). In this regard, Gabaix and Laibson (2006) note that some companies can omit some information to short-sighted consumers, e.g., rates and fees.

An example of this is companies that offer credit cards with no annual fees, omitting the fact that this is only true for the first year of use. This type of argument is matched by Thaler and Tucker (2013), stating that disclosing product information is the key driver of efficiency in consumer markets, with positive externalities to society as a whole. In regard to informal loan sources, most studies analyze moneylending activities (Hoff and Stiglitz 1998; Madestam 2014). However, some studies point out that informal loans among friends and relatives represent a significant economic factor (Turvey et al. 2010; Yuan and Gao 2012). An OECD survey carried out in 14 countries showed that more than one third of those interviewed, in some of these countries, resorted to their network of acquaintances to secure a loan in the 12 months prior to the interview (OECD 2013).

This same report suggests that in some countries, and within some groups, an individual's family and friends represent their first option in case of financial needs. Additionally, this behavior does not necessarily indicate a lack of access to financial services. However, placing excessive trust on one's family and friends can, in turn, exert financial pressure on these groups and on informal networks. Perhaps as a result of the difficulty in obtaining information on credit activities in the informal market, literature on this theme is scarce worldwide and specifically in Brazil. To the knowledge of the authors, the only studies carried out in Brazil focused on the Chinese community (Schiavini et al. 2012; Sheng and Mendes-Da-Silva 2014) and on the state of São Paulo's coffee farming in the late nineteenth century (Tosi et al. 2007, 2011).

Moreover, none of the studies on the informal loan market addressed the topic of financial literacy. However, Cole et al. (2011) report that financial knowledge is an important predictor of financial behavior in emerging markets, while Carpena et al. (2015) highlight the importance of financial literacy for sustainable savings and loan behavior. Lusardi and Tufano (2009), in turn, warn that in spite of the fact that loan decisions have become critical in the face of recent credit crises, little research has been carried out on the relationship between financial literacy and indebtedness. Therefore, a gap exists in analyzing the potential effects of financial literacy in Brazil, especially as related to the financial services used by the lower-income classes. In this sense, a better understanding of financial literacy may be useful, not only for developing better financial products but also for improving public policies in housing, conditional cash transfers, etc.

This study provides a more comprehensive overview of informal credit behaviors than has previously been described in the literature. Most research in this area has used small convenience samples or data from developed markets. This study references a data sample of 1853 individuals in a prominent emerging market, Brazil. This chapter presents highlights from this research to identify specific behaviors regarding around informal credit. These research findings can provide insight for financial professionals, educators, and policymakers to develop more effective financial education for households, especially those who are financially at risk. We provide concluding recommendations, as well as suggestions for future research.

Strategy Employed to Evaluate Financial Literacy

Financial literacy is of interest to many people around the globe, e.g., policymakers, bankers, employers, community groups, and families planning for their future – perhaps due to the rapid creation of a myriad of new financial products, the increasingly global nature of financial markets with all the complexity it brings, and changes in political and demographic characteristics (Rose 2008). For the term "financial literacy," this study used the definition employed by the OECD (2013): "A combination of awareness, knowledge, skill, attitude, and behavior necessary to make sound financial decisions and ultimately achieve individual financial wellbeing" (Atkinson and Messy 2012). The methods used to measure the level of financial literacy vary substantially (Hung et al. 2009; Stolper and Walter 2017). Some researchers use hypothetical financial situations (Lusardi 2008; Lusardi and Mitchell 2009, 2011b) or fictitious financial products (Carlin and Robinson 2012). However, evidence-based financial literacy measures are not unanimous, and a number of criticisms have been made about studies that adopt such methodologies (Stolper and Walter 2017).

Thus, several authors have used proxies for financial literacy. Some have used sociodemographic projections through variables such as income, age, education (Calvet et al. 2007, 2009), or even IQ (Grinblatt et al. 2011, 2012). Others have used outcome-based proxies, such as previous investment experience (Goetzmann and Kumar 2008, Nicolosi et al. 2009, Seru et al. 2009), the composition of the investment portfolio (Goetzmann and Kumar 2008; Grinblatt and Keloharju 2001), and the propensity to invest in complex financial instruments (Genesove and Mayer 2001; Goetzmann and Kumar 2008).

In spite of the fact that financial literacy is a matter of level, this study used a *dummy* variable to identify individuals with little financial literacy. The Brazilian market has a unique and widely available financial product called "capitalization bond," which does not contribute to the financial well-being of consumers, since other available products are as affordable as capitalization bonds – or even more so – offering similar or better benefits at lower costs, with fewer penalties and restrictions

(Melo et al. 2012). Accordingly, this section presents arguments supporting the premise that individuals consuming these bonds have lower financial literacy.

Savings-Based Financial Products

Capitalization bonds are registered securities that can be acquired in a single payment or in installments. Part of the funds invested is used to build capital. Based on the contractual conditions governing each security, this capital is paid back in currency after a given period of time. The other part of the funds invested pays for drawings (capitalization bond holders compete in drawings over the term of the contract and redeem the funds deposited at the end of the period) and administrative expenses.

There are four types of capitalization bonds. According to the National Capitalization Federation (FenaCap 2013), the *traditional* type is the most common, accounting for 81% of all sales in this segment. This type of capitalization bond returns the total amount paid by the underwriter, provided there were no late payments in the installment plan, if this was selected as the form of payment. The second most common is the *incentive* type, which represents 11% of all sales. This bond is intended for businesses, which use it in sales campaigns or loyalty programs, passing the rights to the drawings on to the respective sales staff or clients. The *popular* capitalization bond focuses more on the drawing aspect. Accordingly, the issuer only returns 50% of the payments when the bond matures. This type represents 8% of the segment's sales. Finally, the *planned purchase* bond is associated with a given product or service, but it is no longer offered in the market.

In Brazil, this product is regulated by the Superintendence of Private Insurance (SUSEP), an authority established in 1966 and which responds to the Ministry of Finance. Today, there are 17 companies that offer this type of product in the market (FenaCap 2015a), including the country's most important private and government-owned banks. Table 7.1 shows that revenues from capitalization bonds have grown year after year in Brazil, reaching R$21 billion (R$2 ~ US$1) in 2013, or 0.43% of the country's GDP, which is one of the world's ten largest. According to Portocarrero (2008), capitalization bonds provide individuals with fewer available funds to have access to financial products, as these bonds usually require small contributions. Since traditional capitalization bonds have fixed maturities, usually 12 months, and regular drawings, they attract the savings of individuals who would not otherwise invest their money (FenaCap 2015a, b; Portocarrero 2008).

For this reason, capitalization bonds are usually compared to savings accounts (commonly just called savings, or *poupança*). Savings are Brazil's most popular investment. These accounts are easy to use, have low risk, are exempt from any taxes or bank fees for individuals, and require no minimum amounts for deposits or withdrawals. Before May 3, 2012, savings accounts had their monthly yield fixed at 0.5% plus the daily reference rate (TR) for the period. Federal Provisional Measure no. 567, followed by Law no. 12703, determined new rules for savings

Table 7.1 Brazilian capitalization market across the time

Year	Revenues (R$ thousand)	Share of GDP (%)
2001	4,789,563	0.37
2002	5,217,204	0.35
2003	6,022,577	0.35
2004	6,601,776	0.34
2005	6,910,339	0.32
2006	7,111,434	0.30
2007	7,828,951	0.29
2008	9,015,379	0.30
2009	10,104,143	0.31
2010	11,780,949	0.31
2011	14,081,268	0.34
2012	16,585,517	0.38
2013	20,979,849	0.43

Source: Supervision and Market Monitoring Report – SUSEP (2015)

accounts. Their yield would vary according to the risk-free interest rate (inflation adjustment through the TR was not changed), which is also a proxy for the rate offered to investors in Brazilian treasury notes. Thus, savings deposits after May 4, 2012, earned 70% of the monthly adjusted annual Selic rate when the latter dropped to 8.5% a year or below.

Otherwise, the yield of savings would follow the previous rules. In spite of this rule change, there were few months in which the risk-free interest rate was below that limit. Combined with the fact that the data in this study refer mostly to the year prior to this change and only some months afterwards, the following comparisons use the old rules for savings accounts. But savings accounts and capitalization bonds have one major difference. In the former, the interest rate and the TR apply on the total amount invested. But although capitalization bonds use the same interest and inflation rates, they only apply these rates to the share of the investment actually capitalized, also called the capitalization share.

The Capitalization Bond Rationale

The motivation for an individual to give up earning interest on his or her capital and accept a series of restrictions is, obviously, the chance of winning a prize. To further examine this choice, let us use as example *Ourocap Torcida do Brasil*, a capitalization bond that has a single payment and a 36-month maturity.

These bonds cost between R$600 and R$5000. After buyers make the single payment, for the following 36 months, they are eligible for a prize based on the drawings of Brazil's federal lottery, using a lucky number assigned to each bond, from 000,000 to 999,999. The drawings are divided into five types. Accordingly, each bond is eligible for a total of 199 drawings until maturity. Even if a bond wins a prize under one type of drawing, it is still eligible for a prize under the other drawings.

Assuming a total of n drawings of a same type, which gives a prize of αv, where v is the value (price) of the bond. The probability of the bond winning k times, with $k = 0, 1, \ldots, n$, is given by a binomial distribution of parameters n and p, where p represents the probability of winning one of the drawings. In this case, p is the ratio between the quantity of numbers drawn and the quantity of bonds available (one million). Thus, if r_i denotes the return of type i, the expected value of r_i can be calculated by:

$$E[r_i] = \frac{\sum_{k=0}^{n} k\alpha v \ P(being\ drawn\ k\ times)}{v} = \alpha \sum_{k=0}^{n} k \binom{n}{k} p^k (1-p)^{n-k} = \alpha np \tag{7.1}$$

Under type I, there are drawings on the first four Saturdays of each month ($n = 36 * 4 = 144$), and the prize is ten times the single payment ($\alpha = 10$). Based on the drawings of the federal lottery, ten different lucky numbers are randomly selected in each drawing ($p = 10/1000{,}000$). The value expected by r_1 can be calculated using the formula 7.1, which results in:

$$E[r_1] = 10 \cdot 144 \cdot 0.00001 = 1.44\% \tag{7.2}$$

Under type II, there are monthly drawings on the first Saturday of each month ($n = 36$), and the prize is 20 times the single payment ($\alpha = 20$). Based on the federal lottery drawings, 15 different lucky numbers are selected in each drawing ($p = 15/1{,}000{,}000$). In formula 7.1, the expected value of r_2 is:

$$E[r_2] = 20 \cdot 36 \cdot 0.000015 = 1.08\% \tag{7.3}$$

Type III features quarterly drawings ($n = 12$), and the prizes are equivalent to 200 times the single payment ($\alpha = 200$). Two different lucky numbers are selected in each drawing ($p = 2/1{,}000{,}000$). In Eq. 7.1, the expected value of r_3 is:

$$E[r_3] = 200 \cdot 12 \cdot 0.000002 = 0.48\% \tag{7.4}$$

Type IV drawings select only one number ($p = 1/1000{,}000$), and the prize is equivalent to 1000 times the single payment ($\alpha = 1000$). The drawings happen twice a year ($n = 6$). In formula 7.1, we have:

$$E[r_4] = 1{,}000 \cdot 6 \cdot 0.000001 = 0.60\% \tag{7.5}$$

Finally, type V has only one drawing ($n = 1$) of six different lucky numbers ($p = 6/1000{,}000$), and the prize is equivalent to 2000 the single payment ($\alpha = 2000$). The expected value of r_5, calculated under formula 7.1, is:

$$E[r_5] = 2,000 \cdot 1 \cdot 0.000006 = 1.20\% \tag{7.6}$$

Therefore, the expected return for the drawings in this bond is given by the sum of the values in Eqs. 7.2, 7.3, 7.4, 7.5, and 7.6:

$$E\left[\sum_{i=1}^{5} r_i\right] = \sum_{i=1}^{5} E[r_i] = 4.80\% \tag{7.7}$$

The Brazilian Tax Code imposes a 30-percent income tax rate on prizes obtained through capitalization bond drawings. Accordingly, the expected net amount is:

$$0.7 \cdot \sum_{i=1}^{5} E[r_i] = 0.7 \cdot 4.80\% = 3.36\% \tag{7.8}$$

In comparison with an amount invested in a savings account, and disregarding inflation adjustment (TR) which is common to both investments, considering only the monthly capitalization of 0.5% over 36 months, final earnings net of taxes and fees would result in total interest of:

$$(1 + 0.5\%)^{36} = 19.67\% \tag{7.9}$$

Financial Literacy and Selecting Alternatives

According to the expected utility theory (Neumann and Morgenstem 1947), individuals select lotteries to maximize the expected value of the result. From this perspective, there is no reason for a rational being, even a risk-neutral one, trading a lottery that certainly pays nearly 20% (Eq. 7.9) for another, with a higher risk and an expected return of 3.36% (Eq. 7.8). How, then, can we explain the consumption of a product with a negative prize-risk ratio? Ever since Allais (1952) demonstrated flaws in the assumption of a linear expected utility theory, many economists have investigated this matter. Lopes and Oden (1999) use theory *SP/A* to defend that risk choices are based on two criteria, a risk-return assessment (the *SP* criterion) and a comparison of probabilities, to achieve an aspiration level (the *A* criterion).

According to this approach, an individual could prefer foregoing a certain 20% he or she would earn in a savings account and buy this capitalization bond, if this individual's assessment of the probabilities enables him or her, in some way, to assume the chance of winning a prize above a given level. In other words, based on a personal aspiration and an assessment of the possibility of winning, an individual may behave like a "risk lover." The role of aspiration in selecting lotteries is assessed by experiments in which the distributions of probability of these lotteries are known by the respondents, numerically and/or graphically (Lopes 2013; Lopes and Oden 1999). There seem to be no reasons to believe that the level of aspiration can satisfactorily explain the decision to choose the product described above. First, because the way prizes are presented does not allow an easy assessment of the distributions of probability by the investors, advanced statistical calculation knowledge would be necessary. This is illustrated by the contract that describes the drawing rules for type I bonds (the same product named above, *Ourocap Torcida do Brasil*):

> TYPE I: WEEKLY DRAWINGS HELD ON THE FIRST FOUR (4) SATURDAYS OF EACH MONTH. THIS EVENT WILL OFFER TEN (10) PRIZES EQUIVALENT TO TEN (10) TIMES THE SINGLE PAYMENT TO BONDS WHOSE LUCKY NUMBERS PRINTED ON THE BONDS MATCHES THE FOLLOWING COMBINATIONS:
>
> THE FIRST WINNING BOND WILL BE THAT WHOSE LUCKY NUMBER MATCHES THE NUMBER FORMED BY THE SECOND-TO-LAST ALGARISM OF THE FIRST PRIZE OF THE BRAZILIAN FEDERAL LOTTERY, FOLLOWED BY THE COLUMN COMPRISED OF THE LAST ALGARISM OF THE FIRST TO FIFTH PRIZES IN THE SAME DRAWING OF THE FEDERAL LOTTERY, READ VERTICALLY FROM TOP TO BOTTOM.
>
> THE NINE (9) OTHER WINNING BONDS WILL BE THOSE WHOSE LUCKY NUMBERS MATCH THE NUMBERS FORMED BY ADDING ONE (1) UNIT TO THE FIRST ALGARISM OF THE NUMBER FORMED IN THE PRIOR STEP, AND SO ON.
>
> • ADDING ONE (1) UNIT TO THE ALGARISM NINE (9) OF THE HUNDRED THOUSAND POSITION OF THE NUMBERS FORMED IN THE PRIOR STEPS WILL RESULT IN ZERO (0).

Second, the availability of several federal lotteries with explicitly reasonable prices (between R$1 and R$5) with higher winnings than those offered by capitalization bonds should be analyzed as direct competitors in this choice. By combining an investment in a savings account and federal lotteries, an individual could reap the same benefits at lower costs and with fewer penalties (waiting periods, fines, etc.). In other words, even if the level of aspiration has some influence on that choice, if the buyer cannot compare the chances of winning and the cost of the lottery (associated with the bond) with those of similar products, it would seem more reasonable that financial literacy is playing a more decisive role in this question. There would be two reasons behind this; the first is the way the product is structured and the second the way it is sold.

We should point out that when capitalization bonds adopt a monthly interest rate (0.5%) and an inflation-adjustment rate (TR) similar to that offered by savings accounts, this could bring confusion when the product is purchased. In large banks, internal training documents for sales managers of capitalization bonds warn that it should never be said that these bonds are an investment or even similar to a savings account. Yet these same documents recommend that managers should always emphasize that the interest rate is the same offered by savings accounts and that clients will be able to have all their money back adjusted for inflation and still compete for prizes.

According to the OECD (2013), the way in which individuals choose a product can be influenced by a wide range of factors, including the speed with which they have to make the decision; the availability of alternatives, to the extent that information and advice are available; and their previous experiences. However, if people try to inform themselves when making a purchasing decision, preferably using independent advice, they will therefore be more likely to choose appropriate products that meet their needs at a more efficient cost, less likely to buy something inappropriate, and less subject to a negligent sale where the contract is poorly presented (misselling). This report from OECD (2013) highlights the benefit that financial literacy plays in comparing products, seeking unbiased opinions, and assessing the adequacy of financial products. In this way, the consumption of capitalization bonds will be used to identify individuals with lower levels of financial literacy. However, there are some limitations related to the use of this proxy, which we highlight below.

Limitations About Capitalization Bond as Financial Literacy Proxy

In spite of the fact that the associations between financial literacy and financial results are potentially endogenous, several authors have tried to show the causal mechanism between them (Klapper et al. 2013; Bernheim and Garrett 2001; Lusardi and Mitchell 2009; Lusardi and Mitchell 2011a; Van Rooij et al. 2011; Behrman et al. 2010). However, in this study another source of endogeneity may be identified, because if low levels of financial literacy make the individual more likely to consume bad financial products, the consumption of both savings bonds and informal loans would be affected simultaneously (Fig. 7.1a). On the other hand, we understand that the reasonableness of the proxy for financial literacy and methodological procedures can lessen such concerns (Fig. 7.1b).

First, it should be noted that even if financial literacy affects informal borrowing, it is far from being a single determinant. The availability of credit in the formal market, extraordinary expenses (health, marriage, accidents, etc.), loss of job, or income volatility in general are just some of the possible causes for this choice. Even though financial literacy plays a preponderant role in this selection (as this study

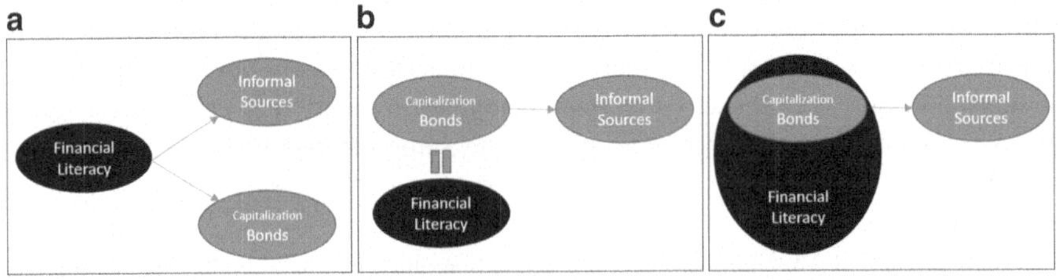

Fig. 7.1 Relation between capitalization bonds, financial literacy, and informal sources. (**a**) Endogeneity. (**b**) Proxy. (**c**) Limitations

intends to show), it is known that a rational decision to resort to the informal market in a moment of despair or lack of alternatives is totally plausible.

On the other hand, the option to buy a capitalization bond is not related to a measure of despair or lack of alternatives. On the contrary, as described previously, these securities are instruments for saving money; and at least one very widespread alternative in the Brazilian market, the savings account, presents less costly contractual conditions, lower acquisition cost, and superior profitability. Still in the list of alternative products, the Brazilian federal government offers several lotteries with very popular prices and higher premiums than the capitalization bonds.

Thus, it seems to us quite reasonable that capitalization bond consumption offers a good way to identify individuals with low levels of financial literacy. However, the main criticism that may arise regarding the adoption of this proxy is due to non-consumers of these securities, when the individuals may have low financial literacy yet not consume capitalization bonds because they have insufficient funds to buy these securities, lack the intention of saving, or are uninterested in the financial market. However, this should not be of major concern; one should keep in mind that any significant effect representing the propensity of financial illiterates in informal lending can and should be underestimated; after all if some individuals who are financially illiterate have not been identified, the effect revealed by this research would then be more relevant than that reported, rather than less (Fig. 7.1c).

In a nutshell, we believe that in the scope of this study, the consumption of capitalization bonds acts as a good substitute for low levels of financial literacy, provided that comparisons can be made to distinguish the different effects that the consumption of these bonds can indicate the inclusion in the financial market, since the securities are mainly traded in bank branches. To this end, individuals will be subdivided into three groups, (i) those who have not borrowed, (ii) those who have borrowed at banks, and (iii) those who have used informal loans, and the effects on the consumption of these contrasted securities in relation to these groups. The details of this method are presented in the following section.

Data and Variables

We used data from a *survey* carried out between August and December 2012 by Bankable Frontier Associates and the Bill & Melinda Gates Foundation called "National survey on financial inclusion and the use of banking correspondents in Brazil." Information was collected using a printed questionnaire, which required an interview of about 1 h to be completed. Participation was voluntary. That survey set out to select a nationally representative sample of Brazilian households. As determined by Cull and Scott (2010), information about financial usage provided by the household head is more complete and accurate than information from an interview with a randomly selected individual. Therefore, a set of initial questions were applied to the first adult encountered at the house in order to select the most financially knowledgeable person as the respondent. Because the respondent was not selected

Table 7.2 Use of credit in the prior 12 months

	Whole sample		Capitalization bond consumers	
Loan	Amount	Share	Amount	Share
Did not use	1142	56.5%	138	12%
Bank	614	30.4%	173	28%
Informal	267	13.2%	101	38%
Acquaintances – WITHOUT	183	9.0%	66	36%
Acquaintances – WITH	64	3.2%	26	41%
Moneylenders	20	1.0%	9	45%
Total	2023	100%	412	20%

Did not use: No type of loan in the past 12 months. Bank: loans or financing from a bank in the prior 12 months (includes face-to-face loan offered through the bank). Acquaintances – WITHOUT: a loan from a friend, neighbor, or relative without interest in the prior 12 months. Acquaintances – WITH: a loan from a friend, neighbor, or relative with interest in the prior 12 months. Moneylenders: a loan from a moneylender in the prior 12 months. Informal: credit from acquaintances, with or without interest, or from moneylenders in the prior 12 months. Consumption of capitalization bonds: reported having, at the time of the interview or before, a capitalization bond. Percentage in relation to the loan category

randomly at the household level, individual results are only representative of the most financially knowledgeable Brazilians.

In section "Concluding Remarks and Future Directions" of that questionnaire, individuals indicated how they used loans from different sources, including the informal market. To build our database, we considered respondents who in the prior 12 months did not use any type of loan or who got loans from at least one of the following sources: banks, moneylenders, or acquaintances, with or without interest charges. The term "acquaintances" means people of the individual's circle, such as friends, family, or even neighbors. Thus, our sample has 2023 loan observations, originating from 1853 different individuals. Table 7.2 shows the share of statements involving the use of loan in relation to the segments surveyed. Money obtained from acquaintances or moneylenders was placed in the *informal* category. The mean age of the interviewees is 48, ranging from 17 to 94. Out of this total, 52% are men and 27% are retirees. Additionally, 92% of the respondents claimed they took household budget decisions. This high percentage is not surprising because one of the recommendations for interviewers was to visit the household up to three times to interview this particular individual. However, only 62% have a personal bank account (simple, current, or savings accounts).

Average reported monthly wage was R$912, which represents 1.47 monthly minimum wages in Brazil. Less than 6% of those interviewed had a college degree, and only 20% graduated from middle (high) school. The average household has 3.4 individuals; there is an average of 0.9 individuals under 16 in each household. Brazil's North Region is home to 20% of the interviewees; the Northeast, 25%; the Center-West, 8%; the Southeast, 32%; and the South, 14%.

Regarding financial behavior, about 42% of the respondents admitted they had already made one late payment, while 9% said they had a poor credit history. Nearly

20% of the interviewees said they held, at the time of the interview or before, capitalization bonds. Table 7.3 shows the percentage of consumption of capitalization bonds within the different credit segments. We see an increase in the percentage of the category of those claiming they had not used loans during the period for the bank loan category.

Table 7.3 Independent variables considered in the model

Variable	Description	Mean	Std. Dev.
Capitalization bond (D)	Do you have or did you have a capitalization bond?	0.197	0.398
Budget decision maker (D)	Do you make most family budget decisions?	0.921	0.270
Bank account (D)	Do you have any personal bank account (simple, current, or savings account)?	0.622	0.485
Late payment (D)	Have you ever made a late payment?	0.418	0.493
Poor credit history (D)	Do you have a poor credit history right now?	0.092	0.288
Age	Age of the respondent (in years)	48.33	15.77
Man (D)	Masculine gender?	0.525	0.499
Retiree (D)	Are you a retiree?	0.272	0.445
Income	Monthly income of the respondent (in reais)[a]	911.75	1424.98
Expenses	Monthly expenses (in reais).[b]	332.89	1275.77
Household members	Number of residents in the household	3.41	1.70
Under 16	Number of residents under 16 in the household	0.878	1.181
National region (D)			
NO	North	0.197	0.398
NE	Northeast	0.250	0.433
CO	Center-West	0.083	0.277
SE	Southeast	0.325	0.468
SU	South	0.144	0.352
Education (D): What was the highest school level you completed?			
Educ 0	Never went to school or never completed primary school	0.241	0.428
Educ 1	Primary school	0.498	0.500
Educ 2	Middle (high) school	0.198	0.398
Educ 3	Higher education	0.059	0.236

Notes: (D) indicates *dummy* variables with value of 1 in case yes and 0 in case no

[a]The *Income* variable considers earnings of the respondent from work, social security, or pension fund, as well as other sources such as rent, the federal severance indemnity fund (FGTS), government scholarships, inheritances, donations, etc. The amount corresponds to the monthly average for the past 12 months

[b]The *Expenses* variable represents the average sum of expenses with utilities, condominium fees, rent, digital service packages, landline telephones, cell phones (prepaid and postpaid), subscription TV, Internet, school tuitions, mortgage payments, consumer loan payments, and insurance payments

This increase might be explained by financial inclusion. Individuals with bank accounts tend to use more bank loans and buy capitalization bonds, which are mostly sold through bank branches (Angst and de Abreu 2007). This argument is supported by the fact that only 48% of those not using loans held bank accounts, whereas 89% of those taking loans at a bank held bank accounts. The second variation we see in Table 7.2, from the bank credit segment to the informal credit segment, matches the hypothesis we would like to test in this study: whether individuals with lower financial literacy levels (consumers of capitalization bonds) are more likely to use informal sources of loan. To confirm this hypothesis, we controlled co-variables that represent the financial and individual behavior, financial inclusion, loan demand and restriction, and social and demographic variables. Table 7.3 describes the variables used in the model.

Empirical Model and Results

The observations were classified into three categories of interest: 0 = no loan, 1 = bank loan, and 2 = informal loan. We used a multinomial logistic regression to analyze the likelihood of these three types. The multinomial logit is ideal for non-ordinal and polytomic category dependent variables. The values attributed to each category (0 = no loan, 1 = bank loan, 2 = informal loan) are arbitrary, i.e., the model does not assume that 0 < 1 < 2. The probability of the y dependent variable assuming the value i is given by:

$$Pr(y = i) = \frac{e^{X\beta_i}}{e^{X\beta_i} + \sum_{j \neq i} e^{X\beta_j}}.$$

So that vectors β_i are uniquely identified, we considered some of them nil, which them becomes the base category. The estimated coefficients represent changes in relation to this base category. Where y assumes three values, such as this in which $i = 0$, 1, and 2, and considering $i = 0$ as the base category, the probabilities are given by:

$$Pr(y = 0) = \frac{1}{1 + e^{X\beta_1} + e^{X\beta_2}},$$

$$Pr(y = 1) = \frac{e^{X\beta_1}}{1 + e^{X\beta_1} + e^{X\beta_2}},$$

$$Pr(y = 2) = \frac{e^{X\beta_2}}{1 + e^{X\beta_1} + e^{X\beta_2}}.$$

Table 7.4 shows the estimates for the multinomial logistic regression coefficients, in which the dependent variable (loan category) assumes three possibilities: 0 = *No loan*, for the individuals who have not reported using any type of loan in the 12 months prior to the completing the questionnaire; 1 = *Bank loan*, for those who reported using bank loans or financing in the 12 months prior to the

Table 7.4 Multinomial logistic regression

Base category	No loan (0)	No loan (0)	Bank loan (1)
Dependent variable	Bank loan (1)	Informal loan (2)	Informal loan (2)
Capitalization bond	0.614***	1.578***	0.963***
Budget decision maker	0.371	−0.509*	−0.879**
Bank account	1.432***	0.619***	−0.813***
Late payment	0.380***	0.859***	0.479**
Poor credit history	−0.048	0.439	0.487*
Age	0.105***	0.047	−0.057
Age^2	−0.00115***	−0.00073*	0.00042
Man	−0.0336	−0.147	−0.113
Retiree	0.755***	−0.076	−0.831***
Household members	0.150**	−0.213**	−0.362***
Under 16	−0.130	0.347**	0.477***
NO	−0.822***	−0.233	1.054***
NE	−0.479**	0.866**	1.345***
CO	−0.610**	0.045	0.655
SE	−0.433**	0.799**	1232***
Ln(income)	0.185*	0.010	−0.175
Ln(expenses)	0.245***	0.195**	−0.050
Educ 0	−0.00371	0.560	0.564
Educ 1	−0.248	0.191	0.439
Educ 2	−0.303	0.075	0.378
Constant	−6.658***	−3.983***	2.675*
N	1463		
Wald chi2(40)	369.90***		
Pseudo R2	0.1740		

Multinomial logistic regression coefficients. Standard errors adjusted to 1326 *clusters* of individuals
p-value: *< 0.10, **< 0.05, ***< 0.01

questionnaire; and 2 = *Informal loan*, for those who reported loans from acquaintances – with or without interest – or from moneylenders in the 12 months prior to the questionnaire. In the first two columns of Table 7.4, we see the coefficients of the model with the *No loan* (0) category used as the base. The last column shows the coefficients of the same model, only changing the base category to *Bank loan* (1). As a result of the base 1 (*Bank loan*) category, the coefficients related to level 0 (*No loan*) were not reported, because they are precisely the same (in magnitude and significance) of the effects estimated in the first column, but with inverted signs.

On the demand side of the loan market, age is one of the most important factors, according to the life-cycle theory (Modigliani and Brumberg 1954). As this theory suggests, people accumulate wealth early in their lives to ease on consumption and maintain their standard of living after retirement. Accordingly, young individuals tend to get into debt because of their expectations of increased income and consumption in the future. As age advances, income increases, and they become less willing to get loans. Consequently, the ratio between loan demand and age will have an inverted U shape. To capture this nonlinear relation, we included the age quadratic and linear terms as independent variables. These estimates are consistent with the theory when we look at bank loan in comparison with those who have not gotten into debt. However, *Age* and Age^2 cannot explain loan taking from informal sources.

Even though studies suggest gender dependence in choosing financial products (Fonseca et al. 2012; Lusardi and Mitchell 2008; OECD 2013), no significant effect was observed for the *Man* variable. The *Retiree* variable indicates the role of consigned credit in encouraging bank credit, to the extent that it reduces interest rates and credit restrictions because it allows payments to be deducted directly from the paycheck. This variable's coefficient in the third column suggests that consigned credit reduces the chances of a retiree in need of credit resorting to informal sources. That is, despite being accessible to any employee, payroll-deductible loans granted to the elderly are encouraged, since the risk of default is practically zero, since the retiree's income is provided by the national pension system.

The family structure is an important predictor to explain loan taking from informal sources. Larger families are less likely to use informal loan than bank loan. However, when these families have children under 16, this situation is inverted, and they become more vulnerable to the informal market. Perhaps this behavior can be explained by household dwellers having a larger (or smaller) share of the family budget. Residents of Brazil's North, Northeast, and Southeast regions are more likely to resort to informal loan than those living in the South Region, who use more formal loan. The South Region of Brazil stands out in terms of the penetration rate of credit unions, more often called cooperatives in Brazil (Lhacer 2012; Garcia and Lhacer 2012). As of 2015, around 90% of South municipalities have credit units, more than twice the average of Brazil as a whole, that was 44% in the same year (Banco Central do Brasil 2016). Therefore, the higher presence of cooperatives seems to be the main reason for having more access to formal credit in the South.

The expected effect of income on loan taking is, to some extent, ambiguous. Individuals with lower income need more loans than those earning more. However, creditors tend to favor borrowers who can better pay their debts. The positive and significant *Ln(income)* coefficient for taking loan at banks in relation to those not taking loan can suggest that income is acting more as a credit restrictor in the market than as a demand leveler. This might make sense for lower-income individuals and is consistent with the mean reported salary, 1.47 minimum monthly wages.

The effect of the *Expenses* is as expected, i.e., families with more expenses are more likely to need loans (formal or informal). However, this variable is not able to explain the choice between these loan alternatives. Note that the estimated model used only 1463 observations. This was because of an expressive flaw in the *Expenses* and *Variable income*. For this reason we reestimate the model by removing these variables. Indeed, education dummies also failed to present significant effects and were removed from the next regression (Table 7.5). According to Lusardi and Mitchell (2011b), education is far from being a good proxy for financial knowledge. It can be noticed that the coefficients and their significance did not change in this reestimation with the complete sample (2021 observations).

Table 7.5 Multinomial logistic regression

Base category	No loan (0)	No loan (0)	Bank loan (1)
Dependent variable	Bank loan (1)	Informal loan (2)	Informal loan(2)
Capitalization bond	0.666***	1.302***	0.637***
Budget decision maker	0.347	−0.401	−0.748**
Bank account	1833***	0.668***	−1.165***
Late payment	0.493***	1.007***	0.514***
Poor credit history	−0.013	0.534**	0.547**
Age	0.083***	0.020	−0.063*
Age^2	−0.00098***	−0.00040	0.00058
Man	−0.056	−0.127	−0.183
Retiree	0.846***	−0.075	−0.921***
Household members	0.143***	−0.017	−0.160**
Under 16	−0.161**	0.105	0.266**
NO	−1.118***	0.015	1.133***
NE	−0.797***	0.683*	1.480***
CO	−0.554**	0.274	0.829**
SE	−0.644***	0.625*	1.269***
Constant	−4.065***	−2.790***	1.275
N	2021		
Wald chi2(40)	444.81***		
Pseudo R2:	0.1664		

Multinomial logistic regression coefficients. Standard errors adjusted to 1851 *clusters* of individuals
p-value: * < 0.10, ** < 0.05, *** < 0.01

Having a bank account is one of the most basic requirements for an individual to take part in the financial market and have access to a wide range of products and services (Banco Central do Brasil 2011; Demirgüç-Kunt and Klapper 2012). The *Bank account* presented significant coefficients in both estimations (Tables 7.4 and 7.5). Individuals with bank accounts are more likely to incur debt, both from banks and from informal sources. But they are much less likely to obtain loans from the informal market than from banks. Individuals with a poor credit history are, as one would expect, more likely to resort to informal sources.

We wrap up this discussion with the three variables that can bring the most information regarding the impact of financial literacy. These are, in addition, of course, to the main *proxy* mentioned above, the consumption of capitalization bonds, the *Late payment* and *Budget decision maker variables.* We would expect that the individual in charge of the household budget has greater knowledge of finances and, probably, the one with the most access to and greatest affinity with financial products and services. We should point out that the individual most familiar with finances in the household does not necessarily have good financial literacy. At any rate, the coefficients point to this individual as the one least likely to use informal sources of loan.

Table 7.6 Marginal effects

Dependent variable	No loan (0)	Bank loan (1)	Informal loan (2)
Capitalization bond	−0.193***	0.029	0.163***
Budget decision maker	−0.012	0.089*	−0.077**
Bank account	−0.245***	0.235***	0.010
Late payment	−0.105***	0.034	0.071***
Poor credit history	−0.021	−0.029	0.051*
Age	0.0029**	−0.0012	−0.0017*
Man	0.013	0.0002	−0.013
Retiree	−0.104**	0.145***	−0.041*
Household members	−0.009	0.037***	−0.028***
Under 16	0.0014	−0.039**	0.041***
NO	0.090*	−0.151***	0.061
NE	0.002	−0.125***	0.123***
CO	0.077	−0.107**	0.030
SE	0.007	−0.112***	0.105***
Ln(income)	−0.026	0.034*	−0.007
Ln(expenses)	−0.045***	0.037***	0.009
Educ 0	−0.034	−0.027	0.062
Educ 1	0.024	−0.054	0.030
Educ 2	0.037	−0.058	0.020
N:	1463		

Mean marginal effects on the probability of observing a result in the dependent variable
p-value: * < 0.10, ** < 0.05, *** < 0.01

Individuals who have paid their bills late are more susceptible to requiring loans from either source, but they are more likely to resort to the informal market than to banks. Since this is controlled by the *Poor credit history* variable, this result can be explained by a fragile financial behavior, in which an individual cannot properly size the volume of debt or the level of interest, jeopardizing the household's finances. In line with these findings are the effects of the consumption of capitalization bonds. To support this analysis, we computed the mean marginal effects on the probability of observing the results for a dependent variable (Table 7.6).

We can see that individuals who buy capitalization bonds are, on average, 16.3 percentage points more likely to resort to the informal loan market. The other estimates are in line with prior discussions. We also calculated the probability of buyers and non-buyers of capitalization bonds using informal sources of loan, maintaining the other variables in their means. The result was 26% ± 6.6%, with 95% of confidence, for capitalization bond consumers, against 8.8% ± 2.6%, also with 95% of confidence, for non-consumers.

The marginal effect of each child under the age of 16 is 4 percentage points. In order to have an idea of the role that the family structure plays in the probability of using informal sources, we reestimate the confidence intervals (for consumers and non-consumers of capitalization bonds) considering a family of five members, with three children under 16 years. The result was 35% ± 12%, with 95% confidence, for capitalization bond consumers, against 13% ± 6%, also with 95% confidence, for non-consumers. Figure 7.2 shows the evolution of these confidence intervals as the family structure changes.

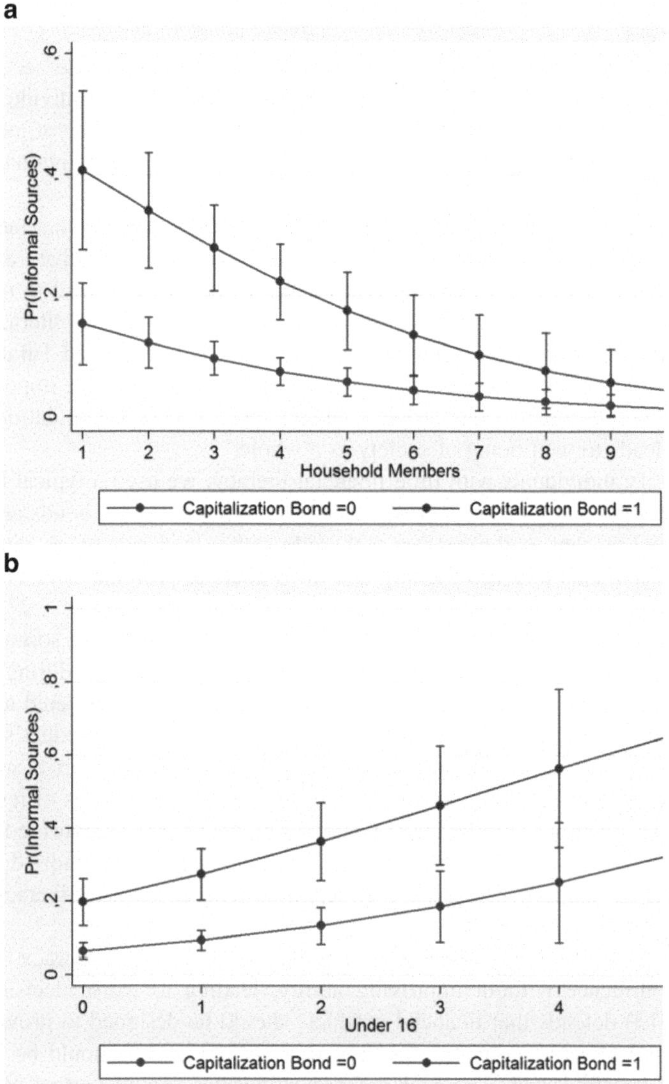

Fig. 7.2 Probability of using informal credit sources. (**a**) Members of the family. (**b**) Under 16 years old. Notes: Prediction of the probability of consumers (1) and non-consumers (0) of capitalization bonds using informal financing. The chart range shows a confidence interval of 95%

Concluding Remarks and Future Directions

The standard literature on the informal loan market considers that information asymmetry is the main driver behind this activity. The idea is that informational asymmetry results in the requirement of collaterals, restricting loan and encouraging informality, which is at an advantage in terms of information and collection techniques. In this study, the authors emphasized the role financial literacy can perform in this process.

Using variables that represent loan demand and restrictions, we see that low financial literacy is responsible for increasing the probability of individuals using informal loan. For example, we find a greater effect on the tendency of individuals with low financial literacy to use informal loan sources than of individuals with a poor credit history.

Our findings are in line with those of OECD (2013), which say that individuals with lower levels of financial literacy are less aware of alternatives and more susceptible to *misselling*, suggesting that for these reasons they tend to rely more on friends and families for their loans. The weight of financial literacy as an important predictor of credit behavior (Cole et al. 2011; Lusardi and Tufano 2009) is, once more, reinforced by our study. Additionally, it reinforces the importance of public policies designed to improve financial literacy of the population, which ultimately leads to well-being of society as a whole.

To identify individuals with little financial literacy, we used a typical Brazilian financial product, *capitalization bonds*, as a *proxy*. Capitalization bonds are mainly sold in bank branches, and managers at these branches in charge of advising clients on their investments undergo training and have goals to promote sales of capitalization bonds.

The product is designed to appear, from different perspectives, as a sort of savings account, with the added benefit of offering prizes through drawings during the term of the bond. In practice, however, the product should not be considered an investment because it only has a return if the bond wins a prize. The product's contract does not describe the cost nor the chances of the buyer winning the prize, something that requires statistical and financial calculations. Moreover, a series of restrictions and penalties are imposed if the buyer interrupts payment or accelerates redemption. Since the proxy variable has the limitation of failing to identify individuals with lower levels of financial literacy, the effects attributed to financial literacy can be assumed to be underestimated.

According to Willis (2008), for some consumers, financial literacy seems to increase confidence without improving ability, leading to worse decisions. The OECD (2013) defends that financial products should be designed to provide users with safe and effective solutions for their needs. Regulations should be the most transparent possible, and consumer defense authorities should protect consumers from any unfair practices.

References

Allais, M. (1952). *The foundations of a positive theory of choice involving risk and a criticism of the postulates and axioms of the American school*. Dordrecht: Springer.

Angst, D., & de Abreu, J. A. P. (2007). Capitalization bonds-effects of anticipated recoveries in profitability and loyalty of customer at a bank in Paraná. *Revista da FAE, 10*(2), 99–113.

Atkinson, A., & Messy, F. A. (2012). *Measuring financial literacy*. Paris: OECD Publishing.

Banco Central do Brasil (2011). *Relatório de inclusão financeira* – Number 2. https://www.bcb.gov.br/Nor/relincfin/RIF2011.pdf. Access: 7 July 2014.

Banco Central do Brasil (2016). palestra proferida na Organização das Cooperativas Brasileiras, disponível em http://www.brasilcooperativo.coop.br/GERENCIADOR/ba/arquivos/cidadania_financeira_parceria_que_da_certo.pdf.

Behrman, J., Mitchell, O. S., Soo, C., & Bravo, D. (2010). *Financial literacy, schooling, and wealth accumulation* (NBER Working Paper No. 16452).

Bernheim, D., & Garrett, D. M. (2001). The effects of financial education in the workplace: Evidence from a survey of households. *Journal of Public Economics, 87*(7–8), 1487–1519.

Bertrand, M., & Morse, A. (2011). Information disclosure, cognitive biases, and payday borrowing. *Journal of Finance, 66*(6), 1865–1893.

Borlea, S. N., Achim, M. V., & Miron, M. G. A. (2017). Corruption, shadow economy and economic growth: An empirical survey across the european union countries. *Studia Universitatis "Vasile Goldis" Arad–Economics Series, 27*(2), 19–32.

Calvet, L. E., Campbell, J. Y., & Sodini, P. (2007). Down or out: Assessing the welfare costs of household investment mistakes. *Journal of Political Economy, 115*(5), 707–747.

Calvet, L. E., Campbell, J. Y., & Sodini, P. (2009). Measuring the financial sophistication of households. *American Economic Review, 99*(2), 393–398.

Campbell, J. Y. (2006). Household finance. *Journal of Finance, 61*(4), 1553–1604.

Carlin, B. I., & Robinson, D. T. (2012). What does financial literacy training teach us? *The Journal of Economic Education, 43*(3), 235–247.

Carpena, F., Cole, S. A., Shapiro, J., & Zia, B. H. (2015). The Abcs of Financial Education: Experimental evidence on attitudes, behaviour, and cognitive biases (Policy Research working paper no. 7413; Impact Evaluation series). Retrieved from World Bank Group website: http://documents.worldbank.org/curated/en/2015/09/25050693/abcs-financial-education-experimen tal-evidenceattitudes-behaviour-cognitive-biases.

Cole, S., Sampson, T., & Zia, B. (2011). Prices or knowledge? what drives demand for financial services in emerging markets? *Journal of Finance, 66*(6), 1933–1967.

Cull, R., & Scott, K. (2010). Measuring household usage of financial services: Does it matter how or whom you ask? *World Bank Economic Review, 24*, 199–233.

Demirgüç-Kunt, A., & Klapper, L. F. (2012). *Measuring financial inclusion: The global findex database*. World Bank Policy Research Working Paper (6025).

FenaCap (2013). *Capitalização: O que você precisa saber*. http://www.cnseg.org.br/fenacap/publicacoes/. Accessed 06 Nov 2015.

FenaCap (2015a). *A capitalização na agenda econômica e social brasileira*. http://www.cnseg.org.br/fenacap/publicacoes/. Accessed 13 Dec 2015.

FenaCap (2015b). *Título de capitalização: O que você precisa saber*. http://www.cnseg.org.br/fenacap/publicacoes/. Accessed 13 Dec 2015.

Fonseca, R., Mullen, K. J., Zamarro, G., & Zissimopoulos, J. (2012). What explains the gender gap in financial literacy? the role of household decision making. *Journal of Consumer Affairs, 46*(1), 90–106.

Gabaix, X., & Laibson, D. (2006). Shrouded attributes, consumer myopia, and information suppression in competitive markets. *Quarterly Journal of Economics, 121*, 505–540.

Garcia, F. G., & Villa Lhacer, P. M. (2012). Maximização de valor pelas cooperativas de crédito brasileiras. *Revista Pensamento & Realidade, 27*(1), 62–76.

Genesove, D., & Mayer, C. (2001). Loss aversion and seller behavior: Evidence from the housing market. *Quarterly Journal of Economics, 116*(4), 1233–1260.
Goetzmann, W. N., & Kumar, A. (2008). Equity portfolio diversification. *Review of Finance, 12*, 433–463.
Grinblatt, M., & Keloharju, M. (2001). How distance, language, and culture influence stockholdings and trades. *Journal of Finance, 56*(3), 1053–1073.
Grinblatt, M., Keloharju, M., & Linnainmaa, J. (2011). IQ and stock market participation. *Journal of Finance, 66*(6), 2121–2164.
Grinblatt, M., Keloharju, M., & Linnainmaa, J. (2012). IQ, trading behavior, and performance. *Journal of Financial Economics, 104*(2), 339–362.
Hoff, K., & Stiglitz, J. E. (1998). Moneylenders and bankers: Price-increasing subsidies in a monopolistically competitive market. *Journal of Development Economics, 55*(2), 485–518.
Hung, A., Parker, A. M., & Yoong, J. (2009). *Defining and measuring financial literacy* (Working paper WR-708, RAND corporation).
Klapper, L., Lusardi, A., & Panos, G. A. (2013). Financial literacy and its consequences: Evidence from Russia during the financial crisis. *Journal of Banking & Finance, 37*(10), 3904–3923.
La Porta, R., Lopez-de Silanes, F., & Schleifer, A. (1999). Corporate ownership around the world. *Journal of Finance, 54*(2), 471–517.
Lhacer, P. M. (2012). *Cooperativas de Credito e Formação de Taxas de Juros nas Operações Bancárias: Tese e evidências empíricas para o Brasil.* Doctoral thesis, Fundação GetúlioVargas, Escola de Administração de Empresas de São Paulo, São Paulo.
Lopes, L. L. (2013). *Goals and the organization of choice under risk* (Working Paper). Available at: http://www.luc.edu/media/lucedu/quinlan-risk/pdfs/Lopes-Final.pdf.
Lopes, L. L., & Oden, G. C. (1999). The role of aspiration level in risky choice: A comparison of cumulative prospect theory and SP/A theory. *Journal of Mathematical Psychology, 43*(2), 286–313.
Lusardi, A. (2008). *Financial literacy: An essential tool for informed consumer choice?* Technical report, NBER.
Lusardi, A., & Mitchell, O. S. (2008). *Planning and financial literacy: How do women fare?* Technical report, NBER.
Lusardi, A., & Mitchell, O. S. (2009). *How ordinary consumers make complex economic decisions: Financial literacy and retirement readiness*. Technical report, National Bureau of Economic Research.
Lusardi, A., & Mitchell, O. S. (2011a). Financial literacy and retirement planning in the United States. *Journal of Pension Economics and Finance, 10*(4), 509–525.
Lusardi, A., & Mitchell, O. S. (2011b). Financial literacy around the world: An overview. *Journal of Pension Economics and Finance, 10*(04), 497–508.
Lusardi, A., & Mitchell, O. S. (2014). The economic importance of financial literacy: Theory and evidence. *Journal of Economic Literature, 52*(1), 5–44.
Lusardi, A., & Tufano, P. (2009). *Debt literacy, financial experiences, and overindebtedness*. Technical report, NBER.
Madestam, A. (2014). Informal finance: A theory of money lenders. *Journal of Development Economics, 107*, 157–174.
Melo, E. F. L., Franklin, S. L., Jr., & Neves, C. R. (2012). Mensuração do risco de sorteio em títulos de capitalização. *Brazilian Review of Finance, 10*(2), 197–213.
Modigliani, F., & Brumberg, R. (1954). Utility analysis and the consumption function: An interpretation of cross-section data. In *The collected papers of Franco Modigliani* (Vol. 6, pp. 3–46). London: MIT Press.
Neumann, L. J., & Morgenstern, O. (1947). *Theory of games and economic behavior*. Princeton: Princeton University Press.
Nicolosi, G., Peng, L., & Zhu, N. (2009). Do individual investors learn from their trading experience? *Journal of Financial Markets, 12*(2), 317–336.

OECD (2013). *Organisation for economic co-operation and development financial literacy and inclusion: Results of oecd/infe survey across countries and by gender*. http://www.oecd.org/daf/fin/financialeducation/.

Pagano, M. (2001). *Defusing default: Incentives and institutions*. Washington, DC: Johns Hopkins University Press.

Portocarrero, H. (2008). Títulos de capitalização e poupança financeira. *Revista Conjuntura Econômica, 62*(5), 64–67.

Rose, L. (2008). Financial literacy: Who cares? *New Zeland Management, 55*(5), 66.

Schiavini, J. M., Scherer, F. L., & Coronel, D. A. (2012). Understanding guanxi and its influence on international relations. *Revista de Economia Contemporânea, 16*(2), 316–332.

Schneider, F., Buehn, A., & Montenegro, C. E. (2010). New estimates for the shadow economies all over the world. *International Economic Journal, 24*(4), 443–461.

Seru, A., Shumway, T., & Stoffman, N. (2009). Learning by trading. *Review of Financial Studies, 23*(2), 705–739.

Sheng, H. H., & Mendes-Da-Silva, W. (2014). The big family: Informal financing of small-and medium-sized businesses by guanxi. *Thunderbird Int'l Business Review, 56*(2), 157–171.

Stolper, O. A., & Walter, A. (2017). Financial literacy, financial advice, and financial behavior. *Journal of Business Economics, 87*(5), 581–643.

SUSEP (2015). *Superintendência de seguros privados*. http://www.susep.gov.br/. Accessed 06 January 2015.

Thaler, R. H., & Tucker, W. (2013). Smarter information, smarter consumers. *Harvard Business Review, 91*, 44–56.

Tosi, P. G., Faleiros, R. N., & Teodoro, R. S. (2007). Crédito e pequena cafeicultura no oeste paulista: Franca/sp 1890–1914. *Revista Brasileira de Economia, 61*(3), 405–426.

Tosi, P. G., Faleiros, R. N., & Fontanari, R. (2011). Modalidades e hierarquias do crédito na cafeicultura paulista (1889–1930). *Revista Brasileira de Economia, 65*(4), 401–412.

Turvey, C. G., Kong, R., & Huo, X. (2010). Borrowing amongst friends: The economics of informal credit in rural China. *China Agricultural Economic Review, 2*(2), 133–147.

Van Rooij, M., Lusardi, A., & Alessie, R. (2011). Financial literacy and stock market participation. *Journal of Financial Economics, 101*, 449–472.

Willis, L. E. (2008). Against financial literacy education. *Iowa Law Review, 94*, 08–10.

Yuan, Y., & Gao, P. (2012). Farmers' financial choices and informal credit markets in China. *China Agricultural Economic Review, 4*(2), 216–232.

Chapter 8
Credit Card Risk Behavior in a High Interest Rate Context

Wesley Mendes-Da-Silva

Abstract College students frequently exhibit little skill for using credit cards in a responsible manner. This chapter examines this issue in an emerging market and in a pioneering manner. University students ($n = 769$), in a high interest rate context, replied to a questionnaire about their habits in credit card use. Logit models revealed associations between personal characteristics and credit card use habits that reflect financially risky behavior. The main results show (i) a larger number of credit cards increase the probability of risk behavior and (ii) those students who alleged awareness of the card's interest rates were less inclined to engage in risk behavior. These results might prove informative to the financial industry as well as university managers and policymakers. This chapter points to the advisability, indeed necessity, to inform students on responsible use of financial products (notably credit cards) emphasizing the associated high interest rates. The findings regarding student behavior for credit card usage in emerging economies are both significant and relevant. Furthermore, financial literature, while stressing the importance of the topic, has not significantly examined emerging economies.

Keywords Credit cards · Young adults · Consumers · Emerging market · Personal finance

JEL Code D14 · E51 · C91

Credit is one of the more interesting topics in financial innovation literature (Beck et al. 2016). Regarding credit, university students frequently face growing responsibilities, and the decisions they make at this point will often define their financial independence and have far-reaching consequences for their future well-being and security. Decision-making methods and citizens' financial habits, especially

Portions of this chapter appeared in the 2012 paper "Credit card risk behavior on college campuses: evidence from Brazil," *Brazilian Administration Review*, vol 47, pp 351–373.

W. Mendes-Da-Silva (✉)
Sao Paulo School of Business Administration (FGV/EAESP), Sao Paulo, SP, Brazil

University of Texas at Austin, Austin, TX, USA

W. Mendes-Da-Silva (ed.), *Individual Behaviors and Technologies for Financial Innovations*, https://doi.org/10.1007/978-3-319-91911-9_8

university students, have received considerable attention from both government and financial industry (Butaru et al. 2016). But, except for the United States, this issue has been studied in less depth in the finance community academic environment, notably in considering emerging markets.

Financial innovation plays a key role to promote societal well-being by reducing capital costs, promoting greater efficiency, and facilitating consumption control and investment decisions and provides considerable benefits for borrowers and investors alike, i.e., families, corporations, and governments (Sánchez 2010:27). Considering the high relevance of understanding future citizens' credit-related behavior, it seems imperative to throw light upon this subject through research. The main study objectives are to (i) identify and characterize which students are at most risk to mismanage and misuse credit cards, (ii) help students recognize the hidden consequences of financial mismanagement, and (iii) provide insight into educational resources and services that might help students better manage their credit card debt and other finances. To develop this research, in 2011 we collected 769 valid questionnaires completed by university students in Sao Paulo, Brazil's main financial center. In this context, the university's relevant role is apparent. Beyond representing a learning environment, the university, by necessity, also exercises certain influences over student behavior beyond academic coursework.

Without doubt, access to credit initiates a strong influence on one's lifestyle, providing convenience, social status, and purchasing power. However, the indiscriminate use of credit cards can have a considerably harmful effect on well-being (Bernthal et al. 2005). Young adults often experience negative reflections caused by poor financial behavior, which can introduce difficulties in academic performance and even compromise their physical and mental health (Lyons 2004, 2007).

According to economic psychology research, high levels of financial stress are highly associated with increased levels of psychological and physical stress (MacFadyen et al. 1996; Lyons and Yilmazer 2005). In this line of thought, studies have documented the high levels of student indebtedness, particularly among those who seek to finance their studies – whether by paying college fees or buying college materials – by placing these purchases against credit card financing (Nellie Mae 2005). Such behavior can result in a panorama of high indebtedness that has, in some cases, even led students to commit suicide. In the United States, government and school managers have introduced restrictions on requests for credit cards on college campuses (Norvilitis and Santa Maria 2002).

This study contributes a pioneering effort in the finance field to provide empirical evidence of the associations between university student profiles and the occurrence of risk behavior in the use of credit cards in an emerging market. From the 769 valid responses collected in São Paulo/Brazil, using logit models, the main results suggest that financial education may contribute to positive behavior for credit card usage. These findings are of essential interest to public policymakers (Mansfield and Pinto 2007), the financial industry (Fogel and Schneider 2011), and school managers (Lyons 2007).

This chapter presents highlights from research referencing a unique data set to examine young adults' credit behavior in a high interest rate environment. The method used in this study is similar to that of Lyons (2004), and the findings provide insight into how financial professionals, educators, and campus administrators can provide more effective financial education to young adults, especially in the context of high interest rates. The chapter closes with recommendations and suggestions for future research.

Background

Over the last two decades, there has been an increase in the use of credit cards by university students (Nellie Mae 2005; US General Accountability Office 2001; Manning 2000), making it necessary to better understand the behavior of this particular public. In the last decade, the volume of credit in the Brazilian economy has grown strongly. According to studies by the Brazilian National Finance System, between January 2004 and January 2011, the bank lending/gross domestic product ratio increased from 24.3% to 46.5%. At the same time, the volume of credit went from ~R$417.8 billion to ~R$1.71 trillion, essentially due to growth in the personal credit portfolio, which represented ~38% of all lending. At the end of this same period, it reached ~46% of the credit stock, at ~R$787.1 billion (Depec 2011). When this is associated with credit card market growth (see Fig. 8.1), it becomes possible to arrive at a reasonable estimate for the size of the card industry.

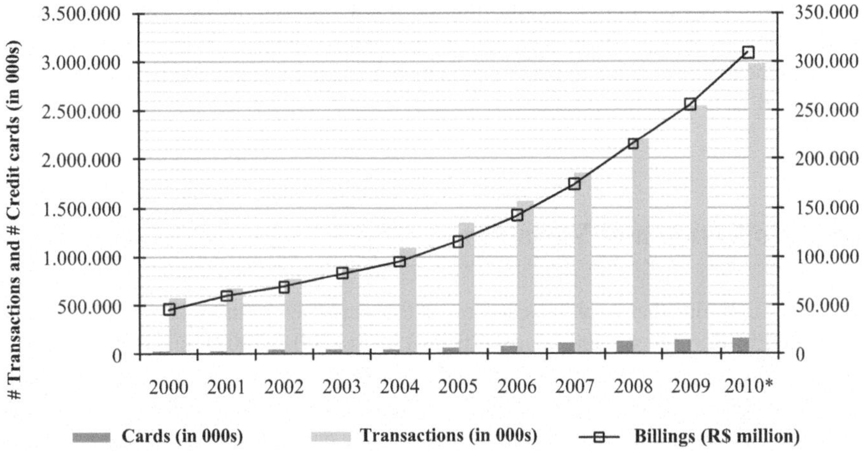

Fig. 8.1 Evolution of credit card use statistics in Brazil. Note: This graph shows the evolution of three measures relating to credit card use in Brazil: # Credit cards (in 000 s); # Transactions (in 000 s); billings (in R$ million). Between 2000 and 2009 (*the numbers for 2010, as at the latest version of this paper, were still estimates), there was a strong growth in the credit card market in Brazil. Throughout this period, therefore, for the # Credit cards: $\Delta\% = 379\%$; # Transactions: $\Delta\% = 346\%$; and billings: $\Delta\% = 460\%$. (Source: Based on data from the ABECS-Brazilian Association of Credit Card and Service Companies (2011))

The line of work that is supported by the traditional life-cycle theory with budgetary restrictions, as proposed by Modigliani (1998), provides provocative insights into citizens' financial decisions, including the intergenerational transfer of financial behavior, i.e., the reasons why students get into debt (Lyons, Scherpf and Neelakantan 2007). The conceptual model of this research assumes that an individual's financial behavior impacts their well-being beyond the personal finance area, including repercussions on their mental and physical health, academic performance, and satisfaction with life (Xiao, Noring and Anderson 1995; Kahneman et al. 2006).

Studies relating to credit card use will usually combine knowledge from different fields, e.g., economics, sociology, and psychology, following a connected domain approach, which is also sought in this study. Two approaches can be found in these works. One line focuses on social and economic psychology to explore student attitudes, perceptions, and behavior vis-a-vis credit cards and money in general (Hayhoe 2002; Roberts and Jones 2001; Kidwell and Turrisi 2000; Danes and Hira 1987; Fan and Xiao 1998; Markovich and Devaney 1997; Masuo et al. 2004; Rindfleisch et al. 1997). The other line of work deals more specifically with student behavior in regard to credit cards, using applied economics concepts to document associations between demographic aspects and habits in credit card use (Allen and Jover 1997; Lawrence et al. 2006; Xiao, Noring and Anderson 1995; Joo et al. 2003; US General Accountability Office 2001; Hayhoe 2002; Lyons 2004, 2007). This work follows the latter line of thinking.

In Brazilian literature no significant attention has yet been paid to the theme of consumer behavior relative to credit card services. To our knowledge, only one piece of research exists in this area, which was carried out by Veludo-de-Oliveira et al. (2004), who concentrate on exploring personal characteristics. There are other studies that support a structured analysis of the formation of financial behavior and how this behavior extends to impact on the well-being of young adults, as presented in Table 8.1.

Data Collection and Variables

The questionnaire that enabled capture of the variables used in this research was translated to Portuguese and adapted from Lyons (2004, 2007) and is accordingly divided into three parts: (i) the use and knowledge of aspects relating to credit, (ii) financial education, and (iii) social profile. Before being applied to the respondent set, the questionnaire was submitted to ten experienced credit card professionals, working in eight different firms that use credit risk analysis, to identify necessary adjustments to the Brazilian reality.

After 15 days of analysis, the senior analysts' views were consolidated into a decision to adapt two variables of risk behavior to the Brazilian market, i.e., (i) the debts retained the balance about R$ 1000.00 and (ii) the number of cards equal to or greater than three. Data were collected in February and March 2011 from university

Table 8.1 Summary of the main empirical works on the credit behavior of university students

Author	Objective	Method	Key results
Fogel and Schneider (2011)	To check associations between the student's profile and risk behavior with money	Application of ANOVA and ANCOVA from a survey of 301 students in New York	The bigger the income, the greater the compulsive buying and money worries
Veludo-de-Oliveira et al. (2004)	To investigate the influence of credit cards on compulsive buying behavior	Exploratory study (using the Likert scale) with 188 young adults in São Paulo/Brazil	Young adults with a propensity for compulsiveness use credit cards more intensely
Masuo et al. (2004)	To analyze the beliefs and behavior of students with regard to money	Factor analysis with 290 Asian and North American university students, exploring intercultural constructs	Three factors were identified: power, security, and finances. Asians strongly believe that money brings power and security
Pinto et al. (2001)	To check if the academic performance of students is in any way associated with their behavior when using credit cards	Survey of 260 students (groups classified as high/low academic performance) from three universities in the United States	No association was found between academic performance and behavior in the use of credit cards
Hayhoe et al. (2000)	To check feelings about the credit cards that students use	OLS regression. $N = 480$, with students in the United States	Women tend to spend more on clothes, while men buy more electronic goods. The gender variable has more influence on the forecast of financial management practices than on the actual attitude to credit
Hayhoe et al. (1999)	To check the reasons for using credit cards	Logit regression and OLS, with 480 students in the United States	The significant predictors were actual attitude to credit, age, the cognitive attitude to credit, and gender
Fan and Xiao (1998)	To study the profile of young adult Chinese as to the way they take buying decisions	Comparative study using factor analysis, taken from 271 questionnaires applied in 5 Chinese universities	There was a similar dimension and profile of the decision-making process between Chinese students and the results obtained with South Korean and US students
Rindfleisch et al. (1997)	To analyze associations between family structure and attitude toward consumption	Analysis by MANOVA, with 138 questionnaires	Family structure is related both to materialism and compulsive consumption
Danes and Hira (1987)	To describe student knowledge of financial administration, explaining their skill differences as a function of this knowledge	Pearson correlation and least squares correlation, from data collected from 323 respondents	On average, students need greater financial knowledge. Their knowledge about insurance, credit, and other areas of finance was superficial

students from different higher education institutions in São Paulo (Brazil's main financial center), who were approached at random on university campuses.

As assumed by Lyons (2004), participating students were classified as being financially risky when at least one of the following four characteristics was found; these constituted the *dependent variables* (dummy, with a value = 1 when risk behavior was found and zero if not): (i) the debit balance on the credit card is currently greater than or equal to R$ 1000.00 (see Q4); while this variable might be better represented as a percentage of household income (or individual), due to students being unwilling to inform the family income in survey, we use the value of $ 1000; we see that choice as problematic in view of homogeneity of the participants demographic group; (ii) delinquency in paying the bill by 60 days or more in the last 2 years (see Q5); (iii) used the full limit of the credit card within the past 2 years (see Q7); and (iv) within the past 2 years, pays the full amount of the statement either sporadically or never (Q6). Based on these four, a fifth dependent variable was obtained: (v) displays at least one of these four behaviors.

As *independent variables* (dummy), 22 factors are used (listed in Table 8.2), organized into three groups, namely, (i) demographic aspects, (ii) financial behavior, and (iii) types of credit card use. It is worth pointing out that some factors may be endogenous. However, data limitations eliminated the ability to obtain instruments for controlling for the possibility of endogeneity. It is therefore assumed that these values can be exogenously determined. The error term, u_i, is assumed as being normally distributed, with a mean of zero and a variance equal to 1.

Empirical Model

We use two test procedures, in addition to descriptive statistics: (i) nonparametric tests of independence (which showed independence between family income and adoption of risky behaviors in the use of credit card) and (ii) analysis of logit models, intended to estimate the likelihood of risky behavior by the respondent profile. As mentioned, binary response nonlinear regression models are used in this research. The two most widely used approaches in financial literature for this purpose are the *logit* and *probit* models, with the first being widely used for convenience (mathematical), bearing in mind the practicality for interpreting the estimated parameters (Dietrich and Sorensen 1984; Aldrich and Nelson 1984).

The estimated parameters in the regressions may be assumed from the descriptive (to the extent that they try to describe the nature of associations between the mean response, i.e., the probability of a student having a high debit balance, e.g., with the 22 regressor variables) and predictive (i.e., to estimate if a student will assume risk behavior, given his demographic profile and his credit card use habits) points of view. The logistic function (for the case of a single predictor variable) is given by the expression (8.1), as follows:

Table 8.2 Frequency (in %) of the profile variables of the respondents (in accordance with the risk extracts of the individuals)

Independent variables of the regressions (all dummies with the value = 1 if the affirmation was seen)	All students ($N = 769$)	Students with cc ($N = 552$)	No risk with cc ($N = 358$)	At risk with cc ($N = 195$)	Groups of students at risk ($N = 195$)			
					Debts on credit card ≥ R$1000 ($N = 104$)	Delay in paying cc bills ($N = 49$)	Does not pay full amount of card bill ($N = 76$)	Uses full limit of credit card ($N = 51$)
Demographics								
Male	49.0	47.5	43.6	54.3	53.8	40.8	44.7	54.9
In relationship	5.0	4.6	3.1	7.1	12.9	6.5	2.7	3.9
Family lives in own home	90.7	91.0	92.7	87.5	90.3	81.6	84.0	88.0
1st generation to do degree	10.1	10.7	9.6	12.3	11.8	17.0	13.5	8.0
Lives in rented property/resid. hall	17.0	16.8	16.0	18.1	16.0	19.6	17.3	18.0
Obtained cc during/after college	44.6	62.2	62.9	60.8	60.6	63.3	60.5	52.9
Financial behavior								
Financially independent of parents	24.1	26.3	22.2	33.3	40.4	38.8	34.7	28.0
Has 3 or more cc	12.2	17.0	12.0	26.1	34.6	28.6	23.7	25.5
Financial situation affects concentration	16.8	17.0	13.1	24.0	26.2	25.5	31.1	26.0
Sleeping diff. because of finances in past	21.1	21.1	16.3	29.2	35.6	31.2	37.3	26.0
Would do pers. finance course online	70.5	70.5	69.5	72.0	76.0	80.4	76.3	76.5
Would do pers. finance course at univ.	81.6	81.5	82.4	79.6	81.0	87.0	81.3	80.4
Knows cc interest rates	30.9	43.3	49.9	31.0	26.2	27.1	24.0	28.6
Uses cc to pay expenses of								
Education (e.g., books)	17.0	23.7	24.6	22.0	31.7	16.3	21.1	19.6
Clothes and pers. items	46.2	63.9	66.8	58.4	65.4	53.1	52.6	60.8
Meals	28.3	39.5	41.6	35.3	40.4	26.5	31.6	29.4
Entertainment (e.g., cinema and theater)	37.7	52.4	53.1	50.7	47.1	46.9	47.4	47.1
Automobiles (e.g., fuel and maintenance)	20.2	27.9	25.1	32.8	44.2	20.4	22.4	27.5
Travel	19.0	26.1	26.0	26.1	40.4	14.3	19.7	19.6

(continued)

Table 8.2 (continued)

					Groups of students at risk ($N = 195$)			
Independent variables of the regressions (all dummies with the value = 1 if the affirmation was seen)	All students ($N = 769$)	Students with cc ($N = 552$)	No risk with cc ($N = 358$)	At risk with cc ($N = 195$)	Debts on credit card ≥ R$1000 ($N = 104$)	Delay in paying cc bills ($N = 49$)	Does not pay full amount of card bill ($N = 76$)	Uses full limit of credit card ($N = 51$)
Rent	1.6	2.2	2.0	2.5	3.8	6.1	2.6	2.0
Payment of accounts generally	4.9	6.9	6.1	8.2	9.6	14.3	10.5	5.9
Diverse expenses	6.5	9.1	6.4	13.8	20.2	12.2	14.5	9.8

Note: % calculated based on valid frequencies (i.e., ignoring missing values). "Students with cc" represents students who have at least one credit card; "No risk with cc" identifies students who have a credit card but who have no risk behavior; "At risk with cc" identifies students who have a credit card and at least one risk behavior. The remaining columns classify students by risk behavior

$$E(Y_i|X_i) = \pi_i = \frac{exp(\beta_0 + \beta_1 X_i)}{1 + exp(\beta_0 + \beta_1 X_i)} \therefore \frac{1}{1 + e^{-(\beta_0 + \beta_1 X_i)}} \quad (8.1)$$

which is equivalent to (8.2):

$$E(Y_i|X_i) = \pi_i = [1 + exp(-\beta_0 - \beta_1 X_i)]^{-1} \quad (8.2)$$

However, in the case of a binary response regression model, comprising k regressors, we have (8.3):

$$E(Y_i|X_i) = \pi_i = [1 + exp(-\boldsymbol{\beta}'\boldsymbol{X})]^{-1} \quad (8.3)$$

with:

$$\boldsymbol{\beta}'\boldsymbol{X} = \beta_0 + \beta_1 X_1 + \beta_2 X_2 + \cdots + \beta_k X_k \quad (8.4)$$

Exploratory Analysis

Examining Fig. 8.2, it can be seen that the whole group ($N = 769$) of respondents (whether they have a credit card or not), both male and female, attributed great relevance to issues relating to (i) investments, (ii) credit cards, and (iii) private pension schemes. Also, there is a broad scope for training citizens in the areas of savings, investments, and private pensions, notably when the group of female respondents is considered. With respect to the relevance and level of alleged knowledge of financial products on the part of the participating students, Fig. 8.2

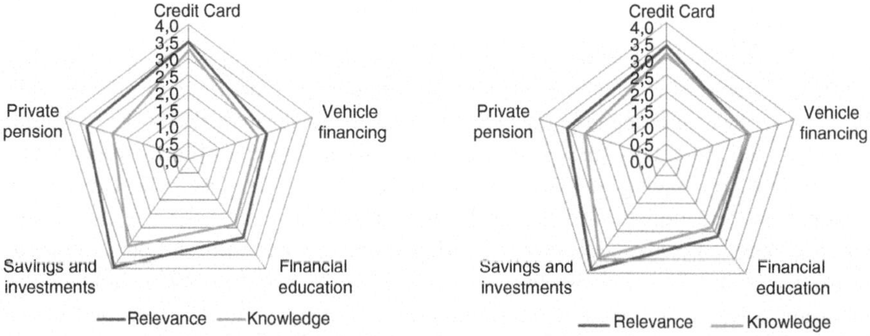

Fig. 8.2 Perception of the relevance and knowledge of financial products (as judged by the respondent students). Note: The graph on the left represents the average values for the relevance and knowledge (self-declared) of financial products on the part of female respondents and on the right are the responses from male students. The points scale considers 1 (no relevance/knowledge) to 5 (a lot of relevance/knowledge). Female respondents ($N = 392[51\%]$); male respondents ($N = 377[49\%]$)

shows the picture for both male and female individuals. The Mann-Whitney U test revealed an independence between *gender* and the *relevance attributed* by the respondents. In the case of financial *product knowledge*, independence was also observed between these variables, with the exception of financing vehicles and savings and investments ($p < 0.01$; $N = 769$). This suggests that male individuals, to a significant extent, tended to allege greater knowledge of these two financial products. Of the 552 students who had credit cards, 195 were classified as having at least one risk behavior, representing approximately 35.3%. In this sense, 136 (~69.7%) of the 195 respondents identified as "at risk" were classified in just 1 of the 4 possible behaviors; 38 students were classified in 2 risk behaviors simultaneously; 16 students had 3 behaviors, and only 5 of the 194 students alleged having four risk behaviors.

Also in Table 8.2, it can be seen that the majority of respondents are female (~51%). Females also comprise the majority of the 552 students observed to have credit cards (~52.5%). However, male students are in the majority (54.6%) – compared with 45.0% found by Lyons (2004) in the North American market – among students who use credit cards and display one or more of the risk behaviors considered in this research.

Logit Regressions

The quality of the results obtained was analyzed, based on four measures: (i) R^2 of MacFadden (Aldrich and Nelson 1984), (ii) percentage of events classified correctly, (iii) likelihood ratio, and (iv) homoscedastic error term test, u_i, of the regression. The first two measures are used to illustrate the adjustment level of the estimated model, and the third indicates whether the explanatory variables have a joint effect on the dependent variable. The last measure is a diagnosis to check the validity of the results obtained.

Tables 8.3 and 8.4 show the simulation results. The upper rows show the estimated coefficients for the explanatory models of the *dependent variables* ($y = 1$): (i) having a negative balance equal to or greater than R$1000, (ii) failing to pay the bill punctually for at least 2 months, (iii) not paying off the credit card bill in full, and (iv) having at least one of the risk behaviors observed. The results obtained in the simulation of the explanatory model of one of the five dependent variables studied were suppressed, i.e., when someone uses full limit of credit card, bearing in mind that their results were judged to be insignificant in light of the measures adopted for diagnosing the quality of the models. The first columns of Tables 8.2 and 8.3 give the 22 *independent variables*. To the right of each independent variable are the respective estimated β_i parameter, the standard error, and the significance, which suggests the marginal effect on the conditional probability of the dependent variable.

With regard to the arguments defended by researchers like Joo et al. (2003), who assume that maintaining significant credit card debt balances constitutes risk behavior on the part of students, Table 8.2 shows substantial signs that students who have

Table 8.3 Probability (logit) of students adopting financial risks with debt and the punctual payment of bills (students with credit cards)

Variable	Credit card debt ≥ R$1000			Payment past due date (more than 2 months)	
	Marginal effect	Standard error		Marginal effect	Standard error
Constant	−3.0360	0.7531	***	−2.0054	0.9308
1. Has more than 3 cc	1.5156	0.3005	***	0.7456	0.3843
2. Obtained cc during/after university	−0.2668	0.2924		0.0886	0.3836
3. Knows cc interest rates	−0.7748	0.2846	***	−0.4886	0.3704
4. Uses cc to pay education expenses	0.0335	0.3387		−0.5533	0.5757
5. Uses cc to buy clothes and personal items	−0.0241	0.3076		−0.5045	0.3997
6. Uses cc to buy meals	−0.1570	0.3470		−0.2931	0.4100
7. Uses cc for entertainment expenses	−0.0595	0.3207		0.1710	0.3900
8. Uses cc for automobile expenses	0.8376	0.2934	***	−0.5176	0.4943
9. Uses cc for travel expenses	0.5517	0.3009	*	−0.8551	0.5728
10. Uses cc for rent expenses	−1.0644	1.0311		1.9090	0.8391
11. Uses cc to pay bills in general	0.5445	0.5041		0.8956	0.5922
12. Uses cc for other expenses	0.9038	0.3371	***	0.4886	0.5137
13. Would take a personal finance course at university	−0.2869	0.4037		0.3633	0.4928
14. Would do an online personal finance course	0.5715	0.3698		0.5950	0.4402
15. Male	0.3679	0.2799		−0.5960	0.3563
16. In a relationship	1.0770	0.6318	*	0.3636	0.8224
17. 1st generation in family to university	−0.3965	0.4737		0.3733	0.4367
18. Financially independent of parents	0.5985	0.3059	*	0.4456	0.3727
19. Lives in residence hall or rented property	0.0092	0.4413		−0.4928	0.5863
20. Family lives in own house	0.5001	0.5057		−0.7554	0.5168
21. Financial situation affects study concentration	0.3990	0.3699		0.4083	0.4065
22. Has had trouble sleeping because of finance situation	0.4161	0.3389		0.0214	0.4002
N with $y = 1$ (Total num. considered in simulation)	95	(496)		41	(496)
R^2 of McFadden	0.1991			0.1310	
% of correct classifications	83.5%			92.1%	
Akaike's information criterion	434.0570			291.8502	
χ^2 likelihood ratio test	96.4727	***		37.0896	**

Notes: This table shows the results obtained for the estimated coefficients for the logit model for the two dependent variables (of the four used in this research). The initial set of data comprised 769 respondents, of whom 552 had a credit card; after discarding incomplete observations, the number N of observations used in the regressions was smaller (reported in the lower part of the Table). The standard error for each marginal effect is indicated in the column to the right of each coefficient

cc credit card

The *p*-values are represented by $*p < 0.10$; $**p < 0.05$; $***p < 0.01$. The estimates were obtained with a robust standard error, using the procedure suggested by Davidson and Mackinnon (2004)

Table 8.4 Probability (logit) being financially risky with regard to full payment and presenting some risk behavior (students with credit cards)

Variable	Partial bill payment only Marginal effect	Standard error		Having risk behavior Marginal effect	Standard error	
Constant	−0.3732	0.7171		−0.5008	0.5428	
1. Has more than 3 cc	0.5047	0.3405		1.2102	0.2914	***
2. Obtained cc during/after university	−0.4944	0.3060		−0.2201	0.2246	
3. Knows cc interest rates	−0.7923	0.3101	**	−0.6555	0.2167	***
4. Uses cc to pay education expenses	0.0496	0.3710		−0.1662	0.2715	
5. Uses cc to buy clothes and personal items	−0.6459	0.2993	**	−0.3295	0.2340	
6. Uses cc to buy meals	−0.3268	0.3573		−0.2889	0.2516	
7. Uses cc for entertainment expenses	−0.2197	0.3340		0.0224	0.2393	
8. Uses cc for automobile expenses	−0.1993	0.3641		0.4834	0.2507	*
9. Uses cc for travel expenses	−0.4895	0.3857		−0.1701	0.2414	
10. Uses cc for rent expenses	−0.1293	0.9516		−0.7683	0.7537	
11. Uses cc to pay bills in general	0.7997	0.5703		0.5068	0.4066	
12. Uses cc for other expenses	0.6159	0.4179		0.6155	0.3296	*
13. Would take a personal finance course at university	−0.5036	0.3537		−0.4505	0.3013	
14. Would do an online personal finance course	0.2541	0.3463		0.3591	0.2703	
15. Male	−0.2309	0.3091		0.4686	0.2215	**
16. In a relationship	−2.0612	0.7731	***	0.3282	0.5349	
17. 1st generation in family to university	0.2567	0.4289		−0.0830	0.3620	
18. Financially independent of parents	0.4515	0.3048		0.4486	0.2421	*
19. Lives in residence hall or rented property	−0.2591	0.4349		0.0844	0.3115	
20. Family lives in own house	−0.3700	0.4520		−0.2310	0.3672	
21. Financial situation affects study concentration	0.8222	0.4034	**	0.6698	0.3480	*
22. Has had trouble sleeping because of finance situation	0.4287	0.3793		0.2265	0.3020	
N with $y = 1$ (total N considered in simulation)	70	(496)		172	(496)	
R^2 of McFadden	0.1254			0.1222		
% of correct classification	86.7%			71.6%		
Akaike's criterion	399,1068			608,0205		
χ^2 Likelihood ratio test	50,6449	***		78,2429	***	

Notes: This table shows the results obtained for the estimated coefficients for the logit model for two dependent variables (not paying off the whole of the bill and having at least one risk behavior in the use of a credit card). The initial set of data comprised 769 respondents, of whom 552 had credit

(continued)

cards; after discarding incomplete observations, the number N of observations used in the regressions was smaller (reported in the lower part of the table). The standard error for each marginal effect is indicated in the column to the right of each coefficient
The *p*-values are represented by $*p<0.10$; $**p<0.05$; $***p<0.01$. Estimates were obtained with a robust standard error, using the procedure suggested by Davidson and Mackinnon (2004). According to the verisimilitude ratio test ($\chi^2 = 19.0521$), the model estimated for use of the full limit of the credit card seemed not to be very significant. *cc* credit card. The parameters estimated for the fourth risk behavior, the fact that the student fully uses his credit card limit, were suppressed because they did not give satisfactory results for the adjustment measures used in this research

more than three credit cards ($\beta_1 \cong 1.5156$; $p < 0.01$) tend to be more likely to have debit balances over R$1,000.00. This result also supports the theory of Black (2001), for whom individuals who have a large numbers of credit cards tend to adopt compulsive purchasing behaviors, acquiring goods and services that are of little use (Roberts and Jones 2001).

Accordingly, in the study of Norvilitis and MacLean (2010) which support the idea that young adults may hold an incentive to use credit cards to increase their well-being, we find that to be financially independent of parents seems to have a marginal positive effect ($\beta_{18} \cong 0.5985$, $p < 0.1$) on the propensity to maintain high outstanding balances on credit card. Therefore, students seem inclined to agree to pay interest on the maintenance of the balance due, even if they do not know the high interest rates charged in Brazil ($\beta_3 \cong -0.7748$, $p < 0.01$) in the name of a possible increase in well-being. This fact is confirmed by the estimated coefficients for the way they use credit cards, i.e., (i) general expenses ($\beta_{12} \cong 0.9038$, $p < 0.01$), (ii) travel expenses, and automobile expenses ($\beta_9 \cong 0.5985$, $p < 0.1$; $\beta_8 \cong 0.8376$, $p < 0.01$).

Therefore, these individuals seem to pursue reducing their high levels of anxiety or even to acquire social status, acceptance, and recognition in their social group by means of consumption that is not very rational (John 1999). In addition, students who are in a relationship seem to have a greater propensity for assuming large debt balances ($\beta_{16} \cong 1.0770$; $p < 0.1$). The estimated model for the probability of maintaining a debit balance equal to or greater than R$1000.00 (see Table 8.3) received a correct classification percentage of events close to 83.5%, and the likelihood ratio test ($\chi^2 = 96.4727$; $p < 0.01$) suggests that the explanatory variables together seem to exercise a significant marginal effect on the dependent variable. As found in the simulations of the model whose dependent variable was the maintenance of balance due on your credit card, when considered in the habit of delaying an invoiced card payment (the fourth column of Table 8.3), individuals possessing three or more cards showed more likely to behave less responsible ($\beta_2 \cong 0.7456$, $p < 0.1$). In this same model, males were less often seen to adopt this behavior ($\beta_{15} \cong -0.5960$, $p < 0.1$), ceteris paribus.

Table 8.4 presents the results for two dependent variables that define the behavior seen as risky: (i) partial payment of the credit card bill and (ii) exhibiting one or more of four risk behaviors. Here we emphasize that one of the behaviors seen as risky did not achieve significant results, so we chose not to report estimates. Among the results obtained for partial payment, we note that individuals who are in a stable relationship were less likely to make partial payments ($\beta_{16} \cong -2.0612, p < 0.01$). And, as found for the maintenance of debit balances, the fact of knowing the interest rates exerted a negative marginal effect on the probability of realizing partial payments of credit card bills ($\beta_3 \cong -0.7923$, $p < 0.05$). This result is in line with the idea of higher levels of financial literacy can lead young adults to engage in more responsible and balanced use of credit card.

Table 8.4 shows that individuals who allege to know the interest rates charged by the credit card administrators seem to have a significant association ($\beta_3 \cong -0.6555$; $p < 0.01$) with at least one of the four risk behaviors considered in this research. In other words, the marginal effect caused by the fact of knowing the interest rates reduces the probability of assuming risk behavior.

This suggests that a better level of education in personal finance may constitute a means of reducing the number of students at risk from using credit cards. Put another way, making students more aware of the cost of capital accessed by credit cards may reduce their likelihood of using this type of funding; this line of argument supports the arguments of authors like Agarwal and Liu (2003). Furthermore, Brazil is considered to be a market whose basic interest rate is one of the highest in the world (see Fig. 8.3).

Also with regard to what is reported in Table 8.3, in line with what Black (2001) suggests, it seems that having a larger number of credit cards is associated with a greater likelihood of the student adopting some risk behavior ($\beta_1 \cong 1.2102$; $p < 0.01$). The number of cards was significantly associated with risk behavior in three of the four models reported in this section. The biggest marginal effect on the dependent variable was found in the explanatory model of the behavior of having a debit balance on the credit card equal to or greater than R$ 1000.00 ($\beta_1 \cong 1.5156$;

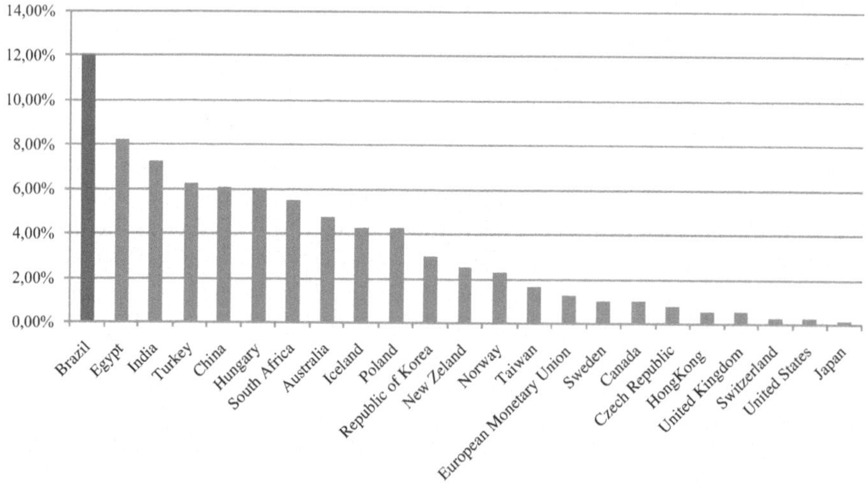

Fig. 8.3 Current annual interest rates around the world in May 2011. (Source: Elaborated by author based data from Bloomberg)

$p < 0.01$), as detailed in Table 8.2. According to Woodruffe (1997), students with this type of behavior look for well-being vis-à-vis a reduction in high levels of anxiety. In short, according to the student's behavioral orientation, the use of the credit card may constitute an attempt to hide difficulties and weaknesses relating to their personality (Faber and Christenson 1996). By way of illustration and interpretation of the coefficients estimated as significant, the probability of an individual having at least one risk behavior (see Table 8.3) would be approximately expressed as follows (8.5):

$$\ln\left(\frac{\pi_i}{1-\pi_i}\right) = -0.5008 + 1.2102\beta_1 + \cdots + 0.6698\beta_{21} \tag{8.5}$$

Therefore, the probability, π_i, that a student ($\beta_{15} = 0$) who is financially independent ($\beta_{18} = 1$), is aware that their financial situation can affect their academic performance ($\beta_{21} = 1$), has more than three credit cards ($\beta_1 = 1$), knows the interest rates charged by their operator ($\beta_3 = 1$), and is used to using their credit card to pay automobile expenses ($\beta_8 = 1$) in addition to other bills ($\beta_{12} = 1$) would adopt at least one of the risk behaviors would be calculated according to the following expression (8.6).

$$\pi_i = \frac{1}{1+e^{-\pi}} \therefore \frac{1}{1+2.718^{-(1.21-0.65+0.48+0.61+0+0.44+0.66)}} \therefore \pi_i \cong 0.9411 \tag{8.6}$$

Along this same line of thinking, in regard to how the financial situation might impact academic performance and well-being, observing the results of the estimates summarized in Table 8.3, it can be noted that the probability of the student not paying off the whole of the bill ($\beta_{21} = 0.8222$; $p < 0.05$) and the probability of having at least one of the risk behaviors being looked at ($\beta_{21} = 0.6698$; $p < 0.1$) are significantly greater among those who perceive that their credit card debts have compromised their concentration.

These results support the ideas argued by Norvilitis and Santa Maria (2002) that individuals who adopt risk behavior tend to have a greater stress level, which in some cases is the reason for them committing suicide. This thinking supports the premise that positive credit card behaviors constitute a means of maximizing well-being, to the extent that this financial instrument can offer convenience (Bernthal, Crockett and Rose 2005).

Regarding the behavior of the subjects according to sex and marital status, the evidence suggests that individuals involved in stable relationships tend to have higher debt balances ($\beta_{16} \cong 1.0770$, $p < 0.1$), but try to keep the full payment of their invoices ($\beta_{16} \cong -2.0612$, $p < 0.01$), and the behavior of keeping outstanding balances was significant, but with $p < 0.1$ and at a lower marginal effect. In addition, male subjects were less likely to delay payments ($\beta_{15} \cong -0.5960$, $p < 0.1$) but more likely to take at least one risk behavior ($\beta_{15} \cong 0.4686$, $p < 0.05$).

Concluding Remarks

The primary research objective in this study was to check for associations between university student profiles in the main financial center of a prominent emerging market, São Paulo/Brazil, and risk behavior in credit card usage. To this end, researchers employed the regressions' procedure with a binary response variable (logit models). Some 769 valid questionnaires were collected, of which 552 respondents alleged to both have and use credit cards. There were two main empirical results.

First, the estimated parameters in the regressions suggest that having multiple credit cards may significantly influence students' likelihood to develop behaviors seen as risky when using this financial instrument, as Black (2001) argues. Second, there are significant indications that financial education can influence students' behavior, vis-a-vis their propensity for adopting risky behavior in credit card use. In other words, students who alleged they knew the interest rates charged by the card administrators were, on average, less likely to adopt risky behaviors. Finally, questions related to the amount of family income met with significant resistance (62% of participants did not respond or did not know). However, only 15% of respondents claimed that their parents pay their credit card bills, suggesting that students are usually responsible to pay for their credit card purchases. Or rather, assuming that the participants are college age, it is understood that control regarding the level of family income does not compromise the results of this study.

Future Directions

Regarding possible research limitations inherent to this study, we have as follows: (i) data collection was restricted to a particular moment in the economy and to a metropolitan region with explicit peculiarities; (ii) a fairly homogenous respondent public, e.g., age and income level, which makes it difficult to generalize from empirical findings; and (iii) the trustworthiness of the responses collected from the respondent public.

Some of the practical implications of this research include (i) financial education on the university campus can promote positive financial behavior, which directly increases student well-being; (ii) students need to better understand the importance of savings and credit management, thus avoiding risky behavior with credit card use; (iii) there is a role for financial teachers, and college administrators can encourage students to develop positive financial behavior, e.g., by developing integration programs between parents and their children; and (iv) financial education programs can pay special attention to how to approach financially at-risk students, e.g., forming groups with specific relevant topics.

The issues previously highlighted, as well as the inherent limitations of the research design, are linked with the lack of studies that consider the Brazilian situation and suggest a promising research field in finance. The following approaches are suggested for future research: (i) test the models presented here by expanding the set of respondents, especially in terms of the age groups and social strata (examining groups other than college students); (ii) check for associations between individual profiles and the decision to use credit card services, since some people decide not to do so, even though there is reasonable consensus that this financial product enables a diversity of aspects that contribute to greater comfort and security in issues relating to consumption; (iii) analyze the role of teaching institutions in delivering financial knowledge to university students; and (iv) explore the behavior differences in the use of credit cards between different markets, as advocated by Allen and Jover (1997) and Butaru et al. (2016).

References

ABECS. (2011). Brazilian Association of Credit Card and Service Companies [Associação Brasileira das Empresas de Cartões de Crédito e Serviços]. Available at: http://www.abecs.org.br/

Agarwal, S., & Liu, C. (2003). Determinants of credit card delinquency and bankruptcy: Macroeconomics factors. *Journals of Economics and Finance, 27*(1), 75–84.

Aldrich, J. H., & Nelson, F. D. (1984). *Linear probability, logit, and probit models*. Beverly Hills: Sage.

Allen, J. L., & Jover, M. A. (1997). Credit card behavior of university students: Ethnic differences. *Consumer Interest Annual, 43*, 162–170.

Beck, T., Chen, T., Lin, C., & Song, F. M. (2016). Financial innovation: The bright and the dark sides. *Journal of Banking & Finance, 72*, 28–51.

Bernthal, M. J., Crockett, D., & Rose, R. L. (2005). Credit cards as lifestyle facilitators. *Journal of Consumer Research, 32*(1), 130–145.

Black, D. (2001). Compulsive buying disorder: Definition, assessment, epidemiology and clinical management. *CNS Drugs, 15*(1), 17–27.

Butaru, F., Chen, Q., Clark, B., Das, S., Lo, A. W., & Siddique, A. (2016). Risk and risk management in the credit card industry. *Journal of Banking & Finance, 72*, 218–239.

Danes, S. M., & Hira, T. K. (1987). Money management knowledge of college students. *Journal of Student Financial Aid, 17*(1), 4–16.

Davidson, R., & Mackinnon, J. G. (2004). *Econometric theory and methods*. New York: Oxford University Press.

DEPEC, Departamento De Pesquisas Econômicas Do Bradesco. (2011). *DestaqueDepec*, No. 10, Year IX, April.

Dietrich, J. K., & Sorensen, E. (1984). An application of logit analysis to prediction of merger targets. *Journal of Business Research, 12*(3), 393 402.

Faber, R., & Christenson, G. (1996). In the mood to buy: Differences in the mood states experienced by compulsive buyers and other consumers. *Psychology & Marketing, 13*(8), 803–819.

Fan, J. X., & Xiao, J. J. (1998). Decision making styles of young Chinese adults. *Journal of Consumer Affairs, 32*(2), 275–293.

Fogel, J., & Schneider, M. (2011). Credit card use: Disposable income and employment status. *Young Consumers: Insight and Ideas for Responsible Marketers, 12*(1), 5–14.

Hayhoe, C. R. (2002). Comparison of affective credit attitude scores and credit use of college student at two points in time. *Journal of Family and Consumer Science, 94*(1), 71–77.

Hayhoe, C. R., Leach, L. J., & Turner, P. R. (1999). Discriminating the number of credit cards held by college students using credit and money attitudes. *Journal of Economic Psychology, 20*(6), 643–656.

Hayhoe, C. R., Leach, L. J., Turner, P. R., Bruin, M. J., & Lawrence, F. C. (2000). Differences in spending habits and credit card use of college students. *Journal of Consumer Affairs, 34*(1), 113–133.

John, D. R. (1999). Consumer socialization of children: A retrospective look at twenty-five years of research. *Journal of Consumer Research, 26*(3), 183–213.

Joo, S. H., Grable, J. E., & Bagwell, D. C. (2003). Credit card attitudes and behaviors of college students. *College Student Journal, 37*(3), 405–419.

Kahneman, D., Krueger, A. B., Schkade, D., Schwarz, N., & Stone, A. A. (2006). Would you be happier if you were richer? A focusing illusion. *Science, 312*(5782), 1908–1910.

Kidwell, B., & Turrisi, R. (2000). A cognitive analysis of credit card acquisition and college student financial development. *Journal of College Students Development, 41*(6), 589–599.

Lawrence, F. C., Cude, B. J., Lyons, A. C., Marks, L., & Machtmes, K. (2006). College students and financial literacy: What have we learned from listening to them? *Journal of Consumer Education, 23*, 13–26.

Lyons, A. C. (2004). A profile of financially at-risk college students. *Journal of Consumer Affairs, 38*(1), 56–80.

Lyons, A. C. (2007). *Credit practices and financial education needs of Midwest college students*. Indianapolis: Networks Financial Institute, Indiana State University.

Lyons, A. C., & Yilmazer, T. (2005). Financial strain and health: Evidence from the survey of consumer finances. *Southern Economic Journal, 71*(4), 873–890.

Lyons, A. C.; Scherpf, E. & Neelakantan, U. (2007). *Intergenerational transfer of financial behaviors from parents to children* (working paper). Indianapolis: Networks Financial Institute, Indiana State University.

MacFadyen, A. J., MacFadyen, H. W., & Prince, N. J. (1996). Economic stress and psychological well-being: An economic psychological framework. *Journal of Economic Psychology, 17*(3), 291–311.

Nellie Mae. (2005). *Undergraduate students and credit cards in 2004: An analysis of usage rates and trends*. Braintree. Available at: http://www.nelliemae.com/library/research_12.html. Accessed 17 Mar 2011.

Manning, R. D. (2000). *Credit card nation: The consequences of America's addiction to credit*. New York: Basic Books.

Mansfield, P. M., & Pinto, M. B. (2007). Marketing credit cards to college students: Will legislations protect them from excessive debt? *Marketing Management Journal, 17*(1), 112–122.

Markovich, C. A., & DeVaney, S. A. (1997). College seniors' personal finance knowledge and practices. *Journal of Family & Consumer Sciences, 89*(3), 61–65.

Masuo, D. M., Malroutu, Y. L., Hanashiro, R., & Kim, J. H. (2004). College students' money beliefs and behaviors: An Asian perspective. *Journal of Family and Economic Issues, 25*(4), 469–481.

Modigliani, F. (1998). The role of intergenerational transfers and life-cycle saving in the accumulation of wealth. *Journal of Economic Perspectives, 2*(2), 15–20.

Norvilitis, J. M., & MacLean, M. G. (2010). The role of parents in college students' financial behaviors and attitudes. *Journal of Economic Psychology, 31*(1), 55–63.

Norvilitis, J. M., & Santa Maria, P. (2002). Credit card debt on college campuses: Causes, consequences and solutions. *College Student Journal, 36*(3), 357–364.

Pinto, M. B., Parente, D. H., & Palmer, T. S. (2001). College student performance and credit card usage. *Journal of College Student Development, 42*(1), 49–58.

Rindfleish, A., Burroughs, J. E., & Denton, F. (1997). Family structure, materialism, and compulsive consumption. *Journal of Consumer Research, 23*(4), 312–325.

Roberts, J. A., & Jones, E. (2001). Money attitudes, credit card use, and compulsive buying among American college students. *The Journal of Consumer Affairs, 35*(2), 213–240.
Sánchez, M. (2010). Financial innovation and the global crisis. *International Journal of Business and Management, 5*(11), 26–31.
U.S. General Accounting Office. (2001). *Consumer finance: College students and credit cards.* Report to Congressional Requesters (GAO-01-773).
Veludo-de-Oliveira, T. M., Ikeda, A. A., & Santos, R. C. (2004). Compra Compulsiva e a Influência do Cartão de Crédito. *Revista de Administração de Empresas, 44*(3), 89–94.
Woodruffe, H. (1997). Compensatory consumption: Why women go shopping when they're fed up and other stories. *Marketing Intelligence& Planning, 15*(7), 325–334.
Xiao, J. J., Noring, F. E., & Anderson, J. G. (1995). College students' attitudes towards credit cards. *Journal of Consumer Studies and Home Economics, 19*(2), 155–174.

Part II
Financial Innovation in the Small Business Level

Chapter 9
Geographic Distance and Reward Crowdfunding Donation

Wesley Mendes-Da-Silva, Luciano Rossoni, Eduardo Francisco, and Cristiane C. Gattaz

Abstract This chapter describes the analysis of a large crowdfunding platform to examine pledges to music production projects and assess the relation between the fundraising accumulation period, the donor-entrepreneur distance, and the donors' propensity to back projects. Our results suggest a significantly negative association between distance and the value of capital pledged to projects, which is consistent with the notion that the entrepreneur's network of close contacts might play a central role in funding. Furthermore, our results contradict the idea that crowdfunding reduces the inhibiting effect of donor-entrepreneur distance. In addition, the results show that a long project exposure is associated with higher values of pledges. These results suggest practical implications for the study of crowdfunding as a financing platform. This study contributes to the literature on the use of crowdfunding as an alternative funding source in a major emerging market.

Keywords Fintech · Crowdfunding · Fundraising · Social networks

JEL Code A13 · D85 · L14

Portions of this chapter appeared in the 2016 paper "The impacts of fundraising periods and geographic distance on financing music production via crowdfunding in Brazil," *Journal of Cultural Economics*, vol 40, pp 75–99.

W. Mendes-Da-Silva (✉)
Sao Paulo School of Business Administration (FGV/EAESP), Sao Paulo, SP, Brazil

University of Texas at Austin, Austin, TX, USA

L. Rossoni
Department of Management, UniGranRio, Rio de Janeiro, RJ, Brazil

E. Francisco
Department of Business Economics, Fundação Getulio Vargas at São Paulo (FGV/EAESP), Sao Paulo, SP, Brazil

C. C. Gattaz
IC² Institute/University of Texas at Austin, Austin, TX, USA
e-mail: cristiane.gattaz@utexas.edu

W. Mendes-Da-Silva (ed.), *Individual Behaviors and Technologies for Financial Innovations*, https://doi.org/10.1007/978-3-319-91911-9_9

Fintechs, where crowdfunding is included, comprises a major line in financial innovation research. Crowdfunding constitutes a way for businesses and other organizations to raise funding from multiple individuals (Strausz 2017). As a kind of fintech, crowdfunding has a high potential for democratization of finance, especially in less structured markets and when reliable financial mechanisms are lacking (Ahlers et al. 2015). This is the case of the Brazilian music market, in which the democratization of crowdfunding itself enables artists to independently finance a record release and thus enter the market without the intermediation of a traditional record label (Galuszka and Brzozowska 2017). Brazil represents a major region for producing and consuming music worldwide, having the eleventh largest market in 2009 (IFPI 2010). Although 58% of the market was national and 90% of the best-selling albums were by local musicians in 2009 (IFPI 2014), music production differs little from the world market, as a few record companies compose the local market (Cassiolato et al. 2008).

As such, the cost of entry for budding musicians is high (Cameron 2015). Although there is often sufficient market demand for Brazilian artists to finance their activities (Lucas 2000), resources for beginners are scarce. Indeed, if we consider musicians as entrepreneurs, at the outset of their initiatives, they find it difficult to attract external capital. Accessing specific financing sources is an inherent problem for musicians in their initial stage (Berger and Udell 1998; Cosh et al. 2009) and places a limiting factor on the entrepreneur's chances of survival and growth – especially given the lack of true guarantees and what potential investors would view as insufficient cash flows or good reputation. It should also be noted that investors are faced with asymmetric information. According to Cosh et al. (2009), entrepreneurs requiring smaller amounts of capital are unable to access venture capital, private equity or banks, which may be available in other stages. Hence, these entrepreneurs tend to find backing from (i) their own resources, (ii) their family, and (iii) their circle of close friends (Parker 2009; Sheng and Mendes-da-Silva 2014).

Crowdfunding has become an innovative method for bringing investors and those requiring capital closer together, especially when the latter are developing artistic, cultural, social, or other types of initiatives (Shiller 2013). This method has enabled relatively small sums pledged by a large number of people to make businesses viable in a more flexible and less costly way that does not require intermediate financiers. A large number of platforms for raising funds through crowdfunding have appeared which enable this phenomenon. One example is *Kickstarter* <https://www.kickstarter.com/>, which is currently the largest crowdfunding platform in the world. This North American website hosts projects including films, games, music, design, and technology. Since its launch in 2009, it has attracted more than R$ 1.5 billion from 5.1 million people to finance more than 50,000 creative projects (Qiu 2013).

Although the World Bank (2013) and specialized consultants point to the rapid growth of this financing model, it still tends to be highly concentrated in North America and Europe (59% and 35% of the total value around the world, respectively) with a negligible presence in developing continents. South America, for example, represented only 0.03% of this market, and that portion exceeded only the corresponding one for the African continent, which represented just 0.003% (Massolution 2013). In addition to crowdfunding's social impact, high interest on part of the financial media and, more recently, the academic business community (Shiller 2013; Bruton et al. 2015; Mollick 2014), various governments have recognized its relevance to developing countries (Royal and Windsor 2014), and consequently, they have given attention to regulating this activity (Agrawal et al. 2014). For example, the US government recently approved the *Jumpstart Our Business Startups Act* (*JOBS Act*), with the main objective to stimulate financial access for companies in the emerging growth stage (Stemler 2013).

In finance, investors tend to demand more information from embryonic businesses, given the high level of risk associated with new businesses (Berger and Udell 1998). Investors in startups also show preference for businesses that are physically closer, which reduces the information asymmetry (Lee et al. 2008). However, crowdfunding facilitates contacting a vast number of geographically dispersed people to obtain small investments to finance a project or enterprise. It also allows business progress to be monitored, even over large distances, which reduces information asymmetries. Moreover, in their mode of pledges, creative entrepreneurs such as musicians can overcome problems of market capitalism as a delivery mechanism (Cameron 2015), which requires a different artists' position in the changing model of music production, promotion, and distribution (Galuszka and Brzozowska 2017).

This chapter presents highlights from research analysis of the data related to 1835 pledges toward 10 music production projects that were judged to be successful on a crowdfunding platform. These research findings provide insight into how fundraising period, geographic distances, and socioeconomic factors impact the pledges made to projects financed through crowdfunding in an emerging economy. These findings can be relevant for financial professionals, policy makers, entrepreneurs, and society overall. The chapter concludes with some recommendations and directions or future research.

Background

The so-called *subprime crisis* was the worst financial crisis since the Great Depression according to Shiller (2013). This crisis has been perceived as due to failings intrinsic to the financial system and the people running it. In particular, financial agents have been seen as one of the principal causes of the crisis by working excessively for their own benefit. According to Shiller (2013), the financial industry needs time to rebuild its reputation with society, and this process is characterized by the emergence of financial innovations, e.g., social impact bonds and crowdfunding. In this sense, crowdfunding is frequently identified as one of the most relevant modern financial innovations (Kuti and Madarász 2014). This financing method has emerged as a novel way of raising capital for entrepreneurial ventures (Macht

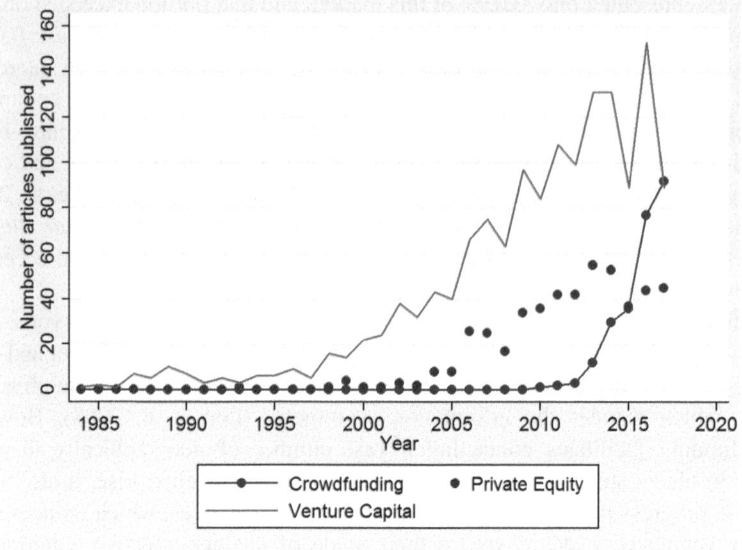

Fig. 9.1 Evolution of the number of published articles about crowdfunding. (Source: Prepared by the authors with Scopus platform data published through 12/18/2017. Each curve represents the number of articles published in Scopus-indexed journals, with titles containing the terms "private equity," "venture capital," or "crowdfunding." The exponential growth in the academic community's interest in the subject of crowdfunding is evident)

2014), and it frequently implements the Internet. Crowdfunding has enabled different business types, such as agribusiness, social projects, technological innovation projects, and particularly cultural production, without the pitfalls of traditional methods of financing (Agrawal et al. 2014; Braet et al. 2013; Lehner 2013; Schwartz 2013). We focus on this novel funding method in the case of music. In addition, the growing interest of the community of researchers in crowdfunding has been accelerated (Fig. 9.1).

Definition and Uses of Crowdfunding

Crowdfunding has been seen as a tool that enables the democratization of financing (Brabham 2008; Galuszka and Brzozowska 2017; Kim and Hann 2014) and as an innovative financing method. It is typically enabled through the Internet by means of social media (Lehner 2013) and allows entrepreneurs to reach geographically dispersed people around the globe who are willing to support the project (Saxton and Wang 2014). Royal and Windsor (2014) describe crowdfunding as the accumulation of small investments in individual projects by a large number of individuals who are supported by a platform – by allowing project initiators to upload projects to the platform online for others worldwide with similar interests to contribute financially.

One characteristic of crowdfunding projects is the existence of a funding target. Often a campaign exceeds 100% of its funding target, which is known as "overfunding"; entrepreneurs are not required to take investment but reserve the right to accept any amount beyond 100%. In this research case, excess funds were delivered to the entrepreneur's musical project.

According to Mollick (2014), the most basic variations in crowdfunding relate to the objectives pursued by the entrepreneurs and investors. By means of these platforms, the entrepreneur can seek a small sum, e.g., a few thousand Brazilian Reals or less, to fund a specific project that is motivated by their own dream or objective. Usually, these types of projects receive the majority of their funding from the entrepreneur's social network, i.e., his or her network of personal contacts (family and friends) (Agrawal et al. 2015; Sheng and Mendes-da-Silva 2014) or his or her network of contacts with that backed their previous campaigns (Butticè et al. 2017; Skirnevskiy et al. 2017). These social networks provide additional support that such funding does not customarily receive from angel investors, such as advice, governance, and prestige (Ferrary and Granovetter 2009). From this starting point, recent studies have highlighted these aspects as pertinent to a relevant research agenda on the theme of crowdfunding (Lehner 2013).

As crowdfunding has evolved, it has reached a growing segment of the public and is no longer restricted to being an alternative way for entrepreneurs or startups to attract funding for their projects. It has evolved so that crowdfunders can perform support roles. By way of illustration, in certain circumstances crowdfunding may be used to achieve the simple objective of raising awareness about a new project as part of a marketing campaign that directly involves consumers (Cameron 2015). The interested company is able to gauge whether there is demand and how much demand there is for a specific product (Schwienbacher and Larralde 2012).

Although crowdfunding can be used with the intention of participating in the equity of the company, this research focused on projects without this characteristic. Among these projects, Agrawal et al. (2014) highlighted seven characteristics in their review: (i) the funding is not geographically concentrated; (ii) the values of pledges are highly asymmetric; (iii) the propensity to invest increases as capital accumulates during the fundraising period of the project, with the risk that investors will follow herd behavior; (iv) friends and family play a key role in the initial stages of the fundraising process; (v) the funding follows concentrations that already existed; (vi) entrepreneurs and investors tend to be highly optimistic at the outset about the results of the project seeking investment; lastly, (vii) the capital attracted by means of crowdfunding might replace traditional financing sources.

In addition to these peculiarities, just as the objectives pursued by entrepreneurs vary, the motivations of the investors may also vary according to the nature of the project (Belleflamme et al. 2014; Cecere et al. 2017; Jancenelle et al. 2018). There are essentially four models for how individuals provide their sponsorship to projects (Kuti and Madarász 2014; Royal and Windsor 2014). The first model is donation, which applies mainly to projects that are characterized as artistic, humanitarian, and socio-environmental and applies to this study. This chapter references investors as "donors" hereafter as the people who are interested in music production projects are not necessarily interested in financial returns, as discussed by Kuti and Madarász (2014), Royal and Windsor (2014), and Zvilichovsky et al. (2018). The sponsorship is in many cases virtually philanthropic. In other words, the investor does not expect a direct personal return from the donation. The second model is based on credit: the funds are provided to the entrepreneur as a loan with an expected return rate.

This model does not (currently) exist in Brazil, as this activity is restricted to financial institutions by law. The third and most widespread crowdfunding model to date is based on nonfinancial compensation: investors receive something in exchange for sponsoring the project. Individuals usually receive the product that was the objective of the appeal, such as books, CDs, DVDs, show tickets, or a wide variety of other things. Finally, there is equity crowdfunding, in which the sponsors are effectively investors and receive a share in the equity of the company they finance. This practice is still rarely found in active use worldwide due to regulatory obstacles (Ahlers et al. 2015; Heminway and Hoffman 2011), and it represented just 5% of the total volume of funds managed through crowdfunding platforms globally in 2013, according to Massolution (2013).

Previous Studies and Hypotheses

Due to the possibilities offered by the Internet, geographic dispersion is probably one of the most common characteristics of crowdfunding operations. Lee et al. (2008) suggest that the arrival of Web 2.0 simplified information sharing across large social networks at reduced costs. This simplification has contributed to establishing governance mechanisms for the enterprise. Put another way, the arrival of online crowdfunding platforms provided a tool to bring the investor and entrepreneur closer together and to share information with greater transparency for project budgets and the necessary details on the destination of the raised funds. Additionally, it became possible: (i) to monitor the whole process (with entrepreneurs having access at any time to all of the investors in the project), (ii) to see the percentage of the fundraising target already achieved, and (iii) to see the remaining time the fundraising period had to run.

From this point of view, based on data covering the period from August 2006 until September 2009, Agrawal et al. (2015) analyzed 34 projects that received 24,862 donations (representing 73% of the total amount invested in the website) in the Dutch platform *Sellaband* <https://www.sellaband.com>, which is a site for musicians seeking funds to launch their albums – to investigate whether crowdfunding is sensitive to the investor-entrepreneur geographic distance. The average investor-entrepreneur distance found by Agrawal et al. (2015) was approximately 4828 km, which is greater than the distance between the most southern and northern parts of Brazil (about 4300 km). In their study, the data indicate that the greater the investor's proximity to the entrepreneur is, the greater the value of the donations will be. According to Agrawal et al. (2015), although crowdfunding suggests a reduced role for spatial proximity, it does play a role.

The authors argue that this geographical effect is driven by investors who likely have a personal connection with the artist-entrepreneur, e.g., family and friends, although they do not present empirical evidence about these social relations. They conclude that the online platform seems to eliminate most distance-related economic frictions, such as monitoring progress, providing input, and gathering information; however, it does not eliminate social frictions. In the same line of thinking, a set of studies, e.g., Sorenson and Stuart (2001), Zook (2002), Mason (2007), and Martins (2015), assume that investors in enterprises in their initial stages tend to demand more information, monitor the business's progress, and also participate in decisions about how the business is run.

These activities result in costs that are sensitive to the investor-entrepreneur distance. Based on a sample of American venture capitalist firms, Sorenson and Stuart (2001) found that the probability of investing in a new venture falls as geographical distance increases. Zook (2002) found similar results for the American Internet industry between 1994 and 2000. According to these authors, although communication technologies and the global financial market have geographically expanded the scope of economic interactions, they tend to occur regionally. Martins (2015) points out that when there are cases of investment outside the domestic sphere, for example, investment in projects in the BRIC countries (Brazil, Russia, India, and China), the risks and costs tend to be mitigated through arrangements established between venture capitalists.

The results of these studies show that the greater the distance between investors and the project, the less likely the investors are to invest, and furthermore, they will probably invest less. However, in the musical production context, we must examine the mechanisms underlying the proximity of the donor and the amount donated. Crowdfunding in the music industry cannot be seen only as an intermediary agent, as it is also the *locus* where social connections between fans and musicians occur (Colombo et al. 2015; Zheng et al. 2014). These fans do more than invest in a musical product: they are meeting the request of people who are part of their social network (Saxton and Wang 2014) or are feeling motivated to act prosocially (Ariely et al. 2009), in which they are probably increasing their financial participation when they believe their contribution is primordial to product success (Zvilichovsky et al. 2018) and, in the case of music, the success of the singer or band who may be seen to have a social identity in itself. For these reasons, we advocate that the mechanisms inherent in the social capital of musicians and the behavioral aspects of donors simultaneously affect the relationship between the geographic distance and the value of a pledge.

According to Nahapiet and Ghoshal (1998, p. 243), social capital can be defined as "the sum of the current and potential resources embedded within, available through, and derived from the social contacts of an individual or an organization." In the crowdfunding context, these personal contacts, such as friends, intense fans, and family, often tend to be closer to the authors of the projects (see McPhearson et al. 2001). Moreover, because the contacts are embedded in the authors' real social networks, it is likely that these contacts are direct targets of funding campaigns. Indeed, using data from *Sellaband*, Agrawal et al. (2015) found that not only did most of the donations occur in the same geographical area or in nearby areas, but these donations also had the highest value. Although they have not considered the distance of ties between donors and musicians, Mollick (2014) and Zheng et al. (2014) identified a positive relationship between the number of social contacts identified on Facebook or other social networks (e.g., Weibo Page, a Chinese social network) with the amount donated and with the musical project's performance. These results are also supported by Saxton and Wang (2014), who found that nonprofit organizations with more Facebook fans receive more donations, and by Colombo et al. (2015), who found that greater numbers of contacts on LinkedIn were associated with both the number of supporters and the volume of capital raised in 669 projects on the *Kickstarter* platform.

In addition to this evidence that more frequent and more valuable donations come from people with personal ties who are geographically closer, it should be noted that relations' networks are also mechanisms of coercion (Coleman 1990; Matzat 2004) in which donors who are socially closer to an entrepreneur whose network is more densely grouped tend to feel more motivated or morally obliged to donate larger amounts. Between these donors the network might include avid fans appealing for recognition by the musicians. The act of giving to musical projects in crowdfunding happens not only for personal reasons or for direct benefits (e.g., received gifts) but also because donors want to obtain a good image or desire the respect and approval of the connected community that is raising money (Ariely et al. 2009). These networks of relations (as we have said) tend to be geographically close to the entrepreneurs. From these arguments, it is relevant to test hypothesis H_1:

H_1 *There is a negative association between the geographic distance separating the entrepreneur and the donor and the value of the music crowdfunding investments.*

Regarding crowdfunding, it should be noted that the literature often lacks an in-depth discussion of the statistical significance of the economic impact of the variables, as described by Drummond and O'Brien (1993) and Miller and Rodgers (2008). In this regard, Agrawal et al. (2015), using models of binary response, indicate that investment propensity increases with funds raised. In a given week, an investor is 2.1 percentage points more likely to invest if the entrepreneur has \$10,000–\$20,000 (compared to the entrepreneur with less than \$10,000 investment) and 8.4 points more likely to invest if they have more than \$40,000.

In addition to evidence of the relationship between the proximity and pledge value, Agrawal et al. (2015), Zhang and Liu (2012), and Kuppuswamy and Bayus (2014) assumed that the volume of accumulated pledges grows as the fundraising time increases. Accordingly, these authors suggest that the propensity for a potential donor/investor to sponsor a project increases, which might suggest some type of herd behavior by investors. Burtch et al. (2013) identified crowd's herding behavior as a possible influencing factor for participation in crowdfunding.

The herding behavior acts as an uncertainty reduction mechanism and may result in greater density in the project supporters' network. The reason is that as the number of donors increases, it becomes more likely that these donors will have links between themselves, which would make them more visible to each other (see Burt 2005).

Indeed, the increased redundancy enables the network to operate as a coercive apparatus (Matzat 2004), as those who have not yet supported an endeavor feel increasingly obliged to contribute (Ariely et al. 2009), particularly in campaigns lacking interest in economic gains (Cecere et al. 2017; Jancenelle et al. 2018). In addition, this sense of obligation, which grows with the project exposure, should affect not only the likelihood of contributing but also the value of the donation. As Ariely et al. (2009) discussed, in the desire to be socially approved, donors feel morally obligated to contribute a proportional or greater value. It should be considered that this behavior is reinforced in social networks, as one of its key features is the reciprocity in trade (Mendes-da-Silva et al. 2008; Zheng et al. 2014).

Still, there is another element to consider: the relationship between the exposure time (time from the announcement of project) and a donation's value. As indicated by Colombo et al. (2015), social capital is important to raising money. Thus, we investigate whether the origin of the actors that promote this social capital matters. At this point, we divide the social capital into two types: (i) external social capital, which is derived from social relations outside of the crowdfunding community, such as friends, family, or intense fans, and (ii) internal social capital, involving those relationships that are established within the crowdfunding community, usually composed by donors and fans and enthusiasts with weaker relationships with entrepreneurs. Colombo et al. (2015) showed that internal social capital significantly affects the number and value of donations in the early stages. These actors belong primarily to the internal network community, and they tend to have faster access to new campaigns in crowdfunding platforms, which increases the chance of them donating in a project's early stages. This effect is temporarily sensitive, for example, in campaigns of serial crowdfunders, that is, entrepreneurs who repeatedly turn to crowdfunding to finance their projects (Butticè et al. 2017). In the case of external social capital, which is designed by the friends, family, and intense fans of the proponents, these contacts are commonly not connected to crowdfunding platforms. Thus, it is expected that the investors who are not socially connected to the entrepreneurs tend to take longer to donate than others. Nevertheless, donors with close ties to the musicians tend to donate larger amounts (Saxton and Wang 2014). Given the above reasons, we believe that the greater the exposure time of the project is, the greater the value of the donations will be. This line of thinking leads to testing hypothesis H_2:

H_2 *There is a positive association between the fundraising accumulation period* via *crowdfunding and the value of the new pledges received by the music entrepreneur.*

Data Collection

In November 2013, when the data analyzed in this study were collected, Brazil had 40 crowdfunding platforms that were listed on specialized sites, e.g., <http://mapadocrowdfunding.tumblr.com>. The majority of sponsored projects were creative and predominantly cultural in nature, although others pursued specific objectives, e.g., financial support for soccer clubs at <http://vascodividazero.com.br>. The dominant site among the 40 crowdfunding platforms is *Catarse*, which was the focus of this study. Only the *Catarse* website was considered, and selection included all of the projects in which (i) the entrepreneurs were musicians who were using the platform to fund the first album of their artistic career and (ii) the target funding was between R$ 10,000 and R$ 30,000 (US$ 1.00 = R$ 2.80), a value selected because 95% of *Catarse*'s hosted projects fall in this monetary range.

The data collection required for constructing the variables under consideration took place in two main phases. The first phase focused on the *Catarse* platform <http://catarse.me>, where two types of data were obtained: data from browsing the website directly and data provided by the platform's founders to its entrepreneurs and sponsors through the privacy policy for the platform. The second data collection phase examined socioeconomic data for the municipalities where the pertinent 1835 pledges originated. These data were obtained from the Brazilian Institute for Geography and Statistics (IBGE – *Instituto Brasileiro de Geografia e Estatística*), and we drew on the most recent Brazilian Census, which was conducted in 2010.

The geographic distance between the entrepreneurs and the donors was obtained for the cities where they were located, referencing Google Maps APIs <http://code.google.com/apis/maps/> to identify the coordinates of each location. The distance was calculated using the procedure adopted by Nichols (2003) with the tool ArcGIS ArcMap 10.0 (ESRI 2010). These tools were chosen in reference of the argument that when the data's spatial distribution is related to the phenomena occurring in the territory, one has a modern way to clarify questions related to various fields of knowledge (Ebner et al. 2009). The use of these techniques in the business field is in an embryonic stage (Goodchild 2010), especially in studies of collaborative phenomena (Sui et al. 2013). In addition, geographical information systems (GISs) could be a tool toward providing a spatial explanation of governance, population, and cultural assets (Redaelli 2012).

Platform Studied

The *Catarse* website <http://catarse.me> launched in January 2011, and it was one of the first crowdfunding platforms in Brazil. It is currently the nation's largest collective financial community and has already raised more than R$ 12 million to finance around 800 projects. The way it works is relatively simple and common to most competing sites: the entrepreneur uses the platform to present their idea to the public, specifying the total investment required and the cut-off date for evaluating whether or not it has been achieved. To be able to use this platform for fundraising, the entrepreneur must meet the requirements given in Table 9.1.

Figure 9.2 shows a typical project page on the platform we studied. On the right, observe (i) the number of sponsors already attracted to the project, (ii) the total

Table 9.1 List of requirements for projects hosted on the Catarse website

#	Requirement
1	The project must be complete and have a clear objective or it will not be accepted on the platform
2	The project must present a realistic fundraising target and account for all of the costs and rates involved in a campaign on the platform; all projects must specify a budget that justifies the fundraising target given
3	Together with the target, projects must have a defined fundraising duration (with a maximum of 60 days[a])
4	The fundraising system is "all or nothing": If the given target is not achieved within the specified timescale, the sponsors receive a credit to back other projects or, if they prefer, a refund of their money; additionally, the project receives nothing
5	All projects must offer rewards as consideration to donors for their sponsorship, for example, copies of the work, CDs of music, innovative experiences, limited editions, and exclusive benefits. Any form of financial return is prohibited
6	All projects must provide certain information that indicates what it is, what will be done, and how the money will be spent
7	A high-quality video explaining the project must be produced

[a]Note: Until 09/30/2013 the *Catarse* platform offered projects that did not achieve full funding (which met certain requirements) a "second chance" on the platform, with a new fundraising period opening once the project had been redesigned to correct any problems. This practice resulted in fundraising periods longer than the 60-day limit. This opportunity was discontinued on 10/01/2013

Fig. 9.2 Schematic view of the Catarse website. (Source: Adapted by the authors from the *Catarse* website http://catarse.me/pt/andreadosguimaraes)

Table 9.2 Profile of pledges made to the projects included in the research

Project[a]	Total raised (in R$)[b]	No. of pledges made to the project[c]	City of the project headquarters[d]	No. of fundraising days[e]
Project No. 1	29,400	377	Curitiba	37
Project No. 2	26,060	112	São Paulo	60
Project No. 3	24,185	189	Niterói	60
Project No. 4	21,180	80	Itapema	56
Project No. 5	20,710	266	São Paulo	51
Project No. 6	20,280	129	São Paulo	60
Project No. 7	15,615	190	Rio de Janeiro	101[f]
Project No. 8	15,452	113	São Paulo	39
Project No. 9	15,070	278	Florianópolis	60
Project No. 10	12,570	101	Curitiba	35

Source: Developed by the authors from the data provided by the crowdfunding platform *Catarse* <http://catarse.em>

Note: This table provides information on the profile of each project included in this research. Observe that the project that attracted the largest number of donors raised a total of R$ 29,400

[a]Name omitted for confidentiality reasons

[b]Total sum in R$ raised by the project over the fundraising period

[c]Number of pledges received by the project during the fundraising period

[d]City in which the candidate project for funds is based

[e]Number of days that the project was visible on the platform to receive pledges (i.e., investments and donations)

[f]One of the projects was resubmitted as a "second chance," and it reached the funding target 101 days after the start of fundraising

pledged so far, (iii) the total requested, (iv) the remaining fundraising period, (v) the project description, and (vi) rewards and other relevant information. Table 9.2 shows a summary of the profiles of the ten projects selected for this study. Notice that these projects raised nearly R$ 200,522.00 from 1835 pledges that originated from 151 different municipalities. The second column of the table shows the project that received the greatest number of investment pledges (377 pledges) achieved its target (through the *Catarse* platform) of R$ 29,400. Project No. 1 originated from the city of Curitiba in Paraná State, Southern Brazil. We do not highlight the pledge rewards because they were extremely similar and had the same pattern. These projects started with online distribution albums after physical distribution and evolved to give autographs and invitations to release shows. Note that Project No. 1 reached this total after 37 days of fundraising. Figure 9.3 shows the geographic distribution of the 377 pledges made to Project No. 1 via the *Catarse* platform, as given in Table 9.2.

Fig. 9.3 Geographic distribution of the pledges received by Project No. 1. This figure shows the geographic distribution of donors pledging capital to Project No. 1, which attracted 396 pledges for a total of R$ 29,400. The most distant donor in Project No. 1, which is located in Curitiba/PR, was in the city of Manaus (Amazonas State); this donor corresponds to a distance of ~2825 km. Country: Brazil. (Source: Produced by the authors from data obtained from the *Catarse* platform using the tool ArcGIS ArcMap 10.0 (ESRI 2010))

Model Estimation

The variables investigated in this study are described in Table 9.3 and were selected by considering the literature on utilizing crowdfunding as a means to fund music production (Agrawal et al. 2015). The empirical model we tested is represented in (1). The four control variables were designed to assess the persistence of the coefficients estimated for the variables of interest, which are intended to test H_1 and H_2.

Table 9.3 Variables in the model

Variable	Description
$Value_i$	Value in R$ of the i-th pledge
Da_i	Number of days from the start of the fundraising period when the i-th pledge was made
$Dist_i$	Geographic distance in kilometers between the entrepreneur-artist and the donor
$GdpCap_i$	GDP per capita in the donor's municipality (in R$)
$Literacy_i$	% literacy in the donor's municipality
HDI_i	HDI in the donor's municipality
$Area_i$	Area of the donor's municipality (in km^2)

The control variables were selected by considering the dataset provided by the *Catarse* website and the arguments in the literature, which indicate that it is possible for the dependent variable be influenced by the control variables (Mason 2007; Agrawal et al. 2014, 2015). Thus, if the control variables have significant correlations with some of the other variables but are not considered in the model, the relationship between the variables of interest would not be adequately demonstrated. The errors ε_i are assumed uncorrelated, and $E(\varepsilon|X) = 0$.

$$Value_i = \beta_0 + \beta_1 Da_i + \beta_2 Dist_i + \beta_3 GdpCap_i + \beta_4 Literacy_i + \beta_5 HDI_i + \beta_6 Area_i + \varepsilon_i \quad (9.1)$$

To test the hypothesis, we used linear regression models based on the ordinary least squares method (OLS model). To check the robustness, first we checked if the dependent variable had an approximately normal distribution. Because the symmetry and kurtosis were relatively high, we also tested the models with standard errors of the patch through the bootstrapping procedure (Preacher and Hayes 2008) and ran the model with the natural logarithm of the variable. In both cases, the results were consistent with the original template. Second, we evaluated the most appropriate functional form for the regression variables. In all of the cases, the linear function was adequate in other ways that did not significantly increase the fit.

Third, we evaluated whether the errors held heteroscedasticity problems through the White test. Fourth, we reviewed the models for multicollinearity problems by assessing the tolerances, which were not less than 0.2, and from the variance inflation factor (VIF), which did not show values greater than 5. Fifth, we evaluated whether the influential observations and atypical cases (cases with standardized residuals greater than 2.5) generated overestimations of the model. To this end, we tested the model after discarding cases with residue greater than 2.5. The direction of the relationship between the variables and the significance remained the same. Sixth, we generated models by replacing the independent variables with their natural logarithms, and the results remained very close to the original model. Seventh, to see if there was any significant influence of the projects on the relationship between the variables, we ran a model with nine dummy variables ($n - 1$ projects) as a control. The results still remained close to what was found in the original model.

Finally, because most of the donations occurred in the municipality in which the project was realized (56.3%), potential for selection bias exists. Therefore, we also used the model selection Heckman (1979) two-stage. In the first stage, we specified the selection variable as the donor-entrepreneur distance with a probit model, where the value 1 was assigned to donations that came from distant cities (802 cases) and 0 was assigned to donations that originated in the same city as the project's location (1033 cases). At this stage, we included the control variables as predictors. In the second stage, we included the inverse Mills ratio variable in the OLS model, which controls the potential effect of selection bias, together with the independent and control variables. It should be noted that since we observed no data from unsuccessful projects, it was not possible to assess empirically whether a selection bias was present in the projects. However, we believe that the relationship between the distance and the exposure time with respect to the value of donations is similar to corresponding relationship of successful projects.

Empirical Results

Table 9.4 shows the general characteristics of the set of projects included in this study. The full initial sample consisted of 1954 pledges to the 10 projects. However, this figure included 119 anonymous pledges, which are allowed by the Catarse platform but do not retain information on the municipality of the donor. Thus, anonymous pledges were excluded, which left 1835 pledges that composed 94% of the original sample. As indicated on Table 9.4, the entrepreneurs received on average more than 183 pledges during the fundraising period. This period lasted an average of 56 days, though one of the projects was submitted as a "second chance" and reached the funding target 101 days after the fundraising launch. Another project achieved its target funding level in just 35 days. The projects attracted on average R$ 19,180.70, with total funds between R$ 10,000 and R$ 30,000, which is in accordance with the inclusion criteria adopted for this study. The average pledge was R$ 104.50, and the pledges varied from R$ 10.00 to R$ 5000.00. The average distance was 0 km, given that the majority of the sponsors (1033 of the total) were located in the same municipality as the project. The most distant sponsor was in Bonfim in Roraima (North of Brazil) for a project based in São Paulo (financial center of Brazil, in the Southeast), which represents a distance of 3297.7 km. In accordance with the study conducted by Agrawal et al. (2015) on the *Sellaband* site, the propensity of sponsors to invest increased as the funds raised by the entrepreneur increased.

From Fig. 9.4, one can see that the distribution of pledges is very homogeneous during the typical project period (up to 60 days). However, a positive correlation between the project maturing and the value of the pledge made is evident; this correlation is observed mainly in the final fundraising phase (50–60 days), with the average pledge made growing by nearly 70% in comparison to the period of 10–20 days (the period with the second-largest average pledge). The pledges after 60 days occurred when the projects were in a "second chance" phase, that is, they

Table 9.4 Descriptive statistics for the variables included in the research

	Average	Median	Min.	Max.	Standarddeviation
Panel A: number of enterprises ($N = 10$)					
No. of pledges considered as received	183.5	159	80	377	96.5
Total funds raised (R$)	19,180.7	18,940	10,810	28,450	5538.8
No. of fundraising days	56	58	35	101	18.9
Panel B: number of pledges ($N = 1835$)					
No. of donors = 1575					
Value of investment (R$)	104.5	50	10	5.000	322.3
Geographic distance (km)	236.7	0	0	3297.7	456.4
GDP per capita in the donor's municipality (R$)	31,298.0	30,400.5	5441.7	115,319.9	10,920.0
Literacy in the donor's municipality (%)	89.9	90.3	73.1	92.0	1.9
HDI in the donor's municipality	0.807	0.805	0.625	0.847	0.029
Area of the donor's municipality (km^2)	1100.8	675	30.8	34,096.4	1420.0

Source: Catarse Website. Demographic indicators: IBGE (Brazilian Institute of Geography and Statistics)

Note: This study considered 10 different music production projects that received 1835 pledges (from across Brazil) *HDI* human development index

were more mature and still had the potential to reach the fundraising target if they were given the opportunity to review some of the problems encountered and make any necessary corrections.

In this period, a drastic increase in the average pledge made can be seen to greater than R$ 250.00, which again suggests the importance of project maturity on the sponsors' decision with regard to the value to be invested. This behavior supports the results obtained by Agrawal et al. (2015). Even though we used OLS models, not models of binary response (such as Agrawal et al. 2015).

Geographic Distribution of Pledges

In the present research, the ten sample projects are based in six cities: four in São Paulo (SP), two in Curitiba (Paraná State), one in Florianópolis (Santa Catarina State), one in Itapema (Santa Catarina State), one in Niterói (Rio de Janeiro State), and one in Rio de Janeiro (Rio de Janeiro State). Pledges were made from 151 Brazilian municipalities and 2 foreign countries: Paris, France, and Neuchatel, Switzerland; these pledges were not included in the analysis. The average distance of the pledges was slightly over 236 km.

As discussed previously, empirical studies suggest that entrepreneurial initiatives tend to be funded by local donors for a range of reasons, such as the following: the monitoring costs are lower, there is better access to information, and active participation in decisions is possible. However, in the study conducted by Agrawal et al. (2015), the majority of pledges made to the projects studied were distant: the average distance between the entrepreneurs and donors was 3000 miles (or about 4828 km), and the donations originated from more than 80 different countries around the world. Figure 9.4 shows the geographic distribution of all of the pledges. The lines represent each sponsor-entrepreneur connection. Table 9.5 shows the geographic distribution of these pledges.

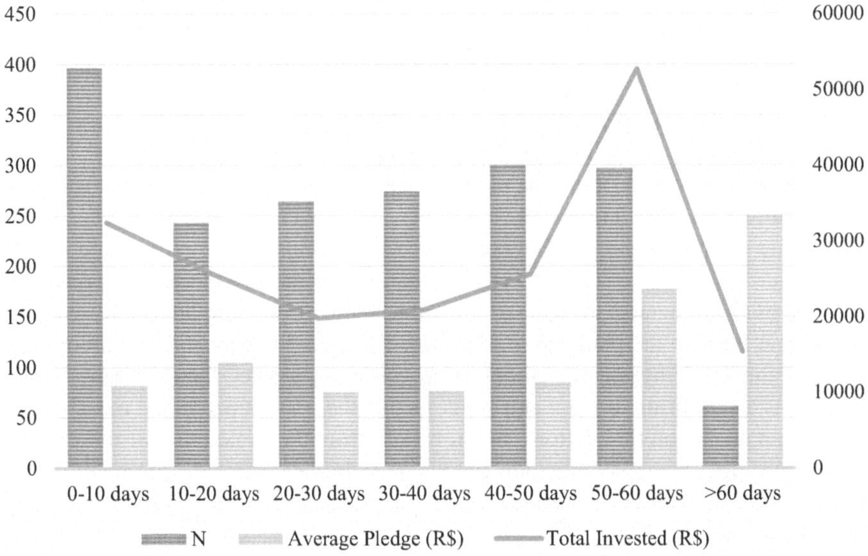

Fig. 9.4 Evolution of pledges over the fundraising period. (Source: Produced by the authors based on data collected on *Catarse* platform). Note: This table shows how the average pledge values changed as the fundraising period progressed. Disregarding the project value of donations over 60 days, observe that as the hosted project matured, the value of the average pledge made via the platform appeared to increase

Table 9.5 Frequency of investments by geographic distance

Distance	N	Average pledge (R$)	Total invested (R$)	% of total invested
0–5 km	1033	109.09	112,694	58.8%
5–50 km	218	166.95	36,395	19.0%
50–500 km	246	63.81	15,698	8.2%
500–1500 km	294	79.54	23,385	12.2%
1500–2500 km	34	60.88	2070	1.1%
> 2500 km	10	156.50	1565	0.8%
Total	1835	104.53	191,807	100%

Source: Produced by the authors from the data they collected

As seen in Fig. 9.5, a majority of pledges originates in regions closer to the project site. Specifically, most pledges are made within a radius of 50 km from the entrepreneur's location, and notably, the majority are within a distance of 5 km. On average, local investments are also greater than more distant ones, suggesting that the shorter the distance to the entrepreneur, the greater the propensity to invest larger sums will be, which agrees with the negative coefficient found for the distance variable in the regression we performed (see Table 9.6). This pattern indicates a negative association with the pledge value. In addition, it is worth noting the similar average pledge in the ten projects from a distance of more than 2500 km.

These data suggest that in Brazil, contrary to the evidence found in the European crowdfunding market (Agrawal et al. 2015), the financing of projects from artists at the start of their careers predominantly revolves around their network of close contacts. The *Catarse* platform states on its website that at least 50% of the funds directed at projects come from the entrepreneur's own network of contacts.

Because of this perception, the platform administrator has advised the managers of hosted projects that, in parallel to posting on the platform, entrepreneurs should also create a supporting social network page for the project. The expectation is that the project's social page followers could help increase the size of the entrepreneur's network of close contacts, which a priori will be more disposed to financially support the project through the platform mechanism. Still, it is fundamental that more than 22% of the total investment comes from distances greater than 50 km, which represents a significant amount and suggests that the best-prepared and most attractive entrepreneurs on the platform might benefit from the availability of these more distant resources by expanding their funding possibilities with the addition of social media presence. Thus, it is more likely that these entrepreneurs will achieve their fundraising targets.

The existence of associations between the pledge value, the fundraising days, and the donor-entrepreneur distance was tested by hypotheses H_1 and H_2. To that end, tests were conducted with respect to Model I, whose parameters were estimated using the OLS and Heckman selection model and are given in Table 9.6. Model I produced the results obtained for the two variables of interest: *days from the start of the fundraising period* and *donor-entrepreneur distance*. It can be confirmed from Model I that H_2 is supported, as *days from the start of the fundraising period* gave a

Fig. 9.5 Geographic distribution of pledges (to projects hosted on the *Catarse* website). (Source: Produced by the authors from the data they collected using the tool ArcGIS ArcMap 10.0 (ESRI 2010)). Note: This figure shows the geographic spread of the 1835 pledges made to the 10 projects we examined, which are based in 6 different Brazilian cities: Curitiba (2), Florianópolis (1), Itapema (1), Niterói (1), Rio de Janeiro (1), and São Paulo (4)

positive and significant parameter ($\widehat{\beta_1} \cong 1.193$; $p - value < 0.01$). Thus, there appears to be a significant association within the values pledged to the hosted projccts. In addition to statistical significance, about the economic importance, as recommended by Miller and Rodgers (2008), note that the effect of another day on the value of each donation is small, around R$ 1.2 (around US $ 0.35), and this value seems to vary little, even considering the other controls adopted. However, as the average value of donations is approximately R$ 50.00, a period of 20 days of exposure could mean an increase of nearly 50% in the value, which is economically relevant.

Table 9.6 Estimated regression parameters (dependent variable: value of pledges)

	Model I		Model II		Model III		Model IV		Model V [a]	
Constant	73.057	***	64.953	**	657.359	*	531.138		318.649	
	(11.348)		(26.685)		(352.548)		(339.560)		(521.386)	
1. Days from the start of the fundraising period	1.193	***	1.203	***	1.218	***	1.185	***	0.937	*
	(0.442)		(0.453)		(0.454)		(0.453)		(0.492)	
2. Donor-entrepreneur distance (in km)	−0.026	**	−0.025	**	−0.039	**	−0.047	***	−0.047	*
	(0.011)		(0.011)		(0.016)		(0.017)		(0.022)	
3. GDP per capita in the donor's municipality (in R$)			0.001		0.001		0.001		−0.002	**
			(0.001)		(0.001)		(0.001)		(0.001)	
4. % literacy in the donor's municipality					−8.271	*	−6.081		7.764	
					(5.023)		(4.903)		(10.024)	
5. HDI in the donor's municipality					196.436		111.506		−1250.150	
					(267.697)		(272.065)		(1174.970)	
6. Area of the donor's municipality (in km^2)							0.009	***	0.014	**
							(0.003)		(0.006)	
7. Inverse Mills ratio (lambda)									149.640	**
									(59.863)	
F	5.369	***	3.747	**	2.323	**	3.130	***		
Akaike criterion	26393.80		26395.67		26398.01		26397.81			
Adjusted R-squared	0.007		0.006		0.006		0.007			
N	1835		1835		1835		1835		802	

Source: Calculated by the authors from the data they collected from the site http://cartase.me and IBGE

Note: This table gives the parameters estimated for the empirical model adopted in this study. It is possible to see from the parameters obtained in the four models that the distance between the investors and the artist-entrepreneurs and the maturity of the fundraising period for the project have a marginally significant effect on the value of the investment made for each *i*-th pledge. This effect can be seen as an indication that being geographically closer to donors induces a greater propensity to attract them. $N = 1835$ investment operations, i.e., pledges to one of the 10 music production projects considered in this study. The regressions were conducted with robust standard error (HC1)

**p*-value <0.1, ***p*-value <0.05, ****p*-value <0.01

The standard errors of the estimated coefficients are given in brackets

[a]Heckman two-step selection model: 1033 censored cases (56.3%) = zero donor-entrepreneur distance. The inverse Mills ratio (IMR) computed by Stata's `heckman` command, and used in the second-stage regression, is *lambda* = $f(x)/F(x)$, where $f(x)$ is the probability density function and $F(x)$ is the complementary cumulative distribution function

These results support the arguments and findings of Agrawal et al. (2015), Zhang and Liu (2012) and Kuppuswamy and Bayus (2014) that greater accumulated time in the fundraising period for the hosted project implies a greater propensity for donors to pledge larger capital sums. This correlation is due to decreases in the uncertainty of the project. The parameters estimated in Model I support hypothesis H_1, as the parameter obtained for the donor-entrepreneur distance was negative and significant ($\widehat{\beta_2} \cong -0.026$; $p - value < 0.05$). This result suggests that there are associations between the donor-entrepreneur distances and the pledge values made to the hosted project, where the increase in one standard deviation in the distribution is related to a decrease of R$ 11.90 on the value of donations, which is also economically relevant.

That is, more distant donors will be less disposed to invest larger sums in the project. This finding does not support the arguments that in the context of an emerging market, crowdfunding can be a sufficiently developed channel to supplant the information asymmetry imposed by the physical donor-entrepreneur distance, as argued by Lee et al. (2008); at a minimum, no support for those arguments was found based on the data gathered from the main crowdfunding platform operating in Brazil. Conversely, concrete social relations networks matter when deciding the amount of a donation (Colombo et al. 2015; Saxton and Wang 2014; Zheng et al. 2014), as even these virtual relationships are, in many cases, supported in person (Wellman 1996).

After testing H_1 and H_2 separately in Model I, the aim was to confirm the effect of the control variables related to the profile of the sponsor's municipality in Models II, III, and IV. Model II shows that the wealth produced in the donor's municipality does not appear to influence the disposition of donors to pledge, i.e., the municipality's GDP per capita is not a significant parameter ($\widehat{\beta_1} \cong 0; p - value > 0.1$). However, Model III produced a counterintuitive result that suggests less awareness among public donors with a higher level of education. Indeed, larger numbers of literate inhabitants imply lower pledges ($\widehat{\beta_4} \cong -827.082$; $p - value < 0.1$). However, this may be a spurious result, as it was not significant in the other models. We note that in Model III, the marginal effects of the variables of interest for the literate group were stronger than the corresponding effects included in Model I. In Model IV, the results suggest that the largest municipalities in terms of area appear to generate larger sums of investment ($\widehat{\beta_6} \cong 0.009; p - value < 0.01$).

In turn, the empirical model we tested (1) suggests that in all of the simulations, there are associations between the donor-entrepreneur distance and the value of each pledge received by the music production projects hosted on the *Catarse* crowdfunding platform, which is currently the largest in Brazil. In addition, significant indications of the effect of the fundraising time on the values of pledges were found when we considered the profile of the donor's municipalities. Finally, as most of the donations occurred within the municipality where the project was located, in Model V we simulated the relationship between the variables after excluding local donations. The results of the Heckman selection model, which served as a robustness check, corroborate the previous results, especially in the relationship between the variables the donor-entrepreneur distance and a donation's value: the greater the distance is, the lower the donated amount will be ($\widehat{\beta_1} \cong 0.041; p - value < 0.1$).

Concluding Remarks

Crowdfunding is an evolving method to secure funds outside of conventional equity markets. This financial innovation has enabled funding for projects for a wide range of purposes, including cultural production projects, social projects, and new technologies (Shiller 2013; Mollick 2014). Because it is supported by the Internet, crowdfunding has the potential to make investment possible without the donors being close to the entrepreneurs. Even when dealing with small and medium investments in companies that are not listed on a stock exchange or in startups, it is only necessary for the entrepreneur to be able to provide relevant information to the donor, which reduces the information asymmetry, and therefore, the risks associated with the project. This fact increases the propensity of donors to pledge capital to the project, being a means of democratizing project financing (Galuszka and Brzozowska 2017).

However, evidence worldwide has suggested that such a project is dependent on the entrepreneur's network of personal contacts, including friends and family (Parker 2009; Agrawal et al. 2015; Sheng and Mendes-da-Silva 2014). In other words, even though crowdfunding has the potential to attract capital from donors who are more distant from the entrepreneur, the maturity level of the crowdfunding industry in particular situations and institutional environments may not provide the necessary conditions for this pattern to happen.

Because it seems there is a lack of studies on how crowdfunding operates as a source of funding for small and medium projects, this chapter examined the existence of associations between the donor-entrepreneur distance and the propensity of donors to sponsor music production projects. In line with the notion that networks of close contacts might play a central role in funding, and simultaneously contradicting the idea that crowdfunding reduces the inhibiting effect of the geographic distance between donors and entrepreneurs, the results point to a significant, negative effect of distance on the amount of capital pledged to projects. These results corroborate hypothesis H_1, which stated that there is a negative association between the donor-entrepreneur distances and the values of pledges to music production projects financed by crowdfunding.

These results support the arguments of Sorenson and Stuart (2001, 2005), Zook (2002), Mason (2007), and Martins (2015). In addition, they contradict the ideas proposed by Lee et al. (2008), for whom the Internet performs a sufficiently expressive role to make the distance between the entrepreneur and donor insignificant in terms of the ability of entrepreneurs to receive pledges for their projects. The data showed that although the Internet allows donations in a wider geographical range, this fact does not impact the values of donations. In addition, the results suggest that as the fundraising period progresses, the pledges to projects tend to increase in value; this pattern corroborates hypothesis H_2, namely, that there is a positive association between the time the project has spent on the platform and the value of the investment received by the entrepreneur. This result supports the arguments made by Zhang and Liu (2012) and by Kuppuswamy and Bayus (2014), for whom donors tend to have a greater propensity to invest in projects that they find hosted for a longer period of time on a crowdfunding platform.

Future Research

The design of this research imposed limits on the work, which may restrict any generalizations that could be made from the results and point to a noteworthy set of issues: (i) the work only considered music projects, (ii) the study was restricted to Brazil, (iii) the time when the data were collected could have coincided with specific behavior for the variables studied, and (iv) there were no individual-level data for donors. The issues investigated in this study add to the contemporary agenda for research into crowdfunding given by Lehner (2013), which appears to provide a promising field of business research. In addition, the results of this study suggest that crowdfunding requires new approaches that could help with the issues of attracting external capital, flexibility and financing costs, and asymmetric information on the part of donors. Accordingly, we encourage effort toward research related to crowdfunding industry development, e.g., (i) business and corporate governance models, (ii) relationships with donors, (iii) networks and the role performed by crowdfunding platforms, (iv) discussions of the legitimacy of crowdfunding, (v) financial metrics, (vi) legal and regulatory barriers, and (vii) recognition of opportunities.

References

Agrawal, A., Catalini, C., & Goldfarb, A. (2015). Crowdfunding: Geography, social networks, and the timing of investment decisions. *Journal of Economics & Management Strategy, 24*(2), 253–274.

Agrawal, A. K., Catalini, C., & Goldfarb, A. (2014). Some simple economics of crowdfunding. *Innovation Policy and the Economy, 14*(1), 63–97. https://doi.org/10.3386/w19133.

Ahlers, G. K., Cumming, D., Günther, C., & Schweizer, D. (2015). Signaling in equity crowdfunding. *Entrepreneurship Theory and Practice, 39*(4), 955–980.

Ariely, D., Bracha, A., & Meier, S. (2009). Doing good or doing well? Image motivation and monetary incentives in behaving prosocially. *American Economic Review, 99*(1), 544–555.

Belleflamme, P., Lambert, T., & Schwienbacher, A. (2014). Crowdfunding: Tapping the right crowd. *Journal of Business Venturing, 29*(5), 585–609. https://doi.org/10.1016/j.jbusvent.2013.07.003.

Berger, A. N., & Udell, G. F. (1998). The economics of small business finance: The roles of private equity and debt markets in the financial growth cycle. *Journal of Banking and Finance, 22*(6–8), 613–673. https://doi.org/10.1016/S0378-4266(98)00038-7.

Brabham, D. C. (2008). Crowdsourcing as a model for problem solving: An introduction and cases. *Convergence: The International Journal of Research into New Media Technologies, 14*(1), 75–90. https://doi.org/10.1177/1354856507084420.

Braet, O., Spek, S., & Pauwels, C. (2013). Crowdfunding the movies: A business analysis of crowdfinanced moviemaking in small geographical markets. *Journal of Media Business Studies, 10*(1), 1–23. https://doi.org/10.1080/16522354.2013.11073557.

Bruton, G., Khavul, S., Siegel, D., & Wright, M. (2015). New financial alternatives in seeding entrepreneurship: Microfinance, crowdfunding, and peer-to-peer innovations. *Entrepreneurship Theory and Practice, 39*(1), 9–26. https://doi.org/10.1111/etap.12143.

Burt, R. S. (2005). *Brokerage and closure: An introduction to social capital.* Oxford: Oxford University Press.

Burtch, G., Ghose, A., & Wattal, S. (2013). An empirical examination of the antecedents and consequences of contribution patterns in crowd-funded markets. *Information Systems Research, 24*(3), 499–519.

Butticè, V., Colombo, M. G., & Wright, M. (2017). Serial crowdfunding, social capital, and project success. *Entrepreneurship Theory and Practice, 41*(2), 183–207.

Cameron, S. (2015). Music in the marketplace: A social economics approach (Routledge advances in social economics). New York: Routledge. ISBN:978-0415723275.

Cassiolato, J. E., Matos, M., & Lastres, H. (2008). The sounds of Brazil: The popular music and the music industry. In D. Barrowclough & Z. Kozul-Wright (Eds.), *Creative industries and developing countries: Voice, choice and economic growth* (pp. 146–173). Oxon: Routledge.

Cecere, G., Le Guel, F., & Rochelandet, F. (2017). Crowdfunding and social influence: An empirical investigation. *Applied Economics, 49*(57), 5802–5813.

Coleman, J. S. (1990). *Foundations of social theory.* Cambridge: Harvard University Press.

Colombo, M. G., Franzoni, C., & Rossi-Lamastra, C. (2015). Internal social capital and the attraction of early contributions in crowdfunding. *Entrepreneurship Theory and Practice, 39* (1), 75–100. https://doi.org/10.1111/etap.12118.

Cosh, A., Cumming, D., & Hughes, A. (2009). Outside entrepreneurial capital. *Economic Journal, 119*(540), 1494–1533.

Drummond, M., & O'Brien, B. (1993). Clinical importance, statistical significance and the assessment of economic and quality-of-life outcomes. *Health Economics, 2*(3), 205–212. https://doi.org/10.1002/hec.4730020303.

Ebner, W., Leimeister, J. M., & Krcmar, H. (2009). Community engineering for innovations: The ideas competition as a method to nurture a virtual community for innovations. *R&D Management, 39*(4), 342–356. https://doi.org/10.1111/j.1467-9310.2009.00564.x.

ESRI. (2010). *ArcGIS ArcMap, version 10.0: Desktop GIS software.* Redlands: ESRI Inc.

Ferrary, M., & Granovetter, M. (2009). The role of venture capital firms in Silicon Valley's complex innovation network. *Economy and Society, 38*(2), 326–359.

Galuszka, P., & Brzozowska, B. (2017). Crowdfunding and the democratization of the music market. *Media, Culture & Society, 39*(6), 833–849.

Goodchild, M. (2010). Twenty years of progress: GIScience in 2010. *Journal of Spatial Information Science*, (1), 3–20. https://doi.org/10.5311/JOSIS.2010.1.2.

Heckman, J. (1979). Sample selection as a specification error. *Econometrica, 47*(1), 153–161.

Heminway, J., & Hoffman, S. (2011). Proceed at your peril: Crowdfunding and the securities act of 1933. *Tennessee Law Review, 78*(4), 879–972.

IFPI. (2010). *Recording industry in numbers 2010.* London: IFPI.

IFPI. (2014). *IFPI digital music report 2014.* London: IFPI.

Jancenelle, V. E., Javalgi, R. R. G., & Cavusgil, E. (2018). The role of economic and normative signals in international prosocial crowdfunding: An illustration using market orientation and psychological capital. *International Business Review, 27*(1), 208–217.

Kim, K., & Hann, I. H. (2014). Crowdfunding and the democratization of access to capital: A geographical analysis. In H. Robert (Ed.), *Smith school research paper.* College Park. https://doi.org/10.2139/ssrn.2334590.

Kuppuswamy, V., & Bayus, B. L. (2014). *Crowdfunding creative ideas: The dynamics of project backers in Kickstarter* (Working Paper N° 2013-15, UNC Kenan-Flagler Research Paper). Chapel Hill. https://doi.org/10.2139/ssrn.2234765.

Kuti, M., & Madarász, G. (2014). Crowdfunding. *Public Finance Quarterly, 59*(3), 355–366.
Lee, S. H., DeWester, D., & Park, S. R. (2008). Web 2.0 and opportunities for small businesses. *Service Business, 2*(4), 335–345. https://doi.org/10.1007/s11628-008-0043-5.
Lehner, O. M. (2013). Crowdfunding social ventures: A model and research agenda. *Venture Capital: An International Journal of Entrepreneurial Finance, 15*(4), 289–311. https://doi.org/10.1080/13691066.2013.782624.
Lucas, M. E. (2000). Gaucho musical regionalism. *British Journal of Ethnomusicology, 9*(1), 41–60. https://doi.org/10.1080/09681220008567291.
Macht, S. A. (2014). Reaping value-added benefits from crowdfunders: What can we learn from relationship marketing? *Strategic Change, 23*(7–8), 439–460. https://doi.org/10.1002/jsc.1988.
Martins, L. V. B. (2015). Syndicated investing in private equity and venture capital industry: Comparing BRICS. *Journal of Financial Innovation, 1*(1), 18–39. https://doi.org/10.15194/jofi_2015.v1.i1.8.
Mason, C. (2007). Venture capital: A geographical perspective. In H. Landström (Ed.), *Handbook of research on venture capital* (pp. 86–112). Cheltenham: Edward Elgar.
Massolution. (2013). *2013CF The crowdfunding industry report*. Los Angeles: Crowdsourcing.
Matzat, U. (2004). The social embeddedness of academic online groups in offline networks as a norm generating structure: An empirical test of the Coleman model on norm emergence. *Computational & Mathematical Organization Theory, 10*(3), 205–226. https://doi.org/10.1023/B:CMOT.0000045369.98848.71.
McPhearson, M., Smith-Lovin, L., & Cook, J. M. (2001). Birds of a feather: Homophily in social networks. *Annual Review of Sociology, 27*, 415–444. https://doi.org/10.1146/annurev.soc.27.1.415.
Mendes-da-Silva, W., Brito, T. F. S., Famá, R., & Liljegren, J. (2008). Effects of friendship in transactions in an emerging market: Empirical evidence from Brazil. *The Icfai University Journal of Behavioral Finance, 5*(2), 25–46.
Miller, J. E., & Rodgers, M. Y. (2008). Economic importance and statistical significance: Guidelines for communicating empirical research. *Feminist Economics, 14*(2), 117–149.
Mollick, E. R. (2014). The dynamics of crowdfunding: An exploratory study. *Journal of Business Venturing, 29*(1), 1–16. https://doi.org/10.1016/j.jbusvent.2013.06.005.
Nahapiet, J., & Ghoshal, S. (1998). Social capital, intellectual capital, and the organization. *Academy of Management Review, 23*(2), 242–266.
Nichols, A. (2003). *Vincenty: Stata module to calculate distances on the Earth's surface*. St Louis: Ideas. Retrieved January 10, 2014, from https://ideas.repec.org/c/boc/bocode/s456815.html.
Parker, S. C. (2009). *The economics of entrepreneurship*. Cambridge: Cambridge University Press.
Preacher, K. J., & Hayes, A. F. (2008). Asymptotic and resampling strategies for assessing and comparing indirect effects in multiple mediator models. *Behavior Research Methods, 40*(3), 879–891. https://doi.org/10.3758/BRM.40.3.879.
Qiu, C. (2013). Issues in crowdfunding: Theoretical and empirical investigation on Kickstarter. *Social Science Research Network*. https://doi.org/10.2139/ssrn.2345872.
Redaelli, E. (2012). Cultural planning in the United States: Toward authentic participation using GIS. *Urban Affairs Review, 48*(5), 642–669. https://doi.org/10.1177/1078087412441158.
Royal, C., & Windsor, G. S. S. (2014). Microfinance, crowdfunding, and sustainability: A case study of telecenters in a South Asian developing country. *Strategic Change, 23*(7–8), 425–438. https://doi.org/10.1002/jsc.1987.
Saxton, G. D., & Wang, L. (2014). The social network effect: The determinants of giving through social media. *Nonprofit and Voluntary Sector Quarterly, 43*(5), 850868. https://doi.org/10.1177/0899764013485159.
Schwartz, A. A. (2013). *Rural crowdfunding* (Working Paper N° 13-18). *Legal studies research paper series*. Boulder. Retrieved 18 Jan 2014, from http://ssrn.com/abstract=2356643.
Schwienbacher, A., & Larralde, B. (2012). Crowdfunding of entrepreneurial ventures. In D. Cumming (Ed.), *The Oxford handbook of entrepreneurial finance* (pp. 369–391). Oxford: Oxford University Press.

Sheng, H. H., & Mendes-da-Silva, W. (2014). The big family: Informal financing of small and medium-sized business by Guanxi. *Thunderbird International Business Review, 56*(2), 157–171. https://doi.org/10.1002/tie.21609.

Shiller, R. (2013). Capitalism and financial innovation. *Financial Analysts Journal, 69*(1), 21–25.

Skirnevskiy, V., Bendig, D., & Brettel, M. (2017). The influence of internal social capital on serial creators' success in crowdfunding. *Entrepreneurship Theory and Practice, 41*(2), 209–236.

Sorenson, O., & Stuart, T. E. (2001). Syndication networks and the spatial distribution of venture capital investments. *American Journal of Sociology, 106*(6), 1546–1588.

Stemler, A. R. (2013). The JOBS act and crowdfunding: Harnessing the power-and money-of the masses. *Business Horizons, 56*(3), 271–275. https://doi.org/10.1016/j.bushor.2013.01.007.

Strausz, R. (2017). A theory of crowdfunding: A mechanism design approach with demand uncertainty and moral hazard. *American Economic Review, 107*(6), 1430–1476.

Stuart, T., & Sorenson, O. (2005). Social networks and entrepreneurship. In S. Alvarez, R. Agarwal, & O. Sorenson (Eds.), *Handbook of entrepreneurship research* (pp. 233–252). New York: Springer.

Sui, D. Z., Elwood, S., & Goodchild, M. (2013). *Crowdsourcing geographic knowledge.* New York: Springer.

Wellman, B. (1996). Are personal communities local? A Dumptarian reconsideration. *Social Networks, 18*(4), 347–354. https://doi.org/10.1016/0378-8733(95)00282-0.

World Bank. (2013). *Crowdfunding's potential for the developing world.* Washington, DC: World Bank.

Zhang, J., & Liu, P. (2012). Rational herding in microloan markets. *Management Science, 58*(5), 892–912. https://doi.org/10.1287/mnsc.1110.1459.

Zheng, H., Li, D., Wu, J., & Xu, Y. (2014). The role of multidimensional social capital in crowdfunding: A comparative study in China and US. *Information & Management, 51*(4), 488–496. https://doi.org/10.1016/j.im.2014.03.003.

Zook, M. A. (2002). Grounded capital: Venture financing and the geography of the Internet industry, 1994-2000. *Journal of Economic Geography, 2*(2), 151–177. https://doi.org/10.1093/jeg/2.2.151.

Zvilichovsky, D., Danziger, S., & Steinhart, Y. (2018). Making-the-Product-Happen: A driver of crowdfunding participation. *Journal of Interactive Marketing, 41*(2018), 81–93.

Chapter 10
Informal Financing of Chinese Entrepreneurs in a Western Environment

Wesley Mendes-Da-Silva

Abstract This chapter discusses the impact of guanxi on the capacity of small- and medium-sized businesses accessing informal financial resources. Entrepreneurs starting a business outside their country of origin can face barriers in accessing capital, customers, or suppliers. Guanxi facilitates interaction between companies and people in Confucianist societies, including when they emigrate to other nations. Does this type of social construct still play the key role, when Confucian entrepreneurs live in Western societies? Based on interviews with Chinese entrepreneurs active in the principal business center of Brazil and nonparametric test data, our results suggest that different levels of guanxi allow SME businesses to access informal financial resources; the entrepreneur's different levels of guanxi, in terms of parental and nonfamily ties, influence the types of informal financing that might be available; unlike the Western literature on the financial cycles of start-ups, this type of informal financing can extend beyond the initial stage of the business; and finally, an entrepreneur's lack of speaking the local language presents a barrier for Chinese entrepreneurs to access formal bank loans.

Keywords Informal financing · Guanxi · Network · Emerging market · Trust

JEL Code L14 · E26 · N15

When the English singer Sting recorded *Englishman in New York* (Sumner 1987) in the late 1980s, his inspiration may have been a sentiment similar to that of a Chinese individual (who has never left his country) might have when visiting a Western country. However, in the Confucian culture, guanxi provides a phenomenon that can lessen the potential difficulty of adaptation in a different culture. Recent studies, such

---

Portions of this chapter appeared in the 2014 paper "The Big Family: Informal Financing of Small- and Medium-Sized Businesses by Guanxi," *Thunderbird International Business Review*, vol 56, pp 157–171.

W. Mendes-Da-Silva (✉)
Sao Paulo School of Business Administration (FGV/EAESP), Sao Paulo, SP, Brazil

University of Texas at Austin, Austin, TX, USA

W. Mendes-Da-Silva (ed.), *Individual Behaviors and Technologies for Financial Innovations*, https://doi.org/10.1007/978-3-319-91911-9_10

as those carried out by Yang and Wang (2011), have defended the idea of guanxi as a governance mechanism. A social construct present in essentially all Confucianist societies, guanxi can be understood as a model of close relationships and exchange of mutual business favors (Kipnis 1997; Lee et al. 2001; Hutchings and Murray 2003).

In this line of argument, Yang (2002) proposes that guanxi has played an increasing role in businesses developed in different economic and institutional contexts. Furthermore, in the last decade, the academic community has paid special attention to guanxi, notably based on its precedents and its antecedents (Dong et al. 2017; Du et al. 2015; Ko and Liu 2017; Opper et al. 2017; Ye and Abosag 2016; Yin and Mattews 2017). Thus, on its precedents, the literature shows evidence that suggests guanxi is negatively associated with opportunism and is positively influenced by uncertainty in decision-making and a perception of similarity. In other words, it would seem that guanxi provides a form for mitigating risk in uncertain environments by means of introducing bonds of trust (Lee et al. 2001).

The literature shows that guanxi contributes to relationship quality, interdependency, and growth of sales, but has less impact on the capacity to generate profits (Park and Luo 2001). Evidence can also be found that in listed companies, guanxi can improve governance mechanisms and the performance of the firm from the market perspective (Yang and Wang 2011; Luo and Chen 1997). Thus the research examining guanxi has covered both the precedents and the consequences (Wong 2010). Furthermore, the studies on guanxi have been characterized by the perusal of the institutional environment in which large multinational companies operate and promote that most guanxi opportunities are restricted to the Confucianist region.

Few studies have focused on the consequences which this Chinese social capital places on the companies' financial profiles, although a wide range of finance literature emphasizes the importance of network ties and social capital for new ventures in obtaining financial resources across the various finance stages of a business (Berger and Udell 1998; Shane and Cable 2002). According to a survey carried out by Li (2006), guanxi can present different types of specific financing. This approach was applied in an exploratory, qualitative, and empirical study of small- and medium-sized Chinese businesses in Brazil by Sheng (2008).

However, various questions still remain open. It is known that different levels of guanxi exist, some stronger and others weaker (Lu and Reve 2011), and that guanxi may involve family or nonfamily ties. Do these differences in levels and intensity of guanxi influence the type of financing? Which type of informal financing are most significant or most used by Chinese entrepreneurs in a more uncertain wider environment (business environment other than their cultural origin)? And what is the role of the different types (or channels) of formal financing in this context?

Given these unknowns, the main objective of this study was to examine how various levels of guanxi influences the ease with which small- and medium-sized businesses obtain informal access to financial resources in a highly uncertain Western business context. To this end, data were collected at the end of 2011 from a community of Chinese entrepreneurs who emigrated to the city of São Paulo,

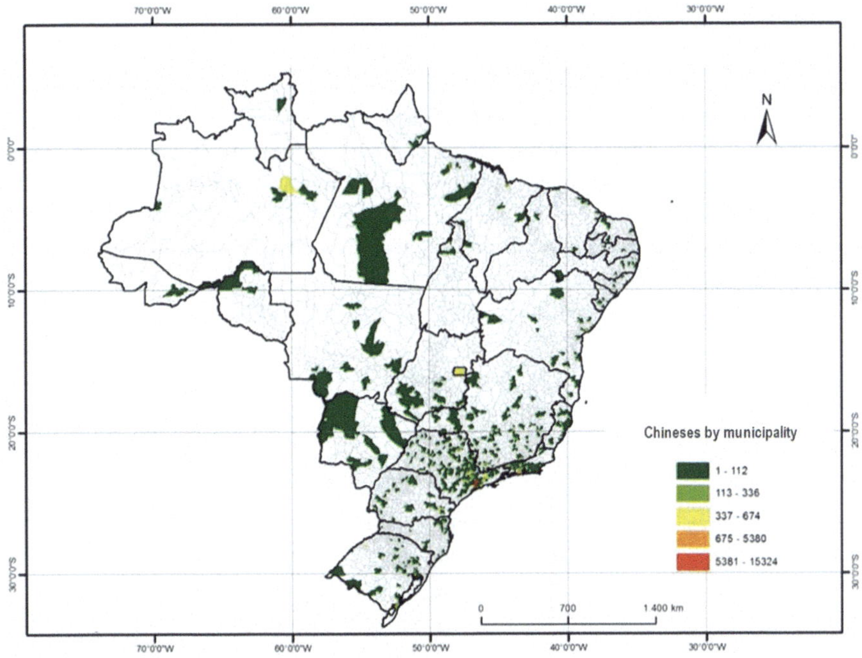

Fig. 10.1 Municipalities of residence of Chinese immigrants in Brazil. Note: Oliveira and Amorim (2016), in the facilities of the Cartography Laboratory PPGG/TIE of PUC/Minas. (Source: SINCRE, Policia Federal do Brazil (2014) and Base cartografica-IBGE (2010))

Brazil, an environment in which the Chinese entrepreneurs are unaccustomed to the language and need to navigate unknown financial institutions in an emerging (yet non-Chinese) economy. Chinese migration to Brazil began two centuries ago, around 1812, and more than 55% of Brazil's Chinese community resides in the state of São Paulo, according to Fig. 10.1 (Amorim 2016).

This study contributes to the financial innovation and entrepreneurial literature inasmuch as it (i) provides empirical evidence of guanxi's characteristics in a Western country with an emerging economy, specifically on the different levels of guanxi; (ii) extends the study of guanxi's role in reducing information asymmetry and conflicts of interest between those needing and those offering capital loans in a non-Confucianist institutional context; and (iii) offers evidence how different forms of guanxi may impact the gathering of informal financial resources for small- and medium-sized businesses. This chapter presents highlights from this research. Our findings provide insight into how financial professionals, financial industry, and entrepreneurs can develop and provide more effective financial strategies based on innovations. The chapter closes with recommendations as well as suggestions for directions in future research.

Comparative Context

According to Lee et al. (2001) and Yang and Wang (2011), guanxi consists as a mechanism for governance and finds more emphatic application in institutional environments characterized by uncertainties, which suggests the relevance of examining the quality of this governance environment. Thus, from data periodically published by Kaufmann et al. (2010), Fig. 10.2 provides an overview of the 2016 governance environment in Brazil and China, compared to other countries in the world considered by Kaufmann et al. (2010).

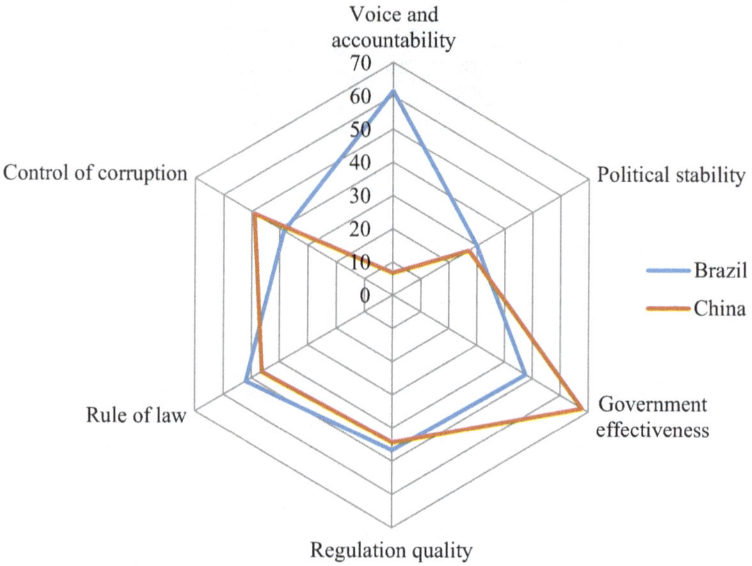

Fig. 10.2 Comparative context of governance Brazil and China (2016). Note: This figure shows the rank (percentile rank among all countries [ranges from 0 {lowest} to 100 {highest} rank}]), characterizing the governance context of Brazil and China in 2016. The six metrics presented are the pillars of the World Governance Index (WGI) published by World Bank (Kaufmann et al. 2010). WGI reports aggregate and individual governance indicators for over 200 countries and territories over the period 1996–2016, for these 6 dimensions of governance: (i) *voice and accountability* = perceptions of the extent to which a country's citizens are able to participate in selecting their government, as well as freedom of expression, freedom of association, and a free media; (ii) *political stability* = perceptions of the likelihood of political instability and/or politically motivated violence, including terrorism; (iii) *government effectiveness* = perceptions of the quality of public services, the quality of the civil service and the degree of its independence from political pressures, the quality of policy formulation and implementation, and the credibility of the government's commitment to such policies; (iv) *regulatory quality* = perceptions of the ability of the government to formulate and implement sound policies and regulations that permit and promote private sector development; (v) *rule of law* = perceptions of the extent to which agents have confidence in and abide by the rules of society and in particular the quality of contract enforcement, property rights, the police, and the courts, as well as the likelihood of crime and violence; (vi) *control of corruption* = perceptions of the extent to which public power is exercised for private gain, including both petty and grand forms of corruption, as well as "capture" of the state by elites and private interests

Li (2006) discusses a particular way to fund business, called *Huei*; it essentially functions as a "consortium," in which an organizing leader invites friends and relations to take part, who, in turn, invite more friends (with guanxi) to join the consortium. This mechanism could perform the role of reason why Asian cultures have such high "family shame" when they fail in a business venture. On the other hand, in the American entrepreneurial context, for example, one thing that Austin Technology Incubator promotes avidly is the *Freedom to Fail* (Gibson and Butler 2015, p. 44). In other words, bankruptcy is bad, but it is personal and, generally speaking, is not expected to affect extended family and friends in a financial manner, while business failure with guanxi funds would have such a devastating personal result.

Brazil presented a better performance than China's governance environment in terms of voice and accountability, which measures the perceptions of the extent to which a country's citizens are able to participate in selecting their government, as well as freedom of expression, freedom of association, and a free media. However, in terms of government effectiveness and control of corruption, China has an advantage over Brazil, according to the data published for the year 2016. Figure 10.3 shows the performance evolution for Brazil and China in the six pillars of the World

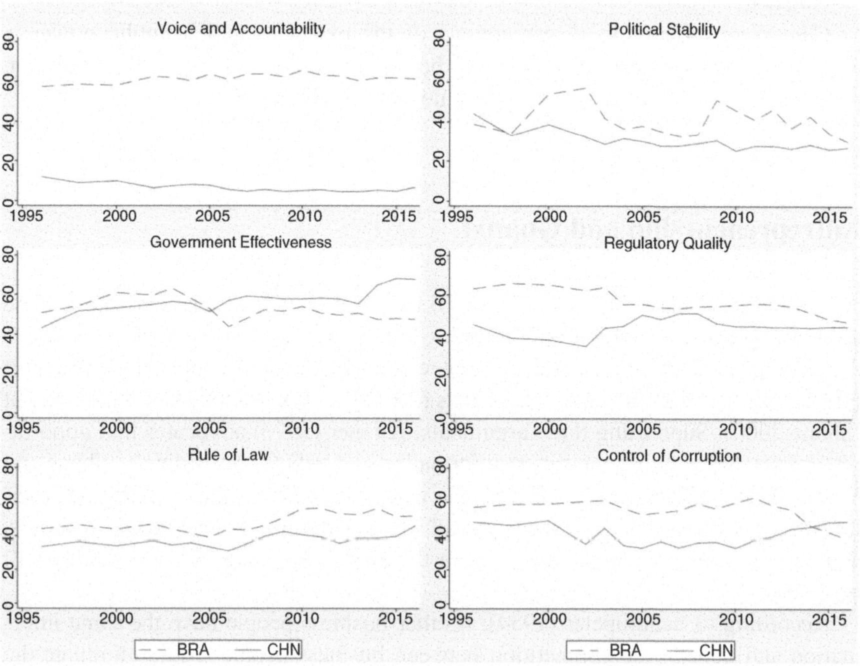

Fig. 10.3 Evolution of the comparative context of governance Brazil and China (1996–2016). Note: This figure shows the evolution in rank (percentile rank among all countries), characterizing the governance context of Brazil and China in the period 1996–2016. The definition of each metric is given in the note in Fig. 10.2

Governance Index (WGI). This index ranks the governance context of all countries, ranging from 0 as lowest to 100 as highest (Kaufmann et al. 2010). WGI reports aggregate individual governance indicators for over 200 countries and territories over the period 1996–2016, for 6 dimensions of governance, as follows:

- *Voice and accountability* = perceptions of the extent to which a country's citizens are able to participate in selecting their government, as well as freedom of expression, freedom of association, and a free media
- *Political stability* = perceptions of the likelihood of political instability and/or politically motivated violence, including terrorism
- *Government effectiveness* = perceptions of the quality of public services, the quality of the civil service and the degree of its independence from political pressures, the quality of policy formulation and implementation, and the credibility of the government's commitment to such policies
- *Regulatory quality* = perceptions of the ability of the government to formulate and implement sound policies and regulations that permit and promote private sector development
- *Rule of law* = perceptions of the extent to which agents have confidence in and abide by the rules of society and in particular the quality of contract enforcement, property rights, the police, and the courts, as well as the likelihood of crime and violence
- *Control of corruption* = perceptions of the extent to which public power is exercised for private gain, including both petty and grand forms of corruption, as well as "capture" of the state by elites and private interests

Entrepreneurship and Guanxi

According to Venkataraman's (1997:120) line of thinking, entrepreneurship can be seen as a process by which opportunities to supply future goods and services are discovered, created, and operated. However, assuming that people have different information and beliefs, some individuals recognize opportunities that others do not (Shane 2000). Supporting these arguments, Kirzner (1973) advocates that opportunities exist due to idiosyncrasies in information and beliefs. Accordingly, Shane and Venkataraman (2000) posit that someone with the resources and the same information and beliefs as an entrepreneur will try to appropriate the business profits, adjusting the price of these resources to the point where the business profits will be eliminated.

According to Schumpeter (1934), if other business people have the same information and beliefs, the competition between business people would eliminate the business opportunity. This line of discussion supports the idea that isolated individuals tend to have less information access or rather that companies with fewer ties in the business environment have less access to the necessary resources, e.g., information, knowledge, status, and capital. Furthermore, companies not linked into business networks tend to make redundant efforts because they lack access to resources already dominated in the business environment.

Thus, as guanxi is essentially a network of companies and people, it is understood that this social construction can influence business performance, notably due to their power over a company's capacity to access resources, including financial ones (Yeung 2006; Hwang 1987). In short, according to Tong (2014), guanxi refers to interpersonal relationships. Chinese businessmen regard guanxi as a crucial facilitator of smooth business transactions, and great effort is expended to build guanxi. Yet if guanxi is, instead, defined as social relationships, then all of us have a large number of guanxi relations. Under Tong (2014), the more compelling question becomes "what are the guanxi bases and how and why are they activated?"

Complexity of the Guanxi Network

In the judgment of Wong (2010), China can be seen as a family formed of high-density relationships. In particular, China is a society based on Confucianism, in which people are highly connected by a variety of guanxi, which can be seen as a network consisting of the huge set of Chinese firms within social and business networks, which has a strong influence on these businesses results (Gibb and Li 2003; Pearce and Robinson 2000). Yet Wong (2010) also states that this definition of guanxi is overly simplistic, given the complex questions involved in this social construct which is based on friendship and affection and on reciprocal obligations to respond with help or assistance on request.

In other words, guanxi networks can be seen as sub-networks (groups defined by people who share some characteristic, and this similarity is recognized as a catalyst in social interaction, in which guanxi can take place most easily) of cells (e.g., organizations such as families or companies) consisting of individuals with guanxi. Such ties can be as simple as two people from the same origin both having affection for their hometown, and the myriad of shared human experiences provides this type of connection, from one individual to another. Such ties help individuals realize connectedness and help strengthen their ties of friendship, so that people come to interact in a small world manner (Hammond and Glenn 2004; Guo and Miller 2010, p. 421).

The small world theorem explains how interpersonal network impacts daily life: an organization or special structure in which people are connected in a regular pattern combined with a chaotic equilibrium (Watts and Strogatz 1998). The small world shows a dynamic underlying the interconnection that reflects the way in which people are, think, and behave (Buchanan 2002). About the intuition of strong and weak ties within a network, if the number of degrees of separation between person A and person B jumps from one to four when a direct link between them is removed, this relationship could be a weak tie, since they are separated by a number of steps. The link is a kind of social bridge, a crucial connection linking the various parts of the social tissue.

In this sense, Granovetter (1973) defends the view that weak ties are more important than strong ties, as the former serve to maintain the connected network. Arguments given by Wong (2010) describe a similar situation in Chinese society and designate these ties (including the weak ones) as guanxi with differing characteristics. In examining the intuition of weak ties formalized by Burt (1992), it could be assumed that weak ties are those which, if broken, can be rebuilt through spanning the distances (degrees of separation) between other existing network participants. Another form of understanding is that if the ties are weak, the level of access to new information is higher. Alternatively, strong ties, if broken, require fewer steps to be rebuilt. For example, family members form a network characterized by strong ties.

Thus, basing himself on the intuition of weak ties introduced by Granovetter (1973), Wong (2010) defends that in China, the tissue of that society is the guanxi arrangement. The principal characteristics of guanxi, according to that author, are: (i) the ties originate within the family (blood ties), also pointing out that this also includes weak ties, which can be seen as a bridge by which outsiders can become insiders; (ii) in Chinese society, once established, strong ties become unbreakable; (iii) frequent interactions with reciprocity strengthen guanxi and bring the participants closer; and (iv) all forms of guanxi are rooted in the family. According to this line of thought, guanxi is understood to be a resource to be managed within the Confucianist business environment (even if not geographically located in countries characterized by this culture), and as in the network, each *guanxi* mechanism acts like a synapse, transmitting resources (e.g., information, knowledge, coordinating activities).

Transaction Costs and Entrepreneurialism

Guanxi can be viewed from the perspective of transaction costs in which the entrepreneurs recognize the need to interact outside the company to attain valuable resources (e.g., information, knowledge, financial resources, status, or reputation), especially when cultural context is minimized. Carlisle and Flynn (2005) share this thinking and add that the accumulation of capital by means of guanxi (legitimacy) helps the business grow in a multicultural environment.

From Shane and Cable's point of view (2002:365), one of the most representative transaction costs for small business success is the asymmetry of information. The authors ask: how can entrepreneurs obtain funding to exploit opportunities when the asymmetry of information that revealed the opportunities is, in itself, a problem? Podolny (1993) assumes that under conditions of uncertainty in the asymmetry of information, direct ties can offer an advantage to people wishing to obtain resources from others. The explanation for this behavior depends largely on two factors: social obligation and access to private information. These two factors are viable in relationships characterized by guanxi. In the perspective of a connected domain, in relating guanxi to the literature on social sciences, we can discuss business capital as a proxy to measure guanxi results. Lastly, Kopnina (2005) confirms various benefits raised for guanxi, for example, the implicit family support at the start of the business – while also pointing to the costs of tradition generated by such relationships when establishing modern small- and medium-sized businesses in Singapore.

Social Capital as a Guanxi Proxy

The concept of social capital has received significant attention in the last decade, both in academic studies and in public debate; and its application to economic problems is still seen with a certain skepticism (Arrow 2000; Dasgupta 2000). Yet some prominent finance researchers accept the concept, incorporate it into the set of economic terms, and pursue appropriate metrics to understand the scale of its importance. Becker (1996), starting from a theoretical perspective, treated social capital as a variable in which an individual's usefulness is considered. Some empirical approaches to social capital have been given by authors such as Knack and Keefer (1997), Knack (1999), Cooke and Wills (1999), Glaeser et al. (2000), and Temple (1999).

There are various conceptions for social capital, and one definition given by Westlund and Bolton (2003) is based on the argument that social capital can be seen as a non-formalized social network (such as guanxi) made up of the agents in a network with rules, values, preferences, and other attributes and social characteristics. Fukuyama (2000) defines social capital as an informal rule that promotes cooperation between the individuals. In the economic sphere, social capital reduces transaction costs, and in the political sphere, it enables the associative life necessary for the success of governments and modern democracy. Arrow (1972) assumes that the central element of commercial transactions is trust and also attributes the lack of such to explain the economic backwardness of some countries around the world.

The literature shows differences in how social capital might be acquired in dissimilar societies, such as the Confucianist collectivist societies and the Western individualist societies. Hamilton (1996) made a clear distinction between Chinese business and Western organizations. Thus, the extensions and the precedents of social capital are analyzed in a comparative approach by Wong and Leung (2001), and Fig. 10.4 summarizes the differences found in these two types of social organizations, as discussed by Lovett et al. (1999) and by Vanhonacker (2004).

Luhmann (1998) assumes that the word trust centers on the ability of certain organizations to function satisfactorily or, rather, the expectation that experts are able to generate in the context of the organizations. In this sense, treating guanxi as a social construct in the form of a network, one can treat social capital as one representation of guanxi, just as social capital supports the formation of networks, i.e., social capital induces trust, which in turn determines the making and maintaining of ties (Buskens 2002). Furthermore, as small- and medium-sized businesses are less formalized and frequently less transparent, they face obstacles

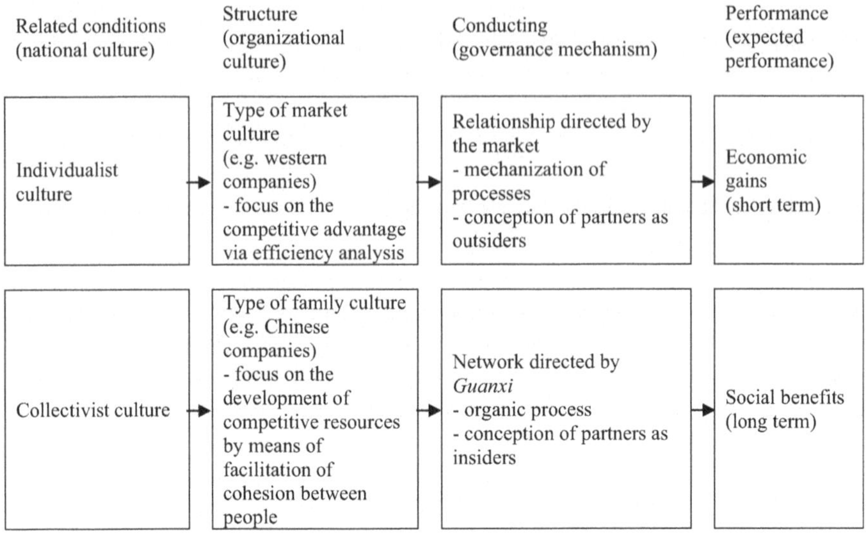

Fig. 10.4 Acquisition of relational capital in the Western world and in Chinese culture. Note: This figure shows the conceptual model of the process of acquisition of relational capital in the Western world and in Chinese culture, in summarized form. One can see that the orientation toward economic gains, the consideration of partners as being outside of the business, due to the priority of the individualist culture in the Western world, is diametrically opposite position to that of Chinese culture. (Source: Adapted from Li et al. (2010, p. 381))

in obtaining access to capital. In this context, personal ties can provide access to resources through a channel characterized by trust and of lower informational asymmetry (Berger and Udell 1998: 622).

Legitimacy and Social Ties

The notion of reciprocity, or sharing something without necessarily expecting something in return, is grounded in the informal exchanges of goods, favors, and work and is a principle that does not extend to the market economies. According to Mauss (1969), reciprocity tends to define social order, as it balances ties and leads to the perception that one individual needs another. This vision is shared from a cultural script. Sahlins (1972) suggests that reciprocity helps establish the relational equilibrium between two close individuals, which is sometimes characterized by the convenience of return.

The actions of reciprocity between friends are not of the "give and take" type (Halpern 1997: 842), but consist of positive reciprocity. Immediate retribution, when strong ties are involved, may even be taken as an offense by the players, as if it were a payment for services rendered, rather than being an alliance. In return, when the ties are weak, in Sahlins' view (1972), the reciprocity is more easily controlled by a negative, i.e., the idea that the players take more than they give.

Self-interest is frequently seen as an a priori motivation in transactions involving distant individuals (strangers/weak ties), meaning that contract violation or other selfish behavior is possible (Castanzias and Helfat 1991). However, when motivational factors other than self-interest are considered, such as the need for affinity, the players may give priority to interests of the other (Seabright et al. 1992). A contribution to behavioral finance is the notion that "friendship," as well as its script, differs from the rational perspective that assumes the maximization of utility to the individual themselves (Mendes-Da-Silva et al. 2008). Put in another way, outside the scope of friendship, a transaction decision will not necessarily benefit the other individual. This is the argument of the traditional view of the economy, based on the rationality of the investor, disputed initially by Tversky and Kahneman (1974).

In exchange relationships between friends, a component to be considered is the socially constructed role that constitutes "friend," which is common in guanxi. Despite the difficulties inherent to defining the term, the behavioral expectations for an individual seen as a "friend" impose certain "scripts" of friendship in transactions, as listed by Halpern (1994, p. 3). In this context, Cummings and Anton (1990) argue that an individual (in the role of agent) may be taken to act in benefit of friends (in the role of principal), even when their friends (principal) do not know they are receiving such attention (from the agents). Thus, the role of "friend" supposes that the individual's conduct will beneficially favor the role of friend over the role of an unknown person or someone outside their circle of personal relationships.

Guanxi and Financing of Business

While interest in guanxi's impact on a firm's access to necessary operational resources is not new (Hwang 1987), guanxi is understood to provide general resources and not just financial ones. Few studies have specifically examined the use of guanxi to finance business activity. On the basis of small- and medium-sized businesses of the Western model, Kopnina (2005) discusses the advantages and disadvantages of guanxi's traditional model for organizational structure and workforce management of small- and medium-sized businesses in Singapore. It has been found that guanxi offers "hidden benefits" to the entrepreneur who manages to obtain start-up capital of this type. This discussion was more directly broached by Li (2006) who carried out a survey on informal company financing in China. This author suggests that informal financing mechanisms such as *Huei* are unstable and tend to be reduced with improved accessibility to the institutional financial environment.

In another study, Sheng (2008) analyzed financing of small- and medium-sized Chinese businesses in Brazil, but this was an exploratory and qualitative study, as the researcher only managed to interview seven entrepreneur cases of Chinese small- and medium-sized businesses in Brazil. The results of Sheng (2008), as well as

Ayyagari et al. (2010), suggest that guanxi enables entrepreneurs to obtain informal financing, reduce the credit costs, prolong the payment periods to local suppliers, and reduce the need for working capital investment. These results also suggest that the institutional environment influences this type of informal loans.

Regarding finance studies with the largest number of observations, most have discussed the question from the perspective of network ties and have pointed to this line of study for potential expansion of the frontier of finance knowledge.

According to Evans and Leighton (1989) and Casson (1982), entrepreneurs often lack sufficient financial resources to exploit identifiable business opportunities. These authors defend the position that seeking external resources is imperative in such situations. Such thinking is foundational to the theory of resource dependence, in which the firm is unlikely to be able to gather all the necessary operational resources from within the company, including the financial and nonfinancial markets resources, whether formally negotiated or not, e.g., reputation, status, and knowledge (Pfeffer and Salancik 1978; Provan 1980).

The consequences of social ties (e.g., friendship and sharing in social circles) on the financing of companies have been widely discussed in the literature on financing new ventures. Shane and Cable (2002) defend that strong network ties are fundamental in the financing of a new business. This strong tie between entrepreneurs and seed-stage investors is based on two mechanisms: information sharing and social obligation.

This idea is also shared by Berger and Udell (1998). In studies of small- and medium-sized businesses, a recurring question is the treatment of information for making financial decisions, i.e., financing and investment. The participation of insider finance (people who know the business and the entrepreneur well) is fundamental for business financing. These authors, in detailing the financing cycles for small- and medium-sized businesses, point out that financial resources from family ties play a limited role in the start-up phase. Similarly, Engelberg, Gao, and Parsons (2012) discuss the role of trust between the investor and the one who seeks resource funds.

Private and public banks in Brazil offer several lines of credit extended to SMEs. Interest rates vary according to a firm's credit rating, and SMEs are provided with support for management orientation as well as with financing. SEBRAE (the Brazilian Service of Support for Micro and Small Enterprises) promotes competitiveness and sustainable development of micro and small enterprises and offers orientation regarding operations management, investment analysis, financing, and production chain.

The Brazilian government also offers financial resources for SMEs at special rates. One priority of BNDES (the Brazilian National Bank for Social and Economic Development) is to support SMEs due to their role in creating jobs and generating national revenue. This type of support is offered to Brazilian enterprises whether they are controlled nationally or internationally. BNDES's financing is offered at lower rates compared to other loans and financing considered good in Brazil and presents different amortization deadlines and grace periods, according to each

SME's profile (Bndes 2012). A lack of awareness of such financial services may be one reason that Chinese entrepreneurs often opt for informal finance sources, i.e., family ties or friendship.

Data and Analysis

This study is based on primary data collected in the second half of 2011. In the city of São Paulo, Brazil, 110 Chinese entrepreneurs were invited to participate. The invitations and entrepreneur questionnaires were conducted by telephone or personal visit. Of these, just 26 were willing to respond to the questionnaire, which was organized in 6 parts: (i) social profile of the entrepreneur and the business; (ii) membership in family networks (first- or second-degree of relationship exclusively) and nonfamily networks (i.e., religious and nonreligious associations); (iii) attributes enabling personal relationships networks (guanxi); (iv) relevance of the finance types (or channels) obtained, both formal and informal; (v) frequency of use of the financing types considered in this study; and (vi) destination of the financial resources obtained by the entrepreneur. The last four parts of the questionnaire collected data according to 10-point Likert scales, where 1 represents *completely irrelevant* aspects and 10 represents *extremely important* aspects.

Difficulty in accessing the entrepreneur participants (even using Mandarin interpreters) resulted in a relatively small data set, considering the intention to subject the data to multivariate treatment. Consequently, nonparametric tests were used, specifically Mann-Whitney U, as an alternative quantitative treatment because of the limited number of observations (Royle 1999). It should be noted that, in seeking information on guanxi (a relationship-based cultural system), our good personal relationships with main Chinese associations in the city of São Paulo contributed to the success of the data collection.

Respondents were informed regarding the nature of the data to be collected and of possible discomfort that might arise, since consent to participate in the study did not imply an obligation to respond to all the questions. The majority (61.5%) were male individuals, 46% spoke only Chinese, 88% had not completed high school, and most owned a bazaar-related establishment. In general, the longer-standing immigrants to Brazil are Chinese from Taiwan (38.5%), whereas more recent immigrants are from Continental China (61.5%). More than 60% are 40 years old, and 80% arrived in Brazil more than 20 years ago.

To test the existence of guanxi associations that included financing for small- and medium-sized businesses, the following procedure was chosen. First, in accordance with the criteria of closeness proposed by Lu and Reve (2011), entrepreneurs were grouped according to their guanxi level in four different ways: degree of family relationship in the city of São Paulo (family ties); strong nonfamily ties, for example, religious and nonreligious associations (strong ties with associations); weak ties whether family or at the level of local associations involving exclusively Chinese (weak guanxi); and accumulated first-degree family ties and belonging to religious associations and simultaneously nonreligious associations (guanxi strong). Second, tests were administered against the possible association between the variables for guanxi level described in the first step, with the aspects measured on the Likert scale (whether in relation to its relevance to the business or the frequency with which the entrepreneur has made use of this in the last 36 months), as follows in Box 10.1:

Box 10.1. Key definitions for funding based on guanxi

Bank loans	A formal instrument by which entrepreneurs obtain financial resources for business activities from banking institutions
Huei	This is the most commonly used type of financing in China. It essentially functions as a "consortium," in which an organizing leader invites friends and relations to take part, who, in turn, invite more friends (with guanxi) to join the consortium. Each consortium member contributes funds, and in the first round, the total amount is to be used by the consortium leader without payment of interest. The nonpayment of interest by the leader represents payment for the administrative services involved in establishing the consortium. After the first round, the leader repays the entire amount, and the total volume may then be auctioned at a monthly interest rate or passed to another individual according to an order predefined at the organization of the consortium as round two. In this organization, due to the good guanxi, the credit risks of all the consortium members are considered equal (Li 2006)
Loans from close relatives	Informal agreement between first- and/or second-degree family relations in order to finance business activities
Loans from friends	Informal agreement between people considered close (or friends), who may have known each other personally in their country of origin and/or in local social activities, in order to finance business activities
Trade credit	Informal commercial agreements established between entrepreneurs and suppliers in order to grant additional periods for payments
Financial assistance from nonreligious associations	Informal agreement by which entrepreneurs belonging to a prescribed circle of personal relationships, predominantly from the same province in their country of origin, obtain financial resources, usually of small amounts

Antecedents of Formation of Guanxi Networks

Of the five guanxi structures described for financing businesses, Chinese entrepreneurs in Brazil tend to favor family relationships. Respondents indicated the following (ranked) order of relevance: (i) close relatives, (ii) business relationships, (iii) of the same origin (region of China), (iv) friendship, and (v) living nearby or previous neighbor. Then, commercial interactions and provincial ties are also valued. Lastly, living close by or having been a neighbor was the aspect with the least contribution. This suggests that the trust necessary for the formation of guanxi seems to be strongly associated with the blood ties between the participants of a guanxi network, at least from the point of view of the study participants.

These results are in line with the studies carried out by Lovett et al. (1999) and Vanhonacker (2004) as a structured view of the differentiated treatments that individuals name as important in establishing types or levels of guanxi. This evidence also corroborates studies describing the intuition of strong and weak ties. Assuming that guanxi is considered to be a significant code in business transactions, this result also supports Thaler's thinking (1985) concerning what he called transactional utility. In other words, individuals may appreciate noneconomic attributes in the formation of *guanxi* networks, and they (in their turn) have influence on business transactions, suggesting that the family ties may be a decisive factor in doing business through *guanxi* networks. Informal financing represented both the more relevant and more used funding mechanism used by the respondents in the last 3 years, compared to formal financing. Table 10.1 shows that the four informal

Table 10.1 Relevance and frequency (average) of use of financial products for financing and investment

		Frequency of use	
Relevance	Relevance in financing	For financing	In investments
Loans from relations	7.24	4.77	
Commercial credit	6.77	5.85	
Consortium (*Huei*)	3.00	1.73	
Bank loan	2.69	2.38	
Loan from friends (*guanxi*)	2.65	1.77	
Help from association	3.08		
Working capital			8.38
Seasonal sales			8.19
Expansion			4.12

Source: Elaborated by the authors from the data collected ($N = 26$)

Note: This table shows the average values found for the types of financing and investment, according to the opinion of the 26 Chinese entrepreneurs participating in the study. If the figures in the second column are examined, we see that the loans obtained from relations were indicated as the most relevant source of business financing, and bank financing as one of the least relevant. The last column shows the average values obtained for the frequency given for the destination of the resources within the businesses, showing that working capital as more frequent than expansion of the business. The values shown in this table refer to the notes attributed by the respondents on a scale of 10 points, where 1 = totally irrelevant and 10 = extremely important sources, such as loans from relatives and trade credit, have a rating greater than 6 on a scale of 10 in terms of relevance.

The formal bank loan was given a rating of just 2.69, a lower rating than the consortium (Huei) and help from associations. For frequency of use, the bank loan (2.38) was also less used in the last 3 years than loans from relations (4.77) and trade credit (5.85). This result is similar to the results obtained by Sheng (2008) and is also in line with Kopnina's (2005) findings for small- and medium-sized businesses in Singapore, where Chinese cultural tradition helps provide seed capital.

This result also contributes to the study by Berger and Udell (1998) which defends the use of insider finance for nontransparent companies (with little information) in the start-up business stage. According to these authors, insider finance consists of a source of capital through loans from the family, friends, or venture capitalists who know the business or entrepreneur very well. In fact, this lack of transparency is present both for suppliers of finance and for Chinese entrepreneurs in Brazil who are unaware of most of the local financial instruments available, which we attribute to difficulty with the local language. Thus, guanxi ensures transparency between the people in a common network and helps businesses obtain informal finance for working capital (rating 8.38) and seasonal sales (rating 8.19).

Experience, Size, and Use of Informal Financing

While the use of informal financing is significant for small- and medium-sized businesses in Brazil, it is not clear whether the entrepreneurs continue to use these methods as they become more experienced in business or increase their businesses. These results apparently suggest bias in the traditional financial studies which stress the importance of informal financing only at the beginning of company life cycles (Berger and Udell 1998) and the use of network ties to finance the initial stage of a new venture (Shane and Cable 2002). These authors seem to assume businesses want to access more formal financing as the business matures and the uncertainties associated with the initial stage of the business diminish over time or with business growth.

The results of this study suggest that, in the case of the immigrant entrepreneur, the importance of informal financing may extend beyond the initial stage. According to preliminary correlations coefficients we checked, only loans from friends lessen significantly, when the entrepreneurs in the sample have more experience and larger number of staff. Despite positive signs, bank loans (formal financing) are not shown to have statistically significant results. The various types of informal financing continue to be used by larger companies. One reason that Chinese entrepreneurs in Brazil extend the importance of informal financing beyond the initial stage could be the entrepreneurs' lack of cultural understanding, where the Chinese small- and medium-sized businesses face difference of language, business practice, culture, and financing environment that impede the use of formal financing.

Guanxi and Type of Financing

Our preliminary results suggested that entrepreneurs perceive a preferential hierarchy of informal guanxi financing choices. Some types of financing are used more often or are considered as more relevant among differing groups of entrepreneurs with various degrees of guanxi (family ties, strong ties with associations, weak guanxi and strong guanxi). The *Huei* type stood out as favored by entrepreneurs with strong guanxi. Entrepreneurs belonging to the group with most guanxi in associations and who had first-degree family relations (strong guanxi) tend to use the type of financing by *Huei* more frequently in comparison with individuals without association-based guanxi and without first-degree family relations in the city of São Paulo, at the level of significance of 10%. It is important to remember that this does not mean that these entrepreneurs use more *Huei* than they do trade credit (in terms of $ volume). This result is in accordance with the characteristics of high credit risk of *Huei* referred to in the previous sections.

This evidence converges with the low frequency of use of *Huei* in Table 10.1 (1.73), as only those entrepreneurs with strong roots in all the forms of social networks had managed to make use of *Huei* in recent years. In fact, according to reports from various entrepreneurs, *Huei* was more widely used in former times (prior to 1999), but with successive economic crises in recent years, the level of credit default among *Huei* participants was very high, and this type of financing became unsustainable. This evidence is in accordance with the argument by Li (2006) that the informal financing mechanism, such as *Huei*, is unstable and liable to suffer from economic crises. The fact that *Huei* is not a family loan also contributes to its instability.

Among Chinese immigrants to Brazil, financing from family members for business loans may often substitute loans that in other contexts might occur between friends. Loans from friends are not considered as relevant by the groups of entrepreneurs with strong family ties and strong guanxi (strong guanxi group). This result suggests that the reciprocity between friends is insufficient to overcome the strength of family ties in a highly uncertain environment. Entrepreneurs belonging to the group with the highest first-degree family guanxi tend to attribute greater relevance to financing by loans from close relatives (family loans) as compared with individuals with second-degree family *guanxi* at the 10% significance level. This evidence complements the literature that uses personal relationships to obtain resources (Engelberg et al. 2012).

Across the group of entrepreneurs with weak guanxi, trade credit is accessed most often. This is explained by the selective composition of this group of entrepreneurs who do not have strong family ties in Brazil and who take relatively little part in religious and nonreligious associations. In this case, they do not consider financing by relatives as relevant to their businesses. Lastly, the results of Table 10.2 also suggest that guanxi can be strengthened by greater involvement of entrepreneurs (with weak family ties) in the religious and nonreligious associations in Brazil. This result is also in line with the discussion of *network initiation* and *network*

Table 10.2 Nonparametric test for independence between relevance and frequency of use of financing, by types of *Guanxi*

	Grouping variables (belonging to Chinese groups in the city of São Paulo)			
Scales of relevance and priority for the channels of access to financial resources*	Family ties[a]	Strong ties with associations	Weak guanxi	Strong guanxi[(d)]
Panel A: relevance of financing types for small- and medium-sized businesses				
Bank loans (financial industry)		✓**		
Huei (guanxi)				
Loans from close relatives (guanxi)	✓*		✓*	
Loans from friends (guanxi)	✓**			✓*
Commercial credit supplier (guanxi)				
Financial assistance granted by association (guanxi)				
Panel B: frequency of use of financing types for small- and medium-sized businesses				
Bank loans (financial industry)		✓*		
Huei (guanxi)				✓*
Loans from close relatives (guanxi)				
Loans from friends (guanxi)				
Commercial credit (guanxi)			✓*	
Panel C: forms of use (investment) of capital in the small- and medium-sized businesses				
Working capital				
Seasonal sales				
Expansion of the company				

Source: Calculations made by the authors on the basis of the data collected in the study

Note: This table gives the results of the nonparametric independence test between types of *guanxi* in relationship to relevance and independence of channels of financing and forms of investment, by means of Mann-Whitney U test

$^{*}p$-value <0.1, $^{**}p$-value <0.05, $^{***}p$-value <0.01

*Panel C refers to the report from the entrepreneurs participating in the study regarding the use of the financial resources within their business (i.e., investment decisions)

✓hypothesis of equality refuted

[a]This variable groups the respondents according to their degree of relationship with their families in Brazil: first and second degrees of relationship

[b]This variable classifies the respondents in two groups: (i) entrepreneurs with weak ties (second-degree relationship or without family relations in Brazil) who participate in the two types of associations (religious and nonreligious) simultaneously and (ii) entrepreneurs in the alternative situation

[c]This variable groups the respondents in two groups: (i) entrepreneurs with second-degree family relations or who have no relations in the city of São Paulo and who participate in at least one association (also includes entrepreneurs who do not participate in any associations involving Chinese)

[d]This variable groups respondents in two groups: (i) entrepreneurs with first-degree family relations in São Paulo and who also maintain links with religious and nonreligious associations in the city of São Paulo and (ii) entrepreneurs who satisfy none of the above premises

maintenance in the study by Lu and Reve (2011). The third column shows that entrepreneurs with "strong ties with associations" not only behave differently to obtain investment than other types of informal financing, they also consider banks loan financing less relevant and use them less frequently than the others.

This unfavorable judgment of the use of bank credit is also related to the entrepreneur's lack of knowledge and the high interest rates for small- and medium-sized businesses in Brazil, in accordance with the responses and comments by entrepreneurs to the final more open questions. Only the younger interviewees with a university education responded as using bank credit for working capital. The others lacked knowledge of bank finance procedures. Although they did not obtain bank financing, some of these entrepreneurs make financial applications (fixed income investment funds) with surplus cash. The main reason for making this application is the rise of the real currency and high interest rate remuneration of funds (current nominal interest rate of Brazilian government bonds in R$ is of around 11% p.a.). This constitutes greater involvement of current Chinese entrepreneurs with the local bank, even if the application is a different result than that of the study by Sheng (2008). In that study, the results suggested that Chinese entrepreneurs avoid all types of banking services.

Concluding Remarks and Future Directions

The results of this study suggest that different guanxi levels enable the small- and medium-sized Chinese businesses with informal access to financial resources in a non-Chinese business and cultural environment (emigrants from one emerging market to another emerging market). These informal financing are relevant and accessed by small- and medium-sized Chinese business entrepreneurs, and guanxi plays a fundamental role as a governance mechanism. This result is presented in details by Sheng (2008) and Sheng and Mendes-Da-Silva (2014).

In the case of Brazil, Chinese entrepreneurs rely on informal loans from family relations (close relatives) and trade credit, rather than bank loans, perhaps because they are unaware of these finance opportunities or lack sufficient language and cultural skills to access formal financing. Consequently, unlike the literatures on the financing cycle and insider finance (Berger and Udell 1998) and on using network ties in financing new ventures (Shane and Cable 2002), this study suggests that the relevance of guanxi's informal financing extends beyond the initial business stage. The results also suggest that entrepreneurs hold a preferential hierarchy of the informal financing choices which guanxi provides. Different types of financing are more commonly used or are considered more relevant, according to the entrepreneurs' degree of guanxi (family ties, strong ties with associations, weak guanxi and strong guanxi).

The *Huei* type is used most often by entrepreneurs with strong guanxi. In recent years, the economic crises affected the level of defaulting among this type of informal loan, and as a result the *Huei* loan has fallen into infrequent use by entrepreneurs, and only those who are deeply rooted in all the forms of social networks have been able to use *Huei*. This evidence agrees with the argument put by Li (2006) that the informal financing mechanisms such as *Huei* (which is not necessarily family) are unstable and liable to suffer from the economic crises. Apparently loans from friends are not considered as relevant by the groups of entrepreneurs with strong family and strong guanxi ties (strong guanxi group). This result suggests that the reciprocity among friends is insufficient to overcome the strength of family ties in a highly uncertain environment. This evidence complements the literature studying personal relationships to obtain resources (Engelberg et al. 2012).

Trade credit is most commonly used by entrepreneurs with weak guanxi. Loans from close relatives are most used by the group of entrepreneurs with strong family ties, i.e., those with first-degree family relations. Bank loans (formal financing), in accordance with our previous discussion, are less used by the entrepreneurs who, despite weaker family ties, are able to acquire more guanxi through their involvement with entrepreneurs in religious and nonreligious associations in Brazil. Thus, although some empirical results are presented in this study, there are data limitations that should be borne in mind. First, not all of the Chinese entrepreneurs contacted in the city of São Paulo wished to give interviews, which introduced some difficulty in collecting data. Second, the low sample size may have led to some bias in the analysis of results.

For future studies, we put forward the following topics:

(i) Conduct similar studies of informal financing as this one, seeking to increase the number of observations over time.
(ii) Compare between Confucianist and Western markets to analyze the impact of personal relationships on small- and medium-sized business capacity to attract financial and nonfinancial resources (e.g., knowledge and technology).
(iii) Analyze the precedents on the formation and acquisition of guanxi in non-Confucianist societies.
(iv) Analyze the relationship between networks of Chinese and Western small- and medium-sized business entrepreneurs, integrating the Western theory of social networks and guanxi (Shane and Cable 2002; Butler and Kozmetsky 2004; Lu and Reve 2011).

References

Amorim, M. S. M. A. (2016). The Chinese immigrant in Brazil and Southeast: An analysis of the data of the demographic census (2010) and SINCRE – federal police (2000-2014). *Caderno de Geografia, 26*(1), 182–196.

Arrow, K. (1972). Gifts and exchanges. *Philosophy and Public Affairs, 1*, 343–362.

Arrow, K. J. (2000). Observations on social capital. In P. Dasgupta & I. Serageldin (Eds.), *Social capital: A multifaceted perspective* (pp. 3–5). Washington, DC: The World Bank.

Ayyagari, M., Demirgüç-Kunt, A., Maksimovic, V., & Smith, R. H. (2010). Formal versus informal finance: Evidence from China. *The Review of Financial Studies, 23*(8), 3048–3097.

Becker, G. S. (1996). *Accounting for tastes*. Cambridge, MA: Harvard University Press.

Berger, A. N., & Udell, G. F. (1998). The economics of small business finance: The roles of private equity and debt markets in the financial growth cycle. *Journal of Banking & Finance, 22*, 613–673.

Bndes (2012). *Cartilha de Orientação ao Pequeno Empresário*. Available at: http://www.bndes.gov.br/SiteBNDES/export/sites/default/bndes_pt/Navegacao_Suplementar/Perfil/Micro_Pequena_e_Media_Empresa_e_Pessoa_Fisica/cartilha_MPME.pdf. Accessed 18 June 2012.

Buchanan, M. (2002). *Nexus: Small worlds and the groundbreaking science of networks*. London: Norton & Co.

Burt, R. S. (1992). *Structural holes: The social structure of competition*. Cambridge: Harvard University Press.

Buskens, V. W. (2002). *Social networks and trust*. London: Klumer Academic Publishers.

Butler, J. S., & Kozmetsky, G. (2004). *Immigrant and minority entrepreneurship: The continuous rebirth of American communities*. London: Praeger Publishers.

Carlisle, E., & Flynn, D. (2005). Small business survival in China: Guanxi, legitimacy, and social capital. *Journal of Developmental Entrepreneurship, 10*(1), 79–96.

Casson, M. (1982). *The entrepreneur*. Totowa: Barnes & Noble Books.

Castanzias, R. P., & Helfat, C. E. (1991). Managerial resources and rents. *Journal of Management, 17*, 12–24.

Cooke, P., & Wills, D. (1999). Small firms, social capital and the enhancement of business performance through innovation programmes. *Small Business Economics, 13*(3), 219–234.

Cummings, L. L., & Anton, R. (1990). The logical and appreciative dimensions of accountability. In S. Srivastra & Cooperider (Eds.), *The functioning of executive appreciation* (pp. 247–437). San Francisco: Jossey-Bass.

Dasgupta, P. (2000). Economic development and the idea of social capital. In I. Serageldin & P. Dasgupta (Eds.), *Social capital – a multifaceted perspective*. Washington: World Bank.

Dong, W., Ma, Z., & Zhou, X. (2017). Relational governance in supplier-buyer relationships: The mediating effects of boundary spanners' interpersonal guanxi in China's B2B market. *Journal of Business Research, 78*, 332–340.

Du, N., Ronen, J., & Ye, J. (2015). Auditors' role in China: The joint effects of guanxi and regulatory sanctions on earnings management. *Journal of Accounting, Auditing and Finance, 30*(4), 461–483.

Engelberg, J., Gao, P., & Parsons, C. A. (2012). Friends with money. *Journal of Financial Economics, 103*, 169–188.

Evans, D., & Leighton, L. (1989). Some empirical aspects of entrepreneurship. *American Economic Review, 79*(3), 519–535.

Fukuyama, F. (2000). *Social capital and civil society* (International Monetary Fund Working Paper, WP/00/74, pp. 1–18).

Gibb, A., & Li, J. (2003). Organizing for enterprise in China: What can we learn from the Chinese micro, small, and medium enterprise development experience. *Future, 35*(4), 403–421.

Gibson, D. V., & Butler, J. S. (2015). Creating and sustaining high-technology development in Austin, Texas. In L. Foss & D. V. Gibson (Eds.), *The entrepreneurial university: Context and institutional change*. New York: Routledge.

Glaeser, E., Laibson, D., Scheinkman, J., & Soutter, C. (2000). Measuring trust. *Quarterly Journal of Economics, 65*(3), 811–846.

Granovetter, M. (1973). The strength of weak ties. *American Journal of Sociology, 78*(6), 1360–1380.

Guo, C., & Miller, J. (2010). Guanxi dynamics and entrepreneurial firm creation and development in China. *Management and Organization Review, 6*(2), 267–291.

Halpern, J. J. (1994). The effect of friendship on personal business transactions. *Journal of Conflict Resolution, 38*(4), 647–664.

Halpern, J. J. (1997). Elements of a script for friendship in transactions. *Journal of Conflict Resolution, 61*(6), 835–868.

Hamilton, G. (1996). *Asian business networks*. Berlin/New York: Walter de Gruyter.
Hammond, S. C., & Glenn, L. M. (2004). The ancient practice of Chinese social networking: Guanxi and social network theory. *E:CO, 6*(1–2), 24–31.
Hutchings, K., & Murray, G. (2003). Family, face, and favours: Do Australians adjust to accepted business conventions in China? *Singapore Management Review, 25*(2), 25–49.
Hwang, K. (1987). Face and favour: The Chinese power game. *American Journal of Sociology, 92*, 944–974.
Kaufmann, D., Kraay, A., & Mastruzzi, M. (2010). *The worldwide governance indicators: A summary of methodology, data and analytical issues* (World Bank Policy Research Working Paper No. 5430). http://papers.ssrn.com/sol3/papers.cfm?abstract_id=1682130.
Kipnis, A. B. (1997). *Producing guanxi: Sentiment, self, and subculture in a North China village*. Durham: Duke University Press.
Kirzner, I. (1973). *Competition and entrepreneurship*. Chicago: University of Chicago Press.
Knack, S. (1999). *Social capital, growth and poverty: A survey of cross-country evidence* (Social Capital Initiative Working Paper No. 4). Washington, DC: The World Bank.
Knack, S., & Keefer, P. (1997). Does social capital have an economic payoff: A cross-country investigation. *Quarterly Journal of Economics, 112*(4), 1251–1288.
Ko, W. W., & Liu, G. (2017). A typology of guanxi-based governance mechanisms for knowledge transfer in business networks of Chinese small and medium-sized enterprises. *Group and Organization Management, 42*(4), 548–590.
Kopnina, H. (2005). Family matters? Recruitment methods and cultural boundaries in Singapore Chinese small and medium enterprises. *Asia Pacific Business Review, 11*(4), 483–499.
Lee, D. J., Pae, J. H., & Wong, Y. H. (2001). A model of close business relationship in China (Guanxi). *European Journal of Marketing, 35*(1/2), 51–69.
Li, C. C. (2006). *Zong Guo Di Xia Jin Ron Diao Cha (Informal finance survey in China)*. XangHai: Popular Publisher.
Li, C. L., Channg, W., & Hsieh, J. (2010). The importance of social capital to the management of multinational firms: Relational networks among Chinese and American firms. In: *Proceedings of the 2nd European Conference on Intellectual Capital Held at ISCTE*, Lisbon University Institute, Lisbon.
Lovett, S., Simmons, L. C., & Raja, K. (1999). Guanxi versus the market: Ethics and efficiency. *Journal of International Business Studies, 30*(2), 231–248.
Lu, R., & Reve, T. (2011). Guanxi, structural hole and closure. *Journal of Strategy and Management, 4*(3), 275–288.
Luhmann, N. (1998). Familiarity, confidence, trust: Problems and alternatives. In D. Gambetta (Ed.), *Trust: Making and breaking cooperative relations*. Oxford: Basil Blackwell.
Luo, Y., & Chen, M. (1997). Does guanxi influence firm performance? *Asia Pacific Journal of Management, 14*, 1–16.
Mauss, M. (1969). *The gifts: Forms and functions of exchange in Archaic societies*. London: Cohen & West.
Mendes-Da-Silva, W., et al. (2008). Effects of friendship in transactions in an emerging market: Empirical evidence from Brazil. *The Icfai Journal of Behavioral Finance, 5*, 25–46.
Opper, S., Nee, V., & Holm, H. J. (2017). Risk aversion and guanxi activities: A behavioral analysis of CEOs in China. *Academy of Management Journal, 60*(4), 1504–1530.
Park, S. H., & Luo, Y. (2001). Guanxi and organizational dynamics: Organizational networking in Chinese firms. *Strategic Management Journal, 22*(5), 455–477.
Pearce, J. A., II, & Robinson, R. B. (2000). Cultivating Guanxi as a foreign investor strategy. *Business Horizons, 43*, 31–38.
Pfeffer, J., & Salancik, G. R. (1978). *The external control of organizations: A resource dependence perspective*. New York: Harper & Row.
Podolny, J. (1993). A status-based model of market competition. *American Journal of Sociology, 98*, 829–872.

Provan, K. (1980). Board power and organisational effectiveness among human service agencies. *Academy of Management Journal, 23*(2), 221–236.

Royle, R. (1999). *Statistical strategies for small sample research*. London: Sage Publications.

Sahlins, M. (1972). *Stone age economics*. Chicago: Aldine Atherton.

Schumpeter, J. (1934). *The theory of economic development: An inquiry into profits, capital, interest, and the business cycle*. Cambridge, MA: Harvard University Press.

Seabright, M. D., Levinthal, D., & Fichman, M. (1992). Role of individual attachments in the dissolution of interorganizational relationships. *Academy of Management Journal, 35*, 122–160.

Shane, S. (2000). Prior knowledge and discovery of entrepreneurial opportunities. *Organization Science, 11*(4), 448–469.

Shane, S., & Cable, D. (2002). Network ties, reputation, and the financing of new ventures. *Management Science, 48*(3), 364–381.

Shane, S., & Venkataraman, S. (2000). The promise of entrepreneurship as a field of research. *Academy of Management Review, 25*(1), 217–226.

Sheng, H. H. (2008). Relationship-based financing models: Experiences of Chinese entrepreneurs in Brazil. *Revista de Administração Contemporânea, 12*, 741–761.

Sheng, H.H., & Mendes-Da-Silva, W. (2014). The big family: Informal financing of small- and medium-sized businesses by Guanxi. *Thunderbird International Business Review, 56*(2), 157–171. https://doi.org/10.1002/tie.21609

Sumner, G. M. T. (1987). *Englishman in New York: Nothing like the Sun*. London: Associated Independent Recording-Air Studios.

Temple, J. (1999). Initial conditions, social capital, and growth in Africa. *Journal of African Economics, 7*(3), 309–347.

Thaler, R. H. (1985). Using mental accounting in a theory of purchasing behavior. *Marketing Science, 4*, 12–13.

Tong, C. K. (2014). *Chinese business: Rethinking guanxi and trust in Chinese business network*. Singapore: Springer.

Tversky, A., & Kahneman, D. (1974). Judgment under uncertainty heuristics and biases. *Sciences, 185*, 1124–1131.

Vanhonacker, W. R. (2004). Guanxi networks in China. *China Business Review, 31*(3), 48–53.

Venkataraman, S. (1997). The distinctive domain of entrepreneurship research. *Advanced Entrepreneurship Research, 3*, 119–138 *Firm Emergence Growth, 78*(6), 1360–80.

Watts, D. J., & Strogatz, S. H. (1998). Collective dynamics of small-world networks. *Nature, 393*, 440–442.

Westlund, H., & Bolton, R. (2003). Local social capital and entrepreneurship. *Small Business Economics, 21*(2), 77–113.

Wong, M. (2010). Guanxi management as complex adaptative system: A case study of Taiwanese ODI in China. *Journal of Business Ethics, 91*, 419–432.

Wong, Y. H., & Leung, T. (2001). *Guanxi-relationship marketing in a Chinese context*. New York: International Business Press.

Yang, M. (2002). Rebuttal: The resilience of Guanxi and its new deployments: A critique of some new Guanxi scholarhip. *China Quarterly, 170*, 459–476.

Yang, Z., & Wang, C. L. (2011). *Guanxi* as a governance mechanism in business markets: Its characteristics, relevant theories, and future research directions. *Industrial Marketing Management, 40*, 492–495.

Yen, D. A., & Abosag, I. (2016). Localization in China: How guanxi moderates Sino–US business relationships. *Journal of Business Research, 69*(12), 5724–5734.

Yeung, M. (2006). Is Guanxi (relationship) a bridge to knowledge transfers. *Journal of Business Research, 59*, 130–139.

Yin, W., & Matthews, K. (2017). Bank lending and bank relationships in China: Guanxi or commercial? *Managerial Finance, 43*(4), 425–439.

Chapter 11
Diversification and Performance of Credit Unions

Laís Karlina Vieira, Valéria Gama Fully Bressan, and Aureliano Angel Bressan

Abstract This chapter evaluates the impact of revenue diversification with expanding products and services upon the financial performance of credit unions. The diversification effect on credit union performance was verified through dynamic panel data models estimated by two-stage system Generalized Method of Moments. Semiannual information (spanning 2009 to 2014) of 525 unique credit unions informed the study. The analysis revealed that nine models estimated with proxies for performance based on profitability indicators showed that diversification does not affect the return of credit unions. However, in three other models, using the growth of adjusted shareholders' equity as a proxy for performance, it was possible to capture the effects of the diversification of revenues. These divergent results may indicate that credit union diversification strategies do not aim to increase dividends or profitability. But it may also suggest that this strategy helps cooperatives meet primary obligations by providing extra resources, maintaining their financial market positions, or even their survival.

Keywords Credit unions · Diversification · Financial performance · Financial innovation

JEL Code L26 · E51 · F45

The purpose of private sector managers, whether in industrial organizations, banks, or cooperatives, is to identify the best strategies and the ideal market conditions, evaluate the competition, and address the interests of the owners. Among institutional strategies, it is a major decision whether or not to diversify activities or business lines. Financial institutions, like other industries, diversify their activities with products and services that go beyond classical financial intermediation, loans, and savings. This chapter focuses on credit unions, and diversification of activities

L. K. Vieira · V. G. F. Bressan · A. A. Bressan (✉)
Department of Business Economics, Federal University of Minas Gerais, Belo Horizonte/MG, Brazil

W. Mendes-Da-Silva (ed.), *Individual Behaviors and Technologies for Financial Innovations*, https://doi.org/10.1007/978-3-319-91911-9_11

will be identified through sources of operating revenue: an institution that derives most of its revenues from credit operations can be considered as concentrated, while an institution that reliably bases its revenues on income from credit operations (denominated interest income) and other sources of operating income (non-interest income) can be considered as diversified. This definition of diversification was based on Esho et al. (2005), Stiroh and Rumble (2006), Mercieca et al. (2007), and Goddard et al. (2008).

Previous studies provide inconclusive empirical results regarding the impact of activity diversification on financial intermediary performance. The literature suggests that banks, when acquiring customer information during the borrowing process, are able to provide other financial services efficiently. Thus, financial conglomerates could leverage economies of scope that drive performance and market assessments. Alternatively, the diversification of activities within a single financial conglomerate may intensify agency problems between business leaders and small shareholders with negative implications for the conglomerate's market value (Laeven and Levine 2007).

Therefore, several studies have explored the relationship between revenues and business strategies that do not arise from credit operations, market conditions, technological changes, and risk-adjusted financial performance in US banks and elsewhere (Goddard et al. 2008). However, the same attention was not given to credit unions, as highlighted by McKillop and Wilson (2011). We highlight some studies that have examined the diversification in credit unions like Esho et al. (2005), Goddard et al. (2008), Mathuva (2016), and Malikov et al. (2017). In developing countries, the topic of diversifying activities in credit unions needs empirical research, since existing work on diversification focused mainly on nonfinancial organizations active in the capital market. Therefore, this analysis will contribute to foment the discussion about diversifying activities of credit unions.

To remain competitive and expand participation in the National Financial System, credit unions can use the strategy of diversifying their activities to offer their members differentiated and more complete financial services. This potential exposes the need to investigate the potential benefits of this strategy for the credit union segment by analyzing the impact of this strategy on credit union performance. Thus, the purpose of this study is to answer the following question: How does diversifying revenues affect financial performance for credit unions in Brazil?

As we join the literature discussion about credit union performance, we note that these institutions stand out within the Brazilian scenario for their reach in the territory, easy access of members to credit and for their cooperative nature, which aims to better serve its members while boosting regional and local businesses. This paper also aims to contribute to the credit unions themselves by providing a study that may assist them to define their strategies. Finally, it contributes to academia by addressing a current theme, on institutions little studied in the Brazilian and international literature, in the context of Brazil constituting an emerging market, filling an under explored research niche.

Performance Credit Unions

Organizational performance is an important construct in management research. The areas of marketing, production, human resources, and strategy are ultimately evaluated for their contribution to organizational performance. However, this construct is often measured in limited ways that do not reflect its multidimensionality (Richard et al. 2009).

Given the various components that impact both performance as well as stakeholders, organizational performance becomes complex to measure satisfactorily in all its dimensions. Therefore, a wide range of information, both financial and non-financial, is needed. Accounting performance measures have been the traditional pillar of quantitative approaches to measure organizational performance (Otley 2002). However, great attention has also been given to the development and use of non-financial performance measures, used to motivate and report organizational performance.

For credit unions, the performance analysis needs to be relevant to the peculiarities involved in managing these institutions. According to Taylor (1971), a credit union, as a cooperative, represents a group organized around a "common bond" that can take various forms, such as people from the same community or the same workplace. Credit unions are nonprofit organizations that rely on voluntary management, elected by its members using the principle of one man, one vote. The foundations of the cooperative enterprise remain unchanged according to the International Co-operative Alliance documents, despite global changes.

In this context, credit unions are different from other financial intermediaries, as they operate to provide services to their members without profit. Both advantages and disadvantages emerge as compared to competing for-profit financial institutions. Its cooperative nature restricts its size, limiting its ability to exploit economies of scope and scale. Yet nonprofit status, coupled with the characteristic of transacting only with its members, provides credit unions with a tax advantage that reduces costs (Fried et al. 1993). One of the great challenges of credit unions is to create management mechanisms that are compatible with this administrative complexity, to meet regulatory requirements, and to operate in accordance with their doctrinal principles (Bressan et al. 2010).

There is a duality in the management of cooperatives: on the one hand, there are cooperative principles, and on the other hand, the market and competition impose certain demands on these institutions. Thus, through democratic management, cooperatives must be efficient and productive to ensure their survival without abandoning their principles (Carvalho et al. 2015). Yet nonprofit organizations exercise a different economic logic in their operation. In this case, it may be strategic that these institutions do not present economic results at the end of the accounting period, but instead they offer more attractive rates to their associate or even a better possible level of services. Therefore, there would be no surpluses of the accounting exercise, but rather, the results would be verified directly in the economic activity of its associates, thus generating value creation for the cooperative (Bialoskorski Neto et al. 2006).

Since the priority of the credit union is to maximize the services provided to its members (owners), this immediately suggests that maximizing profits (or surpluses) is not an appropriate goal as there are no suppliers or customers (nonmembers) to satisfy. Another issue to be highlighted is the possible conflict between borrowing members and savers; while borrowers aim for lower interest rates, savers seek higher deposit rates (Smith 1986; Fried et al. 1993). These characteristics, and others, require a specialized evaluation performance model. It is inappropriate, for example, to treat credit unions as banks and evaluate their performance based on their ability to maximize profit. At the same time, it is also inappropriate to ignore the services offered by other financial institutions, since they often compete in the same markets (Fried et al. 1993).

Diversification of Financial Institutions and Credit Unions

Product diversification, a basic corporate strategy, reflects the scope of the markets and sectors in which an organization competes (Hitt et al. 2008). Diversification occurs when the company expands to manufacture and sell products or a product line that has no market interaction (price elasticity equal to zero) with the company's other products. Such lack of interaction means that the explanations of diversification should focus on the economies of shared factors in production and on the impact of diversity on organizational efficiency (Rumelt 1982).

Organizations diversify for two reasons. First, diversification can improve the organization's efficiency resulting in increased value. Second, if the owners of the organization are not directly involved in the decision to diversify the business, diversification may reflect the managers' preferences (Besanko et al. 2007). While many non-financial corporations around the world have sought to focus on core business practices over the last two decades, financial services firms, and especially banks, have increasingly diversified their businesses (Elsas et al. 2010). Diversification in the banking sector can occur in three ways: (1) between financial products and services (diversification of products or lines of business), (2) through geographical expansion (geographical diversification), and (3) through the combination of geographical diversification and business lines (Mercieca et al. 2007). For the purposes of this study, emphasis is placed on the diversification of products or business lines.

It should be noted that the competitive pressure on current cost gains, attributed in part by financial deregulation, has led US financial institutions to focus on other revenues (not from financial intermediation), including services that incur payment of fees and commissions, insurance, and off-balance sheet business (Goddard et al. 2008). One explanation for diversification in financial institutions is that this business is truly special in the sense that expanding its scope creates value for owners. Such value creation could arise from two sources: economies of scope and changes in the sector due to technological changes and deregulation (Elsas et al. 2010).

Financial institutions that engage in a variety of activities can leverage economies of scope, boosting their performance, and their market assessments. However, empirically it is difficult to measure economies of scope in these financial institutions. In hopes to mitigate this problem, these authors propose an alternative, not to measure economies of scope directly but to investigate whether such financial activities influence the institutions' market assessments. Thus, it is believed that by diversifying activities, a financial institution could provide economies of scope that would improve their assessments (Laeven and Levine 2007).

Diversification can also add value for financial institutions because of industry changes triggered by the technological process and deregulation (Elsas et al. 2010). The banking sector has been transformed by deregulation and rapid technological advances in information flows, information infrastructure and financial markets. Deregulation has promoted competition (previously nonexistent) between banks, non-banking institutions, and financial markets. As a result, many banks have adopted new technologies that have dramatically altered their production and distribution strategies, resulting in large increases in non-interest income (DeYoung and Rice 2004).

Credit unions have received less attention in the literature that studies such diversification. However, such cooperative ventures, classified as financial institutions, may also diversify their activities through the expansion of products and services, to remain competitive in financial markets (Esho et al. 2005). The consequences of non-interest income for the performance of financial institutions are not well understood. The empirical literature has provided conflicting predictions about the impact of greater diversification of activities on the performance of financial intermediaries, requiring further examination (DeYoung and Rice 2004; Esho et al. 2005; Stiroh and Rumble 2006; Laeven and Levine 2007).

Some empirical studies have identified a diversification discount in financial institutions or found no increase in profitability due to diversification. Laeven and Levine (2007) demonstrated the existence of a diversification discount, since the market values of financial conglomerates engaged in various activities were smaller than those financial conglomerates that were classified as specialists in individual activities. Mercieca et al. (2007), when analyzing small credit institutions in the European Union, found no diversification benefits within and between lines of business, as well as an inverse association between noncredit income and bank performance.

The study by Lee et al. (2014) using individual bank data from 22 Asian countries identified non-financial activities of Asian banks as reducing risk but not increasing the profitability of a broad sample base. Jouida et al. (2017) studied the impact of activity and geographical diversification on French financial institutions, and their results demonstrate a negative relationship between performance and diversification (activities or geographic); however, this relationship becomes significantly positive when the institutions implement a strategy of double diversification.

Another line of thought suggests the existence of benefits (or prizes) of diversification for financial institutions. Stiroh and Rumble (2006) examined US financial conglomerates and found benefits from revenue diversification. However, such benefits are offset by the costs generated by increased exposure to activities not arising from financial intermediation, which are more volatile but less profitable than financial intermediation activities. Elsas et al. (2010) analyzed large banks in nine developed countries and found that diversification of revenue increases banks' profitability via higher margins than non-financial corporations and lower cost rates.

Regarding diversification of revenues and the performance of credit unions, Esho et al. (2005) identified that more diversified Australian credit unions presented lower risks and returns. In turn, Goddard et al. (2008) found that larger credit unions should be encouraged to explore more diversification opportunities; on the other hand, smaller credit unions should be encouraged to limit their diversification and continue to operate as simple savings and loan vehicles. Mathuva (2016) examined how revenue diversification influences the performance of Kenya's credit and savings cooperatives, to find that a greater reliance on noncredit income is associated with higher returns, with revenue diversification beneficial to small cooperatives.

Malikov et al. (2017) confirmed that credit unions in the United States enjoy economies of diversification. Their approach to studying the benefits/costs of diversification differs from others, inasmuch as diversification economies are based on microeconomic theory and are measured in terms of cost savings due to the increase in the scope of products through the multiple processes of production. In addition, they focus on diversifying products within a group of interest-generating activities (different types of loans).

Data Collection

Of the 650 individual credit unions operating in December 31, 2014, in Brazil, 525 credit unions belonging to the Sicoob, Sicredi, and Unicred systems were analyzed in the period from 2009 to 2014, representing 81% of this population. The 125 cooperatives were excluded from the sample because, during the period of analysis, they (i) did not collect deposits from their associates, (ii) changed their activity or classification with the Central Bank of Brazil, or (iii) did not present information in any analyzed period, including any credit union that went through the merger process during that time.

The semiannual credit union accounting data of the Accounting Plan of the Institutions of the Brazilian National Financial System and the report of incorporations and divisions of credit unions were obtained from the Central Bank of Brazil (2014), and the data referring to the semiannual national gross domestic product (GDP) were collected in the Brazilian Institute of Geography and Statistics.

Econometric Model

The literature on the relationship between diversification and performance has highlighted the potential problems of endogeneity of the variables that may arise in these models and that may result in inconsistent estimates (Campa and Kedia 2002; Stiroh and Rumble 2006; Goddard et al. 2008; Park and Jang 2012; Lee et al. 2014; Jouida et al. 2017). In addition, some studies have emphasized the persistence of financial performance indicators, suggesting that static models may be inadequate and so recommending the use of dynamic models (Goddard et al. 2004; Athanasoglou et al. 2008; Carvalho et al. 2010; Migliardo and Forgione 2015; Jouida et al. 2017).

Thus, in order to control the potential problems of endogeneity in the estimates and also to consider the temporal persistence of performance, a dynamic panel was estimated by the System Generalized Method of Moments (System GMM). Initially, the description of the variables used in the System GMM is presented, and later, the equations that were estimated are presented. To evaluate the performance of cooperatives, which is the dependent variable investigated in the models, several performance proxies were used to validate the results found and are described in Table 11.1.

In order to capture the effect of revenue diversification on the performance of cooperatives, the Herfindahl-Hirschman index adjusted for revenue was constructed based on the accounts of the Accounting Plan of the Institutions of the Brazilian National Financial System (APIBNFS). According to APIBNFS, the various activities of Brazilian credit unions result in income obtained through five portions of operating revenues (ORev): (1) Loan from Credit Operations (CREDOp), (2) Income

Table 11.1 Definition of dependent variables used in the study

Acronyms	Definition of dependent variables	Authors who used performance metrics
ROA_{it}	Return on total assets $ROA = \frac{\text{Surpluses}}{\text{Total assets}}$	Esho et al. (2005), Stiroh and Rumble (2006), Mercieca et al. (2007), Goddard et al. (2008), Bressan et al. (2011), Lee et al. (2014), and Francisco (2014)
ROE_{it}	Return on equity $ROE = \frac{\text{Surpluses}}{\text{Equity}}$	DeYoung and Rice (2004), Goddard et al. (2004, 2008), Stiroh and Rumble (2006), Mercieca et al. (2007), Bressan et al. (2011), Lee et al. (2014), and Francisco (2014)
ROI_{it}	Return on investment $ROI = \frac{\text{Operational result}}{\text{Expensive resources}}$	Francisco (2014)
EqG_{it}	Equity growth (adjusted) $EqG = \left(\frac{\text{Equity of the current month}}{\text{Equity of the previous month}}\right) - 1$	Bressan et al. (2011) and Gollo and Silva (2015)

from Interbank Liquidity Investments (IILI), (3) Income from Securities and Derivative Financial Instruments (ISDFI), (4) Income from Service (ISERV), and (5) Other Operating Revenues (OTHER).

In addition to these, Non-Operating Income from Credit Operations (NonCRED) was obtained, which is the sum of the accounts: Income from Interbank Liquidity Investments, Income from Securities and Derivative Financial Instruments, Income from Services, Other Operating income. Thus, to ensure robust results, two different calculation methods were used, as indicated in the literature, to obtain the diversification index based on Herfindahl-Hirschman. These measures aim to assign a numerical value to describe the diversity of a credit union's portfolio. A third measure of diversification is also used in this study, but this is not supported by the Herfindahl-Hirschman index. This measure referred to herein as RNOC verifies the proportion of revenues not derived from credit operations, due to the total operating income of the cooperatives. The diversification measures are presented in Table 11.2.

Table 11.2 Definition of diversification and expected signal variables

Acronym	Definition of dependent variables	Expected sign	Authors who used the diversification measure
DIVA it	One minus the Herfindahl-Hirschman index (1-HHI). HHI obtained by the composition of the operating income in two categories $DIV_A = 1 - \left(\left(\frac{CREDOp}{ORev}\right)^2 + \left(\frac{NonCRED}{ORev}\right)^2\right)$	Uncertain	Stiroh and Rumble (2006), Mercieca et al. (2007), and Goddard et al. (2008)
DIVB it	One minus the Herfindahl-Hirschman index (1-HHI). HHI obtained through the composition of revenue into five categories $DIV_B = 1 - \left(\left(\frac{CREDOp}{ORev}\right)^2 + \left(\frac{IILI}{ORev}\right)^2 + \left(\frac{ISDFI}{ORev}\right)^2 + \left(\frac{ISERV}{ORev}\right)^2 + \left(\frac{OTHER}{ORev}\right)^2\right)$	Uncertain	Esho et al. (2005) to measure the concentration of revenues (HHI); Elsas et al. (2010) to measure diversification (1-HHI)
RNOCit	Ratio of income not derived from loans and operating revenues $RNOC = \frac{NonCRED}{ORev}$	Uncertain	Stiroh and Rumble (2006), Mercieca et al. (2007), Goddard et al. (2008), and Lee et al. (2014)

Source: Prepared by the authors

Table 11.3 Definition of the explanatory variables used for control and expected signal

Acronym	Definition of dependent variables	Expected sign	Authors who adopted the variables
$Y_{i,t-1}$	Deviation dependent variable (ROA, ROE, ROI, or EqG). It is the dynamic model variable	Positive	Goddard et al. (2004), Athanasoglou et al. (2008), and Migliardo and Forgione (2015)
LNA_{it}	Natural logarithm of total assets	Positive	Stiroh and Rumble (2006), Goddard et al. (2008), and Lee et al. (2014)
ΔlnA_{it}	Variation of the natural logarithm of the asset	Positive	Stiroh and Rumble (2006), Mercieca et al. (2007), Goddard et al. (2008), and Lee et al. (2014).
$(\Delta lnA)^2_{it}$	Quadratic transformation of the natural logarithm of the asset	Negative	Stiroh and Rumble (2006), Mercieca et al. (2007), and Goddard et al. (2008)
EqA_{it}	Ratio between shareholders' equity and total assets $EqA = \frac{\text{Equity}}{\text{Total assets}}$	Uncertain	Goddard et al. (2004, 2008), Stiroh and Rumble (2006), Mercieca et al. (2007), and Lee et al. (2014)
LA_{it}	Ratio between loans and total assets $LA = \frac{\text{Loans}}{\text{Total assets}}$	Uncertain	Stiroh and Rumble (2006), Mercieca et al. (2007), Goddard et al. (2008), and Lee et al. (2014).
$\Delta lnGDP_{it}$	Variation in the natural logarithm of the gross domestic producer every 6 months	Positive	Goddard et al. (2008)
$Incorporation_{it}$	Dummy that assumes value equal to 1 when total and/or partial incorporation occurs and 0 otherwise	Uncertain	Pessanha et al. (2012) and Bortoluzzo et al. (2014)

Source: Prepared by the authors

Other explanatory variables were included in the models to capture the persistence of performance (dynamic variable) and also to control the other factors that also impact the performance of credit unions, in addition to diversification. These variables are described in Table 11.3.

The dynamic panel data models were estimated by system GMM according to the following structures:

$$Y_{it} = \lambda Y_{i,t-1} + \beta_1 \text{RNOC}_{it} + \beta_2 \text{LNA}_{it} + \beta_3 \Delta lnA_{it} + \beta_4 [\Delta \ln A]^2_{it} + \beta_5 \text{EqA}_{it} + \beta_6 \text{LA}_{it} + \beta_7 \text{lnGDP}_{it} + \beta_8 \text{Incorporation}_{it} + u_{it} \quad (11.1)$$

$$Y_{it} = \lambda Y_{i,t-1} + \beta_1 \text{DIV}_{A\,it} + \beta_2 \text{LNA}_{it} + \beta_3 \Delta \text{lnA}_{it} + \beta_4 [\Delta \text{lnA}]^2_{it} + \beta_5 \text{EqA}_{it} + \beta_6 \text{LA}_{it} + \beta_7 \text{lnaGDP}_{it} + \beta_8 \text{Incorporation}_{it} + u_{it} \quad (11.2)$$

$$Y_{it} = \lambda Y_{i,t-1} + \beta_1 \mathrm{DIV}_{Bit} + \beta_2 \mathrm{LNA}_{it} + \beta_3 \Delta\mathrm{lnA}_{it} + \beta_4 [\Delta\mathrm{lnA}]^2_{it} + \beta_5 \mathrm{EqA}_{it} + \beta_6 \mathrm{LA}_{it} + \beta_7 \mathrm{lnGDP}_{it} + \beta_8 \mathrm{Incorporation}_{it} + u_{it} \tag{11.3}$$

where Y = ROA, ROE, ROI, or EqG; $i = 1, ..., N$ credit unions affiliated to the Sicoob, Sicredi, and Unicred systems; $t = 1, ..., T$ semesters and refers to the period from 2009–2 to 2014–2; β is the estimated coefficient for each independent variable; λ is the estimated persistence coefficient for the lagged dependent variable; and $u_{it} = \alpha_i + \varepsilon_{it}$ is the compound error term where α_i is the individual effect which is not observed and ε_{it} is the random error term. In these models there is no intercept, since the individual heterogeneity of each cooperative is captured by means of the difference between the intercepts and included in the compound error term. The description of the variables was presented in Tables 11.1, 11.2, and 11.3.

For the estimation of the models in dynamic panels, the system GMM was used, since this estimator is an improvement of the GMM estimator in differences that presents more robust estimates to deal with endogeneity problem present in the dynamic variable and also in other variables of the model. The system GMM is estimated with two stages and with the correction of Windmeijer, for greater robustness. In order to validate the use of the system GMM estimator, the following tests were applied: (i) Sargan/Hansen test of overidentifying restrictions, (ii) Arellano–Bond test for autocorrelation, (iii) Difference Hansen Test (Dif-Hansen), and (iv) Unit Root Test.

Procedures Adopted in the Estimation of the Econometric Model

To identify more suitable models for each performance and diversification variable, a procedure was adapted to fit the models as used by Lane et al. (1986) and Bressan et al. (2011). This procedure was used in the system GMM methodology so as to elaborate models that would keep only the significant control variables, always maintaining the diversification and dynamic variables, while considering the principle of parsimony that presupposes the simplicity of regression models. Subsequently, when faced with restricted and unrestricted models that met the validation required by the system GMM, the Wald test was used to decide the final model most suitable for analysis. The following procedures were used to validate the models: (i) restriction in the number of instruments (Roodman 2009; Cameron and Trivedi 2009) and (ii) utilization, as instruments for the endogenous variables, only the lags of the first differences (Blundell and Bond 1998; Baum 2006).

Diversification and Performance Analysis in Credit Unions

We will first discuss the validation of the GMM model and follow with discussion of the specific findings the impact of diversifying financial products for credit unions. The system GMM estimator imposes the assumption that the first differences of the instrumental variables are not correlated with the unobserved individual effect. This condition is ensured if the stochastic process that generates x_{it} is stationary (Blundell and Bond 1998). Thus, first, the stationarity of the series was verified applying the unit root test in the regressor variables, as presented in Table 11.4.

Chi-square statistics were calculated by two tests: augmented Dickey-Fuller (ADF) and Phillips-Perron (PP). In the case of the PP test, the null hypothesis of unit root was rejected for all independent variables, showing stationary series and validated condition for the use of system GMM. The ADF test also rejected the null hypothesis for all variables, except for LNA. Separate Dickey-Fuller and Phillips-Perron tests were performed for the variable ΔlnGDP, which is not a data panel, but a time series. Thus, Z statistics were calculated by PP and ADF, as presented in Table 11.5. In the case of the variable ΔlnGDP, the PP test showed the rejection of the null hypothesis of unit root; however, in the ADF test, the null hypothesis was not rejected.

Table 11.4 Unit root tests of the regressor variables

	Augmented Dickey-Fuller		Phillips–Perron	
Variables	Statistic χ^2 χ^2	*P*-value	Statistic χ^2 χ^2	*P*-value
DIV_A	2271.74	0.0000	3227.74	0.0000
DIV_B	1758.04	0.0000	2175.23	0.0000
RNOC	1844.83	0.0000	2205.51	0.0000
LNA	1103.88	0.1209	1367.61	0.0000
ΔlnA	2054.50	0.0000	8486.70	0.0000
$(\Delta \ln A)^2$	2439.17	0.0000	7641.00	0.0000
EqA	1846.46	0.0000	3280.02	0.0000
LA	1946.91	0.0000	2688.30	0.0000

Source: Research data

Note: H_O, all panels contain unit root; H_a, at least one panel is stationary. We present the test statistic χ^2 and its level of significance (*p*-value)

Table 11.5 Unit root tests for ΔlnGDP

	Augmented Dickey-Fuller	Phillips–Perron		
Variables	Statistic Z	*P*-value	Statistic *Z*	*P*-value
ΔlnGDP	−2.22	0.1995	−6.05	0.0000

Source: Research data

Note: H_O, all panels contain unit root; H_a, at least one panel is stationary. We present the *Z* test statistic and its level of significance (*p*-value)

Therefore, the results analyzed provide a condition for model estimation by system GMM. The Phillips-Perron test showed that all independent variables have stationary series; the expanded Dickey-Fuller test indicated that the variables that had unit root are control variables and the variables of most interest in the research (DIV_A, DIV_B, and RNOC) have stationary series and the fact that the stochastic stationary process is a sufficient condition, but not necessary for the estimation of the system GMM.

Six different types of models will be analyzed to verify the relationship between performance and diversification, considering traditional performance metrics. The diagnostic analyses of the models 1 to 6 (Table 11.6), considering the system GMM method, signal the exogeneity of the instruments, thus indicating the validity of the same for the estimation process. When analyzing the credit unions' performance persistence through the lagged dependent variables ($ROA_{i,t-1}$ and $ROE_{i,t-1}$), one of the six models analyzed was statistically significant and negative, indicating that the previous period's return negatively affects the return of the current period. This result differs from that found by Goddard et al. (2004) and by Athanasoglou et al. (2008) for banks, since the authors find a significant persistence of abnormal profit from one period to the other. However, it resembles the findings of Jouida et al. (2017) for French financial institutions. This result seems reasonable, since credit unions do not aim to maximize their surpluses, and a period in which there are no surpluses is not an indicator of poor performance.

However, the variables of interest in the research, which deal with diversification (DIV_A, DIV_B, and RNOC), were not statistically significant to explain the return of credit unions, considering the traditional performance metrics in models 1 to 6 (Table 11.6). In other words, it is the indirect effect of the diversification captured through the adaptation of the Herfindahl-Hirschman index for revenue (DIV_A and DIV_B), or through the use of direct income diversification (RNOC), which reflects the difference between credit activities and activities not resulting from credit operations; it is not possible to infer any relation between the diversification and the performance of the cooperatives obtained through traditional metrics. It should be noted that Stiroh and Rumble (2006), Goddard et al. (2008), and Lee et al. (2014) assessed financial institutions and used the same traditional proxies for performance, and all of these authors corroborated the findings of this study, since they indicated that overall improvement in the profitability of financial institutions is not associated with increased diversification.

The size of the credit union (LNA) had a significant and positive relationship in only two models, and in the others it was not used, or it was not significant. As expected, the significant results indicate that larger cooperatives have a higher return, perhaps due to the benefits of economies of scale that are more often seen in large institutions, as also diagnosed by Stiroh and Rumble (2006), Mercieca et al. (2007), and Jouida et al. (2017). The variable ΔlnA, which measures the growth of the assets, was significant to explain the performance and presented a positive signal in all models (Table 11.6), according to the expected sign for this relation, demonstrating that the growth strategies of credit unions are favorable for their performance.

Table 11.6 Estimates by GMM system – models 1 to 6

Model	(1)	(2)	(3)	(4)	(5)	(6)
Variable dependent (Y)	ROA	ROA	ROA	ROE	ROE	ROE
$Y_{i,t-1}$	−0.6035***	−0.6154***	−0.6562***	−0.3652*	−0.3777**	−0.1726
	(0.1060)	(0.1192)	(0.1100)	(0.1892)	(0.1829)	(0.1680)
DIV_A	−0.0340	–	–	−0.1192	–	–
	(0.0505)	–	–	(0.1689)	–	–
DIV_B	–	−0.0055	–	–	−0.1442	–
	–	(0.0374)	–	–	(0.1367)	–
RNOC	–	–	0.0146	–	–	0.1462
	–	–	(0.0547)	–	–	(0.1095)
LNA	–	–	0.0003	0.0168***	0.0183***	0.0031
	–	–	(0.0012)	(0.0036)	(0.0039)	(0.0050)
ΔlnA	0.0239***	0.0170***	0.0263***	0.1199***	0.1234***	0.1205***
	(0.0045)	(0.0035)	(0.0077)	(0.0238)	(0.0225)	(0.0258)
$(\Delta \ln A)^2$	−0.0210**	–	−0.0243***	−0.1192***	−0.1230***	−0.1322***
	(0.0082)	–	(0.0091)	(0.0389)	(0.0352)	(0.0477)
EqA	–	–	0.0135	–	–	−0.0833*
	–	–	(0.0211)	–	–	(0.0438)
LA	0.0238**	0.0267**	0.0348	–	–	0.1193*
	(0.0111)	(0.0120)	(0.0257)	–	–	(0.0703)
ΔlnGDP	−0.0154***	−0.0184**	−0.0187	–	–	−0.1234***
	(0.0059)	(0.0082)	(0.0115)	–	–	(0.0337)
Incorporation	−0.0035***	−0.0059***	−0.0034**	−0.0150**	−0.0154***	−0.0128**
	(0.0011)	(0.0012)	(0.0015)	(0.0060)	(0.0055)	(0.0064)
Constant	0.0234	0.0097	−0.0128	−0.1636***	−0.1705***	−0.0851

(continued)

Table 11.6 (continued)

Model	(1)	(2)	(3)	(4)	(5)	(6)
Variable dependent (Y)	ROA	ROA	ROA	ROE	ROE	ROE
	(0.0286)	(0.0261)	(0.0339)	(0.0413)	(0.0372)	(0.0566)
AR(1) (z)	−1.05	−0.92	−0.75	−1.00	−0.99	−1.87*
AR(2) (z)	−1.64	−1.61	−1.72*	−1.20	−1.26	−0.46
Sargan test (χ^2)	134.77***	107.26***	166.88***	8.33	7.47	32.71***
Hansen test (χ^2)	15.38	16.99	16.4665	6.53	4.91	24.03*
Dif-Hansen test (χ^2)	4.24	6.79	3.35	3.15	2.58	5.20
Wald test (χ^2)	1.55	6.60*	9.89**	5.35	6.79*	16.00***
# of observations	5250	5250	5250	5250	5250	5250
# of groups	525	525	525	525	525	525
# of instruments	20	19	28	15	15	25

Source: Research data

Notes: The first differences of the lagged dependent variables (ROA and ROE), DIV_A, DIV_B, RNOC, and EqA were used as instruments. It is assumed that the other regressors are exogenous. The Sargan tests indicate that the instruments are correlated with the residuals in models 1, 2, 3, and 6, while the Hansen tests indicate that the instruments are not correlated with the residues. AR(1) and AR(2) show that there is no first- and second-order autocorrelation in the models. The Dif-Hansen tests attest to the orthogonality conditions of the instrument subassembly. The Wald tests indicate that models 3 and 6 are unrestricted, the others being restricted. The standard errors are in parentheses; in the tests the value of the statistic is presented, and the statistical significance is indicated by the symbols * 10%, ** 5%, and *** 1%

The quadratic term of the active growth $(\Delta \ln A)^2$ was significant and negative in five models.

This result indicates a concave relationship, in the form of inverted "U." It is assumed that the growth of the asset has a positive impact on cooperative performance until an optimum point that, when exceeded, would have a negative impact on performance. The variable that captures the level of equity, the ratio of shareholders' equity to total assets (EqA), was used in only two models and presented as nonsignificant. Therefore, it was not possible to make inferences as to their effect on cooperative performance. The variable LA, the ratio between loans and total assets, presented a positive sign and was significant in two models. This variable is considered as a measure of credit union specialization and demonstrates that such specialization increases profitability. This significant result is in line with that expected in the banking literature, since specialization in lending has been shown to add benefits such as economies of scale in lending operations, lending expertise, credit risk reduction, and increased marketing effectiveness (Kimball 1997).

The macroeconomic variable, the variation of the logarithm of GDP (ΔlnGDP) that analyzes whether the growth of national income impacts credit union performance, produced a result that was contrary to expectations, being significant and negative in three models (Table 11.6); in the others it was not used, or it was not significant. The negative relationship between GDP growth and the return of credit unions suggests that in lower growth scenarios, cooperatives become more viable alternatives and consequently obtain a better return. In this sense, the International Labor Organization report by Birchall and Ketilson (2009) emphasized that cooperatives have proved resilient in times of crisis, in which financial cooperatives remain financially sound.

Regarding the merger dummy, it can be observed that mergers carried out by credit unions affect return in a negative way (Table 11.6). This result agrees with the findings of Bauer et al. (2009). The authors identified benefits from mergers for members of the merged cooperatives and for regulatory agents, but not for the incorporating cooperative. This suggests that the acquiring credit unions may encounter regulatory pressure to undertake the merger or incorporation. Also, members of the acquiring credit union may seek to avoid insecurity in the merged cooperative environment if a target credit union were to fail. This would explain the lack of improvement in the cooperative performance.

After evaluating traditional performance measures not related to diversification, credit union performance was also verified using alternative proxies, so that these proxies were not based on surpluses as the ROA and the ROE, to verify if the results would be convergent. Therefore, the return on investment (ROI) was used as a measure of performance: a variable that measures the operating result obtained by the resources invested by creditors and quotaholders and the growth of the shareholders' equity (EqG), since growth in shareholders' equity is expected to result from good institutional performance, given that this growth can be obtained through the remainder of the fiscal years, the increase of the capital stock, the increase of reserves, and also the payment of shares.

In the diagnostic analysis of the system GMM, in the 7 to 12 models that deal with the alternative performance variables, the Arellano and Bond tests for autocorrelation prove that there is no autocorrelation in the residuals of the first- and second-order first differences. The instruments are considered jointly valid, according to the Hansen tests. Finally, the difference Hansen tests confirm that the instrument subsets are exogenous (Table 11.7). The dynamic variable was significant and negative in the models that used ROI as a proxy for performance. This result was contrary to expected, indicating that the top return of the previous period has a negative impact on the return of the current period. In the models where performance measures are EqG, the lagged dependent variables did not present statistical significance. This shows that the previous quarter's net asset growth (EqG) does not impact the growth of current equity for credit unions.

Regarding the relationship between diversification and credit union performance, considering ROI as a proxy for performance, we observe that DIV_A, which captures the indirect effect of diversification through the adaptation of the Herfindahl-Hirschman for revenue divided into two categories, was not significant. The income diversification measure (DIV_B), which is also based on the Herfindahl-Hirschman index, with the difference that the income was broken down into five main sources, was similarly not significant. Also, the RNOC diversification measure was not significant, which shows that a higher proportion of rents not resulting from credit operations does not affect the return on investment of credit unions (Table 11.7). Therefore, it is not possible to make inferences about the relationship between diversification and return on investment of credit unions, as was verified when traditional performance measures were used.

The effect of revenue diversification on the equity growth (EqG) for credit unions is both significant and positive for the three models analyzed (Table 11.7), which confirms that a cooperative's income diversification is associated with a higher growth in shareholders' equity. This effect was positive for the indirect diversification measured by the diversification indices based on the Herfindahl-Hirschman index (DIV_A and DIV_B), indicating that a more diversified product portfolio positively affects the cooperatives' performance. In addition, diversification shows a positive direct effect, demonstrating that the increase in a noncredit income component is related to stockholders' equity growth. This result agrees with findings of Elsas et al. (2010) for financial institutions and is consistent with exploitation of economies of scale and scope through diversification in the financial sector, noting that in this case, the authors worked with another proxy for performance. The authors also point out that market uncertainty increases the attraction and justification for diversification strategy for financial institutions.

Regarding the control variables (Table 11.7), the effects of size (LNA) on credit union performance were shown as significant and positive in models 7 and 8, confirming that larger cooperatives have a return on the top investment, that is, the size of cooperatives influences their performance. In the other models, this variable was not significant or was not used.

Asset growth, measured by the variation of the natural logarithm of the total assets (ΔlnA), was found to be significant and positive in the models that used ROI

Table 11.7 Estimates by system GMM: models 7 to 12

Model	(7)	(8)	(9)	(10)	(11)	(12)
Variable dependent (Y)	ROI	ROI	ROI	EqG	EqG	EqG
$Y_{i,t-1}$	−0.5548***	−0.5487***	−0.6397***	0.0292	0.0251	0.0444
	(0.1178)	(0.1105)	(0.1167)	(0.0686)	(0.0758)	(0.0870)
DIV_A	0.0395	–	–	0.9321**	–	–
	(0.0856)	–	–	(0.3833)	–	–
DIV_B	–	0.0486	–	–	0.5997**	–
	–	(0.0633)	–	–	(0.2766)	–
RNOC	–	–	0.1030	–	–	0.4726**
	–	–	(0.0834)	–	–	(0.2366)
LNA	0.0042***	0.0040***	–	−0.0049	−0.0028	−0.0060
	(0.0015)	(0.0015)	–	(0.0087)	(0.0076)	(0.0090)
ΔlnA	0.0366***	0.0369***	0.0471***	0.1503	0.1451	0.1445
	(0.0100)	(0.0103)	(0.0092)	(0.1087)	(0.1159)	(0.1053)
$(\Delta lnA)^2$	−0.0273**	−0.0269**	−0.0394***	0.8039**	0.8488*	0.8749**
	(0.0114)	(0.0116)	(0.0103)	(0.4028)	(0.4428)	(0.4168)
EqA	0.0342	0.0375	–	0.0048	0.0181	−0.0104
	(0.0306)	(0.0300)	–	(0.1081)	(0.0708)	(0.0756)
LA	0.0520***	0.0595***	0.1145**	0.3126***	0.3116***	0.3619**
	(0.0176)	(0.0203)	(0.0477)	(0.0985)	(0.1150)	(0.1490)
ΔlnGDP	−0.0186**	−0.0221**	−0.0347**	0.5980***	0.6109***	0.6006***
	(0.0089)	(0.0098)	(0.0162)	(0.0893)	(0.0995)	(0.0951)
Incorporation	−0.0077***	−0.0078***	−0.0085***	0.0610*	0.0526	0.0514
	(0.0022)	(0.0022)	(0.0024)	(0.0367)	(0.0356)	(0.0344)
Constant	−0.0930	−0.1021*	−0.0675	−0.4674**	−0.3978***	−0.2503***

(continued)

Table 11.7 (continued)

Model	(7)	(8)	(9)	(10)	(11)	(12)
Variable dependent (Y)	ROI	ROI	ROI	EqG	EqG	EqG
	(0.0577)	(0.0528)	(0.0603)	(0.2020)	(0.1311)	(0.0923)
AR(1) (z)	−1,20	−1,33	−0,84	−1,24	−1,22	−1,23
AR(2) (z)	−1,42	−1,4	−1,93*	−0.31	−0.33	−0.12
Sargan test (χ^2)	227,79***	230.43***	163,27***	20.5	15,94	18,2
Hansen test (χ^2)	25,91	26,5*	16,98	17,32	17,47	21,48
Dif-Hansen test (χ^2)	5,86	7,56	8,37	5,52	4,10	5,63
Wald test (χ^2)	8,82**	5,34**	1,72	19,51***	48,04***	22,48***
# of observations	5250	5250	5250	5250	5250	5250
# of groups	525	525	525	525	525	525
# of instruments	28	28	20	25	25	25

Source: Research data

Notes: The first differences of the lagged dependent variables (ROI and EqG), DIV_A, DIV_B, RNOC, and EqA were used as instruments. It is assumed that the other regressors are exogenous. Sargan's tests indicate that the instruments are correlated with the residuals in models 7, 8, and 9, while the Hansen tests indicate exogenous instruments in all models. AR (1) and AR (2) demonstrate that there is no autocorrelation. Dif-Hansen attests the orthogonality conditions of the instrument subassembly in all models. The Wald tests indicate that only the 9 model is restricted, with the others unrestricted. The standard errors are in parentheses; in the tests, the value of the statistic is presented, and the statistical significance is indicated by the symbols * 10%, ** 5%, and *** 1%

as a proxy for performance, indicating that asset growth is associated with a return on investment. Yet the quadratic form of total asset growth $(\Delta \ln A)^2$ was significant and negative in ROI models, showing a nonlinear relationship between asset growth and return on investment, in the form of an inverted "U." This indicates that asset growth has a positive impact on return on investment to a certain optimal level and then declines. The relation between the growth of the asset squared $(\Delta \ln A)^2$ and the growth of the net equity was positive, except in model 11, being contrary to the results found in the literature for other measures of performance.

While a positive quadratic relationship was identified between asset growth and net equity growth, these models did not reveal an optimal range for asset growth. Regarding the variable EqA, ratio between net equity and total assets, it is not possible to make inferences as to its effect on performance, since this variable was not significant in all models.

However, the variable LA, the ratio of loans to total assets, was significant and positive in all models (Table 11.7), demonstrating that the loan specialization is associated with better credit union performance. This result is in line with that expected in the banking literature and the study by Stiroh and Rumble (2006) for US banking institutions. When analyzing the association between national income growth (ΔlnGDP) and return on investment, it is estimated that the result was significant and negative (Table 11.7), suggesting that the increase in national income negatively impacts the return on the investment of credit unions, as has occurred with other models whose performance measures were based on return. However, in using equity growth as a proxy for performance, ΔlnGDP was significant and positive, indicating that the growth of the Brazilian economy is associated with a higher growth of the credit unions' net equity.

This result suggests that the growth of national income is related to the superior performance of credit unions, since the financial system is expected to respond positively to the population's income, that is, the higher the income of the people, the greater the volume of financial transactions, the greater the demand for deposits and credit, and therefore, the greater the demand for financial intermediation (Central Bank of Brazil 2015). Regarding the incorporation dummy, it was obtained that this variable was significant and negative in relation to the ROI, suggesting that the mergers negatively affect the return on investment of credit unions. The dummy is not significant when considering the EqG as a dependent variable.

In general, when considering the results of the models that used traditional performance measures (ROA and ROE), it was found that the diversification of credit unions' revenues by providing a portfolio of broader products and services does not affect their profitability (Table 11.8). Another measure of profitability used as a proxy for the performance of credit unions was the return on investment (ROI), which measures the operating result of credit unions due to the investments made by creditors and quotaholders. In this case, the models were also unable to capture the relationship between credit union diversification and performance, as did ROA and ROE.

Therefore, when considering measures of profitability as proxies for credit union performance, the results show that income diversification has no affect.

Table 11.8 Synthesis of the model estimates by system GMM

Y	ROA			ROE			ROI			EqG		
Model	1	2	3	4	5	6	7	8	9	10	11	12
$Y_{i,t-1}$	–	–	–	NS	–	NS	–	–	–	NS	NS	NS
DIV_A	NS			NS			NS			+		
DIV_B		NS			NS			NS			+	
RNOC			NS			NS			NS			+
LNA			NS	+	+	NS	+	+		NS	NS	NS
ΔlnA	+	+	+	+	+	+	+	+	+	NS	NS	NS
$(\Delta\ln A)^2$	–		–	–	–	–	–	–	–	+	NS	+
EqA			NS			NS	NS	NS		NS	NS	NS
LA	+	+	NS			NS	+	+	+	+	+	+
ΔlnGDP	–	–	NS			–	–	–	–	+	+	+
Incorporation	–	–	–	–	–	–	–	–	–	NS	NS	NS

Source: Research data

Notes: Blank fields indicate that the variable was not used for a given model. *NS*, not significant at 5%

Improvement in profitability of these institutions is not associated with diversification of activities. It is perhaps worth reiterating in this context that the credit union is, by definition, a nonprofit institution. Furthermore, when equity growth (EqG) is considered the proxy for credit union performance, the metrics reveal a positive effect of income diversification on performance, demonstrating that providing a variety products and services has a beneficial effect on credit union performance, in context of increasing adjusted shareholders' equity.

The suggested explanation for the positive effect on performance is that credit unions can take advantage of economies of scale and scope obtained by diversifying their activities, exploiting synergies and boosting the growth of their adjusted equity. In addition, delivering a full portfolio of products and services can make the institution more attractive to its associates and provide significant revenue streams, positively reflecting the institution's performance and making it more competitive. The 12 performance models are summarized in Table 11.8.

Conclusions

Credit unions, as nonprofit financial institutions, can diversify their products and services to better compete in the financial market and serve their associates. This potential instilled curiosity to analyze the effects of such diversification in the cooperative segment of credit. Therefore, this paper sought to answer the following question: What is the effect of income diversification on the performance of credit unions in Brazil? In the present analysis, one of the nine estimated models used proxy-to-measure return measures; all models showed that diversification does not affect the return of credit unions. Yet it is still possible to make inferences in this inquiry. In three models that incorporated a proxy for credit union performance of credit unions, growth of equity as proxy provided consistent and significant results. All these models indicate that diversification of income sources is positively related to the growth of equity for credit unions, that is, diversification provide credit unions with benefits that drive growth.

These divergent results may indicate that the use of the diversification strategy by credit unions does not aim to increase their surpluses or their returns. However, it may suggest that this strategy is used to help the cooperative meet its core obligations, develop synergies and managerial skills, provide an extra source of resources, and maintain its financial market position or even its survival. We also highlight the result found in the models in which the dynamic variables reference returns as performance proxies. These suggest that the upper return of the current period negatively affects the return of the next period of the credit union, a result that is contrary to that found in the literature for profit-seeking institutions, although this can be considered consistent with the main objectives of credit unions. This is associated with the fact that credit unions do not aim to maximize their surpluses, and the amount of abnormal surpluses may signal to the need for changes in in order to provide superior benefits to its members.

Another interesting result was seen in the variable to monitor the performance effects of total or partial incorporation of cooperatives. Models that used measures of return as a performance proxies showed that total or partial incorporation negatively affects credit union performance. This suggests that cooperative incorporation processes are not motivated by increased returns but may be linked to strategic factors such as maintaining a cooperative environment consolidated or related to the regulatory requirements imposed by the Central Bank of Brazil. Finally, the present study sought to contribute to a discussion about the effects of product and services diversification of and services in credit unions in an emerging country, such as Brazil, seeking to reduce the gap in the banking literature on the effects of diversification in the context of credit unions.

Future Directions

There is a paucity of studies on the question of how financial product diversification affects credit unions, and these findings remain polarized on the subject. Informative future research on this topic might experiment with using different proxies to measure both the performance and the diversification of financial products in credit unions. Another interesting possibility for future research might propose performance metrics to measure the cooperative's outcome, in terms of both social and economic benefits to its cooperative, given the mutualistic nature of this type of organization. In addition, results obtained in the present study may be compared with results found in other studies; besides examining the main determinants of the credit union diversification might empirically determine whether credit unions that exhibit high surpluses respondingly change their rates, both for loan and for member savings, to provide greater value creation for their members.

Other noteworthy trends for future studies might be to verify the effects of geographical diversification on credit unions, jointly analyze the diversification of activities and geographical diversification in credit unions, identify the importance of the interaction between these strategies on performance, identify whether there is a diversification economy in financial institutions located in emerging countries, and finally investigate how emerging financing sources might affect credit union performance.

References

Athanasoglou, P. P., Brissimis, S. N., & Delis, M. D. (2008). Bank-specific, industry-specific and macroeconomic determinants of bank profitability. *Journal of International Financial Markets, Institutions and Money, 18*(1), 121–136. https://doi.org/10.1016/j.intfin.2006.07.00.

Bauer, K. J., Miles, L. L., & Nishikawa, T. (2009). The effect of mergers on credit union performance. *Journal of Banking and Finance, 33*(12), 2267–2274. https://doi.org/10.1016/j.jbankfin.2009.06.00.

Baum, C. F. (2006). *A introduction to modern econometrics using Stata*. College Station: Stata Press.

Besanko, D., Dranove, D., Shanley, M., & Schaefer, S. (2007). *A Economia da Estratégia* (5th ed.). Porto Alegre: Bookman.

Bialoskorski Neto, S., Nagano, M. S., & Moraes, M. B. C. (2006). Utilização de redes neurais artificiais para avaliação socioeconômica: Uma aplicação em cooperativas. *Revista de Administração (USP), 41*(1), 59–68.

Birchall, J., & Ketilson, L. H. (2009). *Resilience of the cooperative business model in time of crisis*. Geneva: Sustainable Enterprise Programme, International Labour Organization.

Blundell, R., & Bond, S. (1998). Initial conditions and moment restrictions in dynamic panel data models. *Journal of Econometrics, 87*(1), 115–143. https://doi.org/10.1016/S0304-4076(98)00009-8.

Bortoluzzo, A. B., Garcia, M. P. D. S., Boehe, D. M., & Sheng, H. H. (2014). Desempenho de Fusões e Aquisições Cross Border: Análise Empírica do Caso Brasileiro. *ERA – Revista de Administração de Empresas, 54*(6), 659–671 https://doi.org/10.1590/S0034-759020140606.

Bressan, V. G. F., Braga, M. J., Bressan, A. A., & Resende Filho, M. D. A. (2010). Uma Proposta de Indicadores Contábeis Aplicados às Cooperativas de Crédito Brasileiras. *Revista Contabilidade e Controladoria, 2*(3), 58–80. https://doi.org/10.5380/rcc.v2i3.19625.

Bressan, V. G. F., Braga, M. J., Bressan, A. A., & Resende Filho, M. D. A. (2011). Uma aplicação do sistema PEARLS às cooperativas de crédito brasileiras. *Revista de Administração, 46*(3), 258–274. https://doi.org/10.5700/rausp1011.

Cameron, A. C., & Trivedi, P. K. (2009). *Microeconometrcs using Stata*. College Station: Stata Press.

Campa, J. M., & Kedia, S. (2002). Explaining the diversification discount. *The Journal of Finance, 57*(4), 1731–1762. https://doi.org/10.2307/3094522.

Carvalho, F. D. M., Kayo, E. K., & Martin, D. M. L. (2010). Tangibilidade e intangibilidade na determinação do desempenho persistente de firmas Brasileiras. *Revista de Administração Contemporânea, 14*(5), 871–889. https://doi.org/10.1590/S1415-65552010000500007.

Carvalho, F. L., de Diaz, M. D. M., Bialoskorski Neto, S., & Kalatzis, A. E. G. (2015). Saída e Insucesso das Cooperativas de Crédito no Brasil: Uma Análise do Risco. *Revista de Contabilidade e Finanças, 26*(67), 70–84. https://doi.org/10.1590/1808-057x201411390.

Central Bank of Brazil (2014). *Relação de Instituições em Funcionamento no País: Sedes de cooperativas de crédito sob a supervisão do BACEN, em funcionamento no país 31 dez.* http://www.bcb.gov.br/?RELINST. Accessed 19 May 2015.

Central Bank of Brazil (2015). *Relatório de Inclusão Financeira*. http://www.bcb.gov.br/Nor/relincfin/RIF2015.pdf. Accessed 26 Jan 2016.

DeYoung, R., & Rice, T. N. (2004). Noninterest income and financial performance at U.S. commercial banks. *The Financial Review, 39*(1), 101–127. https://doi.org/10.1111/j.0732-8516.2004.00069.x.

Elsas, R., Hackethal, A., & Holzhäuser, M. (2010). The anatomy of bank diversification. *Journal of Banking & Finance, 34*(6), 1274–1287. https://doi.org/10.1016/j.jbankfin.2009.11.02.

Esho, N., Kofman, P., & Sharpe, I. G. (2005). Diversification, fee income, and credit union risk. *Journal of Financial Services Research, 27*, 259–281. https://doi.org/10.1007/s10693-005-1804-0.

Francisco, J. R. d. S. (2014). *Índice de Governança Corporativa: Criação de Valor e Desempenho nas Cooperativas de Crédito. Tese de Doutorado*. Belo Horizonte: Universidade Federal de Minas Gerais.

Fried, H. O., Knox Lovell, C. A., & Eeckaut, P. V. (1993). Evaluating the performance of US credit unions. *Journal of Banking & Finance, 17*(2–3), 251–265. https://doi.org/10.1016/0378-4266(93)90031-8.

Goddard, J., Molyneux, P., & Wilson, J. O. S. (2004). The profitability of European banks: A cross-sectional and dynamic panel analysis. *The Manchester School, 72*(3), 363–381. https://doi.org/10.1111/j.1467-9957.2004.00397.x.

Goddard, J., McKillop, D., & Wilson, J. O. S. (2008). The diversification and financial performance of US credit unions. *Journal of Banking & Finance, 32*(9), 1836–1849. https://doi.org/10.1016/j.jbankfin.2007.12.015.

Gollo, V., & Silva, T. P. (2015). Eficiência global no desempenho econômico-financeiro de cooperativas de crédito brasileiras. *Revista de Contabilidade e Organizações, 25*, 43–55. https://doi.org/10.11606/rco.v9i25.88099.

Hitt, M. A., Ireland, R. D., & Hoskisson, R. E. (2008). *Administração estratégica: Competitividade e globalização* (2th ed.). São Paulo: Thomson Learning.

Jouida, S., Bouzgarrou, H., & Hellara, S. (2017). The effects of activity and geographic diversification on performance: Evidence from French financial institutions. *Research in International Business and Finance, 39*, 920–939. https://doi.org/10.1016/j.ribaf.2016.01.028.

Kimball, R. C. (1997). Specialization, risk, and capital in banking. *New England Economic Review*, 51–73.

Laeven, L., & Levine, R. (2007). Is there a diversification discount in financial conglomerates? *Journal of Financial Economics, 85*(2), 331–367. https://doi.org/10.1016/j.jfineco.2005.06.00.

Lane, W. R., Looney, S. W., & Wansley, J. W. (1986). An application of the cox proportional hazards model to bank failure. *Journal of Banking and Finance, 10*(4), 511–531. https://doi.org/10.1016/S0378-4266(86)80003-6.

Lee, C.-C., Yang, S.-J., & Chang, C.-H. (2014). Non-interest income, profitability, and risk in banking industry: A cross-country analysis. *The North American Journal of Economics and Finance, 27*, 48–67. https://doi.org/10.1016/j.najef.2013.11.002.

Malikov, E., Zhao, S., & Kumbhakar, S. C. (2017). Economies of diversification in the US credit union sector. *Journal of Applied Econometrics, 32*(7), 1329–1347. https://doi.org/10.1002/jae.2569.

Mathuva, D. (2016). Revenue diversification and financial performance of savings and credit co-operatives in Kenya. *Journal of Co-Operative Organization and Management, 4*(1), 1–12. https://doi.org/10.1016/j.jcom.2015.11.001.

McKillop, D., & Wilson, J. O. S. (2011). Credit unions: A theoretical and empirical overview. *Financial Markets, Institutions & Instruments, 20*(3), 79–123. https://doi.org/10.1111/j.1468-0416.2011.00166.x.

Mercieca, S., Schaeck, K., & Wolfe, S. (2007). Small European banks: Benefits from diversification? *Journal of Banking and Finance, 31*(7), 1975–1998. https://doi.org/10.1016/j.jbankfin.2007.01.004.

Migliardo, C., & Forgione, A. F. (2015). Extra profits in the healthcare factoring industry: Evidence from panel data analysis. *Economics Bulletin, 35*(1), 322–337.

Otley, D. (2002). Measuring performance: The accounting perspective. In A. Neely (Ed.), *Business performance measurement: Theory and practice*. New York: Cambridge University Press.

Park, K., & Jang, S. S. (2012). Effect of diversification on firm performance: Application of the entropy measure. *International Journal of Hospitality Management, 31*(1), 218–228. https://doi.org/10.1016/j.ijhm.2011.03.011.

Pessanha, G. R. G., Calegario, C. L. L., Sáfadi, T., & Ázara, L. N. (2012). Impactos das Estratégias de Fusão e Aquisição na Rentabilidade dos Bancos Adquirentes: Uma Aplicação dos Modelos de Intervenção no Setor Bancário Brasileiro. *RAM – Revista de Administração Mackenzie, 13*(5), 101–134. https://doi.org/10.1590/S1678-69712012000500005.

Richard, P. J., Devinney, T. M., Yip, G. S., & Johnson, G. (2009). Measuring organizational performance: Towards methodological best practice. *Journal of Management, 35*(3), 718–804. https://doi.org/10.1177/0149206308330560.

Roodman, D. (2009). How to do xtabond2: An introduction to difference and system GMM in Stata. *Stata Journal, 9*(1), 86–136.

Rumelt, R. P. (1982). Diversification strategy and profitability. *Strategic Management Journal, 3*(4), 359–369.

Smith, D. J. (1986). A test for variant objective functions in credit unions. *Applied Economics, 18*(9), 959–970. https://doi.org/10.1080/00036848600000053.

Stiroh, K. J., & Rumble, A. (2006). The dark side of diversification: The case of US financial holding companies. *Journal of Banking and Finance, 30*(8), 2131–2161. https://doi.org/10.1016/j.jbankfin.2005.04.030.

Taylor, R. A. (1971). The credit union as a cooperative institution. *Review of Social Economy, 29*(2), 207–217. https://doi.org/10.1080/00346767100000033.

Chapter 12
Transactions Among Friends

Wesley Mendes-Da-Silva

Abstract This chapter addresses the inclusion of human behavioral aspects and implications of cognitive psychology and anthropology in decisions relating to the field of behavioral finance. It offers a broad literature review toward identifying opportunities for financial innovations that are based on the notion of friendship. This chapter also presents and discusses empirical results from two evidence-based studies, referencing 400 questionnaires answered by young adults. Principal results suggest that individuals assume different behaviors in transactions among friends rather than among strangers—friends agree about the price attributed to an asset, while strangers show the propensity to bargain. In addition, agents acting on behalf of a friend appear to devote more enforcement, even if they are not receiving any reward or are being monitored.

Keywords Trust · Friendship · Social networks · Decision-making · Financial decisions

JEL Code C91 · L14 · D23

Recently researchers on behavioral finance and decision-making have been recognized for contributions to the literature that addresses the potential effects of social cognition (how people think about the way they interact with one another) in financial transactions (Shefrin 2015). The classical economic approach assumes that decisions would not be made by considering the other people involved. Yet cognition, based in personal interaction, would have the potential to influence transaction results.

Portions of this chapter appeared in the 2008 paper 'Effects of Friendship in Transactions in an Emerging Market: Empirical Evidence From Brazil', *Icfai Journal of Behavioral Finance*, vol 5, pp 25–46.

W. Mendes-Da-Silva (✉)
Sao Paulo School of Business Administration (FGV/EAESP), Sao Paulo, SP, Brazil

University of Texas at Austin, Austin, TX, USA

W. Mendes-Da-Silva (ed.), *Individual Behaviors and Technologies for Financial Innovations*, https://doi.org/10.1007/978-3-319-91911-9_12

Following the notion of rationality assumed by the classical economic approach, these effects do not exist or are at least controlled. Few studies have considered the effects that another individual involved in the transaction has on decision-making. Thus, literature that deals with the potential effects of friendship on transactions, or on inherent pricing of transactions that occur in similar contexts, has not yet been expressed. Some of the results obtained in this research suggest that such effects occur in a systematic and visible way.

Professional or personal decisions can assume various forms, such as decisions about the financing of small projects, loans for the acquisition of equipment, purchases, and service contracts, among others. Organizational processes related to a particular transaction can be affected by interpersonal interactions (i.e., friendship). In other words, this could occur in consequence of the use of cognitive models in transactions in which friends negotiate. This chapter discusses a relevant topic in part of the literature of behavioral finance, which suggests that people employ mental models or "cognitive structures," also called scripts (Halpern 1992, 1994, 1997; Ramirez-Fernandez et al. 2017), that change in a transaction, according to whether information is being traded with friends or strangers. I present empirical evidence of friendship's effects on price expectations in certain business transactions and discuss extensions of this phenomenon to the finance area.

Empirical evidence suggests that individuals assume different behaviors when involved in transactions carried out between friends rather than strangers. Friends tend to more readily agree to the price attributed to an asset, while strangers show the propensity to define prices through a bargaining process, if they have not already agreed a priori. Moreover, it is seen that when individuals act as agents for others, they assume different behaviors in the protection of the principal's interest, conforming to the level of friendship between the principal and agent. This chapter presents highlights from this research and analyzes the data set to identify friendship's influence over individual behavior in business transactions. The methodology used in this study is similar to that of Halpern (1994), which Mendes-Da-Silva et al. (2008) follows as well. These research findings provide insight into how financial professionals, executives, families, and business people can develop and make more effective decisions. In addition to these recommendations, I offer suggestions and directions for future research.

Trust and Networks in Transactions

Although individuals take part in transactions largely governed by the economic concept of utility maximization, social networks are also involved in many of these transactions in which negotiators adhere to a variety of functional rules of these same networks (Granovetter 1974). These social norms are frequently implicit; however, those who share them are capable of recognizing them, when they represent an access code to the group (Hällsten et al. 2017).

Granovetter (1974), upon reflecting the maintenance of social networks, opposed the traditional sociological perception by affirming that weak social ties are more effective in maintaining a network than strong ties formed by parents and close friends and that weak ties can better stimulate the flow of new information within a network of professionals or organizations (Mendes-Da-Silva 2011). Friends and close relatives with whom individuals construct stronger ties, by themselves, only guarantee the support of this nucleus/group. However, the weaker ties are between work colleagues, school friends, and even acquaintances, who, in principle, do not deposit a genuine trust. According to Granovetter (1974), they are important inasmuch as they serve as a connecting link to a variety of others, thus amplifying the circle of influence and negotiations.

According to Granovetter (1974), social networks, besides being inclusive, are random and dynamic. The network is a system in which there is no prioritization or hierarchy in contacts, exchanges, or influence but rather a multiple dimension in which the relationship between people is defined in terms of processes that are constructed at the moment of the perception of reality (i.e., transactions), by way of cognition. There is an ontological construction, in the context of which, the behaviors are elaborated by way of human and nonhuman relations. The contribution to behavioral finance, therefore, consists in perceiving, by way of scripts, the behavior of the player, his/her relation to the other players, the fair behavior, and the mode by which an individual affects the financial result of a transaction (Coleman 1990). In addition, Fiske and Taylor's (1991) economic theory generally ignores the effects of cognitive structures that guide behavior, to suggest the concept of a script as a model of behavior in related-party transactions.

According to Fiske and Taylor (1991), the script refers to adequate behaviors in known situations, related to the purposes and inherent expectations of specific social positions in which individuals are placed (i.e., friends and strangers, father and son, boss and subordinate, teachers and students). The object of this study is to understand the characteristics, behaviors, and strategies carried out to perpetuate the relationship between individuals referred to as friendship. The script is influenced by cultural norms or the shared experiences of people (Franken et al. 2017). The area of finance has received research contributions from other fields of knowledge that examine human behavior in trade situations. However, I can give prominence to the necessity of examining how social relations that involve friendship affect the behavior of the players in commercial practice and in other possible relations that are developed by way of friendship.

Malinowski (1926) dealt with issues related to the rules of trade. In this context, the notions of propriety and reciprocity among individuals were examined, emphasizing mutual obligations and the recognition of the necessity for cooperation (Labun et al. 2016). Malinowski (1926) transposes the classical economic vision when he discusses alternative forms of punishment by not fulfilling a financial obligation. In other words, shame and the exclusion from social order would be lesser forms of severe punishment for an individual. To Canary et al. (1995), the cognition of transactions with friends can be investigated as a multivariate phenomenon that, in a complex form, presents the elements that constitute friendship, which establish the scripts to a mutual exchange: (i) interaction by way of a joint history, (ii) similarity of shared values, (iii) mutual respect, (iv) disposition to the truth, and (v) affection.

It is supposed that there is decisive differentiation in the treatment with those who are friends and those who are not. Individuals, when negotiating with friends, behave differently than when doing transactions with others they do not know. Those differences are systematic and predictable, even when players are not necessarily under direct observation of one another. From the concept of script, the differences of behavior between friends and strangers, in business negotiations, can be understood by way of rules of behavior, formed of objects and expectations. In transactions with strangers, scripts are also used. However, trust in the other party's commitment and honesty, in principal, is reduced, and consequently the capacity of formatting the script is less than between those who establish themselves as friends in transactions, in which context, those expectations are more explicit, as supported by the arguments of Williamson (1985) and Husted (1990).

Friendship

Adult relationships that involve friendship may be formed by people who play many roles (Demir et al. 2017; Plummer et al. 2016), i.e., family, work, or friends from the same fraternity (Canary et al. 1995). Kelley (1979) argues that daily interactions include negotiations with friends or colleagues, and in these situations, trades and favors occur, incurring reciprocity, albeit there is no proximity as intense as those that exist among relatives or in the case of some type of interest of sexual order. The important thing, according to Pinker (1997, p. 529), is to recognize that if "there is an exchange of favors, both parties benefit, since that value that they obtain is greater than what they give."

Models of cooperation promote the continuity of relationships. A partnership is established when players perceive that they are involved in an interaction that is positive and that the person with whom they are negotiating demonstrated trust and reciprocity in another time. According to anthropology, negotiations and the share are governed "by a cost-benefit analysis and by a meticulous mental account book of retributions." However, Schuster and Copeland (1996) maintain that the relationship between players is not guided by interests of personal relationship or even by ties of loyalty.

Mauss (1969) observed such behaviors in the ritual ceremony of potlatch, in North America, that occurred in marked periods of life, the so-called rites of passage: birth, marriage, and funerals. In these ceremonies, after a grand banquet, the homaged delivered the presents that they had received to those invited. Thus, the offering of goods and riches among partners dealt with a political, economic, and social exchange, regulating the social order (Demir et al. 2017). In potlatch, donation is considered a gift and a reward for spiritual obligation. Pinker (1997) observes that in close relationships, especially when dealing with friends and spouses, there is a feeling of continual debt; nevertheless, the effort of settling the debt is pleasurable because it tends to exponentially, and not immediately, bring rewards, strengthening familial bonds in the process.

The context of friendship and its involvement in economic models have not been substantially contemplated since the reasoning presented by Hirschman (1986). These previous models are essentially developed assuming an ideal market, with perfect competition, which functions without the necessity of prolonged social contact. From the classical economics' point of view, the models based on the assumption of rationality suggest that individuals could receive or pay similar prices in situations that involve the same goods, independent of who is exchanging.

The notion of a contract, according to McNeil (1974) and Rousseau and McLean Parks (1992), offers a comprehensive model of the differences between the behavior of friends and strangers in a transactional situation. McNeil (1986) proposes that long-term contracts are distinct for (i) specificity, (ii) scope, (iii) flexibility, and (iv) monitorability. In essence, transactional contract, on the one hand, can be seen as monetary agreements characterized by limited involvement of the personal life of players and, on the other hand, relational contracts directed toward other purposes, considering socioemotional exchanges and monetary elements. Exchanges between strangers can be characterized as transactional, and exchanges between friends can be considered relational. McNeil (1974) and Rousseau and McLean Parks (1992) even describe the relational contract as a psychological contract, a description which recognizes that two parties of the same contract can interpret the content in different ways. That is, it seems that there exists a certain component of subjectivity in the interpretation of contracts.

In this study, like that conducted by Halpern (1997), we use a definition of friendship, based on prior consultation with the participants. In other words, the definition of "friend" was used based on the interpretation of the study participants. The players were instructed regarding many recurrent terms in the relative literature on friendship (as illustrated in a following section describing the experiments). The decision process has been a topic of concern in many diverse research areas (Tversky and Kahneman 1974; Carroll et al. 1988; Loewenstein et al. 1989). However, to my knowledge, there does not exist in the current literature a study regarding the effects of friendship in financial transactions in the Western emerging market's context. The main contribution of this study is how participants react in relation to those they consider as friends.

Friendship and Pricing Behavior

Although financial results are frequently considered, in the classical economic theory which is immune to nonpecuniary considerations, there exists evidence that friendship itself exerts an effect on pricing behavior. In this context, Baker (1984) found results that support the idea that "small panels of friends," who operate in the stock market, influence the volatility of the assets in which they transact. With respect to the impacts of friendship in financial transactions, Halpern (1992, 1994) indicates that friendship affects the anticipated appraisal of goods. He found that friends readily agree to the price for a product or service, even without discussion. However, strangers disagree: salesmen request more for goods, while buyers offer less, an indication of the propensity to bargain.

Cognitive Structures for Friendship in Transactions

Cognitive structures (scripts) help individuals make judgments in various situations, guiding their strategies for interaction (Schank and Abelson 1977). In these terms of information processing, a script is a set of specific estimates, based on common understanding of how a person will interact with others in various situations (Schank and Abelson 1977). As social actors, the individuals use these estimates to establish future behaviors (Taylor et al. 2016).

As defined by Fiske and Taylor (1991), events of a script describe a sequence of steps in well-known situations, for example, in restaurants (there exist subscripts for elegant establishments, which are not the same as those for the environment of fast food) or in the work environment. Rules of a script guide the set of behaviors expected of a person in a specific social status (i.e., a boss with an employee, a father with a son, or between friends and strangers). Scripts can also interact, such as having dinner in a restaurant with friends versus with business-oriented partners. In turn, the script of friendship is a function of numerous characteristics, strategies, and behaviors that generally need to be present for the friendship to exist.

In this context, the script of friendship that we reference for this chapter is from Halpern (1992, 1994, 1997) who includes universal agreements on maintenance of (i) friendship in the future, (ii) voluntary nature of the relation, (iii) links of association in the relation, as well as acquisition and maintenance of fairness, reciprocal auto-disclosure, and future interaction (Blau 1964; Morgan and Sawyer 1967; Boulding 1973; Rubin 1973; Shapiro 1975; Austin and McGinn 1977). Some aspects of scripts of friendship can be influenced by cultural norms or shared experiences. For example, friends interact according to a particular set of shared histories, similar values, mutual respect, confidence, and previous affection for the other.

There are also scripts for interaction with strangers. Strangers are people whom you do not know and with whom (at least in the context of this study) you do not expect to interact with again. The scripts of relationships with strangers suggest a more protective approach for a negotiation, rather than a relationship of confidence, more common between friends. Generally, in a relationship with a stranger, larger interests do not exist. Similarly, it is anticipated that strangers will not place confidence in one's attitudes (even though it is not pleasant to recognize this aspect) nor do people expect their interests to receive priority with a stranger.

Friendship and Financial Innovation

Individuals frequently act in situations in which preexisting friendships could influence the management of a company. In public companies, for example, work performed with the members of the board of directors (including the compensation of executives and disciplining them when necessary) could become compromised due to friendships that exist between board members and executives (Adams and Ferreira 2007; Mendes-Da-Silva 2011; Fracassi and Tate 2012).

Regarding corporate governance, the finance literature has identified a certain difficulty in achieving the independence of the board of directors. Independence is a necessary condition for preserving the disciplinary capacity of the board of directors with respect to the executives (agents), protecting the interests of the shareholders (principals), and maximizing the value of the firm. Described from the economic point of view of Jensen and Meckling (1976), friendships may exert nonprofessional influence in a typical principal-agent relationship, which is often cited as one of the major risks in private equity, venture capital, or equity crowdfunding (Turan 2015).

From an organizational view, aspects of the administration process (e.g., acquisition of materials) assume a form of transaction in which individuals interact to establish prices and conditions that satisfy the two sides. In the individual sphere, the purchase of an apartment or an automobile, for example, is also a transaction that requires a negotiation in which individuals can perceive themselves as friends or strangers. This aspect can impact the result of the transaction. Thus, friendship can influence the transactions by means of its components—confidence, anticipation of future interactions, empathy, interdependence, or expectation of "fairness" (Williamson 1985).

Based on this understanding, a purchaser may pay more for an identical product acquired from a friend than from a stranger; this may be due to the confidence in the honesty of the friend, who caused the purchaser to pay a premium for this confidence. These consequences were also evident in the studies of Baker (1984) and Greenhalgh and Chapman (1994), when they verified that the volatility of stock prices in the stock market is affected by friendship, which reflects the behavior of the investors in their propensity to pay or to accept prices proposed for a stock. In this regard, Mendes-Da-Silva et al. (2016) found results that contradict the premise that investments in crowdfunding are insensitive to the distance between investor and entrepreneur. With the advent and advancement of the Internet and communication technologies, friendship relationships have assumed a central role in new virtual structures, which have made possible phenomena ranging from crowdsourcing (Liang et al. 2017; Lu et al. 2017) to crowdfunding (Hellmann and Thiele 2015). These relationships, in turn, enable networks that support the emergence and consolidation of financial innovations, from which markets await changes in society, including the redefinition of the safe way in which banks operate and offer financial products, such as insurance and loans (Powell 2017).

Harmony

There is a tendency that in "friendship," the individuals work to maintain the goodwill and harmony, perpetuating the bond and the voluntary nature of their relationships, including when discussing the negotiation of assets. This must occur in a reciprocal fashion. This understanding has been debated by Mauss (1969), Boulding (1973), Austin (1980), and Malinowski (1926).

Morgan and Sawyer (1967) defend that friends might divide a set of rewards in equal parts, when they are presented to them in a unified manner, despite possible asymmetries in individual merit. As indicated by Fry et al. (1983), friends generally prefer to maintain the goodwill and harmony in the long run, rather than getting an immediate pecuniary return in a transaction. In summary, some individuals, to promote the bonds of friendship, might accept suboptimal agreements in order to prevent conflicts. This behavior is debated by Thaler (1985), where he refers to the behavior of "players" in analogous situations as "utility transactional." This can be empirically tested by examining if the individuals are willing to offer more money for a specific product in a transaction involving friends than in a transaction involving strangers and similarly if the salesmen require less money from friends than from strangers.

The purchaser will be cautiously interested in the merchandise (of a stranger), assuming a defensive position. By extension, the purchaser will tend to appraise goods below its value based on the estimate that the salesman requires a greater value for the goods, as a result of the salesman's perception of the purchaser's capacity to pay. In turn, the purchaser would like to avoid financial losses in the transaction. From this scenario, a bargain zone would be created (Raiffa 1982). The bargain, inherent to the transaction, occurs as a process through which the "players" (buying and selling) become related. As McNeil (1986) describes, when strangers negotiate in extreme cases, they use threats, ultimatums, or other related techniques. Intuitively, strangers are more inclined to offer and to perceive risk, each in relation to the other, which is different from the inclination of friends. However, a friend with an expectation of a price for goods, using the same bargaining processes used in transactions between strangers, could be perceived as inadequate in the "script" of friendship.

Obligation of Reciprocity and Accountability

The basis of the notion of reciprocity is not imposed on market economies but in the informal exchanges of goods, favors, and work. In principle, it relates to sharing something with somebody without necessarily expecting something in exchange. Reciprocity according to Mauss (1969) tends to keep the social order, since it establishes bonds and it awakens the perception that one individual needs another. In some cultures, such as Chinese, the notion of reciprocity acquires explicit, if

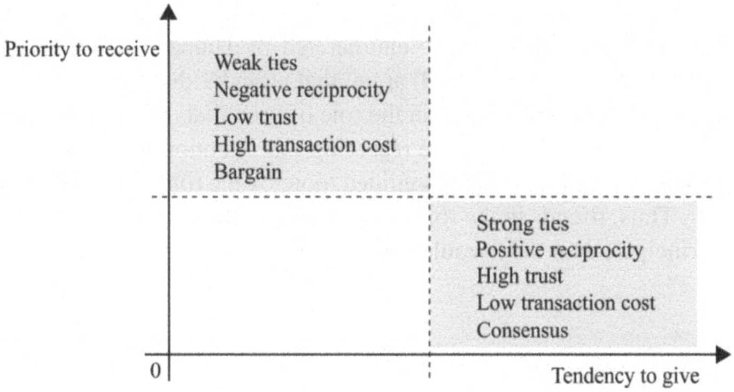

Fig. 12.1 Behavior matrix for transactions involving "close" individuals (strong ties) and "distant" individuals (weak ties)

informal, contours. This is the case with *guanxi*, without which business does not occur as easily and quickly as it could (Hennart 2015; Qin and Deng 2016).

This vision is shared from the cultural "script." Sahlins (1972) suggests that reciprocity is responsible for establishing the balance of the relation between two close individuals characterized, at times, by the convenience of return. Reciprocal actions between friends are not "give-and-take" (Halpern 1997, p. 842) but consist of a positive reciprocity. Also when one is discussing strong ties, immediate repayment can be viewed as an offense by players, as if it were a payment for the given services, rather than constituting an alliance. On the other hand, in discussing weak ties, in view of Sahlins (1972), the reciprocity is more easily controlled by a refusal or the idea that players take more than they give. The maintenance of strong ties also has the potential to contribute to the perception of well-being of the individuals involved in the transactions (Elmer et al. 2017). This argument is represented in a schematic form in Fig. 12.1.

One's own interest, instead of the interest of the other, is frequently considered as a motivation a priori in transactions involving distant individuals (strangers/weak ties), creating the possibility for egoistic contract breaking or other behaviors (Castanzias and Helfat 1991). However, when motivational factors beyond one's own interests are considered, as is required for affinity of friendship, players can assume a behavior in which they prioritize the interests of the other (Seabright et al. 1992). A contribution to behavioral finance is that the notion of "friendship," much like its script, differs from the rational perspective that assumes the maximization of the individual's own utility. In other words, the decisions in transactions would not necessarily be guided by the well-being of a friend. This is the argument of the traditional view of the economy, based on the rationality of the investor, contested initially by Tversky and Kahneman (1974). In trade relations between friends, one component needs to be considered—the social construct of "friend."

Despite the inherent difficulties to define the term according to arguments from Hällsten et al. (2017) and Iannone et al. (2017), the expectations in transaction, when generated for the behavior of an individual perceived as a "friend," include aspects that establish scripts of "friendship," enumerated by Halpern (1994, p. 3). In this context, Cummings and Anton (1990) argue that an individual (in the role of agent) is led to act to the benefit of friends (in the role of principals), even when the friends (principals) do not know that they are receiving this attention (of the agents). In this manner, the behavior of individuals is guided more by the role of "friend" than by the role of player. Thus, friends in the role of agents are willing to do more for friends, in the role of principal, than they would for strangers.

Subjects and Procedure

After examining and concatenating theoretical arguments found in the literature, together with a few colleagues, based on Halpern (1994), I initiated an attempt to empirically test the impact of friendship on transactions, which began with data collection (Mendes-Da-Silva et al. 2008), which were later analyzed to verify whether the arguments were accurately reflected by human behavior. Thus, data collection was conducted in two distinct phases. First, we explored the social construct of "friendship," to verify that friendship, as viewed by the participants, would include (i) persons whom they like a great deal (without being romantically involved), (ii) someone they trust, and (iii) a relationship they desire to maintain for an indefinite time. From this first phase, we adapted two experiments from Halpern (1994) to test impacts of friendship on transactions. In the second phase, we administered three experiments to graduate students registered in eight business administration courses at each of three timeframes (morning, afternoon, and evening).

Three experiments were conducted jointly during the second fortnight of the month of March in 2007 in the city of Sao Paulo, Brazil, one of the financial centers of South America. Of the 165 participants, 44.60% individuals were female, and 55.40% were male; the average (median) age was of 21.15 (20.00), with standard deviation of 3.53 years. After a preliminary verification, the 400 instruments used to collect the data from the experiments, we discovered that 30 had not been answered completely and so were not included. The respondents' gender was not correlated in relation to the experiments.

Experiments

Two experiments were conducted to test impacts of friendship on transactions. This study essentially follows the structure of the test used by Halpern (1994). The participants in Experiment 1 were randomly assigned the role of player based on two aspects: (i) the role to be played in the transaction (whether buying or selling) and (ii) the relationship between players (whether stranger or friend). In this manner, there were four possibilities of roles in the experiment: (i) a buying friend, (ii) a selling friend, (iii) a buying stranger, or (iv) a selling stranger of some hypothetical goods with which the students were familiar. Moreover, players were instructed to assume that the business-oriented transaction was with someone of the same gender, who was described as a "friend" (*someone whom the individual likes a great deal and trusts and with whom the player desires to maintain relations for indefinite time*) or "colleague" (*somebody that they did not know very well, nor had the expectation to maintain a relationship for an extended period of time*). The players read the description of eight goods and then indicated how much they were willing to offer (if buying) or require (if selling), for each good. The descriptions of each good also included a range for its expected market price,[1] which was based on the available prices of goods similar to those offered to the players. This range was established by visiting retail stores and by consulting websites specialized in quotes for consumer products.

The eight goods, with their respective price ranges, were:

English dictionary: R$23–R$85
Ticket to a show: R$30–R$160
MP3 player: R$90–R$195
Cellular telephone: R$169–R$629
Financial calculator: R$339–R$635
Television: R$350–R$450
Digital camera: R$539–R$1,198
Mountain bike: R$950–R$1,650

The goods were selected in order to create a continuous scale of prices, allowing to verify whether friendship exerts a different effect in agreements based on the level of prices. The researchers instructed the participants to assume the role of players in which they would decide to sell/buy from a hypothetical individual (stranger/friend), assuming that the price to be received/paid in the transaction was just, based on the roles played in Experiments 1 and 2.

Experiment 1

Instructions to the Participant

You decided to buy/to sell from/to a friend/colleague the indicated good, assuming that the price is just. You simply need to decide which price that he/she needs to pay/receive for the listed good. In some cases, you may want to know more information on this product or situation. However, for the purpose of this experiment, concentrate on making a decision based solely on the supplied information. Do not try to examine the hypothesis with great detail;

(continued)

[1] In that time: 1.00US$ = 2.12R$.

we are simply interested in the first price that comes to mind. You have only one chance to make an offer for this good; the buyer/seller may or may not accept. As a buyer/seller, assume that no other comparable items are available; even so, you should not propose a value that is not just.

Sample of the Scene Considered by the Player

You desire to buy/to sell, from/to a friend/colleague, a ticket for one show. You have only one chance to make an offer for this highly desirable ticket to the show. Your friend/colleague bought the ticket, but he will not be able to attend nor obtain a profit by selling it. The price of the show is not printed on the ticket, and your friend/colleague does not recall with any certainty the exact amount paid. The market price of the ticket is between R$3,000 and R $16,000. Your friend/colleague is not obligated to accept offers. But, for your knowledge, he/she does not plan to offer it to anyone else. (Remember: You do not have any chance to bargain and will not have a second possibility of negotiation) How much would you offer to your friend/colleague for the ticket? The value you offered was R$________.

Experiment 2

Instructions to the Participant

You decided to try to sell a determined good on behalf of your friend/ colleague and agreed to the procedure of sale and will act in accordance with the agreement. For this exercise, you need to decide the final value that you will accept for the good on behalf of your friend/colleague. Your desire is that he/she receives a good deal; therefore, you are acting on good faith (this means that you will search for an offer that is reasonable). At the same time, your friend/colleague trusts you and desires that you sell it well. Moreover, he/she does not want to have a substantial financial loss.

Sample of the Scenario Proposed to the Player

Your friend is currently away from home and is unable to return in the near future; you will take care of your friend's dearest pet Rex. Rex is a very pretty dog with good pedigree. The dog is happy and healthy and has the papers of pedigree in sequence. During his/her last visit, your friend/colleague passed little time with Rex, and he/she did not seem as attached to the dog. Your friend/colleague is not certain whether he would return and does not know if he would be able to keep the dog. Therefore, he/she asks you to sell the dog. You agree that selling the dog is favorable for your friend/colleague. This should happen as fast as possible, since the older the animal, the harder it is to sell it. In addition, you have your own affairs to attend to so you don't have much time. The market value for a similar animal is between R$450 and R $2,300. What is the final value what you would be willing to accept when negotiating to sell Rex? The final value that you accepted for Rex was R $________.

Analysis Procedure

The appropriate use of parametric estimation methods requires, in general, a normal distribution of the population and a constant variance. Often, it is impossible to correctly ascertain the distribution of the probabilities of assumed values with a stochastic variable in a given population. Therefore, without being able to clarify the exact mathematical distribution of the population, nonparametric estimation methods appear to be a better alternative. The t test for differences between means assumes that the distribution of random variables is normal. To verify this assumption we used the Kolmogorov-Smirnov test, which compares the function of the observed distribution of a variable with its theoretically determined distribution. After testing the distributions of the continuous variables, it was not possible to assume that the random variables do not exhibit a normal distribution (at a 99% confidence level). Nonparametric statistics were used for the necessary tests for the remainder of the study. As an alternative to the t test for differences between means, a Mann-Whitney U test was used.

Empirical Results

Experiment 1

The analysis of the results indicates that friends and strangers differ in their pricing behavior. Strangers disagree, while friends agree on prices attributed to a good, supporting that people agree more easily with friends than strangers during a negotiation. Schuster and Copeland (1996) claim that the interests of personal relationships are irrelevant to the negotiation process. As shown in Panel A of Table 12.1, except for the digital camera ($p < 0.05$), with its price interval between R$539 and R$1198, and the bicycle ($p < 0.01$), there was no observed difference between the values attributed by the players in the position of seller or buyer when the two are friends.

Reinforcing the results found in Panel A of Table 12.1, Panel B (at a 1% significance level) shows that for all eight hypothetical goods, the prices required by the sellers and the propensity of the buyers (in the absence of friendship) to accept the price is significantly different than when friendship exists between the two. That is, when strangers engage in a negotiation, the equilibrium price is more difficult to arrive at than when the buyer and seller are friends. The indication that strangers tend to disagree on the price of a good, according to Halpern (1994), would encourage a bargaining process in the transaction between the two parties. The fact that friend-buyers and friend-sellers appear to agree upon the value of a hypothetical good is perhaps due to mutual trust, partnership, or even the desire to maintain a good relationship between the two parties (Rubin 1973).

Table 12.1 Nonparametric tests for buying/selling to friend/stranger

	Dictionary	Ticket	MP3 player	Cellular phone	Calculator	Television	Digital camera	Bicycle
Panel A: Prices proposed by buyers and sellers with a relationship of friendship								
U	3533	3897.5	3601.5	3868.5	3459.5	3827.5	3262.5	3018.5
Z	−1.372	−0.313	−1.175	−0.397	−1.589	−0.530	−2.155	−2.869
p-value	0.17	0.754	0.24	0.691	0.112	0.596	0.031**	0.004***
Panel B: Prices proposed by buyers and sellers who have no relationship								
U	2627	3022.5	2975.5	2854	3252	3320.00	2575.5	2876
Z	−5.090	−4.055	−4.18	−4.48	−3.44	−3.34	−5.22	−4.43
p-value	0***	0***	0***	0***	0.001***	0.001***	0***	0***
Panel C: Prices required in sales to friends and to strangers								
U	2816	2908.5	3432. 00	3080	3670	3531	3274.5	3649.5
Z	−4.120	−3.880	−2.44	−3.39	−1.78	−2.25	−2.87	−1.84
p-value	0***	0***	0.015**	0.001***	0.075*	0.024**	0.004***	0.065*
Panel D: Prices offered when purchasing from friends and from strangers								
U	3960.5	4190	4112.5	3995	4108	4051.5	4199	4198.5
Z	−0.746	−0.105	−0.322	−0.648	−0.334	−0.498	−0.079	−0.081
p-value	0.456	0.917	0.748	0.517	0.738	0.618	0.937	0.936

Source: Adapted from Mendes-Da-Silva et al. (2008)

Panel A: presents the results of the Mann-Whitney U test of the prices proposed by the buyers and sellers (players) when the two have a relationship of friendship. These results suggest that when the two sides are friends, there is greater agreement in the price given by both sides a priori. Panel B: presents the results for the difference in means between the prices proposed by the buyers and sellers (players) when the two are strangers. These results suggest that when the two parties are strangers (not friends), there exists a greater disagreement in the price given by both sides a priori. Panel C: presents the results of the test for the difference in means between the prices required by the players in the selling position to a friend or stranger. The statistics suggest that when individuals are selling a good to a friend, they are likely to require lower values for the goods than if they were selling to a stranger. Panel D: presents the results for the difference in means between the prices offered for a good by the players in the buying position from a friend or stranger. The statistics suggest that when individuals are buying a good, they do not offer different prices to friends and strangers

*p-value <0.1; **p-value <0.05; ***p-value <0.01

Surprisingly, the players made their pricing decisions, with friends tending to agree and strangers tending to disagree a priori, entirely independent of one another and without the opportunity to confer (i.e., negotiate) with each other. Moreover, the deals agreed upon are not simply in the middle of the price interval suggested in the experiment. Thus, the results shown in Panel A of Table 12.1 and those presented in Panel B support the arguments and corroborate the findings of Halpern (1992, 1994). Panel C indicates, at a significance level of 10%, that the required prices given to the hypothetical goods when selling to a friend are significantly different from the required prices when selling to a stranger. In other words, the results support the idea that the individual in the selling position requires a lower price for the product from a friend than from a stranger (selling price to friend < selling price to stranger). This conforms to the rationale proposed by Fry et al. (1983).

On the whole, in the light of the results of Panel D, no significant differences exist in the prices that the players in the buying position are willing to pay for the hypothetical goods. This is independent of whether they are buying from a friend or stranger. These results go contrary to the argument which posited that buyers would offer more to friends than strangers. An alternative explanation for this finding, according to the data collected, is that people would be more reluctant to part with money than to gain assets of similar value. Panel A (left side) of Fig. 12.2 presents a comparison between the prices proposed by the players in the positions of buyer or seller, acting as friends or strangers in a negotiation transaction involving a cellular telephone. The different treatment that friends and strangers employ in this experiment support the arguments developed by Thaler (1985) with respect to "transactional utility." The individuals in the experiment demonstrated different behaviors in analogous situations, depending on their personal relationship with the other party in the transaction.

Experiment 2

In Experiment 2 the participants sought to obtain the best results possible in a sales transaction while acting as agents for principals with whom a relationship of friendship either exists or does not exist. The friend or stranger (principal) in the experiment is unaware of the behavior of the agent during the transaction. We begin with descriptive statistics of the proposed sale prices deemed acceptable by the agent. The results shown in Table 12.2 suggest that the prices reached higher values when the agent was acting on behalf of a friend instead of a stranger.

After analyzing the descriptive statistics, a nonparametric test was used (since the data does not meet the necessary assumptions for parametric tests) to verify the independence of the relationship of friendship and the price that the player (seller) seeks for on behalf of the principal (friend or stranger). The test results (Mann-Whitney $U = 14606.50$; $p < 0.05$) provide evidence for a difference between the prices proposed by agents in a sales transaction on behalf of principals where friendship exists and those transactions where the principal is a stranger. Panel B

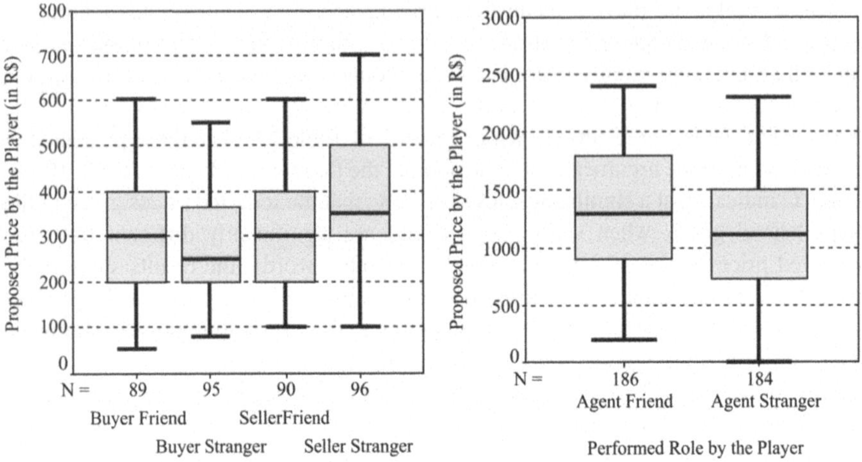

Fig. 12.2 Box plots of prices in transactions between friends and strangers. Note: this figure illustrates the results obtained in the two experiments conducted. Panel A: box plot of the prices (in R$) proposed and required by the players in the position of buyer and seller (with relationships varying between friends and strangers) of a hypothetical cellular telephone; this exhibit presents the comparison between the values that players propose to pay for the purchase of a cellular phone (from a friend/stranger) and receive for the sale of the phone (from a friend/stranger). It is apparent that individuals demand less of friends in sales transactions as well as offer more to friends than strangers in purchase transactions (however, the nonparametric tests did not support this last idea). Panel B: box plot of the price proposed by the seller agent (according to the relationship); this exhibit presents the comparison between the values that the players propose to obtain in the sale of the pet, according to the type of relationship the seller agent has with the pet owner. It is apparent that when a player is selling an item as an agent for someone who is a friend, the player proposes to obtain a higher price than if the agent is acting on behalf of a stranger. (Source: Adapted from Mendes-Da-Silva et al. 2008)

Table 12.2 Values (in R$) that the player in the position of seller is willing to sell a pet that belongs to another individual

Statistics	When the owner is a friend	When the owner is a stranger	*t*
N	186	184	
Mean	1301.83	1160.03	***
Std dev.	553.51	538.49	

Source: Adapted from Mendes-Da-Silva et al. (2008)
This table presents the values assumed by the prices for which the players were willing to sell a pet as cited in Experiment 2. The table is divided into two columns, those that have a relationship of friendship with the owner of the animal and those that have no relationship with the owner. The results of the nonparametric test suggest that when the owner of the animal is a friend to the individual who is charged with selling the animal, the individual seeks a higher price for the animal than if the owner were a stranger. ***$p < 0.01$

of Fig. 12.2 illustrates that the price for which people are willing to sell another person's pet varies depending on the relationship between the person selling and the owner of the pet. People who sell pets for others are more likely to seek a higher price for an animal that belongs to a friend than a stranger. These results support the idea that agents attempt to assist friends more, even if the results of the transaction are required to be reported to the principal. This is consistent with the implied obligation that friendship takes on in the script for a transaction. In other words, the results suggest that during a transaction, friends respond to forces other than those that are solely economic. These other motivations are a part of the script implied when agents and principals have a relationship of friendship.

These results provide evidence that individuals are more likely to seek better results in a transaction when acting on behalf of a friend, even if the friend does not have an explicit knowledge of how the transaction is being handled (no accountability). This view is also shared by Krackhardt and Stern (1988) and Zand (1972) who state that friends involved in a particular culture enjoy mutual loyalty and expect honesty and transparency (self-disclosure) from one another. In other words, friends tend to expect reciprocity for their deeds, notwithstanding according to Halpern (1997, p. 842) that the mutual expectation in the relationship may be one of "give-and-take." At the same time, these results go against the view of Castanzias and Helfat (1991) which assumes as wholly valid the premise of agency theory discussed by Jensen and Meckling (1976), in which an agent that works under conditions of low accountability and low expectations of value by the principal should not attempt to obtain significantly greater value for friends over strangers.

Concluding Remarks

Some studies in behavioral finance have sought to understand how the mind categorizes information, an area of study which is concentrated in social cognition research. Behavioral finance is a fast-growing field of research, mainly explaining agent behavior through heuristics and their consequent cognitive slants, together with their repercussions on the market (Thaler 1999). However, little discussion has focused on human behavior apart from research in social psychology and anthropology, both of which have proven helpful in understanding individual behavior in making financial decisions (Shefrin 2015; Fracassi 2017). In practical terms, behavioral finance research seeks to establish a link between the psychological sciences and economic theory and thus better understand the choices made to manage wealth.

Under the premise that individuals adhere to social norms, cognitive structures (or scripts) exist that incorporate behavior rules between individuals for multiple situations (Meuwese et al. 2017). This chapter examines the effects of friendship on a player's price expectations in certain transactions. There are two principal results that point to the existence of scripts for the behavior of friends in negotiation transactions.

First, individuals involved in transactions where the two parties are friends will act differently than when the two parties are strangers. Friends will tend to agree on a price attributed to a product, while strangers will be more willing to disagree and bargain with respect to the price. Second, when an individual conducts a transaction on behalf of a friend, results point to the existence of a different script than when acting on behalf of a stranger. When friendship with the principal exists, the agent will seek to better protect the principal's interests. In addition, despite the interesting evidence found regarding friendship's influence on transactions, no less important are the implications the evidence has for transactions with strangers. Indeed, individuals are more likely to transact with potential players in an environment of weak ties rather than only transacting with friends.

Future Directions

It is apparent that friendship influences an individual's behavior scripts in the context of negotiation transactions. These scripts are comprised of social norms that restrict the full exercise of rational behavior in a transaction, according to the concept of rational behavior as outlined in classical economic theory. The methods used to inform this chapter possess limitations worth discussing. The tests were performed within a specific age group and geographic region, thus limiting, in some form, the results obtained. Similar limitations are found throughout the behavioral finance literature, and together they suggest a vast field of study for future exploration. Future studies might replicate this study in greater numbers across a more diverse group of players, introducing different transactions, as well as employ other experimental designs to test the hypotheses. Finally, it is apparent that finance research is moving toward the acquisition of a new construct that will further strengthen and complete the current models used in the research. Furthermore, according to Thaler (1999), the concept of behavioral finance tends to be incorporated within modern finance. While friendship is widely discussed in the literature, it is a subject that implores empirical evidence (Schuster 2015). For this reason it is understood that this topic constitutes a modern research agenda in financial innovation.

References

Adams, R. B., & Ferreira, D. (2007). A theory of friendly boards. *Journal of Finance, 62*(1), 217–250.

Austin, W. (1980). Friendship and fairness: Effects of type of relationship and task performance on choice of distribution rules. *Personality and Social Psychology Bulletin, 6*, 402–408.

Austin, W., & McGinn, N. C. (1977). Sex differences in choice of distribution rules. *Journal of Personality, 45*, 379–394.

Baker, W. E. (1984). Floor trading and crowd dynamics. In P. Adler & P. Adler (Eds.), *The social dynamics of financial markets* (pp. 107–128). Greenwich: JAI Press.

Blau, P. M. (1964). *Exchange and power in social life*. New York: Wiley.

Boulding, K. E. (1973). *The economy of love and fear*. Belmont: Wadsworth.

Canary, D. J., Cupach, W. R., & Messman, S. J. (1995). *Relationship conflict: Conflict in parent-child, friendship, and work relationships*. Thousand Oaks: Sage.

Carroll J. S., Bazerman, M. H., & Maury, R. (1988). Negotiator cognitions: A descriptive approach to negotiators' understanding of their opponents. *Organizational Behavior and Human Decision Processes, 41*(3), 352–370. https://doi.org/10.1016/0749-5978(88)90034-9.

Castanzias, R. P., & Helfat, C. E. (1991). Managerial resources and rents. *Journal of Management, 17*, 12–24.

Coleman, J. S. (1990). *The foundations of social theory*. Cambridge: Harvard University Press.

Cummings, L. L., & Anton, R. (1990). The logical and appreciative dimensions of accountability. In S. Srivastra & D. L. Cooperider (Eds.), *The functioning of executive appreciation* (pp. 247–437). San Francisco: Jossey-Bass.

Demir, M., Haynes, A., & Potts, S. K. (2017). My friends are my estate: Friendship experiences mediate the relationship between perceived responses to capitalization attempts and happiness. *Journal of Happiness Studies, 18*(4), 1161–1190.

Elmer, T., Boda, Z., & Stadtfeld, C. (2017). The co-evolution of emotional well-being with weak and strong friendship ties. *Network Science, 5*(3), 278–307.

Fiske, S. T., & Taylor, S. E. (1991). *Social cognition*. New York: Random House.

Fracassi, C. (2017). Corporate finance policies and social networks. *Management Science, 63*(8), 2420–2438.

Fracassi, C., & Tate, G. (2012). External networking and internal firm governance. *Journal of Finance, 67*(1), 153–194.

Franken, A., Keijsers, L., Dijkstra, J. K., & ter Bogt, T. (2017). Music preferences, friendship, and externalizing behavior in early adolescence: A SIENA examination of the music marker theory using the SNARE study. *Journal of Youth and Adolescence, 46*, 1839–1850.

Fry, W. R., Firestone, I. J., & Williams, D. L. (1983). Negotiation process and outcome of stranger dyads and dating couples: Do lovers lose? *Basic and Applied Social Psychology, 4*(1), 1–16.

Granovetter, M. (1974). *Getting a job: A study of contacts and careers*. Cambridge: Harvard University Press.

Greenhalgh, L., & Chapman, D. (1994). Characteristics of relationships between disputants: Impact and empirical assessment. Unpublished Manuscript.

Hällsten, M., Edling, C., Rydgren, J. (2017). Social capital, friendship networks, and youth unemployment. Social Science Research, 61, 234–250. https://doi.org/10.1016/j.ssresearch.2016.06.017

Halpern, J. J. (1992). The effect of friendship on bargaining: Experimental studies of personal business transactions. In J. L. Wall & L. R. Jauch (Eds.), *Best paper proceedings* (pp. 64–68). Las Vegas: Academy of Management.

Halpern, J. J. (1994). The effect of friendship on personal business transactions. *Journal of Conflict Resolution, 38*(4), 647–664.

Halpern, J. J. (1997). Elements of a script for friendship in transactions. *Journal of Conflict Resolution, 61*(6), 835–868.

Hellmann, T., & Thiele, V. (2015). Friends or foes? The interrelationship between angel and venture capital markets. *Journal of Financial Economics, 115*(3), 639–653.

Hennart, J. F. (2015). Leveraging Asian institutions to deepen theory: A transaction cost perspective on relational governance. *Asian Business & Management, 14*(4), 257–282.

Hirschman, A. O. (1986). *Rival views of market society*. New York: Viking.

Husted, B. (1990). Interorganizational trust (Unpublished dissertation, University of California, Berkeley).

Iannone, N. E., McCarty, M. K., & Kelly, J. R. (2017). With a little help from your friend: Transactive memory in best friendships. *Journal of Social and Personal Relationships, 34*, 812–832.

Jensen, M. C., & Meckling, W. (1976). Theory of firm: Managerial behavior, agency costs and ownership structure. *Journal of Financial Economics, 3*, 305–360.

Kelley, H. H. (1979). *Personal relationships: Their structures and processes*. Hillsdale: Lawrence Erlbaum.

Krackhardt, D., & Stern, R. N. (1988). Informal networks and organizational crises: An experimental simulation. *Social Psychology Quarterly, 51*(2), 123–140.

Labun, A., Wittek, R., Steglich, C. (2016). The co-evolution of power and friendship networks in an organization. *Network Science, 4*(3), 364–384.

Liang, Y., Lv, W., Wu, W., Xu, K. (2017). Friendship-aware task planning in mobile crowdsourcing. *Frontiers of Information Technology and Electronic Engineering, 18*(1), 107–121.

Loewenstein, G. F., Thomson, L., & Bazerman, N. H. (1989). Social utility and decision making in interpersonal contexts. *Journal of Personality and Social Psychology, 57*(3), 426–441.

Lu, D., Sang, J., Chen, Z., Xu, M., & Mei, T. (2017). Who are your "Real" friends: Analyzing and distinguishing between offline and online friendships from social multimedia data. *IEEE Transactions on Multimedia, 19*, 1299–1313.

Malinowski, B. (1926). *Crimeny Costumbre en la Sociedad Salvage*. Barcelona: Editora Ariel.

Mauss, M. (1969). *The gifts: Forms and functions of exchange in Archaic societies*. London: Cohen & West.

McNeil, I. R. (1974). The many futures of contracts. *Southern California Law Review, 47*, 691–816.

McNeil, I. R. (1986). Exchange revisited: Individual utility and social solidary. *Ethnics, 96*, 567–593.

Mendes-Da-Silva, W. (2011). Small worlds and board interlocking in Brazil: A longitudinal study of corporate networks, 1997–2007. *Brazilian Review of Finance, 9*(4), 521–548.

Mendes-Da-Silva, W., Brito, T., Famá, R., & Liljegren, J. T. (2008). Effects of friendship in transactions in an emerging market: Empirical evidence from Brazil. *Icfai Journal of Behavioral Finance, 5*, 25–46.

Mendes-Da-Silva, W., Rossoni, L., Conte, B.S., Gattaz, C.C. (2016). *Journal of Cultural Economics, 40*(1), 75–99. https://doi.org/10.1007/s10824-015-9248-3

Meuwese, R., Cillessen, A. H. N., & Güroğlu, B. (2017). Friends in high places: A dyadic perspective on peer status as predictor of friendship quality and the mediating role of empathy and prosocial behavior. *Social Development, 26*(3), 503–519.

Morgan, W. R., & Sawyer, J. (1967). Bargaining, expectations and the preference of equality over equity. *Journal of Personality and Social Psychology, 6*, 139–149.

Pinker, S. (1997). *How the mind works*. New York: W.W. Norton & Company.

Plummer, D.L., Stone, R.T., Powell, L., Allison, J. (2016). Patterns of adult cross-racial friendships: A context for understanding contemporary race relations. *Cultural Diversity and Ethnic Minority Psychology, 22*(4), 479–494.

Powell, J. H. (2017). Financial innovation: A world in transition. In *41st Annual Central Banking Seminar, Sponsored by the Federal Reserve Bank of New York*, New York. Available at: https://www.federalreserve.gov/newsevents/speech/powell20171018a.htm.

Raiffa, H. (1982). The art and science of negotiation. Cambridge, MA: Harvard University Press/Belknap.

Qin, Z., & Deng, X. (2016). Government and family Guanxi in Chinese private firms: Perceptions and preference. *Review of Managerial Science, 10*(1), 35.

Ramirez-Fernandez, J., Ramirez-Marin, J. Y., & Munduate, L. (2017). I expected more from you: The influence of close relationships and perspective taking on negotiation offers. *Group Decision and Negotiation*. https://doi.org/10.1007/s10726-017-9548-4.

Rousseau, D. M., & Mclean Parks, J. (1992). The contracts of individuals and organizations. In L. L. Cummings & B. M. Staw (Eds.), *Research in organizational behavior* (pp. 1–43). Greenwich: JAI.

Rubin, Z. (1973). *Liking and loving*. New York: Holt, Rinehart & Wiston.

Sahlins, M. (1972). *Stone age economics*. Chicago: Aldine Atherton.

Schank, R. C., & Abelson, R. P. (1977). *Scripts, plans and understanding*. Hilsdale: Lawrence Erlbaum.

Schuster, C. (2015). Your family and friends are collateral: Microfinance and the social. Theorizing the Contemporary, Cultural Anthropology website, March 30. https://culanth.org/fieldsights/660-your-family-andfriends-are-collateral-microfinance-and-the-social.

Schuster, C., & Copeland, M. (1996). *Global business: Planning for sales and negotiations*. Fort Worth: Dryden.

Seabright, M. D., Levinthal, D., & Fichman, M. (1992). Role of individual attachments in the dissolution of interorganizational relationships. *Academy of Management Journal, 35*, 122–160.

Shapiro, E. G. (1975). Effects of expectations of future interactions on reward allocation in dyads: Equity or equality? *Journal of Personality and Social Psychology, 31*, 873–880.

Shefrin, H. (2015). The behavioral paradigm shift. *Revista de Administração de Empresas, 55*(1), 95–98.

Taylor, R. J., Mouzon, D.M., Nguyen, A.W., Chatters, L.M. (2016). Reciprocal family, friendship and church support networks of African Americans: Findings from the national survey of American life. *Race and Social Problems, 8*(4), 326–339.

Thaler, R. H. (1985). Using mental accounting in a theory of purchasing behavior. *Marketing Science, 4*, 12–13.

Thaler, R. H. (1999). The end of behavioral finance. *Financial Analyst Journal, 55*(6), 12–17.

Turan, S. S. (2015). Stakeholders in equity-based crowdfunding: Respective risks over the equity crowdfunding lifecycle. *Journal of Financial Innovation, 1*(2). https://doi.org/10.15194/jofi_2015.v1.i2.34.

Tversky, A., & Kahneman, D. (1974). Judgment under uncertainty heuristics and biases. *Sciences, 185*, 1124–1131.

Williamson, O. E. (1985). *The economic institution of capitalism*. New York: Free Press.

Zand, D. E. (1972). Trust and managerial problem solving. *Administrative Science Quarterly, 17*, 229–239.

Part III
Financial Innovation in the Corporate Level

Chapter 13
Corporate Sustainability, Capital Markets, and ESG Performance

Alexandre S. Garcia, Wesley Mendes-Da-Silva, and Renato J. Orsato

Abstract This chapter discusses associations between the financial profile of a firm and superior environmental, social, and governance (ESG) performance, considering firms from Brazil, Russia, India, China, and South Africa (the so-called BRICS countries). In particular, the study analyzes ESG performance in sensitive industries, i.e., those subject to systematic social taboos, moral debates, and political pressures and those that are more likely to cause social and environmental damage. We applied linear regressions with a data panel collected from 365 listed companies between 2010 and 2012. Our results suggest the market capitalization as the main predictor of ESG performance. In general, larger companies have higher levels of performance. We also found that companies in sensitive industries present superior environmental performance even when controlling for size and country. Our conclusions provide insights for future studies around ESG performance.

Keywords Corporate social responsibility (CSR) · Environmental, social, and governance (ESG) performance · Sustainability index · BRICS

JEL Code F18 · G34 · M14

Portions of this chapter appeared in the 2017 paper "Sensitive industries produce better ESG performance: Evidence from emerging markets," *Journal of Cleaner Production*, vol 150, pp135–147.

A. S. Garcia (✉)
Centro Universitario Fecap, Sao Paulo, SP, Brazil
e-mail: garcia@fecap.br

W. Mendes-Da-Silva
Sao Paulo School of Business Administration (FGV/EAESP), Sao Paulo, SP, Brazil

University of Texas at Austin, Austin, TX, USA

R. J. Orsato
Department of Operations Management, Fundação Getulio Vargas at São Paulo (FGV/EAESP), Sao Paulo, Brazil
e-mail: renato.orsato@fgv.br

W. Mendes-Da-Silva (ed.), *Individual Behaviors and Technologies for Financial Innovations*, https://doi.org/10.1007/978-3-319-91911-9_13

When companies such as Lonmin, Samarco, BP, or Petrobras make headlines for wrong reasons, it is often the result of environmental, social, or governance (ESG) mismanagement (Hayat 2015), which has become increasingly important for business, policy makers, and investors (Dyllick and Hockerts 2002; Halt and Milstein 1999). A central reason companies seek recourse in capital markets is the possibility of raising money at low costs. This depends, however, on the ability of firms to remunerate investors, who prioritize companies that provide a better return per unit of risk. In this regard, the quality of institutional communication with the market via reports containing accurate, extensive, and reliable information is central for firms (Mendes-Da-Silva and Onusic 2014; Mendes-Da-Silva et al. 2014). Hence, the search for growing returns is likely to coexist with better governance, social, and environmental practices (Cheng et al. 2014).

Previous studies found that a company's commitment to sustainability and corporate social responsibility (CSR)[1] reduces uncertainty, business risk, and, by extension, the cost of capital (Bassen et al. 2006; Orlitzky and Benjamin 2001). If a company operates responsibly, the risk is reduced for consumer boycotts or other penalties, rendering it more interesting for investors. Assuming business risk as the probability that the company will not meet its objectives, firms that pollute or have unfair employee relations may suffer penalties and fines or even be forced to halt operations, leading to financial losses. In the view of Bassen et al. (2006), a major risk of irresponsible corporate behavior is reputational loss. Incidents caused by irresponsible behavior can reduce the trust and loyalty among company stakeholders. The *Deepwater Horizon* oil spill of BP in the Gulf of Mexico in 2010 is exemplary (Roberto 2011). Likewise, bad CSR performance may motivate consumers to boycott the products of a firm, as occurred with Shell in the Brent Spar incident in 1995 (Dickson and McCulloch 1996).

CSR in firms operating in "sensitive industries" is trickier; many question whether they can be socially responsible. Sensitive industries are characterized by social taboos, moral debates, and political pressure, including sinful industries, such as tobacco, gambling, alcohol, and adult entertainment (Cai et al. 2012). In the last 40 years, studies examining the relationship between corporate social performance (CSP) and corporate financial performance (CFP) focused on sensitive industries operating in developed countries (Rahdari 2016), with most showing a positive CSP-CFP relationship (Griffin and Mahon 1997; Orlitzky et al. 2003; Margolis et al. 2009).

Such outcome does not seem valid, however, for companies from emerging economies (Allouche and Laroche 2005; Rettab et al. 2009; Aras et al. 2010; Lu et al. 2014; Chetty et al. 2015; Martínez-Ferrero and Frías-Aceituno 2013). Indeed, as the study of Orsato et al. (2015) suggests, the ESG literature is not only scarcer but also controversial. For this reason, the research presented in this chapter analyzes the relationship between the financial performance of companies listed in emerging

[1]While acknowledging the different terms that many practitioners and academics have coined, in this chapter, we use the terms corporate social responsibility and ESG interchangeably.

markets belonging to the group of BRICS (Brazil, Russia, China, India, and South Africa) and their ESG performance. In such contexts, ESG practices are expected to be in greater demand than in mature markets (Dobers and Halme 2009; Baughn et al. 2007) due to the deprived social and environmental demands in BRICS countries. In this respect, our study contributes to better understanding ESG performance in countries where it matters most. In addition to this research gap, we investigate the ESG performance of companies in these countries operating in sensitive sectors.

The study is relevant for three reasons. First, according to Friede et al. (2015) and Lewandowski (2017), associations between corporate financial performance (CFP) and ESG performance remain fragmented. Studies that analyzed differences in CFP and ESG across regions (Jamali and Karam 2016; Rodrigo et al. 2016) were inconclusive. Some found strong correlation between ESG and CFP in the emerging market group, significantly higher than in developed markets. Second, part of the literature ascertains that lower ratings for ESG imply lower disclosure and/or lower adherence to ESG standards, which can induce riskier and more unstable investment environments. Yet, countries with higher economic growth, like the BRICS, may enable companies to invest more in ESG practices to limit the impact of ESG-related costs in the long term (Peiró-Signes and Segarra-Oña 2013). Third, since the 1970s, most studies have pointed out a positive ESG-CFP correlation (Friede et al. 2015), but there is no agreement that sensitive industries always entail low ESG performance (Statman and Glushkov 2009; Hong and Kacperczyk 2009). Since our study addresses these three issues, as well as the scarcity of empirical evidence from emerging countries, from BRICS in particular, it contributes to the ESG literature. With data collected from 365 listed BRICS companies, it provides one of the most comprehensive overviews of ESG performance about emerging markets.

This chapter presents highlights from our research and uses this large data set to discuss associations between financial profile and ESG performance. Our findings—i.e., the effect of market capitalization on ESG performance is assumed to be identical across all the groups, while the regression reports the average within-group effect—provide insight into how financial professionals, educators, managers, policy makers, and other stakeholders can develop more effective initiatives about corporate report toward a new point of view about the company-society relationship. We make recommendations for future research at the end of the chapter.

Environmental, Social, and Governance (ESG), Risk, and Financial Performance

In one of the initial studies on corporate social responsibility (CSR), Carrol (1979) proposed a model for testing CSR investments in organizations based on the economic, legal, and ethical domains (environmental issues were embedded in the economic and legal domain). Since then, expressions such as sustainability, corporate responsibility, corporate governance, socio-environmental governance, as well as environmental, social, and governance (ESG) have been used synonymously. From a generic perspective, Bassen et al. (2006:16) state that CSR is "a dynamic concept, and its ethical content depends largely on theoretical paradigms, regional economic traditions, business-level specifics and the time period involved." Other authors (i.e., Arya and Zhang 2009; Child 2005) agree with the argument that business organizations operating in different nations also experience different degrees of coercive pressures to engage in CSR activities. Overall, the lack of consensus about a definition, among other problems, has limited empirical testing. Numerous definitions of CSR have been proposed, and often no clear definition is given, rendering theoretical development and measurement difficult (McWilliams et al. 2006).

Stakeholder theory has been central for the topic of CSR. Freeman and McVea (2000) argue that companies should make decisions that align with the interest of groups or individuals who can be affected by the activities of the company: the so-called stakeholders. In a nutshell, stakeholder theory states that the capacity of a firm to generate sustainable wealth is determined by its relationships with its various stakeholders. Following this line of thinking, the company should disclose financial and nonfinancial information to be as transparent as possible. Such practices will reduce informational asymmetry with the general public, resulting in greater confidence levels by investors. As Cheng et al. (2014:16) stated, "Higher levels of transparency reduce informational asymmetries between the firm and investors, thus mitigating perceived risk." In a meta-analysis, Orlitzky and Benjamin (2001) confirmed such a proposition: better CSR performance reduces company risk.

Overall, research on the association between financial and socio-environmental performance has been inconclusive (Griffin and Mahon 1997; Roman et al. 1999). Studies on the subject seek to identify the influences of ESG factors on companies' financial performance and vice versa (Surroca et al. 2010; Lourenço and Branco 2013). Orlitzky and Benjamin (2001), for instance, argue that managers and financial analysts still consider that social performance increases company risk and is, therefore, a "punishable offense." Although they are not explicit, this perspective is based on the neoclassical view that ESG practices constitute a source of inefficiency, introducing the potential to reduce shareholders' returns. In contrast, Bassen et al. (2006) and Cheng et al. (2014) found positive associations between best ESG practices and a company's risk profile.

Lam et al. (2012) found that increasing investments in companies with good ESG performances can also reduce systematic market risk. Such reduction is due to these companies, on average, being better capitalized in the market and presenting better ESG performances. Sassen et al. (2016), on the basis of a large European panel dataset of 8752 firm-year observations covering the period 2002–2014, found that a higher CSP decreases total and idiosyncratic risk. Other studies have investigated the impact on company risk and cost of capital, based on ESG practices. For instance, Kim et al. (2015) concluded that companies' efforts to reduce carbon productivity are compensated by the reduction of capital costs, and, accordingly, the firm's value increases. When investigating if the voluntary disclosure of nonfinancial information has an impact on the risk of the company and its capital cost, Dhaliwal et al. (2011) concluded that companies that had a high capital cost in a particular year obtained a reduction in their cost of capital when, in the following year, they publicized their ESG activities. Serafeim (2014) reached similar conclusions in his study of North American companies between 2002 and 2010.

By preparing an integrated report (i.e., a report that combines financial and sustainability data), companies attract investors who value long-term investments. The systematic risk has a negative correlation with the ESG indicators, suggesting that CSR disclosure reduces risk and, consequently, the cost of capital (Serafeim 2014). Controversially, Richardson and Welker (2001) concluded that there is no relationship between the disclosure of social practices and the cost of capital among companies whose return on capital is higher than the average. In sum, the association between the ESG, risk, and financial performance of companies remains an open question.

BRICS and Sensitive Industries

The British economist Jim O'Neill created the term BRIC in 2001, suggesting that, together, the economies of Brazil, Russia, India, and China (South Africa would be added later) would overtake the economies of the West by 2040 (O'Neill 2012). The aggregated gross domestic product (GDP) of these countries quadrupled in the decade of 2000–2010, jumping from US$3 trillion to US$12 trillion. According to O'Neill (2012), the opportunity for productivity growth is greater in the BRICS than in developed countries. In other words, countries with a younger and growing labor force have higher potential to generate GDP growth.

Nevertheless, pressure is growing for less orthodox development—one that includes ESG practices in BRICS companies. Such a trend can already be seen in the capital markets of South Africa and Brazil, for instance, which have created sustainability indexes in their stock exchanges, giving visibility to companies that excel in ESG practices (Orsato et al. 2015). ESG attributes are starting to show impact on both the risk profile and the financial returns of companies—even if the results are still inconclusive (Orlitzky and Benjamin 2001; Bassen et al. 2006; Hong and Kacperczyk 2009; Cheng et al. 2014) and if the majority of studies about the influence of ESG practices on the business risk use companies operating in developed economies (Richardson and Welker 2001; Dhaliwal et al. 2011; Serafeim 2014). Few works have been developed using data from emerging economies (Dobers and Halme 2009; Baughn et al. 2007).

Lockett et al. (2006) found that 89% of theoretical CSR papers are non-normative, whereas for the CSR in the literature on developing countries, the balance is more evenly split. This is largely due to the relatively large number of papers on the role of business in development, which tend to adopt a normative, critical perspective (Blowfield and Frynas 2005; Willi et al. 2011). In developing countries, responsible management of companies generally develop initiatives characterized by contributions to local urgent causes and community religious values, and are often based on philanthropy or charity (Raynard and Forstater 2002). Managers responsible for companies located in these countries experience a great challenge: meeting international standards of global markets while facing legal infrastructure failures and a culture of support for responsible business.

The IDH—Institutional Difference Hypothesis (Campbell 2006)—uses institutional theory as the primary theoretical basis (DiMaggio and Powell 1991; Meyer and Rowan 1977) and argues that institutional differences between developed and emerging economies have important effects on strategic decision-making in organizations (Hoskisson et al. 2000). According to Julian and Ofori-Dankwa (2013), institutional weaknesses in emerging markets, such as the quality of capital markets, affect the relationship between CFP and CSP. The logic of the IDH suggests that, in the context of emerging countries, firms are more likely to prioritize capital accumulation and not recognize the potential strategic benefit of CSR investments (Frynas 2005; Ofori and Hinson 2007).

Different economies are at different stages of development, with varying sophistication in civil society; so are companies at different stages of CSR. Likewise, the stakeholder demand for CSR can vary substantially across nations, regions, and lines of business (McWilliams et al. 2006). Sensitive industries constitute a particular group requiring attention in the BRICS. Social taboos, moral debates, and political pressure typically characterize sensitive industries (or controversial industries, as they have also been called). This is an overarching term that includes sinful industries, such as tobacco, gambling, alcohol, and adult entertainment, as well as industries involved with emerging environmental, social, or ethical issues, such as weapons, nuclear, oil, cement, and biotech (Baron et al. 2009).

Traditionally, socially responsible funds have used negative screening (also called ethical screening or exclusion) as the criterion to leave companies operating in such sectors out of investment portfolios (Orsato et al. 2015). Some studies suggest a positive association between firm size and industry membership with social disclosure (e.g., Deegan and Gordon 1996; Baron et al. 2009). However, whether firms of sensitive industries can become socially responsible remains an open question (Moura-Leite et al. 2014; Rodrigo et al. 2016). In particular, research about the ESG performance and the financial profile of companies from sensitive industries operating in BRICS countries is very scarce.

In a nutshell, the review of the literature suggests that differences exist between the institutional context and company profiles of advanced economies, when compared with emerging economies, in terms of attributes such as (i) the capital market (Khanna and Palepu 1997), (ii) the risk profile of companies (Cheng et al. 2014), and (iii) the environmental legitimacy (Ioannou and Serafeim 2014). These differences in attributes may impact the research results of different countries. As observed by Jamali and Karam (2016), the nuanced forms of CSR in the developing world are invariably contextualized and locally shaped by multilevel factors and actors embedded within wider formal and informal governance systems. Because institutional context and culture can play an important role in determining appropriate CSR priorities and initiatives, other scholars (Visser 2005; Hamann 2006) note that models such as Carrol's (1991), which was developed in an American context, may not be relevant for emerging economies.

ESG and Financial Performance

Based on the literature, we depart from the premise that there is no association between best ESG practices and financial performance in companies operating in the BRICS. This is because companies operating in these countries have limited sources of finance due, in part, to the weakness of the local capital markets and the trade-off between investing in ESG and other, often more lucrative, activities (López Iturriaga and Crisóstomo 2010). Together with economic issues, the institutional framework of a country can influence the nature and degree of adoption of ESG practices (Dobers and Halme 2009).

National institutional environments, such as weak and contracted governments; gaps in public governance and transparency; arbitrary enforcement of rules, regulations, and policies; and low levels of safety and labor standards, affect how CSR is conceived and practiced in developing countries. Hence, in most of the developing world, CSR continues to be equated with philanthropy, where substantive engagement with CSR is the exception rather than the norm (Jamali and Neville 2011). Therefore, we do not expect ESG practices to be capable of increasing the investment returns of companies operating in BRICS countries.

As the review of the literature also indicated, associations between the financial and ESG performances of companies belonging to sensitive industrial sectors, such as oil, gas chemicals, mining, steelmaking, and paper and pulp, are inconclusive. For instance, according to Richardson and Welker (2001), whereas companies in sensitive industries have better financial and social disclosure rates, they present inferior financial performance and lower cost of capital than their counterparts in nonsensitive industries. In contrast, Baron et al. (2009) found that the coefficients of Kinder, Lydenberg, Domini & Co. (KLD) exclusionary (alcohol, gambling, firearms, military, nuclear power, and tobacco) are positive and statistically significant, indicating better financial performance for firms operating in such sensitive industrial sectors. In addition to such contentious findings, most studies include only samples of North American and European companies.

In our research (details below), we followed the definition of sinful industries (e.g., tobacco, gambling, weapons, alcohol, adult entertainment) based on Baron et al. (2009). For other sensitive sectors in environmental or ethical terms, we followed the suggestion of Richardson and Welker (2001), who included oil, gas, chemicals, mines, metals, and forestry products. Finally, our classification set of firms belonging to sensitive industries followed previous research that classified firms according to Standard Industrial Classification (SIC) codes (Cowen et al. 1987;

Patten 2002) for industries often classified as environmentally sensitive, which include mining, oil and gas, paper, chemicals (excluding pharmaceuticals), and metals.

An example of the social and environmental impacts of such industries is the accident caused by the Brazilian mining firm Samarco Mineração S.A. In a nutshell, a dam holding mineral sludge managed by Samarco collapsed, releasing an avalanche of sludge that buried a rural village, killing 17 people and traveling more than 400 miles. Considered one of Brazil's worst environmental disasters ever, the incident (on November 5, 2015) triggered a criminal investigation and a roughly $5 billion civil lawsuit by authorities against Samarco and its parent companies, mining giants Vale SA and BHP Billiton Ltd. (Kiernan 2016).

Environmentally sensitive firms are more likely to disclose their environmental performance (Cormier and Magnan 2003; Kilian and Hennigs 2014) and as a result tend to show better performance than firms that belong to nonsensitive sectors (Lin et al. 2015; Cai et al. 2012). Companies with manufacturing processes that negatively impact the environment will have greater disclosure, when compared with companies in other industries. In general, industries including mining, petroleum, and chemical companies will emphasize—and often communicate in the media—their environmental, health, and safety efforts (Jenkins and Yakovleva 2006; Line et al. 2002).

Nonetheless, the question of whether firms of sensitive industries can become socially responsible remains largely unanswered. Because large firms and firms in these industries have their social and environmental performance closely scrutinized, research on the firms of developed countries suggests a positive association between industry membership and the interaction of firm size and industry membership with social disclosure (Deegan and Gordon 1996; Baron et al. 2009). Contrary to this rationale, our hypotheses assume that there are no differences between the ESG performance and the financial profile of companies belonging to sensitive industries, versus nonsensitive industries, operating in BRICS countries.

Data and Variables

Two criteria were employed in selecting firms for this study. First, we considered only companies listed in emerging economies, particularly the group known as BRICS, comprising Brazil, Russia, India, China, and South Africa. Second, we did not consider financial companies because of the specificity of their operational activity. After this filter, the total sample was composed of 1095 observations from 365 companies, distributed in 8 different sectors, identified based on the North American Industry Classification System (NAICS) 3-digit code: mining and construction (19%); manufacturing of food, textile, lumber, chemicals, and petroleum products and publishing (18%); manufacturing of plastics, leather, concrete, metal products, machinery, and equipment (18%); transportation, communications, electricity, gas, and sanitary services (20%); trade (9%); diversified industrials, retail, and diversified real estate investment trust (REITS[2]) (8%); personal, business, and entertainment services (4%); and professional services (4%).

Our variables were collected from two databases. Data were collected first from Thomson Reuters Eikon™ to compose our dependent variables, namely, the ESG (environmental, social, and governance) performance of the company. In other words, we collected data about the performance of the company in environmental, social, and corporate governance terms. We used the *DataStream* database to collect data about the company profile, which composed our independent variables. The reliability of these databases has neither been questioned in the academic community nor among users of corporate information, as Cheng et al. (2014) argue. Thomson Reuters Eikon™ offers a comprehensive platform for establishing customizable benchmarks (e.g., sector and country) for the assessment of corporate performance. The list of variables is presented in Table 13.1.

Annually, 400 data points are used as inputs to a default equal-weighted framework to calculate 70 key performance indicators (KPIs), to be further organized into 18 categories within three pillars[3]: (a) the environmental performance score, (b) social performance score, and (c) corporate governance performance score. Thomson Reuters Eikon™ integrates economic research and strategy development with asset analysis. Because we were dealing with component variables of the empirical model, four dependent variables were used: *overall ESG performance*, *environmental performance*, *social performance*, and *performance in corporate governance*. Regarding the independent variables at the company level, we used variables usually adopted in the finance literature (Dowell et al. 2000; Maury and Pajuste 2005; Cheng et al. 2014): *Systematic risk index, the firm's financial leverage index, the firm's free cash flow, market capitalization*, and *return on assets*.

Control variables were added to the model so that the results could be moderated for a vaster number of factors. The literature also frequently controls for firm size and sector (Dhaliwal et al. 2011; Richardson and Welker 2001). All these variables were extracted from DataStream, a global financial and macroeconomic database covering equities, stock market indices, currencies, company fundamentals, fixed income securities, and key economic indicators. Based on the Thomson Reuters Eikon™ database, we used a general performance score for each company, which is categorized into three pillars: social, environmental, and governance. We selected companies from BRICS countries from this database. Although the database of ESG indicators dates back to 2001, only in 2007 the ESG scores for companies from BRICS countries were introduced. However, considering the limited quantity of

[2]REIT is a company that owns, operates, or finances income-producing real estate. For a company to qualify as a REIT, it must meet certain regulatory guidelines. REITs often trade on major exchanges like other securities and provide investors with a liquid stake in real estate. More about REIT, please see Feng et al. (2011).

[3]http://financial.thomsonreuters.com/en/products/data-analytics/company-data/esg-research-data.html, Sept. 2016.

Table 13.1 Variables definitions and measures

Variable	Definition	Theoretical foundations
ESG performance	= Measure that varies from 0% to 100%. It is based on information grouped into governance, economic, environmental, and social pillars, as compiled by Thomson Reuters. It reflects the average performance of a company in these four areas. Data: Thomson Reuters Eikon™	Sassen et al. (2016) and Cheng et al. (2014)
Environmental performance	= Measure that varies from 0% to 100%. It measures the impact of a company on natural systems, including air, soil, and water, as well as on natural ecosystems. There are 57 indicators. Among the environmental factors that make up this rating is information about the use of energy, the reuse of water, carbon dioxide emissions, and waste recycling. Data: Thomson Reuters Eikon™	Sassen et al. (2016) and Cheng et al. (2014)
Social performance	= Measure that varies from 0% to 100%. It measures the company's capacity to generate trust and loyalty in its workers, customers, and society, through the use of best management practices. There are 60 indicators that include information about employee turnover, work-related accident rates, hours of training, health programs, and worker safety. Data: Thomson Reuters Eikon™	Sassen et al. (2016) and Cheng et al. (2014)
Performance in corporate governance	= Measure that varies from 0% to 100%. It measures the systems and processes of a company, which guarantee that its board members and executives act in the best interests of its shareholders, with a long-term view of the operations. There are 48 information indicators, such as the rights of minority shareholders, executive remuneration, independent board members, and audit committees. Data: Thomson Reuters Eikon™	Sassen et al. (2016) and Cheng et al. (2014)
Systematic risk index	= Obtained from the *beta* index of companies, considering a time frame of 24 months. It is calculated by the covariance between the asset returns of the company and the return on the share portfolio of the market, divided by the variation in the return of the share portfolio of the market. Data: DataStream database	Maury and Pajuste (2005) and Sassen et al. (2016)
Financial leverage index of the firm	= Calculated by dividing total liabilities by total assets. Data: DataStream database	Barnett and Salomon (2012)
Free cash flow of the firm	= This is the value in US$, based on the series of cash receipts that comprise the cash flow divided by the average weighted cost of capital. Data: DataStream database	Mishra and Modi (2013)

(continued)

Table 13.1 (continued)

Variable	Definition	Theoretical foundations
Firm size	= Continuous variable that reflects the size of the company. It was measured by two different proxies, one accounting Ln of net revenue, measured in US dollars, of the *i*-nth company in the *t*-nth year and another from the market, Ln of market capitalization. Data: DataStream database	Dhaliwal et al. (2011)
Asset profitability	= Calculated by dividing the result by the total assets. Data: DataStream database	Dowell et al. (2000)
Industry	= Dummy variable that identifies whether the company belongs to an industry that is seen as sensitive (major socio-environmental impact: energy—including oil and gas—chemicals, paper and pulp, mining and steelmaking). Receives the value 1 if yes and 0 otherwise. Data: DataStream database	Richardson and Welker (2001) and Lee and Faff (2009)

companies from these countries in the database in the period from 2007 to 2009, for the purposes of the sample of this work, we decided to use the period of 2010 to 2012.

Empirical Model

In spite of the relevance of studies of a causal nature, around which literature in the field of ESG still presents itself, our objective in this research is to check for associations between the financial profile of listed companies in BRICS countries and their ESG performance by way of panel data (static and unbalanced) regressions, and based on the set of variables chosen, the model to be tested is (1), with $N = 1095$ and $T = 3$.

$$\text{Firm performance}_{it} = \beta_0 + \beta_1 \text{Roa}_{it} + \beta_2 \text{Industry}_{it} + \beta_3 \text{FCF}_{it} + \beta_4 \text{Risk}_{it} + \sum_{j=1}^{k} \delta_j CV_{ji} + \varepsilon_{it} \tag{13.1}$$

in which the value of the *i*-nth firm, in the *t*-nth year, $Performance_{it}$, depends on K exogenous variables, $(x_{1it}, \cdots, x_{Kit})$, which differ between the firms at a given moment in time and vary over time. The error term, ε_{it}, which is assumed to be an IID (independent and identically distributed) random variable, with a mean of zero and variance σ_u^2, independent of $(x_{1i}, \cdots, x_{iT})$, represents the effects of the omitted variables that are peculiar both to the firms as well as to the period studied. This work uses linear regressions with a data panel. Three different methods are used for estimating the model: pooled regression, random effects, and fixed effects. The constant coefficients model presupposes that both the intercept and inclinations do not vary. This model is also called a pooled regression.

The individual fixed effects model presupposes that the inclinations are maintained but that the intercepts are different for each unit. In this case, no temporal effects influence the regression, just individual ones. These effects can be observable or not and are normally correlated with the regressors. In other words, they are endogenous (Baltagi 2001). The random effect model presupposes that, if there are effects that do not form part of the model, they will be exogenous and not correlated with the regressors. No indications were found for the correlation between regressors and the regression error, which suggests the nonexistence of problems of endogeneity (Hsiao 2005; Petersen 2009).

Empirical Results

Before performing panel data regressions, we provide some descriptive statistics in Table 13.2 Panel A. The average for the ESG general performance score in the sample is 45.9, with a standard deviation of 30.7, suggesting significant variation in the practice of the ESG general performance. Figure 13.1 shows ESG indicators of Brazil and Russia increased over the period, whereas India's and South Africa's ESG indicators showed reductions. Some of the indicators for China increased, such as governance, and some stagnated, such as environmental and social indicators. The analysis indicates that even with a drop in its indicators over 3 years, South Africa is the BRICS country that has the highest ESG and is three times better than China (the overall performance index in 2010). China has the lowest rates in the sample, with the exception of its governance index, which beats India's.

Table 13.2 Panel B shows the matrix of correlations for the variables used in the study. The bivariate correlations reveal no unexpected standards but show a positive relationship between social and environmental indicators and the value of the firm, as observed in the market capitalization variable, which is similar to what we find in Lam et al. (2012). Corporate governance seems to be the only ESG factor that has no positive relationship with the value of a firm, but this is mainly the result of Russian companies that present a negative relationship between these indicators. As can also be observed in Table 13.2 Panel B, the dependent variables point to a low correlation with the independent variables, corroborating Lattin et al. (2011).

Table 13.3 shows descriptive statistics of the studied variables, for which Table 13.2 (Panel A) showed the existence of differences between the groups of companies belonging to the industries judged to be sensitive (oil, gas, chemicals, mining, steelmaking, and paper and pulp) relative to those companies belonging to industries in an alternative situation ($p < 0.05$). Companies in sensitive industries have better ESG indicators for the three dimensions considered: environmental, social, and governance. The average overall ESG performance is 57.44 in companies

Table 13.2 Descriptive statistics and correlations

Panel A: descriptive statistics	N	Mean	Median	Std. dev.	Min.	1Q	3Q	Max.	Skewness
General performance	904	45.96**	46.32	30.75	3.10	13.95	75.44	96.51	0.05
Environmental performance	904	47.17**	44.00	27.93	8.64	20.39	72.96	94.67	0.19
Social performance	904	56.21**	61.00	31.03	4.09	25.18	86.76	97.08	−0.27
Governance performance	904	34.11**	29.17	24.56	1.73	12.23	52.21	94.13	0.58
Systematic risk	525	0.53**	0.49	0.53	−0.89	0.18	0.82	2.22	0.40
Leverage	1078	33.00**	31.36	22.62	0.00	14.74	49.37	103.60	0.37
Market capitalization	1067	17.30**	17.09	1.88	13.52	15.82	18.73	22.22	0.31
Return on assets	1060	9.34**	8.02	8.66	−28.63	4.52	12.62	118.74	3.04
Free cash flow	1039	1.70**	0.41	14.72	−39.39	−0.46	2.69	73.34	1.74
Panel B: correlations	1	2	3	4	5	6	7	8	9
1. General performance									
2. Environmental performance	0.870**								
3. Social performance	0.933**	0.807**							
4. Governance performance	0.660**	0.440**	0.533**						
5. Systematic risk	0.07	0.103*	0.105*	0.00					
6. Leverage	−0.087**	−0.01	−0.05	−0.06	0.05				
7. Market capitalization	0.158**	0.242**	0.138**	−0.06	0.233**	−0.04			
8. Free cash flow	0.099**	0.076*	0.087*	0.078*	0.124**	−0.227**	0.119**		
9. Return on assets	0.148**	0.067*	0.122**	0.04	−0.05	−0.331**	0.161**	0.193**	

Source: Author's calculations

Note: Panel A shows the descriptive statistics of the variables studied. The column that shows the mean values also points to the existence of significant differences between companies in sensitive industries and industries in an alternative situation

*p-value < 0.1; **p-value < 0.05

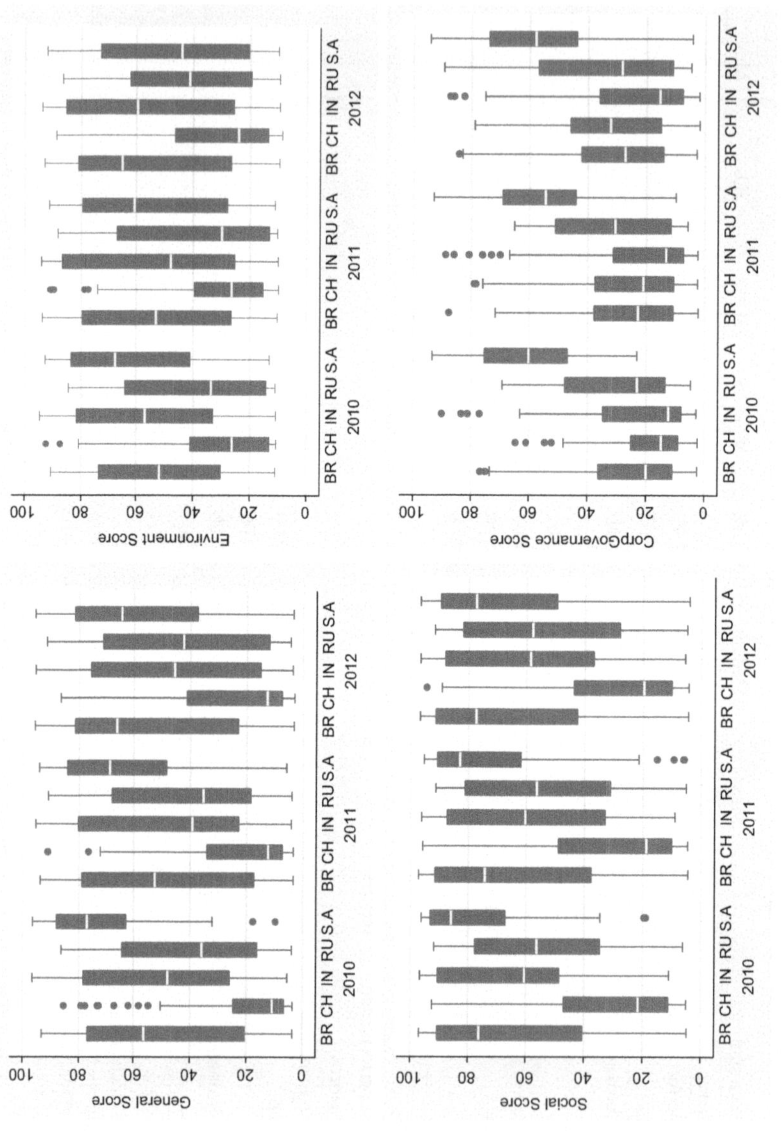

Fig. 13.1 ESG performance of firms across BRICS countries. Note: *BR* Brazil, *CH* China, *IN* India, *RU* Russia, *SA* South Africa

Table 13.3 Descriptive statistics segregated by industry type

Panel A: Sensitive industries	N	Average	Std Dev.	Min.	Max.
General performance	191	57.44	28.16	4.46	96.46
Environmental performance	191	58.71	25.01	10.25	94.02
Social performance	191	68.85	25.94	5.93	96.73
Governance performance	191	39.98	26.31	2.87	94.13
Systematic risk	102	0.78	0.50	−0.63	1.59
Leverage	214	29.02	19.64	0.00	77.00
Market capitalization	213	17.88	2.08	13.56	22.22
Return on assets	211	8.50	8.87	−12.18	63.98
Free cash flow	211	1.11	14.50	−39.39	73.34
Panel B: Nonsensitive industries					
General performance	713	42.88	30.70	3.10	96.51
Environmental performance	713	44.07	27.88	8.64	94.67
Social performance	713	52.82	31.42	4.09	97.08
Governance performance	713	32.53	23.84	1.73	91.66
Systematic risk	423	0.47	0.52	−0.89	2.22
Leverage	864	33.99	23.20	0.00	103.60
Market capitalization	854	17.16	1.81	13.52	21.89
Return on assets	849	9.55	8.60	−28.63	118.74
Free cash flow	828	1.85	14.78	−39.39	73.34

from sensitive industries, compared with 42.88 in companies from other industries. The financial indicators are also consistent with the literature (Richardson and Welker 2001; Deegan and Gordon 1996), with companies from sensitive sectors having a larger systematic risk (average 0.78 on the *beta* index, compared with 0.47) and smaller return on assets (ROA) index than companies from nonsensitive sectors (8.50 versus 9.55). The two sector groups have similarities in terms of company size, measured by the logarithm of their market capitalization value (with averages of 17.88 in sensitive sectors and 17.16 for other sectors).

Regressions

The impacts on corporate social performance was estimated by three different procedures (ordinary least squares, OLS; random effects, RE; and fixed effects, FE). The dependent variables are *general performance, environmental performance, social performance*, and *corporate governance* of the firm. As it can be seen in Table 13.4, we report only the results via estimation with fixed effects and robust standard error.

To identify the estimation method that best adjusts to each model, we chose the regression model controlling for FE (as a result of the existence of unobserved variables that probably affect the ESG performance of the company), since FE was

Table 13.4 Estimated coefficients for panel data regression (fixed effects)

	Model I	Model II	Model III	Model IV
	Overall ESG	Environmental	Social	Corporate gov.
Constant	−72.302*	−46.518	−24.163	17.639
	(40.592)	(35.396)	(32.909)	(40.901)
Return on assets	0.21	−0.096	−0.079	−0.191
	(0.261)	(0.189)	(0.297)	(0.269)
Free cash flow	0.026	0.139	0.002	−0.006
	(0.113)	(0.111)	(0.144)	(0.109)
Market capitalization	7.741***	6.071***	5.608***	1.632
	(2.554)	(2.209)	(2.063)	(2.549)
N [#companies]	384 [172]	384 [172]	384 [172]	384 [172]
R^2 adjust	93.30%	93.90%	92.50%	90.81%
Akaike criterion	3008.2	2903.2	3020.9	2997.6
F	16.026	18.694	14.733	11.883

Source: Author's calculations based on data collection

Notes: This table shows the results obtained for estimates of the panel data regression parameters in four different models, being a model for each of the four dependent variables considered in this study—overall ESG, environmental, social, and corporate governance. Our results suggest that fixed effects (in fixed effect (FE) models, the effect of each predictor variable (i.e., the slope) is assumed to be identical across all the groups, and the regression merely reports the average within-group effect) and robust standard error are adequate

*$p < 0.1$; **$p < 0.05$; ***$p < 0.01$

more appropriate to consider the fit tests of the models (Hsiao, 2005).[4] The associations between ESG and CFP found in the literature are inconclusive, requiring further research (Friede et al. 2015). Thus, the consideration of different time

[4] In fixed effect (FE) models, the effect of each predictor variable (i.e., the slope) is assumed to be identical across all the groups, and the regression merely reports the average within-group effect. It is recommended to use FE in situations in which the interest is concentrated only in analyzing the impact of variables that vary across time. FE models focus the relationship between predictors and dependent variables within an entity, e.g., country, industry, company, or person. Each entity has its own individual characteristics that may or may not influence the predictor variables, e.g., whether a person is male or female can influence one's opinion on a particular issue. When using FE, we assume that something within the entity/individual can affect or predispose the predictor or dependent variables, and we must control that. This is the logic behind the assumption of correlation between the entity's error term and the predictors. FE removes the effect of these characteristics that do not vary across time, so that it is possible to evaluate the net effect of the predictors on the dependent variable. Furthermore, it is assumed that in the FE model, these characteristics that do not vary across time are unique to the individual/entity and are not correlated with other individual characteristics. It is assumed that each entity is different. Thus, the entity error term and the constant (which captures individual characteristics) should not be correlated with the others. Consequently, in cases where the error terms are correlated, FE models are inadequate, since the inferences may not be correct, which is the main reason for modeling this relation by the Hausman test. The FEs will not work well with the data that reflects minimal variation within the cluster. It is also recommended to control for time effects whenever unexpected variation, or special events, affects the dependent variable. In short, fixed-effect models are designed to analyze the causes of changes within an entity/individual (Angrist and Pischke 2009).

periods, the use of different methods, the use of new variables, and the study of different institutional environments can be contributive. Considering the scope and the design adopted for the present research, we are not concerned about causation. Instead, we focused our discussion on associations between the variables studied in the emerging markets context. As a result, our study signals empirical associations, rather than causation. However, according to Angrist and Pischke (2009) and Morgan and Winship (2014), even studies supported in the verification of associations may be relevant to research of a causal nature.

Assuming the results via fixed effects, only the size of the firm seems to have an influence on ESG performance in overall $(\widehat{\beta} = 7.741; p < 0.01)$, environmental $(\widehat{\beta} = 6.071; p < 0.01)$, and social $(\widehat{\beta} = 5.608; p < 0.01)$ issues; larger companies tend to have a better performance, as already found in previous works (Cheng et al. 2014; Surroca et al. 2010; Richardson and Welker 2001; Bansal and Clelland 2004; Dhaliwal et al. 2011). According to Lam et al. (2012), large companies have more resources for carrying out activities that enhance their performance in ESG, and socially responsible investment portfolios have a tendency to prefer companies with a larger market capitalization. Only the governance performance proxy was not associated with market capitalization $(\widehat{\beta} = 1.632; p > 0.1)$.

According to the specialized literature, there are reasons to believe in the possibility of nonlinear associations between the systematic risk of a company (i.e., the performance capacity of the company being impacted by the behavior of the economy generally) and economic results. This line of thinking assumes that moments of stress in the financial system can amplify the fundamental adverse shocks and result in depressions or crises. However, the absence of stress does not necessarily trigger a macroeconomic boom (Gertler and Kiyotaki 2010; Mendoza 2010; He and Krishnamurthy 2012; Giglio et al. 2016).

Therefore, understanding that a company's performance is not simply summed up in its economic and financial performance, it is assumed that there are reasons to test the nonlinearity potential of systematic risk with the ESG performance of the firm. The results obtained for auxiliary regressions, which include quadratic terms for each of the independent variables considered, point to possible nonlinearity between the systematic risk of the firm and its ESG performance. The results of these auxiliary regressions suggest the existence of a relationship that can be described by way of an "inverted U-shaped" curve. Put another way, it seems that companies with greater or less systematic risk have poorer ESG performance; in other words, the results suggest that there are values for systematic risk that maximize ESG performance and that these values are also close to 1. Therefore, companies with a systematic risk that is similar to the portfolio of market assets seem to exhibit the best aggregate ESG performance.

A number of recent studies have estimated a U-shaped relationship between corporate social performance and corporate financial performance, such that better financial returns are associated with the highest and lowest levels of corporate social performance (e.g., Barnett and Salomon 2012; Brammer and Millington 2008). The associations between systematic risk and the sustainability of a business have already proven to be a topic of interest to the business media and regulatory agents in mature markets (Krosinsky 2013). However, it is understood that while the question of sustainability constitutes determinants for business performance, investors and the regulatory agents still seem to pay little attention to this issue, despite the fact that some representative investors have already alleged they are adopting structures for analyzing companies using ESG concepts (CalPERS 2014).

Future Directions

ESG performance has emerged as a research theme in recent years (Hayat 2015). The literature about motivations for superior performance in corporations has concentrated on developed economies (Bassen et al. 2006; Cheng et al. 2014; Dhaliwal et al. 2011). Emerging markets, despite representing a significant proportion of the businesses around the word, have yet to find an expressive presence in the literature that addresses ESG performance (Dobers and Halme 2009; Baughn et al. 2007). In part, this is because reliable data were not available until quite recently. In this respect, this study is both timely and relevant because it addresses ESG practices in emerging markets.

As we presented in the previous session of this chapter, our research was based on data from 365 companies listed in the BRICS countries. We used four different ESG performance proxies (overall ESG and environmental, social, and corporate governance performance) to hypothesize that the financial profile of the BRICS firms has no impact on their ESG performance. Our hypotheses for the BRICS companies deny the counterintuitive evidence that companies in sensitive industries could have better ESG performance than companies from other sectors—including cleaner, nonsensitive industries. However, even when the size of the company and the country in which the firm is listed are controlled, we found that the best environmental performance is predominantly in those companies that are seen as sensitive or are more likely to cause damage to society, as observed by a regression with random effects. Such findings support the studies on corporate environmental legitimacy for firms from sensitive industries, which tend to disclose their ESG performance to protect their reputation.

Evidence was found that the association between the systematic risk of the firm and its ESG performance could be described as an inverted U-shaped curve, indicating the existence of a maximum value for ESG performance, by way of the firm's systematic risk level. This result sheds light into the timely role of investors and regulatory agents in systemic risks. If investors continue to largely ignore systemic risks, such as those arising from climate change (environment), inequality, and working conditions in poor countries (social), they will effectively be indicating that these risks are irrelevant. In addition, regulatory market agents, such as the SEC in the United States, are taking the opinion of investors as the basis for determining who deserves the attention and actions of public regulatory agents.

In terms of academic contribution, our research adds to the numerous efforts researchers have made to further understand the relationship between CSP and CFP, with the advantage that we tested firms of emerging countries. Our results indicate that the profitability of the firm's assets is associated with only one of the ESG performance proxies (environmental performance), as observed by the regression with random effects. The negative sign of this association indicates that the companies with the best ESG performance tend to be less profitable. In particular, the main contribution of our study relates to unprecedented evidence and the description of the mechanism through which these associations can occur. This may be preponderant for future studies focusing on the causal relationships between ESG and CFP. Studies indicating a negative association between ESG and CFP are a minority in the literature. In this regard, there is an expectation that "good companies," i.e., those with the best ESG rating, achieve better productivity and better market valuation. However, belonging to an industry with controversial reputation, such as alcohol, gambling, tobacco, firearms, military, and nuclear industries, does not necessarily imply low ESG performance. Although firms that operate in sensitive industries generally run higher risks (Sassen et al. 2016), they are subject to more scrutiny internally and externally and often achieve higher financial performance (Hong and Kacperczyk 2009). Therefore, they have an incentive to seek higher productivity and performance, including ESG.

The design chosen for this research imposes some limitations that are worth registering. First, the dataset includes only companies listed in the BRICS countries and at a particular moment in time. With regard to the period of time, we worked with the data available at the time this research was carried out. Second, the econometric techniques adopted may have resulted in biases because of variables that are important but were not studied; however, the use of different estimation techniques may moderate this limitation. Finally, the lack of studies on the topic discussed here points toward a research agenda that might include the following: (i) to replicate this study to include companies listed in other emerging countries; (ii) to expand the period studied, in view of the availability of more recent applicable data; and (iii) to employ alternative estimation methods to identify causal effects and address endogeneity problems arising from various causes, such as simultaneity, measurement error, bad controls, and omitted variables.

References

Allouche, J., & Laroche, P. (2005). A meta-analytical investigation of the relationship between corporate social and financial performance. *Revue de Gestion des Ressources Humaines, 57*(1), 8–41.

Angrist, J. D., & Pischke, J. S. (2009). *Mostly harmless econometrics: An empiricist's companion*. Princeton/Oxford: Princeton University Press.

Aras, G., Aybars, A., & Kutlu, O. (2010). Managing corporate performance: Investigating the relationship between corporate social responsibility and financial performance in emerging markets. *International Journal of Productivity and Performance Management, 59*(3), 229–254.

Arya, B., & Zhang, G. (2009). Institutional reforms and investor reactions to CSR announcements: Evidence from an emerging economy. *Journal of Management Studies, 46*(7), 1089–1112.

Baltagi, B. H. (2001). *Econometric analysis of panel data*. West Sussex: Wiley.

Bansal, P., & Clelland, I. (2004). Legitimacy, impression management, and unsystematic risk in the context of the natural environment. *Academy of Management Journal, 47*(1), 93–103.

Barnett, M., & Salomon, R. (2012). Does it pay to be really good? Addressing the shape of the relationship between social and financial performance. *Strategic Management Journal, 33*, 1304–1320.

Baron, D. P., Harjoto, M. A., & Jo, H. (2009). *The economics and politics of corporate social performance* (Working paper no. 45), Stanford University Graduate School of Business.

Bassen, A., Meyer, K., & Schlange, J. (2006). *The influence of corporate responsibility on the cost of capital* (Working paper series), University of Hamburg.

Baughn, C. C., Bodie, N. L. D., & McIntosh, J. C. (2007). Corporate social and environmental responsibility in Asian countries and other geographical regions. *Corporate Social Responsibility and Environmental Management, 14*(4), 189–205.

Blowfield, M., & Frynas, J. G. (2005). Setting new agendas: Critical perspectives on corporate social responsibility in the developing world. *International Affairs, 81*(3), 499–513.

Brammer, S. J., & Millington, A. I. (2008). Does it pay to be different? An analysis of the relationship between corporate social and financial performance. *Strategic Management Journal, 29*, 1325–1343.

Cai, Y., Jo, H., & Pan, C. (2012). Doing well while doing bad- CSR in controversial industry sectors. *Journal of Business Ethics, 108*, 467–480.

CalPERS. (2014). *Towards sustainable investment and operations: Making progress – 2014 report*. Available at: http://www.calpers.ca.gov/eip-docs/about/pubs/esg-report-2014.pdf.

Campbell, J. L. (2006). Institutional analysis and the paradox of corporate social responsibility. *American Behavioral Scientist, 49*(7), 925–938.

Carrol, A. B. (1979). A three-dimensional conceptual model of corporate performance. *Academy of Management Review, 4*(4), 497–505.

Carrol, A. B. (1991). A. The pyramid of corporate social responsibility: Toward the moral management of organizational shareholders. *Business Horizon, 34*, 39–48.

Cheng, B., Ioannou, I., & Serafeim, G. (2014). Corporate social responsibility and access to finance. *Strategic Management Journal, 35*, 1–23.

Chetty, S., Naidoo, R., & Seetharam, Y. (2015). The impact of corporate social responsibility in firms' financial performance in South Africa. *Contemporary Economics, 9*(2), 193–214.

Child, J. (2005). The dynamic between firms' environmental strategies and institutional constraints in emerging economies: Evidence from China and Taiwan. *Journal of Management Studies, 42* (1), 95–125.

Cormier, D., & Magnan, M. (2003). Environmental reporting management: A continental European perspective. *Journal Accounting Public Policy, 22*, 43–62.

Cowen, S. S., Ferreri, L. B., & Parker, L. D. (1987). The impact of corporate characteristics on social responsibility disclosure: A typology and frequency-based analysis. *Accounting, Organizations and Society, 12*(2), 111–122.

Deegan, C., & Gordon, B. (1996). A study of environmental disclosure practices of Australian corporations. *Accounting and Business Research, 26*, 187–199.

Dhaliwal, D. S., Li, O. Z., Tsang, A., & Yang, Y. G. (2011). Voluntary nonfinancial disclosure and the cost of equity capital: The initiation of corporate social responsibility reporting. *American Accounting Association, 86*(1), 59–100.

Dickson, L., & McCulloch, A. (1996). Shell, the Brent spar and Greenpeace: A doomed tryst? *Environmental Politics, 5*(1), 122–129.

Dimaggio, P., & Powell, W. (1991). *The new institutionalism in organizational analysis*. Chicago: The University of Chicago Press.

Dobers, P., & Halme, M. (2009). Corporate social responsibility and developing countries. *Corporate Social Responsibility and Environmental Management, 16*(5), 237–249.

Dowell, G., Hart, S., & Yeung, B. (2000). Do corporate global environmental standards create or destroy market value? *Management Science, 46*(8), 1059–1074.

Dyllick, T., & Hockerts, K. (2002). Beyond the business case for corporate sustainability. *Business Strategy and the Environment, 11*(2), 130–141.

Feng, Z., Price, S. M., & Sirmans, C. F. (2011). An overview of equity real estate investment trusts (REITs): 1993–2009. *Journal of Real Estate Literature, 19*(2), 307–343.

Freeman, R. E., & McVea, J. (2000). A stakeholder approach to strategic management. In M. Hitt, E. Freeman, & J. Harrison (Eds.), *Handbook of strategic management*. Oxford: Blackwell Publishing. Available at: http://papers.ssrn.com/paper.taf?abstract_id=263511.

Friede, G., Busch, T., & Bassen, A. (2015). ESG and financial performance: Aggregated evidence from more than 2000 empirical studies. *Journal of Sustainable Finance & Investment, 5*(4), 210–233. https://doi.org/10.1080/20430795.2015.1118917.

Frynas, J. G. (2005). The false developmental promise of corporate social responsibility: Evidence from multinational oil companies. *International affairs, 81*(3), 581–598.

Gertler, M., & Kiyotaki, N. (2010). Financial intermediation and credit policy in business cycle analysis. *Handbook of Monetary Economics, 3*, 547–599.

Giglio, S., Kelly, B., & Pruitt, S. (2016). Systemic risk and the macroeconomy: An empirical evaluation. *Journal of Financial Economics, 119*(3), 457–471.

Griffin, J. J., & Mahon, J. F. (1997). The corporate social performance and corporate financial performance debate. *Business and Society, 36*(1), 5–31.

Halt, S., & Milstein, M. (1999). Global sustainability and the creative destruction of industries. *Sloan Management Review, 41*(1), 23–33.

Hamann, C. (2006). Can business make decisive contributions to development? Toward a research agenda on corporate citizenship and beyond. *Development Southern Africa, 23*, 175–195.

Hayat, U. (2015). ESG issues and investment practice. *CFA Institute Magazine, 26*(5), 50–50. https://doi.org/10.2469/cfm.v26.n5.17.

He, Z., & Krishnamurthy A. (2012). A *macroeconomic framework for quantifying systemic risk* (Working paper), Chicago Booth.

Hong, H., & Kacperczyk, M. (2009). The price of sin: The effects of social norms on markets. *Journal of Financial Economics, 93*, 15–36.

Hoskisson, R. E., Eden, L., Lau, C. M., & Wright, M. (2000). Strategy in emerging economies. *Academy of Management Journal, 43*(3), 249–267.

Hsiao, C. (2005). *Analysis of panel data*. New York: Cambridge University Press.

Ioannou, I., & Serafeim, G. (2014). *The consequences of mandatory corporate sustainability reporting: Evidence from four countries* (Working paper). Harvard Business School.

Jamali, D., & Karam, C. (2016). Corporate social responsibility in developing countries as an emerging field of study. *International Journal of Management Reviews, 20*, 1–30.

Jamali, D., & Neville, B. (2011). Convergence versus divergence of CSR in developing countries: An embedded multi-layered institutional lens. *Journal of Business Ethics, 102*, 599–621.

Jenkins, H., & Yakovleva, N. (2006). Corporate social responsibility in the mining industry: Exploring trends in social and environmental disclosure. *Journal of Cleaner Production, 14*, 271–284.

Julian, S. D., & Ofori-Dankwa, J. C. (2013). Financial resource availability and corporate social responsibility expenditures in a sub-Saharan economy: The institutional difference hypothesis. *Strategic Management Journal, 34*(11), 1314–1330.

Khanna, T., & Palepu, K. (1997). Why focused strategies may be wrong for emerging markets. *Harvard Business Review, 75*, 41–51.

Kiernan, P. (2016). Samarco warned of problems at dam, engineer says. *The Wall Street Journal* Retrieved from http://on.wsj.com/1Q7D2AK.

Kilian, T., & Hennigs, N. (2014). Corporate social responsibility and environmental reporting in controversial industries. *European Business Review, 26*, 79–101.

Kim, Y.-B., An, H.-T., & Kim, J.-D. (2015). The effect of carbon risk on the cost of equity capital. *Journal of Cleaner Production, 93*, 279–287.

Krosinsky, C. (2013). Sustainability and systemic risk: What's the SEC's role? *The Guardian*. October 23th, 2013. Available at: http://www.theguardian.com/sustainable-business/sustainability-risk-investors-sec.

Lam, S. S., Jacob, G. H., & Yee, T. S. (2012). *Socially Responsible Investment Styles: Equity Risk, Return and Valuation, PRI-CBERN Academic Conference*, Toronto, October 1–3.

Lattin, J. M., Carroll, J. D., & Green, P. E. (2011). *Análise de dados multivariados* (p. xix, 455p). São Paulo: CENGAGE Learning.

Lee, D. D., & Faff, R. W. (2009). Corporate sustainability performance and idiosyncratic risk: A global perspective. *Financial Review, 44*, 213–237.

Lewandowski, S. (2017). Corporate carbon and financial performance: The role of emission reductions. *Business Strategy and the Environment, 26*, 1196–1211.

Lin, C. S., Chang, R. Y., & Dang, V. T. (2015). An integrated model to explain how corporate social responsibility affects corporate financial performance. *Sustainability, 7*, 8292–8311.

Line, M., Hawley, H., & Krut, R. (2002). The development of global environmental and social reporting. *Corporate Environmental Strategy, 9*, 69–78.

Lockett, A., Moon, J., & Visser, W. (2006). Corporate social responsibility in management research: Focus, nature, salience, and sources of influence. *Journal of Management Studies, 43*(1), 115–136.

López Iturriaga, F. J., & Crisóstomo, V. L. (2010). Do leverage, dividend payout and ownership concentration influence firms' value creation? An analysis of Brazilian firms. *Emerging Markets Finance and Trade, 46*(3), 37–52.

Lourenço, I. C., & Branco, M. C. (2013). Determinants of corporate sustainability performance in emerging markets: The Brazilian case. *Journal of Cleaner Production, 57*, 134–141.

Lu, W., Chau, K. W., Wang, H., & Pan, W. (2014). A decade's debate on the nexus between corporate social and corporate financial performance: A critical review of empirical studies 2002–2011. *Journal of Cleaner Production, 79*, 195–206.

Margolis, J., Elfenbein, H., & Walsh, J. (2009). *Does it pay to be good... and does it matter? A meta-analysis of the relationship between corporate social and financial performance* (Working paper), Harvard Business School.

Martínez-Ferrero, J., & Frías-Aceituno, J. V. (2013). Relationship between sustainable development and financial performance: International empirical research. *Business Strategy and Environment, 24*, 20–39.

Maury, B., & Pajuste, A. (2005). Multiple large shareholders and firm value. *Journal of Banking & Finance, 29*(7), 1813–1834.

McWilliams, A., Siegel, D. S., & Wright, P. M. (2006). Corporate social responsibility: Strategic implications. *Journal of Management Studies, 43*, 1–18.

Mendes-Da-Silva, W., & Onusic, L. M. (2014). Corporate e-disclosure determinants: Evidence from the Brazilian market. *International Journal of Disclosure and Governance, 11*, 54–73.

Mendes-Da-Silva, W., Onusic, L. M., & Bergmann, D. R. (2014). The influence of e-disclosure on the ex-ante cost of capital of listed companies in Brazil. *Journal of Emerging Market Finance, 13*(3), 1–31.

Mendoza, E. (2010). Sudden stops, financial crises, and leverage. *American Economic Review, 100* (5), 1941–1966.

Meyer, J. W., & Rowan, B. (1977). Institutionalized organizations: Formal structure as myth and ceremony. *American Journal of Sociology, 83*(2), 340–363.

Mishra, S., & Modi, S. B. (2013). Positive and negative corporate social responsibility, financial leverage, and idiosyncratic risk. *J Bus Ethics, 117*, 431–448.

Morgan, S. L., & Winship, C. (2014). *Counterfactuals and causal inference*. Cambridge: Cambridge University Press.

Moura-Leite, R. C., Padgett, R. C., & Galán, J. I. (2014). Stakeholder management and nonparticipation in controversial business. *Business and Society, 53*, 45–70.

O'Neill, J. (2012). *O mapa do crescimento-oportunidades nos BRICs e além deles*. São Paulo: Globo.

Ofori, D. F., & Hinson, R. E. (2007). Corporate social responsibility (CSR) perspectives of leading firms in Ghana. *Corporate Governance: The international Journal of Business in Society, 7*(2), 178–193.

Orlitzky, M., & Benjamin, J. D. (2001). Corporate social performance and firm risk: A meta-analytic review. *Business and Society, 40*(4), 369–396.

Orlitzky, M., Schmidt, F., & Rynes, S. (2003). Corporate social and financial performance: A meta-analysis. *Organization Studies, 24*(3), 403–441.

Orsato, R. J., Garcia, A. S., Mendes-Da-Silva, W., Simonetti, R., & Monzoni, M. (2015). Sustainability indexes: Why join in? A study of the 'corporate sustainability index (ISE)' in Brazil. *Journal of Cleaner Production, 96*(1), 161–170.

Patten, D. M. (2002). The relation between environmental performance and environmental disclosure: A research note. *Accounting, Organizations and Society, 27*(8), 763–773.

Peiró-Signes, A., & Segarra-Oña, M. V. (2013). Trends in ESG practices: Differences and similarities across major developed markets. In M. G. Erechtchoukova, P. A. Khaiter, & P. Golinska (Eds.), *Sustainability appraisal: Quantitative methods and mathematical techniques for environmental performance evaluation* (pp. 125–140). https://doi.org/10.1007/978-3-642-32081-1_6.

Petersen, M. A. (2009). Estimating standard errors in finance panel data sets: Comparing approaches. *Review of Financial Studies, 22*, 435–480.

Rahdari, A. H. (2016). Developing a fuzzy corporate performance rating system: A petrochemical industry case study. *Journal of Cleaner Production, 131*, 421–434.

Raynard, P., & Forstater, M. (2002). *Corporate social responsibility: Implications for small and medium enterprises in developing countries*. United Nations Industrial Development Organization. Retrieved on August 11, 2016 from www.unido.org/userfiles/BethkeK/csr.pdf.

Rettab, B., Brik, A. B., & Mellahi, K. (2009). A study of management perceptions of the impact of corporate social responsibility on organizational performance in emerging economies: The case of Dubai. *Journal of Business Ethics, 89*(3), 371–390.

Richardson, A. J., & Welker, M. (2001). Social disclosure, financial disclosure and the cost of equity capital. *Accounting, Organizations and Society, 26*, 597–616.

Roberto, M. A. (2011). BP and the gulf of Mexico oil spill. *Harvard Cases*, Product #W11366-PDF-ENG.

Rodrigo, P., Duran, I. J., & Arenas, D. (2016). Does it really pay to be good, everywhere? A first step to understand the corporate social and financial performance link in Latin American controversial industries. *Business Ethics: A European Review, 25*(3), 286–309.

Roman, R. M., Haybor, S., & Agle, B. R. (1999). The relationship between social and financial performance. *Business and Society, 38*(1), 109–125.

Sassen, R., Hinze, A. K., & Hardeck, I. (2016). Impact of ESG factors on firm risk in Europe. *Journal of Business Economics, 86*(8), 867–904. https://doi.org/10.1007/s11573-016-0819-3.

Serafeim, G. (2014). *Integrated reporting and investor clientele* (Working paper), Harvard Business School.

Statman, M., & Glushkov, D. (2009). Equity investments: The wages of social responsibility. *Financial Analysts Journal, 65*(4), 33–46.

Surroca, J., Tribó, J. A., & Waddock, S. (2010). Corporate responsibility and financial performance: The role of intangible resources. *Strategic Management Journal, 31*, 463–490.

Visser, W. (2005). Corporate citizenship in South Africa: A review of progress since democracy. *Journal of Corporate Citizenship, 18*, 29–38.

Willi, A., Brammer, S., & Millington, A. (2011). Corporate social responsibility in developing countries: An institutional analysis. In Academy of Management Conference, August 2011, San Antonio.

Chapter 14
Board of Directors and Corporate Networks

Wesley Mendes-Da-Silva

Abstract Social network analysis (SNA) is an emerging research field in finance. This chapter references SNA and knowledge of corporate governance, to deal with a similarly emerging topic in finance, board interlocking, and shall examine the validity of the small-world model in a relevant emerging market and the existence of associations between the firm's worth and its network of corporate relationships. This study references official data relating to more than 400 listed companies. The main results suggest that the network configuration of the relationships between board members and companies reflects the small-world model. Furthermore, there seems to be a significant relationship between the firm's worth and its network centrality, described according to an "inverted U" type curve, which suggests optimum values exist for social prominence in the corporate network.

Keywords Corporate governance · Corporate networks · Social networks · Board interlocking

JEL Code G34 · L14 · C91

An element of finance literature has assumed that the frontier expansion of this field of knowledge is associated with research development characterized by connected domain approaches, which integrates various areas of knowledge. In this context, for example, works on behavioral finance and economic sociology stand out. Along this same line of thinking, the corporate governance area has proved to be a fertile field for connected domain research, because the topic has developed through contribution from various professionals from different disciplinary areas. It has to be emphasized that the corporate board is a central theme in the study of corporate

---

Portions of this chapter appeared in the 2011 paper "Small Worlds and Board Interlocking in Brazil: A Longitudinal Study of Corporate Networks 1997–2007", *Brazilian Review of Finance*, vol 9, pp521–548.

W. Mendes-Da-Silva (✉)
Sao Paulo School of Business Administration (FGV/EAESP), Sao Paulo, SP, Brazil

University of Texas at Austin, Austin, TX, USA

W. Mendes-Da-Silva (ed.), *Individual Behaviors and Technologies for Financial Innovations*, https://doi.org/10.1007/978-3-319-91911-9_14

governance and financial innovations (Yermack 2017). Since Mills (1956) published *The Power Elite*, critics have argued that the North American corporate environment can be seen as an insular, politically powerful network of "old boys." According to this logic, attribute sharing enables the establishment of ties between board members of the major publicly quoted companies, which initiates a network configuration (a set of nodes linked by nodes). This network has frequently been seen as a small world of mutual knowledge, characterized by the sharing of activities on company boards (board interlocking).

Is corporate Brazil a small world? Do members of the boards of listed companies know each other? The replies to questions like these can offer insight to information flow, innovation, and management practices (Kang et al. 2018). A small world is understood to be an environment that is characterized by a network whose actors are close to one another (few degrees of separation), resulting in an environment in which the actors are strongly clustered. This suggests a simultaneous sharing of worldviews and standards of professional conduct on the part of the board members (Stafsudd 2009). According to financial literature, in the context of the roles the corporate board is tasked to undertake, the network formed by its members has shown itself to be a powerful means of propagating corporate management practices, from how to acquire a firm (Haunschild 1993) to how firms respond to takeovers (Davis and Greve 1997). And recently researchers have made contributions from technology to governance mechanisms, for instance, Yermack (2017) discusses interactions between Blockchains and corporate governance and indicates this field as a track for future research on financial innovations.

According to the arguments of Leitner (2005) and Davis et al. (2003:301), the contagion process (via the network) within individual boards is clear: members meet frequently (almost on a monthly basis), to share knowledge and ideas, possibly obtained from some other boards, based on member interactions with directors of other boards. Therefore, the topography of corporate social networks and the firm's positioning in these networks are important, in view of this contagion dynamic and information flow (Coleman 1990; Martínez-Jaramillo et al. 2010). Therefore, if the network structure of relationships among board directors has an impact on the information flow between companies, it is expected that changes in network structures will have important consequences on strategies, including the financial strategies adopted by organizations.

In Brazil, studies into board interlocking, the central subject of this research, which are characterized by extensive longitudinal studies, are still unknown, especially with describing the small world of company boards of directors (Lazzarini 2007). The "neighborliness" of the corporate elite is assumed to be the network of interlocks created when boards share one or more common directors (Schonlau and Singh 2009; Bouwman 2011). In turn, board directors are connected by the common service they provide on one or more corporate boards. They also have attributes in common, e.g., courses and the universities where they were educated (Cohen et al. 2010). In the Brazilian experience, significant company changes might have been caused by events such as (i) internationalization processes; (ii) a more active stance by institutional investors; (iii) mergers and acquisitions; (iv) redefinition of government practices, seen as highly recommendable; (v) reclassification of the Brazilian economy regarding public security risk; and (vi) the supposed stability of the Brazilian economy (in a context of global crisis).

While it is rarely questioned that such factors drive changes in how top administrators, and by extension the companies, establish ties in the corporate environment, analysts have never documented a representative number of the net results of these transformations. The main contribution of this article is based on the attempt to develop a point of reference for future works, whose purpose is to expand the frontiers of knowledge in finance, using social network analysis (SNA).

This chapter presents highlights from this research and references this large data set of listed firms and describes research in the area of corporate governance using a connected domain approach, an aspect that is widely recognized in constructing and advancing scientific knowledge, particularly in the field of finance. In view of the above arguments, initiating a small-world approach, the purpose of this article is to analyze how the configuration of the global relationship network evolved between Brazilian listed companies and their board directors between 1997 and 2007, using SNA to do so. Furthermore, the study also observes the manner in which the firm's position within the corporate relationships network impacts the firm's worth.

The main results were obtained: (i) the network of relationships between board members (and also between companies) reflects a small-world model. In other words, the average distance between board directors (and the company) is sufficiently small. At the same time, the values for the clustering coefficient of the board members are high. In addition, evidence points to the existence of a relationship between the firm's network centrality and its worth that may be described as an "inverted U" type curve. In other words, within the scope of the corporate relationships network, evidence points to the existence of companies' centrality values that maximizes their worth. These research findings provide insight into how corporate networks can impact firm performance. At the end of this chapter, some recommendations are provided, including directions for future research.

The Composition of Boards and Interlocking

Significant interest in the topic of board interlocking, both by academia and the business community, is not a recent phenomenon (Bearden et al. 1975). However, definition of the term "board interlocking" has not been unanimous. Among the various opinions that exist on the topic, the most frequent argument found in the literature posits that board interlocking exist if at least one company board member simultaneously occupies a place on another company's board of directors (Mizruchi 1996). However, it was not until the end of 2009 that this topic was included in the discussion agenda about best practices in Brazil's corporate governance environment (IBGC 2015). In this research, it is assumed that the occurrence of board interlocking leads to the rise of personal and corporate networks. Figure 14.1

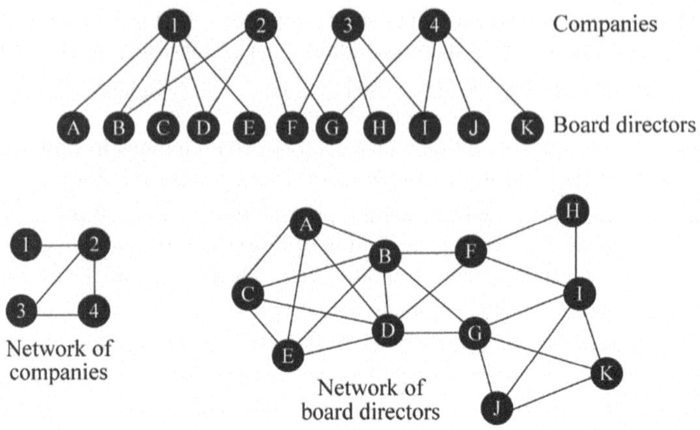

Fig. 14.1 Schematic representation of corporate networks. Note: This figure represents a typical scheme for a nondirectional network of 4 companies (nodes/vertices 1–4), linked by 11 board directors (nodes/vertices *A* to *K*). The top part of the figure illustrates the two-mode projection of companies with shared board members. In the lower left, the set of *X* nodes = {1,2,3,4} represents the one-mode network of companies (network of companies). On the lower right, the *Y* node = {*A*, *B*,. . .. . .,*J*,*K*} shows the network of board directors (linked by companies in common). In this research the one-mode analysis structure was adopted, or rather, it was either assumed that the network was formed by board directors or merely by companies. However, literature already offers discussion of two-mode approaches (Robins and Alexander 2004). (Source: Prepared by the author, Adapted from Newman et al. 2001)

shows a basic scheme in which four companies (nodes) are linked by ties that reflect the sharing of attributes, in this case sharing company board members as nodes linked by ties that form a network.

The Small-World Model

Recent advances in mathematics and computing and, specifically, developments in graph theory (based on knowledge of SNA) have resulted in a widespread increase of research regarding social networks. In particular, the small-world model is a powerful tool to scrutinize the phenomenon of network formation (Conyon and Muldoon 2006). The small-world phenomenon was initially analyzed in the work of Milgram (1967), which consisted of an experiment that involved sending letters to various people who forwarded them, via a network of people they knew.

The study concluded that apparently distant people may be in actual fact connected by a very short chain of known intermediaries. Milgram (1967) found this close chain was essentially limited to a critical path of 6 (six) steps. In other words, according to this author, there is a great tendency that an individual known by one person will also form part of the circle of relationships of a second known individual or mutual acquaintance. The theoretical small-world model is described in detail by Newman et al. (2001). Two global characteristics of this theoretical network model, which has profound consequences for the social phenomenon, must be observed with particular attention in the characterization of a small world: (i) *the distance between actors* (L) and (ii) *the clustering coefficient* (C_Δ).

In social networks such as corporate networks (i.e., companies or board directors), locally grouped and globally connected actors are expected; or rather, many less prestigious companies are linked to others that have greater social prominence. So, Baum et al. (2004) emphasize the relevance of studying network properties, as well as their evolution over time, in view of their impacts on small-world consequences, since this type of configuration can significantly affect the speed of interaction between the component companies of a network of corporate relationships, for example Davis et al. (2003).

The first property of the small-world model is that pairs of randomly chosen nodes may be unexpectedly close to each other. A graph/network with N nodes contains $N\ (N-1)/2$ pairs of nodes. If they are numbered 1, 2. . ., N and $d_{i,j}$ is the distance between nodes i and j, then someone can calculate the typical distance between the component nodes of the network, using the following Eq. (14.1):

$$L = \frac{2}{N(N-1)} \sum_{i<j} d_{i,j} \tag{14.1}$$

In the context of corporate boards (and in accordance with the analysis unit, firms or board members), the term L measures the (typical) number of steps necessary to move from one actor to another within the context of the network. Put another way, in a network of corporate relationships, information will reach a director after being passed on by L intermediary members, since typically there are L directors separating director i from director j. The second property of the small-world model is the high clustering coefficient, a measure of the density of the network. According to Newman et al. (2001), the *clustering coefficient* for the (global) network is calculated as follows (14.2):

$$C_\Delta = \frac{3 \times \text{number of triangles in the graph}}{\text{number of connected links}} \tag{14.2}$$

where a triangle is a set of three different nodes, j, k, and l, in which each node (or actor) is connected to two others. A connected link consists in a set of three nodes, j, k, and l, in which j is connected to k and k is connected to l (l need not be connected to j); the factor 3 in the numerator is necessary to ensure that $0 \lesssim C_\Delta \lesssim 1$, as each triangle contributes to the increase in the three connected links. Figure 14.2 illustrates this notion. To the right of the figure, there are 2 complete triangles (6–8–9) and (4–6–9), but 13 connected links (6–4–7; 6–4–9; 7–4–9; 4–6–8; 4–6–9; 8–6–9; 4–7–8; 6–8–9; 6–8–7; 7–8–9; 4–9–6; 4–9–8; 6–9–8), so $C_\Delta = 3 \times \frac{2}{13} = \frac{6}{13}$. The distance ($L$) between node 6 and node 9 is 2 (2° of separation).

Small-world validity can be checked by comparing the values obtained for these two measures relative to the networks being analyzed, starting from the values for

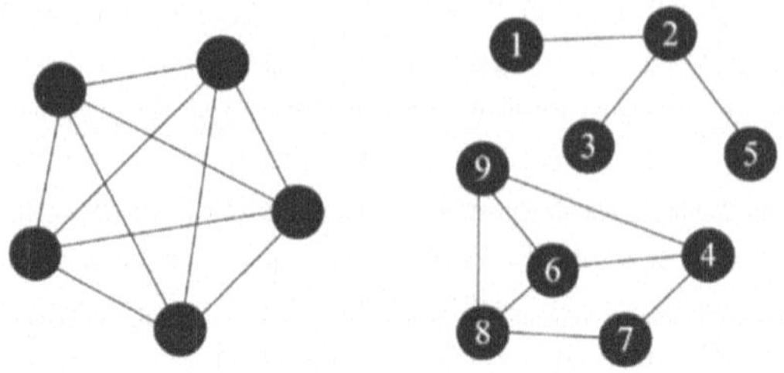

Fig. 14.2 Examples of simple graphs. Note: The left-hand side of the figure shows a complete graph (all the nodes are interconnected), illustrating a component/cluster. On the right-hand side of this figure, two connected components/clusters are shown. By way of illustration, in any network, if three nodes, *j*, *k*, and *l*, form a connected link, then *j* is connected to *k* and *k* is connected to *l*, and, if "is connected to" were a strictly transitive relationship, then the conclusion is that node *j* is connected to node *l*. Therefore, in the network shown in this figure, node 9 is linked to node 8, and node 8, in turn, is linked to node 7. So, by transitivity, node 9 is linked to node 7. Therefore, the clustering coefficient C_{Δ}, computed according to the expression (2), represents the proportion of links for which the transitive conclusion is verified. It needs to be emphasized that there is a local clustering coefficient measure (for each component node in the network), as proposed by Watts and Strogatz (1998). (Source: Prepared by the author)

these two parameters in random networks (simulated) with a same number of actors, *n*, and ties, *k*. For random networks, $L_{\text{expected}} \sim ln(n)/ln(k)$ and $C_{\Delta\text{expected}} \sim k/n$, where *n* is the number of nodes (or actors) in the network and *k* is the average degree centrality (average number of adjacent ties) of each component actor in the network (Watts and Strogatz 1998). So in the light of the measures found, the strictly typical finding of small world will be seen if $L_{\text{observed}} \sim L_{\text{expected}}$, while $C_{\Delta\text{observed}} \gg C_{\Delta\text{expected}}$. However, like the procedure assumed by Baum et al. (2004) and Davis et al. (2003), in this research verification of the existence of a small world in the context of personal and corporate networks will be satisfied when $Q_{sw} = (C_{\Delta\ \text{observed}}/L_{\text{observed}}) \times (L_{\text{expected}}/C_{\Delta\text{expected}}) \gg 1$.

The Small-World Model in the Corporate Environment

The board of directors is an important social network, especially in the fields of economics, finance, and management. Some (few) recent studies have documented that, even in Brazil, directors frequently hold more than one position on corporate boards. Fama and Jensen (1983) emphasize that, at least in the North American economy, outside board members (outsiders) act as executives in other companies or are important decision-making agents in other organizations. However, in the Brazilian experience, there seems, as yet, to be no research to inform this phenomenon within the national context.

In this sense it is expected that the connectivity of companies leads to consequences, such as dissemination of executive remuneration practices (Subrahmanyam 2008) and the adoption of anti-takeover measures, poison pills, and the spread of golden parachutes (Davis and Greve 1997). Over the last few years, both the capital markets specialist media (including in Brazil) and academic publications have discussed the supposition that certain corporate boards are configured like a type of "closed club." Concerning the application of the small-world approach to the study of the board interlocking phenomenon, the clustering coefficient measure is a way of investigating the "clique" or "clubby" aspects of boards (Conyon and Muldoon 2006; Yermack, 2006).

A limited number of studies examine the small-world properties of social networks within the context of corporate governance. These works typically compare small-world characteristics (the L and C_{Δ} measures) with those that are expected from a family of random graphs, originally introduced in the work done by Erdös and Rényi (1959). Only one study (Mendes-Da-Silva and Vidal 2010) was found that considers the Brazilian market in this regard.

Among the works that deal with small-world properties in the context of company boards, Davis et al. (2003) examine a sample of US corporate boards at three points in time; the results obtained by these authors suggest that the North American corporate environment can truly be understood as a "small world." Conyon and Muldoon (2006) found that the small-world concept applies to the United States, Germany, and the United Kingdom.

The small-world approach has also been used in other studies on networks comprising ties and actors, which go beyond board interlocking. The link between companies resulting from sharing controlling shareholders in Brazil was studied by Lazzarini (2007), who recommends research of corporate boards such as this study has undertaken. The small-world concept within the corporate environment was also used by Baum et al. (2004) to study the network formed by banks that underwrite operations for raising funds in the Canadian capital market.

Positioning in the Corporate Network and the Firm Value

There are two basic classes of measures for understanding social networks: the positioning of each node/actor in the network and the topography of the network (Wasserman and Faust 1994). The first category illustrates the measures of social prominence (centrality), which describe how influential a node/actor may be within the context of its/his/her network. It was decided to use two of these measures: *degree centrality* (*degree*), the number of adjacent ties to each actor, and *betweenness centrality* (*betweenness*), the capacity to intermediate contacts between various actors in the network.

Pfeffer and Salancik (1978) start from the assumption that firms create ties to obtain desired resources and manage uncertainties in the corporate environment. Therefore, networks are seen as a way for firms to access organizations with the required resources and the capacity to help the firms support the restrictions imposed by the external environment. Bunderson (2003) also notes that groups seem to achieve higher performance levels (take better decisions) when board members share an accurate understanding of the others' expertise. Pirson and Turnbull (2011) present a structured analysis of the gains that networked boards enjoy relative to isolated boards, e.g., a reduction in the judgment bias in decisions, better risk control, and a greater capacity to react to crisis. It is therefore expected that the greater a company's influence in a corporate network, the greater its access to resources will be, whether they are negotiated in the market or not. Given these findings, it is reasonable to test the following hypothesis:

H_{1a}: *There is a significant association between degree centrality and the firm value.*

H_{1b}: *There is a significant association between centrality and the firm value.*

Literature offers arguments and evidence, however, that point to the existence of trade-offs with regard to the firm's centrality. In this line of thinking Harris and Shimizu (2004) underline the idea that boards may be so occupied (an increased number of connections may result in directors overaccumulating functions) that they compromise their role within the company environment, i.e., monitoring executive activities and considering the adequacy of the management decisions relative to shareholder expectations, ultimately reducing the firm's value. Fich and Shivdasani (2006) found results that point to the idea that firms with boards who keep "busy" (*busy boards*) which, according to these authors, means essentially outsiders who hold three or more places on boards, have poor corporate governance. Labianca and Brass (2006) also highlight the negative role of relationships within the context of social networks, which may reduce the firm value.[1] Given these arguments that suggest there are value limits for the firm's centrality, the following hypothesis is tested:

H_2: *There are values associated with the firm's centrality that maximize its worth.*

Over and above centrality in the network, there are other interesting measures, including the efficiency of the links (structural holes). According to the arguments from Burt (1992) and Noyes (2007), we examined the relationships between the firm's structural holes and the identification of investment alternatives, as well as Yang et al. (2010). In constructing nonredundant ties (coming from positioning itself in the corporate relationships network in such a way as to optimize structural holes, a procedure shown in Fig. 14.3), the company can benefit from its access to information that enables it to identify new investment opportunities (whose proxy adopted here is Tobin's Q). The right-hand side of Fig. 14.3 shows the expectation of value creation due to the greater efficiency of the firm's ties. In order to consider whether the efficiency of the firm's ties is a consequence of the firm's greater inclination to

[1]Along this line of thinking, Fracassi and Tate (2012), based on data relating to North American companies for the 2000–2007 period, deal with the firm's external ties, as constituted between board directors and executives. In this study the conclusion is that (i) firms whose CEOs are more powerful tend to elect directors linked to the CEO; (ii) CEO-director ties reduce the firm's worth; and (iii) firms in which there are CEO-director ties have a greater tendency to become involved with acquisitions that have a negative net present value.

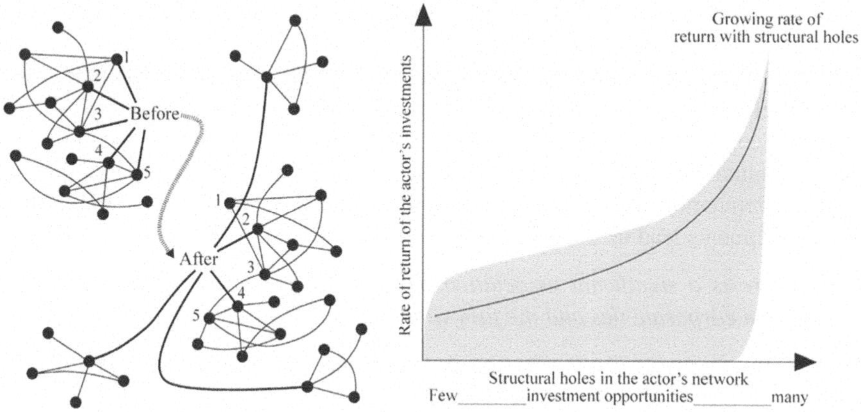

Fig. 14.3 Structural holes and the firm value. Note: The left-hand side of this figure illustrates a procedure to optimize the firm's structural holes (redefine its position in the network in such a way as to reduce the inefficiency of the ties that are constituted). On the right-hand side of the figure is an illustration of the expected association between the firm's structural holes and the return for shareholders. (Source: Adapted from Burt 1992, p. 22 and p. 37)

invest, it is expected that the market will judge the firm's investment opportunities in a better light, as reflected in its market worth, which motivates a test of the following hypothesis:

H$_3$: *There is a significant association between the firm's structural holes and its value.*

According to Scott (2001), informal social networks between board members can resolve problems associated with a lack of team spirit, coordination, and cooperation. Such informal networks may result from various types of relationship. For example, ties formed at academic institutions may facilitate an approximation between directors, thus increasing their linking capacity in various network types. A similar educational background may also facilitate dialogue, since professions serve as approximation mechanisms between executives, given the cultural cognitive affinity attributed to a shared identity.

With regard to the relevance of personal characteristics to strategy and corporate performance, Labianca and Brass (2006:606) emphasize that social networks research, especially if company-focused, has ignored the relevance of individual personality and personal characteristics on corporate performance. In this regard, Cohen et al. (2008) presented an in-depth discussion on how the firm's performance relates to the ties constituted by executives sharing courses and schools, a thinking that is also shared by Kilduff (1992) and Mehra et al. (2001). In these terms, the prevalence of the board directors in sharing personal characteristics, e.g., the company in which they serve as director (*corporate ties*), their graduate school (*university ties*), and/or their professional qualifications (*similarity in educational background*), would be a source of competitive advantage on some occasions, in view of the increase in mutual trust, integration of behavior, and cooperation between board directors.

Using these arguments, the owning of share capital by board directors also supplies elements that might increase an organization's legitimacy in terms of their actions (Scott 2001; Westlund and Adam 2010), since it starts from the assumption that influential directors tend to have more access to information as well as enjoying a greater reputation with financing mechanisms and market regulators (Lin 2001). These arguments lead us to test the following hypotheses:

H_{4a}: *There is a significant association between the centrality of the board that comes from corporate ties and the firm value.*

H_{4b}: *There is a significant association between the centrality of the board that comes from university ties and the firm value.*

H_{4c}: *There is a significant association between the centrality of the board that comes from a similar educational background and the firm value.*

In addition, Coleman (1990) and Pirson and Turnbull (2011) argue that by acquiring competences, improving information access, minimizing redundant efforts, and identifying investment opportunities and by leveraging the social capital that comes from greater cohesion, the company can be expected to enhance its worth through its greater density/local clustering position, which leads to the following hypothesis:

H_5: *There is a significant and positive association between the local clustering coefficient of the firm and its value.*

Data Collection and Variables

Official annual data was made available by the Brazilian Securities Commission (*CVM*) and by consultancy company, Economatica®. The unit of analysis used here was either the boards of directors of companies listed on the stock exchange or board directors themselves within the Brazilian context between 1997 and 2007. Information was collected about the actual board directors from 415 companies (forming an unbalanced panel), resulting in a group of thousands of board directors. The collection and database preparation phase included extensive manual and computer procedures to ensure date quality as it related to the boards, aimed to ensure accuracy in identifying the ties between individuals/firms. This included reading and standardizing each individual's name across companies while at the same time eliminating any ambiguities. For example, one board director was found with different renderings of his name: (i) Antonio Carlos Augusto R. Bonchistiano, (ii) Antonio Carlos A. R. Bonchistiano, and (iii) Antonio Carlos Augusto R. Boncristiano. For the panel data regression, the Tobin's Q index was used as a dependent variable for the firm's proxy value, which was estimated in accordance with a procedure proposed by

Chung and Pruitt (1994). The independent variables used in the panel data regression were organized in three groups, namely, measures relating to the positioning of the firm in the corporate network, structure of the firm's board of directors, and control variables.

Measures relating to the positioning of the firm in the corporate network: A specific SNA software application, Ucinet 6.0 for Windows, was used to obtain the variables relating to the positioning of the firm in the corporate network. *Degree centrality* (*degree*) in absolute terms, an actor included in a network comprising g actors, can achieve $g - 1$ ties, at most. *Degree* considers only adjacent relationships or, rather, the local centrality of the players. According to Freeman (1979), the degree centrality index, defined by $C_D(n_i)$ of an actor n_i participating in a network, is given by (14.3):

$$C_D(n_i) = d(n_i) = x_{i+} = \sum_j x_{ij} = \sum_j x_{ji} \tag{14.3}$$

In this work the normalized form of *degree centrality* was used, expressed in a percentage form (degree divided by the maximum number of ties possible, expressed as a %). In Fig. 14.1, for example, board director G has *degree centrality* = 5 and normalized *degree centrality* = 50%.

However, interaction between two nonadjacent actors may depend on a group of other actors, who may exercise some control over the interactions between two nonadjacent actors. Therefore, in order to put two actors, n_2 and n_3, in contact with each other, the shortest path is $n_2 \rightarrow n_1 \rightarrow n_4 \rightarrow n_3$, then it can be said that actors $n_1$and n_4 control interactions between actors n_2 and n_3. This is, therefore, the concept of *betweenness centrality* (*betweenness*), which considers the interaction between nonadjacent actors. If all distance communications $d(n_j, n_k)$, which go through actor k, are counted, this provides a measure of "stress." When there is more than one possible path between j and k, all paths that pass through actor i are considered equiprobable. Therefore, the *betweenness centrality* for n_i is the sum of the estimated probabilities for all pairs of actors, not including the i-th actor. This is given by the Eq. (14.4):

$$C_B(n_i) = \sum_{j<k} \frac{g_{jk}(n_i)}{g_{jk}} \tag{14.4}$$

where g_{jk} is the number of paths that link two actors. Therefore, if all these paths are equiprobable in terms of choice for establishing communication, the probability of a path being chosen is simply $\frac{1}{g_{jk}}$. In short, this measure indicates the number of pairs of nodes that an actor is capable of linking. In this research the normalized form (expressed as a %) was used. For example, in Fig. 14.1, board director G has *betweenness centrality* = 12.5 and normalized *betweenness centrality* = 27.77%.

The third variable of the positioning of the firm is *structural holes*, which are types of nonredundant relationship between two contacts (Burt 1992). Therefore, the smaller the number of redundant ties, the greater the number of structural gaps, there being less information redundancy. We specifically use the efficiency measure of the ties (Burt 1992:53), which measures the number of nonredundant contacts, *EffSize*, relative to the total number of contacts n of an actor i.

The fourth positioning variable of the firm is the *local clustering coefficient*: C_i to the i-th node is given by the proportion of ties between the vertices in its neighborhood, divided by the number of ties that could exist between them. By way of illustration, in Fig.14.1 the node G has $C_i = 0.40$. According to a procedure by Watts and Strogatz (1998), a graph $G = (V, E)$ formally consists in a set of nodes $V$and the ties E between them. A tie, e_{ij}, connects node i to node j. Neighborhood N to the vertex $v_i$is defined as those immediately connected neighbors. Therefore, if node v_i has k_i neighbors, $\frac{k_i(k_i-1)}{2}$ ties would exist between the neighborhood nodes. So C_i is formally defined in (14.5):

$$C_i = \frac{2|\{e_{jk}\}|}{k_i(k_i-1)} : v_j, v_k \in N_i, e_{jk} \in E. \tag{14.5}$$

The three other independent variables, *corporate degree centrality*, *university centrality*, and *knowledge centrality*, consist in the average degree centrality of board directors in the networks of directors formed by these three ways of establishing ties, which led to H_{4a}, H_{4b}, and H_{4c}.

Structure of the firm's board of directors: (i) *Size of the board,* expressed by the *ln* of the number of directors of the firm in each year studied; (ii) *outsiders*, expressed by the percentage of board members that are external to the firm (Yermack 1996).

Control variables: selected on the basis of the possible influence they exercise over the dependent variable (the firm value) and the independent variables. If the control variables have a correlation with some of these variables and are not considered in the model, the relationship between the variables of interest cannot be shown in an adequate manner: *age of the firm* (ln of the number of months between registering the firm with the *CVM* until the end of the financial year t), *superior performance* (difference between the Ebit index/total sales of the i-th firm and the Ebit index/total sales of the economic sector to which the firm belongs), ln of *quick ratio* of the i-th firm in the t-th year, and ln of *total assets of the* i-th firm in the t-th year.

Empirical Model

In view of the purpose of this research, the data analysis is organized into two main blocks: (i) verification of the validity of small worlds to the Brazilian market (using a procedure suggested by Davis et al. (2003) and by Stafsudd 2009) and (ii) verification of the existence of associations between the positioning (of the company) in the corporate relationships network and the firm value, using panel data regression (unbalanced statistic). From the set of variables detailed on previous section of this chapter, the model to be tested is (14.6), with $N = 415$ and $T = 11$.

$$\text{Value}_{it} = \beta_0 + \sum_{k=1}^{K} \beta_k x_{kit} + u_{it}, \quad \begin{matrix} i=1,\ldots,N, \\ t=1,\ldots,T, \end{matrix} \tag{14.6}$$

in which the value of the i-th firm in the t-th year, Value_{it}, depends on K exogenous variables, $(x_{1it}, \cdots, x_{Kit})$, which differ between the firms at two given moments in time and also vary over time. The error term, u_{it}, which is assumed as an IID random variable, with an average of zero and variance σ_u^2, independent of $(x_{1i}, \cdots, x_{iT})$, represents the effects of the omitted variables that are specific to both the firms and to the period studied.

Verification of the Small-World Phenomenon in Board Director Networks

According to Davis et al. (2003), the results obtained (summarized in Tables 14.1 and 14.2) are indicative of the existence of the small-world phenomenon between listed companies and between board members, respectively. It has to be emphasized that the strength of this configuration, Q_{SW}, grew over the period and maintained values that were considerably greater than 1 ($Q_{SW} \gg 1$), whether for the network of directors or the network of companies.

The results in Table 14.2 suggest that board directors are highly grouped from the local point of view, but maintain their distance (between each other) in the network, which does not impede the finding that their world is considered to be "as small as" could be expected. This indicator illustrates the structural consistency of the conditions of the small-world phenomenon. These results comprise empirical evidence of the cooperation between board directors in terms of companies' links, rather than a deliberate effort on the part of the directors to constitute this network configuration. Therefore, one can understand that the Brazilian corporate environment has operated within the described parameters of a small world. In other words, it seems that the Brazilian capital market has grown in such a way that demand for directors from outside the firm has led to choice mechanisms of board members being selected in such a way as to establish a network in which distances between people are smaller (consequently the companies will be closer).

Obviously, this does not provide sufficient elements to imply, with any degree of certainty, that there is a development of relationships between board directors within the environment of the Brazilian capital market. However, it does lead to an important reflection about the corporate environment: while relationships between board directors have not been very close globally, the high clustering coefficients (C_Δ) revealed in the data indicate the formation of "neighborhoods" and, therefore,

Table 14.1 Small-world statistics of the network of relationships between listed companies in Brazil (1997–2007)

Parameters for diagnosis of small world	1997	1998	1999	2000	2001	2002	2003	2004	2005	2006	2007
Panel A: Parameters observed in the network											
Density[a] (Δ)	0.049	0.031	0.031	0.024	0.029	0.032	0.034	0.026	0.022	0.019	0.018
# of companies in the network	222	299	294	324	323	318	319	329	344	383	385
# of companies in the main component (n)	57	133	146	171	152	146	139	161	182	230	237
Average no. of ties per company (k)	3.263	4.617	5.137	4.959	5.184	5.164	5.223	4.783	4.407	4.652	4.599
$C_{\Delta observed}$: Clustering coefficient observed (global)	0.449	0.552	0.546	0.516	0.531	0.596	0.586	0.528	0.501	0.520	0.501
$L_{observed}$: Average distance observed	4.098	5.948	5.080	5.641	7.270	5.681	6.168	6.079	5.667	5.242	5.349
Maximum distance (diameter)	11	18	15	14	18	13	15	16	16	18	19
Panel B: Expected parameters for the network											
$C_{\Delta\ expected}$: Clustering coefficient expected (k/n)	0.057	0.034	0.035	0.029	0.034	0.035	0.037	0.029	0.024	0.020	0.019
$L_{\ expected}$: Average distance expected ($\ln(n)/\ln(k)$)	3.42	3.20	3.05	3.21	3.05	3.04	2.99	3.25	3.51	3.54	3.58
Panel C: Calculation of the small-world coefficient (Q_{SW})											
Small-world indicators											
$C_{\Delta\ observed}/L_{observed}$	0.11	0.09	0.11	0.09	0.07	0.10	0.10	0.09	0.09	0.10	0.09
$L_{expected}/C_{\Delta\ expected}$	59.72	92.09	86.55	110.73	89.52	85.82	79.44	109.29	144.90	174.89	184.68
$Q_{SW} = [C_{\Delta\ observed}/L_{observed}] \times [L_{expected}/C_{\Delta\ expected}]$	6.54	8.55	9.30	10.13	6.54	9.00	7.55	9.49	12.81	17.35	17.30

Source: Prepared by the author and based on data collected in the research

Note: This table shows (for the period from 1997 to 2007) the parameters actually observed in the network (Panel A) and the parameters obtained by simulation (Panel B) for diagnosis of the small-world phenomenon, according to Watts and Strogatz (1998). To do so, data relative to all companies listed on the Bovespa [São Paulo stock exchange] were used, with data relating to the composition of the boards of directors published by the Securities Commission, the Brazilian market regulatory agent. Comparing the results of Panels A and B, it is possible (using established premises) to assess in Panel C the feasibility of admitting that the network of relationships in listed companies in Brazil is similar to a small-world model, bearing in mind the values obtained for its indicator ($Q_{SW} >> 1$), which suggests the existence of strong indications that its configuration is similar to that of a small world. The measures shown in this table relate to the main component of the network of companies for each of the years studied

[a]Density is a structural measure of the network, which expresses the relationship between the possible and observed number of ties between the actors

Table 14.2 Small-world statistics for the network of relationships between board members of listed companies in Brazil (1997–2007)

Parameters for diagnosis of small world	1997	1998	1999	2000	2001	2002	2003	2004	2005	2006	2007
Panel A: Parameters observed in the network											
Density (Δ)[a]	0.0200	0.0145	0.0141	0.0136	0.0175	0.0152	0.0153	0.0131	0.0107	0.0080	0.0175
# of directors in the network	1.140	1.472	1.449	1.617	1.594	1.572	1.505	1.569	1.680	1.879	1.941
# of directors (n)	494	683	712	766	577	681	625	726	866	1140	1191
Average no. of ties per director (k)	10.07	9.87	10.04	10.39	10.07	10.36	9.54	7.46	9.25	7.56	9.22
$C_{\Delta observed}$: Clustering coefficient observed (global)	0.914	0.903	0.897	0.900	0.904	0.897	0.895	0.893	0.896	0.898	0.899
$L_{observed}$: Average distance observed	5.048	6.373	6.102	6.362	8.055	6.153	6.344	6.898	6.383	6.319	6.503
Maximum distance (diameter)	11	14	15	15	19	14	16	17	14	19	19
Panel B: Expected parameters for the network											
$C_{\Delta expected}$: Clustering coefficient expected (k/n)	0.0204	0.0145	0.0141	0.0136	0.0174	0.0152	0.0153	0.0103	0.0107	0.0066	0.0077
$L_{expected}$: Average distance expected ($\ln(n)/\ln(k)$)	2.686	2.850	2.847	2.837	2.753	2.790	2.854	3.278	3.040	3.480	3.189
Panel C: Calculation of the small-world coefficient (Q_{SW})											
Small-world indicators											
$C_{\Delta observed}/L_{observed}$	0.18	0.14	0.15	0.14	0.11	0.15	0.14	0.13	0.14	0.14	0.14
$L_{expected}/C_{\Delta expected}$	131.82	197.15	201.88	209.19	157.82	183.31	187.02	318.96	284.47	525.01	412.12
$Q_{SW} = [C_{\Delta\ observed}/L_{observed}] \times [L_{esxpected}/C_{\Delta expected}]$	23.87	27.93	29.68	29.59	17.71	26.72	26.38	41.29	39.93	74.61	56.97

Source: Prepared by the author and based on data collected in the research

Note: This table shows (for the period from 1997 to 2007) the parameters actually observed in the network (Panel A) and the parameters obtained by simulation (Panel B) for diagnosis of the small-world phenomenon, according to Watts and Strogatz (1998). To do so, data relative to all companies listed on the Bovespa [São Paulo stock exchange] were used, with data relating to the composition of the boards of directors published by the Securities Commission, the Brazilian market regulatory agent. Comparing the results of Panels A and B, it is possible (using established assumptions) to assess in Panel C the feasibility of admitting that the network of relationships in listed companies in Brazil is similar to a small-world model, bearing in mind the values obtained for its indicator ($Q_{SW} >> 1$), which suggests the existence of strong indications that its configuration is similar to that of a small world. The measures shown in this table relate to the main component of the network of companies for each of the years studied

[a]Density is a structural measure of the network, which expresses the relationship between the possible and observed number of ties between the actors

the possibility of forming social capital via cohesion (Coleman 1990). To calculate small-world statistics, it is necessary to assume the existence of a totally connected network. Therefore, the main component of the complete network was adopted. By way of illustration, Fig. 14.4 shows the segregation of a main component.[2]

In Table 14.1 it can be seen that the Q_{SW} index for the network of companies is considerably greater than 1 throughout the whole period, highlighting that in addition to being bigger than the unit value, it has been growing. In other words, in 1997 it assumed the value ~6.54, and by 2007 it had tripled this value to ~17.30. In light of the measures found for the corporate relationships network and considering the small-world checking procedures suggested by Watts and Strogatz (1998) and the experiences applied to capital markets by Baum et al. (2004:312) and Davis et al. (2003), it seems that the Brazilian market, even though it grew between 1997 and 2007, behaved in the manner of a small-world environment. This characteristic has been particularly strong in recent years.[3]

This type of finding suggests that contagion power may have increased as a result of the speed of communication, which is the function of the power of dissemination of management practices, driven by board interlocking. Put another way, the Brazilian corporate environment, while it has grown significantly, as shown in Tables 14.1 and 14.2 (Δ%# of companies and Δ%# of board directors), is a cohesive network, in which contact between companies is ever closer, thus increasing the relevance of the reputation of the firm in its access to resources that are judged to be essential to its operation. In this sense, and according to the thinking of Subrahmanyam (2008), it is to be expected that the companies' connectivity results in consequences, such as the dissemination of executive remuneration practices. It has to be emphasized that management practices will depend on the firm's performance level and, by extension, its value in the perception of market agents.

[2]The main component is the largest cluster of interconnected nodes. By way of illustration, in Panel A in Table 14.2, it can be seen that of the 1941 directors in the network in 2007, 1191(~61.4% of the directors belonged to the same cluster) were interconnected (see Fig. 14.4).

[3]In the study of Stafsudd (2009:72), small-world statistics are shown for company networks connected by their shareholders. In this research the author presents Q_{SW} statistics for Denmark, Germany, Sweden, the United Kingdom, and the United States. Because the tie between companies was through their shareholders and not board interlocking, here it was decided not to report such values comparatively. However, by way of illustration, the values computed by Stafsudd (2009:72) are in the interval [1.04;5.65], with the exception of Germany, which according to this author has a network of companies linked by its shareholders with $Q_{SW} \approx 87.96$, which suggests the validity of the small-world model for that market. According to this result, in the opinion of Stafsudd (2009:72), Germany, which has limited investor protection and considerable small-world strength, may not generate sufficient control to complete/substitute the formal mechanisms for protecting the interests of minority shareholders. A recent illustration of this in Brazil was made by Lazzarini (2007).

Regressions

The results of the impact of the chosen independent variables on the company's value were estimated using three different procedures: OLS, random effects (RE), and fixed effects (FE), as presented in Table 14.3; FE with a robust standard error was found to be adequate (Hsiao 2005; Petersen 2009)[4]. Since (i) the Breusch-Pagan test ($p < 0.001$) rejected the adequacy of the pooled OLS, suggesting the use of RE; (ii) the F test ($p < 0.001$) suggested that the coefficients generated by the pooled OLS are not consistent (suggesting greater consistency when controlling for FE); (iii) the White test indicated problems of heteroscedasticity ($p < 0.001$); and (iv) the Hausman test ($p < 0.001$) contradicted the null hypothesis that the parameters' model controlling for RE was consistent.

So, as Yermack (1996) assumed, and following the recommendations of Hsiao (2005), in this research, the regression model controlling for Feb (as a result of the existence of non-observed variables that probably affect the firm value) was more consistent in terms of its parameters. In situations like this, the FE model controls the variables omitted from the regression. In addition, the FE model allows a single intercept for each firm, being thus indicated for modeling panel data when the intercept α_i is dealt with as a fixed parameter. It is equally desirable to use FE when observations are obtained from the whole population (SNA does not admit use of samples) and it is wished to make inferences for the individuals (firms) for which data are available. All these conditions apply to this work.[5]

Assuming the fixed effects model as being the most suitable, discussion of the results using panel data regression diagnosis revolves around the estimated parameters in Model 3, although all the simulated models are reported in this particular table. With regard to the nine position regressors of the firm in the corporate network, the results obtained in the FE model indicate that there are signs of the existence of values for the degree centrality of the firm[6] that maximize its value. In other words, if the linear coefficient, $\beta_1 \approx 0.1798$ ($p < 0.01$), is positive and the quadratic coefficient $\beta_1' \approx -0.0496$ ($p < 0.05$) is negative, it is understood that there may be an association between degree centrality in the corporate network and the firm value, described as an "inverted U" type curve (existence of the point of maximum curvature).

It seems that the value of both those companies with lower centrality values and with higher centrality values reduces, probably for different but similar worth-reducing reasons. This result is in line with the arguments of Bunderson (2003) and Labianca and Brass (2006) and supports not rejecting the H_{1a} and H_2 hypotheses. It is understood, therefore, that there will be a combined effect between the

[4]No indications were found of the correlation between regressors and regression error, which suggests the nonexistence of problems of endogeneity.

[5]These arguments are supported by the assumptions assumed by Jackson (2008:434–58).

[6]Bearing in mind the transversal character of this research and the growth in corporate networks over the period studied, it was decided to use centrality in its normalized form.

Table 14.3 Estimated parameters for the worth of the firm

Independent variables	Model 1 Coefficients for OLS	Standard error		Model 2 Coefficients for RE	Standard error		Model 3 Coefficients for FE	Standard error	
Constant	2.3336	0.2205	***	2.4088	0.3931	***	2.3787	1.8334	
Position of the firm in the network									
1. Normalized degree centrality (degree)[a]	0.5593	0.0894	***	0.3705	0.0639	***	0.1798	0.0591	***
Normalized degree centrality^2	−0.1411	0.0300	***	−0.0990	0.0219	***	−0.0496	0.0204	**
2. Normalized betweenness centrality[b]	0.0331	0.0378		0.0097	0.0277		0.0121	0.0257	
3. Structural holes by board interlocking of the firm (SH)[c]	0.0952	0.0747		0.1249	0.0640	*	0.1198	0.0618	*
4. Clustering coefficient (local)[d]	−0.1336	0.0772	*	−0.1358	0.0648	**	−0.1643	0.0828	**
5. Corporate degree centrality[e]	−1.7104	0.4583	***	−0.3184	0.3979		0.4992	0.4198	
6. University degree centrality[f]	−0.0027	0.0029		−0.0006	0.0020		0.0007	0.0016	
7. Knowledge degree centrality[g]	0.0053	0.0044		0.0045	0.0046		0.0031	0.0061	
8. Interaction term degree * SH	0.0216	0.0219		0.0347	0.0164	**	0.0332	0.0178	*
Board composition									
9. Ln of the # of directors of the firm	0.0249	0.0677		0.0176	0.0766		0.0081	0.1083	
10. % of outside directors of the firm	0.0041	0.0012	***	−0.0008	0.0011		−0.0031	0.0013	**
Control variables									
11. Ln of the firm's age	−0.1721	0.0237	***	0.1060	0.0334	***	0.4781	0.0848	***
12. Firm's superior performance	−0.0132	0.0075	*	−0.0017	0.0066		0.0069	0.0099	
13. Ln of the firm's quick ratio	−0.3139	0.0287	***	−0.1702	0.0294	***	−0.1741	0.0471	***
14. Ln of the firm's total assets	−0.1027	0.0155	***	−0.1270	0.0280	***	−0.1933	0.1460	
Akaike's criterion		4277.17			4526.03			2803.38	
R^2(R^2 adjusted)	0.1487	(0.1409)					0.7650	(0.7030)	
F		19.1344	***					12.3475	***

Source: Prepared by the author, based on collected data

Note: This table shows the results obtained for estimates of the panel data regression parameters in three different models (Model 1, minimum ordinary squares; Model 2, random effects; Model 3, fixed effects). It was found that Model 3 is adequate: fixed effects and robust standard error (with the dependent variable being Tobin's Q index), since these tests of premises suggested that this method was convenient (1659 observations of 332 companies over a period of 11 years). (i) Breusch-Pagan test = 614.725 ($p < 0.001$); (ii) White test, with LM statistic = 284.104 ($p < 0.001$); (iii) Hausman test = 181.131 ($p < 0.001$); (iv) F test for examining group differences in the intercepts = 10.3982 ($p < 0.001$).

OLS ordinary least squares, *RE* random effects, *FE* fixed effects, *SH* structural holes

$^{*}p < 0.1$; $^{**}p < 0.05$; $^{***}p < 0.01$

[a]# of ties adjacent to each firm

[b]Capacity to intermediate contacts between firms

[c]Strength of the firm's ties

[d]# of ties established by the firm relative to the number of ties that would be possible

[e]Average degree of board directors of the firm in the network of boards (board directors who serve the same companies)

[f]Average degree of board directors of the firm in the network of universities (board directors from the same university)

[g]Average degree of board members of the firm in the knowledge areas' network (board directors with the same profession)

linear and quadratic terms of the independent variable. The optimum point will therefore be seen when $\partial E(\gamma)/\partial(x) = 0$.

According to the estimated parameters for *degree centrality* (*normalized degree*), the point of maximum curvature for degree centrality is around 1.8125; in other words, provided the other estimated coefficients in Model 3 are respected, with the dependent variable being Tobin's Q, it seems that a value for normalized *degree centrality* $\approx$ 1.8125% indicates a maximum for Tobin's Q index vis-à-vis the estimated parameters in the regression obtained in Model 3, all things being equal. Put another way, according to the estimated coefficients for normalized degree centrality, a firm can maximize its value if it establishes, on average, a value close to 1.8% of the possible adjacent ties with other companies. Therefore, in 2007, when 385 companies were found to be in the corporate network, the degree (via interlocking) that maximizes the firm value is around seven companies, i.e., [0.018125 × (385–1)], all things being equal.

On the other hand, with regard to betweenness centrality, no results were found that support the idea that this positioning measure of the firm in the network exercises a significant influence on its worth ($\beta_2 \approx 0.0121$; $p > 0.1$), which leads to rejection of hypothesis H_{1b}, thus contradicting the arguments of Bunderson (2003) and Labianca and Brass (2006).

In line with the defense of Burt (1992) and Yang et al. (2010), the structural holes of the firm are positive and significantly associated with its value ($\beta_3 \approx 0.1198$; $p < 0.1$). This suggests that those companies whose board interlocking ties are less redundant achieved greater worth. In other words, it seems that the companies that optimized structural holes increased their worth. This supports non-rejection of H_3. A result along these same lines is that the firm's clustering coefficient proved to be negatively associated with its worth ($\beta_4 \approx -0.1643$; $p < 0.05$) and this suggests that companies with a greater degree of local alignment tend to be worth less. A reasonable understanding is that there are value limits to the firm's centrality and the level of local alignment. This was demonstrated by the significance of the quadratic term of the firm's *centrality degree* (β_1' ≈ -0.0496; $p < 0.05$). Hypotheses H_{4a}, H_{4b}, and H_{4c} were rejected, indicating the nonsignificance of the association of the firm's worth with the relative densities of the ties of the board directors which result from sharing boards, universities, and areas of knowledge, respectively, thus contradicting the arguments of Lin (2001) and Cohen et al. (2008).

Put another way, based on the arguments of Burt (1992), the information flow in personal relationships and social groups presumes that the probability of a piece of information being propagated in a network grows with the strength of its ties, which from the empirical point of view is estimated by two independent dimensions: (i) the frequency of the ties and (ii) emotional closeness (Burt 1992). But the results obtained did not support this argument. In the view of Labianca and Brass (2006), the existence of ties (e.g., having attended the same university and/or having done the same course), despite the asymmetry of values and preferences of the network actors, would produce negative results for the firm (negative externalities), vis-a-vis the difficulty of maintaining common objectives.

The interaction term between the firm's degree centrality and structural holes (*degree* vs. *SH*) received a positive and significant coefficient ($\beta_8 \approx 0.0332; p < 0.1$), strengthening the idea that companies with a larger number of ties, and better ones, tend to achieve higher levels of worth in the view of market agents. This indication supports the assumptions of Burt (1992) that a larger and less redundant number of ties enable identification of new investment opportunities, which lead to an increase in the firm's worth.

In observing the results obtained for the two variables relative to the composition of the board, it is found that board size did not prove to be significantly associated with the firm's worth ($\beta_9 \approx 0.0081; p > 0.1$), which contradicts the results obtained by Yermack (1996). In addition, the number of outside directors, even though it obtained a significant coefficient, has a small marginal effect on the firm's Tobin's Q ($\beta_{10} \approx -0.0031; p < 0.05$). Therefore, an innovative result and one that may merit greater attention from the academic community is that, rather than the size of the board, the way in which this board is linked by board interlocking to other companies may have a greater influence on the firm's worth. Among the four control variables, both the *firm's age* ($\beta_{11} \approx 0.04781; p < 0.01$) and the *quick ratio* ($\beta_{13} \approx -0.1741; p < 0.01$) were significant.

The results obtained in the panel data regressions support the idea that the firm's degree centrality and structural holes are resources the company can and must manage with a view to achieving its corporate objectives. Therefore, the way in which the firm configures its board will determine its positioning in the network and consequently will have an impact on its access to market resources, whether formally negotiated or not, through board interlocking.

Concluding Remarks

Based on the graph theory, this research has attempted to check the validity of the small-world model for the capital market and to verify the existence of associations between the firm's worth and its position in the corporate relationships network, by means of board interlocking. This study is most relevant in the context of the roles of corporate boards and their impact on the flow of resources (whether negotiated or otherwise in the markets), such as capital, status, prestige, and legitimacy within the corporate environment.

In the light of these results supported by a data set relating to 415 nonfinancial companies listed on the BM&FBovespa [São Paulo Stock Exchange] in the 1997–2007 period, it can be supposed that the top administration of hundreds of publicly quoted companies listed in Brazil essentially consists of people who know one another very well. According to the findings of Milgram (1967), over the 11 years studied, the board directors belonging to the main component of the network of relationships ($\sim$50%) proved to be separated by a number of personal ties close to 6° of separation, meaning that the small-world properties were seen as being valid in the relationship networks that comprised both board directors and companies.

This supports the argument that in collaboration networks, individuals with an outstanding reputation, or who represent access to resources, experience, or knowledge, for example, tend to be more sought after. Consequently, they increase their prestige while at the same time exercising an influence on the governance practices of other companies via articulation and the sharing of prospects (Merton 1996; Moody 2004). Further, because of their career paths in different institutions over time and their peers in these institutions, they can promote a stratified connection between corporate boards, especially across companies that seek independent board members.

Such aspects raise questions as to the role exercised by certain companies in corporate governance via the activities of their board directors. Some companies may be more attractive in terms of establishing new relationships, thus increasing their influence in regard to their power to participate more actively in the flow of resources (financial and nonfinancial, whether formally negotiated in the markets, or otherwise) in the corporate relationships network; they act as key links between those companies that are around them.

Regarding company's worth, results indicate the existence of optimum levels of centrality, and optimum social prominence levels of the firm (in terms of its degree centrality), which maximize the company's worth. In line with the relevance of the firm's position in the network to the firm's worth, a positive association was found between structural holes and Tobin's Q index. This reaffirms the arguments of Burt (1992), which defend the opinion that a reduction in redundant ties can improve access to new investments and new ways of mobilizing resources (not only financial ones) through board interlocking.

The results obtained with the firm's position in the network, in comparison with the parameters estimated for the variables related to the corporate board composition, particularly the board's size and the number of outside directors, support the idea that establishing parameters for ways in which a firm's corporate power establishes ties with other boards is just as important as managing the board's characteristics.

Directions for Future Research

The current discussion does not bring this topical debate to an end. Rather, the growth in the area of social network analysis and financial networks suggests an innovative field of research, with valuable insight to explain the phenomena that intervene in corporate governance questions. While the present study contributes expansion of the field of corporate governance, recently published works in the finance area have pointed to the contribution that such research describing the informal mechanisms of governance (as corporate networks are) can lead to a better understanding of governance models around the world, based on the complexity of corporate networks (Rossoni et al., 2018).

In addition, the dynamics of those networks shows an explicit growth across the time; this can be observed in Figs. 14.4 (2007) and 14.5 (2015). For an elucidatory

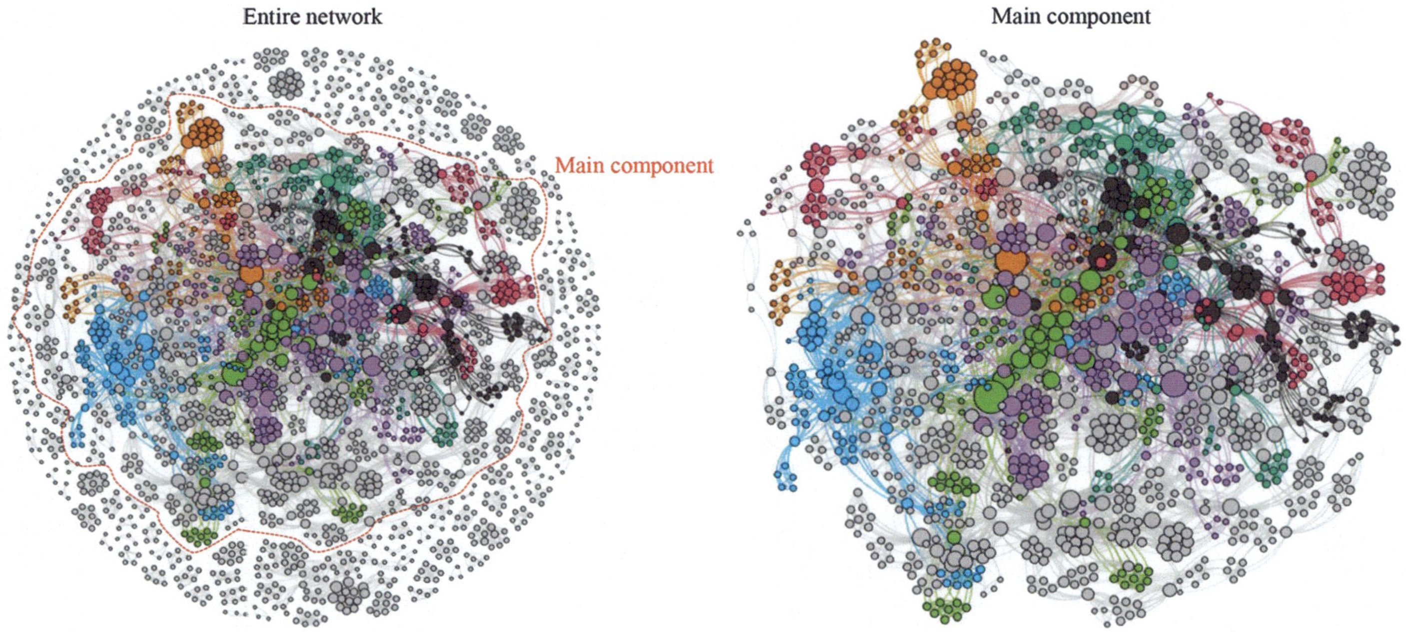

Fig. 14.4 Segregation of the main component of the network of board directors in 2007. Source: Prepared by the author, based on official data collected from the IAN/CVM. Notes: (i) This figure illustrates the segregation of the main component of the network of relationships between board directors in 2007; (ii) on the left-hand side is the complete network arrangement of directors (1941 professionals grouped in 134 components/clusters); (iii) on the right is the main component of the network (a component that brings together the greatest number of interconnected nodes), in which 1191 directors participate; (iv) each node represents a director belonging to the network of corporate relationships, and the size of each node indicates the *degree centrality* of each director; and (v) it is worth emphasizing that this research considered the board directors and executives (those who are also board directors in other companies) of the companies participating in the research. The intention was not to fail to compute a tie between two companies when an executive simultaneously performs director functions in at least one other company (to do so a function was developed in Visual Basic that can be obtained on request from the author of this study)

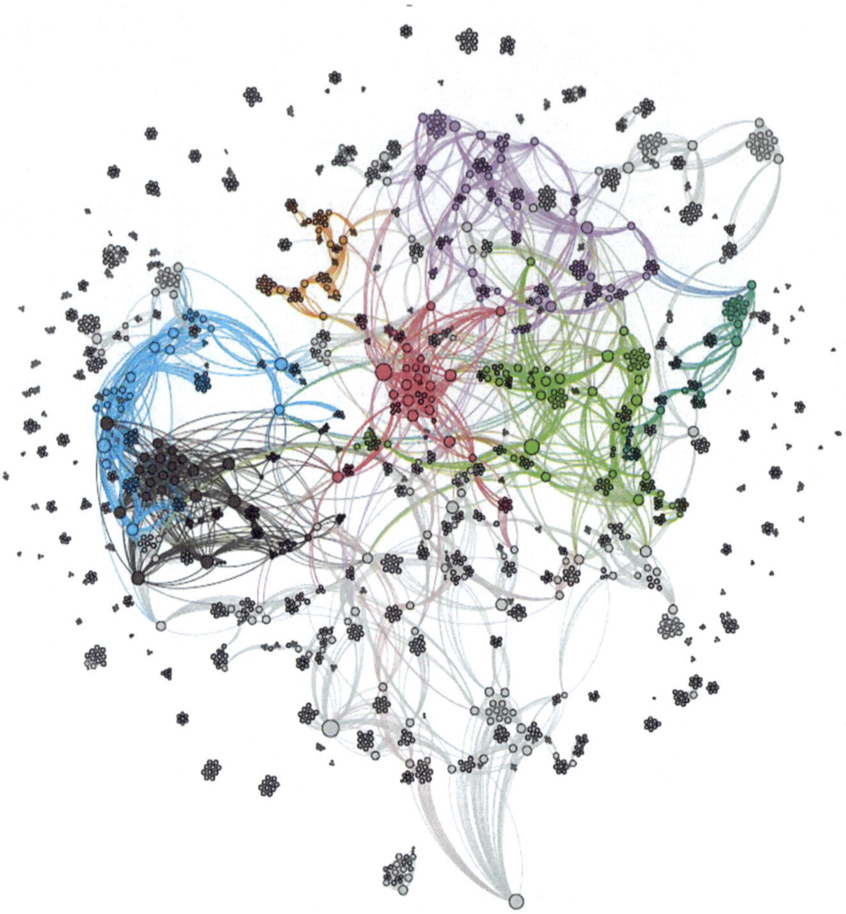

Fig. 14.5 Board members network in the Brazilian capital market (2015). Note: Each node represents one of the 1992 board members on listed firms in Brazil in 2015, and each tie implies at least a board shared between the board members

discussion of this view, it is recommended that the texts of Fracassi and Tate (2012), Cohen et al. (2010), and Stafsudd (2009) be reviewed. Among aspects that might contribute to a better understanding of interlocking phenomenon, one can mention the presence of board directors who represent the interests of investors and economic groups (this was not dealt with in this research).

References

Baum, J. A. C., Rowley, T. J., & Shipilov, A. V. (2004). The small world of Canadian capital markets: Statistical mechanics of investment Bank syndicate networks, 1952–1989. *Canadian Journal of Administration Sciences, 21*(4), 307–325.

Bearden, J., Atwood, W., Freitag, P., Hendricks, C., Mintz, B., & Schwartz, M. (1975). *The nature and extent of bank centrality in corporate network*. In J. Scott (Ed.), *Social networks* (Vol. 3). London: Sage 2002.
Bouwman, C. H. S. (2011). Corporate governance propagation through overlapping directors. *Review of Financial Studies, 24*(7), 2358–2394.
Bunderson, J. S. (2003). Recognizing and utilizing expertise in work groups: A status characteristics perspective. *Administrative Science Quarterly, 48*(4), 557–591.
Burt, R. S. (1992). *Structural holes: The social structure of competition*. Cambridge, MA: Harvard University Press.
Chung, K. H., & Pruitt, S. W. (1994). A simple approximation of Tobin's Q. *Financial Management, 23*, 70–74.
Cohen, L., Frazzini, A., & Maloy, C. (2008). The small world of investing: Board connections and mutual fund returns. *Journal of Political Economy, 116*(5), 951–979.
Cohen, L., Frazzini, A., & Maloy, C. (2010). Sell-side school ties. *The Journal of Finance, 65*, 1409–1437.
Coleman, J. S. (1990). *Foundations of social theory*. Chicago, IL: University of Chicago Press.
Conyon, M. J., & Muldoon, M. R. (2006). The small world of corporate boards. *Journal of Business Finance & Accounting, 33*, 1321–1343.
Davis, G. F., & Greve, H. R. (1997). Corporate elite networks and governance changes in the 1980's. *American Journal of Sociology, 103*, 1–37.
Davis, G. F., Yoo, M., & Baker, W. E. (2003). The small world of corporate elite, 1982–2001. *Strategic Organization, 1*(3), 301–326.
Erdös, P., & Rényi, A. (1959). On random graphs. *Publicationes Mathematicae Debrecen, 6*, 290–297.
Fama, E. F., & Jensen, M. C. (1983). Separation of ownership and control. *Journal of Law Economics, 26*, 301–325.
Fich, E. M., & Shivdasani, A. (2006). Are busy boards effective monitors? *Journal of Finance, 61*, 689–724.
Fracassi, C., & Tate, G. (2012). External networking and internal firm governance. *Journal of Finance, 67*(1), 153–194.
Freeman, L. C. (1979). Centrality in social networks: Conceptual clarification. *Social Networks, 1*, 215–239.
Harris, I. C., & Shimizu, K. (2004). Too busy to serve? An examination of the influence of overboarded directors. *Journal of Management Studies, 41*, 775–798.
Haunschild, P. R. (1993). Interorganizational imitation: The impact of interlocks on corporate acquisition activity. *Administrative Science Quarterly, 38*, 564–592.
Hsiao, C. (2005). *Analysis of panel data* (2nd ed.). New York: Cambridge University Press.
Instituto Brasileiro de Governança Corporativa. (2015). *Código de Melhores Práticas de Governança Corporativa*. Available at: http://www.ibgc.org.br/userfiles/2014/files/codigoMP_5edicao_web.pdf.
Jackson, M. O. (2008). *Social and economic networks*. Princeton, NJ: Princeton University Press.
Kang, J. K., Liu, W. L., Low, A., & Zhang, L. (2018). Friendly boards and innovation. *Journal of Empirical Finance, 45*, 1–25.
Kilduff, M. (1992). The friendship network as a decision-making resource: Dispositional moderators of social influences on organizational choice. *Journal of Personality and Social Psychology, 62*, 168–180.
Labianca, G., & Brass, D. J. (2006). Exploring the social ledger: Negative relationships and negative asymmetry in social networks in organizations. *Academy of Management Review, 31*, 596–614.
Lazzarini, S. G. (2007). Changing to stay the same: Analyzing the dynamics of owner networks in Brazil as 'small worlds'. *RAE Eletron, 6*(1), Art. 6.
Leitner, Y. (2005). Financial networks: Contagion, commitment, and private sector bailouts. *Journal of Finance, 60*, 2925–2953.

Lin, N. (2001). *Social capital: A theory of social structure and action*. Cambridge: Cambridge University Press.
Martínez-Jaramillo, S., Pérez, O. P., Embriz, F. A., & Dey, F. L. G. (2010). Systemic risk, financial contagion and financial fragility. *Journal of Economic Dynamics and Control, 34*(11), 2358–2374.
Mehra, A., Kilduff, M., & Brass, D. J. (2001). The social networks of high and low self-monitors: Implications for workplace performance. *Administrative Science Quarterly, 46*, 121–146.
Mendes-Da-Silva, W., & Vidal, P. (2010). Lost in space? The topography of social relationship network of board members in the Brazilian capital market. In *Proceedings from 10th Brazilian Finance Conference*, São Paulo.
Merton, R. K. (1996). *On social structure and science*. Chicago, IL: University Press Chicago.
Milgram, S. (1967). The small world problem. *Psychology Today, 2*, 60–67.
Mills, C. W. (1956). *The power elite*. Oxford: New York.
Mizruchi, M. S. (1996). What do interlocks do? An analysis, critique, and assessment of research on interlocking directors. *The Annual Review of Sociology, 22*, 271–298.
Moody, J. (2004). The structure of a social science collaboration network: Disciplinary cohesion from 1963 to 1999. *American Sociological Review, 69*, 213–238.
Newman, M. E. J., Strogatz, S. H., & Watts, D. J. (2001). Random graphs with arbitrary degree distributions and their applications. *Physical Rev E, 64*, 026118-1–026118-17.
Noyes, E. A. (2007). Interlocking Boards and Patterns of Corporate Entrepreneurship in the S&P500: 1996–2006. PhD Dissertation, Boston University.
Petersen, M. A. (2009). Estimating standard errors in finance panel data sets: Comparing approaches. *Review of Financial Studies, 22*, 435–480.
Pfeffer, J., & Salancik, G. R. (1978). *The external control of organizations: A resource dependence perspective*. New York: Harper & Row.
Pirson, M., & Turnbull, S. (2011). Toward a more humanistic governance model: Network governance structures. *Journal of Business Ethics, 99*, 101–114.
Robins, G., & Alexander, M. (2004). Small worlds among interlocking directors: Network structure and distance in bipartite graphs. *Computational & Mathematical Organization Theory, 10*, 69–94.
Rossoni, L., Aranha, C. E., & Mendes-Da-Silva, W. (2018). The complexity of social capital: The influence of board and ownership interlocks on implied cost of capital an emerging market. *Complexity*. Article ID 6248427.
Schonlau, R., & Singh, P. V. (2009). *Board network and merger performance. Tepper school of business* (Paper 449). Available at: http://repository.cmu.edu/tepper/449.
Scott, W. R. (2001). *Institutions and organizations* (2nd ed.). Thousand Oaks: Sage.
Stafsudd, A. (2009). Corporate networks as informal governance mechanisms: A small worlds approach to Sweden. *Corporate Governance: An International Review, 17*, 62–76.
Subrahmanyam, A. (2008). Social networks and corporate governance. *European Financial Management, 14*, 633–662.
Wasserman, S., & Faust, K. (1994). *Social network analysis: Methods and applications*. Cambridge, UK: Cambridge University Press.
Watts, D. J., & Strogatz, S. H. (1998). Collective dynamics of small-world networks. *Nature, 393*, 440–442.
Westlund, H., & Adam, F. (2010). Social capital and economic performance: A meta-analysis of 65 studies. *European Planning Studies, 18*, 893–919.
Yang, H., Lin, Z., & Lin, Y. (2010). A multilevel framework of firm boundaries: Firm characteristics, dyadic differences, and network attributes. *Strategic Management Journal, 31*, 237–261.
Yermack, D. L. (1996). Higher evaluation of companies with a small board of directors. *Journal of Financial Economics, 40*, 185–211.
Yermack, D. (2006). Flights of fancy: Corporate jets, CEO perquisites, and inferior shareholder returns. *Journal of Financial Economics 80*(1), 211–242.
Yermack, D. (2017). Corporate governance and blockchains. *Review of Finance*, 7–31. https://doi.org/10.1093/rof/rfw074.

Chapter 15
Corporate Disclosure via the Internet and Implied Cost of Capital

Wesley Mendes-Da-Silva and Daniel Reed Bergmann

Abstract The classical literature of finance establishes arguments that emphasize the negative impact of corporate transparency on the level of return required by investors, or the cost of capital of the firm. However, even as the growing sophistication of technologies at the disposal of listed companies, the corporative communication with its stakeholders is still predominantly supported in the technological device that precedes the Internet. Therefore, this chapter discusses the relationship between voluntary disclosure via corporate websites and the implied cost of equity capital of listed companies. Based on data from more than 300 companies, our main results are three. First, on average, the companies listed on the New Market showed a lower cost of capital. Second, the companies deemed to be the most aggressive showed a higher cost of capital (≈3% points higher than the conservative companies. Third, the metrics of corporate website disclosure did not appear to be related to cost of capital.

Keywords Disclosure · Cost of capital · Financial statements · Corporate governance · Accounting policy

JEL Code G34 · D24 · O14

Among the financial decisions made by a firm, such as financing and investment, there is a governing factor, the cost of capital, known as the return demanded by investors adjusted to company risk. Accordingly, it is understood that there is a constant search for less expensive costs of capital, as these work together to increase

---

Portions of this chapter appeared in the 2014 paper "The Influence of E-disclosure on the Ex-Ante Cost of Capital of Listed Companies in Brazil", *Journal of Emerging Market Finance*, vol 13, pp 335–365.

W. Mendes-Da-Silva (✉)
Sao Paulo School of Business Administration (FGV/EAESP), Sao Paulo, SP, Brazil

University of Texas at Austin, Austin, TX, USA

D. R. Bergmann
University of São Paulo, São Paulo, SP, Brazil

W. Mendes-Da-Silva (ed.), *Individual Behaviors and Technologies for Financial Innovations*, https://doi.org/10.1007/978-3-319-91911-9_15

the firm's value (Copeland et al. 2005). Grossman (1981) and Milgrom (1981) argue for the full disclosure of relevant information to the buyer, e.g., M&A acquirers or investors. If potential buyers know what content is relevant but suspect that the seller is withholding relevant content, then, in the absence of disclosure, the buyers will reasonably discount the value of the seller's assets to the worst case (Scott 1994). This discounting imposes an expressive cost on the seller, who then has an incentive to make more relevant information available (Chen et al. 2010). Financial innovations, e.g., Blockchain and the Internet, can contribute to improve the corporate governance, including corporate disclosure (Yermack 2017). In addition, the cost of capital can be increased as the growth of frictions in the context in which the company operates (Cheynel 2013).

However, in current practice, sellers often do not behave in this manner. That is, firms often do not have the informational content that is of interest to the market. In the last few decades, several authors have concentrated their efforts on advancing arguments that focus on factors that could mitigate the arguments of Grossman (1981) and Milgrom (1981). Verrecchia (1983) and Dye (1985) proposed models highlighting the role of buyer uncertainty as the reason for management not revealing corporate data. A matter cited as among the most relevant in the context of decisions associated with investor relations are the potential benefits that a firm could obtain by providing higher levels of disclosure (Espinosa and Trombetta 2007).

One of the advantages of disclosing would be a decrease in the firm's cost of capital. However, the evidence surrounding this relationship remains inconclusive (Souissi and Khlif 2012). Examining the lack of a conclusion, Espinosa and Trombetta (2007) cite two methodological aspects, the first of which are difficulties of measurement. Neither the cost of capital nor the quality of disclosure can be directly and expressly observed by the researcher, often rendering it necessary to fall back on individual perceptions and leading tests of this association to start from a considerable degree of subjectivity. Representing the second methodological aspect to consider are questions associated with the specification of the model; supporting the arguments put forward by Gietzman and Trombetta (2003), empirical tests have erred by disregarding the different choices companies make in terms of accounting policies.

Providing our discussion on this chapter, we contribute to the literature on the effects of web disclosure on the cost of capital by discussing these two methodological issues. To measure disclosure, many authors employ indices, but the nature of these indices varies considerably among the studies. Consequently, proposals can be found based on the voluntary and mandatory aspects of disclosure (Giner 1997). Furthermore, it is unusual to find studies that effectively consider the relevance of the information for the users, e.g., investors, analysts, and managers (Mendes-Da-Silva et al. 2009; Mendes-Da-Silva and Onusic 2012). Therefore, in our research, efforts were focused in three areas: (i) the use of a disclosure index that includes financial and corporate management data and considers the relevance of this information for the market; (ii) an estimate of the implied cost of equity capital (ICC), or ex ante cost of equity capital; and (iii) the consideration of differences in accounting policies between the companies listed on the Sao Paulo Stock Exchange, called [B][3], and the classification of these policies as aggressive or conservative.

This chapter assesses the empirical validity of the interaction equilibrium advanced by Gietzman and Trombetta (2003), which considers the cost of capital to be jointly determined by the company's level of disclosure and its accounting policy. Studies testing the empirical validity of the argument that greater disclosure implies a lower cost of capital have obtained inconclusive results (Botosan 1997; Botosan and Plumlee 2002). One explanation for this finding is the existence of a possible omission of variable bias, that is, accounting policy. According to the defense of Espinosa and Trombetta (2007), if the accounting policy is relevant, then the relationship between disclosure and the cost of capital is not monotonic.

This relationship would be negative for aggressive companies but insignificant when considering conservative companies (Artiach and Clarkson 2011). Another belief present in the literature is that the weak link between disclosure and the cost of capital in more developed economies is due to the high degree of disclosure that is practiced in these countries and that is not observed in emerging economies (Xiao et al. 2004; Souissi and Khlif 2012; Garay et al. 2013). The objective of this research is to verify the existence of negative and significant associations between corporate disclosure and the cost of capital. Therefore, four disclosure proxies are used (three by means of the corporate website and one dummy variable taken from the [B][3]'s New Market listing), and four other proxies of the calculation of the ICC are used in accordance with Espinosa and Trombetta (2007).

Our results suggest: (i) no association at all was found between disclosure via a corporate website and the cost of capital; (ii) companies listed in the differentiated segment of corporate governance, known as the New Market, and classified as conservative on average have a cost of capital that is 6% points lower than other companies; and (iii) results were found supporting the argument that a firm's accounting policy (aggressiveness) could play a significant role in the detection of relationships between the cost of capital and disclosure.

The relationship between a company's level of corporate disclosure and its cost of capital has attracted significant interest from the global academic community. In the theoretical field, the negative relationship between the two variables is shown to be reasonably consolidated (Diamond and Verrechia 1991; Easly and O'Hara 2004). Overall, since the groundbreaking work of Botosan (1997), several empirical studies on this subject have obtained results regarded in the literature as inconclusive (Espinosa and Trombetta 2007).

In this context, the technology camp has produced new and relatively inexpensive communication mechanisms, notably the Internet (Patten and Crampton 2003; Gajewski 2015). Simultaneously, there is an increasing number of studies on the use of the Internet for disclosure activities and investor relations without addressing the impact of the use of the web on the firm's cost of capital (Déjean and Martinez 2009). Therefore, in view of the needs of market-listed companies and investors, it has been deemed relevant to understand the associations between voluntary disclosure through a firm's corporate website and its ICC.

This study collected data from over 300 listed companies in an emerging market, i.e., where frictions as consequence of low disclosure are present (Carvalho and Castro 2016); we tested the sensitivity of the implied cost of capital (ICC) to disclosure through the corporate website. For this we consider the opinion of market analysts, both to calculate the ICC and to obtain a disclosure index via corporate website. This chapter presents highlights from this research and uses this data set to identify differences in propensity to provide information, according to the accounting policy adopted by the company. The findings from this research provide insight into how financial professionals, managers, board members, and policy makers can develop and provide more effective financial statements disclosure strategy to the stakeholders, especially firms which accounting policy is more aggressive. At the end of this chapter, some recommendations are made. Directions for future research are also included.

Advantages and Disadvantages of Voluntary Disclosure

The disclosure of information is one of the most important decisions made by the top management of listed companies because it has potential consequences. This choice assumes the need to identify net benefits arising from the trade-off between the advantages and disadvantages of the voluntary disclosure of information about the company (Sánchez et al. 2011). In the opinion of Jensen and Meckling (1976), the information that is made available can be useful in the decision-making process of shareholders and managers and can help shareholders and other stakeholders to monitor the activities of the top management. From the perspective of the signaling theory, according to Baiman and Verrecchia (1996), the availability of information can be recognized as a signal to the capital markets. By decreasing information asymmetry, the company can optimize financing costs and thus increase its value (Espinosa and Trombetta 2007).

However, the determinants of access to capital at reduced costs remain a controversial aspect in the literature. Along this line of discussion, whereas Francis et al. (2008) obtained results supporting the idea that more open companies achieve less burdensome access to capital, Botosan (1997) and Wang et al. (2008), analyzing the associations between disclosure and the cost of capital, did not obtain evidence of benefits for the company resulting from voluntary disclosure expressed by means of a lower cost of capital. Other benefits for the company could originate in the behavior underlying the more voluntary provision of relevant information to the market, i.e., corporate image and increased investor confidence (Babío et al. 2003); such benefits may lead to an increase in the liquidity of shares on the stock exchange (Healy et al. 1999) and access to larger amounts of financial resources (Marr and Gray 2002). However, an optimal level of voluntary disclosure assumes the identification of liquid benefits arising from the trade-off between the costs and benefits as a result of the disclosure of corporate information (Hayes and Lundholm 1996).

However, producing and disclosing information voluntarily can lead to disadvantages that outweigh the benefits (Sánchez et al. 2011, p.474). Gray et al. (1990) highlight the costs associated with competitive disadvantages and political costs (e.g., taxes and limits imposed by the government on the company operations) and thus justify the reluctance of top management to disclose corporate information at levels higher than those required by law. Furthermore, with regard to the disadvantages of engaging in behavior that is more inclined to provide information to the market, Gallhofer et al. (2007) argue that the costs associated with the disclosure of corporate information include the production and disclosure of information to the market. Therefore, these costs would be significantly reduced by disclosing information via the Internet. In addition, executives can try to avoid an information disclosure precedent that will be difficult to maintain in the future (Graham et al. 2005).

Information Disclosure via the Internet

Interest in the matter of corporate disclosure via the Internet is neither new nor restricted to the academic community. Several initiatives in the business environment can be cited as examples, e.g., in 1996, Electronic Data Gathering, Analysis, and Retrieval (EDGAR) appeared in the United States as an attempt to standardize procedures. System for Electronic Document Analysis and Retrieval (SEDAR) was created in Canada, and eXtensible Business Reporting language (XBRL) appeared as a language extension of eXtensible Markup Language (XML) for use in the presentation and exchange of information, principally financial. As an example of the interest of the regulatory agencies, one can cite the FASB (2000) guidelines and the Portuguese securities commission CMVM (2000). Examination of the financial literature shows significant growth in the interest of the international academic community in the matter of corporate disclosure via the Internet, as shown by Petravick and Guillet (1998) in the United States, Craven and Marston (1999) in the United Kingdom, Hedlin (1999) in Switzerland, Sánchez et al. (2011) in Spain, Lattemann (2005) in Germany, and Malarvizhi and Yadav (2009) in Canada. However, in Brazil, few studies can be found, especially when compared to the international scene (Mendes-Da-Silva et al. 2009; Mendes-Da-Silva and Onusic 2012).

Assessments by researchers such as Gallhofer et al. (2007) reveal clear potential advantages for companies that provide adequate and timely investor-friendly information via their website. A complementary view of these findings is that, compared to traditional printed means, the Internet provides many opportunities for corporate communication. Furthermore, it provides a wealth of critical and nonofficial information that competes with official communication channels (Paisey and Paisey 2006). Moreover, Noack (1997) highlights the fact that both the corporate costs of printing and correspondence by mail as well as investors' cost of accessing information can be significantly reduced. In contrast, the Internet enables a company to control the context with regard to the presentation of the data, emphasizing the positive aspects and enabling the interpretation of potentially negative information with regard to the company (Cho and Roberts 2010).

The Cost of Capital and Disclosure

The association between the cost of capital and disclosure has been the target of several works worldwide in the area of corporate finance, e.g., Botosan (1997) in the United States, Richardson and Welker (2001) in Canada, Hail (2002) and Botosan and Plumlee (2002) in Switzerland, and Gietzmann and Ireland (2005) in the United Kingdom. All these works begin with the belief that the disclosure negatively influences the level of the capital cost of the company. Furthermore, other works defend the idea that this association has been confirmed as negative, above all in markets characterized by low-level institutional transparency, e.g., Zhang and Ding (2006) in China, Espinosa and Trombetta (2007) in Spain, Déjan and Martinez (2009) in France, and Lopes and Alencar (2010) in Brazil.

This configuration of the institutional environment (i.e., civil law countries) would motivate managers to voluntarily provide relevant information as a means of reducing uncertainty among investors, thus contributing to a greater tradability of the securities issued by the company. To that end, Brazil, an economy where little disclosure is practiced, such as China and France and contrary to the United States, Canada, and the United Kingdom (Souissi and Khlif 2012, p. 53), represents an interesting research subject, given its growing importance for the world economy, which so far has not led to studies in this field.

Data and Variables

From the same list of 40 items of market interest discussed in detail by Mendes-Da-Silva and Onusic (2012), this work uses four disclosure variables, 3 of them obtained from a check of 40 items made available by the companies studied on their corporate websites, weighted by the mean score obtained from consultation (using an electronic questionnaire on the Internet) with 18 analysts registered on the Sao Paulo Stock Exchange, called [B][3]. Following the method adopted by Mendes-Da-Silva and Onusic (2012), indices of the disclosure of financial information (*Ifin*), which included 17 items, and governance information (*Igov*), which included 23 items, were constructed for a total of 40 corporate disclosure (*e-Disc*) items, all of which are listed in Table 15.1. For example, all companies that disclose quarterly reports, including financial reports, count 10.1 points, because each item was judged according to a scale from 0 to 11 points, where 0 = irrelevant item and 11 = very relevant item.

Table 15.1 Indices of voluntary disclosure via the corporate website

#	Information	Freq.	%	χ^2	Mean weight for disclosure[a]
	Panel A: Categories of financial information				
1	Quarterly reports, including financial reports	120	93.8		10.1
2	General view of the performance of the company (FAQ, recent facts, quick news)	120	93.8		9.9
3	Calendar of events of interest to the investor (e.g., dividend distribution)	120	93.8	*	10
4	Financial information in a language other than Portuguese	119	93		9.7
5	Full annual report	117	91.4		10
6	Other CVM (securities commission) files (e.g., reference form)	117	91.4		9.6
7	Coverage by analysts	113	88.3		8.7
8	Text of the most recent financial news	110	85.9		10
9	Commentaries and presentations (e.g., quarterly performance road shows)	106	82.8		8.9
10	Current share prices of the company in markets where they are traded	103	80.5		9.7
11	History of share prices	101	78.9		9.6
12	Most recent monthly financial data	95	74.2		10.6
13	Link to the securities commission – CVM website	79	61.7	*	6.9
14	Information detailing a profit reinvestment plan	66	51.6		10.1
15	Discussion of the advantages for an investor of holding shares in the company	51	39.8		8
16	Information about their broker(s) (address or direct link)	41	32		7.3
17	Link to share data on another website	28	21.9		6.7
	Panel B: Categories of corporate governance				
1	Text on the concept of corporate governance	116	91		7
2	Names of the members of the board of directors	115	90		8.8
3	Structure of the board of directors	115	90		9.9
4	Composition of the share capital of the company	111	87		10.2
5	Investor portal on the home page	107	84		9
6	Information disclosure policy to the markets	105	82		9
7	Professional qualification of the directors and advisors	105	82		9.7
8	Reference to good corporate governance practices adopted	104	81		9.6
9	Rules of conduct for executive directors	96	75		8.1
10	Reports on the social responsibility of the company	92	72		8.1
11	Working rules of the board of directors	90	70		9.6
12	Procedures for the selection and election of directors and advisors	88	69		9.1
13	Ratings assigned (classification of corporate governance and securities issued)	76	59		9.7

(continued)

Table 15.1 (continued)

#	Information	Freq.	%	χ^2	Mean weight for disclosure[a]
14	Explicit description of the powers of the directors	66	52		9
15	Investor kit (basket of information of interest to the investor)	64	50		9.6
16	Where the company is listed and financial statements in accordance with national standards	60	47		101
17	Publication of the role and position of the board members	57	45		7.2
18	Description of the conditions of independence of the board members	52	41		9.2
19	Fees paid to audit firms	43	34		7.7
20	Description of the relationship between directors and shareholders	40	31		9.2
21	Disclosure of positions of board members in other companies	32	25		7
22	Remuneration (detailed) of directors and advisors	27	21		9.6
23	Directors' interests in the capital of the company	24	19		9.6

Source: Constructed by the authors based on an examination of corporate websites (N = 128) conducted between August and October 2011

Note: This table shows the frequency (in descending order) with which the information categories were found on the corporate websites and the average relevance scores assigned (between August and October 2011) to each information category in the opinion of the corporate information users, i.e., rating agencies, securities brokers, and pension funds. The last column shows the test statistic of χ^2 for independence with regard to the listing of the company in the trading sector of the New Market

$^{*}p < 0.1$; $^{**}p < 0.05$; $^{***}p < 0.01$

[a]This column shows the average relevance score for each corporate information category given by market agents (eight brokers, two rating agencies, and eight fund managers). 0 = irrelevant item; 11 = very relevant item

In this way, between August and October 2011, 300 websites were examined, yielding a total of 5210 examined items (40 × 128 corporate websites). The fourth dependent variable is a dummy that is given a value of 1 if the company is listed on the New Market and zero otherwise. It is worth highlighting that each website was visited simultaneously by the researchers as a means of minimizing possibly ambiguous interpretations of the content provided by the companies. In June 2011, 525 companies were listed on the [B][3], of which 193 were not considered (because they were more regulated and thus were under more obligations with regard to disclosure, which could bias the results).

The websites of 17 companies were not identified. *Thomson Reuters* provided data on future profit estimates for only 128 of the remaining 314 companies. Therefore, the final group comprised 128 nonfinance companies, 83 (64.8%) of which were listed on the New Market, that were distributed between 17 industrial sectors. A maximum time of 15 min was given for the exploration of each corporate website, as the items must be available and organized in such a way as to be easily found by those interested. Responses from users of corporate information were collected using an electronic questionnaire sent over the Internet.

Procedure of ICC Estimate

In accordance with the arguments of Francis et al. (2005), the cost of equity capital (a dependent variable in this research) is an ex ante metric that reflects expectations about the returns offered by the company and thus is not directly observable. The various works concentrating their efforts on obtaining estimates of the cost of equity capital use price and profit estimates made by analysts, implementing these metrics in the evaluation model (Gebhardt et al. 2001; Pástor et al. 2008; Hou et al. 2012; Ashton and Wang 2013; Dittmar and Lundblad 2017). Therefore, from these estimates are drawn the values for the cost of equity capital with an internal rate of return equal to the current prices of the shares and to a sequence of expected earnings derived from analysts' expectations. In this study, for the purposes of the proxy of the ICC, four different calculation procedures were used, e.g., r_{riv}, r_{pef}, r_{peg}, and r_{mpeg}, detailed below.

The cost of capital calculated by the CAPM is based on realized or ex post values. As mentioned by Jenkinson (2006): "Much of the complexity associated with estimating the cost of capital derives from the difficulty of observing the expectations of investors." Elton (1999) and Fama and French (2002) argue that realized returns are biased to measure expected returns. They state that the difference between realized and expected returns derive from recent market information. To overcome this problem, ICC deals with the predicted values of the company's earnings and their growth in the short and long term.

Malkiel (1979) and Gordon and Gordon (1997) developed the first approach that estimates the cost of capital based on the dividend discount model. The traditional Gordon and Gordon (1997) model, also known as the dividend discount approach, proposes that the expected return on an asset is given by the discount rate that equates the market price with the expected future dividend flow. Assuming that the expectation of future dividend flow can initially be represented by the expectation for the next period and that, from then on, a constant dividend growth rate in perpetuity, the model can be represented by the Eq. (15.1):

$$P_o = \sum_{t=1}^{\infty} \frac{dps_t \times (1+g)^{t-1}}{(1+K_e)^t} = \frac{dps_1}{K_e - g} \tag{15.1}$$

where:

P_o is the market price of the asset at the current date.

dps_t is the expected dividend per share.

K_e is the cost of equity of the firm.

g is the perpetuity of the dividend rate.

This equation leads to the implied cost of equity by: $K_e = \frac{dps_1}{P_o} + g$.

For a few decades, the calculation of the cost of capital based on Gordon's model has fallen into disuse because it is focused on the distribution of value based on the dividends rather than the generation of value produced by the company's earnings. In 2001, a few implied cost of capital models start to emerge, which will improve the Gordon's model. As an alternative to calculate the cost of capital, Gebhardt et al. (2001), Claus and Thomas (2001), Easton (2006), and Ohlson and Juettner-Nauroth (2005) adopt the use of expected returns based on projections of market analysts. The idea, common to the four models, is to find the cost of equity as the rate of return that equalizes the market price with a future sequence of the company's earnings. Easton and Sommers (2007) state that the main difference between these models is the treatment given to the long-term growth rate of abnormal earnings. Hail and Leuz (2006), Dhaliwal, Krull, and Li (2007), and Hou et al. (2012) apply the model to estimate the ex ante. This approach calculates the implied cost of capital of a firm using different ICC models, and then, it calculates the average between the results.

A fifth measurement was also used, obtained from the average of the four metrics (r_{avg}). Among the various procedures suggested for the estimate of the company's ICC, e.g., Botosan (1997), one of the least expensive in terms of necessary data is that adopted by Espinosa and Trombetta (2007) and formalized in (15.2):

$$P_t = \frac{\widehat{x}_{t+2} - \widehat{x}_{t+1}}{\left(r_{\text{peg}}\right)^2} \tag{15.2}$$

in which r_{peg} = the ex ante cost of equity capital, where *peg* refers to the price-profit growth model (Ohlson and Juettner-Nauroth 2005), $\widehat{x}_{t+1}$ = the average earnings per share (*EPS*) (estimated by analysts for the company in the following financial year), and $\widehat{x}_{t+2}$ = the average earnings per share estimated by analysts for the company in the second following financial year. In this way, the ex ante cost of equity capital in December 2011 is calculated starting from the estimated EPS for the end of 2012 and 2013, available on the *Thomson Reuters* database.

In this example, the price P_t of the share belonging to the *i*th company is observed on the last business day of 2011. In the same manner used by Espinosa and Trombetta (2007), four measures of the ex ante cost of equity capital were assumed based on the forecast earnings of the company, initially by means of the procedures recommended by Gebhart et al. (2001). According to these authors, the price of the company's shares, P_{it}, could be expressed as the book value (bv_t), adding the residual earnings (x_t), discounted from the cost of capital (r_e) of the company, as shown in (3). For the practical purpose of estimating r_e, it is necessary to have an explicit definition of a forecast period. The relationship between the cost of equity capital, future earnings and company's share price at a determined date can be expressed by (15.3):

$$P_{it} = bv_t + \sum_{\tau=1}^{+\infty} \frac{E_t[x_{t+\tau} - r_e bv_{t+\tau-1}]}{(1+r_e)^\tau} \tag{15.3}$$

$$P_{it} = bv_t + \sum_{\tau=1}^{+\infty} \frac{E_t[(ROE_{t+\tau} - r_e)bv_{t+\tau-1}]}{(1+r_e)^\tau} \tag{15.4}$$

where:

bv_t = the book value at time t

E_t [˙] = the expectation based on information available at time t

$x_{t+\tau}$ = the net earnings for the period $t + \tau$

r_e = the cost of equity capital

$ROE_{t+\tau}$ = the return on the net equity of the company for the period $t + \tau$.

Equations (15.3) and (15.4) are identical to the discounted dividend model but express the value of the company in terms of accounting numbers in an infinite series. This limitation requires a "terminal value" (*TV*) to obtain a value of r_e. Therefore, according to Gebhardt et al. (2001), a three-phase approach is used to calculate intrinsic value. First, explicit estimates of earnings were used (a consensus of EPS used by analysts) for the next 3 years (2012–2014). Second, earnings forecasts were obtained for the years 2015 and 2016 by means of a linear interpolation comparing the ROE of the company in question (i) with the moving average of the ROE of the sector for the 5 preceding years ($EPS_{i,2015} = FROE_{i,2015}{*}bv_{2014}$). Finally, for the third step, a total period of 5 years was used to calculate the cost of equity capital, as it addresses the reference period of company evaluations made in Brazil and, according to Espinosa and Trombetta (2007), the results obtained had not differed significantly over a period of 5–15 years. An estimate of the infinite horizon for each company is shown in (15.5):

$$P_t = bv_t + \frac{FROE_{t+1} - r_e}{(1+r_e)} bv_t + \frac{FROE_{t+2} - r_e}{(1+r_e)^2} \widehat{bv}_{t+1} + TV \tag{15.5}$$

where:

bv_t = the book value for year t.

$\widehat{bv}_{t+\tau} = bv_{t+\tau-1} + FEPS_{t+\tau} - FDPS_{t+\tau}$, where *FDPS* is the forecast for dividends per share for year $t + \tau$ estimated using the current payout rate (k). Specifically, it is assumed that $FEPS_{t+\tau} = FEPS{*}k$.

r_e – the estimated cost of capital.

$FROE_{t+\tau}$ = the estimated ROE for year $t + \tau$. For the first 2 years, this variable is calculated as $FRPS_{t+\tau}/bv_{t+\tau-1}$ where FEPS is the average of the EPS estimates gathered from the I/B/E/S platform made available by *Thomson Reuters* for year $t + \tau$ and $bv_{t+\tau-1}$ is the book value per share for year $t + \tau - 1$. Beyond the third year, the FROE is estimated using a linear interpolation with the average ROE for the industry.

For a T horizon, the terminal value is given by (15.6):

$$TV = \sum_{\tau=3}^{T-1} \frac{\widehat{x}_{t+\tau} - r_e}{(1+r_e)^{\tau}} bv_{t+\tau-1} + \frac{FROE - r_e}{r(1+r)^{T-1}} bv_{t+T-1} \tag{15.6}$$

This relation was solved by an iterative process using Mathematica© software and produced an estimate of the ex ante cost of capital (r_{riv}) conditioned by the information currently available. After the proxy suggested by Gebhardt et al. (2001) was calculated, starting from the same data, another three alternative measures were calculated for the ex ante cost of capital based on the procedures detailed by Ohlson and Juettner-Nauroth (2005). In addition to r_{peg} and r_{riv}, two more proxies of the ex ante cost of capital were calculated, one obtained following the Price to Forward Earnings Model (r_{pef}) and the other following the Modified Price to Earnings Growth Model (r_{mpeg}), in accordance with Eqs. (15.7) and (15.8), respectively, shown below:

$$P_t = \frac{\widehat{x}_{t+1} + r_e d_{t+1} + \widehat{x}_{t+2}}{(r_e + 1)^2 - 1} \tag{15.7}$$

$$P_t = \frac{\widehat{x}_{t+2} + r_e d_{t+1} - \widehat{x}_{t+1}}{(r_e)^2} \tag{15.8}$$

Frank and Shen (2016) developed a study to evaluate the relationship between investment levels (high and low) and the measurement of the cost of capital. When the CAPM is used, companies with a high cost of capital invest higher values. When the ICC is used, companies with a high cost of capital invest lower amounts. The authors assert that the implied cost of capital may better reflect the temporal variation of the returns demanded by the shareholders. According to Li, Ng, and Swaminathan (2013), the implied cost of capital may be a good approximation to the expected returns over time. The authors concluded that the ICC strongly predicts future market returns over a period of 1 month to 4 years, and this predictive power is persistent, even at different stages of the business cycles.

Hou et al. (2012) developed two methodologies for calculating the implied cost of capital based on the forecast of future earnings of US companies. The first uses a regression model with the following independent variables: total assets, dividends paid, historical earnings, and discretionary accruals. The second methodology uses the earnings forecast through the projections provided by market analysts. Hou et al. (2012) showed an advantage in using the econometric model, though is not possible to discard the analysts' projection as proxy of the cost of capital, according to the results pointed out in Li, Ng, and Swaminathan (2013) and Frank and Shen (2016). Gasparini (2015) shows that there is a reduction in the cost of equity due to the adoption of the provisions of IFRS in Brazil in 2010. The conclusion was that Easton's model (2004) was adequate to evaluate the cost of capital of publicly held companies compared to other figures of equity models.

Accounting Policy

Accruals are defined as the difference between net earnings and the net operating cash flow; i.e., they are accounts that can affect the amount of earnings without necessarily changing the amount of cash in hand (cash and cash equivalents) and can be divided into discretionary accruals and non-discretionary accruals. In the opinion of Martinez (2008), there is nothing wrong with not recording accruals unless the manager increases or decreases them with the objective of changing earnings. The intention of this procedure is to enable a distinction to be made between aggressive and conservative companies, such as that adopted in the Espinosa and Trombetta (2007) study, which departs from the procedure proposed by Dechow et al. (1995) which effectively addresses the modified Jones model. Once the classification of the companies was completed, the discretionary accruals for the *i*th company were calculated (DA_i) as follows:

$$\mathrm{Cons}_{i\tau}\begin{cases} DA_{i\tau} > 0 \rightarrow \mathrm{Cons} = 1\ (\mathrm{agressive}) \\ DA_{i\tau} < 0 \rightarrow \mathrm{Cons} = 0\ (\mathrm{conservative}) \end{cases}$$

The modified Jones model uses a variation of net revenue and the value of the fixed assets, starting from the assumption that non-discretionary accruals depend on these variables that are measured according to the total assets. The modified Jones model seeks to measure total discretionary accruals (current or noncurrent) using the variables that comprise (15.9) as described by Dechow et al. (1995).

$$\mathrm{NDA}_{it} = \beta_1\left(\frac{1}{\mathrm{Assets}_{it-1}}\right) + \beta_2\left(\frac{\Delta\mathrm{Rev}_{it}}{\mathrm{Assets}_{it-1}} - \frac{\Delta\mathrm{Rec}_{it}}{\mathrm{Assets}_{it-1}}\right) + \beta_3\left(\frac{Ppe_{it-1}}{\mathrm{Assets}_{it-1}}\right) + \varepsilon_{it} \tag{15.9}$$

where:

NDA_{it} = non-discretionary accruals of firm *i* in year *t*

$\Delta\mathrm{Rev}_{it}$ = the variation in the gross revenue of firm *i* between the years t and t − 1

$\Delta\mathrm{Rec}_{it}$ = the variation in accounts receivable (customers) of firm i between the years *t* and t− 1

Ppe_{it} = the fixed assets of firm *i* in year *t*

Assets_{it-1} = the total assets of firm *i* in year t − 1

ε_{it} = the regression residuals of the *i*th firm in year *t*

β_1, β_2,β_3 = specific parameters of the *i*-th firm

By using the estimates of the parameters β_1, β_2, and β_3 in (15.9), we can obtain DA_{it} according to 15.10 as follows (Espinosa and Trombetta 2007):

$$DA_{it} = \frac{TA_{it}}{\text{Assets}_{it-1}} - \hat{\beta}_1\left(\frac{1}{\text{Assets}_{it-1}}\right) - \hat{\beta}_2\left(\frac{\Delta\text{Rev}_{it}}{\text{Assets}_{it-1}} - \frac{\Delta\text{Rec}_{it}}{\text{Assets}_{it-1}}\right) - \hat{\beta}_3\left(\frac{Ppe_{it-1}}{\text{Assets}_{it-1}}\right) \quad (15.10)$$

The total accruals are calculated on the basis of the balance sheet approach, which is set out in (15.11):

$$TA_{it} = \frac{\Delta CA_{it} - \Delta CL_{it} - \Delta\text{Cash}_{it} + \Delta\text{Std}_{it} - \text{Dep}_{it}}{\text{Assets}_{it-1}} \quad (15.11)$$

where:

ΔCA = the variation in the amount of current assets
ΔCL = the variation in the amount of current liabilities
ΔCash = the variation in the amount of cash in hand (and cash equivalents)
ΔStd = the variation in the amount of short-term financing and loans
Dep = *depreciation* and amortization expenses
Assets = total assets

Discretionary accruals (*DA*) are based on the calculation of the difference between total accruals (*TA*) and non-discretionary accruals (*NDA*) following the procedure of DeAngelo (1986) adopted by Jones (1991, p. 207). As a matter of fact, the total accruals of a previous period ($\tau - k$) are used as a measure of normal total accruals. Abnormal accruals (ΔTA) are defined as the difference between the current total accrual and the normal total accrual, which in turn can be broken down into discretionary accruals (*DA*) and non-discretionary accruals (*NDA*), as shown in (15.12):

$$TA_{it} = NDA_{it} + DA_{it} \therefore DA_{it} = TA_{it} - NDA_{it} \quad (15.12)$$

Other Independent Variables

The ex ante cost of capital is only an empirical proxy for the non-observable cost of equity capital. According to Espinosa and Trombetta (2007, p. 1383), Gebhardt et al. (2001), and Hail (2002), one means of justifying the validity of this proxy is to study its relationship to other variables that reflect the firm's risk factors as perceived by investors. Therefore, the chosen control variables are derived from works found in the literature. The following risk characteristics were considered in the analyses using a specific rationale.

Leverage: The cost of equity capital is an increasing function of the amount of debt in the capital structure of the firm, considering that the debt increases the volatility of future earnings. Several works document this assumption, e.g., Hail (2002), Espinosa and Trombetta (2007), Botosan and Plumlee (2002), and Gebhardt et al. (2001).

Beta: The CAPM (capital asset pricing model) suggests that the non-diversifiable risk coefficient (systematic) of a share could be positively correlated with the firm's cost of capital. Previous studies are not unanimous in showing this relationship in a consistent manner, as in the study of Gebhardt et al. (2001), whereas others, such as Hail (2002), confirm the positive relationship. In this research, the beta of each share was obtained by using a market model, assuming that at least 12 observations of monthly returns are necessary over 60 months up to month *t*.

Size: The size of the firm was used as a proxy of information availability on the assumption that information is more available in large companies than smaller companies. Following this line of thought, if the company provides more information, future earnings tend to be perceived by investors and analysts as less risky, which implies a lower cost of capital. As Espinosa and Trombetta (2007) observe, this effect could be stronger in developing markets. Therefore, the expectation is a lower cost of capital for large companies than for smaller ones. The natural logarithm of the capitalization of the firm in the market in 2011 was used as a proxy of the size of the firm.

Specification of the Model

To test the existence of a significant association between the ex ante cost of capital and disclosure, the OLS (ordinary least squares) method was used by means of the model shown in (15.13).

$$\begin{aligned} r_{it} = \alpha &+ \varphi_1 \text{Disclosure}_{it-1} + \varphi_2 \text{Beta}_{it} + \varphi_3 \text{Leverage}_{it-1} \\ &+ \varphi_4 \text{lnMkt}t\text{Value}_{it-1} + \varphi_5 \text{Agressiveness}_{it-1} + \varepsilon_{it} \end{aligned} \tag{15.13}$$

where:

r_{it} = the proxy for the ex-ante cost of capital ($r_{\text{pef}}, r_{\text{peg}}, r_{\text{mpeg}}, r_{\text{riv}}$).

Disclosure = the *proxy* for voluntary disclosure via the web indicator (*eDisc, IGov, IFin*).

Beta = the *coefficient* of systematic risk.

Leverage = the *financial* leverage index.

lnMarket Value = the *natural* logarithm of market capitalization

Aggressiveness = the *dummy* variable that assumes a value of 1 for aggressive companies (positive discretionary accruals, i.e., $DA_{i\tau} > 0$) and 0 otherwise. The standardized *DA* value in z-scores was used.

Table 15.2 Descriptive statistics for estimates of the implicit ex ante cost of capital

					Percentile			
Variable	N	Mean	Min.	Q_1	Q_2	Q_3	Max.	Std dev.
r_{peg}	128	0.146	0.037	0.109	0.138	0.175	0.529	0.062
r_{pef}	73	0.084	0.006	0.056	0.078	0.107	0.363	0.047
r_{mpeg}	68	0.145	0.067	0.113	0.132	0.161	0.414	0.057
r_{riv}	44	0.173	0.007	0.041	0.085	0.158	3.088	0.459

Source: Authors' calculations
Notes: r_{pef} is the estimate obtained from the Price to Forward Earnings Model, r_{peg} is obtained from the Price to Earnings Growth Model, and r_{mpeg} is derived from the Modified Price to Earnings Growth Model. All of these estimates are obtained by means of the use of some restrictive assumptions for the parameter used to evaluate the Abnormal Earnings Growth Model

Table 15.3 Descriptive statistics of the independent variables

				Percentile				
Variable	N	Mean	Min.	25	50	75	Max.	Std dev.
Disclosure index eDisc	128	247.75	0	204.08	251.05	301.43	354.10	68.96
Disclosure index I_Fin	128	120.29	0	105.83	124.10	139.10	155.80	29.41
Disclosure index I_Gov	128	127.46	0	97.65	130.65	160.50	198.30	43.51
Beta risk coefficient	128	0.90	−0.20	0.60	0.90	1.18	1.80	0.39
Financial leverage	128	1.696	−52.37	1.529	2.100	3.041	30.677	8.415
Ln market capitalization	128	14.67	12.17	13.78	14.64	15.44	18.28	1.18

Source: Authors' calculations
Notes: This table shows the descriptive statistics of the independent variables used in the research

Discussion

With regard to the empirical results attained, initially the estimate of the cost of capital highlighted by the method adopted in the model for r_{pef} (the lower of the four calculations) suggests that, on average, the cost of capital was in the region of 8.4%, as shown in Table 15.2.

Table 15.3 shows the descriptive statistics of the independent variables adopted in the research.

Table 15.4 shows the matrix correlations between the variables (dependent and independent) used in the study. Note that among the various proxies for the ex ante cost of capital, only mpeg was significantly correlated with two others, r_{peg} and r_{pef}. This finding suggests a certain independence between these metrics.

Table 15.4 Correlation matrix between the variables studied

	r_{riv}	r_{peg}	r_{pef}	r_{mpeg}	*eDisc*	*I_Fin*	*I_Gov*	*Beta*	*Lev*	*lnMktVal*	*DAGG*
r_{riv}											
r_{peg}	0.132										
r_{pef}	−0.16	0.085									
r_{mpeg}	−0.02	0.280**	0.742***								
eDisc	−0.13	0.066	−0.038	−0.019							
I_Fin	−0.05	0.089	−0.038	−0.08	0.919***						
I_Gov	−0.16	0.044	−0.035	0.017	0.964***	0.781***					
Beta	0.002	0.241***	−0.033	−0.02	−0.016	−0.004	−0.023				
Lev	−0.02	−0.061	0.109	0.106	0.128	0.132	0.114	−0.04			
lnMktVal	−0.17	−0.286***	−0.148	−0.159	0.086	0.079	0.083	0.057	0.086		
DAGG	−0.10	0.037	0.197*	−0.005	−0.009	0.021	−0.029	−0.02	−0.16*	−0.103	
NM	0.093	0.024	−0.21*	−0.293**	0.028	0.011	0.036	0.036	−0.096	−0.179**	0.259***

Source: Authors' calculations
*$p < 0.1$; **$p < 0.05$; ***$p < 0.01$

Table 15.5 Estimated parameters for the ex ante cost of equity capital

	Proxies of ex-ante cost of capital					
Independent variables	r_{pef}		r_{peg}		r_{mpeg}	
Constant	0.195	***	0.349	***	0.343	***
	(0.072)		(0.068)		(0.093)	
1. Beta risk coefficient	−0.002		0.041	***	−0.008	
	(0.013)		(0.013)		(0.016)	
2. Financial leverage	0.001		0.000		0.001	
	(0.001)		(0.001)		(0.001)	
3. Ln market capitalization	−0.007		−0.016	***	−0.012	*
	(0.005)		(0.005)		(0.006)	
4. Aggressiveness (discretionary accruals)	0.030	**	0.002		0.012	
	(0.011)		(0.011)		(0.014)	
5. New Market listing	−0.033	***	−0.006		−0.044	***
	(0.012)		(0.011)		(0.015)	
R^2 adjusted	0.115		0.116		0.095	
N	73		128		68	
F	2.871	**	4.335	***	2.403	**
Akaike information criterion (AIC)	−240.29		−357.5		−197.5	

Source: Authors' calculations

Notes: This table shows a summary of the estimated parameters (regression by the OLS method) for three cost of equity capital proxies: r_{pef}, r_{peg}, and r_{mpeg} (no significant parameters for the proxy r_{rif} were obtained). r_{pef} is the estimate obtained from the Price to Forward Earnings Model, r_{peg} is obtained from the Price to Earnings Growth Model, and r_{mpeg} is derived from the Modified Price to Earnings Growth Model. All of these estimates are obtained using some restrictive assumptions for the parameter of the evaluation of the Abnormal Earnings Growth Model. $^{*}p < 0.1$; $^{**}p < 0.05$; $^{***}p < 0.01$. The bracketed figures are the standard error in the estimate of the coefficient of each independent variable

Among disclosures via corporate website proxies, none showed an association with any of the metrics of the cost of capital. However, the listing of the firm on the $[B]^3$'s New Market, the fourth disclosure proxy, showed significant correlation coefficients with r_{pef} and r_{mpeg}. These results may suggest that a greater propensity to provide corporate information via the corporate website does not entail a decrease in the cost of capital.

A more aggressive accounting policy expressed by discretionary accruals (*DA*) shows the correlation of only one cost of capital metric, r_{pef}. With regard to the regression analysis, it should be considered that for the fit diagnosis of the estimated regressions, the metrics adjusted R-squared, Akaike information criterion (AIC), and the significance of the F statistic were employed and are reported in the lower portion of Table 15.5 for each estimated model. Statistics for evaluation of multicollinearity, i.e., VIF (variance inflation factor) and tolerance were examined, and no findings suggested the existence of problems of this nature in any of the models reported in Table 15.5.

In the case of the estimated regressions, none of the three Internet disclosure proxies (*eDisc*, *Igov*, and *Ifin*) showed estimates of significant parameters when

Table 15.6 Regressions for the ex ante cost of capital

	Aggressiveness of the firm			
Independent variables	Conservative		Aggressive	
Constant	0.176	***	0.240	
	(0.062)		(0.151)	
1. Beta risk coefficient	−0.024	*	0.010	
	(0.014)		(0.022	
2. Financial leverage	0.000		0.002	
	(0.001)		(0.002)	
3. Market capitalization index	−0.005		−0.008	
	(0.004)		(0.010)	
4. New Market listing	−0.020	*	−0.053	**
	(0.010)		(0.024)	
R^2 adjusted	0.099		0109	
N	40		33	
F	2.210	**	2.102	**

Source: Authors' calculations

Notes: This table shows the results of the OLS regressions setting the ex ante cost of capital as a dependent variable to the r_{pef} proxy (the only variable for which disclosure and aggressiveness were simultaneously significant). The second column shows the estimated coefficients when considering only the subgroup of companies classified as conservative. The third column shows the estimates for the subgroup of companies classified as aggressive. Comparing the results in this table provides indications that supporting the idea that consideration of company accounting policy is a relevant variable for testing the existence of associations between the cost of capital and corporate disclosure, taking into account the increase (and greater significance) of the independent variable coefficient, New Market listing (disclosure proxy), when considering the aggressive companies

regressed against any of the four metrics of the cost of capital, r_{rif}, r_{pef}, r_{peg}, and r_{mpeg}. However, as shown by Table 15.6, the proxy of the cost of capital that obtained results from the explanatory model closest to the idea of negative association of the level of disclosure was r_{pef}, even though the most aggressive companies tend to experience a greater level of demand for return by investors. Note that on average, the companies listed on the New Market obtained estimated values for their cost of capital that were 3.3% points lower ($\widehat{\varphi_5} \approx -0.033; p < 0.01$) than companies listed outside this special [B][3] segment.

Furthermore, on average, the companies judged to be more aggressive showed a cost of capital 3% points above the companies judged to be conservative. This result supports the notion that a greater willingness to provide corporate information reduces the cost of capital and, furthermore, that this relationship is more significant among aggressive companies ($\widehat{\varphi_4} \approx 0.03; p < 0.05$). With regard to the explanatory model of r_{peg}, a positive and significant association of the beta coefficient of the firm with the cost of capital measured by this proxy was found ($\widehat{\varphi_1} \approx 0.041; p < 0.01$), suggesting, as indicated in the literature, a positive correlation between the systematic risk coefficient of the firm with its cost of equity capital.

These results support the indications found by Lopes and Alencar (2010) in the Brazilian market, although those authors only considered companies with the highest liquidity on the stock market, which in itself could constitute a bias in the selection because trade ability is associated with company size. Moreover, in the explanatory model of r_{peg} (Table 15.5), it is noted that larger companies (ln *Market Capitalization*) obtained a lower cost of capital ($\widehat{\varphi_1} \approx -0.016; p < 0.01$), thus also supporting the argument of Espinosa and Trombetta (2007) that firm size is a proxy for information availability and thus the tendency for future earnings to be perceived as less risky by investors, leading to less discounting of the firm's future cash flows.

Furthermore, according to these authors, this relationship would be more pronounced in developing markets such as Brazil. On considering the explanatory model of proxy r_{mpeg} as estimated for r_{pef}, a positive signal was found for the estimated coefficient of the New Market variable ($\widehat{\varphi_1} \approx -0.041$; $p < 0.01$). In addition, similarly to that found in the estimates obtained for the explanatory model of r_{peg}, the size of the firm, expressed by market capitalization, was found to be significantly and negatively associated with the cost of capital ($\widehat{\varphi_3} \approx -0.012$; $p < 0.1$), supporting the arguments of Espinosa and Trombetta (2007) for the validity of company size as a proxy for the availability of information to the market, as previously discussed in the results obtained for the explanatory model of r_{peg}.

Table 15.6 is presented to discuss the assertion of Espinosa and Trombetta (2007) on the complementarity between the choices of accounting policy and voluntary corporate disclosure, according to which exclusive focus on only one of these channels of communication could compromise the results of tests of the association between disclosure and cost of capital (Dhaliwal et al. 1979).

In other words, from finding associations with a small marginal effect to insignificant signals, works on this association could suffer from omitted variable bias. In fact, the results reported on Table 15.5 indicate that, considering the subgroup of companies classified as conservative, and the cost of capital measured by proxy r_{pef}, the marginal effect of the New Market listing is less than that found for this variable for the subgroup of companies classified as aggressive. Furthermore, among the aggressive companies, the coefficient is greater and more significant. This result supports the argument of Espinosa and Trombetta (2007) on the relevance of considering the aggressiveness of the firm in tests of a negative relationship between disclosure and the cost of capital.

Future Directions

Starting from the assumption that corporate disclosure could be significantly associated with the firm's cost of capital as advocated by Diamond and Verrechia (1991) and Easly and O'Hara (2004), the objective of this study was to confirm the existence of associations between voluntary disclosure and the ex ante cost of equity capital (so-called ICC) of the firm. The main contribution of this research is supported by the paucity of research on the various means of estimating the ex ante cost of equity capital as well as its relation with disclosure via the corporate website, especially when considering emerging economies such as Brazil.

According to Gietzmann and Trombetta (2003), firms could reduce the component of adverse selection in their cost of capital by following two channels of communication: first, by choosing a specific accounting policy from the alternatives offered by the accounting rules (Dechow et al. 2010) and, second, by choosing a level of disclosure of relevant corporate information (Botosan and Plumlee 2002).

In the same manner as that adopted by Espinosa and Trombetta (2007), Gietzmann and Trombetta (2003) advocated that these two channels of communication could interact insofar as the choice of disclosure could depend significantly on the choice of accounting policy. Therefore, according to these authors, firms that adopt conservative accounting policies may deem it unnecessary to provide high levels of disclosure due to having pursued an accounting policy that is less prone to financial crises. Alternatively, firms that adopt aggressive accounting policies could use additional channels of disclosure as a means of mitigating the negative effect that their choice of accounting policy may have in a capital market environment. To conduct these tests, data were used from 128 companies listed in Brazil, on [B][3], at the end of 2011. From a review of the literature, using dependent variables, 4 different metrics of disclosure were adopted, 3 through the corporate website, considering the relevance of 40 items of corporate information in accordance with the opinion of the market analysts registered with the stock exchange and New Market listings as proxies of disclosure. Accordingly, for greater robustness, four different methods of calculating the ex ante cost of equity capital were employed.

In the case of the empirical results of this research, it should be emphasized that of the four variables intended to express the ex ante cost of capital, only three showed parameters indicative of the significance of the model. Therefore, when the estimates for the proxy r_{pef} are observed, indications of the negative association between corporate disclosure (only when the New Market listing was assumed as a proxy of disclosure) and the aggressiveness of the firm are found, confirming the results and arguments of Espinosa and Trombetta (2007), who stated that these two channels of communication (corporate disclosure and accounting policy) must be considered jointly in the models because otherwise an omitted variable bias is incurred, resulting in nonsignificant parameters for the negative association between disclosure and the cost of capital. To summarize, on average, companies listed in the differentiated corporate governance segment, known as the New Market, and classified as conservative reduced their cost of capital by 6% points. Nonetheless, in opposition to the argument of some works in the recent literature, e.g., Mendes-Da-Silva et al. (2009) and Mendes-Da-Silva and Onusic (2012), or even guidelines issued by regulatory agencies around the world, e.g., FASB (2000) and the CMVM (Securities Commission) (2000), on the existence of a negative relationship between disclosure via the corporate website and the firm's cost of capital, none of the disclosure variables obtained a significant and negative signal when regressed against any of the four cost of capital metrics. One interpretation of this finding is that investors do not attach sufficient importance to the use of the website by the company for investor relations activities and use other sources of corporate information or even advice on the allocation of assets from professional investment guidance services.

In view of the relevance of the field research examined here, it is worth noting the limitations of this study. Given that websites do not have long-term memories (or files), it is difficult to analyze consistently the evolution of each firm's disclosure over time, which makes it difficult to conduct longitudinal studies. With regard to the coverage of Brazilian market analysts, few companies are the target of future analyst estimates, which makes the ex ante cost of capital difficult to obtain unless the four methodologies employed here are taken into consideration. Other dimensions that require investigation can be noted, such as the following: (i) an analysis of the history of propensity toward corporate disclosure, such as the makeup of the board of directors, (ii) a comparative analysis of the propensity of controlled and family-managed companies to provide financial information on their corporate websites and the impact of such disclosure on the firm's cost of capital, (iii) an asymmetric cross-industry investigation into the willingness to provide information to the market, and (iv) an analysis of the questions discussed in this study using a comparative approach to explore differences between institutional environments.

References

Artiach, T. C., & Clarkson, P. M. (2011). Disclosure, conservatism and the cost of equity capital: A review of the foundation literature. *Accounting & Finance, 51*(1), 2–49.

Ashton, D., & Wang, P. (2013). Terminal valuations, growth rates and the implied cost of capital. *Review of Accounting Studies, 18*(1), 261–290.

Babío, M. R., Muíño, M. F., & Vidal, R. (2003). La actitud de lãs empresas cotizadas ante la presentación de la información voluntária. Uma referencia a la naturaleza de la información. *Revista Europea de Dirección y Economía de la Empresa, 17*.

Baiman, S., & Verrecchia, R. (1996). The relation among capital markets, financial disclosure, production efficiency, and insider trading. *Journal of Accounting Research, 34*(1), 1–22.

Botosan, C. A. (1997). Disclosure level and the cost of equity capital. *The Accounting Review, 72* (3), 323–349.

Botosan, C. A., & Plumlee, M. A. (2002). A re-examination of disclosure level and the expected cost of equity capital. *Journal of Accounting Research, 40*(1), 21–40.

Carvalho, F. A., & Castro, M. R. (2016). A Brazilian perspective on Macropudential and monetary policy interaction. In L. I. Jacome, Y. Carriere-Swallow, H. Faruqee, & K. Srinivasan (Eds.), *Challenges for central banking: Perspectives from Latin America*. Washington, DC: International Monetary Fund (IMF).

Chen, Z., Dhaliwal, D. S., & Xie, H. (2010). Regulation fair disclosure and the cost of equity capital. *Review of Accounting Studies, 15*(1), 106–144.

Cheynel. (2013). A theory of voluntary disclosure and cost of capital. *Review of Accounting Studies, 18*(4), 987–1020.

Cho, C. H., & Roberts, R. W. (2010). Environmental reporting on the internet by America's Toxic 100: Legitimacy and self-presentation. *International Journal of Accounting Information Systems, 11*(1), 1–16.

Claus, J., & Thomas, J. (2001). Equity Premia as Low as Three Percent? Evidence from Analysts' Earnings Forecasts for Domestic and International Stock Markets. *The Journal of Finance, 56* (5), 1629–1666.

Comissão De Mercados De Valores Mobiliários. (2000). Entendimentos e Recomendações da CMVM Sobre a Utilização da Internet.

Copeland, T. E., Weston, J. F., & Shastri, K. (2005). *Financial theory and corporate policy* (4th ed.). Boston: Pearson.
Craven, B. M., & Martson, C. L. (1999). Financial reporting on the internet by leading UK companies. *European Accounting Review, 8*(2), 321–333.
DeAngelo, L. E. (1986). Accounting numbers as market valuation substitutes: A study of management buyouts of public stockholders. *The Accounting Review, 61*(3), 400–420.
Dechow, P. M., Sloan, R. G., & Sweeney, A. P. (1995). Detecting earnings management. *The Accounting Review, 70*(2), 193–225.
Dechow, P., Ge, W., & Schrand, C. (2010). Understanding earnings quality: A review of the proxies, their determinants and their consequences. *Journal of Accounting and Economics, 50* (2&3), 344–401.
Déjean, F., & Martinez, I. (2009). Environmental disclosure and the cost of equity: The French case. *Accounting in Europe, 6*(1), 57–80.
Dhaliwal, D., Krull, L., & Li, O. Z. (2007). Did the 2003 Tax Act reduce the cost of equity capital?. *Journal of Accounting and Economics, 43*(1), 121–150.
Dhaliwal, D. S., Spicer, B. H., & Vickrey, D. (1979). The Quality Of Disclosure And The Cost Of Capital. *Journal of Business Finance & Accounting, Summer, 6*(2), 245–266.
Diamond, D. W., & Verrechia, R. (1991). Disclosure, liquidity and cost of equity capital. *The Journal of Finance, 46*(4), 1325–1360.
Dittmar, R. F., & Lundblad, C. T. (2017). Firm characteristics, consumption risk, and firm-level risk exposures. *Journal of Financial Economics, 125*(2), 326–343.
Dye, R. A. (1985). Disclosure of non proprietary information. *Journal of Accounting Research, 23* (1), 123–145.
Easton, P. (2006). Use of Forecasts of Earnings to Estimate and Compare Cost of Capital Across Regimes. *Journal of Business Finance & Accounting, 33*(3–4), 374–394.
Easton, P. D., & Sommers, G. A. (2007). Effect of Analysts' Optimism on Estimates of the Expected Rate of Return Implied by Earnings Forecasts. *Journal of Accounting Research, 45*(5), 983–1015.
Easly, D., & O'Hara, M. (2004). Information and cost of capital. *The Journal of Finance, 59*(4), 1553–1583.
Elton, E. J. (1999). Expected returns, realized returns and asset pricing tests. *The Journal of Finance, 54*(4), 1199–1220.
Espinosa, M., & Trombetta, M. (2007). Disclosure interactions and the cost of equity capital: Evidence from the Spanish continuous market. *Journal of Business Finance & Accounting, 34* (9), 1371–1392.
Fama, E., & French, K. (2002). Testing Trade-Off and Pecking Order Predictions about Dividends and Debt. *The Review of Financial Studies, 15*(1), 1–33.
FASB-Financial Accounting Standards Board. (2000). Electronic distribution of business reporting information. Available at: http://www.fasb.org/brrp/brrp1.shtml. Accessed May 29 2018.
Francis, J. R., Khurana, I. K., & Pereira, R. (2005). Disclosure incentives and effects on cost of capital around the world. *Accounting Review, 80*(4), 1125–1162.
Francis, J., Nanda, D., & Olsson, P. (2008). Voluntary Disclosure, Earnings Quality, and Cost of Capital. *Journal of Accounting Research, 46*(1), 53–99.
Frank, M. Z., & Shen, T. (2016). Investment and the weighted average cost of capital. *Journal of Financial Economics, 119*(2), 300–315.
Gajewski, J. F. (2015). Can internet-based disclosure reduce information asymmetry? *Advances in Accounting, 31*(1), 115–124.
Gallhofer, S., Haslam, J., Monk, E., & Roberts, C. (2007). The emancipator potential of online reporting: The case of counter accounting. *Accounting, Auditing & Accountability Journal, 19* (5), 681–718.
Garay, U., González, M., Guzmán, A., & Trujillo, M. A. (2013). Internet-based corporate disclosure and market value: Evidence from Latin America. *Emerging Markets Review, 17*, 150–168.

Gasparini, V. M. R. (2015). A adoção completa do IFRS e seus impactos no custo de capital próprio, calculados a partir de modelos de custo implícito de capital. Master's Dissertation, Faculdade de Economia, Administração e Contabilidade de Ribeirão Preto, University of São Paulo, Ribeirão Preto. https://doi.org/10.11606/D.96.2015.tde-21072015-102627. Retrieved 2018-05-29, from http://www.teses.usp.br

Gebhardt, W. R., Lee, C. M., & Swaminathan, B. (2001). Toward an implied cost-of-capital. *Journal of Accounting Research, 39*(1), 135–176.

Gietzmann, M., & Ireland, J. (2005). Cost of capital, strategic disclosures and accounting choice. *Journal of Business Finance and Accounting, 32*(3), 559–634.

Gietzmann, M., & Trombetta, M. (2003). Disclosure interactions: Accounting policy choice and voluntary disclosure effects on the cost of rising outside capital. *Accounting and Business Research, 33*(3), 187–205.

Giner, B. (1997). The influence of company characteristics and accounting regulations on information disclosed by Spanish firms. *European Accounting Review, 6*(1), 45–68.

Gordon, J. R., Gordon, M. J. (1997). The Finite Horizon Expected Return Model. *Financial Analysts Journal, 53*(3), 52–61

Graham, J. R., Harvey, C. R., & Rajgopal, S. (2005). The economic implications of corporate financial reporting. *Journal of Accounting and Economics, 40*(1), 3–73.

Gray, S. J., Radebaugh, L. H., & Roberts, C. B. (1990). International perceptions of cost constraints on voluntary information disclosures: A comparative study of UK and US multinationals. *Journal of International Business Studies, 21*(4), 597–622.

Grossman, S. (1981). The role of warranties and private disclosure about product quality. *Journal of Law and Economics, 24*(3), 461–483.

Hail, L., & Leuz,C. (2006). International Differences in the Cost of Equity Capital: Do Legal Institutions and Securities Regulation Matter?. *Journal of Accounting Research, 44*(3), 485–531.

Hail, L. (2002). The impact of voluntary corporate disclosure on the ex-ante cost of capital for Swiss firms. *The European Accounting Review, 11*(4), 741–773.

Hayes, R., & Lundholm, R. (1996). Segment reporting to the capital market in the presence of a competitor. *Journal of Accounting Research, 34*(2), 261–279.

Healy, P., Hutton, A., & Palepu, K. (1999). Stock performance and intermediation changes surrounding sustained increases in disclosure. *Contemporary Accounting Research, 16*(3), 485–520.

Hedlin, P. (1999). The internet as a vehicle for investor relations: The Swedish case. *European Accounting Review, 8*(2), 373–379.

Hou, K., van Dijk, M. A., & Zhang, Y. (2012). The implied cost of capital: A new approach. *Journal of Accounting and Economics, 53*(3), 504–526.

Jenkinson, T. (2006). Regulation and the cost of capital. In: M. Crew, & D. Parker, *International handbook on economic regulation*. Cambridge MA, Edward Elgar. ISBN 978.1843766711.

Jensen, M. C., & Meckling, W. H. (1976). Theory of the firm: Managerial behavior, agency costs and ownership structure. *Journal of Financial Economics, 3*(4), 305–360.

Jones, J. J. (1991). Earnings management during import relief investigations. *Journal of Accounting Research, 29*(2), 193–228.

Lattemann, C. (2005). The Use of ICT in Annual Shareholder Meetings and Investor Relations: An Examination of the German Stock Market. *Corporate Reputation Review, 8*(2), 110–120.

Li, Y., Ng, T., & Swaminathan, B. (2013). Predicting market returns using aggregate implied cost of capital. *Journal of Financial Economics, 110*(2), 419–436.

Lopes, A. B., & Alencar, R. C. (2010). Disclosure and cost of equity capital in emerging markets: The Brazilian case. *International Journal of Accounting, 45*(4), 443–464.

Malarvizhi, P., & Yadav, S. (2009). Corporate Environmental Disclosures on the Internet: An Empirical Analysis of Indian Companies. *Issues in Social & Environmental Accounting, 2*(2), 211–232.

Marr, B., & Gray, D. (2002). Measuring intellectual capital – The internal and external drivers for measuring and reporting the intangibles of an organization. In *Proceedings of the Transparent Enterprise. The Value of Intangibles, Conference,* Madrid, November 2002

Martinez, A. L. (2008). Detectando *Earnings Management* no Brasil: Estimando os *Accruals* Discricionários. *Revista de Contabilidade e Finanças, 19*(46), 7–17.

Mendes-Da-Silva, W., & Onusic, L. M. (2012). Corporate e-disclosure determinants: Evidence from the Brazilian market. *International Journal of Disclosure and Governance.* https://doi.org/10.1057/jdg.2012.14.

Mendes-Da-Silva, W., Ferraz-Andrade, J. M., Famá, R., & Maluf Filho, J. A. (2009). Disclosure Via Website Corporativo: Um Exame De Informações Financeiras e de Governança no Mercado Brasileiro. *Revista de Administração de Empresas, 49*(2), 190–205.

Malkiel, B. G. (1979). The capital formation problem in the United States. *Journal of Finance, 34*(2), 291–306.

Milgrom, P. (1981). Good news and bad news: Representation theorems and applications. *Bell Journal of Economics, 12*(2), 380–391.

Noack, D. (1997). Web pages help build investor relations. *Investors' Bus Daily, 10,* A1.

Ohlson, J. A., & Juettner-Nauroth, B. (2005). Expected EPS and EPS growth as determinants of value. *Review of Accounting Studies, 10*(2 & 3), 349–365.

Paisey, C., & Paisey, N. J. (2006). And they all lived happily ever after? Exploring the possibilities of mobilizing the internet to promote a more enabling accounting for occupational pension schemes. *Accounting, Auditing & Accounting Journal, 19*(5), 719–758.

Pástor, L., Sinha, M., & Swaminathan, B. (2008). Estimating the intertemporal risk-return tradeoff using the implied cost of capital. *Journal of Finance, 63*(6), 2859–2897.

Patten, D. M., & Crampton, W. (2003). Legitimacy and the internet: An examination of corporate web page environmental disclosures. In *Advances in environmental accounting & management* (Advances in environmental accounting & management, Vol. 2, pp. 31–57). Emerald Group Publishing Limited. https://www.emeraldinsight.com/doi/abs/10.1016/S1479-3598%2803%2902002-8.

Petravick, S., & Guillet, J. (1998). Distribution earnings reports on the internet. *Management Accounting, 80,* 54–56.

Richardson, A., & Welker, M. (2001). Social disclosure, financial disclosure and the cost of equity capital. *Accounting Organisations and Society, 26*(7&8), 597–616.

Sánchez, I. M. G., Domínguez, L. R., & Álvarez, I. G. (2011). Corporate governance and strategic information on the internet. *Accounting, Auditing & Accountability Journal, 24*(4), 471–501.

Scott, T. W. (1994). Incentives and disincentives for financial disclosure: Voluntary disclosure of defined benefit pension plan information by Canadian firms. *The Accounting Review, 69*(1), 26–43.

Souissi, M., & Khlif, H. (2012). Meta-analytic review of disclosure level and cost of equity capital. *International Journal of Accounting and Information Management, 20*(1), 49–62.

Verrecchia, R. E. (1983). Discretionary disclosure. *Journal of Accounting and Economics, 5*(1), 179–194.

Wang, K., Sewon, O., & Claiborne, M. C. (2008). Determinants and consequences of voluntary disclosure in an emerging market: Evidence from China. *Journal of International Accounting, Auditing and Taxation, 17*(1), 14–30.

Xiao, J. Z., Yang, H., & Chow, C. W. (2004). The determinants and characteristics of voluntary internet-based disclosures by listed Chinese companies. *Journal of Accounting and Public Policy, 23*(3), 191–225.

Yermack, D. (2017). Corporate governance and blockchains. *Review of Finance,* 7–31. https://doi.org/10.1093/rof/rfw074.

Zhang, L., & Ding, S. (2006). The effect of increased disclosure on cost of capital: Evidence from China. *Review of Quantitative Finance and Accounting, 27*(4), 383–401.

Chapter 16
Stock Exchange Listing and Capital Budgeting Practices

Wesley Mendes-Da-Silva and Richard Saito

Abstract This chapter compares capital budgeting techniques employed in listed and unlisted companies. We surveyed the chief financial officers (CFOs) of 398 listed companies and 300 large unlisted companies, and based on 91 respondents, the results suggest that the CFOs of listed companies tend to use less simplistic methods more often, for example: NPV and CAPM; while CFOs of unlisted companies are less likely to estimate the cost of equity, despite being large companies. These findings indicate that stock exchange listings may require greater sophistication of the capital budgeting process.

Keywords Capital budgeting · Finance survey · Financial decisions · Corporate finance

JEL Code G31 · G34 · C91

Studies that use surveys can contribute to knowledge creation in Finance, due to the possibility of obtaining data often unavailable elsewhere (Rea and Parker 1997; Baker and Mukherjee 2007; Neuhauser 2007). There are important issues concerning financial decisions that remain scarcely investigated, especially in the emerging markets (Lazardis 2004; Hermes et al. 2007; Andor et al. 2015). Among such financial decisions, capital budgeting is a significant topic, regarding practices adopted by financial managers to determine which projects might maximize shareholder value. In recent years, authors such as Levine (1997) have indicated

---

Portions of this chapter appeared in the 2014 paper "Stock Exchange Listing Induces Sophistication of Capital Budgeting", *Revista de Administracao de Empresas*, vol 54, pp560–574.

W. Mendes-Da-Silva (✉)
Sao Paulo School of Business Administration (FGV/EAESP), Sao Paulo, SP, Brazil

University of Texas at Austin, Austin, TX, USA

R. Saito
Department of Finance, Fundação Getulio Vargas at São Paulo (FGV/EAESP), Sao Paulo, Brazil
e-mail: richard.saito@fgv.br

W. Mendes-Da-Silva (ed.), *Individual Behaviors and Technologies for Financial Innovations*, https://doi.org/10.1007/978-3-319-91911-9_16

decreased demand for more simplistic financial decisions, e.g., Payback and accounting ratios. This would be due to economic growth, which increases the sophistication of the financial markets (Scott and Petty 1984; Canace and Salzsieder 2016). In the last 20 years, some emerging markets have experienced: (i) relative economic and political stability; (ii) capital market growth above the global average; (iii) increased adoption of good corporate governance practices (Mendes-Da-Silva and Onusic 2012). Nevertheless, surveys reveal that the company decision-making process is rarely studied at the level of companies listed on the stock exchange, and even rarer for unlisted companies (Balbinotti et al. 2007). This gap in literature provides an interesting opportunity to investigate the impact of sophistication of management quality, e.g., capital budgeting. This study assumes the argument found in the literature, that public companies (listed on the stock exchange) tend to have more sophisticated decision-making mechanisms, or rather, less simplistic than unlisted (or private) companies, due to the need to provide market reports (Booth 1996; Drury and Tayles 1996; Lazaridis 2004). Finance literature has provided evidence from around the world concerning the capital budgeting of companies, e.g., Graham and Harvey (2001), Lazaridis (2004), Du Toit and Pienaar (2005), and Hermes et al. (2007). This chapter is similar to the latter, and uses an adaptation of its data collection instrument. Also, according to Graham (2011), this study constitutes a tool for teaching Corporate Finance.

This chapter presents insight drawn from research data captured by surveying 698 companies (398 listed and 300 unlisted). The primary research objective is to compare the use of capital budgeting techniques by large companies, listed and unlisted. Based on 91 responding companies, the main findings suggest that the chief financial officers (CFOs) of listed companies tend to use less simplistic techniques, e.g., NPV and CAPM, compared to the CFOs of major unlisted companies, who tend to not estimate the cost of capital, suggesting some level of precariousness in the capital budgeting process, and supporting recent arguments by Jacobs and Shivdasani (2012). These research findings provide insight into how financial professionals can develop and provide more effective decisions about capital budgeting. At the end of this chapter, some recommendations and directions for future research are included.

Previous Studies

From a modern standpoint, the cost of capital for companies is one of the most important aspects in capital budgeting decision making (Jacobs and Shivdasani 2012). Surveys about emerging markets practices are still scarce, among which Balbinotti et al. (2007) focused on the methodological aspects of a survey about financial decisions, i.e., translation and validation of questionnaires. Among the Finance studies featuring surveys, one of the categories found in the literature focuses on company practices and techniques for capital budgeting (Gitman and Forrester 1977; Schall et al. 1978; Bierman 1993; Ryan and Ryan 2002). This chapter contributes to the literature by focusing on the determinants of capital budgeting practices, comparing listed and unlisted companies.

According to Hermes et al. (2007), this research primarily deals with four capital budgeting techniques: (i) *Net Present Value* (NPV); (ii) *Internal Rate of Return* (IRR); (iii) *Payback* (PB); and (iv) *Accounting Rate of Return* (ARR), often used for research in the field of Finance, although there are other techniques used less frequently, e.g., Real Options (Brounen et al. 2004). An opportunity worthy of attention in Finance research is the verification of the CFOs' levels of interest in these traditional capital budgeting techniques, considering that since the 1960s, the literature has documented the interest of practitioners around the world (Miller 1960; Istvan 1961; Graham and Harvey 2001; Du Toit and Pienaar 2005; Hermes et al. 2007). Frezatti et al. (2012) indicate the limited number of studies conducted in Brazil on capital budgeting practices, even though this subject is important for companies' performance and competitiveness, regardless of their level of maturity and size (Vos and Vos 2000; Danielson and Scott 2005).

The international literature exploring different managerial techniques for capital budgeting have typically described economies whose characteristics differ significantly from emerging markets context (Bierman 1993; Graham and Harvey 2002), although studies in emerging economies can be found (Du Toit and Pienaar 2005). In example, the research conducted by Gitman and Forrester (1977), in the United States; Brounen et al. (2004), in Europe; Hermes et al. (2007), who compared the practices adopted in China and the Netherlands.

Hermes et al. (2007) support the viewpoint that, over time, implementation of sophisticated capital budgeting methods has become more common. These authors argue that this is mainly due to: (i) the financial markets having developed over time, leading to the use of more relevant, convenient and necessary methods, e.g., Discounted Cash Flow (DCF); (ii) CFOs' training has increased over time; (iii) advancement of the computational apparatus available to the CFOs; iv) reduced costs associated with acquiring technology.

Determinants of the Capital Budgeting Practices

Assuming that investment decisions are made by individuals, would it be a mistake to assume that the managers' personal preferences and environmental conditions may influence the capital budgeting decision (Hermes et al. 2007) and, by extension, the company's value? The literature has documented a wide range of motives that determine the choice of capital budgeting practices. According to Klammer (1972), in the late 1950s, less than 20% of North American companies used DCF techniques as the primary method of selecting projects. In the early 1970s, this percentage was already 57%. In the following decade, Hendricks (1983) noted that 76% of companies used DCF methods as the primary decision tool.

The number of companies that used more simplistic methods, for example PB, was reduced from 34% in 1959, to 11% of North American companies in 1981

(Hendricks, 1983). Along the same lines, Trahan and Gitman (1995) considered companies listed in the North American financial media, to show that larger companies tend to make greater use of more sophisticated capital budgeting techniques, e.g., DCF techniques. In Asia, Kester et al. (1999) obtained results suggesting an increasing relevance of DCF techniques, but a predominant practice non-DCF techniques, i.e., PB.

Research Design

To collect data for this study, we accessed the questionnaire used by Hermes et al. (2007, pg. 636), composed of seven questions. First, we adapted the survey instrument as recommended by Balbinotti et al. (2007, pg. 29–33) in regard to the translation and validation of financial survey questionnaires. Specifically, the changes included: (i) translation from English to Portuguese, done by a qualified professional; (ii) pre-test with 5 CFOs, members of the Brazilian Institute of Finance Executives; (iii) inclusion of the Governance variable, missing from the original questionnaire. The questionnaire was distributed to 398 companies listed in the B^3 and 300 major companies not listed on the stock exchange, but listed in a traditional business media publication in the Brazilian market: Revista Exame (2012). In September and November of 2012, the questionnaires were sent/received (by mail) to/from CFOs of these companies. Each packet contained: the questionnaire; a letter describing the study, its voluntary nature and the assurance of respondent anonymity; a stamped envelope to return the CFOs' responses.

Of the 698 letters, 17 were returned due to the company's change of address (9 were from listed companies), 52 valid responses were received from listed companies, and another 39 from unlisted companies. This response rate (~13.4%) compares well to previous studies of the same topic, e.g., Trahan and Gitman (1995), 12%; Kester et al. (1999), 15.5%; Graham and Harvey (2001), 9%; and Brounen et al. (2004), 5%. To verify the respondents' representativeness of the group of respondent companies, albeit less detailed (since the respondents had been promised anonymity to encourage participation), we verified listed company respondents by their governance level. We checked, through a non-parametric independent test, and did not find significant evidence of self-selection biases among listed companies, which was impossible to test among unlisted companies.

The survey consisted of: (i) closed questions about the company's capital budgeting techniques; (ii) specific questions about the company's characteristics, e.g., size, sales to international markets, type of ownership and operating sector; (iii) questions regarding the CFO's profile, e.g., age and educational level. Regarding capital budgeting techniques, the CFOs were to indicate: (i) the frequency of using different project evaluation techniques (using a scale of 1–6, where 1 = Never and 6 = Always); (ii) the method most commonly used to estimate cost of capital; (iii) the methods used to estimate cost of equity; (iv) problems associated with the use of

DCF methods; and (v) reasons for using non-DCF methods. The dependent (dummy) variables related to the capital budgeting methods (Table 16.6) and the methods of estimating cost of capital (Table 16.7) will receive the value = 1 if the score given by the respondent was ≥5 (on a scale of 1–6, where 1 = Never and 6 = Always), and zero if otherwise. Based on the variables related to the profiles of the company and the CFO, we used binary response regressions (1) to verify the existence of associations between these variables and the company's tendency to use certain capital budgeting techniques.

$$\pi_i = \pi(Y = 1|X) = F(Z_i) = \frac{1}{1 + e^{-Z_i}} = \frac{1}{1 + e^{-(\beta_0 + \beta Z_i)}} \tag{16.1}$$

The dependent variables related to the problems with using DCF and reasons for using non-DCF techniques (Table 16.8) will receive the value = 1 when indicated by the respondent, and zero when they were not chosen by the CFO. The independent variables used were:

Listed Company	= 1 if the company is listed on the stock exchange (BM&FBovespa), and zero if otherwise
Firm size	= 1 if the company's annual sales equal or exceed BRL$300 million and zero if otherwise
CFO's education	= 1 if the company's CFO has a doctorate or masters degree, and zero if neither
CFO's age	= 1 if the company's CFO is at least 49 years old, or zero if the CFO is younger
Governance	= 1 if the company is listed on the new market of BM&FBovespa, and zero if otherwise
Industry	= 1 if the company is a manufacturer, and zero if otherwise

With explicitly listed the four most common capital budgeting techniques in the questionnaire (Brounen et al. 2004; Hermes et al. 2007). The respondent was provided the opportunity to indicate other techniques employed, as well as their frequency of use. As expected, few reported other techniques, e.g., Real Options or Sensitivity Analysis; and therefore, we chose to disregard the rare use of these analysis method.

Empirical Results

The results are reported in five subsections. The first describes the company and CFO profiles and the second examines the determinants of the use of capital budgeting techniques. The third presents the frequency of use of cost of capital estimation techniques. The fourth reports the results of the logit regressions for capital budgeting techniques. The fifth shows logit regressions related to obstacles for the use of DCF techniques, as well as reasons for using non-DCF techniques.

Characteristics of the Companies and the CFOs

Table 16.1 displays the respondents' company and CFO characteristics. More than half of the listed companies indicated that their products are not marketed internationally; while 40% of the unlisted companies reported having no export activities. Approximately one third of the listed companies are manufacturers; and almost half of the unlisted companies. Close to 80% of the CFOs claimed to have a graduate degree.

Regarding the independence between company characteristics and stock exchange listing, a nonparametric test indicated that dependency existed in two classes of characteristics, i.e., *Operational sector* ($X^2 = 10.876$; p-value <0.1) and *CFO's Age* ($X^2 = 7.515$; p-value <0.1). With regards to company size, the unlisted companies exhibited higher sales. Or rather, while 80% of the listed companies show sales over BRL$90 million, nearly 90% of unlisted companies are in this sales range. Approximately 54% of the listed companies do not make international sales, while 43.6% of unlisted companies sell only to the domestic market.

As for the CFOs' characteristics, in general, there seems to be a greater frequency of professionals with a graduate level education in the listed companies, i.e., 21.2% of the CFOs of these companies claim to have a masters or doctorate degree. This percentage is similar to that found by Hermes et al. (2007, pg. 637) for the Chinese market, and lower than that found in the Netherlands, 33%. Among the 39 unlisted companies, only 15.4% have this education level; in other words, it seems that private companies, there is a predominance of professionals with an educational level equivalent to MBAs, i.e., training programs with an executive focus.

Thus, we noted that 64.1% of private company executives have at most an MBA. On the other hand, this percentage fell to 59.6% in publicly traded companies. As for the CFOs' age, we noted that ~80% of the private company executives are between 40 and 59 years old; while this percentage was less than 56% for public companies. Finally, with regards to the adoption of corporate governance practices identified as recommended, 25 companies (~48% of the listed companies) belong to the New Market.

Capital Budgeting Techniques Adopted by the Companies

Table 16.2 shows CFO capital budgeting techniques. Like Graham and Harvey (2001), Brounen et al. (2004), and Hermes et al. (2007), we asked how often various capital budgeting methods are used, using a 6-point scale (where 1 = Never and 6 = Always). This provides both information regarding which methods CFOs use for capital budgeting decisions, as well as the relative importance of these different methods. Respondents indicated they used DCF methods of NPV and IRR, and the non-DCF methods PB and ARR; and other techniques listed by the respondents, e.g., EBITDA. From a technical standpoint, the NPV is the least simplistic

Table 16.1 Characteristics of the companies and the responding CFOs

	Listed		Unlisted		χ^2
	N	%	N	%	
Gross revenue					4.018
Less than 2.4 mil BRL$	6	11.5	3	7.7	
Between 2.4 mil BRL$ and 16 mil BRL$	3	5.8	1	2.6	
Greater than 16 mil BRL$ and up to 90 mil BRL$	1	1.9	0	0.0	
Greater than 90 mil BRL$ and up to 300 mil BRL$	5	9.6	1	2.6	
Greater than 300 mil BRL$	37	71.2	34	87.2	
% of sales abroad					3.231
There are no sales for the international market	28	53.8	17	43.6	
1–24%	15	28.8	9	23.1	
25–50%	5	9.62	7	17.9	
50–90%	3	5.77	5	12.8	
100%	1	1.92	1	2.56	
Industry					10.876*
Industrial/manufacturing	18	34.6	19	48.7	
Transportation/infrastructure	7	13.5	6	15.4	
Technology	1	1.92	1	2.56	
Financial services	5	9.62	0	0	
Energy	10	19.2	1	2.56	
Wholesale/retail	11	21.2	12	30.8	
CFO's education					2.303
No degree	2	3.85	0	0	
Degree	8	15.4	8	20.5	
Masters/PhD	11	21.2	6	15.4	
MBA	31	59.6	25	64.1	
CFO's age					7.515*
$\leq$ 40 years	16	30.8	6	15.4	
Between 40 and 48 years	16	30.8	17	43.6	
Between 49 and 59 years	13	25	15	38.5	
$\geq$ 60 years	7	13.5	1	2.56	
Governance (BM&FBovespa criteria)					–
Traditional	18	34.6	0	0	
Bovespa+	2	3.85	0	0	
Level 1	5	9.62	0	0	
Level 2	2	3.85	0	0	
New market	25	48.1	0	0	

Source: Developed by the authors. N Listed companies = 52; N Unlisted companies = 39. *p-value <0.1. The test statistic χ^2 suggests the existence of dependence between stock exchange listing and two company characteristics, i.e., *Operational sector* ($\chi^2 = 10.876$) and *CFO's Age* ($\chi^2 = 7.515$)

Table 16.2 Intensity of use of different capital budgeting methods by CFOs

	DCF		Non-DCF		
Panel A: Listed ($N = 52$)	NPV	IRR	PB	ARR	Others
% scores 5 or 6	84.6%	75.0%	50.0%	13.4%	13.5%
Average score	5.30	4.90	4.00	2.50	2.0
Company size					
Annual revenue ≤ BRL$ 300,000,000	5.50	4.70	3.70	2.50	1.33
Annual revenue > BRL$ 300,000,000	5.20	5.00	4.20	2.50	1.84
CFO's education					
Yes	5.36	4.91	4.00	2.27	1.82
No	5.32	4.90	4.02	2.56	1.66
CFO's age					
<49 years	5.40	5.00	4.00	2.3	1.56
≥49 years	5.30	4.80	4.00	2.9	1.90
Operational sector					
Manufacturing	5.17	5.39	4.61*	2.72	1.28
Others	5.41	4.65	3.71	2.38	1.91
International sales					
≤50%	5.27	4.81*	3.88*	2.50	1.69
>50%	6.0	6.0	5.75	2.50	1.75
Governance					
Yes	5.6	5.5	4.5	2.5	1.8
No	5.0	4.3	3.6	2.5	1.6
Panel B: Unlisted ($N = 39$)					
% scores 5 or 6	61.5	61.5	56.4	20.50	15.3
Average score	4.60 (*720*) ***	4.50 (*809*) *	4.40	2.50	1.74
Company size					
Annual revenue ≤ BRL$ 300,000,000	5.40	5.40	5.20	1.40	1.00
Annual revenue > BRL$ 300,000,000	4.50	4.40	4.40	2.70	1.85
CFO's education					
Yes	5.0	4.80	4.80	2.20	2.50
No	4.60	4.50	4.40	2.60	1.61
CFO's age					
<49 years	4.52	4.13*	4.30	2.83	1.61
≥49 years	4.81	5.06	4.69	2.13	1.94
Operational sector					
Manufacturing	4.70	4.30	4.90	2.10	1.79
Others	4.60	4.70	4.00	3.00	1.70
International sales					
≤50%	4.55	4.48	4.58	2.70	1.73

(continued)

Table 16.2 (continued)

	DCF		Non-DCF		
Panel A: Listed ($N = 52$)	NPV	IRR	PB	ARR	Others
>50%	5.17	4.67	3.83	1.67	1.83

Source: Developed by the authors
Note: The line "% Scores 5 or 6" shows the percentage of companies that indicated using a capital budgeting method *Always* (score = 6) or *Almost always* (score = 5). The line "Average score" presents the average score given by the CFOs, using a scale of 0 (*never*) to 6 (*always*). The other lines show the average score for different categories, based on the company's characteristics. We checked for independence (Mann-Whitney test) between the company and CFO profiles, and the intensity of use of the capital budgeting techniques (significance indicated beside each average value). The numbers in italics and between parentheses are nonparametric test statistics, comparing the average values between listed companies and unlisted companies. The averages for the company categories were different from each other. The results indicate that the two groups of companies use DCF techniques, i.e., NPV and IRR, with different levels of intensity
$^{*}p$-value <0.1; $^{**}p$-value <0.5; $^{***}p$-value <0.01

technique, followed by the IRR (Hermes et al. 2007). Moreover, the non-DCF techniques are regarded as less accurate and less sophisticated, in particular the PB. We found that 84.6% of the CFOs of listed companies claimed to use the NPV always or almost always (scores $\geq$5).

This percentage is close to that found by Hermes et al. (2007) for the Dutch market (89%), and higher than that found in China (49%). However, in Brazil, according to the responses provided by the CFOs of unlisted companies, this percentage falls to 61.5%. Nevertheless, regardless or being listed or unlisted on the Stock Exchange, the companies seem to indicate NPV as the most used method, making it the most popular among respondents. It is worth noting, however, that according to the responses for unlisted companies, the scores given to the NPV are very close to those obtained by the IRR. That is, both the NPV and the IRR were indicated by ~61.5% of the CFOs. This response was not found with the listed companies, among which the IRR was found to be less commonly used than the NPV. We also found that non-DCF techniques seem to be more heavily used by the CFOs of unlisted companies. This observation is consistent with the lower educational level of the CFOs. In other words, the findings suggest an association between the CFO's educational level and their preference for certain capital budgeting techniques. As such, it seems that the non-DCF techniques, which are less accurate and more simplistic, may be preferred by the CFOs with a lower educational level.

Estimating Cost of Capital

With regard to the methods for estimating the cost of capital, which is an important and necessary aspect for DCF techniques, e.g., NPV and IRR, we asked that the CFOs indicate which methods they most often used to estimate the cost of capital (Table 16.3). It is understood that, the cost of capital adjusted to the risk of each

Table 16.3 Most commonly used methods for measuring the cost of capital (% of total)

	Rates used as a proxy for cost of capital				
	Specific k/ project	*WACC*	k_d	k_e	Other methods
Panel A: Listed (N = 52)	5.0	37.0	4.0	6.0	0.0
	9.6	71.2	7.7	11.5	0.0
Company size					
Annual revenue ≤ BRL$ 300,000,000	13.3	80.0	6.7	0.0	0.0
Annual revenue > BRL$ 300,000,000	8.1	67.6	8.1	16.2	0.0
CFO's education					
No	9.8	68.3	7.3	14.6	0.0
Yes	9.1	81.8	9.1	0.0	0.0
CFO's age					
<49 years	6.3	75.0	9.4	9.4	0.0
≥49 years	15.0	65.0	5.0	15.0	0.0
Operational sector					
Others	11.8	73.5	5.9	8.8	0.0
Manufacturing	5.6	66.7	11.1	16.7	0.0
International sales > 50%					
No	10.4	72.9	8.3	8.3	0.0
Yes	0.0	50.0	0.0	50.0	0.0
Governance					
No	18.5	63.0	14.8	3.7	0.0
Yes	0.0	80.0	0.0	20.0	0.0
Panel B: Unlisted (N = 39)	5.0	24.0	2.0	3.0	5.0
	12.8	61.5	5.1	7.7	12.7
Company size					
Annual revenue ≤ BRL$ 300,000,000	20	20	20	40	0
Annual revenue > BRL$ 300,000,000	11.8	67.6	5.9	5.9	8.9
CFO's education					
No	12.1	57.6	6.1	9.1	15.1
Yes	16.7	83.3	0	0	0
CFO's age					
<49 years	13.0	65.2	4.3	4.3	13.1
≥49 years	12.5	56.25	6.25	12.5	12.5
Operational sector					
Others	70.0	5.0	15.0	10.0	
Manufacturing	26.3	52.6	5.3	0.0	15.8
International sales > 50%					
No	12.1	60.6	6.1	9.1	12.1
Yes	16.7	66.7	0.0	0.0	16.7

(continued)

Table 16.3 (continued)

	Rates used as a proxy for cost of capital				
	Specific k/ project	*WACC*	k_d	k_e	Other methods
Governance					
No	12.8	61.5	5.1	7.7	12.8
Yes	0	0	0	0	0

Note: This table presents the percentage of companies in each of the categories that indicates that a certain discount rate is used more often. The total percentages for different company categories may total more than 100% due to rounding

project, as well as the *WACC* constitute less simplistic techniques. The cost of debt (k_d) is explicitly less sophisticated than both of these, despite situations in which projects are fully financed with debt issuances. Table 16.3 shows that 37% of the listed companies claim to use the *WACC* as the discount rate for cash flows in evaluating their projects. Table 16.4, on the other hand, presents the responses obtained for different methods that companies use to calculate their cost of equity (k_e). It is noteworthy that 11% of the listed companies claim to not calculate k_e. Among the unlisted companies, this percentage is ~31%. This suggests a certain precariousness of the decision-making process for capital budgeting, to the extent that the unfamiliarity of k_e may lead to significant mistakes in decision making, whether by accepting or rejecting investment projects.

Jacobs and Shivdasani (2012) recently observed a similar phenomenon in the North American market. In these authors' opinion, most companies have used erroneous premises to calculate the cost of capital. Therefore, they tend to make financial decisions that are not aligned with the goal of creating value for the company. This becomes more problematic when dealing with smaller companies in the domestic market. Perhaps, unfamiliarity with the k_e is greater, when considering the set of unlisted companies. However, considering other emerging economies, the number of companies that pay no attention to calculating the k_e is even greater. Thus, Hermes et al. (2007) indicates that over 64% of the Chinese companies do not. It should be noted that this work does not explore the advantages of more complex methods, such as Real Options, over DCF methods, such as NPV (Copeland and Antikarov 2003).

Capital Budgeting Techniques, Cost of Capital and Estimating the Cost of Equity: Bivariate and Multivariate Analysis

This subsection addresses the results obtained from the logit models (Tables 16.6, 16.7 and 16.8), according to (16.2), which expresses the probability π_i of the i-th company using certain capital budgeting techniques. To verify robustness, OLS regressions were performed, as an alternative to the logit model, with no differences found between the two test methods.

Table 16.4 Most frequently used methods for estimating the cost of equity (***K***$_e$) in % of total

	Historical avg. return	CAPM	k_e+ Premium + growth	Does not estimate k_e	Other methods
Panel A: Listed ($N = 52$)	3.0	27.0	8.0	6.0	8.0
	5.8	51.9	15.4	11.5	15.4
Company size					
Annual revenue ≤ R $300,000,000	13.3	33.3	26.7	13.3	13.3
Annual revenue > R $300,000,000	2.7	59.5	10.8	10.8	16.2
CFO's education					
No	4.9	51.2	14.6	12.2	17.1
Yes	9.1	54.5	18.2	9.1	9.1
CFO's age					
<49 years	3.1	56.3	15.6	12.5	12.5
≥49 years	10.0	45.0	15.0	10.0	20.0
Operational sector					
Others	5.9	61.8	11.8	8.8	11.8
Manufacturing	5.6	33.3	22.2	16.7	22.2
International sales > 50%					
No	6.3	50.0	14.6	12.5	16.7
Yes	0.0	75.0	25.0	0.0	0.0
Governance					
No	7.4	51.9	3.7	14.8	22.2
Yes	4.0	52.0	28.0	8.0	8.0
Panel B: Unlisted ($N = 39$)	1.0	13.0	4.0	12.0	9.0
	2.6	33.3	10.3	30.8	23.1
Company size					
Annual revenue ≤ R$ 300,000,000	0.0	0.0	0.0	40.0	60.0
Annual revenue > R$ 300,000,000	0.0	38.2	11.8	29.4	20.6
CFO with masters/PhD					
No	0.0	33.3	12.1	33.3	21.2
Yes	0.0	33.3	0.0	16.7	50.0
CFO's age					
<49 years	0.0	34.8	13.0	34.8	17.4
≥49 years	0.0	31.3	6.3	25.0	37.5
Operational sector					
Others	0.0	40.0	10.0	25.0	25.0
Manufacturing	0.0	26.3	10.5	36.8	26.3
International sales > 50%					
No	0.0	30.3	12.1	30.3	27.2
Yes	0.0	50.0	0.0	33.3	16.7

(continued)

Table 16.4 (continued)

	Historical avg. return	CAPM	k_e+ Premium + growth	Does not estimate k_e	Other methods
Governance					
No	0.0	0.0	0.0	0.0	0.0
Yes	0.0	0.0	0.0	0.0	0.0

Note: This table presents the percentage of companies in each of the categories that indicates that a certain discount rate is used more often. The total percentages for different company categories may total more than 100% due to rounding

Table 16.5 Correlation matrix for independent variables used in the estimates

	Listed company		Company size	CFO's education	CFO's age	Operational sector
Company size	−0.192	*				
CFO's education	0.073		−0.018			
CFO's age	−0.026		−0.059	0.016		
Operational sector	−0.142		−0.155	−0.110	0.108	
Governance	0.533	***	0.029	0.084	−0.095	−0.108

Source: Developed by the authors
*p-value <0.1; **p-value <0.05; ***p-value <0.1

$$\pi_i = \ln\left(\frac{P_i}{1-P_i}\right) = \varphi_1 + \varphi_2\text{Listed company}_i + \varphi_3\text{Firm size}_i + \varphi_4\text{CFO education}_i + \varphi_5\text{CFO's age}_i + \varphi_6\text{Industry}_i + \varphi_7\text{Governance}_i + u_i \tag{16.2}$$

Where: *Listed Company* is the dummy variable that indicates if the i-th company is listed in the stock exchange (value = 1) or not (value = 0), and other independent variables: *Firm size, CFO's education, CFO's age, Governance* and *Industry* with u_i as the stochastic disturbance term. Table 16.5 presents the correlation coefficients between the independent variables, noting that only *Firm size* showed significant correlation with *Listed companies*. No multicollinearity problems were found in the regressions.

In Table 16.6, the dependent variables were created as follows: NPV = 1 if the score given by the company for the NPV method was ≥5, and NPV = 0 if otherwise; IRR = 1 if the score given by the company for the IRR method was ≥5, and IRR = 0 if otherwise; PB = 1 if the score given by the company for the PB method was ≥5, and PB = 0 if otherwise. Model I suggests that stock exchange listing increases the company's likelihood to use NPV more commonly as a capital budgeting technique ($\widehat{\varphi_2} \approx -1.235$; p – value < 0.05). This could corroborate Levine (1997), who argues that listed companies tend to maintain structures and practices

Table 16.6 Determinants of the capital budgeting methods (logit)

	NPV				IRR			PB		
	I		II		III	IV		V	VI	
Constant	0.470		1.689	*	0.470	0.550		0.258	−0.776	
	(0.329)		(0.883)		(0.329)	(0.713)		(0.323)	(0.720)	
Listed company	1.235	**	0.506		0.629	−0.035		−0.258	−0.845	
	(0.506)		(0.614)		(0.459)	(0.534)		(0.426)	(0.566)	
Company size			−1.396	*		−0.390			−0.053	
			(0.787)			(0.581)			(0.560)	
CFO's education			1.076			0.387			0.853	
			(0.819)			(0.660)			(0.556)	
CFO's age			0.111			0.325			0.829	*
			(0.540)			(0.501)			(0.487)	
Industry			−0.349			0.158			1.366	***
			(0.526)			(0.484)			(0.500)	
Governance			1.392			1.576	**		1.424	**
			(0.895)			(0.735)			(0.639)	
#observations	91		91		91	91		91	91	
McFadden R^2	0.060		0.135		0.016	0.070		0.002	0.139	
Akaike's criterion	100.61		103.02		114.45	118.45		129.51	122.30	
% correct classification	74.7%		74.7%		69.2%	69.2%		52.7%	68.1%	
χ^2 likelihood test	6.27		13.86		1.88	7.87		0.37	17.57	

Source: Authors' calculations

Note: All of the models presented in this table were estimated using the logit method. In parentheses, under each coefficient, is the standard error of the estimate of each coefficient obtained. The estimates were obtained with a robust standard error using the procedure suggested by Davidson and Mackinnon (2004, pg. 250)

*p-value <0.01; **p-value <0.05; ***p-value <0.1

aimed at greater sophistication of the capital budgeting decision-making process. In other words, with the development of capital markets, the investors' demand for quality financial decisions is expected to grow.

However, when considering the other independent variables (Model II), the *Company's Size* $(\widehat{\varphi_2} \approx -1.396; p - \text{value} < 0.1)$ seems to have a more expressive and significant effect on the tendency to use the NPV, highlighting that smaller companies tend to use the NPV less often. It is worth noting that the unlisted companies are the largest (Tables 16.1 and 16.5). Model VI shows that there seems to be an association between the *CFO's Age* and their preference for greater use of more simplistic techniques, e.g., PB $(\widehat{\varphi_5} \approx 0.829,\ p - \text{value} < 0.1)$. Table 16.7 presents the estimated coefficients for the models whose dependent

Table 16.7 Determinants of the methods for estimating the cost of equity (logit)

	CAPM				k_d+ premium + growth					
	VII		VIII		IX	X		XI		XII
Constant	−0.693	**	−1.420	**	−2.170***	−1.480		−0.811	**	−0.640
	(0.340)		(0.704)		(0.932)	(1.976)		(0.346)		(1.188)
Listed company	0.770	*	1.086	*	0.464	−1.317		−1.226	**	−0.936
	(0.439)		(0.562)		(0.653)	(1.138)		(0.556)		(0.676)
Company size			1.293	**		−0.959				−0.210
			(0.628)			(0.704)				(0.648)
CFO's education			0.041			−0.342				−0.635
			(0.642)			(0.812)				(0.873)
CFO's age			−0.279			−0.203				−0.598
			(0.477)			(0.742)				(0.632)
Industry			−0.790			0.420				0.659
			(0.496)			(0.717)				(0.591)
Governance			−0.309			2.580	**			−0.707
			(0.621)			(1.034)				(0.894)
#observations	91		91		91	91		91		91
McFadden R^2	0.025		0.099		0.007	0.133		0.057		0.095
Akaike's criterion	125.65		126.34		74.44	75.476		89.338		95.88
% correct classifications	58.2%		70.3%		86.8%	86.8%		80.2%		81.3%
χ^2 likelihood test	3.16		12.47		0.52	9.48		5.17		8.63

Source: Authors' calculations

Note: All of the models presented in this table were estimated using the logit method. In parentheses, under each coefficient, is the standard error of the estimate of each coefficient obtained. The estimates were obtained with a robust standard error using the procedure suggested by Davidson and Mackinnon (2004, pg. 250)

*p-value <0.01; **p-value <0.05; ***p-value <0.1

variables use different methods for obtaining the cost of equity, as well as not calculating the k_e. The results obtained in Models VII and VIII suggest that the listed companies on the Stock Exchange are more likely to indicate CAPM as a method to calculate the cost of equity. Thus, considering the coefficients obtained in Model VII, we observed that the effect of stock exchange listing ($\widehat{\varphi_2} \approx 0.770$; $p -$ value < 0.1) on the probability of using CAPM as a method to calculate the cost of equity is ~18.59% points.

This impact is even more significant ($\widehat{\varphi_2} \approx 1.086$; $p -$ value < 0.1) when considering the effect of *Company Size*, i.e., Model VIII suggests an increase of ~25.46% points. A detailed discussion regarding interpretation of the estimated coefficients in the logit model can be found in Wooldridge (2011, pg. 535–548). In other words, the results show that company size also determines the decision to use CAPM to calculate the cost of equity; together, these two variables significantly affect the likelihood of a company using the CAPM more often. This also means that smaller companies, not listed on the stock exchange, are less likely to use the CAPM to calculate the cost of equity. This finding supports the arguments and findings of Hermes et al. (2007). Also on Table 16.7, Model XI presents coefficients that suggest that stock exchange listing may lead to greater willingness to calculate the cost of equity ($\widehat{\varphi_2} \approx -1.226$; $p -$ value < 0.05). But, when considering the other independent variables (Model XII), this effect was no longer significant, despite maintaining the coefficient sign ($\widehat{\varphi_2} \approx -0.936$; $p -$ value > 0.1).

Obstacles for the Use of DCF Techniques and Reasons for Using Non-DCF Techniques

Table 16.8 presents the results obtained for problems identified in using DCF techniques, and the advantages of using non-DCF techniques (models XVII and XVIII). According to the results obtained in model XIV, it seems that the older CFOs (over age 50) less commonly perceive the difficultly in estimating risk as a factor that could discourage the use of DCF techniques ($\widehat{\varphi_5} \approx -1.272$; p-value <0.05). However, the perception that the difficulty in estimating risk may be a factor that constitutes an obstacle for using DCF techniques, is also explained by the company's operational sector. Or rather, the manufacturing companies seem to have a greater propensity to understand the estimation of risk as an obstacle for using DCF techniques ($\widehat{\varphi_6} \approx 1.678$; p-value <0.01). Nevertheless, contrary to that obtained in Model XIV, the explanatory model of the difficulty of contemplating strategic factors in project evaluation, the manufacturing companies demonstrated a less restrictive view regarding the use of DCF techniques.

Table 16.8 Determinants of problems and obstacles for using the DCF and determinants of the motivation for using non-DCF methods

	Difficulty estimating risk			Difficulty including strategy in the project			Other advantages of using non-DCF techniques		
	XIII	XIV		XV	XVI		XVII	XVIII	
Constant	−0.154	−1.074		0.154	0.731		−1.204***	−2.610	***
	(0.321)	(0.712)		(0.321)	(0.741)		(0.380)	(0.869)	
Listed company	0.308	0.711		−0.308	−0.098		0	−0.719	
	(0.425)	(0.618)		(0.425)	(0.559)		(0.503)	(0.796)	
Company size		0.747			−0.194			1.180	*
		(0.563)			(0.595)			(0.714)	
CFO's education		−0.347			−0.177			0.801	
		(0.639)			(0.528)			(0.612)	
CFO's age		−1.272	**		0.271			0.332	
		(0.508)			(0.463)			(0.545)	
Operational sector		1.678	***		−0.995	**		0.115	
		(0.513)			(0.483)			(0.586)	
Governance		0.043			−0.814			1.428	*
		(0.635)			(0.603)			(0.776)	
#observations	91	91		91	91		91	91	
McFadden R^2	0.004	0.142		0.004	0.058			0.089	
Akaike's criterion	129.61	122.15		129.61	132.79		102.31	103.56	
% correct classifications	53.8	65.9%		53.8%	61.5%		76.9%	76.9%	
χ^2 likelihood test	0.52	17.99		0.53	7.35		–	8.75	

Source: Authors' calculations

Note: All of the models presented in this table were estimated using the logit method. In parentheses, under each coefficient, is the standard error of the estimate of each coefficient obtained. The estimates were obtained with a robust standard error using the procedure suggested by Davidson and Mackinnon (2004, pg. 250)

**p*-value <0.01; ***p*-value <0.05; ****p*-value <0.1

Concluding Remarks

This article aimed to compare the use of capital budgeting techniques among companies listed in the stock exchange with large companies not listed in the stock exchange, in an emerging economy, Brazil. Based on the arguments presented in the literature, we expected that the company's level of development, e.g., stock exchange listing, would impact the capital budgeting practices adopted by the companies. The motivation for this study is based on three important factors. First, the financial markets have shown explicit development over time, including the Brazilian market (Mendes-Da-Silva and Onusic 2012). Therefore, one would expect the use of DCF methods to be the most suitable, convenient and necessary (Hermes et al. 2007). Second, CFOs training level has increased over time, which may support the adoption of more sophisticated capital budgeting techniques (Graham 2011). Third, the increased availability of computer tools, coupled with reduced technology costs, may also facilitate and encourage the use of more advanced techniques.

This study was based on a survey of 698 Brazilian companies, of which 398 were listed and 300 unlisted. Thus, from a response rate of around 13%, the data set consisted of 91 companies, including both listed and unlisted. The data analysis was conducted based on nonparametric tests and logit models, which focused on the potential effect that the need to report to the market (listed companies) could have on the capital budgeting practices. In other words, the goal was to verify whether capital budgeting practices differ significantly between listed companies and unlisted companies; and if so, whether these differences can be explained by the characteristics of the company and the CFO. Brazil's growing market lends particular significance to this study, since previous studies of this type have mainly been conducted in developed economies, or in the Asian markets.

The findings suggest that the CFOs of listed companies tend to use more sophisticated techniques, e.g., NPV (when not considering the full set of independent variables) and CAPM (even considering all of the independent variables), when compared to CFOs of the largest unlisted companies. This finding supports the arguments presented in previous works, such as Hermes et al. (2007) Or rather, taking into account the need to report to company stakeholders, the CFOs of listed companies seem to more commonly use more sophisticated capital budgeting techniques. This suggests the explicit need to intensify the training for those CFOs who employ less sophisticated methods for capital budgeting decision-making (Kester et al. 1999; Coleman 2007; Graham 2011).

These findings highlight two issues to consider. First is to increase CFO education to encourage more sophisticated capital budgeting practices, notably among listed companies, in view of the need to report to the market. Second is to prioritize governance structures, i.e., the Board, investors and shareholder to promote less simplistic capital budgeting practices. The growth and specificities of the Brazilian capital market increases the importance that corporate governance structures, notably the company's Board, and the shareholders influence the CFO's performance, to maximize company value. Moreover, recent studies link the use of inappropriate capital budgeting techniques to value destruction. That is, neither adopting projects with low potential, nor rejecting projects with promise for value creation is desirable for the company (Dixit and Pindyck 1995; Cassimon et al. 2011).

It is important to highlight the possibility of self-selection biases in the set of respondent companies. This could possibly disto research findings, i.e., companies that employ more simplistic methods of investment analysis may be less willing to respond to the survey, since they could attribute less value to the topic. Thus, this study may be, at least to some degree, overstated in terms of the sophistication level of the capital budgeting process of large Brazilian companies.

Future Directions

While several limitations may be attributed to this study (i.e., it deals with only an emerging country, possible selection biases based on the willingness to respond to the questionnaire, the relatively small number of observations, the current national and global economy) inquiries regarding CFO capital budgeting practices, especially in emerging economies, may be relevant and contributory for future research, such as: (i) replicating this study in the future, checking the progress in the adoption of capital budgeting practices; (ii) develop similar studies in other emerging economies to explore the effect of market development on CFO practices; (iii) expand this study to explore potential effects of various capital budgeting techniques on the company's value; iv) given the possibility that poor decisions can destroy company value, we suggest analyzing the effects of corporate governance structures and shareholder activism on capital budgeting practices employed by CFOs (Park and Park 2004). These issues are beyond the scope of this study, but they undoubtedly constitute good potential for future research in the area of Finance.

References

Andor, G., Mohanty, S. K., & Toth, T. (2015). Capital budgeting practices: A survey of Central and Eastern European firms. *Emerging Markets Review, 23*, 148–172.

Baker, H. K., & Mukherjee, T. K. (2007). Survey research in finance: Views from journal editors. *International Journal of Managerial Finance, 3*(1), 11–25.

Balbinotti, M. A. A., Benetti, C., & Terra, P. R. S. (2007). Translation and validation of the Graham-Harvey survey for the Brazilian context. *International Journal of Managerial Finance, 3*(1), 26–48.

Bierman, H. (1993). Capital budgeting in 1992: A survey. *Financial Management, 22*(3), 24.

Booth, L. (1996). Making capital budgeting decisions in multinational corporations. *Managerial Finance, 22*(1), 3–18.

Brounen, D., De Jong, A., & Koedijk, K. (2004). Corporate finance in Europe: Confronting theory with practice. *Financial Management, 33*(4), 71–101.

Canace, T. G., & Salzsieder, L. (2016). The timing of asset purchases to achieve earnings thresholds. *Journal of Management Accounting Research, 28*(1), 81–106.

Cassimon, D., Backer, M. D., Engelen, P. J., Wouwe, M. V., & Yordanov, V. (2011). Incorporating technical risk in compound real option models to value a pharmaceutical R&D licensing opportunity. *Research Policy, 40*(9), 1200–1216.

Coleman, L. (2007). Risk and decision making by finance executives a survey study. *International Journal of Managerial Finance, 3*(1), 108–124.

Copeland, T., & Antikarov, V. (2003). *Real options: Practitioner's guide*. New York: Cengage.

Danielson, M. G., & Scott, J. A. (2005). *The capital budgeting decisions of small businesses*. Philadelphia, PA. Available at: https://astro.temple.edu/~scottjon/documents/CapitalBudgetinginSmallFirms_June2006_final.pdf

Davidson, R., & Mackinnon, J. G. (2004). *Econometric theory and methods*. New York: Oxford University Press.

Dixit, A. K., & Pindyck, R. S. (1995). The options approach to capital investment. *Harvard Business Review*, 105–115. Available at: https://hbr.org/1995/05/the-options-approach-to-capital-investment

Drury, C., & Tayles, M. (1996). UK capital budgeting practices. Some additional survey evidence. *European Journal of Finance, 2*, 371–388.

Du Toit, M. J., & Pienaar, A. (2005). A review of the capital budgeting behavior of large South African firms. *Meditari Accountancy Research, 13*(1), 19–27.

Revista Exame (2012). Exame Melhores e Maiores 1000 Maiores Empresas do Brasil Edição Especial, Editora Abril, São Paulo.

Frezatti F, de Souza Bido D, Da Cruz APC, Barroso MFG, de Camargo Machado MJ (2012) Investment decisions on long-term assets: Integrating strategic and financial perspectives. *European Accounting Review, 22*(2), 297–336. https://doi.org/10.1080/09638180.2012.718672

Gitman, L. J., & Forrester, J. R. (1977). A survey of capital budgeting techniques used by major US firms. *Financial Management, 6*(3), 66–71.

Graham, J., & Harvey, C. (2001). The theory and practice of corporate finance: Evidence from field. *Journal of Financial Economics, 60*(2–3), 187–243.

Graham, J. R. (2011). Using CFO surveys as a motivational tool to teach corporate finance. *Financial Review, 46*(2), 193–205.

Graham, J., & Harvey, C. (2002). How do CFOs make capital budgeting and capital structure decisions? *Journal of Applied Corporate Finance, 15*(1), 8–23.

Hendricks, J. A. (1983). Capital budgeting practices including inflation adjustments: A survey. *Managerial Planning, 31*(4), 22–28.

Hermes, N., Smid, P., & Yao, L. (2007). Capital budgeting practices: A comparative study of the Netherlands and China. *International Business Review, 16*(5), 630–654.

Istvan, D. F. (1961). The economic evaluation of capital expenditures. *Journal of Business, 34*(1), 45–51.

Jacobs, M. T., & Shivdasani, A. (2012). Do you know your cost of capital? *Harvard Business Review, July-August*, 1–8.

Kester, G., Chang, R. P., Echanis, E. S., Haikal, S., ISA, M. M., & Skully, M. T. (1999). Capital budgeting practices in the Asia-Pacific region: Australia, Hong Kong, Indonesia, Malaysia, Philippines, and Singapore. *Financial Practice Education, 9*(1), 25–33.

Klammer, T. P. (1972). Empirical evidence on the application of sophisticated capital budgeting techniques. *Journal of Business, 45*(3), 387–397.

Lazaridis, I. T. (2004). Capital budgeting practices: A survey in the firms in Cyprus. *Journal of Small Business Management, 42*(4), 427–433.

Levine, R. (1997). Financial development and economic growth: Views and agenda. *Journal of Economic Literature, 35*, 688–726.

Mendes-Da-Silva, W., & Onusic, L. M. (2012). Corporate e-disclosure determinants: Evidence from the Brazilian market. *International Journal of Disclosure and Governance*. https://doi.org/10.1057/jdg.2012.14.

Miller, J. H. (1960). A glimpse at practice in calculating and using return on investment. *NAA Bulletin (now Management Accounting), XLII,* June 20, 65–76.
Neuhauser, K. (2007). Survey research in finance. *International Journal of Managerial Finance, 3* (1), 5–10.
Park, Y., & Park, G. (2004). A new method for technology valuation in monetary value: Procedure and application. *Technovation, 24*, 387–394.
Rea, L. M., & Parker, R. A. (1997). *Designing and conducting surveys research* (2nd ed.). San Francisco, CA: Josey-Bass Publishers.
Ryan, P. A., & Ryan, G. P. (2002). Capital budgeting practices of the fortune 1000: How have things changed? *Journal of Business and Management, 8*(4), 355–364.
Schall, L. D., Sundem, G. L., & Geijsbeek, W. R., Jr. (1978). Survey and analysis of capital budgeting methods. *Journal of Finance, 33*(1), 281–287.
Scott, D., Jr., & Petty, W., II. (1984). Capital budgeting practices in large American firms: A retrospective analysis and synthesis. *Financial Review, 19*(1), 111–123.
Trahan, E. A., & Gitman, J. L. (1995). Bridging the theory-practice gap in corporate finance: A survey of chief financial officers. *Quarterly Review of Economics and Finance, 35*(1), 73–87.
Vos, A., & Vos, E. (2000). Investment decision criteria in small New Zealand businesses. *Small Enterprise Research, 8*(1), 44–55.
Wooldridge, J. M. (2011). *Introdução à Econometria*. São Paulo: Cengage.

Index

W. Mendes-Da-Silva (ed.), *Individual Behaviors and Technologies for Financial Innovations*, https://doi.org/10.1007/978-3-319-91911-9

The manufacturer's authorised representative in the EU is Springer Nature Customer Service Centre GmbH, Europaplatz 3, 69115 Heidelberg, Germany. If you have any concerns regarding our products, please contact ProductSafety@springernature.com

Printed and bound by CPI Group (UK) Ltd, Croydon, CR0 4YY
05/10/2026
02228144-0014